AFRICAN AMERICAN LITERATURE

A Brief Introduction and Anthology

Al Young

The HarperCollins Literary Mosaic Series
Ishmael Reed
General Editor
University of California, Berkeley

HARPERCOLLINS*COLLEGEPUBLISHERS*

Acquisitions Editor: Lisa Moore
Cover Design: Kay Petronio
Cover Illustration: Rupert Garcia, "Shadow Nose History: Diaspora African," Copyright Rupert
Garcia and courtesy of artist and Sammi Madison-Garcia, Rena Bransen Gallery (SF), Galerie
Claude Samuel (Paris), and Daniel Saxon Gallery (LA)
Electronic Production Manager: Laura Chavoen
Electronic Page Makeup: Kay Spearman/The Resource Center
Printer and Binder: RR Donnelley & Sons Co.
Cover Printer: The LeHigh Press, Inc.

African American Literature

Library of Congress Cataloging-in-Publication Data

African American literature : a brief introduction and anthology / Al
  Young.
      p.   cm. -- (The HarperCollins literary mosaic series)
   Includes bibliographical references and index.
   ISBN 0-673-99017-6 (alk. paper)
   1. American literature--Afro-American authors--History and
criticism. 2. Afro-Americans--Intellectual life. 3. Afro-Americans
in literature. I. Young, Al, 1939-   . II. Series.
PS153.N5A336 1995
810.8'0896073--dc20   95-33074
                                                              CIP

95 96 97 9 8 7 6 5 4 3

"The purpose of all art is
to lay bare the questions
which have been hidden
by the answers."

—James Baldwin

Contents

FICTION

POETRY

Foreword

by Ishmael Reed, General Editor

I abandoned the use of textbooks early in my teaching career and developed my own "reader." I was frustrated with textbooks in which the preponderance of prose and poetry was written by people of similar backgrounds and sensibilities—the white-settler-surrounded-by-infidels-and-savages theme common to Euro-American literature. In these textbooks we seldom got information about how the Native Americans or the Africans felt. Female and minority writers were left out. There was slack inclusion of contemporary writers, and little space devoted to the popular American culture of our century. These textbooks seemed slavishly worshipful of the past, such that every mediocre line by a past "great" was treated with reverence while the present was ignored.

Of course, there are many worthwhile ideas to be gained from what in our sound-bite culture—in which complicated ideas are dumbed down for instant consumption—is referred to as "Western Civilization." But as Asian American writer Frank Chin points out when referring to the Cantonese model, after the ability of the Cantonese to absorb every culture with which they've come into contact, one doesn't have to abandon the styles of one's own tradition in order to embrace styles from other traditions. As I have mentioned elsewhere, the history of modern art would be quite different had not artists been receptive to or borrowed from the traditions of others. This creative give and take between artists of different cultures particularly characterizes the arts of the twentieth century.

Things have improved over the years, especially with the outbreak of textbooks labeled "multicultural," a term that has become a football in the struggle between the politically correct of the left and the right. However, even the new and improved multicultural texts appear to have added African American, Native American, Hispanic American, and Asian American writers as an afterthought. The same writers and the same—often unrepresentative—works show up again and again.*

The HarperCollins Literary Mosaic Series

The HarperCollins Literary Mosaic Series was created as an antidote to this version of multiculturalism whose fallibility becomes evident when talented writers, well-known and respected in their communities, are ignored. The HarperCollins Literary Mosaic Series includes not only those writers who have made it into the canon but also writers undeservedly neglected in today's crop of texts.

* *For more information on the arbitrariness of this selection process, see Michael Harper's excellent <u>Every Shut Eye Aint Sleep</u>.*

In his autobiographical remarks, *Asian American Literature* editor Shawn Wong makes an important point that teachers should consider when adopting texts for their ethnic literature, multiculturalism, American literature, and introductory literature courses. Wong writes that his study of Asian American literature occurred outside of the university. "At no time," he writes, "in my English and American literature undergraduate education or in my entire public school education had any teacher ever used (or even mentioned) a work of fiction or poetry by a Chinese American or any Asian American writer." This observation could be made by all the editors of the HarperCollins Literary Mosaic Series: Al Young for *African American Literature*, Gerald Vizenor for *Native American Literature*, Nicolás Kanellos for *Hispanic American Literature*, and of course Shawn Wong for *Asian American Literature*. They had to go outside of the academy—which has committed an intellectual scandal by excluding these major traditions of our common American heritage.

The Series Editors: Pioneers for an Inclusive Tradition

These editors are among the architects of a more inclusive tradition. Indeed, this series is unique because the four editors are not only writers and scholars in their own right but are among the pioneers of American literature of the latter part of this century! It's hard to imagine a list of talented insiders who are as informed about the currents and traditions of their ethnic literatures as the editors of the HarperCollins Literary Mosaic Series. These texts provide teachers with an opportunity to employ material in their classrooms that has been chosen by writers who have not only participated in the flowering of their literatures but also have assisted in the establishment of a tradition for their literatures.

Al Young

Al Young is a multitalented artist who has distinguished himself as a poet, novelist, screenwriter, editor, and writing instructor. His presence is very much in demand at writing workshops and conferences. He has taught at a number of universities and colleges, including Stanford University, Crown College, the University of California at Berkeley, the University of California at Santa Cruz, Rice University, and most recently at the University of Michigan. Among his honors are a Wallace Stegner Writing Fellowship, a Joseph Henry Jackson Award, a Guggenheim Fellowship, an American Book Award, and a PEN/Library of Congress Award for Short Fiction. Al Young and I were editors of the Yardbird Reader series, which has been recognized as the first national publication of its kind devoted to presenting new multicultural literature.

Gerald Vizenor

Pulitzer Prize–winner N. Scott Momaday has said that Gerald Vizenor "has made a very significant contribution to Native American letters and also to American literature in general. He's innovative, he has the richest sense of humor of anyone I know, and in addition he's the most articulate person—he's a man to be reckoned with." Among his innovative novels are *Heirs of Columbus* and *Griever: An American Monkey King in China.* An American Book Award winner, Vizenor insists that the story of Native Americans in the United States should be told by Native Americans and not by intermediaries or translators. His *Native American Literature* anthology in The HarperCollins Literary Mosaic Series will provide students and readers with an entirely different slant on Native American literature from the one they have become accustomed to in standard texts.

Nicolás Kanellos

Author of a number of scholarly works and articles, Nicolás Kanellos is the founder and director of Arte Público Press, the oldest and largest publisher of United States Hispanic literature, as well as the *Americas Review* (formerly *Revista Chicano-Reguena*), the oldest and most respected magazine of United States Hispanic literature and art. A full professor at the University of Houston, he is a fellow of the Ford, Lilly, and Gulbenkian foundations and of the National Endowment for the Humanities. He is also the winner of an American Book Award and is a formidable essayist with an unrivaled knowledge of the intersections of African, European, and Native American cultures.

Shawn Wong

It is not surprising that Shawn Wong and Frank Chin, Lawson Inada, and Jeffery Chan have become known as "the four horsemen of Asian American literature" by both their admirers and detractors. One wonders how Asian American literature would look without their efforts. It was they who began the painstaking construction of a tradition whose existence had been denied by the academy. In *Aiiieeeee! An Anthology of Asian American Writers* and its successor, *The Big Aiiieeeee! An Anthology of Chinese American and Japanese American Literature,* the four editors gave permanent status to an Asian American literary tradition. Wong is also the author of *Homebase,* the first novel published in the United States by an American-born Chinese male. This novel received the Pacific Northwest Booksellers Award for Excellence and the Fifteenth Annual Governor's Writer's Day Award. Among his many other honors, Wong has also received a fellowship from the National Endowment for the Arts. He has taught writing at the University of Washington since 1984.

Remapping Our Tradition

Although the four editors are from different backgrounds, the issues raised in their introductions are those with which a few generations of multicultural scholars, writers, and artists have grappled. With *African American Literature,* Al Young has both a literary and humanistic purpose. He believes that readers and writers will be able to learn from their exposure to some of the best writing in the United States that there are experiences all of us share with the rest of humanity. Like the classic critic F. R. Leavis, Al Young believes that writing can make people better. The writers included in Gerald Vizenor's *Native American Literature* are not outsiders writing about Native Americans or colonial settlers promoting the forest as a tough neighborhood full of high-risk people, a threat to civilized enclaves, but rather works by Native Americans themselves, beginning in 1829 with William Apess's autobiography, *A Son of the Forest.* Nicolás Kanellos's *Hispanic American Literature* represents a literary tradition, part European and part African, that existed in the Americas prior to the arrival of the English. The situation in Asian American literature, one of the youngest of American literatures, is as turbulent as that of the atmosphere surrounding a new star. Shawn Wong's introduction addresses the continuing debate over issues about what constitutes Asian American literature and the role of the Asian American writer.

The books in the HarperCollins Literary Mosaic Series give a sampling of the outstanding contributions from writers in the past as well as the range of American writing that is being written today. And the anthologies in this series contain a truly representative sampling of African American, Native American, Hispanic American, and Asian American writing at the end of this century so that students can become acquainted with more than the few European and European Americans covered by traditional texts or the same lineup of token ethnic writers found in the policy issue multicultural books. It should be welcome news to instructors looking for new ways to teach that such a distinguished group committed themselves to producing three-to-five-hundred-page textbooks that can either be used as the primary text in a course, supplemented with novels, combined for a single class, or used to supplement other texts that don't have the desired coverage of ethnic literature. While each book is designed to be brief enough for flexible uses in the classroom, each volume does represent the breadth of major literary genres (autobiography, fiction, poetry, and drama) that characterizes the literary contribution of each tradition, even if—as in the case of drama—the short format of the series would accommodate only a single example. The four volumes of The HarperCollins Literary Mosaic Series constitute nothing less than a new start for those who are interested in remapping our writing traditions.

Writing for Our Lives

> The genius of the United States is not best or most in its executives
> or legislatures, nor in its ambassadors or authors or colleges or
> churches or parlors, nor even in its newspapers or inventors ... but
> always most in the common people. Their manners, speech, dress,
> friendships—the freshness and candor of their physiognomy—the
> picturesque looseness of their carriage ... their deathless attachment
> to freedom (Walt Whitman, "Leaves of Grass," 1855 Preface).

Whitman said that these qualities and others await the "gigantic and generous
treatment worthy of it." Though American authors from the eighteenth century to
the present day have talked about a body of writing that would be representative of
these attributes of democracy, one could argue that "the gigantic and generous
treatment worthy of it" is a recent and critical development because until recently
many points of view have been excluded from United States literature. The Literary
Mosaic Series also demonstrates that, for authors of a multicultural heritage, literature
often provides an alternative to the images of their groups presented by an often-
hostile media.

Of all the excellent comments made by Al Young in his introduction, one is
crucial and strikes at the heart of why the writing is so varied in The HarperCollins
Literary Mosaic Series. He writes,

> and if you think people are in trouble who buy the images of who
> they are from the shallow, deceitful versions of themselves they see
> in mass media, think what it must feel like to be a TV-watching
> African-American male. Pimp, thug, mugger, drug dealer, crackhead,
> thief, murderer, rapist, absentee father, welfare cheat, convict, loser,
> ne'er-do-well, buffoon. Think of these negative images of yourself
> broadcast hourly all over the globe.

When African Americans, Native Americans, Hispanic Americans, and Asian
Americans write, they're not just engaging in a parlor exercise—they are writing
for their lives. The twentieth century has shown that unbalanced images can cost
groups their lives. That is why The HarperCollins Literary Mosaic Series came to
be—to trumpet these lives, lives that are our national heritage. And once these
voices have been heard, there is no turning back.

Acknowledgments

This is a series that has been taken the time, talents, and enthusiasm of its editors—Al Young, Gerald Vizenor, Nicolás Kanellos, and Shawn Wong—and I am excited that they chose to be a part of this project. In addition, the editors and I wish to thank those people who helped us prepare the series, particularly those instructors who reviewed this material in various drafts and offered their expertise and suggestions for making the books in this series even more useful to them and their students: Joni Adamson Clarke, University of Arizona; Herman Beavers, University of Pennsylvania; A. Lavonne Brown Ruoff, University of Illinois at Chicago; William Cain, Wellesley College; Rafel Castillo, Palo Alto College; Jeffrey Chan, San Francisco State University; King-Kok Cheung, University of California at Los Angeles; Patricia Chu, George Washington University; Robert Combs, George Washington University; Mary Comfort, Moravian College; George Cornell, Michigan State University; Bruce Dick, Appalachian State University; Elinor Flewellen, Santa Barbara City College; Chester Fontineau, University of Illinois at Champaign-Urbana; Sharon Gavin Levy, University of Minnesota at Duluth; Shirley Geok-Lin Lim, University of California at Santa Barbara; Tom Green, Northeastern Junior College; James Hall, University of Illinois at Chicago; Lynda M. Hill, Temple University; Lane Hirabayashi, University of Colorado; Gloria Horton, Jacksonville State University; Ketu H. Katrak, University of Massachusetts at Amherst; Josephine Lee, Smith College; Russell Leong, University of California at Los Angeles; Michael Liberman, East Stroudsberg University; Paulino Lim, Jr., California State University at Long Beach; Kenneth Lincoln, University of California at Los Angeles; Marcus "C" Lopez, Solano Community College; Shirley Lumpkin, Marshall University; Barbara McCaskill, University of Georgia; Nelly McKay, University of Wisconsin at Madison; Lucy Maddox, Georgetown University; Thomas Matchie, North Dakota State University; Joyce Middleton, University of Rochester; Alice Moore, Yakima Valley Community College; Eric Naylor, University of the South; Jon Olson, Oregon State University at Corvallis; Ernest Padilla, Santa Monica College; David Payne, University of Georgia; Joyce Pettis, North Carolina State University; David Robinson, Winona State University; Don Rothman, Oakes College, University of California at Santa Cruz; Leonard A. Slade, Jr., State University of New York at Albany; Stephen Sumida, University of Michigan; Brian Swann, Cooper Union; John Trimbur, Worcester Polytechnical Institute; Hari Vishwanadha, Santa Monica College; Marilyn Nelson Waniek, University of Connecticut; Shelly Wong, Cornell University; Jackie Valdez, Caspar College; Richard Yarborough, University of California at Los Angeles.

Acknowledgments

The editor wishs to thank the following persons whose assistance was invaluable in preparing this volume:

Sumi Hahn,
Lynn Huddon,
Clarence Major,
Lisa Moore,
Ishmael Reed,
Michael Young

Introduction

Literature does not die unless its creators become the victims of genocide and silence of the grave, and until its creations are erased from the mind's ear and the mind's eye and calcined in bonfires.

—Jan Carew
"Moorish Culture-Bringers: Bearers of Enlightenment"
(Essay published in *Golden Age of the Moor,*
edited by Ivan Van Sertima)

Testify v. (1840s–1990s) to confess one's sins, bad deeds, life story (originally in church but now in music, literature, and through other forms of art); to ritually comment upon any cultural experience understood by all black people; a secular or religious confession ... Example: "I want to testify this evening to the goodness of my Lord and to the fact he directed me away from a life of sin."

Juba to Jive:
A Dictionary of African-American Slang,
Clarence Major, editor

Those "twenty Negars" sold by Dutch seamen to Captain John Smith, who brought them to Jamestown, Virginia, in 1619 (one year before the Pilgrims landed at Plymouth Rock), did not step off the boat singing "Sometimes I Feel Like a Motherless Child," or "We Shall Overcome," or "Say It Loud (I'm Black and I'm Proud)." Neither did they moan a chorus of slow blues, or cakewalk in ragtime, or break into some spirited jazz classic, or quickstep their way, all motion and flash, through Marvin Gaye's "Make Me Wanna Holler" or Aretha Franklin's "I Wonder How It Feels to Be Free." Nor did any one of them shout, "I have a dream!"

As silly as that may sound, it has to be said. Why? Because we live in a streamlet of time that sometimes seems to have been dammed off from the natural, oceanic flow of history. The emergence of those North American peoples of color—variously knows as Negroes, Blacks, and Afro-Americans—who now call themselves African Americans was not an overnight occurrence. Centuries have gone into shaping the outlook and cultural legacy of African Americans, who are, in fact, an altogether new race of human beings—biologically and culturally. And if the term *homo americanus* is taken seriously, the story of their experience and their contributions to North American and global culture is nothing less than vast.

From pre-colonial times and the Revolutionary War through the cataclysmic wars of the twentieth century—World War I, World War II, the Cold War of the McCarthy Era, the Korean War, Vietnam, the so-called Persian Gulf War—Black Americans have served and been sacrificed. And from the Civil War of the 1860s through the Civil Rights struggle of the 1960s, Black Americans, the essential American, have laid their hearts and souls and bodies on the line—and usually without forgetting their status as second-class citizens in what professes to be the world's greatest democracy.

So great has been the restlessness of our unreflective times and the republic we cherish that many citizens have serious trouble distinguishing between TV-Hollywood versions of history and the real thing. And since the majority of Americans are the descendants of slaves, indentured servants, migrant workers, immigrants, or refugees, we have much to gain from knowing even just a little about our country's true origins.

You may think you are reading and thinking about African American literature, but, in reality, it is America herself you will be exploring and experiencing through literature. And whatever else literature may turn out to be, it is surely a form of testifying.

Myth and History: Literature and Reality

Africa herself in African American culture and lore is frequently fictionalized and romanticized to the point of seeming more Africanesque than African. For example, African Americans favor Swahili as an African language to study. But many would never guess that Swahili, which, in Eastern Africa, has long served as a sort of *lingua franca*, was actually heavily influenced by Arab traders who intermarried with native women and colonized that eastern coast. Swahili, a Bantu-based language, enabled peoples of linguistically disparate cultures to talk with one another, and this included those whose lucrative business it was to literally sell others among them down the river.

Kunta Kinte, immortalized in Alex Haley's bestselling book and celebrated TV miniseries *Roots,* has come to symbolize all young Africans that slave-runners, with help from other Africans, captured and shipped to America. But Kunta Kinte was a fiction, while those "twenty Negars"—as Captain John Smith spelled them out in his *General Histories of Virginia*—were the real thing, even though we still know pitifully little about them.

In fact, we are only beginning to place in meaningful perspective information about the histories, economies, philosophies, governments, religions, and cosmologies of ancient civilizations and empires (Benin, Ashanti, Ghana, Mali, Hausa, Kanem-Bornu, Mossi, Oyo, Songhay) that flourished in regions we now know by other names.

Americans at all familiar with geography can now identify those locations as Ghana (dubbed the Gold Coast by European profiteers), the Ivory Coast, Nigeria, Togo, Cameroon, the Congo, Guinea, Sierra Leone, Senegal, Upper Volta, Chad, Gabon, Gambia, or Dahomey. It was from such cultures, grounded on Africa's west coast, that most plantation-bound natives were plucked.

Captain Smith's "twenty Negars," and all the Africans who followed, brought with them to America the cultures of West Africa—Yoruba, Ibo, Angolan, Akan. It would be seven years before the Dutch would import the first indentured African slaves, eleven of them, to New Amsterdam. As for the New England slave trade—which, along with rum and opium, turned the kind of get-rich-quick profits in its day that international drug trafficking does now—that industry would not be launched until 1638, when the first Africans arrived in Boston on the slave ship *Desire*.

Desire. What an apt name for a vessel jammed, fore and aft, with human cargo, without whom the building of what was to become thought of as the richest nation on earth, the United States of America, would have been clearly impossible.

Not only would African culture survive in the Americas, the African heritage itself would enable African Americans to withstand a terrifying experience, an experience whose dramatic unfoldment continues to this day.

The experience of peoples of African descent in the United States would seem unbearably harsh had we not grown accustomed to hearing about it repeatedly, rhetorically. Perhaps self-preservation plays a role in the way human beings learn to disconnect themselves emotionally from disturbing imagery and its meanings. We hear again and again about the settler slaughter of Indians, the millions executed under Stalin in the Soviet Union, Nazi Germany's systematic annihilation of Jews, the nuclear destruction of Hiroshima and Nagasaki, the violence-shrouded politics of the Vietnam Era, "ethnic cleansing" in Bosnia-Herzegovina, or the monumental scale of the political massacre in Rwanda.

These are historic events we often talk about and *hear* talked about ritualistically. What such prolonged nightmares tell us about human behavior, our own behavior, sometimes seems to be more than we can either accept or even stand to hear. And such events and experiences get packaged into formulaic, antiseptic versions, which we prefer to the real thing.

That ancient Europe really did owe much of her wisdom, know-how, material resources, and riches to Africa is vividly documented by historians, poets, and philosophers of ancient Greece and Rome—Herodotus, Plato, Thucydides, Cicero, Tacitus. That North America, in her dizzying rise to power as a global leader in little more than a century, owed a great deal to Africa, and to slaves and their descendants, might largely remain a quietly kept secret were it not for the rich and powerful body of imaginative literature—autobiography, fiction, poetry, and drama—that African American writers continue to create.

From the sixteenth through the nineteenth centuries, the importation of African slaves into the New World to feed flourishing plantation economies would bring Europe wealth of immeasurable proportions. With gold, silver, pearls, ivory, cotton, sugarcane, tobacco, and rum so plentiful, and with land and labor so cheap, neither Western civilization nor the known world would ever be the same.

"There is always something new from Africa," was what the ancient Roman writer, soldier, and statesman Pliny the Elder had to say about this fabled continent. But slavery was nothing new. Greek and Roman society had been slave-based. While slaves in Athens and Rome often tutored or educated their masters, however, literacy and reading among slaves in the United States was not only discouraged, it was punishable by law.

"Fortunate for the slave," historian Sterling Stuckey reminds us in his brilliant *Slave Culture,* "the retention of important features of the African cultural heritage provided a means by which the new reality could be interpreted and spiritual needs at least partially met, needs often regarded as secular by whites but as often considered sacred to blacks. The division between the sacred and the secular, so prominent a feature of modern Western culture, did not exist in black Africa in the years of the slave trade, before Christianity made real inroads on the continent."

Olaudah Equiano, an African and, so far as we know, the first to write a whole book in English, published in 1789, *The Interesting Narrative of the Life of Olaudah Equiano, or Gustavas Vassa the African, Written by Himself,* had this to say about his homeland: "We are almost a nation of dancers, musicians, and poets. Thus every great event, such as a triumphant return from battle, or other cause for public rejoicing, is celebrated in public dances, which are accompanied with songs and music suited to the occasion."

European colonials in New Amsterdam, New England, or Virginia regarded dancing and singing as pure devilment. The physical expression of joyfulness or celebration, so crucial to sacred ceremonies and devotional worship in African cultures, was punished in the colonies. Dance, especially, was sinful.

Consider that fact alone of the Negro past: the clash of cultures, in which a people found themselves not only enslaved, but among people who rejected them as human beings. Slavemasters could neither see nor could they afford to see slaves, that is, their very possessions, as possessing any culture whatever. When you begin to understand that most slavemasters viewed their slaves as cattle or livestock, then you begin to understand why so much of slave religious practices and African-derived culture had to be communicated secretly.

Once the very first of the so-called Black Codes—legal statutes that legitimized slavery as an institution—took effect in Virginia in 1661, languages and linguistic communication itself became endangered. Under slavery, not only was it against the law to teach a slave to read or write, it was illegal for slaves to teach themselves.

"Sometimes," one ex-slave recounted in *The Unwritten History of Slavery* (Nashville: Fisk University; on microfilm: Harbor Side, Maine: Social Science Institute), "the masters would let us have evenings in the church ... We'd sit in front with the patrolers behind us. The colored preachers would tell us to obey our masters. That's all they knew to say. If they said something else, the patrolers might stop them. One time we were singing: Ride on, king Jesus, no man can hinder thee, when the patrolers told us to stop or they would show whether we could be hindered or not."

Coded Meanings: The Secret Language of Communication

After she escaped North from the Maryland plantation where she was born of African parents around 1820, Harriet Tubman, a leading conductor of the Underground Railroad, slipped back into the South at least fifteen times to lead more than three hundred other women, men, and children to freedom. Easing her way around by night through southern backwoods, Tubman, destined to become known as the "Moses of her race," softly sang a special song to signal slaves bent on escaping that she was nearby and ready to roll.

This gutsy woman—who couldn't read or write—was convinced that God guided and gave her safe passage. In her heart, as she told fellow conductor Thomas Garrett, she "ventured only where God sent." And this is what Harriet Tubman sang to slaves ready to run to freedom:

> *Dark and thorny is the pathway*
> *Where the pilgrim makes his ways;*
> *But beyond this vale of sorrow*
> *Lie the fields of endless days.*

And there were other songs, each of which had two, three or many meanings, depending on who was singing, and who was listening. "Follow the Drinking Gourd," for example, urged fleeing slaves to guide themselves along their escape route by the position of the Big Dipper in the sky:

> *Follow the drinking gourd!*
> *Follow the drinking gourd!*
> *For the old man is a-waiting*
>   *for to carry us to freedom*
> *If you follow the drinking gourd.*

Other songs included "Brother Moses Gone to de Promiseland," "Steal Away to Jesus," and "Swing Low, Sweet Chariot."

In the soil of such experiences the masked or dual aspect of African American culture took root. W. E. B. Du Bois, the eminent sociologist and political strategist, called it "double-consciousness" in his eloquent classic, *The Souls of Black Folk:* " An American, a Negro, two souls, two thoughts, two unreconciled strivings; two warring ideals in one dark body whose dogged strength alone keeps it from being torn asunder."

Even though these now-classic Negro spirituals spoke at one level of Jesus and heaven and chariots and angels, they also told other stories and expressed other sentiments beyond the surface meaning of their texts. In other words, spirituals themselves comprise a vital portion of African American literature. To this day, a relatively modern gospel song such as Clara Ward's "How I Got Over" exemplifies the inspirational intentions of African American storytelling.

One hundred years after Harriet Tubman and others conducted fugitive slaves on the Underground Railway to safe-passage, another kind of conductor—a composer, arranger, pianist, and all-around musical genius—testified in another way to the complexity and depth of the Black American experience. Ellington wrote an orchestral suite that he called *Black, Brown and Beige.*

And what did Edward Kennedy "Duke" Ellington wish to convey by this title?

"Black, Brown and Beige was planned as a tone parallel to the history of the American Negro," Ellington wrote in his controversial autobiography, *Music Is My Mistress,* "and the first section, 'Black,' delved deeply into the Negro past. In it I was concerned with the close relationship between work songs and spirituals.... The second section, 'Brown,' recognized the contribution made by the Negro to this country in blood. We begin with the heroes of the Revolutionary War.... The third section, 'Beige,' [referred] to the common view of the people of Harlem, and the little Harlems around the U.S.A."

What discoveries do we make when we delve into the African American past? Have African Americans made any contributions to the United States? Do African Americans come at all close to sharing anything that resembles a "common view"?

Because the answers to questions we ask are usually found curled around the questions themselves, it might be enlightening to pause and look at each of those three questions prompted by Duke Ellington's *Black, Brown and Beige.*

First of all, the African American past, thanks to literature, is enormously recoverable. The Senegal-born slave-servant Phillis Wheatley, whose poems are ripe-to-bursting with metaphor, may very well have been thinking about the meaning or even the attainment of freedom when she sat in her master's Boston house and wrote these lines of "On Imagination":

From star to star the mental optics rove,
Measure the skies, and range the realms above,
There in one view we grasp the mighty whole,
Or with new worlds amaze th' unbounded soul.
  Though Winter frowns to Fancy's raptur'd eyes
The fields may flourish, and gay scenes arise;
The frozen deeps may break their iron bands,
And bid their waters murmur o'er the sands.

Sifting through the sands of New World time in search of the Negro past, we come upon a unique body of literary works by writers of African descent whose backgrounds and temperaments crisscross political, esthetic, ideological, social, and geographic zones. From altogether unpredictable perspectives and temperaments, African American poets, novelists, short story writers, playwrights, essayists, memoirists, and scholarly critics represent the exciting sweep of diverse personalities that has always characterized the Black literary scene.

From the slave narratives and biographies of the abolitionist movement and the twelve-year post-Civil War era of Reconstruction when ex-slaves were elected to high political office in the South, from Booker T. Washington's classic autobiography, *Up From Slavery,* in which he calls for the "Talented Tenth" to lead the Negro population in bettering themselves materially through education and not through agitation; from World War I, which saw the return of Negro troops who had sacrificed their lives for their country in "the war to end all wars" and returned home from frontline duty in France and elsewhere, now more eager than ever to change their condition, from the days and nights of the Harlem Renaissance of the 1920s, which ended with the Great Depression, on through World War II, the thunderous years of the Civil Rights movement, the Black Power sixties, the anti-affirmative action eighties, and the neo-Nazi nineties—through all of these developments, African American writing has thrived and told its story.

The complexity, the range, the beauty and savvy of African American literature is stunning. If you have ever wondered what it might be like to walk in someone else's shoes, to see and think and feel through the eyes, mind, or the heart of another, then you have come to the right place. To read and listen with the mind's ear to what abolitionist activist Frederick Douglass, a runaway slave, had to say about his life and times is to step inside his body and soul.

Selling Stereotypes: A Way of Not Seeing

That we have on record written transcriptions of hundreds of stories told by the survivors of slavery seems a blessing. Such stories used to be told in family and communal gatherings, on front porches, in backyards, kitchens, at the dinner table, at bedtime. Now we mostly get our stories from television and films.

Just think. If people buy the images of who they are from the shallow, deceitful versions of themselves they see depicted in mass media, imagine what it must feel like to be, say, a television-watching African American male. Pimp, thug, thief, mugger, murderer, drug dealer, drug addict, rapist, absent father, welfare slave, welfare cheat, convict, loser, ne'er-do-well, buffoon—these are the images, the negative depictions, broadcast hourly all over the globe.

Sterling A. Brown, the writer and teacher regarded as *the* folk poet of the Harlem Renaissance, described these kinds of stereotypes in his book *The Negro in American Fiction.* Roughly, Brown broke down these White-generated images of Blacks into seven categories: (1) The Contented Slave, (2) The Wretched Freeman, (3) The Comic Negro, (4) The Brute Negro, (5) The Tragic Mulatto, (6) The Local Color Negro, and (7) The Exotic Primitive.

Toms, Coons, Mulattoes, Mammies and Bucks is the title that film and popular culture historian Donald T. Bogle gave his landmark study of Blacks in Hollywood films. Along the way, Bogle informed us that Hollywood stereotypes not only African Americans, but absolutely everyone. The impact of mass media depictions on public consciousness cannot be minimized or trivialized. In his own long autobiographical essay, *The Devil Finds Work,* the eminent James Baldwin tells us that his stepfather hated Baldwin's "frog-eyes," his mother's eyes, and had always told the boy he was ugly. This is how the writer recalls the effect on him, as a child, of seeing Bette Davis in a film: "So, here, now, was Bette Davis, on that Saturday afternoon, in close-up, over a champagne glass, pop-eyes popping. I was astounded. I had caught my father, not in a lie, but in an infirmity. For, here, before me, after all, was a *movie star; white;* and if she was white and a movie star, she was *rich;* and she was *ugly.*"

Of course, an African American male may also see himself depicted on television as an entertainer, athlete, mayor, police chief, or Congressman. But if you crave the kind of rich, textured depictions, the nuances of subtle complexities of personality (contradictions, eccentricities, inconsistencies) that characterize real-life, breathing men and women—then you will have to put down your remote-control and pick up a poem, or a novel, or a short story.

Storytelling, which works through metaphor, is the battery that powers myth. The late Joseph Campbell, a compelling mythologist, reminded us that the first function of any mythology "is to awaken in the individual a sense of awe, wonder and participation in the inscrutable mystery of being." Poet Langston Hughes opens his moving poem "Consider Me" with the lines: "Consider me/descended also from/the Mystery." It is the stories told by these descendants of "the Mystery," the descendants of those "twenty Negars"— whispered, shouted, chaptered, rhymed, and acted out—

that make up the literature of African America, a literature popular all over the freedom-starved world, where it is translated, studied, and devoured.

The Black Cultural Achievement

By the 1920s, the Harlem that figures so prominently in the Duke Ellington musical portrait of "Negro America" had become a focal point for African American culture. Poetry, fiction, criticism, music, dance, sociology, history, education—each of these was flourishing full force after World War I in this relatively small area of uptown Manhattan.

In fact, achievements of African Americans, not only in the arts, but in practically every sphere of American life, were vast. The lawn sprinkler, the golfing tee (prior to whose invention golfers had to scoop and pile up dirt for every tee-off), the mechanical pencil-sharpener are "little inventions" for which African Americans took out patents. A. C. Roebuck, a founder of the famed Sears & Roebuck stores, was an African American. There were Black scientists such as Benjamin Banneker, the mathematician, astronomer, almanac editor, and publisher who in 1753 built America's first clock and who, at Thomas Jefferson's behest, laid out the city of Washington, D.C.

There was Norbert Rillieux, whose pan evaporator revolutionized the sugar industry; Jan Ernst Matzeliger, inventor of the shoe-lasting machine; Elijah McCoy, the mechanical engineer who is known as "the father of lubrication" and whose automatic lubrication devices inspired the phrase "the real McCoy"; Granville T. Woods, known as "the Black Edison," George Washington Carver, botanist and agricultural chemist, known worldwide for his work with peanuts; Garrett Morgan, inventor of both the gas mask and the traffic light; D. Charles Drew, who gave the world blood plasma; Dr. Percy L. Julian, the soybean chemist, the pioneer who synthesized cortisone; Dr. Ernst E. Just, revolutionary marine biologist.

But, the myth of Harlem in the 1920s was that of a place fueled, like the rest of the country during Prohibition, by bootleg booze and gangster-run speakeasies, a place where jazz and blues ran nonstop and where the literati (novelist Wallace Thurman waggishly referred to his uptown writerly crowd as "the niggerati") boogied down year-round from midnight to noon, then went home to nurse a hangover and write about the night.

The names alone practically tell the story: poets Langston Hughes, Claude McKay, Countee Cullen, Jean Toomer; novelists Wallace Thurman, Rudolph Fisher, Zora Neale Hurston, Jessie Fauset; singers Ma Rainey, her protegée Bessie Smith, Ethel Waters, the dancer Bill "Bojangles" Robinson; multi-talented performers such as Paul Robeson, Florence Mills, vaudevillian Bert Williams; musicians such as Louis Armstrong, his pianist wife, Lil Hardin, Willie "The Lion" Smith, Earl "Fatha" Hines, Don Redman, the young Fats Waller, and Duke Ellington.

If ever there was an image that shows no sign of fading, it is the picture of Harlem and the fictitious version of the Cotton Club we get from the old movie and publicity stills. While a bubbling, slick-haired Duke Ellington—all got up in white, and all smiles—suavely bobs and sways in front of a smooth but snappy jazz band, sophisticated nightclub patrons sip their smart cocktails and pat their feet in time to what has been billed as "Jungle Music." The band itself, which seems a bit too jolly, backs up elaborately choreographed flocks of swivel-hipped, high-kicking chorus girls, shapely and comely, but leaning in complexion closer to Beige than Black. The truth is this: Black people, with rare exception, were only allowed *on stage* at the Cotton Club, not in the audience. And the painful irony of that situation is dealt with again and again in the literature produced by African American writers during this exciting period of American history.

It was a time when Prohibition was still going full-force, when Americans of all colors mostly still lived on farms, and when country and urban blues singers sang about outlaws and gangsters such as Chicago-based Al Capone. The Texas-bred blues singer Sam "Lightnin'" Hopkins, in one set of impishly poetic lyrics he wrote and recorded, has Capone telling the President of the United States" "You can run the country, / But I'm gonna run the city."

As for the cities themselves, they grew at a dizzying clip. By 1929, when the Great Depression all but destroyed the relative prosperity the United States had enjoyed, poor Blacks and Whites were already beginning to migrate from southern farms and small towns to industrialized northern cities.

One small-town girl, Zora Neale Hurston, the novelist and folklorist, who made her way from the all-Black town of Eatonville, Florida, up through Baltimore and New York City, where she became a prominent but not always visible member of the Harlem literary scene, had her own, unfashionable notions about how Black Americans should express themselves on paper. Hurston believed that it was perfectly fine to write about Black people without reference to the Black-White struggle; that is, it was necessary neither to depict African Americans as victims or losers, nor as martyrs or saints. In her celebrated novel, *Their Eyes Were Watching God*, the story of one woman's full-circle search for happiness, Hurston showed what she meant. Not only did she express her opinion in the 1930s, at a time when African Americans were being socially savaged, excluded, and lynched in record numbers, she said it at a time when women of *any* color were, like children, largely expected to be seen, but not heard.

As the economy streamlined itself, however, national interest in Black culture, the Negro Renaissance, and other human rights struggles dissipated. America was catapulted into a global war against fascism. When the war was over, the American population had shifted from rural to urban, and the industrialization mobilization of those emergency years had shifted the American economy into high gear. It took close to half a century for the United States' war economy to run out of gas.

Because culture—the lasting, ennobling product of any society—remains priceless, America is a far richer nation than it realizes. Unlike peoples of Africa, Asia, or Europe, Americans are often oblivious of their true cultural treasures. Settler-colonial nations tend to measure wealth in terms of money and military clout. As worshipers of the new, such nations-in-progress either dismiss or ignore the past, including their own history. Industrialist Henry Ford spoke for a nation when he said: "History, bunk!"

But a debunking of our history reveals that it is the stories, the art and the culture, that enrich us. As for African American literature, it is not something that was "bused" into American classrooms during the Civil Rights struggles of the sixties. Rather, African American literature is a distillation of the ways in which once-whole communities, families, lovers and strugglers, joiners and loners of African descent have experienced the United States. That is what makes this body of literature so overwhelmingly American.

From the close of World War II in 1945 to the dawn of our own age, the world changed. Germany and Japan—America's wartime enemies and postwar allies—became world economic powers. And now, as we move into the twenty-first century, young Americans of all colors and cultural backgrounds are painfully learning that they may not be able to live as well as their parents.

Something happened, but what?

As strange as it may seem, many answers to this complex question can be found in the stories, and drama, the poems and reflections of imaginative writers. "Poetry is truer than history," said Aristotle. Those poets, storytellers, dramatists, and memoirists whose works give this book its life are, in effect, sharing with the world the fruits of their experience. And, like all literature, African American literature presents an invaluable record of what lies beyond man's purely animal existence. It is the inner life of human beings, mankind's spiritual life, that literature explores. Can there ever be a more lasting or more beautiful way to testify than this?

Nurtured with sweat, watered with tears, sowed in the fertile soil of human imagination, tilled with sorrow and blood, scrap-irony and wit, paradox and hope, the bountiful crop of African American literature continues to take root and flower in the sunshine and shadow of love.

AUTOBIOGRAPHY

Jourdon Anderson

(19th Century)

This letter, written in 1865 by Jourdon Anderson to his former master, expresses all the previously checked bitterness that Anderson could not voice before he became a freedman. Besides the information found in this letter, there is very little that historians know about this former slave.

To my old Master

Dayton, Ohio, August 7, 1865.
To my old Master, Colonel P. H. Anderson, *Big Spring, Tennessee.*

Sir: I got your letter, and was glad to find that you had not forgotten Jourdon, and that you wanted me to come back and live with you again, promising to do better for me than anybody else can. I have often felt uneasy about you. I thought the Yankees would have hung you long before this, for harboring Rebs they found at your house. I suppose they never heard about your going to Colonel Martin's to kill the Union soldier that was left by his company in their stable. Although you shot at me twice before I left you, I did not want to hear of your being hurt, and am glad you are still living. It would do me good to go back to the dear old home again, and see Miss Mary and Miss Martha and Allen, Esther, Green, and Lee. Give my love to them all, and tell them I hope we will meet in the better world, if not in this. I would have gone back to see you all when I was working in the Nashville Hospital, but one of the neighbors told me that Henry intended to shoot me if he ever got a chance.

I want to know particularly what the good chance is you propose to give me. I am doing tolerably well here. I get twenty-five dollars a month, with victuals and clothing; have a comfortable home for Mandy—the folks call her Mrs. Anderson—and the children—Milly, Jane, and Grundy—go to school and are learning well. The teacher says Grundy has a head for a preacher. They go to Sunday school, and Mandy and me attend church regularly. We are kindly treated. Sometimes we overhear others saying, "Them colored people were slaves" down in Tennessee. The children feel hurt when they hear such remarks; but I tell them it was no disgrace in Tennessee to belong to Colonel Anderson. Many darkeys would have been proud, as I used to be, to call you master. Now if you will write and say what wages you will give me, I will be better able to decide whether it would be to my advantage to move back again.

As to my freedom, which you say I can have, there is nothing to be gained on that score, as I got my free papers in 1864 from the Provost-Marshal-General of the

---

1.   northern province in China

Department of Nashville. Mandy says she would be afraid to go back without some proof that you were disposed to treat us justly and kindly; and we have concluded to test your sincerity by asking you to send us our wages for the time we served you. This will make us forget and forgive old scores, and rely on your justice and friendship in the future. I served you faithfully for thirty-two years, and Mandy twenty years. At twenty-five dollars a month for me, and two dollars a week for Mandy, our earnings would amount to eleven thousand six hundred and eighty dollars. Add to this the interest for the time our wages have been kept back, and deduct what you paid for our clothing, and three doctor's visits to me, and pulling a tooth for Mandy, and the balance will show what we are in justice entitled to. Please send the money by Adam's Express, in care of V. Winters, Esq., Dayton, Ohio. If you fail to pay us for faithful labors in the past, we can have little faith in your promises in the future. We trust the good Maker has opened your eyes to the wrongs which you and your fathers have done to me and my fathers, in making us toil for you for generations without recompense. Here I draw my wages every Saturday night; but in Tennessee there was never any pay-day for the negroes any more than for the horses and cows. Surely there will be a day of reckoning for those who defraud the laborer of his hire.

In answering this letter, please state if there would be any safety for my Milly and Jane, who are now grown up, and both good-looking girls. You know how it was with poor Matilda and Catherine. I would rather stay here and starve—and die, if it come to that—than have my girls brought to shame by the violence and wickedness of their young masters. You will also please state if there has been any schools opened for the colored children in your neighborhood. The great desire of my life now is to give my children an education, and have them form virtuous habits.

Say howdy to George Carter, and thank him for taking the pistol from you when you were shooting at me.

From your old servant,
Jourdon Anderson.

Harriet A. Jacobs

(1813–1897)

    Born a slave in Edenton, North Carolina, Harriet A. Jacobs was the mother of two when she ran away from her "master" after rejecting his sexual advances. Desperate to remain near her children so that she could protect them, Jacobs remained in hiding for seven years before escaping to the North, where she eventually joined her brother, also a fugitive slave, in the abolitionist movement. Jacobs's close friendship with Quaker reformers Issac and Amy Post enabled her to meet other such notable activists as Harriet Beecher Stowe, whom she disliked, and Lydia Marie Child, who eventually became Jacobs's editor. By the time Jacobs contacted Child, **Incidents in the Life of a Slave Girl, Written by Herself** *was complete and needed only a willing publisher, which Childs was able to secure. After some initial setbacks,* **Incidents** *was published in 1861 in Boston, and a British edition appeared a year later. Because of the constraining influence of popular contemporary genteel standards,* **Incidents** *could only hint at the sexual indignities that Jacobs suffered as a female slave: "Slavery is terrible for men; but it is far more terrible for women." After enjoying some modest fame as the author of* **Incidents**, *Jacobs devoted herself to relief work for freedmen and slaves who fought for the Union Army. Although she lost track of her son after he moved to Australia in 1853, her daughter lived and worked with her until 1897, the year Jacobs died. Along with praising her accomplished writing style, modern scholars have emphasized the importance of Jacobs's accomplishment as a woman writer who, despite struggling to protect her motherhood and her sexual independence from oppressive historical forces, nonetheless transformed herself into an unforgettable literary voice.*

from
Incidents in the Life of a Slave Girl

    A small shed had been added to my grandmother's house years ago. Some boards were laid across the joists at the top, and between these boards and the roof was a very small garret, never occupied by any thing but rats and mice. It was a pent roof, covered with nothing but shingles, according to the southern custom for such buildings. The garret was only nine feet long and seven wide. The highest part was three feet high, and sloped down abruptly to the loose board floor. There was no admission for either light or air. My uncle Phillip, who was a carpenter, had very skillfully made a concealed trap-door, which communicated with the storeroom. He had been doing this while I was waiting in the swamp. The storeroom opened upon a piazza. To this hole I was conveyed as soon as I entered the house. The air was stifling; the darkness total. A bed had been spread on the floor. I could sleep quite comfortably on one side; but the slope was so sudden that I could not turn on the other without hitting the roof. The rats and mice ran over my bed; but I was weary, and I slept such sleep as the wretched may, when a tempest has passed over them. Morning came. I knew it only by the noises I heard; for in my small den day and night were all the same. I suffered for air even more than for light. But I was not comfortless. I heard the voices of my children. There was joy and there was sadness in the sound. It made my tears flow. How I longed to speak to them! I was eager to look on their faces; but there was no hole, no crack, through which I could peep. This continued darkness was oppressive. It seemed horrible to sit or lie in a cramped position day after day, without one gleam of light. Yet I would have chosen this, rather than my lot as a slave, though white people considered it an easy one; and it was so compared with the fate of others. I was never cruelly over-worked; I was never lacerated with the whip from head to foot; I was never so beaten and bruised that I could not turn from one side to the other; I never had my heel-strings cut to prevent my running away; I was never chained to a log and forced to drag it about, while I toiled in the fields from morning till night; I was never branded with hot iron, or torn by blood-hounds. On the contrary, I had always been kindly treated, and tenderly cared for, until I came into the hands of Dr. Flint. I had never wished for freedom till then. But though my life in slavery was comparatively devoid of hardships God pity the woman who is compelled to lead such a life!

My food was passed up to me through the trap-door my uncle had contrived; and my grandmother, my uncle Phillip, and aunt Nancy would seize such opportunities as they could, to mount up there and chat with me at the opening. But of course this was not safe in the daytime. It must all be done in darkness. It was impossible for me to move in an erect position, but I crawled about my den for exercise. One day I hit my head against something, and found it was a gimlet. My uncle had left it sticking there when he made the trap-door. I was as rejoiced as Robinson Crusoe could have been at finding such a treasure. It put a lucky thought into my head. I said to myself, "Now I will have some light. Now I will see my children." I did not dare to begin my work during the daytime, for fear of attracting attention. But I groped round; and having found the side next to the street, where I could frequently see my children, I stuck the gimlet in and waited for evening. I bored three rows of holes, one above another; then I bored out the interstices between. I thus succeeded in making one hole about an inch long and an inch broad. I sat by it till late into the night, to enjoy the little whiff of air that floated in. In the morning I watched for my children. The first person I saw in the street was Dr. Flint. I had a shuddering, superstitious feeling that it was a bad omen. Several familiar faces passed by. At last I heard the merry laugh of children, and presently two sweet little faces were looking up at me, as though they knew I was there, and were conscious of the joy they imparted. How I longed to *tell* them I was there!

My condition was now a little improved. But for weeks I was tormented by hundreds of little red insects, fine as a needle's point, that pierced through my skin, and produced an intolerable burning. The good grandmother gave me herb teas and cooling medicines, and finally I got rid of them. The heat of my den was intense, for nothing but thin shingles protected me from the scorching summer's sun. But I had my consolations. Through my peeping-hole I could watch the children, and when they were near enough, I could hear their talk. Aunt Nancy brought me all the news she could hear at Dr. Flint's.

From her I learned that the doctor had written to New York to a colored woman, who had been born and raised in our neighborhood, and had breathed his contaminating atmosphere. He offered her a reward if she could find out any thing about me. I know not what was the nature of her reply; but he soon after started for New York in haste, saying to his family that he had business of importance to transact. I peeped at him as he passed on his way to the steamboat. It was a satisfaction to have miles of land and water between us, even for a little while; and it was a still greater satisfaction to know that he believed me to be in the Free States. My little den seemed less dreary than it had done. He returned, as he did from his former journey to New York, without obtaining any satisfactory information. When he passed our house next morning, Benny was standing at the gate. He had heard them say that he had gone to find me, and he called out, "Dr. Flint, did you bring my mother home? I want to see her." The doctor stamped his foot at him in a rage, and exclaimed, "Get out of the way, you little damned rascal! If you don't, I'll cut off your head."

Benny ran terrified into the house, saying, "You can't put me in jail again. I don't belong to you now." It was well that the wind carried the words away from the doctor's ear. I told my grandmother of it, when we had our next conference at the trap-door; and begged of her not to allow the children to be impertinent to the irascible old man.

Autumn came, with a pleasant abatement of heat. My eyes had become accustomed to the dim light, and by holding my book or work in a certain position near the aperture I contrived to read and sew. That was a great relief to the tedious monotony of my life. But when winter came, the cold penetrated through the thin shingle roof, and I was dreadfully chilled. The winters there are not so long, or so severe, as in northern latitudes; but the houses are not built to shelter from cold, and my little den was peculiarly comfortless. The kind grandmother brought me bed-clothes and warm drinks. Often I was obliged to lie in bed all day to keep comfortable; but with all my precautions, my shoulders and feet were frostbitten. 0, those long, gloomy days, with no object for my eye to rest upon, and no thoughts to occupy my mind, except the dreary past and the uncertain future! I was thankful when there came a day sufficiently mild for me to wrap myself up and sit at the loophole to watch the passers by. Southerners have the habit of stopping and talking in the streets, and I heard many conversations not intended to meet my ears. I heard slave-hunters planning how to catch some poor fugitive. Several times I heard allusions to Dr. Flint, myself, and the history of my children, who, perhaps, were playing near the gate. One would say, "I wouldn't move my little finger to catch her, as old Flint's property." Another would say, "I'll catch *any* nigger for the reward. A man ought to have what belongs to him, if he *is* a damned brute." The opinion was often expressed that I was in the Free States. Very rarely did any one suggest that I might be in the vicinity. Had the least suspicion rested on my grandmother's house, it would have been burned to the ground. But it was the last place they thought of. Yet there was no place, where slavery existed, that could have afforded me so good a place of concealment.

Frederick Douglass

(1817–1895)

Frederick Douglass was an exceptionally accomplished journalist and orator and a fiery force in the abolitionist movement at a time when slaves were forbidden to read or write. His **Narrative of the Life of Frederick Douglass, An American Slave** *(Written by Himself; published at the Anti-Slavery Office, No. 25 Cornhill, Boston, 1845) is probably the most widely read work of its kind. The slave narrative was a popular form of literature in the eighteenth and nineteenth centuries. More than one hundred book-length slave narratives were published before the Civil War ended. Citing scholar Marion Wilson Starling's estimate that 6,000 former slaves—in interviews, essays, and books brought out between 1703 and 1944—had recounted their lives and experiences, Harvard's Henry Louis Gates, Jr. has written: "No group of slaves anywhere, at any other period of history, has left such a large repository of testimony about the horror of becoming the legal property of another human being." Born to a Black slave mother and a White planter, at Tuckahoe, Maryland, Frederick Augustus Washington Bailey assumed the name "Douglass" after escaping a Baltimore plantation by train. His remarkable life as a ship caulker, sailor, and day laborer took him to New York and Massachusetts, where his rhetorical genius came to the attention of the Massachusetts Anti-Slavery Society. His subsequent lecture tours took him throughout New England and the Midwest, and from 1845 to 1847, still technically a fugitive slave, Douglass "toured" England, Scotland, and Ireland. On his return, he founded the* **North Star***, a weekly abolitionist journal later known as* **Frederick Douglass's Paper***. A firebrand in his youth, Douglass became an éminence grise following the Civil War (he called for the deployment of Black troops by Union forces). From 1889 to 1891 he was American Minister Resident and Consul-General in the Republic of Haiti.*

from
Narrative of the Life of Frederick Douglass, An American Slave

I have already intimated that my condition was much worse, during the first six months of my stay at Mr. Covey's, than in the last six. The circumstances leading to the change in Mr. Covey's course toward me form an epoch in my humble history. You have seen how a man was made a slave; you shall see how a slave was made a man. On one of the hottest days of the month of August, 1833, Bill Smith, William Hughes, a slave named Eli, and myself, were engaged in fanning wheat. Hughes was clearing the fanned wheat from before the fan. Eli was turning, Smith was feeding, and I was carrying wheat to the fan. The work was simple, requiring strength rather than intellect; yet, to one entirely unused to such work, it came very hard. About three o'clock of that day, I broke down; my strength failed me; I was seized with a violent aching of the head, attended with extreme dizziness; I trembled in every limb. Finding what was coming, I nerved myself up, feeling it would never do to stop work. I stood as long as I could stagger to the hopper with grain. When I could stand no longer, I fell, and felt as if held down by an immense weight. The fan of course stopped; every one had his own work to do; and no one could do the work of the other, and have his own go on at the same time.

Mr. Covey was at the house, about one hundred yards from the treading-yard where we were fanning. On hearing the fan stop, he left immediately, and came to the spot where we were. He hastily inquired what the matter was. Bill answered that I was sick, and there was no one to bring wheat to the fan. I had by this time crawled away under the side of the post and rail-fence by which the yard was enclosed, hoping to find relief by getting out of the sun. He then asked where I was. He was told by one of the hands. He came to the spot, and, after looking at me awhile, asked me what was the matter. I told him as well as I could, for I scarce had strength to speak. He then gave me a savage kick in the side, and told me to get up. I tried to do so, but fell back in the attempt. He gave me another kick, and again told me to rise. I again tried, and succeeded in gaining my feet; but, stooping to get the tub with which I was feeding the fan, I again staggered and fell. While down in this situation, Mr. Covey took up the hickory slat with which Hughes had been striking off the half-bushel measure, and with it gave me a heavy blow upon the head, making a large wound, and the blood ran freely; and with this again told me to get up. I made no effort to comply, having now made up my mind to let him do his worst. In a short time after receiving this blow, my head grew better. Mr. Covey had now left me to my fate. At this moment I resolved, for the first time, to go to my master, enter a complaint, and ask his protection. In order to do this, I must that afternoon walk seven miles; and this, under the circumstances, was truly a severe undertaking. I was exceedingly feeble; made so as much by the kicks and blows which I received, as by the severe fit of sickness to which I had been subjected. I, however, watched my chance, while Covey was looking in an opposite direction, and started for St. Michael's. I succeeded in getting a considerable distance on my way to the woods, when Covey discovered me, and called after me to come back, threatening what he would do if I did not come. I disregarded both his calls and his threats, and made my way to the woods as fast as my feeble state would allow; and thinking I might be overhauled by him if I kept the road, I walked through the woods, keeping far enough from the road to avoid detection, and near enough to prevent losing my way. I had not gone far before my little strength again failed me. I could go no farther. I fell down, and lay for a considerable time. The blood was yet oozing from the wound on my head. For a time I thought I should bleed to death; and think now that I should have done so, but that the blood so matted my hair as to stop the wound. After lying there about three quarters of an hour, I nerved myself up again, and started on my way, through bogs and briers, barefooted and bareheaded, tearing my feet sometimes at nearly every step; and after a journey of about seven miles, occupying some five hours to perform it, I arrived at master's store. I then presented an appearance enough to affect any but a heart of iron. From the crown of my head to my feet, I was covered with blood. My hair was all clotted with dust and blood; my shirt was stiff with blood. My legs and feet were torn in sundry places with briers and thorns, and were also covered with blood. I suppose I looked like a man who had entered a den of wild beasts, and barely escaped them. In this state I appeared before my master, humbly entreating him to interpose his authority for my protection. I told him all the circumstances as well as I could, and it seemed, as I spoke, at times to affect him. He would then walk the floor, and seek to justify Covey by saying he expected I deserved it. He asked me what I wanted. I told him, to let me get a new home; that as sure as I lived with Mr. Covey again, I should live with but to die with him; that Covey would surely kill me; he was in a fair way for it. Master Thomas ridiculed the idea that there was any danger of Mr. Covey's killing me, and said that he knew Mr. Covey; that he was a good man, and that he could not think of taking me from him; that, should he do so, he would lose the whole year's wages; that I belonged to Mr. Covey for one year, and that I must go back to him, come what might; and that I must not trouble him with any more stories, or that he would himself *get hold of me*. After threatening me thus, he gave me a very large dose of salts, telling me that I might remain in St. Michael's that night, (it being quite late,) but that I must be off back to Mr. Covey's early in the morning; and that if I did not, he would *get hold of me*, which meant that he would whip me. I remained all night, and, according to his orders, I started off to Covey's in the morning (Saturday morning), wearied in body and broken in spirit. I got no supper that night, or breakfast that morning. I reached Covey's about nine o'clock; and just as I was getting over the fence that divided Mrs. Kemp's fields from ours, out ran Covey with his cowskin, to give me another whipping. Before he could reach me, I succeeded in getting to the cornfield; and as the corn was very high, it afforded me the means of hiding. He seemed very angry, and searched for me a long time. My behavior was altogether unaccountable. He finally gave up the chase, thinking, I suppose, that I must come home for something to eat; he would give himself no further trouble in looking for me. I spent that day mostly in the woods, having the alternative before me—to go home and be whipped to death, or stay in the woods and be starved to death. That night, I fell in with Sandy Jenkins, a slave with whom I was somewhat acquainted. Sandy had a free wife who lived about four miles from Mr. Covey's; and it being Saturday, he was on his way to see her. I told him my circumstances, and he very kindly invited me to go home with him. I went home with him, and talked this whole matter over, and got his advice as to what course it was best for me to pursue. I found Sandy an old adviser. He told me, with great solemnity, I must go back to Covey; but that before I went, I must go with him into another part of the woods, where there was a certain *root*, which, if I would take some of it with me, carrying it *always on my right side*, would render it impossible for Mr. Covey, or any other white man, to whip me. He said he had carried it for years; and since he had done so, he had never received a blow, and never expected to while he carried it. I at first rejected the idea, that the simple carrying of a root in my pocket would have any such effect as he had said, and was not disposed to take it; but Sandy impressed the necessity with much earnestness, telling me it could do no harm, if it did no good. To please him, I at length took the root, and, according to his direction, carried it upon my right side. This was Sunday morning. I immediately started for home; and upon entering the yard gate, out came Mr. Covey on his way to meeting. He spoke to me very kindly, bade me drive the pigs from a lot near by, and passed on towards the church. Now, this singular conduct of Mr. Covey really made me begin to think that there was something in the *root* which Sandy had given me; and had it been on any other day than Sunday, I could have attributed the conduct to no other cause than the influence of that root; and, as it was, I was half inclined to think the *root* to be something more than I at first had taken it to be. All went well till Monday morning. On this morning, the virtue of the *root* was fully tested. Long before daylight, I was called to go and rub, curry, and feed, the horses. I obeyed, and was glad to obey. But whilst thus engaged, whilst in the act of throwing down some blades from the loft, Mr. Covey entered the stable with a long rope; and just as I was half out of the loft, he caught hold of my legs, and was about tying me. As soon as I found what he was up to, I gave a sudden spring, and as I did so, he holding to my legs, I was brought sprawling on the stable floor. Mr. Covey seemed now to think he had me, and could do what he pleased; but at this moment—from whence came the spirit I don't know—I resolved to fight; and, suiting my action to the resolution, I seized Covey hard by the throat; and as I did so, I rose. He held on to me, and I to him. My resistance was so entirely unexpected, that Covey seemed taken all aback. He trembled like a leaf. This gave me assurance, and I held him uneasy, causing the blood to run where I touched him with the ends of my fingers. Mr. Covey soon called out to Hughes for help. Hughes came, and, while Covey held me, attempted to tie my right hand. While he was in the act of doing so, I watched my chance, and gave him a heavy kick close under the ribs. This kick fairly sickened Hughes, so that he left me in the hands of Mr. Covey. This kick had the effect of not only weakening Hughes, but Covey also. When he saw Hughes bending over with pain, his courage quailed. He asked me if I meant to persist in my resistance. I told him I did, come what might; that he had used me like a brute for six months, and that I was determined to be used so no longer. With that, he strove to drag me to a stick that was lying just out of the stable door. He meant to knock me down. But just as he was leaning over to get the stick, I seized him with both hands by his collar, and brought him by a sudden snatch to the ground. By this time, Bill came. Covey called upon him for assistance. Bill wanted to know what he could do. Covey said, "Take hold of him, take hold of him!" Bill said his master hired him out to work, and not to help whip me; so he left Covey and myself to fight our own battle out. We were at it for nearly two hours. Covey at length let me go, puffing and blowing at a great rate, saying that if I had not resisted, he would not have whipped me half so much. The truth was, that he had not whipped me at all. I considered him as getting entirely the worst end of the bargain; for he had drawn no blood from me, but I had from him. The whole six months afterwards, that I spent with Mr. Covey, he never laid the weight of his finger upon me in anger. He would occasionally say, he didn't want to get hold of me again. "No," thought I, "you need not; for you will come off worse than you did before."

This battle with Mr. Covey was the turning-point in my career as a slave. It rekindled the few expiring embers of freedom, and revived within me a sense of my own manhood. It recalled the departed self-confidence, and inspired me again with a determination to be free. The gratification afforded by the triumph was a full compensation for whatever else might follow, even death itself. He only can understand the deep satisfaction which I experienced, who has himself repelled by force the bloody arm of slavery. I felt as I never felt before. It was a glorious resurrection, from the tomb of slavery, to the heaven of freedom. My long-crushed spirit rose, cowardice departed, bold defiance took its place; and I now resolved that, however long I might remain a slave in form, the day had passed forever when I could be a slave in fact. I did not hesitate to let it be known of me, that the white man who expected to succeed in whipping, must also succeed in killing me.

From this time I was never again what might be called fairly whipped, though I remained a slave four years afterwards. I had several fights, but was never whipped.

It was for a long time a matter of surprise to me why Mr. Covey did not immediately have me taken by the constable to the whipping post, and there regularly whipped for the crime of raising my hand against a white man in defence of myself. And the only explanation I can now think of does not entirely satisfy me; but such as it is, I will give it. Mr. Covey enjoyed the most unbounded reputation for being a first-rate overseer and negro-breaker. It was of considerable importance to him. That reputation was at stake; and had he sent me—a boy about sixteen years old—to the public whipping-post, his reputation would have been lost; so, to save his reputation, he suffered me to go unpunished.

Lorenzo Ezell

(WPA Archives)

*At the time of this interview—conducted by an unidentified WPA Federal Writers'
Project interviewer at Beaumont, Texas—ex-slave Lorenzo Ezell was 87 years of age.
Collected between 1936 and 1939,* **Slave Narratives, a Folk History of Slavery in the
United States from Interviews with Former Slaves** *was preserved in typewritten
pages by the Federal Writers' Project, Washington, D.C., in 1941. The eldest of seven
children, Lorenzo Ezell was reared on the South Carolina plantation he so vividly
describes. This account of his early upbringing and migrations typified the experience
of many slaves whose lives were changed by the Civil War. The hymns and folk songs
with which he peppers his spoken narrative are poetically rich in mythical significance.*

I Could Be a Conjure Doctor and Make Plenty Money

Us Plantation was just east from Pacolet Station on Thicketty Creek, Spartanburg
County, in South Carolina. Dat near Little and Big Pacolet Rivers on de route to Limestone
Springs, and it just a ordinary plantation with de main crops cotton and wheat.

I belong to de Lipscombs and my mamma, Maria Ezell, she belong to 'em too.
Old Ned Lipscomb was amongst de oldest citizens of dat county. I'se born dere on
July 29, in 1850, and I be eighty-seven year old dis year. Levi Ezell, he my daddy, and
he belong to Landrum Ezell, a Baptist preacher. Dat young massa and de old massa,
John Ezell, was de first Baptist preecher I ever heered of. He have three sons, Landrum,
and Judson, and Bryson. Bryson have gift for business and was right smart of a orator.

Dey's fourteen niggers on de Lipscomb place. Dey's seven of us chillen, my
mamma, three uncle, and three aunt, and one man what wasn't no kin to us. I was
oldest of de chillen, and dey called Sallie and Carrie and Alice and Jabus and Coy and
LaFate and Rufus and Nelson.

Old Ned Lipscomb was one de best massa in de whole county. You know dem
old patterollers, dey call us "Old Ned's free niggers," and sure hate us. Dey cruel to
us, 'cause dey think us have too good a massa. One time dey cotch my uncle and beat
him most to death.

Us go to work at daylight, but us wasn't abused. Other massas used to blow de
horn or ring de bell, but Massa, he never use de horn or de whip. All de man folks was
allowed raise a garden patch with tobaccy or cotton for to sell in de market. Wasn't
many massas what allowed dere niggers have patches and some didn't even feed 'em
enough. Dat's why dey have to get out and hustle at night to get food for dem to eat.

De old massa, he insisted us go to church. De Baptist church have a shed built behind de pulpit for cullud folks, with de dirt floor and split log seat for de women folks, but most de men folks stands or kneels on de floor. Dey used to call dat de coop. De white preacher back to us, but iffen he want to he turn around and talk to us awhile. Us makes up songs, 'cause us couldn't read or write. I 'member dis one:

> De rough, rocky road what Moses done travel,
> I'se bound to carry my soul to de Lord;
> It's a mighty rocky road but I must done travel,
> And I'se bound to carry my soul to de Lord.

Us sing "Sweet Chariot," but us didn't sing it like dese days. Us sing:

> Swing low, sweet chariot,
> Freely let me into rest,
> I don't want to stay here no longer;
> Swing low, sweet chariot,
> When Gabriel make he last alarm
> I wants to be rollin' in Jesus arm,
> 'Cause I don't want to stay here no longer.

Us sing another song what de Yankees take dat tune and make a hymn out of it. Sherman army sung it, too. We have it like dis:

> Our bodies bound to morter and decay,
> Our bodies bound to morter and decay,
> Our bodies bound to morter and decay,
> But us souls go marchin' home.

Before de War I just big enough to drop corn and tote water. When de little white chillen go to school about half mile, I wait till noon and run all de way up to de school to run base when dey play at noon. Dey several young Lipscombs, dere Smith and Bill and John and Nathan, and de oldest son, Elias.

In dem days cullud people just like mules and hosses. Dey didn't have no last name. My mamma call me after my daddy's massa, Ezell. Mamma was de good woman and I 'member her more dan once rockin' de little cradle and singin' to de baby. Dis what she sing:

Milk in de dairy nine days old,
Sing-song Kitty, can't you ki-me-o?
Frogs and skeeters gittin' mighty bold
Sing-song, Kitty, can't you ki-me-o?

(Chorus)

Keemo, kimo, darro, wharro,
With me hi, me ho;
In come Sally singin'
Sometime penny winkle,
Lingtum nip cat,
Sing-song, Kitty, can't you ki-me-o?

Dere a frog live in a pool,
Sing-song, Kitty, can't you ki-me-o?
Sure he was de biggest fool,
Sing-song, Kitty, can't you ki-me-o?

For he could dance and he could sing
Sing-song, Kitty, can't you ki-me-o?
And make de woods around him ring
Sing-song, Kitty, can't you ki-me-o?

Old massa didn't hold with de way some mean massas treat dey niggers. Dere a place on our plantation what us call "de old meadow." It was common for runaway niggers to have place along de way to hide and rest when dey run off from mean massa. Massa used to give 'em somethin' to eat when dey hide dere. I saw dat place operated, though it wasn't knowed by dat den, but long time after I finds out dey call it part of de "underground railroad." Dey was stops like dat all de way up to de North.

We have went down to Columbia when I about eleven year old and dat where de first gun fired. Us rush back home, but I could say I heered de first guns of de War shot, at Fort Sumter.

When General Sherman come across de Savannah River in South Carolina, some of de soldiers come right across us plantation. All de neighbors have brung dey cotton and stack it in de thicket on de Lipscomb place. Sherman's men find it and set it on fire. Dat cotton stack was big as a little courthouse and it took two months burnin'.

My old massa run off and stay in de woods a whole week when Sherman men come through. He didn't need to worry, 'cause us took care of everything. Dey a funny song us make up about him runnin' off in de woods. I know it was make up, 'cause my uncle have a hand in it. It went like dis:

> White folks, have you seed old massa
> Up de road, with he mustache on?
> He pick up he hat and he leave real sudden
> And I believe he's up and gone.
>
> Old massa run away
> And us darkies stay at home.
> It must be now dat Kingdom's comin'
> And de year of Jubilee.
>
> He look up de river and he seed dat smoke,
> where de Lincoln gunboats lay.
> He big 'nough and he old 'nough and he orter know better,
> But he gone and run away.
>
> Now dat overseer want to give trouble
> And trot us 'round a spell.
> But we lock him up in de smokehouse cellar,
> With de key done throwed in de well.

Right after dat I start to be boy what run mail from camp to camp for de soldiers. One time I was capture by a bunch of deserters what was hidin' in de woods along Pacolet River. Dey didn't hurt me, though, but dey most scare me to death. Dey parole me and turn me loose.

All four my young massas go to de War, all but Elias. He too old. Smith, he kilt at Manassas Junction. Nathan, he get he finger shot at de first round at Fort Sumter. But when Billy was wounded at Howard Gap in North Carolina and dey brung him home with he jaw split open, I so mad I could have kilt all de Yankees. I say I be happy iffen I could kill me just one Yankee. I hated dem 'cause dey hurt my white people. Billy was disfigure awful when he jaw split and he teeth all shine through he cheek.

After war was over, Old Massa call us up and told us we free but he advise not leave de place till de crop was through. Us all stay. Den us select us homes and move to it. Us folks move to Sam Littlejohn's, north of Thicketty Creek, where us stay two year. Den us move back to Billy Lipscomb, de young massa, and stay dere two more year. I'se right smart good banjo picker in dem day. I can 'member one dem songs just as good today as when I pick it. Dat was:

Early in de mornin'
Don't you head de dogs a-barkin'?
Bow, wow, wow!

Hush, hush, boys,
Don't make a noise,
Massa's fast a-sleepin'.
Run to de barnyard,
Wake up de boys,
Let's have banjo pickin'.

Early in de mornin'
Don't you hear dem roosters crowin'?
Cock-a-doodle-do.

I came in contact with de Klu Klux. Us left de plantation in '65 or '66 and by '68 us was havin' such a awful time with de Klu Klux. First time dey come to my mamma's house at midnight and claim dey soldiers done come back from de dead. Dey all dress up in sheets and make up like spirit. Dey groan around and say dey been kilt wrongly and come back for justice. One man, he look just like ordinary man, but he spring up about eighteen feet high all of a sudden. Another say he so thirsty he ain't have no water since he been kilt at Manassas Junction. He ask for water and he just kept pourin' it in. Us think he sure must be a spirit to drink dat much water. Course he not drinkin' it, he pourin' it in a bag under he sheet. My mamma never did take up no truck with spirits so she knowed it just a man. Dey tell us what dey gwine do iffen we don't all go back to us massas and us all agrees and den dey all disappear.

Den us move to New Prospect on de Pacolet River, on de Perry Clemmons place. Dat in de upper edge of de county and dat where de second swarm of de Klu Klux come out. Dey claim dey gwine kill everybody what am republican. My daddy charge with bein' a leader amongst de niggers. He make speech and instruct de niggers how to vote for Grant's first election. De Klu Klux want to whip him and he have to sleep in a hollow log every night.

Dey's a old man name Uncle Bart what live about half mile from us. De Klu Klux come to us house one night, but my daddy done hid. Den I hear dem say dey gwine go kill old man Bart. I jump out de window and shortcut through dem wood and warn him. He get out de house in time and I save he life. De funny thing, I knowed all dem Klu Klux spite dey sheets and things, I knowed dey voices and dey saddle hosses.

Dey one white man name Irving Ramsey. Us play fiddle together lots of time. When de white boys dance dey always wants me to go to play for dey party. One day I say to dat boy, "I done knowed you last night." He say, "What you mean?" I say, "You one dem Klu Klux." He want to know how I know. I say, "Member when you go under the chestnut tree and say, "Whoa, Sont, whoa, Sont, to your hoss?" He say, "Yes." And I laugh and say, "Well, I'se right up in dat tree." Dey all knowed I knowed dem den, but I never told on dem. When dey seed I ain't gwine to tell, dey never try whip my daddy or kill Uncle Bart no more.

I ain't never been to school but I just picked up readin'. With some my first money I ever earn I buy me a old blue-back Webster. I carry dat book wherever I goes. When I plows down a row I stop at de end to rest and den I overlook de lesson. I 'member one de very first lessons was, "Evil communications corrupts good morals." I knowed de words "evil" and "good" and a white man explain de others. I been done use dat lesson all my life.

After us left de Pacolet River us stay in Atlanta a little while and den I go on to Louisiana. I done left Spartanburg completely in '76 but I didn't git into Texas till 1882. I finally get to Brenham, Texas and marry Rachel Pinchbeck two year after. Us was marry in church and have seven chillen. Den us separate. I been batching about twenty year and I done lost track most dem chillen. My gal, Lula, live in Beaumont, and Will, he in Chicago.

Every time I tells dese niggers I'se from South Carolina dey all say, "Oh, he bound to make a heap." I could be a conjure doctor and make plenty money, but dat ain't good. In slavery time dey's men like dat regarded as bein' dangerous. Dey make charms and put bad mouth on you. De old folks wears de rabbit foot or coon foot and sometime a silver dime on a fishin' string to keep off de witches. Some dem old conjure people make lots of money for charm against ruin or cripplin' or dry up de blood. But I don't take up no truck with things like dat.

Marriah Hines

(WPA Archives)

Marriah Hines's straightforward remembrance of life on the plantation where she grew up assures us that slavemasters were individuals; they were not all like Simon LeGree, the cruel, degenerate planter who terrorized the good-hearted Uncle Tom and innocent Little Eva in Harriet Beecher Stowe's 1852 classic novel, **Uncle Tom's Cabin**. *Hines was 102 years old when WPA Federal Writers' Project interviewer David Hoggard, himself African American, spoke with her near Norfolk, Virginia, in the late 1930s. The tone of Marriah Hines's narrative about her "good white folks" is in ways remindful of the anti-affirmative action sentiments of certain officially endorsed Black writers in the post-Civil Rights Eighties.*

My White Folks Treated Us Good

I lived with good people. My white folks treated us good. There was plenty of 'em that didn't fare as we did. Some of the poor folks almost starved to death. Why, the way their masters treated them was scandalous, treated them like cats and dogs. We always had plenty of food, never knowed what it was to want food bad enough to have to steal it like a whole lot of 'em. Master would always give us plenty when he give us our rations. Of course we slaves were given food and clothing and just enough to keep us goin' good. Why, master would buy cloth by the loads and heaps, shoes by the big boxful; den he'd call us to the house and give each of us our share. Plenty to keep us comfortable. Course it weren't silk nor satin, no ways the best there was, but 'twas plenty good 'nough for us, and we was plenty glad to get it. When we would look and see how the slaves on the joining farm was faring, 'twould almost make us shed tears. It made us feel like we was getting along most fine. Dat's why we loved and respected Master, 'cause he was so good to us. 'Cause Master was good and kind to us, some of the other white folks used to call him "nigger lover." He didn't pay dat no mind, though. He was a true Christian man, and I mean he sure lived up to it. He never did force any of us to go to church if we didn't want to. Dat was left to us to decide. If you wanted to you could; if you didn't you didn't have to. But he'd always tell us, you ought to go.

Not only was Master good but his whole family was, too. When the weather was good we worked in the fields and on other little odd jobs that was needed done. We slaves would eat our breakfast, and go to the fields; dere weren't no hurry-scurry. Lots o' times when we got in the fields the other slaves had been in the field a long time. Dere was times, though, we had to get to it early, too. 'Specially if it had been rainy weather and the work had been held up for a day or so. Master didn't make us work at all in bad weather, neither when it got real cold. The men might have to get in firewood or somethin' of that sort but no all day work in the cold—just little odd jobs. We didn't even have to work on Sundays, not even in the "house." The master and the preacher both said dat was the Lord's day and you weren't supposed to work on that day. So we didn't. We'd cook the white folks victuals on Saturday and lots o' times dey eat cold victuals on Sundays.

Master would sometimes ask the preacher home to dinner. "You plenty welcome to go home with me for dinner, but you'll have to eat cold victuals 'cause there ain't no cooking on Sundays at my house." Lots of times we slaves would take turns on helping 'em serve Sunday meals just 'cause we liked them so much. We hated to see Missus fumbling round in the kitchen all out o' her place. We didn't have to do it; we just did it on our own free will. Master sometimes gives us a little money for it, too, which made it all the better. Master and Missus was so good to us we didn't mind working a little on Sunday, in the house.

Master had prayer with the whole family every night, prayed for us slaves too. Any of the slaves that wanted to join him could. Or if they wanted to pray by demselves they could. Sundays we went to church and stayed the biggest portion of the day. Nobody had to rush home.

On our plantation we had general prayer meeting every Wednesday night at church. 'Cause some of the masters didn't like the way we slaves carried on we would turn pots down and tubs to keep the sound from going out. Den we would have a good time, shouting, singing, and praying just like we pleased. The patterrollers didn't pay us much attention 'cause they knew how Master let us do. Dey would say nasty things about Master 'cause he let us do like we did.

We had plenty time to ourselves. Most of the time we spent singing and praying 'cause Master was such a good Christian and most of us had confessed religion. Evenings we would spin on the old spinning wheel, quilt, make clothes, talk, tell jokes, and a few had learned to weave a little bit from Missus. We would have candy pulls from cooked molasses and sing in the moonlight by the tune of an old banjo picker. Chillen was mostly seen, not heard, different from younguns of today talking backward and forward cross their mammies and pappies. Chillen dat did dat would get de breath slapped out on 'em. Your mammies didn't have to do it, either; any old person would and send you home to get another lickin'.

We slaves had two hours off for dinner, when we could go home and eat before we finished work about sundown. We ain't had no colored overseers to whip us nor no white ones. We just went along so and did what we had to, without nobody watching over us. Everybody was just plumb crazy about Master. During the day you could see him strutting down the field like a big turkey gobbler to see how the work was going on. Always had a smile and a joke with you. He always tell us we was doing fine, even sometimes when we weren't. We'd always catch up our work, so he wouldn't have to fuss. We loved Missus and the chillen so much we wouldn't even let 'em eat hardly, Missus didn't have to do nothing, hardly. Dere was always some of us round the house.

About a year before we heard about freedom, Master took sick and the slaves wouldn't a-looked sadder if one of their own younguns had been sick. Dey 'spected him to die, and he kept calling for some cabbage. Missus finally let me cook him some cabbage and let him have some "pot likker" (the water the cabbage was cooked in). He didn't die den, but a few years later he did die. Dat was the first and the last time any cooking ever was done in that house on Sunday.

When Master told us we was free it didn't take much effect on us. Told us we could go where we pleased and come when we pleased, that we didn't have to work for him any more 'less we wanted to. Most of us slaves stayed right there and raised our own crops. Master helped us much as he could. Some of us he gave a cow or a mule or anything he could spare to help us. Some of us worked on the same plantation and bought our own little farms and little log cabins, and lived right there till Master died and the family moved away. Some of us lived there right on. Master married me to one of the best colored men in the world, Benjamin F. Hines. I had five chillen by him, four girls and one boy; two of the girls and the boy are dead. Dey died about 1932 or '33. I stay with one a while, den I go and stay a while with the other one.

Lizzie Williams

(WPA Archives)

The Selma, Alabama, where Lizzie Williams was born before the Civil War in the 1860s, and the Selma, Alabama, of the Civil Rights movement of the 1960s seem, by her account, to have shared much in common. Williams' account of her treatment as a slave is particularly striking. The picture of slavery she paints is complex and nuanced, especially as she shares her observations about mulatto offspring, the burning of Selma, and the Ku Klux Klan. Williams was interviewed at the age of 90 at Asheville, North Carolina, by the Federal Writers' Project's Marjorie Jones.

Don't Guess Names Matter Much No Way

I'se born in Selma, Alabama, I can't mind how long ago, but just about ninety years. I come to dis country about 1882. I'se purty poorly dese days and I'se gettin' homesick for my old home.

I'se born and live on old man Billy Johnson's plantation—thousands acres of ground and plenty of niggers. My pappy, he always belong to old man Billy. He not such a bad man but de Lord knows I'se seed better ones. When I'se right smart size, Missy Mixon, she was Marse Billy's wife's sister, she get Marse Billy to let her have me. She was a good woman. She took me to town to live and make a little white girl out of me. Y'all knows what I means. I got treated more like de white folks dan de rest of de niggers.

But 'twarn't long afore Missy send me to New Orleans to nurse de sick child of her sister. I never was satisfied down dere. Everybody so different. But de next year we go back to Alabama.

I went to Marse Ellis Mixon's. He terrible mean to his niggers. But I belong to de missus, she always treat me good. All de little niggers have to learn to work when dey little; get out and pull weeds. Dey never had no time to play. Most dem niggers was scared to death, just like de ones on Billy Johnson's plantation. Dey know dey get whipped just like a mule if dey act like dey don't wanna work. Dey never get much to eat, just side meat, corn bread and 'lasses. Old Billy he had overseers what was mean to de poor niggers. Sometime dey ties dem up and dey strip dem and dey whips dem with cowhide, else dey lets other niggers do it.

All de niggers have to go to church, just like de white folks. Dey have a part of de church for demselfs. After de War we have a church of our own. All de niggers love to go to church and sing. I mind a lot of de songs we used to sing in de fields. I mind

my pappy used to sing in de field: "Get on Board, Little Chillen, Get on Board."
Sometimes dey baptize in de river. Den dey sing:

> I wanna be ready,
> I wanna be ready,
> I wanna be ready, good Lord, to walk in Jerusalem just like John.
> John say de city was just four square,
> To walk in Jerusalem just like John,
> But I'll meet my mother and father dere,
> To walk in Jerusalem, just like John.

I 'members about de patterrollers. De niggers have to get a pass from de massa
or de missus if dey go anywhere. De patterrollers just like police. About dozen of
dem ride along together. First thing dey say: "Where you pass?" Den if you have one
dey lets you go but if you don't have one dey strips you to de waist and dey lams you
good till de blood comes. Sometimes dey rolls you over a barrel and lams you while
de barrel rolls.

I mind a tale my pappy tell about one time he see de patterrollers comin'. He
scared to death 'cause he didn't have no pass. He know if dey finds him what dey do.
So Pappy he gets down in de ditch and throw sand and grunts like a hog. Sure 'nough,
dey thinks he a hog and dey pass on, 'cept one who was behind de others. He say,
"Dat am de gruntin'est old hog I ever hear. I think I go see him." But de others dey
say: "Just let dat old hog alone and mind you own business." So dey pass on. Pappy
he laugh about dat for long time.

I mind old Mose, he have monthly pass from de massa but he forget it one day
and de patterrollers whip him and throw him in de calaboose. In de mornin' when de
massa wake and find no fresh water and no fire in de stove and de cows not milked, he
say: "I know Mose in de calaboose," and he have to go after Mose.

Lots of de poor niggers run away, but 'twarn't no use. Dere weren't no place to
go. Dey was always lookin' for you and den you had to work harder dan ever, besides
all kinds of punishment you got. Den dey nearly starve you to death, just feed you on
bread and water for long time.

De niggers never know nothin' about learnin', just work all dey's fit for. De only
thing I ever do with a book is just to dust it off. I mind two little niggers whose missy
teach dem to read. Emily, she look like a white gal. She was treated just like she
white. Her daddy was a white man. Emily was a smart gal. She belong to one of de
Johnson mens. She do all de sewin' for her missy. When de missy go to buy clothes
for de chillen she always take Emily along. Her pappy pay no more attention to her
dan to de rest of de niggers. But de missy she was good to her. She never stay in de

quarters; she stay in de house with de white folks. But Emily had de saddest look on her yaller face 'cause de other niggers whisper about her pappy. Many de poor nigger women have chillen for de massa, dat is if de massa a mean man. Dey just tell de niggers what to do and dey know better dan to fuss.

Old Missus she good to me. I mind one time I got terrible mad and say some ugly words. Marse Ellis he come up behind me and he say: "Lizabeth I gwine to wallop you good for dat." I commence cryin' and run to de missus and she say: "Look here, Ellis Mixon, y'all mind you own business and look after you own niggers. Dis one belongs to me." Just de same, when de missus went upstairs Marse Ellis take me in de smokehouse and start to hit me. I yell for de missus and when she come she plenty mad. Marse say he never meant to whip me, just scare me a little.

I mind about de War. We niggers never know what it about. We just go on and work. Never see nothin', never hear nothin', never say nothin', but de War all round. Every day we hear dat de Yankee soldiers comin'. De plantations was gettin' robbed. Everybody kept a-hidin' things. It was a terrible time. I mind plain when dey comes to Selma. All de folks was at church when de Yankees come. Dey weren't no fightin' much, dey didn't have time. Dey just march in and take de town. But Oh lordy, dat night dey burn de stores and houses and take all de things dey want. Cannons and guns all round, it was terrible sight.

Marse Ellis' plantation about fifteen mile from Selma on Pea Ridge. I mind one night Marse come home from town and he say: " 'Lizabeth." I say, "Yes sir." He say: "Bring me some fresh water from de spring." I run as fast as I can and bring de water and give it to him. Den he say: "'Lizabeth, de Yankees am comin' soon, and I knows you's gwine to tell 'em where I hide all my belongings, guns and everything."

"No," I says, "just why would I tell where you hide you guns and things?" Missy come in den and she say: "Go on and let Lizzie alone, better be feared dem niggers you done so mean to gwine tell, dat's all you got to be feared of. But you let Lizzie alone, she belong to me."

Marse Ellis he go out and hide some more stuff. Dat night de soldiers burn Selma. Dat were on Sunday. Next night we wake up in de middle of de night and de house where we keep de best carriage and horse was a-burnin'. De poor horse done break out of de barn and was a-runnin' round all over de place a-screamin' with her poor back burnt terrible. We never find out if de Yankees set de barn fire or not. Guess dey did. Dey done set Marse Hyde's house afire and burn it to de grownd with Marse Hyde in it. Marse Hyde, he had plantation in New Orleans and when de Yankees take de town Marse Hyde, he promise not to leave, but when de soldiers know he escape dey come to his house on Pea Ridge. When de Yankees find him here, dey burn him in de house with all his belongings.

On de Tuesday mornin' after dey burn Selma I wake up to see Marse Ellis' plantation all surrounded with Yankee soldiers. I was nigh scared to death. I so afraid dey hurt me and Missy but dey didn't, dey just march through de house and when dey see Marse Ellis dey ask him for he guns and things dey want. Marse Ellis show dem where de things were. 'Twarn't no use to do anything else. I take Marse Frank's tobacco and hide it in de missus' trunk. Den when de soldiers get what dey want dey laugh and march away on de hill.

After de surrender all de niggers just lost. Nowhere to go, nothin' to do, unless dey stay with de massa. Nobody have anything but 'Federate money and it was no good. My pappy had about three hundred dollars but 'twarn't no good at all.

All some of de white folks think of was killin' de poor niggers what worked for dem for years. Dey just scour de country and shoot dem, especially de young men. One day dey come down de road towards my pappy. Dey start askin' questions about what he gwine to do now he free. "What I gwine to do?" says Pappy. "What can I do? I just stay on de plantation and help Old Massa if I can get an old mule and a piece of an old plow." One of de boys look at Pappy and say "I like take you head for a target," but de old man with dem say, "No," so dey leave my pappy alone.

Dey have de commissary where de folks get food; it belong to de Yankee soldiers. Food scarce like everything. Folks say now dey have hard times; dey won't know nothin' about hard times 'less day live in wartime and be slave to white folks.

Den dey was de Ku Klux Klan. Dey were frightful lookin' critters. My pappy say dey go out in de country and tie poor niggers to de tree and beat 'em to death. Dey dress all kinds of fashions. Most of dem look like ghosts. Dey never go like de patterrollers; dey just sneak round at night when de poor niggers in bed. Den about twelve o'clock dey tie up all de niggers dey catch and after dey through beatin' dem, dey leaves dem with dey hands tied in de air and de blood a-streamin' out of dey backs.

After freedom I come here to live with my folks de Williams. Dat's how I come to be Williams. Never had no chillen of my own. Dey calls me 'Lizbeth Johnson before I went to live with de Mixons. Den I be one of de Mixon niggers, den later I be a Williams. Don't guess names matter much no way.

Louis Armstrong

(1900–1971)

Not only was New Orleans-born Louis Armstrong America's premier creative musician-composer (jazz trumpeter, vocalist, bandleader, recording sensation, actor, comic) and cultural ambassador. He was bon vivant, storyteller, and lover of life, whose hobby was typing. Armstrong's idea of relaxing was to sit and type, which is how he came to write his own autobiography, **Satchmo: My Life in New Orleans***, first published in 1954. Citing his birthdate as July 4, 1900, Armstrong reminisces affectionately and dramatically about his early days at the Colored Waifs' Home for Boys, where he started out blowing bugle and ended up learning cornet under his teacher, Mr. Peter Davis.*

from Satchmo

Chapter 1

When I was born in 1900 my father, Willie Armstrong, and my mother, May Ann—or Mayann as she was called—were living on a little street called James Alley. Only one block long, James Alley is located in the crowded section of New Orleans known as Back o' Town. It is one of the four great sections into which the city is divided. The others are Uptown, Downtown and Front o' Town, and each of these quarters has its own little traits.

James Alley—not Jane Alley as some people call it—lies in the very heart of what is called The Battlefield because the toughest characters in town used to live there, and would shoot and fight so much. In that one block between Gravier and Perdido Streets more people were crowded than you ever saw in your life. There were churchpeople, gamblers, hustlers, cheap pimps, thieves, prostitutes and lots of children. There were bars, honky-tonks and saloons, and lots of women walking the streets for tricks to take to their "pads," as they called their rooms.

Mayann told me that the night I was born there was a great big shooting scrape in the Alley and the two guys killed each other. It was the Fourth of July, a big holiday in New Orleans, when almost anything can happen. Pretty near everybody celebrates with pistols, shot guns, or any other weapon that's handy.

When I was born my mother and father lived with my grandmother, Mrs. Josephine Armstrong (bless her heart!), but they did not stay with her long. They used to quarrel something awful, and finally the blow came. My mother moved away, leaving me with grandma. My father went in another direction to live with another woman. My mother went to a place at Liberty and Perdido Streets in a neighborhood filled with cheap prostitutes who did not make as much money for their time as the whores in Storyville, the famous red-light district. Whether my mother did any hustling, I cannot say. If she did, she certainly kept it out of my sight. One thing is certain: everybody from the churchfolks to the lowest roughneck treated her with the greatest respect. She was glad to say hello to everybody and she always held her head up. She never envied anybody. I guess I must have inherited this trait from Mayann.

When I was a year old my father went to work in a turpentine factory out by James Alley, where he stayed till he died in 1933. He stayed there so long he almost became a part of the place, and he could hire and fire the colored guys who worked under him. From the time my parents separated I did not see my father again until I had grown to a pretty good size, and I did not see Mayann for a long time either.

Grandmother sent me to school and she took in washing and ironing. When I helped her deliver the clothes to the white folks she would give me a nickel. Gee, I thought I was rich! Days I did not have to go to school grandmother took me with her when she had to do washing and housework for one of the white folks. While she was working I used to play games with the little white boys out in the yard. Hide-and-go-seek was one of the games we used to play, and every time we played I was It. And every time I would hide those clever little white kids always found me. That sure would get my goat. Even when I was at home or in kindergarten getting my lessons I kept wishing grandma would hurry up and go back to her washing job so I could find a place to hide where they could not find me.

One real hot summer day those little white kids and myself were having the time of our lives playing hide-and-go-seek. And of course I was It. I kept wondering and figuring where, oh where was I going to hide. Finally I looked at grandma who was leaning over a wash tub working like mad. The placket in the back of her Mother Hubbard skirt was flopping wide open. That gave me the idea. I made a mad dash over to her and got up under her dress before the kids could find out where I had gone. For a long time I heard those kids running around and saying "where did he go?" Just as they were about to give up the search I stuck my head out of grandma's placket and went "P-f-f-f-f-f!"

"Oh, there you are. We've found you," they shouted.

"No siree," I said. "You wouldn't of found me if I had not stuck my head out."

Ever since I was a baby I have had great love for my grandmother. She spent the best of her days raising me, and teaching me right from wrong. Whenever I did something she thought I ought to get a whipping for, she sent me out to get a switch from the big old Chinaball tree in her yard.

"You have been a bad boy," she would say. "I am going to give you a good licking."

With tears in my eyes I would go to the tree and return with the smallest switch I could find. Generally she would laugh and let me off. However, when she was really angry she would give me a whipping for everything wrong I had done for weeks. Mayann must have adopted this system, for when I lived with her later on she would swing on me just the same way grandmother did.

I remember my great-grandmother real well too. She lived to be more than ninety. From her I must have inherited my energy. Now at fifty-four I feel like a young man just out of school and eager to go out in the world to really live my life with my horn.

In those days, of course, I did not know a horn from a comb. I was going to church regularly for both grandma and my great-grandmother were Christian women, and between them they kept me in school, church and Sunday school. In church and Sunday school I did a whole lot of singing. That, I guess, is how I acquired my singing tactics.

I took part in everything that happened at school. Both the children and the teachers liked me, but I never wanted to be a teacher's pet. However, even when I was very young I was conscientious about everything I did. At church my heart went into every hymn I sang. I am still a great believer and I go to church whenever I get the chance.

After two years my father quit the woman he was living with, and went back to Mayann. The result was my sister Beatrice, who was later nicknamed "Mama Lucy." I was still with my grandmother when she was born, and I did not see her until I was five years old.

One summer there was a terrible drought. It had not rained for months, and there was not a drop of water to be found. In those days big cisterns were kept in the yards to catch rain water. When the cisterns were filled with water it was easy to get all the water that was needed. But this time the cisterns were empty, and everybody on James Alley was frantic as the dickens. The House of Detention stables on the corner of James Alley and Gravier Street saved the day. There was water at the stable, and the drivers let us bring empty beer barrels and fill them up.

In front of the stables was the House of Detention itself, occupying a whole square block. There prisoners were sent with "thirty days to six months." The prisoners were used to clean the public markets all over the city, and they were taken to and from their work in large wagons. Those who worked in the markets had their sentences reduced from thirty days to nineteen. In those days New Orleans had fine big horses to pull the patrol wagons and the Black Maria. I used to look at those horses and wish I could ride on one some day. And finally I did. Gee, was I thrilled!

One day when I was getting water along with the rest of the neighbors on James Alley an elderly lady who was a friend of Mayann's came to my grandmother's to tell her that Mayann was very sick and that she and my dad had broken up again. My mother did not know where dad was or if he was coming back. She had been left alone with her baby—my sister Beatrice (or Mama Lucy)—with no one to take care of her. The woman asked grandmother if she would let me go to Mayann and help out. Being the grand person she was, grandma consented right away to let me go to my mother's bedside. With tears in her eyes she started to put my little clothes on me.

"I really hate to let you out of my sight," she said. "I am so used to having you now."

"I am sorry to leave you, too, granny," I answered with a lump in my throat. "But I will come back soon, I hope. I love you so much, grandma. You have been so kind and so nice to me, taught me everything I know: how to take care of myself, how to wash myself and brush my teeth, put my clothes away, mind the older folks."

She patted me on the back, wiped her eyes and then wiped mine. Then she kind of nudged me very gently toward the door to say good-bye. She did not know when I would be back. I didn't either. But my mother was sick, and she felt I should go to her side.

The woman took me by the hand and slowly led me away. When we were in the street I suddenly broke into tears. As long as we were in James Alley I could see Grandma Josephine waving good-bye to me. We turned the corner to catch the Tulane Avenue trolley, just in front of the House of Detention. I stood there sniffling, when all of a sudden the woman turned me round to see the huge building.

"Listen here, Louis," she said. "If you don't stop crying at once I will put you in that prison. That's where they keep bad men and women. You don't want to go there, do you?"

"Oh, no, lady."

Seeing how big this place was I said to myself: "Maybe I had better stop crying. After all I don't know this woman and she is liable to do what she said. You never know."

I stopped crying at once. The trolley came and we got on.

It was my first experience with Jim Crow. I was just five, and I had never ridden on a street car before. Since I was the first to get on, I walked right up to the front of the car without noticing the signs on the backs of the seats on both sides, which read: FOR COLORED PASSENGERS ONLY. Thinking the woman was following me, I sat down in one of the front seats. However, she did not join me, and when I turned to see what had happened, there was no lady. Looking all the way to the back of the car, I saw her waving to me frantically.

"Come here, boy," she cried. "Sit where you belong."

I thought she was kidding me so I stayed where I was, sort of acting cute. What did I care where she sat? Shucks, that woman came up to me and jerked me out of the seat. Quick as a flash she dragged me to the back of the car and pushed me into one of the rear seats. Then I saw the signs on the backs of the seats saying: FOR COLORED PASSENGERS ONLY.

"What do those signs say?" I asked.

"Don't ask so many questions! Shut your mouth, you little fool."

There is something funny about those signs on the street cars in New Orleans. We colored folks used to get real kicks out of them when we got on a car at the picnic grounds or at Canal Street on a Sunday evening when we outnumbered the white folks. Automatically we took the whole car over, sitting as far up front as we wanted to. It felt good to sit up there once in a while. We felt a little more important than usual. I can't explain why exactly, but maybe it was because we weren't supposed to be up there.

When the car stopped at the corner of Tulane and Liberty Streets the woman said:

"All right, Louis. This is where we get off."

As we got off the car I looked straight down Liberty Street. Crowds of people were moving up and down as far as my eyes could see. It reminded me of James Alley, I thought, and if it weren't for grandma I would not miss the Alley much. However, I kept these thoughts to myself as we walked the two blocks to the house where Mayann was living. In a single room in a back courtyard she had to cook, wash, iron and take care of my baby sister. My first impression was so vivid that I remember it as if it was yesterday. I did not know what to think. All I knew was that I was with mama and that I loved her as much as grandma. My poor mother lay there before my eyes, very, very sick … Oh God, a very funny feeling came over me and I felt like I wanted to cry again.

"So you did come to see your mother?" she said.

"Yes, mama."

"I was afraid grandma wouldn't let you. After all I realize I have not done what I should by you. But, son, mama will make it up. If it weren't for that no-good father of yours things would have gone better. I try to do the best I can. I am all by myself with my baby. You are still young, son, and have a long ways to go. Always remember when you're sick nobody ain't going to give you nothing. So try to stay healthy. Even without money your health is the best thing. I want you to promise me you will take a physic at least once a week as long as you live. Will you promise?"

"Yes, mother," I said.

"Good! Then hand me those pills in the top dresser drawer. They are in the box that says Coal Roller Pills. They're little bitty black pills."

The pills looked like Carter's Little Liver Pills, only they were about three times as black. After I had swallowed the three my mother handed me, the woman who had brought me said she had to leave.

"Now that your kid is here I've got to go home and cook my old man's supper."

When she had gone I asked mama if there was anything I could do for her.

"Yes," she said. "Look under the carpet and get that fifty cents. Go down to Zattermann's, on Rampart Street, and get me a slice of meat, a pound of red beans and a pound of rice. Stop at Stahle's Bakery and buy two loaves of bread for a nickel. And hurry back, son."

It was the first time I had been out in the city without my grandma's guidance, and I was proud that my mother trusted me to go as far as Rampart Street. I was determined to do exactly as she said.

When I came out of the back court to the front of the house I saw a half a dozen ragged, snot-nosed kids standing on the sidewalk. I said hello to them very pleasantly.

After all I had come from James Alley which was a very tough spot and I had seen some pretty rough fellows. However, the boys in the Alley had been taught how to behave in a nice way and to respect other people. Everyone said good morning and good evening, asked their blessings before meals and said their prayers. Naturally I figured all the kids everywhere had the same training.

When they saw how clean and nicely dressed I was they crowded around me.

"Hey, you. Are you a mama's boy?" one of them asked.

"A mama's boy? What does that mean?" I asked.

"Yeah, that's what you are. A mama's boy."

"I don't understand. What do you mean?"

A big bully called One Eye Bud came pretty close up on me and looked over my white Lord Fauntleroy suit with its Buster Brown collar.

"So you don't understand, huh? Well, that's just too bad."

Then he scooped up a big handful of mud and threw it on the white suit I loved so much. I only had two. The other little ashy-legged, dirty-faced boys laughed while I stood there splattered with mud and rather puzzled what to do about it. I was young, but I saw the odds were against me; if I started a fight I knew I would be licked.

"What's the matter, mama's boy, don't you like it?" One Eye Bud asked me.

"No, I don't like it."

Then before I knew what I was doing, and before any of them could get ready, I jumped at him and smashed the little snot square in the mouth. I was scared and I hit as hard as I possibly could. I had his mouth and nose bleeding plenty. Those kids were so surprised by what I had done that they tore out as fast as they could go with One Eye Bud in the lead. I was too dumbfounded to run after them—and besides I didn't want to.

I was afraid Mayann would hear the commotion and hurt herself struggling out of bed. Luckily she did not, and I went off to do my errands.

When I came back mother's room was filled with visitors: a crowd of cousins I had never seen. Isaac Miles, Aaron Miles, Jerry Miles, Willie Miles, Louisa Miles, Sarah

Ann Miles, Flora Miles (who was a baby) and Uncle Ike Miles were all waiting to see their new cousin, as they put it.

"Louis," my mother said, "I want you to meet some more of your family."

Gee, I thought, all of these people are my cousins?

Uncle Ike Miles was the father of all those kids. His wife had died and left them on his hands to support, and he did a good job. To take care of them he worked on the levees unloading boats. He did not make much money and his work was not regular, but most of the time he managed to keep the kids eating and put clean shirts on their backs. He lived in one room with all those children, and somehow or other he managed to pack them all in. He put as many in the bed as it would hold, and the rest slept on the floor. God bless Uncle Ike. If it weren't for him I do not know what Mama Lucy and I would have done because when Mayann got the urge to go out on the town we might not see her for days and days. When this happened she always dumped us into Uncle Ike's lap.

In his room I would sleep between Aaron and Isaac while Mama Lucy slept between Flora and Louisa. Because the kids were so lazy they would not wash their dishes we ate out of some tin pans Uncle Ike bought. They used to break china plates so they would not have to clean them.

Uncle Ike certainly had his hands full with those kids. They were about as worthless as any kids I have ever seen, but we grew up together just the same.

As I have said my mother always kept me and Mama Lucy physic minded.

"A slight physic once or twice a week," she used to say, "will throw off many symptoms and germs that congregate from nowheres in your stomach. We can't afford no doctor for fifty cents or a dollar."

With that money she could cook pots of red beans and rice, and with that regime we did not have any sickness at all. Of course a child who grew up in my part of New Orleans went barefooted practically all the time. We were bound to pick up a nail, a splinter or a piece of glass sometimes. But we were young, healthy and tough as old hell so a little thing like lockjaw did not stay with us a long time.

Mother and some of her neighbors would go to the railroad tracks and fill baskets with pepper grass. She would boil this until it got really gummy and rub it on the wound. Then within two or three hours we kids would get out of bed and be playing around the streets as though nothing had happened.

As the old saying goes, "the Lord takes care of fools," and just think of the dangers we kids were in at all times. In our neighborhood there were always a number of houses being torn down or built and they were full of such rubbish as tin cans, nails, boards, broken bottles and window panes. We used to play in these houses, and one of the games we played was War, because we had seen so much of it in the movies. Of course we did not know anything about it, but we decided to appoint officers of different ranks anyway. One Eye Bud made himself General of the Army. Then he made me Sergeant-at-Arms. When I asked him what I had to do he told me that whenever a man was wounded I had to go out on the battlefield and lead him off.

One day when I was taking a wounded comrade off the field a piece of slate fell off a roof and landed on my head. It knocked me out cold and shocked me so bad I got lockjaw. When I was taken home Mama Lucy and Mayann worked frantically boiling up herbs and roots which they applied to my head. Then they gave me a glass of Pluto Water, put me to bed and sweated me out good all night long. The next morning I was on my way to school just as though nothing had happened.

Ralph Ellison

(1914–1994)

Widely regarded in the second half of the twentieth century as the preeminent African American novelist and essayist, Ralph Ellison is the author of the classic **Invisible Man**, *which received the 1953 National Book Award, and two collections of essays,* **Shadow and Act** *and* **Going to the Territory**. *Born Ralph Waldo Ellison in Oklahoma City seven years after Oklahoma had been admitted to the Union, Ellison, a trumpet-player, attended Tuskegee Institute to study music. In the middle of the Great Depression he abandoned his studies and moved to New York, where he became friends with the writers Langston Hughes and Richard Wright. Driven by abiding interests—philosophy, politics, folklore, literature, jazz, esthetics, psychology—he became a stunningly successful writer and social observer. Always eloquent, astute, and provocatively expressive, Ralph Ellison is representative of the kind of all-around intellectual who began to fade from the American scene during the McCarthy era.*

Remembering Richard Wright

Earlier today while considering my relationship with Richard Wright, I recalled Heraclitus' axiom "Geography is fate," and I was struck by the ironic fact that in this country, where Frederick Jackson Turner's theory of the frontier has been so influential in shaping our conception of American history, very little attention has been given to the role played by geography in shaping the fate of Afro-Americans.

For example, Wright was a Mississippian who migrated to Chicago and then to New York. I, by contrast, am an Oklahoman and by geographical origin a Southwesterner. Wright grew up in a part of what was the old Confederacy, while I grew up in a state which possesses no indigenous tradition of chattel slavery. Thus, while we both grew up in segregated societies, mine lacked many of the intensities of custom, tradition, and manners which "colored" the institutions of the Old South, and which were important in shaping Wright's point of view. Both of us were descendants of slaves, but since my civic, geographical, and political circumstances were different from those of Mississippi, Wright and I were united by our connection with a past condition of servitude, and divided by geography and a difference of experience based thereupon. And yet it was that very difference of experience and background which had much to do with Wright's important impact upon my sensibilities.

And then there was New York. I met Wright there in 1937, and it was no accidental encounter. It came about because through my reading and working in the library at Tuskegee Institute, I'd become fascinated by the exciting developments that were taking place in modern literature. Somehow in my uninstructed reading of Eliot and

Pound, I had recognized a relationship between modern poetry and jazz music, and this led me to wonder why I was not encountering similar devices in the work of Afro-American writers. Indeed, such reading and wondering prepared me not simply to *meet* Wright, but to seek him out. It led, in other words, to a personal quest. I insist upon the "seeking out" because, you see, I too have an ego and it is important to me that our meeting came about through my own initiative. For not only is it historically true, but it has something to do with my being privileged to be here on what I consider to be a very important moment in the history of our literature. Perhaps Richard Wright would have dismissed such a moment as impossible, even as late as 1957, but still, here we are, gathered in the hot summertime to pay him honor. *I* would not have been surprised, since it was my reading of one of Wright's poems in the *New Masses* which gave me a sense of his importance. I had arrived in New York on July 5, 1936— a date of no broad symbolic importance, but one highly significant to me because it made a meeting with Wright a possibility. For although the *New Masses* poem was not a masterpiece, I found in it traces of the modern poetic sensibility and technique that I had been seeking.

The morning after my arrival in New York, I encountered standing in the entrance of the Harlem YMCA two fateful figures. They were Langston Hughes, the poet, and Dr. Alain Locke, the then head of the philosophy department at Howard University. I had never seen Langston Hughes before, but regardless of what is said about the quality of education provided by the old Negro schools (ours was named for Frederick Douglass), we were taught what is now termed "Black History" and were kept abreast of current events pertaining to our people. Thus, as early as the sixth grade we were made aware of the poetry of Langston Hughes along with the work of the other Negro Renaissance writers. So I recognized Hughes from his photographs. But I recognized Dr. Locke because he had been at Tuskegee only a few weeks prior to my arrival in New York, having gone there to visit with Hazel Harrison, a teacher in the music department, and a very fine pianist who had been one of Ferruccio Busoni's prize pupils ... Here I'm trying to provide a bit of historical background to give you an idea of the diverse cultural forces at play in the lives of Afro-Americans from the early 1920s to 1936.

Miss Harrison was a friend of Prokofiev, and possessed some of his scores at a time when few would have imagined that a Russian master's music was being made a part of the musical consciousness of an Afro-American college. And certainly not in such a college as Tuskegee—even though Tuskegee's musical tradition was actually quite rich and quite varied. But then, this is but another example of the contradictions of American culture which escape our attention because they are obscured by racism. And yet, thanks to Miss Harrison, I could, like any eager, young, celebrity-fascinated college junior, walk straight up to Dr. Locke and say, "Dr. Locke, do you remember me?" And to my delight he said, "Why, of course I do." He then introduced me to Langston Hughes and told Hughes of my interest in poetry.

Langston Hughes had with him copies of Malraux's *Man's Fate* and *The Days of Wrath*, and after a few moments' conversation he said, "Since you like to read so much, maybe you'd like to read these novels and then return them to their owner"— and so I did. And the returns were tremendous. This incident and this meeting later made it possible for me to ask Langston Hughes if he knew Richard Wright. "Yes, he said, "and it so happens that he's coming here from Chicago next week." And with his great generosity, and without telling me, Hughes wrote Richard Wright that there was a young Negro something-or-the-other in New York who wanted to meet him. The next thing I knew I received a postcard—which I still have—that said, "Dear Ralph Ellison, Langston Hughes tells me that you're interested in meeting me. I will be in New York ... " on such and such a date in July ... signed Richard Wright. Thus I was to meet Wright on the day after his arrival in New York in July of 1937.

At the time I still thought that I would return to Tuskegee to take my degree in music, but I was not to make it. I had come to New York to earn expenses for my senior year, but it was during the Depression and I was unable to make the money. Then, in talking with Wright, my plans and goals were altered; were, in fact, fatefully modified by Wright's.

Wright had come to New York for two purposes, one which was talked about openly, and the other quietly underplayed. The first was to become the editor of the magazine *New Challenge*. The other was to work in the Harlem Bureau of the Communist newspaper *The Daily Worker*. With Wright's presence in the *Worker's* 135th Street office, my introduction to the craft of writing leaped ahead. For it was there that I read many of his unpublished stories and discussed his ideas concerning literature and culture.

Wright was quiet concerning his assignment to the *Worker's* staff because he had left Chicago under a cloud. In 1936 he had been thrown out of the May Day parade—sacred to all Communists—for refusing to carry out some assignment. And the fact that he had been publicly humiliated by both white *and* black Communists had left him quite bitter. However, someone higher up in the hierarchy recognized his value and was able to persuade him to go to New York—which proved to be to my good fortune.

Being unemployed much of the time, I began to hang around the Harlem Bureau, not so much for the ideology being purveyed there—although I found it fascinating— but because of Wright and the manuscripts of a sheaf of novelettes (later published as *Uncle Tom's Children*) that lay in an open desk drawer. Of all those who visited the office, I was the only one who bothered to read those now-famous stories. Perhaps this was because his comrades looked upon Wright as an intruder. He was distrusted not only as an "intellectual" and thus a potential traitor, but as a possible "dark horse" in the race for Harlem party leadership; a "ringer" who had been sent from Chicago to cause them trouble. Wright had little sense of humor concerning their undisguised hostility, and this led, as would be expected, to touchy relationships. Despite his obvious organizational and journalistic abilities—the *Worker* featured his reportage—the members of the Communist rank and file sneered at his intellectuality, ridiculed his writings, and dismissed his concern with literature and culture as an affectation. In brief, they thought him too ambitious, and therefore a threat to their own ambitions as possible party functionaries.

Being a true outsider, I was amused by this comedy of misperception, for Wright seemed anything but a threat to their petty ambitions. Besides, I was absolutely intrigued by his talent and felt privileged to read his writings. I'd never met anyone who, lacking the fanfare of public recognition, could move me with the unpublished products of his fictional imagination. Of course, I read Wright's work uncritically, but there was no doubt in my mind that he was an exceptional writer. Even better, he was delighted to discuss the techniques, the ideological and philosophical implications of his writings, and this with one who'd never attempted to write anything beyond classroom assignments and a few poems. Evidently Wright wished to exchange ideas with someone of his own general background, and I was fortunate in being able to contribute more than curiosity to our discussion. For I had studied with creative musicians, both classical and jazz, and had been taught to approach the arts analytically. I had also read fairly widely on my own. But to encounter the possessor of such literary talent and have him make me his friend and confidant—that was indeed an exciting and inspiring experience.

Nor did it end with mere talk. As editor of *New Challenge*, Wright asked me to contribute a book review in its first issue. To one who had never attempted to write anything, this was the wildest of ideas. But still, pressed by his editorial needs, and sustained by his belief that an untapped supply of free-floating literary talent existed in the Negro community, Wright kept after me, and I wrote a review and he published it. But then he went even further by suggesting that I write a short story!

I said, "But I've never even tried to write a story ... "

He said, "Look, you talk about these things, you've read a lot, and you've been around. Just put something down and let me see it ... "

So I wrote a story, titled "Hymie's Bull," that was based upon experiences that I'd had a few years before when riding freight trains from Oklahoma to Alabama. I was dubious over the outcome, but to my delight Wright accepted the story and sent it to the printer.

Ah, but fate, as they say, was in the wings and *New Challenge* was not to appear again. I hasten to add that this was not a disaster created by my first attempt at fiction. Rather, it had to do with an aspect of Afro-American cultural history and involved certain lingering echoes of the Negro Renaissance, a movement which "ran out of gas" with the Crash of 1929. As the period ended, a number of figures important to the movement had died, and with the Great Depression upon them, those members of the white community who had sponsored the Renaissance were unable to continue. The money was no longer available, and so the movement languished. However, with the deepening of the Depression there came a significant development in the form of the federal projects for the arts that were organized by the Works Progress Administration. These projects were most important to the continuing development of Afro-American artists. For although a reaction to a national disaster, they provided— as have most national disasters—the possibility for a broader Afro-American freedom. This is a shocking thing to say, but it is also a very *blues*, or tragicomic, thing to say, and a fairly accurate description of the manner in which, for Negroes, a gift of freedom arrived wrapped in the guise of disaster. It is ironic, but no less true, that the most tragic incident of our history, the Civil War, was a disaster which ended American slavery.

Wright himself worked on both the Chicago and the New York Federal Writers' Project, and I could not have become a writer at the time I began had I not been able to earn my board and keep by doing research for the New York project. Through Wright's encouragement, I had become serious about writing, but before going on the project I sometimes slept in the public park below City College because I had neither job nor money. But my personal affairs aside, the WPA provided an important surge to Afro-American cultural activity. The result was not a "renaissance," but there was a resuscitation and transformation of that very vital artistic impulse that is abiding among Afro-Americans. Remember that our African forefathers originated in cultures wherein even the simple routines of daily living were highly ritualized and that even their cooking utensils were fashioned with forms of symbolism which resonated with overtones of godhead. And though modified, if not suppressed, by the experience of American slavery, that tradition of artistic expressiveness has infused the larger American culture. Afro-American cultural style is an abiding aspect of our culture, and the economic disaster which brought the WPA gave it an accelerated release and allowed many Negroes to achieve their identities as artists.

But now, back to Wright and *New Challenge*. *New Challenge* was organized by people active in the Negro Renaissance and whose outlook was in many ways at odds with Wright's. Thus, according to Wright, *New Challenge* ended publication because the two young women who were in charge before he came on the scene were afraid that his connection with the Communist party would lead to its being taken over. So rather than lose control, they got rid of Wright.

History has no vacuum. There are transformations, there are lesions, there are metamorphoses, and there are mysteries that cloak the clashing of individual wills and private interests. *New Challenge* faded, but Wright went on to publish *Uncle Tom's Children* and, shortly afterward, *Native Son*. When Richard Wright came to

New York his talents as a writer were, to a large extent, already formed. Indeed, even before 1927, when he migrated to Chicago, he had published fiction in Robert S. Abbott's magazine *The Bronzeman*. So it isn't true, as has been said, that the Communist party "discovered" his talent. Wright was literary in an informed way even in Jackson, Mississippi. But what happened to him in Chicago resulted from his coming into contact with an organized political group which possessed a concept of social hierarchy that was a conscious negation of our racially biased social system. Thus, through his political affiliation Wright was able to identify his artistic ambitions with what was, for him, a totally new conception of social justice. In the discussions that took place in the Chicago John Reed Club he sharpened his conception of literary form and the relationship between fictional techniques and the world view of Marxism. And he came to see art and society in terms of an ideology that was concerned with power, and willing to forgo racial differences in order to take over the world. I realize that this is all rather abstract, but I am trying to suggest the tenor of our discussions. Fortunately, Wright's interest in literary theory was not limited to areas prescribed by the party line.

For instance, I was very curious as to how one could put Marx and Freud together. No real problem now, I suppose. But coming from where I did, it was puzzling. And I was to discover that it was also a problem for Communist intellectuals and for many of their opponents. Either Marx was raised up and Freud put down, or Freud raised up and Marx put down. So for me, all of this was pretty strange. But at least with Richard Wright, I could discuss such matters. This was very important for a young writer (and of course I became a young writer, for I soon realized that I wasn't going back to Tuskegee and to music). And since Wright had assured me that I possessed a certain talent, I decided that writing was the direction I would take. I don't know whether he was satisfied with my talent or not; I suspect not. This was interesting, for while I possessed more formal education, it was he who encouraged me and gave me a sense of direction. I'd like you to appreciate the irony of this development: Here was a young Afro-American who had gone only to grade school, but who had arrived in Chicago possessing a certain articulateness and an undeveloped talent for writing. He had no further formal education—although he was aware of the University of Chicago and came to associate with a number of its intellectuals—but he gave himself over to the complex reality of late 1927 Chicago and made it his own. Chicago, the city where after years of Southern Negro migration the great jazz was being played and reinvented, where the stockyards and railroads, and the steel mills of Gary, Indiana, were transforming a group of rural, agricultural Americans into city people and into a *lumpenproletariat*, a class over whom we now despair.

Wright found the scene challenging. He learned that in this country wherever one wanders, one must pay his dues to change and take advantage of possibility by asserting oneself. You'll recall my saying earlier that "geography is fate"; now let me say that one's fate is also determined by what one does and by what one does *not* do. Wright set out to come into a conscious possession of his experience as Negro, as political revolutionary, as writer, and as citizen of Chicago.

Somehow, in getting into the John Reed Club, Wright had learned the techniques of agitprop art—which he came later to despise—and before he went to Harlem he had been a contributing editor of the original *Partisan Review* and a founder of such magazines as *Anvil*. He had been poor in accepting discipline and had had his political troubles in the Communist party, but when I knew him he was not shrinking from the challenges of his existence. Nor complaining that he'd been " 'buked and scorned." Nor did he feel that he had handicaps that could not be overcome because of his identity as a Negro writer. Instead, he was striving to live consciously—at least artistically and intellectually—at the top of his times. Wright's spirit was such, and his sense of possibility was such, that even during the time when he was writing *Native Son* he was concerned with learning the stylistic and dialectical fine points found in the work of Steinbeck, of Hemingway, of Malraux, and of Thomas Mann; for these he viewed as his competitors. I warn you that this is only *my* interpretation, but it was as though Wright was thinking, "I have a finer sense, a more basic knowledge of American reality than Hemingway, or Steinbeck, or anybody else who is writing." He had the kind of confidence that jazzmen have, although I assure you that he knew very little about jazz and didn't even know how to dance. Which is to say that he didn't possess the full range of Afro-American culture. But having the confidence of his talent, having the sense (which he gained from Marxism) that he was living in a world in which he did not have to be confused by the mystifications of racism, Wright harnessed his revolutionary tendencies to a political program which he hoped would transform American society. Through his cultural and political activities in Chicago he made a dialectical leap into a sense of his broadest possibilities, as man and as artist. He was well aware of the forces ranked against him, but in his quiet way he was as arrogant in facing up to them as was Louis Armstrong in a fine blaring way.

To a young Oklahoman this attitude of Wright's was affirmative—and again, "geography is fate." For out there our people fought back. We seldom won more than moral victories, but we fought back—as can be seen from the many civil rights victories that were initiated there. And as can be heard in the Southwestern jazz and in the performances of the Jimmy Rushings, the Hot Lips Pages, the Count Basies, the Benny Motens, and Charlie Christians. We were an assertive people, and our mode of social assertion was artistic, mainly music, as well as political. But there was also the Negro church, wherein you heard the lingering accents of nineteenth-century rhetoric with its emphasis upon freedom and individual responsibility; a rhetorical style which gave us Lincoln, Harriet Tubman, Harriet Beecher Stowe, and the other abolition-preaching Beechers. Which gave us Frederick Douglass and John Jasper and many other eloquent and heroic Negroes whose spirit still moves among us through the contributions they made to the flexibility, the music, and the idealism of the American language. Richard Wright was a possessor of that tradition. It is resonant in his fiction and it was a factor in his eager acceptance of social responsibility.

But now I should add that as far as Negroes in New York were concerned, Wright was for the most part friendless. Part of this was due to the fact that he kept to Communist circles and was intensely involved with writing and political activities. But as far as his rapid development as a writer is concerned, it would not have been possible but for the Chicago John Reed Club. This required an intellectual environment, and in Negro communities such were few and far between. Thus, given his talent and driving ambition, it was fortunate that he found the necessary associations among other young writers, many of whom were not Communists. Within such integrated groups he could question ideas, programs, theories. He could argue over philosophical interpretations of reality and say, if he chose, "Well, dammit, I'm black, and this concept of this program doesn't seem valid to me." This was most important for Wright, and since he affirmed many impulses which I felt and understood in my own way, it proved important to me. And no less important was his willingness to discuss problems encountered within the Communist party, and especially his difficulty in pursuing independent thought.

Because there, too, he was encountering a form of intellectual racism. It was not couched in the rhetoric of Negro inferiority *à l'americain*, but in the form of an insistence upon blind discipline and a constant pressure to follow unthinkingly a political "line." It was dramatized in the servile attitudes of certain black Communist functionaries who regarded Wright—with his eloquence and his tendency toward an independence of thought—as a dangerous figure who had to be kept under rigid control.

And of course, Wright's personality would not allow him to shun a battle. He fought back and was into all kinds of trouble. He had no interest in keeping silent as the price of his freedom of expression. Nor was he so dazzled by his freedom to participate in the councils of newspapers and magazines as to keep his mouth shut. Instead, he felt that his experience, insight, and talent were important to the party's correct assessment of American reality. Thus he fought to make his comrades understand that *they* didn't know a damn thing about the complexities of the South, whether black or white, and insisted that they could not possibly understand America's racial situation by approaching it through such facile slogans as "Black and White Unite and Fight." Not when the white workingman was doing us the greatest face-to-face damage, and when the unions were practicing policies of racial exclusion. In trying to get this across, in saying, as it were, "Your approach is too simple," Wright met all kinds of resistance, both ideological and personal. But at least he made the fight, and I bring it up here by the way of offering you something of the background of emotional and intellectual conflict out of which *Native Son* was written.

I read most of *Native Son* as it came off the typewriter, and I didn't know what to think of it except that it was wonderful. I was not responding critically. After all, how many of you have had the unexpected privilege of reading a powerful novel as it was, literally, ripped off the typewriter? Such opportunities are rare, and being young, I was impressed beyond all critical words. And I am still impressed. I feel that *Native Son* was one of the major literary events in the history of American literature. And I can say this even though at this point I have certain reservations concerning its view of reality. Yet it continues to have a powerful effect, and it seems to me a mistake to say, as was said not long ago in *Life* magazine, that *Native Son* is a "neglected" novel. And here I should remind those of you who were too young to remember, that *Native Son* was such a popular work that the dust jacket of the Book-of-the-Month Club edition could consist of a collage made of accolades written by critics and reviewers from throughout the country. It was a financial as well as a critical success, and with its publication Wright became a famous man.

But its success was by no means to still his burning passion—not simply for justice, but to become the author of other compelling works of literature. His response to the reception of *12 Million Black Voices*, which is, I think, his most lyrical work, is an example. He was much bemused by the fact that this work could move his white readers to tears, and saw this as an evasion of the intended impact of his vision. Thus he began to talk over and over again of forging such hard, mechanical images and actions that no white reading them could afford the luxury of tears.

But here I must turn critic. For in *my* terms, Wright failed to grasp the function of artistically induced catharsis—which suggests that he failed also to understand the Afro-American custom of shouting in church (a form of ritual catharsis), or its power to cleanse the mind and redeem and rededicate the individual to forms of ideal action. Perhaps he failed to understand—or he rejected—those moments of exultation wherein man's vision is quickened by the eloquence of an orchestra, an actor or orator or dancer, or by anyone using the arts of music or speech or symbolic gesture to create within us moments of high consciousness; moments wherein we grasp, in the instant, a knowledge of how transcendent and how abysmal and yet affirmative it can be to be human beings. Yet it is for such moments of inspired communication that the artist lives. The irony here is that Wright could evoke them, but felt, for ideological reasons, that tears were a betrayal of the struggle for freedom.

I disagreed with his analysis, for tears can induce as well as deter action. Nevertheless, it is imperative that I say that through his writings Richard Wright achieved, here in the social and racial chaos of the United States, a position of artistic equality. He insisted upon it. And not only in his own political party—with which he eventually broke—but internationally. He was never at peace. He was never at rest. The restlessness which sent our forefathers hurtling toward the West Coast, and which now has us climbing up all sorts of walls, was very much within him. In 1956, in Paris, when we were leaving the headquarters of the magazine *Presence Africaine* (and this is the first time I've revealed this and I hope he won't mind, since it might be meaningful to some scholar), he said to me, "Really, Ralph, after I broke with the Communist party I had nowhere else to go ... " This was said in resigned explanation of his continued presence in Europe. And I think he was telling me that his dedication to communism had been so complete and his struggle so endless that he had had to change his scene, that he had had to find a new ground upon which to struggle. Because as long as he stayed within the framework of his political party, he had to struggle on two fronts: asserting on one the principles of equality and possibility (which the Communists stood for, or *pretended* to stand for), and on the other, insisting upon the fact *not* that it took a Negro to tell the truth about Afro-American experience, but that you had to at least get down into the mud and live with its basic realities to do so. And that you could not deal with its complexities simply from a theoretical perspective. *Black Boy* was an attempt to depict some of those complexities.

So much of *Black Boy* (originally entitled *American Hunger*) is exaggerated, I think, precisely because Wright was trying to drive home, to dramatize—indeed, because of its many fictional techniques he could with justice have called it a "nonfiction" novel—the complexity of Negro American experience as he knew it and had lived it. The fictional techniques were not there in order to "con" anyone, but to drive home to Americans, black and white, something of the complexity and cost in human terms, in terms of the loss to literature and to art, and to the cause of freedom itself, imposed by racial discrimination; the cost, that is, of growing up in a society which operated on one side of its mind by the principle of equality while qualifying that principle severely according to the dictates of racism. Wright was thinking and fighting over these issues at close quarters—fighting with the Communists especially because he had thought that they offered a viable solution. Instead, he discovered that they were blind.

But now to more delightful relationships with Wright. He had as much curiosity about how writing is written as I had about how music is composed, and our curiosity concerning artistic creation became the basis of our friendship. Having studied music from the age of eight, and having studied harmony and symphonic form in our segregated school, I was also interested in how music related to the other arts. This, combined with my growing interest in literary creation, made my contact with Wright's enthusiasm an educational and spirit-freeing experience. Having read Pound and Eliot and Shaw and the criticism of Harriet Monroe and I. A. Richards—all available in

Tuskegee's excellent little library—it was important that in Wright, I had discovered a Negro American writer who possessed a working knowledge of modern literature, its techniques and theories. My approach to literature was by no means racial, but Wright was not only available, he was eager to share his interests, and it gave me something of that sense of self-discovery and exaltation which is implicit in the Negro church and in good jazz. Indeed, I had found it in baseball and football games, and it turns up in almost any group activity of Afro-Americans when we're not really thinking about white folks and are simply being our own American selves.

I'm reminded of a discussion that another Tuskegeean and I were having with a group of white friends. The discussion had to do with our discovery of Hemingway (whom I discovered in a Negro barbershop) and Conrad (another writer I often discussed with Wright), and suddenly the Tuskegee graduate said to me, "Aren't you glad that we found those guys on our own at Tuskegee?"

Now, that was not Negro chauvinism, but a meaningful observation about the relationship between social scene and experience, and I concurred. Because I had had the same reaction when I first talked with Wright about fictional technique and we had gone on to discuss some of the complications and interconnections between culture and society that claimed our conscious attention despite the fact that we were segregated. The question reminded me of how wonderful it was to have read T.S. Eliot in the context of Tuskegee. The question was not raised to celebrate a then-segregated college in a violently segregated state, but to inform our white friends that racism aside, there are other important relationships between scenes, ideas, and experience. Scene and circumstance combined to give ideas resonance and compel a consciousness of perspective. What one reads becomes part of what one sees and feels. Thus it is impossible for me to reread certain passages from Joyce or Eliot or Sir Thomas Browne without seeing once again the deep magenta skies that descend upon the Tuskegee campus at dusk in summer. The scene, then, is always a part of personality, and scene and personality combine to give viability to ideas. Scene is thus always a part, the ground, of action—and especially of *conscious* action. Its associations and implicit conflicts provide the extra dimension which anchors poetry in reality and structures our efforts toward freedom.

Richard Wright was trying to add to our consciousness the dimension of being a black boy who grew up in Jackson, Mississippi (a scene that was not always so rugged, even for him, as he pictured it artistically), but a boy who grew up and who achieved through his reading a sense of what was possible out there in the wider world. A boy who grew up and achieved and accepted his own *individual* responsibility for seeing to it that America become conscious of itself. He insisted that it recognize the interconnections between its places and its personalities, its act and its ideals. This was the burden of Richard Wright and, as I see it, the driving passion of Richard Wright.

It led to his triumphs as it led, inevitably, to some of his defeats. But one thing must be said of Richard Wright: In him we had for the first time a Negro American writer as randy, as courageous, and as irrepressible as Jack Johnson. And if you don't know who Jack Johnson was, I'll tell you that when I was a little boy that early heavyweight boxing champion was one of the most admired underground heroes. He was rejected by most whites and by many respectable Negroes, but he was nevertheless a hero among veterans of the Spanish-American War who rejoiced in the skill and élan with which Johnson set off the now-outrageous search for a "White Hope."

This suggests that we literary people should always keep a sharp eye on what's happening in the unintellectualized areas of our experience. Our peripheral vision had better be damned good. Because while baseball, basketball, and football players cannot really tell us how to write our books, they *do* demonstrate where much of the significant action is taking place. Often they are themselves cultural heroes who work powerful modification in American social attitudes. And they tell us in nonliterary terms much about the nature of possibility. They tell us about the cost of success, and much about the nonpolitical aspects of racial and national identity, about the changing nature of social hierarchy, and about the role which individual skill and excellence can play in creating social change.

In this country there were good Negro writers before Wright arrived on the scene—and my respects to all the good ones—but it seems to me that Richard Wright wanted more and dared more. He was sometimes too passionate, I think now as I offer you the memories of a middle-aged man. But at least Wright wanted and demanded as much as any novelist, any artist, should want: He wanted to be tested in terms of his talent, and not in terms of his race or his Mississippi upbringing. Rather, he had the feeling that his vision of American life, and his ability to project it eloquently, justified his being considered among the best of American writers. And in this crazy, mixed-up country, as is witnessed by this conference dedicated to his works and to his memory, it turns out that he was right.

Al Young

(b. 1939)

Born in Ocean Springs, Mississippi, in 1939, Al Young learned to read at the age of three. His father, a professional bassist and tuba-player, filled the house with records and music, and music continues to be one of the main metaphors that drives Young's poetry, fiction, and essays. He is the author of more than fifteen books, including **Heaven: Collected Poems 1956–1990**, **Straight No Chaser** *(1994), the novels* **Sitting Pretty** *(1976) and* **Seduction by Light** *(1988), and the musical memoirs* **Mingus Mingus** *(with Janet Coleman, 1989), and* **Drowning in the Sea of Love** *(1995). Following his childhood and adolescence in Mississippi and Michigan, Young migrated to California, where he completed his Bachelor of Arts degree in Spanish at the University of California, Berkeley. Language in all its written and spoken inflections, philosophy, music, science, cultural ideology, mysticism, and travel are his lifetime fascinations. He has written numerous screenplays for such popular performers as Richard Pryor, Sidney Poitier, and Bill Cosby. A tireless writer and lecturer, who often performs his work with jazz artists, Young has taught at Stanford, University of California, Santa Cruz, the University of Washington, and the University of Michigan, and traveled widely. Translations of his work have appeared in Latin America, Asia, and Europe, and he is the recipient of numerous awards as well as Guggenheim, Fulbright, National Endowment for the Arts, and Lila Wallace-Reader's Digest fellowships. In whatever genre he happens to be working, Al Young's focus is always on the human heart, the human spirit, and a largely neglected, shared global destiny.*

Somebody Done Hoodoo'd the Hoodoo Man

Junior Wells, 1967

I grew up in homes where the verbal jam session was a floating and usually festive fixture. Clusters of people were forever talking with one another, telling stories, sharing experiences, observations, jokes, riddles, conundrums, and swapping lies. Our talk was musical. The old folks often quoted scripture and we all mimicked the voices and gestures of others, marbling the fat of our utterance with lean strips of proverbial wisdom: "A dog that'll *carry* a bone will *bring* you one." Much later I would become aware of the Kenyan proverb that goes: "Talking with one another is loving one another." For then it was enough to take delight in the pictures and emotions that flooded my imagination as I went about learning, by ear and by heart, the nature of the world that lay beyond my childhood walls and fields.

I used to curl up on floor pallets in a corner or in warmly quilted beds with the door ajar and, while pretending to be asleep, listen to the grown folks carry on into the night by kerosene lamplight—with crickets or rain or wind in the background—way back up in rural Pachuta, Mississippi, and other distant settings.

Language and its stitched-together patterns of sound and beat and melody and pitch was real for me. Those crazy-quilt patches of bright and somber and giddy sound formed the literal fabric of my tender world. They were to be taken every bit as seriously as the very tree stump by the side of the dust road winding into town; that stately chinaberry stump where Uncle John, my maternal grandfather's brother, boasted that he'd once seen a hair-raising haint trot past one autumn long ago, hundreds of midnights before I was born. "He was ridin on a moon-white steed," said Uncle John, "and he was as close to me as you sittin from me now. Old Jack seen it too, like to sked him half to death. Rared back, commence to buckin and jeckin so bad I got gooseflesh!"

But I knew Old Jack. He was still alive and he was Uncle John's favorite riding mule. And I knew what Papa, my grandfather, meant when he'd haul off and say in the dead of winter, "I'm tireda hurryin down there to see bout John's mules. Only thing John's mules sufferin from is the miss-meal colic."

It was all as clear and mysteriously evident as lightning bugs pinpointing the summer-starved nights, winking out their starry morsels of code. My cousin Jesse and the other kids even held long discussions about this. That was probably the way fireflies talked with one another. We figured there had to be some luminous cipher involved that was none of people's business. All the same, we spent hours trying to break the lightning bug code; that is, when we weren't dashing around trapping them in Mason jars to make our own special flashlights. The rise and fall of locust choirs on sizzling afternoons was equally magnetizing. Locusts, in fact, provided the background music for a signal incident that buzzes through my memory circuits to this day.

I'd just finished feeding the chickens and was resting on the edge of the back porch, lazily scrawling letters in the yard dirt with a prized stick, when an old, raggedy, smiling hobo appeared out of nowhere. He wore a faded, floppy straw hat and was carrying a burlap croaker sack. I stood, startled, and looked at once to see what Claude was going to do. Claude was our sleek, black farm dog whose jet keen nose usually picked up everything. But Claude didn't stir; he didn't let out so much as a low growl. That tattered stranger, armed with nothing but a grin, crouched at the porch steps where Claude had been dozing and, nodding a friendly "Hi do?" in my direction, patted the dog on his tick-tortured head just as gently as anyone in the family might have done.

Mama, my grandmother, was coming from her garden with an apronful of fresh-cut okra, snapbeans and green tomatoes. I could see she was as puzzled as I was. Nevertheless, she put on a smile, walked around to where we were and she and the hobo exchanged pleasantries. He wasn't asking for a handout or odd jobs to do; he was only passing through and had somehow lost his way. Mama, her gold tooth fittings flashing in the late sunlight, patiently re-routed him, invited him to pluck a few figs and gather some pecans, then sent him on his way. He seemed harmless enough. But when he was gone, she studied Claude and looked at me, then stepped into the shadows of the porch. Narrowing her lucent brown eyes, she said, "I do believe that old rascal musta hoodoo'd that dog." She said this low under her breath, just loud enough for me to hear.

"Hoodoo!" I said. I must've been seven, maybe eight, and I'd heard the term but never from her lips until now. Its meaning had long been hidden from me. "What's hoodoo, Mama?"

"Hoodoo?" she repeated with a slow smirk that wasn't easy to read. "Aw, that's a kinda magic, whatchacall conjure. You burn candles, you mix these powders, get a holt to a locka somebody's hair or a piece of they clothes, say these words over and over. It's magic, but it's the Devil's magic. See, God got his magic and the Devil got his. Myself, I don't like to be foolin with them hoodoo people, never did."

"Well, how come you say that man done hoodoo'd Claude?"

"Cause that dog ain't got no business layin up and lettin that Negro pet him like that. Didn't bark, didn't even budge hardly."

"But how could the man put a hoodoo on him if he hadn't even seen Claude before?"

"That's what we don't know. He coulda slipped round here one night while we was sleep and sprinkled around some goofer dust. Mighta even had some in his hand or up his sleeve just now for all we know."

"But, Mama, wouldn't we'da heard him sneakin round the house here at night?"

"Don't know that either. Them kinda folks know all this lowdown stuff; that's all they study. The man coulda run up on Claude back there in the woods someplace and hoodoo'd him then."

"But why would he wanna hoodoo Claude in the first place?"

Mama trained her gaze on the chickens and the chicken coop and said, "Can't answer that neither, but I can tell you one thing. If I hear any kinda devilment goin on in the night, yall'll hear me shootin my pistol."

This was the same woman who moaned and hummed and sang spirituals all day long while she worked, and who taught me table blessings and the beautiful Twenty-Third Psalm.

It was in such settings that poetry began for me. Perhaps it is children who understand poetry best. I know for certain that, unlike most people, I never outgrew the need or magic or the curative powers of language. The quiescent greenness of those pastures in which I pictured myself lying down is more vivid than ever, and I can see the shapes of cloud and sky reflected in those still waters. I do not take John lightly when he declares, "In the beginning was the Word, and the Word was with God, and the Word was God." Even now in the Nuclear Era when we're constantly only a micro-chip blip away from graceless extinction; even at a time when the functions of poetry have been denigrated and trivialized, when post-literate societies largely regard poetic expression as a mere amusement at best, I've come to view Creation itself as the actualized speech of the Divine; the unnameable, dream-like essence of some marvelous cosmic presence. Sustained and intensive personal experience and involvement with language has opened both my ears and eyes to the magnitude of the Word and its power to transmute perception and consciousness: reality, if you will.

Such lofty realizations have never been uncommon among traditional pre-literate peoples, nor among the so-called civilized. Hindu, Taoist, Christian, Buddhist and Islamic cosmologies abound with them. Leslie Silko opens *Ceremony*, her fecund novel about Indian life on a New Mexico reservation, with a poem that begins: "Ts'its'tsi'nako, Thought-Woman is sitting in her room/and whatever she thinks about/appears." And in his moving book, *Eskimo Realities*, the humanist anthropologist and filmmaker Edmund Carpenter notes: "In Eskimo the word 'to make poetry' is the word 'to breathe'; both are derivatives of *anerca*—the soul, that which is eternal, the breath of life. A poem is words infused with breath of spirit. 'Let me breathe of it,' says the poet-maker and then begins: 'I have put my poem in order on the threshhold of my tongue.'"

It took me quite some time to learn how poetry has always functioned and flourished among all peoples in all times and places, customarily as a natural component of song, dance, work, play, prophecy, healing, exorcism, ceremony, ritual or communal worship. It was the printing press, among other innovations—to say nothing of altered notions about the place of the individual in the scheme of things—that helped change the way we think about poetry and the Word.

Long before the printed word and stuffy ideas about literature turned up in my life, and certainly long before I became the willing ward of schoolteachers, I was sleeping with words. I fondled and sniffed and placed my ear to their secret meanings. I soaked up the silences between syllables, tested them, tasted the saltiness or sweetness of them, and stared off into their bottomless eyes and down their dark, rosy throats. In a world innocent of ABC's, I dreamed in word-pictures and word-objects and word-feelings. And, like most children who live poetry all day long, I disappeared in between the spaces words made. It is this early enchantment with electrifying speech that abides with me still, inspite of the literature industry, inspite of poet-careerists and their ambitions, and quite inspite of the poetry scene itself.

"I always knew you were gonna be strange," Mama reminded me recently. She lived to be one hundred years and six months; a tough and beautiful little country woman whose light-drenched eyes can still see clean through me. My father's long gone from this world, and my mother just slipped away too. I've wandered and rambled from Mississippi to Michigan to California; all over this country, all over the world. And Mama's still here, telling me things I need to hear. "Always knew you were gonna be strange. From the time you could babble, you had your own way of talkin and understandin. We would put you on the floor with a funnybook or a magazine while you was still a baby, and you'd start turnin pages and feelin on em, and drift right off into some other world. Never would cry hardly. Long as you had them books to look at, you was happy. I never seen anything like it."

All my life I've been trying to hold onto and expand the joyous purity of those early moments and the magical talk that nourished it. Word by word, line by line, season upon season, poetry keeps teaching me that the only time there is is now.

Samuel R. Delaney

(b. 1942)

Frequently described as one of the most famous and controversial science fiction writers of the late twentieth century, Samuel R. Delaney is the author of more than twenty-five books of fiction and nonfiction, including the novels **Babel 17**, **The Einstein Intersection**, **Dhalgren**, **Stars in My Pocket Like Grains of Sand**, *and* **The Bridge of Lost Desire**. *These pages are selected from his controversial but highly readable autobiography,* **The Motion of Light in Water**, *1988. Subtitled* **Sex and Science Fiction Writing in the East Village, 1957-1965**, *it deals with the writer's unusual childhood, adolescence, and early adulthood in Manhattan, where he was born in 1942. A youthful folksinger, who worked with Bob Dylan, a budding scientist who met and spoke with Albert Einstein, a teenage father and groom who knew even then that he was gay. Delaney attended the Bronx High School of Science and the City College of New York. Imaginative, pithy, and mythic describe Delaney's open-minded approach to autobiographical narrative in which metaphor and conscious re-invention and manipulation of the "verifiable" past play emphatically exciting roles.*

from The Motion of Light in Water

8.0 I've often asked myself why Marilyn and I married. At different times I've given myself different answers. Since age ten or so, I'd known my major sexual preferences were homosexual. Through my adolescence, as I'd explored this personally difficult (as all sex is) and socially confused (as most sex is) situation—at least as it awaited young people in the fifties, who then had little chance of any parental support—Marilyn had been among my few confidantes, as I'd soon become one of hers for her own heterosexual explorations.

But who were we, this Jew from the Bronx, this black from Harlem?

In many ways, neither of us was typical of the image the preceding sentence evokes—yet the truth it tells, under its bipartite interrogation, is necessary for any understanding.

Where had we come from?

How had we come together?

For all new marriages, I suspect, afford their moments of retrospection and account taking, their late-night hours, their hours at early dawn, when we survey and choose among the elements of the past that have, most likely, brought us to the present—as much as a month spent in a mental hospital.

8.01 As a child, I was fascinated by science and math. Like so many kids of those years, I'd made crystal radios and wound high-frequency coils and designed primitive computer circuits to play nim and add numbers in binary notation. I looked up various topics of mathematics on my own and, in my manner, tried to study them. The private, progressive Dalton School I'd attended since I was five didn't actively dissuade me—and called that lack of dissuasion encouragement. I wrote plays and tried to write novels and was stunned, at eight, when a classmate, a girl named Gabby, wrote a beautiful letter from the hospital in the form of a rebus, illustrated with words and pictures cut from magazines (" ... Life [the colophon from a *Life* magazine] here in the *Hospital* [the word cut from a piece of letterhead stationery] is no *Bed* [picture of a bed] of *Roses* [picture of a bunch of red roses] ... "), then died; and learned how to do splits and cartwheels from Wendy and memorized "The Raven" and "Jabberwocky" and Gilbert and Sullivan lyrics with Priscilla; and—after seeing a high school production of it one week and the next an Old Vic presentation at the ancient Metropolitan Opera House, with Robert Helpmann as Oberon and fiery-haired Moira Shearer as Titania, with impossibly ornate sets and a wonderfully obscene homoerotic Puck—learned long slabs of *A Midsummer Night's Dream* with Peter; and *The Waste Land* and "The Love Song of J. Alfred Prufrock"—because Sue-Sue, in the high school division, told me Eliot was impossible to understand and I'd show them—and read science fiction with Robert and Johnny; and borrowed Priscilla's *Mad* comic book to read in the boys' john, cover to cover, and called her nightly to ask her how were things in Afghanistan; and drew maps of imaginary lands; and listened to Tom Lehrer records with my friend Mike, who, like Johnny and Robert, was an inveterate nail-biter and was the one other kid from Dalton who would also be going on, with me, to the Bronx High School of Science.

And in the afternoons, after swimming, my nose still sharp with chlorine, my ears still wet, I left the ten-story red-brick school building just off Park Avenue to take the bus home to the three-story private house, well above 110th Street—Harlem's southern boundary—in which my father's funeral home filled the first floor, with Mr. Onley's Grocery just to our left and Mr. Lockley's Hosiery and House Paint Store to our right, as every morning I left that house, in my early years to be driven, and later to wait on the corner for the No. 2, to transect that boundary once again: in social terms a journey of near ballistic violence, carried out each day in more or less indifferent silence.

8.02 I'd begun to play the guitar at summer camp. After half a dozen years of violin lessons, and three years in my elementary school orchestra as first-chair violinist, a position (and desk) I shared with an older boy named Tony, the new instrument was very easy. Though when I'd begun, he'd played the violin no more than I did, my father had gotten a set of elementary books and for the first six months had been my teacher—for he was a man who could get music out of just about any instrument he picked up. He'd played the cornet until shortly before I was born and, when much younger, had sat in a few times with Cab Calloway's band. He and my mother had been close friends of Cab and his wife, Lady Constance, and Christmas—Cab's birthday—would see the four of them at an annual hockey game with which Cab celebrated, before his party, later, up at his home, the recreation room set up in a replica of the Cotton Club, the only way that anyone black who was not a performer working there could ever get to see it, as Negroes were not allowed in as audience.

But now my father ran a Seventh Avenue funeral home.

He was a tall man, and a number of distant female cousins or young women friends of the family would confide to me, after his death, that they'd always thought him dashingly handsome. My father was also a very nervous man. My mother's sister, Virginia, frequently put it: "If there's any way to worry about it at all, don't worry, Sam will find it." His intense anxieties put a constant strain on my mother, and certainly on my sister and me—which, in my case, led to frequent arguments and general hostility.

For my twelfth birthday, my father's best friend (another tall, good-looking black man), Bebe, made me a hand-carved sailboat. It was nearly two and a half feet long. Bebe had cast the keel in lead himself. The deck had been scored with burn lines from a soldering iron to suggest planking. The rudder was functional; under the removable cabin, down inside, was a sponge to soak up any water that slopped down in it; and its single mast carried the triangular sails, forward and aft, of a tall schooner. Indeed, the boat was not actually finished by April, though I was taken to see it, and there was a promise that, as soon as it was done, Bebe, my father, and I would go out to sail it in the lake in Central Park, below the walls and minarets of Castle Belvedere. A few months later, on a Sunday morning with the boat, that's where we were.

Bebe had never built a boat for sailing before, and even with the lead on the keel, the balance was not right. The moment it went in the water, the mast listed a good twenty degrees. My suggestion was to put a couple of rocks, which I dug up from the grasses beside the lake, down in with the sponge. It corrected the list till the mast was only about five or ten degrees off plumb. Then we began the endless adjusting of the sails.

All around us, people were sailing other boats—some with remote-control motors—easily and neatly. But beautiful job of carving that it was, Bebe's boat would move out, turn sharply, come back, and bump the shore. Or if the breeze had any strength at all, the boat would simply turn on its side and drop its mast to the water. Bebe was an easygoing guy—all my father's close friends had to be—and was sitting back while Dad sputtered and pulled at this string, and tried to tighten the other bit of slack. That's when I looked up and saw the elderly man standing a few feet off, watching.

He was just about my height, was wearing a gray sweater, somewhat baggy pants, and cloth shoes. His white hair tufted from both sides of his head. He had a full, gray mustache, and he stood with a pipe held up against his chest, in one rather slender hand. I recognized him immediately, from endless pictures in *Life*, in *Newsweek*, in *Time*. Now he stepped up, and when he spoke, the German accent confirmed what I was already sure of. "Excuse me," he said. "Perhaps I can help give you a little hand?"

Without looking up, my father launched into an explanation of what, if he could just get … this thing here over there … he was trying … to do.

Bebe asked, "Do you sail boats?"

The man smiled and nodded.

"He built that one himself," I said. "All by hand."

"That's very nice," the man said with evident appreciation.

"It's my birthday present," I went on. "But they're playing with it."

"Ah!" The man laughed. He looked down over my father's shoulder. "Excuse me," he said. "If you will loosen the back sail there, you won't have such a problem with the way it leans … "

My father looked up.

"May I … ?" the man said.

A little flustered, my father said, "Well, all right … go ahead, if you want."

The man knelt down at the boat. As soon as he took it in his hands, he frowned. "Oh," he said, looking up at us. "Well, you do have a problem here. It really is just too top-heavy." He sighed and loosened the sail anyway.

"That's what I told him," Bebe said, meaning my father.

"This probably won't help then," the man said, finishing his knot and standing, while the boat bobbed at the lake's edge, "very much. But it certainly looks nice."

"Thank you anyway," I said and held out my hand. I was not going to let our visitor get away without a handshake. He took my hand firmly in his. "Thank you," I said again.

The ritual once started, Bebe shook hands with him, and finally, standing, my father did too.

The man smiled, nodded, gestured with his pipe, and turned away. I didn't think my father knew who he was, but I was sure Bebe had recognized him. But Bebe was looking over my dad's shoulder again; and Dad was again squatting over the boat. I glanced back at the man, who was now thirty yards away and almost invisible through the park's Sunday strollers.

"Hey," I said, "do you know who that *was*?"

"Huh?" Dad said.

"That old guy?" Bebe asked.

"That was Albert Einstein!"

Bebe looked up, with a big frown. "Oh, no, it couldn't ... " Then he strained to see through the crowd. "You know, it did look like him, some."

"Not 'some,' " I said. "It *was* him!"

Now my father was frowning too. "What would Albert Einstein be doing in Central Park on Sunday morning, playing with boats?"

"I'm not kidding," I said. "I know it was him. I've seen pictures." And twenty years later I first read about the famous physicist's hobby: model sailboats.

8.03 In June 1956, I left Dalton and got ready to go on to the Bronx High School of Science, a city public school (yes, in the Bronx) of megacephalic reputation, where, already, some of my older cousins went. One, Nanny, a year before, had written a couple of brief, reflective essays, one of which dealt with the time years before that, when she, her younger brothers, and my aunt (my father's older sister) and uncle had lived upstairs from us in the building on Seventh Avenue. The essay had been published in the school's literary magazine, *Dynamo*, for January 1955. My family made much of it, and I sat in my cousins' dark living room, on Fish Avenue in the Bronx, reading it again and again, now looking at other pieces in the magazine, even memorizing some of the other poems in the issue by students I'd never heard of.

Nanny had written:

> LEVY AND DELANEY FUNERAL HOME was the sign that always greeted me when I came home from school. My uncle was Delaney. Levy was dead and had been even before I was born. This always used to remind me of "Scrooge and Marley," except that my uncle was no Scrooge. He was tall, mild-mannered, and quite the opposite of Scrooge or any stereotyped mortician. He and his family lived on the second floor, while we lived on the third floor of the small brick house that seemed out of place between the towering Harlem apartments ... At times I wished I didn't live over a funeral home, especially when my friends teased me about ghosts and other horrible apparitions of the dead. Although I laughed with them to hide my self-consciousness, I never could see how a corpse could harm anyone ... My young brother, my cousin [that was me, I knew], and I thought nothing of playing hide-and-seek in the basement among the new coffins on display ...
> There were two entrances to the building. The door to the left led directly upstairs and the door on the right to the funeral parlor. Sometimes I used the right-hand door. Once inside the funeral parlor, members of the family

could use another door which opened into the hallway leading to the stairs. One day, when I came home from school, I walked through the funeral parlor toward the door to the hallway and saw two large screens near this door. My curiosity was aroused, and by climbing up the stairs and holding on to the banister, I was able to peer around the doorway and over the screen. I caught my breath, for lying amid white satin was a most beautiful woman. She wore a long blue gown: a red rose was fastened in her dark hair ...

As I read and reread my cousin's account of a memory of ten or more years before, while I recognized the tone and the timbre of her description of "the small brick building" where I now lived (my family now had both the second and third floors), I found myself curious over two things. First, how could she have described my father as "mild-mannered"? To me he was always an angry, anxious man. Perhaps, I thought, because he might read it, she'd had to say something nice. (Her own father, my Uncle Ed, had been, in my own memories of that earlier time, the mild and gentle man in the house.) Also (and oddly this bothered me even more), though the two doors into the building she'd mentioned in her essay were just as she'd described, she'd committed a fundamental distortion of the architecture.

Opening from one of the offices into the stairway up to the second floor (yes, that office had once been a viewing room: I could remember the screens with their maroon crushed velvet in their wooden frames standing beside the caskets), that door was much too far from the foot of the stairs, by three or four feet, to allow you, in the hall stair, to look through it while standing on the steps themselves.

Nanny was tall, almost six feet. But—and, back at home, I tried it again and again—you would have to have been at least nine or even ten feet tall to stand on the bottom step and lean forward far enough to see around the jamb and through the door into the other room. And of course with each step you went up, you'd have to be even taller. As I stood on the bottom step, holding the end of the banister and leaning out to test it, I found myself reflecting: Nanny's clear and lucid memory was of a beautiful brown-skinned young woman with a rose in her hair, lying in one of the satin-lined caskets. Mine, from no more than a year back, was of walking, by myself, into the little morgue behind the chapel, where a dark, ordinary-looking black man, in his late twenties or thirties, lay, naked, on the white-enamel embalming table with its drain grooves leading to the trough around it. I walked around him a bit, looking at his genitals, his slightly turned-out feet, his lightly closed eyes, watching him under the fluorescent lights for a minute. Fascinated by what I wasn't sure, I reached over and took the cool and wholly limp hand in mine—and found myself getting an erection ...

Surely somewhere a reality lay behind Nanny's account—an account that, indeed, presented itself as real. The family was terribly proud of her piece, passing it around from one to the other; and my father said, again and again, how touched he was by her memory. (Would I, I wondered—a full year before I entered the school—ever have anything published in *Dynamo*?) But whatever that reality was, it had been sealed outside of, and by, the text. I would never have dared question it, to Nanny or anyone else—because I did not want anyone to question mine. Whatever had actually happened was held, in some other time and place, safely outside any language that I could bring myself to initiate, or that anyone else even thought to.

That seemed to be, if anything, the power of writing—to hold sway over memory, making it public, keeping it private, possibly, even keeping it secret from oneself—for I was sure Nanny felt (ten years after the fact) that the impossible feat of elongation she'd described at the foot of the stairs was as true as—many years on—I would come to feel my sentence was about my father's death.

Itabarí Njeri

(b. 1954)

A graduate of Boston University and the Columbia School of Journalism, Itabarí Njeri has worked as a professional actress and singer (from opera to rhythm and blues doo-wop). Presently a staff reporter for the **Los Angeles Times***, she did her rookie reporting for the* **Greenville News** *and for National Public Radio in Boston, where she was also a producer. As a reporter for the* **Miami Herald***, Njeri wrote features, arts criticisms, and essays—personal and social, such as the award-winning "Granddaddy," an amazing almost cinematic account of how she tracked down and confronted the all-but-forgotten murderers of her grandfather, a Georgia physician.* **Every Good-Bye Ain't Gone; Family Portraits and Personal Escapades***, her acclaimed first book, drew raves from Charles Johnson, Trey Ellis, and the* **New York Times** *Book Review.*

Born in Brooklyn in 1954, where her life began "in a neighborhood of Caribbean immigrants and African American migrants from the South," Njeri writes with exhilarating warmth, power, verve, and irony about contemporary conflicts, whether they be cultural, communal, familial, sexual, professional, or spiritual.

Granddaddy

I drove along a road in southern Georgia. It was a night without a moon. Beyond the pine trees and farmland I could see fire in the distance. Farmers had torched their fields to clear the earth for planting. Bark and grass smoldered at the edge of the road. I saw a tall pine ablaze, and I could not suppress the thought of a burning cross as I drove to the house of the man who killed my grandfather twenty-three years ago.

I had heard the tale all of my life: Drunken white boys drag racing through a small southern town in 1960 had killed my granddaddy. Nobody, I was told, knew their names. Nobody, I was told, knew what happened to them. Things were hushed up. Those were the rumors. What everyone knew was this: Granddaddy was a black doctor in Bainbridge, Georgia. Late on the night of October 30 his phone rang. It was an emergency. A patient was gravely ill. Granddaddy left his home in his robe and pajamas, drove to the small infirmary he ran in town and treated his patient. As he was returning home, a car collided with his. My grandfather was thrown to the pavement. His ribs were broken; his skull was cracked.

Several hours later, the telephone call came to my parents' apartment in Harlem. Granddaddy was dead.

During my childhood, my grandfather was the only adult male I remember openly loving me. Yet, oddly, I seemed unable to absorb the meaning of his death. I felt no grief. Nineteen sixty had been filled with confusing events that disturbed the calm childhood I had known. The distant and accidental violence that took my grandfather's life could not compete with the psychological terror that had begun to engulf my own. The year my grandfather died, my own father returned, and I began to sleep each night with a knife under my pillow.

As I grew older, my grandfather assumed mythic proportions in my imagination. Even in absence, he filled my room like music and watched over me when I was fearful. His fantasized presence diverted thoughts of my father's drunken rages. With age, my fantasizing ceased, the image of my grandfather faded. What lingered was the memory of his caress, the pain of something missing in my life, wrenched away by reckless white youths. I had a growing sense—the beginning of an inevitable comprehension— that this society deals blacks a disproportionate share of pain and denial.

With time, I felt compelled to find out what really happened in Bainbridge that night in 1960.

My family wasn't much help. My stepgrandmother, Madelyn, had suffered a nervous breakdown after the accident and to this day is unyielding in her refusal to discuss it. "It's been twenty-three years," she says. "It took me a long time to get past that. I don't want to open old wounds."

She also feared that, if I stirred things up, "they might desecrate" my granddaddy's grave. If she still held such fears after so much time, I needed no other reason to return to Bainbridge, and so I did.

Black people in Bainbridge had told me my grandfather was buried in Pineview Cemetery. "It's the black cemetery in the white part of town," said Anne Smith, seventy-eight, an elegant, retired schoolteacher. Granddaddy had delivered her baby. "The white cemetery is in the black part of town," she said.

I headed for the white part of town.

The streets were unfamiliar. I had only been to Bainbridge twice before, in 1957 and 1958.

Mama and I had flown to Tallahassee from New York City. Granddaddy had picked us up and driven the forty-two miles north to Bainbridge, Georgia's "first inland port," population 12,714, then. The town lies in the southwest corner of the state, north of Attapulgus, south of Camilla.

My grandfather had moved there in 1935 after his residency at Brewster Hospital in Jacksonville, Florida. Shortly before, he'd divorced my Jamaican-born grandmother, Ruby Duncombe Lord, to marry Madelyn Parsons, a much younger woman. Ruby never had a kind word to say about Granddaddy. Their marital problems were myriad, but among them was her refusal to move to the Jim Crow South from New York. "I'll not step aside for any white people," she boldly claimed. What she really felt, I suspect, was justifiable fear of a life filled with terrorism. But Bainbridge needed a black doctor, so Granddaddy went.

I spent two summers with my grandfather, and a few holidays. I was about four the first time we met, and properly outfitted for the occasion in a brilliant yellow, silk-and-satin-trimmed peignoir. I believed myself devastating. But the straps kept slipping. The sleeves kept sliding. I didn't care. Granddaddy hugged me and chased me in circles around the house till we fell down laughing on the floor.

"Oh, Granddaddy, I don't feel so well," I'd tease.

"We can't have that," he'd say, then run and get his black bag and pretend to prepare an injection.

"No, no. I'm fine, Grandpa." He'd chase me again.

"Sure you're fine now?"

"I'm sure." I squealed and ran myself silly. He'd catch me, hug me and tickle me to tears.

Now I was searching for his grave.

The weather was windy, cold, very gray. In the car, outside the cemetery, I sat searching for my sunglasses. I kept fumbling for them, in my purse, under the seat. I had not cried once.

It was my third day in town. I had talked to dozens of people who knew him, trying to reconstruct his life and death. I wanted to be professionally detached, unemotional. I cursed the missing sunglasses.

Thirteen minutes later I gave up and stepped out of the rented car.

I began walking around the southern rim of the graveyard. His would be a big tombstone, I was sure.

"Was he good?" repeated L.H.B. Foote incredulously. "One of the best. He never stopped trying to learn medicine and that makes any doctor good." Leonard Hobson Buchanan Foote, M.D., did not look his eighty-five years. We had sat in his Tallahassee home on the Florida A&M University campus. For forty years he had been the director of student medical services there. He had been one of my grandfather's closest friends.

They entered Howard University the same year. "The freshman class of 1918," Foote said. The year before, my grandfather had immigrated to the United States from Georgetown, Guyana, then a British colony.

"I was just a boy from Maryland," Foote said, "born and reared just north of Baltimore." Granddaddy, he recalled, "was tall, slender, a nice-looking young colored man with a foreign accent. I'd say, 'Man, I can't understand you. What are you saying?' He'd say, 'You just listen real good. I speak the King's English.' I said, 'What king?' He said, 'The King of England.' 'You're one of those West Indians, huh?' 'Yeah, what's wrong with that?' 'Not a thing,' I said. 'Welcome here, brother.'"

"I felt like I had lost a brother when he died. He had a lot of whites who were his friends, some of them were his patients."

But, he said, Granddaddy had been the object of some resentment. There are, explained Foote, *"three things that the southern white man has tried over the years to keep out of the hands of blacks—education, money and social rank. Your grandfather had all that."*

As I walked to the western edge of the graveyard, I heard voices nearby. Several houses lined the western perimeter of the cemetery. I stared at the windows looking out on the tombstones.

"Rumor was, one of the boys in the car could look out his kitchen window and see Daddy's grave," my aunt Earlyne had told me.

I searched for nearly an hour. Finally, I reached the north end. About fifty feet ahead of me I spotted a gray marble headstone.

I stepped closer to the tombstone, a solitary monument in a twenty-foot-square plot. It was the biggest headstone in the cemetery: The Family of Dr. E A R Lord.

I started standing in the cold. I wiped my nose. In the crevice of the chiseled letters that formed the word "of," dirt and rain had left a sooty streak. It was the only smudge on the stone. Unconsciously, I leaned forward and began to wipe the stain with the pink Kleenex in my hand. I rubbed hard against the marble. The tissue frayed and disintegrated in the wind.

On the slab of marble that covered his grave was the symbol of the medical profession, the caduceus with its entwined serpents on a winged staff. Engraved in the stone was his full name: Edward Adolphus Rufus Lord Sr. M.D.

They called him Earl Lord for short. He was born July 26, 1897, in Georgetown, Guyana. He died October 30, 1960, in Bainbridge, Georgia.

"Wasn't from around here," Bernice Busbee drawled. The man across from her stood gnomelike behind the rocking chair in his office, smiled like Puck and softly proclaimed himself "the oldest living white person in Bainbridge." Then Mortimer Alfred Ehrlich, M.D., eighty-nine, sat down and rocked.

He was retired. As a younger man Dr. Ehrlich had often come to my grandfather's infirmary to help with surgery. He was one of the few whites in Bainbridge whom my family thought of as a genuine friend.

I told him only that I was a newspaper reporter doing a story about small-town doctors; I wanted him to speak freely. Then I asked him about Dr. Lord.

Dr. Ehrlich regarded me thoughtfully.

"I don't want to talk bad of the dead," he said. I switched off the tape recorder and smiled my encouragement.

"He was a bad man," Ehrlich finally said. The old chair groaned with each rock.

"Blacks didn't like him either," Busbee offered. She had been Ehrlich's receptionist for thirty-one years. Now they spent their days making quilts for comfort when it's cold. "He was an undermining, sneaky fellow," she said. "He tried to bring the NAACP in here."

"Lord was for integration," Ehrlich elaborated.

"He just didn't fit in," she said. "Didn't understand the people. Didn't know our ways. We were all glad when he was gone."

My smile was beginning to ache.

"If he hadn't been killed in the accident, he would have been shot," Ehrlich said. "Better he was killed that way so we didn't have the bother of a trial for whoever shot him."

We spoke for a few more minutes. Then I rose to leave and shake his hand. He offered the tips of his fingers.

I left him rocking.

That old white southerners would have believed that the NAACP was subversive, and condemned my grandfather for belonging to it, did not surprise me. That my grandfather was political at all did.

I had thought my family in Bainbridge to be insulated, apolitical members of the southern black bourgeoisie under segregation. I recall going to a movie theater with my uncle Paul and my aunt Pat, the youngest of the five children Granddaddy had with Madelyn. I wandered to the "wrong" side of the theater lobby to read the posters advertising the coming attractions.

"No, come here," Aunt Pat said, tugging me gently.

"Why?" I boomed, pulling her to where I wanted to be.

"You just can't," Uncle Paul told me with no further explanation. He was tall, handsome and dark brown like Granddaddy, while Aunt Pat was so pale she could have gone into the "whites only" section of the theater unnoticed. But I recall no signs that announced the Jim Crow seating plan. I had never heard of him, and my aunt had to put a hand over my mouth to quiet my protests from the balcony.

"Why are we up here? Why can't we sit downstairs?"

I remembered that night in the theater when I called Aunt Earlyne to tell I was going back to Bainbridge.

"We always grew up so secure," she insisted. "We could just walk into any store and say 'Charge it.'" As she spoke, I envisioned the delicate string of pearls, my first and only, that she sent to me when I was just a toddler. The Lords, she said, could take clothes out of a store on approval at any time. This was when most southern blacks weren't allowed to try on a pair of shoes. You bought them and suffered if they didn't fit. "We never really felt any open hostility toward us," she mused. "But it was always something you knew was there. You knew how far you could go in raising an issue. Some things you could get away with. Others, you knew you could not. It was a KKK city and KKK members ran it along with a few politicians from the town's first families."

I would find out later that my grandfather had spoken out for equal pay for black and white teachers in Bainbridge long before the 1954 U.S. Supreme Court ruled that separate could not be equal. He wanted black and white students to use the same textbooks. He wanted black students to ride buses, not walk miles to school.

"All of these inequities were addressed by Dr. Lord," said S. B. Bryant, the retired assistant principal of Hutto High, once all black. Now it is an integrated junior high school. He is seventy-one and blind.

"No one liked the disparities, but there were those who sat supinely by and took it. And there were those, like Dr. Lord, who were concerned." As schoolteachers, "we couldn't openly contribute to the NAACP and keep our jobs."

"Dr. Lord, however, *stayed* in the superintendent's office pleading the cause, so much so that when they got ready to name the swimming pool, it was named after him."

It was the only city-owned swimming facility that allowed blacks. It wasn't integrated until 1970.

There was also a street named after him, in the black part of town. Lord Avenue. It's still there. Still in the black part of town.

Granddaddy's name is still painted on the window of the infirmary he once ran. It is a flophouse now.

Bainbridge seemed a little town locked in time.

The downtown streets were mostly vacant, empty of traffic. An old white man sat on a bench, muttering to himself in front of the gazebo.

The city built the latticed structure a few years ago. In Chamber of Commerce literature costumed southern belles adorn it, but on this day no one was there but the self-absorbed old man and some goldfish. The fish swam in a pool at the base of a statue of a Confederate soldier. Along the marble rim of the pool in gold was: Bainbridge, Incorporated 1829.

I felt like an alien there.

I was born in Brooklyn, the daughter of a Marxist historian and a nurse. I had studied most of my life to be a musician, an opera singer. In the 1970s I embraced what was considered to be radical black politics. I rejected my slave name for an African one. I began to wear only traditional African clothes. I abandoned classical music because it was incompatible with my newly aroused sense of cultural identity. In time I would come to see that black nationalism almost inevitably leads to a kind of cultural chauvinism indistinguishable from racism, the very thing I thought I was fighting.

But no moderation of my political views could make me tolerate the stifling atmosphere of Bainbridge. On my first day in town I spoke with some of the city's young blacks. They spoke with bitterness about the professional opportunities denied them in their hometown. And they laughed dryly at the social outlets Bainbridge offered them: Skatetown, the roller rink, its six nights of rock set aside for soul on Sundays, the unspoken invitation that let blacks know that night—and only that night— was theirs. Meanwhile, their white counterparts got to go to the country club, to which no black belonged. And like the generations of blacks who lived there during and before my grandfather's day, they all said: What do you do if you're black in Bainbridge and you've got ambition? Go to Tallahassee.

"Some nights, a chilling silence would fall on the town," my mother told me, recalling one particularly stark image she maintained of Bainbridge. "It was that time of evening after supper, when the dishes were done and families would gather in the parlor before bed." It seemed as though the town had gasped, held its breath, then minutes later released it with a shudder, she said. "The next morning, word would come that someone had been lynched."

As I walked through the town, I imagined how much more cruel a place it was when my grandfather, elegant and worldly, lived and died there.

I remembered his house on Planter Street in the way a child recalls a beautiful, festive dream. All the room! Lots of space to dance whenever music played; music that poured down on me from above. Granddaddy had installed an elaborate music system with speakers in the ceiling of each room.

In the front of the house was a circular driveway that led to the porch. A dark blue canopy stretched from the front door to the street, to protect guests from inclement weather. Art deco glass bricks framed the windows in each room. A glass brick bar stood on the circular patio in the rear of the house. Four giant white columns grandly marked the boundaries of his property.

What an impertinence that house must have been for a black man in Bainbridge in 1942.

I wondered how many whites in Bainbridge had mourned his death? Who among them would have stepped forward to demand punishment for his killers?

How do you unlock a twenty-three-year-old mystery? Without much hope, I visited the newspaper, the *Bainbridge Post-Searchlight*, published twice weekly, to see if their morgue contained any reference to my grandfather's death, any leads I could follow. I expected to find nothing, but I was wrong.

On the front page, November 3, 1960, where a week later the newspaper would report the election of John F. Kennedy, was a four-paragraph story: "Dr. E.A.R. Lord, well known colored physician, died early Sunday ... " My eyes raced down the column. " ... enroute to Memorial Hospital of injuries sustained ... The accident, according to Bainbridge police officers, occurred ... intersection of Planter and Scott ... "

"Dr. Lord, driving a '53 Ford ... The other vehicle ... '57 Dodge driven by ... "

Nothing quite registered. I had always been told no one ever found out who did it, that the killer had been protected by the white establishment.

But here was his name, on the front page.

John Lawrence Harper, twenty-two.

I jumped for the phone book. Harper wasn't listed, but I felt it didn't matter. If he was still alive, I knew I could find him.

And ask him—what?

I needed more information before I could confront him. How had the accident happened? Was he drunk? If his name was known, might he even have been punished?

With a name, I thought I could find these things out. I hurried across the street to the courthouse.

The files for 1960 showed that John Lawrence Harper had never been charged with a crime. Expecting nothing, I checked the civil court records. A clerk pulled the dockets for the 1960-61 term for me. There was a case styled *Madelyn P. Lord vs. John Lawrence Harper*.

I stared at the page in disbelief.

My grandmother, who had been silent all these years, had not only known the identity of the driver, but sued for damages in 1961. One hundred thousand dollars in damages.

In the file, I found a police report. Under the "apparent cause of accident," it said Harper was "exceeding lawful speed." There was no mention of alcohol.

The case had gone to trial. Harper had alleged the accident was my grandfather's fault; my grandmother had claimed Harper was to blame. On May 5, 1961, a jury had reached a verdict: six thousand dollars for Madelyn Lord.

I called my aunt Earlyne. She was shocked. She knew nothing about a civil suit. She only knew her mother never tried to press any criminal charges both because she was so "traumatized" by Granddaddy's death and because of "politics." It was a Klan town, she reminded me.

But if my grandmother was so traumatized, how did she find the wherewithal to proceed with a civil suit?

Her friends pressed her to do it, said Anne Smith, the retired teacher who told me where to find my grandfather's grave. My grandmother was so upset, she recounted, she let strangers take my grandfather's car away.

My aunt recalled the same story. "Someone took it after the accident, fixed it up and was driving around town in it."

After Granddaddy died, Smith said, my grandma Madelyn was still going into stores charging things for which she could not pay. "I'd go to the house, get the jewelry and have to take it back to the store," Smith said. My grandmother lived in a daze, she told me.

I knew the fog had lifted for my grandmother, but not the fear.

I searched for transcripts of the trial. If they ever existed, they were gone. All that was left, except for routine paperwork, was the list of jurors.

They would be all white. Blacks weren't called for jury duty in Bainbridge, Georgia, in 1961. How would these jurors react to me, a black woman from Miami, on their doorstep asking questions about the local boy who had killed her grandfather?

I wanted the truth, and in this particular town complete honesty didn't seem to be the way to get it. As with Dr. Ehrlich, I decided not to mention I was Dr. Lord's granddaughter. Further, I decided to interview the jurors by telephone. I did not want them to know I was black.

I wanted to be fair. But more important, I wanted the truth.

I wanted to know why Granddaddy died.

Juror James F. Steadham, now seventy-four:

"It was the middle of the night," he remembered. "Lord was half drunk, half asleep ... The boys had gone out to the Dog and Gun Club and I think they were about half drunk and they just run together ... " How good was his memory? The police report made no allegations about alcohol. There was no mention of a blood test for Harper or an autopsy report for my grandfather. I thought it unlikely that Granddaddy had been drinking. He had been aroused from bed by a phone call, had driven to the infirmary and treated a patient. Would he have stopped at a bar on the way home in his pajamas?

I asked Steadham if he knew Dr. Lord.

"Yeah, I just knew him when I saw him. He was a nigger and ... wasn't much association between white and niggers at that time. I had nigger friends that I think just about as much of as white friends."

But "Lord," he said, "was kinda arrogant. Sooner or later somebody would have shot him. He didn't understand the people here ... Bainbridge was a good town to live in for both black and white. He just didn't get along too well with the public. I think he must of come in from the North."

How, I asked him, was the six-thousand-dollar figure arrived at? It seemed a small sum to me even for 1961.

"We kicked that around a bit. Money was scarce and hard to get," he said. He said he thought the award was just. The jury had discussed it, he said, and one juror had pointed out:

"'Never saw a hundred-thousand-dollar nigger.'"

In the next few days I would reach four other jurors, Bainbridge police chief James "Jabbo" Duke, the lawyer who had represented my grandmother in the suit, the former police officer who had investigated the accident, the former district attorney.

No one agreed on anything.

Two of the four jurors I could still find said they remembered nothing of the case. The third said my grandfather had been at fault. The fourth said Harper had been at fault. My grandmother's former lawyer remembered almost nothing about the case, nor did the cop on the scene ("I can hardly remember what happened a week ago"). Chief Duke was also hazy, but he remembered my grandfather well. He said he had been well respected by blacks and whites alike, and a fine doctor.

It was the first kind word about my grandfather that I had heard from a white person, but I could not shake off a skepticism about his sincerity. He hadn't offered his hand to me when we met or parted, either; nor had I offered mine to him.

The police accident report listed two witnesses, though it didn't specify how they happened to be involved. One had left Bainbridge. "That's my son you're talking about," said Benson Woodbery's mother. "No one knows where he is. When the accident happened, he was living with his grandmother." Last she heard, he was living in Florida. " . . . But he's just the kind that drifts," the mother said.

The other witness was Lee Parker, Bainbridge's postmaster. I called him.

"I don't know why they would have my name as a witness. I passed by the accident after it happened. Maybe a half hour, an hour later. Yes, I knew Larry Harper. I grew up in Bainbridge. His father still lives here," Parker told me. The father's name was C. E. Harper.

A short, plump, white-haired man answered the door. He looked like a man perpetually on the verge of telling a joke. In his living room he pointed to a plaster of paris bust swathed with red cloth. He undraped it. It was a woman with cascading, shoulder-length hair and bare breasts big enough to suckle a nation. He laughed. His wife covered it again.

The father of the man who had killed my grandfather was sixty-nine. He seemed genuinely friendly, but clearly uncomfortable. Again, I told him only that I was a reporter writing about small-town doctors, and that during my interviews, Earl Lord's name had been mentioned repeatedly as a physician who'd had some influence in Bainbridge. I asked about Dr. Lord's death.

He said he didn't remember much about the accident. I asked if he knew of any witnesses.

"Lee Parker was in the car with Larry," he volunteered.

Lee Parker. The man who'd been listed as a witness to the accident but denied knowing anything about it. What was he hiding?

I said nothing.

Harper's wife, Estelle, sat staring at the black reporter and white photographer in her living room.

"This isn't going to stir up any racial thing?" Harper asked. He looked genuinely concerned.

"I used to sell insurance, you know," he went on. "I have lots of black friends. Always got along well. I called Larry to tell him you were coming. He wasn't home. He's in Albany, Georgia, now, selling insurance.

"This is not going to stir up a black-white thing?" he asked again. "I know Larry really hated it when it happened," the father assured me.

Perhaps he really did, I thought, looking at the genial man who was his father, a man who had never been deliberately unkind to a black person in his life, probably. Perhaps his son was like him. Probably. Perhaps.

I went back to my motel room and telephoned John Lawrence Harper in Albany.

I kept rehearsing my tone of voice—calm, businesslike, detached. I was trying to keep the nerves and anger out.

His voice was pleasant, youthful. I said that in the course of my story on doctors I had become interested in Dr. Lord, and that I was trying to reconstruct the events of his life and the accident that caused his death.

"So ... what do you want from me?"

"I'm trying to find out what happened," I told him.

"I wouldn't even be interested, it happened so long ago."

I asked if he ever thought about the accident.

"Naw," he said. "The case that happened then was then. I had a lot of feelings then, none now."

I told him there are no official records explaining what actually happened.

"Yeah, probably never will be either, will it?" he tossed out cockily. " ... Probably wasn't important enough to."

I stiffened. "Someone *did* die."

"So, people die in accidents every day."

"What were the circumstances?" I repeated.

"Oh, gosh, it could be a million circumstances ... Good heavens ... "

There was a click. The line went dead. I called back.

"I thought we were through. It's so irrelevant now. You think there's some mystery here to be unwound. I was in a car. Another man was in a car. We met under a red light ... "

"Your father ... told me that Mr. Parker was in the car with you."

"He remembers more about it than I do."

"Why did Mr. Parker say he wasn't involved then?"

"I'm sure he looks back on that thing ... " He paused. "It was a trying experience for all of us. I don't imagine he *wanted* to be involved at the time, and his feelings, probably, when you called him, came back. He probably doesn't recollect the event hardly either.

"There was nobody in the car with me," he said.

"So you father was incorrect?"

"Ah, probably so if he said that."

"So Mr. Parker was not there?"

"Uh, when did you talk to Daddy, today?"

"Yes."

"Yeah, he remembers more about it than I do," Harper repeated sarcastically.

He was understandably defensive, shaken to have an incident half his lifetime old resurrected. That was the reason for the cockiness, the sarcasm, I tried to convince myself. I knew I was upsetting him badly but still I pressed him.

"Do you go to bed with a clear conscience about this?"

"Clear conscience—now wait a minute ... " He raised his voice for the first time. "You went too far there. That thing was cleared up twenty-three years ago and you're asking me something about a conscience. Hey, don't call me anymore." He hung up.

I sat there on the bed of my motel room, trembling. Around me were all my pens and notebooks, all the trappings of the dispassionate journalist.

No, Harper was wrong. It was not "cleared up."

I had to see him in person.

We drove past one-blink-and-gone towns built around railroad tracks, grazing cows and pecan orchards to get to Albany. It was close to dusk when we arrived. The only gas station open downtown had no maps of the city. I found Harper's address in an old phone book at the service station and asked for directions. We got sent to an area of dilapidated shacks near an old railroad station. It was the wrong place.

We turned back toward town and checked into a Holiday Inn. A more recent telephone directory had a different address.

The house was in a well-to-do subdivision with nicely trimmed lawns and lamps at the front door. No lights were on at Harper's address. It was 9:10 P.M. We drove around and returned twenty minutes later. The house was still dark. The photographer stayed in the car while I got out to look closer. The house was empty, recently vacated, it appeared. Newspapers were still in the driveway.

Frustrated, I returned to the motel and dialed information. The operator gave me the same telephone number for Harper that was listed in the current phone directory, but at another address. I resorted to a cab company for directions.

We drove miles past the city limits unable to find it. The absent moon and clouds made the night sky seem opaque. The sudden flicker of light in the woods was startling. I'd never seen torched farmland before. The deeper we drove into the countryside, the more widespread the flames. The fields the farmers set afire posed no danger on the damp earth. It was the glowing branches at the road's edge, overlapping like a cross, that made me shudder ... drift ... into a psychic film noir replay of the past twenty-three years.

We had driven twenty miles and were lost. We turned back. Fifteen miles toward town, I spotted it, Harper's street, just before a railroad crossing. The house was in a tract of modest single-family homes and duplexes. It was midnight. We'd have to return in the morning.

We went back to the Holiday Inn. I drank a shot of cognac and smoked half a pack of cigarettes. I don't care much for liquor. I don't smoke.

At 7:40 A.M., I stepped from my car into the rain at the home of the man I wanted to see. The photographer remained in the car. We knew a camera would make things more difficult.

The house was divided into two apartments. Harper's was on the left. The heels of my black pumps sank in the red mud that covered what should have been a lawn. I entered a dark foyer and pressed the bell. Gloria Harper, his wife, answered the door. I told her my name and gave her my card.

"We have nothing to say to you." She was five feet two inches at most, plump, had brown hair and wore glasses. She pulled the floor-length robe tighter around her.

I told her only her husband could tell me what happened the night of the accident. She stared at me as I stood in the dimly lit hallway dressed all in black, my hands in my pockets, the collar of my coat turned toward my beige cheeks.

"My husband's getting dressed for work. He has nothing to say to you." She shut the door in my face. I stood there for a few moments, breathed deeply, then pressed the bell again.

"Look, I told you—"

I interrupted. I told her what I had heard about the accident.

She stood there framed by the open door. A young boy walked behind her and stood slightly to her left. He was not more than sixteen, bare-chested and dressed in jeans. His hair looked ash blond. One could not be sure in the pale light. But his face was clearly beautiful. He looked pained and perplexed at my presence.

"I'd like to hear your husband's version of what happened."

"He has nothing to tell you," she said.

"Let *him* tell me that, Mrs. Harper." Then I told them. "I'm not interested just as a reporter," I said. "I am Dr. Lord's granddaughter."

"I knew it," Harper exclaimed. He had been standing at the side of the door, out of sight, listening.

He had on a yellow shirt and tan slacks and wore glasses. He looked older than forty-five. Perhaps because his hair was so white. His wife and son formed a zigzag line of defense in front of him.

"I knew it had to be someone from the family," he said excitedly. His hands were stiffly at his sides. He stared at me from behind his child. I realized my stance may have looked threatening. I took my hands out of my pockets.

"You just stay right there," the wife said. "We're calling the police."

"I knew it, I knew it … " Harper kept saying. I heard him pick up the phone. The wife shut the door in my face again. I stood there for a moment, wondering what would happen to me if I stayed to be taken to some small southern city jail. I left.

We drove past groves of nut trees in the drizzling rain and away from Albany. The landscape and the graying light pushed thoughts of John Lawrence Harper from my mind. And my heart slowed, enough for me to think and take stock of what had happened.

I had stood on a man's doorstep and humiliated him in front of his wife and child. For what? What had he done?

Twenty-three years ago he had the misfortune to be in an auto accident that claimed a life.

The rumors had been wrong. There was no evidence of drag racing, none I could find. If there had been a cover-up, it had been pretty inept. Harper's name was front-page news in the local paper. If there had been an injustice, hadn't it been mitigated by a six-thousand-dollar award by a white jury to a black woman?

Despite the pain that induced it, hadn't my grandmother's silence for twenty-three years kept alive in my family a hurtful distortion?

And yet I felt like screaming. Because nothing was resolved, nothing was settled. Absolutely nothing.

I came to Bainbridge, Georgia, hoping to find and expose a killer who had been protected by a white racist society for twenty-three years. That, or something else: to discover that the man who killed Granddaddy had been punished, and that he and the people of his town, whites and blacks, had mourned the loss of a man such as E.A.R. Lord.

But I found neither thing. I found no clear-cut guilt or innocence, nor did I find my grandfather warmly remembered.

In Bainbridge, Georgia, 1983, I found a town that had changed very little in the last twenty-three years, one that had entered this quarter century only reluctantly, dragged by the courts, pouting, without guilt. Yes, it does have integrated schools and a lone black city councilman. And it named a street after a dead black doctor. But it is still strangled by plantation-style racism: gentle-voiced, genteel whites unabashedly talking of niggers, white people still so contemptuous of blacks that they would not soil their hands by touching mine. There is still a black part of town and a white part of town. A black cemetery and a white cemetery. Skatetown rock on weekdays and Skatetown soul on Sundays. Opportunities for whites, a bus ticket out of town for blacks.

And who is to blame?

I came, tried to find blame, and I failed. I wanted to stay in Bainbridge longer. I wanted to go back once I returned to Miami. With more reporting, I argued, I could find an answer; the truth. My editors said no. Then they suggested that Bill Rose, a white reporter born and raised in the South, try to talk to Harper, just to see if he'd feel less threatened. I agreed.

Harper ran to the men's room in his office building when Rose came to see him and would not talk.

At the paper, we struggled with this story for months, arguing over its point of view and the need to dig deeper. It was the only way to find the truth, I bellowed. Finally, I was compelled to write.

A woman whose family had lived in Bainbridge walked into the newsroom months after my return. She was a Miami writer. She told an editor she had something to tell me. Her uncle had been killed by "rednecks" in the town, she said. They had found him walking in the woods, beat him and left him to die. It was the 1930s, she said; about the time my grandfather came to Bainbridge; about the time my mother remembers the chilling silence that fell on the town some evenings. Her uncle's murder, said the woman, almost destroyed her grandmother's life, contributed to her own mother's mental breakdown. The pain becomes "generational," said Marjorie Klein, whose uncle was a Jew.

There is so much blood on the land, who will ever know The Truth?

And so, as a matter of law and justice, I am compelled to consider the whites of Bainbridge to be innocent: the man who drove the car, the jurors who had "never seen a hundred-thousand-dollar nigger" and awarded six thousand dollars, the white town that did not prosecute.

Yet I cannot.

In the absence of proof of guilt, I need some proof of innocence. Or I am left, against the backdrop of my life and the lives of so many others, to wariness.

Would John Lawrence Harper have been prosecuted had he been black and my grandfather white? Can you really expect me to assume otherwise? On that night in Bainbridge, Georgia, twenty-three years ago, even if just for a moment, did John Lawrence Harper heave a sigh of relief that it was only a black man who had died?

How could I assume otherwise?

I feel the suspicion in me. I feel the hatred creeping up. Those feelings are so powerful, they cannot be extinguished by trustingly extending to the town, to the man, the benefit of a doubt. Trust requires more than a failure to prove guilt; it requires a belief in innocence.

The night my grandfather's skull cracked against the pavement, my grandmother Madelyn flew through the street, her white nightgown, her pale, pale skin streaks of light against the darkness. She tried to push through the crowd, a witness told me months after I returned from Bainbridge. A white cop pushed her back gently. "Don't worry yourself, ma'am," he told her. "It's just a nigger."

Against a backdrop of personal loss, against the evidence of history that fills me with a knowledge of the hateful behavior of whites toward blacks, I see people of Bainbridge. And I cannot trust them. I cannot absolve them.

Perhaps you will argue that this is intemperate. Perhaps you will call me a racist. I do not think that I am.

But I am weary of the collective amnesia of most white Americans. I am not responsible for what Daddy or Granddaddy did, they say; and as long as they are innocent of perpetuating the evils of the past, they are right. I read history as a child, not fiction. I understand how insidious was the impersonal social system that had coldly denied opportunity to blacks, and seemingly left no one to blame, as if systems do not bear the marks of their creators.

I saw what it did to my father. It helped shatter him, a classical scholar with a doctorate in philosophy and few options for a black intellectual in America in the 1930s. He spent his life writing about liberty denied because of race and class. He spent his life galled that he was confined to traditional Negro colleges, unrecognized as an important scholar by the white academic establishment, his intellect always defined by the parameters of race.

I found him naked and bloated, lying on his apartment floor, dying, an alcoholic in a diabetic coma, the bills from the liquor store stuck in the pages of his books. I was twenty-five and he was sixty-nine, the anger between us unresolved at his death. I am bitter when I think what society denied him and me. And I am bitter when I think of my grandfather, and the white people of Bainbridge.

In going back to Bainbridge I felt I was tracking down a thousand anonymous bigots whose acts would never be known, whose guilt or innocence would never be judged. Men who killed a black man and laughed. Even men who, without malice, killed a black man and sighed, knowing it ultimately did not matter.

When I returned home, my aunt Earlyne told me that if she met Harper today, she would shake his hand. "That's what Daddy would have wanted," she said. "Turn the other cheek. We can't live in this world with hate."

I know no such charity.

I want a thousand anonymous bigots to know that somebody's grandchild might someday knock at their door, too.

FICTION

Charles W. Chestnutt

(1858–1932)

Born in Cleveland, Ohio, and raised in Fayetteville, North Carolina, Charles Waddell Chestnutt was a precociously gifted student who became a school teacher at the age of fourteen and a principal at the age of twenty-two. In addition to his teaching responsibilities, Chestnutt was frustrated with the limitations imposed upon Blacks in the South. He therefore moved in 1883 to New York, where he briefly worked for a Wall Street news agency before relocating to Cleveland, his birthplace. While working for a railroad company there, Chestnutt began studying the law and publishing short stories, poems, and humorous sketches in local periodicals. These avocational efforts soon paid off: in 1887 Chestnutt not only passed the Ohio state bar but received national attention when his story "The Goophered Grapevine" appeared in the Atlantic Monthly. *The 1989 publication of two short-story collections,* **The Conjure Woman and Other Tales** *and* **The Wife of His Youth and Other Stories of the Color Line,** *inspired Chestnutt to concentrate on his fiction, resulting in three novels over the next six years:* **The House Behind the Cedars** *(1900),* **The Marrow of Tradition** *(1901), and* **The Colonel's Dream** *(1905). Successful in business, active in civic affairs, and engaged in the raising of his family, Chestnutt also managed to write six other novels after 1905; none of them, however, was accepted for publication. Clearly his fictional denunciations of "the unjust spirit of caste"—symbolized in the problems and prejudices of those Blacks who could "pass" for White—did not make for easily publishable reading. Despite this long silencing, Chestnutt received the Springarn Achievement Award in 1928 for his "pioneer work as a literary artist depicting the life and struggles of Americans of Negro descent."*

The Wife of His Youth

Mr. Ryder was going to give a ball. There were several reasons why this was an opportune time for such an event.

Mr. Ryder might aptly be called the dean of the Blue Veins. The original Blue Veins were a little society of colored persons organized in a certain Northern city shortly after the war. Its purpose was to establish and maintain correct social standards among a people whose social condition presented almost unlimited room for improvement. By accident, combined perhaps with some natural affinity, the society consisted of individuals who were, generally speaking, more white than black. Some envious outsider made the suggestion that no one was eligible for membership who was not white enough to show blue veins. The suggestion was readily adopted by those who were not the favored few, and since that time the society, though possessing a longer and more pretentious name, had been known far and wide as the "Blue Vein Society," and its members as the "Blue Veins."

The Blue Veins did not allow that any such requirement existed for admission to their circle, but, on the contrary, declared that character and culture were the only things considered; and that if most of their members were light-colored, it was because such persons, as a rule, had had better opportunities to qualify themselves for membership. Opinions differed, too, as to the usefulness of the society. There were those who had been known to assail it violently as a glaring example of the very prejudice from which the colored race had suffered most; and later, when such critics had succeeded in getting on the inside, they had been heard to maintain with zeal and earnestness that the society was a life-boat, an anchor, a bulwark and a shield—a pillar of cloud by day and of fire by night, to guide their people through the social wilderness. Another alleged prerequisite for Blue Vein membership was that of free birth; and while there was really no such requirement, it is doubtless true that very few of the members would have been unable to meet it if there had been. If there were one or two of the older members who had come up from the South and from slavery, their history presented enough romantic circumstances to rob their servile origin of its grosser aspects.

While there were no such tests of eligibility, it is true that the Blue Veins had their notions on these subjects, and that not all of them were equally liberal in regard to the things they collectively disclaimed. Mr. Ryder was one of the most conservative. Though he had not been among the founders of the society, but had come in later, his genius for social leadership was such that he had speedily become its recognized adviser and head, the custodian of its standards, and the preserver of its traditions. He shaped its social policy, was active in providing for its entertainment, and when the interest fell off, as it sometimes did, he fanned the embers until they burst again into a cheerful flame.

There were still other reasons for his popularity. While he was not as white as some of the Blue Veins, his appearance was as to confer distinction upon them. His features were of a refined type, his hair was almost straight; he was always neatly dressed; his manners were irreproachable, and his morals above suspicion. He had come to Groveland a young man, and obtaining employment in the office of a railroad company as messenger had in time worked himself up to the position of stationery clerk, having charge of the distribution of the office supplies for the whole company. Although the lack of early training had hindered the orderly development of a naturally fine mind, it had not prevented him from doing a great deal of reading or from forming decidedly literary tastes. Poetry was his passion. He could repeat whole pages of the great English poets; and if his pronunciation was sometimes faulty, his eye, his voice, his gestures, would respond to the changing sentiment with a precision that revealed a poetic soul and disarmed criticism. He was economical, and had saved money; he owned and occupied a very comfortable house on a respectable street. His residence was handsomely furnished, containing among other things a good library, especially rich in poetry, a piano, and some choice engravings. He generally shared his house with some young couple, who looked after his wants and were company for him; for Mr. Ryder was a single man. In the early days of his connection with the Blue Veins he had been regarded as quite a catch, and young ladies and their mothers had maneuvered with much ingenuity to capture him. Not, however, until Mrs. Molly Dixon visited Groveland had any woman ever made him wish to change his condition to that of a married man.

Mrs. Dixon had come to Groveland from Washington in the spring, and before the summer was over she had won Mr. Ryder's heart. She possessed many attractive qualities. She was much younger than he; in fact, he was old enough to have been her father, though no one knew exactly how old he was. She was whiter than he, and better educated. She had moved in the best colored society of the country, at Washington, and had taught in the schools of that city. Such a superior person had been eagerly welcomed to the Blue Vein Society, and had taken a leading part in its activities. Mr. Ryder had at first been attracted by her charms of person, for she was very good-looking and not over twenty-five; then by her refined manners and the vivacity of her wit. Her husband had been a government clerk, and at his death had left a considerable life insurance. She was visiting friends in Groveland, and, finding the town and the people to her liking, had prolonged her stay indefinitely. She had not seemed displeased at Mr. Ryder's attentions, but on the contrary, had given him every proper encouragement; and indeed, a younger and less cautious man would long since have spoken. But he had made up his mind, and had only to determine the time when he would ask her to be his wife. He decided to give a ball in her honor, and at some time during the evening of the ball to offer her his heart and hand. He had no special fears about the outcome, but, with a little touch of romance, he wanted the surroundings to be in harmony with his own feelings when he should have received the answer he expected.

Mr. Ryder resolved that this ball should mark an epoch in the social history of Groveland. He knew, of course—no one could know better—the entertainments that had taken place in past years, and what must be done to surpass them. His ball must be worthy of the lady in whose honor it was to be given, and must, by the quality of its guests, set an example for the future. He had observed of late a growing liberality, almost a laxity, in social matters, even among members of his own set, and had several times been forced to meet in a social way persons whose complexions and callings in life were hardly up to the standard which he considered proper for the society to maintain. He had a theory of his own.

"I have no race prejudice," he would say, "but we people of mixed blood are ground between the upper and the nether millstone. Our fate lies between absorption by the white race and extinction in the black. The one doesn't want us yet, but may take us in time. The other would welcome us, but it would be for us a backward step. 'With malice towards none, with charity for all,' we must do the best we can for ourselves and those who are to follow us. Self-preservation is the first law of nature."

His ball would serve by its exclusiveness to counteract leveling tendencies, and his marriage with Mrs. Dixon would help to further the upward process of absorption he had been wishing and waiting for.

The ball was to take place on Friday night. The house had been put in order, the carpets covered with canvas, the halls and stairs decorated with palms and potted plants; and in the afternoon Mr. Ryder sat on his front porch, which the shade of a vine running up over a wire netting made a cool and pleasant lounging place. He expected to respond to the toast "The Ladies" at the supper, and from a volume of Tennyson—his favorite poet—was fortifying himself with apt quotations. The volume was open at "A Dream of Fair Women." His eyes fell on these lines, and he read them aloud to judge better of their effect:

> At length I saw a lady within call,
>   Stiller than chisell'd marble, standing there;
> A daughter of the gods, divinely tall,
>   And most divinely fair.

He remarked the verse, and turning the page read the stanza beginning

> O sweet pale Margaret.
> O rare pale Margaret.

He weighed the passage a moment, and decided that it would not do. Mrs. Dixon was the palest lady he expected at the ball, and she was of a rather ruddy complexion, and of lively disposition and buxom build. So he ran over the leaves until his eyes rested on the description of Queen Guinevere:

> She seem'd a part of joyous Spring:
> A gown of grass-green silk she wore,
> Buckled with golden clasps before;
> A light-green tuft of plumes she bore
> Closed in a golden ring.
>
> She look'd so lovely, as she sway'd
> The rein with dainty finger-tips,

A man had given all other bliss,
And all his worldly worth for this,
To waste his whole heart in one kiss
Upon her perfect lips.

As Mr. Ryder murmured these words audibly, with an appreciative thrill, he heard the latch of his gate click, and a light footfall sounding on the steps. He turned his head, and saw a woman standing before his door.

She was a little woman, not five feet tall, and proportioned to her height. Although she stood erect, and looked around her with very bright and restless eyes, she seemed quite old; for her face was crossed and recrossed with a hundred wrinkles, and around the edges of her bonnet could be seen protruding here and there a tuft of short gray wool. She wore a blue calico gown of ancient cut, a little red shawl fastened around her shoulders with an old-fashioned brass brooch, and a large bonnet profusely ornamented with faded red and yellow artificial flowers. And she was very black, so that her toothless gums, revealed when she opened her mouth to speak, were not red, but blue. She looked like a bit of the old plantation life, summoned up from the past by the wave of a magician's wand, as the poet's fancy had called into being the gracious shapes of which Mr. Ryder had just been reading.

He rose from his chair and came over to where she stood. "Good afternoon, madam," he said.

"Good evenin', suh," she answered, ducking suddenly with a quaint curtsy. Her voice was shrill and piping, but softened somewhat by age. "Is dis yere whar Mistuh Ryduh lib, suh?" she asked, looking around her doubtfully, and glancing into the open windows, through which some of the preparations for the evening were visible.

"Yes," he replied, with an air of kingly patronage, unconsciously flattered by her manner, "I am Mr. Ryder. Did you want to see me?"

"Yas, suh, ef I ain't 'sturbin' of you too much."

"Not at all. Have a seat over here behind the vine, where it is cool. What can I do for you?"

"Scuse me, suh," she continued, when she had sat down on the edge of a chair, 'scuse me, suh, I's lookin' for my husban'. I heerd you wuz a big man an' had libbed heah a long time, an' I 'lowed you would n't min' ef I'd come roun' an' ax you ef you'd ever heerd of a merlatter man by de name er Sam Taylor 'quirin' round' in de chu'ches ermongs' de people fer his wife 'Liza Jane?"

Mr. Ryder seemed to think for a moment.

"There used to be many such cases right after the war," he said, "but it has been so long that I have forgotten them. There are very few now. But tell me your story, and it may refresh my memory."

She sat back farther in her chair so as to be more comfortable, and folded her withered hands in her lap.

"My name's 'Liza," she began, "'Liza Jane. W'en I wuz young I us'ter b'long ter Marse Bob Smif, down in ole Missoura. I wuz bawn down dere. W'en I wuz a gal I wuz married ter a man named Jim. But Jim died, an' after dat I married a merlatter man named Sam Taylor. Sam wuz fre-bawn, but his mammy and daddy died, an' de w'ite folks 'prenticed him ter my marster fer ter work fer 'im 'tel he wuz growed up. Sam worked in de fiel', an' I wuz de cook. One day Ma'y Ann, ole miss's maid, came rushin' out ter de kitchen, an' says she, ' 'Liza Jane, old marse gwine sell yo' Sam down de ribber.'"

" 'Go way f'm yere, says I; 'my husban's free!'"

"Don' make no diff'ence. I heerd ole marse tell ole miss he wuz gwine take yo' Sam 'way wid 'im ter-morrow, fer he needed money, an' he knowed whar he could git a t'ousan' dollars fer Sam an' no questions axed.'"

"W'en Sam come home f'm de fiel' dat night, I tole him 'bout ole marse gwine steal 'im, an' Sam run erway. His time wuz mos' up, an' he swo' dat w'en he wuz twenty-one he would come back an' he'p me run erway, er else save up de money ter buy my freedom. An I know he'd 'a' done it, fer he thought a heap er me, Sam did. But w'en he come back he did n'fin' me, fer I wuzn' dere. Ole marse had heerd dat I warned Sam, so he had me whip' an' sol' down de ribber.

"Den de wah broke out, an' w'en it wuz ober de cullud folks wuz scattered. I went back ter de ole home'; but Sam wuzn' dere, an' I could n' l'arn nuffin' 'bout 'im. But I knowed he'd be'n dere to look fer me an' had n' foun' me, an' had gone erway ter hunt fer me.

"I's be'n lookin' fer 'im eber sence," she added simply, as though twenty-five years were but a couple of weeks, "an' I knows he's be'n lookin' fer me. Fer he sot a heap er sto' by me, Sam did, an' I know he's be'n huntin' fer me all dese years—'les'n he's be'n sick er sump'n, so he could n' work, er out'n his head, so he could n' 'member his promise. I went back down de ribber, fer I 'lowed he'd gone down dere lookin' fer me. I's be'n ter Noo Orleens, an' Atlanty, an' Charleston, an' Richmon'; an' w'en I'd be'n all ober de Souf I come ter de Norf. Fer I knows I'll fin' 'im some er dese days," she said softly, "er he'll fin' me, an' den we'll bofe be as happy in freedom as we wuz in de ole days befo' de wah." A smile stole over her withered countenance as she paused a moment, and her bright eyes softened into a far-away look.

This was the substance of the old woman's story. She had wandered a little here and there. Mr. Ryder was looking at her curiously when she finished.

"How have you lived all these years?" he asked.

"Cookin', suh. I's a good cook. Does you know anybody w'at needs a good cook, suh? I's stoppin' wid a cullud fam'ly roun' de corner yonder 'tel I kin git a place."

"Do you really expect to find your husband? He may be dead long ago."

She shook her head emphatically. "Oh, no, he ain' dead. De signs an' de tokens tells me. I dremp three nights runnin' on'y dis las' week dat I foun' him."

"He may have married another woman. Your slave marriage would not have prevented him, for you never lived with him after the war, and without that your marriage doesn't count."

"Wouldn't make no diff'ence wid Sam. He would n' marry no yuther 'ooman 'tel he foun' out 'bout me. I knows it, she added. "Sump'n's be'n tellin' me all dese years dat I's gwine fin' Sam 'fo' I dies."

"Perhaps he's outgrown you, and climbed up in the world where he wouldn't care to have you find him."

"No, indeed, suh," she replied, "Sam ain' dat kin' er man. He wuz good ter me, Sam wuz, but he wuzn' much good ter nobody e'se, fer he wuz one er de triflin'es' han's on de plantation. I 'spec's ter haf ter suppo't 'im w'en I fin' im, fer he nebber would work 'less'n he had ter. But den he wuz free, an' he did n' git no pay fer his work, an' I don' blame 'im much. Mebbe he's done better sence he run erway, but I ain' 'spectin' much.

"You may have passed him on the street a hundred times during the twenty-five years, and not have known him; time works great changes."

She smiled incredulously. "I'd know 'im 'mongs' a hund'ed men. Fer dey wuzn' no yuther merlatter man like my man Sam, an I could n' be mistook. I's toted his picture roun' wid me twenty-five years."

"May I see it?" asked Mr. Ryder. "It might help me to remember whether I have seen the original."

As she drew a small parcel from her bosom he saw that it was fastened to a string that went around her neck. Removing several wrappers, she brought to light an old-fashioned daguerreotype in a black case. He looked long and intently at the portrait. It was faded with time, but the features were still distinct, and it was easy to see what manner of man it had represented.

He closed the case, and with a slow movement handed it back to her.

"I don't know of any man in town who goes by that name," he said, "nor have I heard of any one making such inquiries. But if you will leave me your address, I will give the matter some attention, and if I find out anything I will let you know."

She gave him the number of a house in the neighborhood, and went away, after thanking him warmly.

He wrote the address on the fly-leaf of the volume of Tennyson, and when she had gone, rose to his feet and stood looking after her curiously. As she walked down the street with mincing step, he saw several persons whom she passed turn and look back at her with a smile of kindly amusement. When she had turned the corner, he went upstairs to his bedroom, and stood for a long time before the mirror of his dressing-case, gazing thoughtfully at the reflection of his own face.

At eight o'clock the ballroom was a blaze of light and the guests had begun to assemble; for there was a literacy programme and some routine business of the society to be gone through with before the dancing. A black servant in evening dress waited at the door and directed the guests to the dressing rooms.

The occasion was long memorable among the colored people of the city; not alone for the dress and display, but for the high average of intelligence and culture that distinguished the gathering as a whole. There were a number of school teachers, several young doctors, three or four lawyers, some professional singers, an editor, a lieutenant in the United States Army spending his furlough in the city, and others in various polite callings; these were colored, though most of them would not have attracted even a casual glance because of any marked difference from white people. Most of the ladies were in evening costume, and dress coats and dancing pumps were the rule among the men. A band of string music, stationed in an alcove behind a row of palms, played popular airs while the guests were gathering.

The dancing began at half past nine. At eleven o'clock supper was served. Mr. Ryder had left the ballroom some little time before the intermission, but reappeared at the supper table. The spread was worthy of the occasion, and the guests did full justice to it. When the coffee had been served, the toastmaster, Mr. Solomon Sadler, rapped for order. He made a brief introductory speech, complimenting host and guests, and then presented in their order the toasts of the evening. They were responded to with a very fair display of after-dinner wit.

"The last toast," said the toastmaster, when he reached the end of the list, "is one which must appeal to us all. There is no one of us of the sterner sex who is not at some time dependent upon a woman—in infancy for protection, in manhood for companionship, in old age for care and comforting. Our good host has been trying to live alone, but the fair faces I see around me tonight prove that he is too largely dependent upon the gentler sex for most that makes life worth living—the society and love of friends—and rumor is at fault if he does not soon yield entire subjection to one of them. Mr. Ryder will now respond to the toast—'The Ladies.' "

There was a pensive look in Mr. Ryder's eyes as he took the floor and adjusted his eye-glasses. He began by speaking of woman as the gift of Heaven to man, and after some general observations on the relations of the sexes he said:

"But perhaps the quality which most distinguishes woman is her fidelity and devotion to those she loves. History is full of examples, but has recorded none more striking than one which only today came under my notice."

He then related, simply but effectively, the story told by his visitor of the afternoon. He gave it in the same soft dialect, which came readily to his lips, while the company listened attentively and sympathetically. For the story had awakened a responsive thrill in many hearts. There were some present who had seen, and others who had heard their fathers and grandfathers tell, the wrongs and sufferings of this past generation, and all of them still felt, in their darker moments, the shadow hanging over them. Mr. Ryder went on:

"Such devotion and confidence are rare even among women. There are many who would have searched a year, some who would have waited five years, a few who might have hoped ten years; but for twenty-five years this woman has retained her affection for and her faith in a man she has not seen or heard of in all that time.

"She came to me today in hope that I might be able to help her find this long-lost husband. And when she was gone I gave my fancy rein, and imagined a case I will put to you.

"Suppose that this husband, soon after his escape, had learned that his wife had been sold away, and that such inquiries as he could make brought no information of her whereabouts. Suppose that he was young, and she much older than he; that he was light, and she was black; that their marriage was a slave marriage, and legally binding only if they chose to make it so after the war. Suppose, too, that he made his way to the North, as some of us have done, and there, where he had larger opportunities, had improved them, and had in the course of all these years grown to be as different from the ignorant boy who ran away from fear of slavery as the day is from the night. Suppose, even, that he had qualified himself, by industry, by thrift, and by study, to win the friendship and be considered worthy of the society of such people as these I see around me to-night, gracing my board and filling my heart with gladness; for I am old enough to remember the day when such a gathering would not have been possible in this land. Suppose, too, that as the years went by, this man's memory of the past grew more and more indistinct, until at last it was rarely, except in his dreams, that any image of this bygone period rose before his mind. And then suppose that accident should bring to his knowledge the fact that the wife of his youth, the wife he had left behind him— not one who had walked by his side and kept pace with him in his upward struggle, but one upon whom advancing years and a laborious life had set their mark—was alive and seeking him, but that he was absolutely safe from recognition or discovery, unless he chose to reveal himself. My friends, what would the man do? I will presume that he was one who loved honor, and tried to deal justly with all men. I will even carry the case further, and suppose that perhaps he had set his heart upon another, whom he had hoped to call his own. What would he do, or rather what ought he to do, in such a crisis of a lifetime?

"It seemed to me that he might hesitate, and I imagined that I was an old friend, a near friend, and that he had come to me for advice; and I argued the case with him. I tried to discuss it impartially. After we had looked upon the matter from every point of view, I said to him, in words that we all know

> This above all: to thine own self be true,
> And it must follow, as the night the day,
> Thou canst not then be false to any man.

Then, finally, I put the question to him, 'Shall you acknowledge her?'

"And now, ladies and gentlemen, friends and companions, I ask you, what should he have done?"

There was something in Mr. Ryder's voice that stirred the hearts of those who sat around him. It suggested more than mere sympathy with an imaginary situation; it seemed rather in the nature of a personal appeal. It was observed, too, that his look rested more especially upon Mrs. Dixon, with a mingled expression of renunciation and inquiry.

She had listened, with parted lips and streaming eyes. She was the first to speak: "He should have acknowledged her."

"My friends and companions," responded Mr. Ryder, "I thank you, one and all. It is the answer I expected, for I knew your hearts."

He turned and walked toward the closed door of an adjoining room, while every eye followed him in wondering curiosity. He came back in a moment, leading by the hand his visitor of the afternoon, who stood startled and trembling at the sudden plunge into this scene of brilliant gayety. She was neatly dressed in gray, and wore the white cap of an elderly woman.

"Ladies and gentlemen," he said, "this is the woman, and I am the man, whose story I have told you. Permit me to introduce to you the wife of my youth."

Zora Neale Hurston

(1881–1960)

Zora Neale Hurston died in Fort Pierce, Florida, broke and forgotten. Although she had been active in New York from the 1920s through the 1940s as a writer, journalist, folklorist, and anthropologist, she spent her last years working as a maid. Renowned for her lyrical, myth-rich prose and poetic storytelling, Hurston was deeply fascinated by Black culture—folklore, religion, Black oral traditions—but the theme of Black-White conflict simply did not interest her. Having grown up female in the all-Black town of Eatonville, Florida, where her father, a minister, had been elected mayor for three successive terms, Hurston differed radically in her social and political outlook from such contemporaries as Langston Hughes and Richard Wright. After attending Howard University and Barnard College in New York, where she was a student of anthropologist Franz Boas, Hurston published **Mules and Men** *in 1935. A colorful and prolific writer of plays, novels, short stories, and articles, she could not interest publishers in her final writings. Not until the seventies was her second novel,* **Their Eyes Were Watching God** *(1937), reprinted, gradually to become recognized as an American classic.*

Sweat

1.

It was eleven o'clock of a Spring night in Florida. It was Sunday. Any other night, Delia Jones would have been in bed for two hours by this time. But she was a washwoman, and Monday morning meant a great deal to her. So she collected the soiled clothes on Saturday when she returned the clean things. Sunday night after church, she sorted and put the white things to soak. It saved her almost a half-day's start. A great hamper in the bedroom held the clothes that she brought home. It was so much neater than a number of bundles lying around.

She squatted on the kitchen floor beside the great pile of clothes, sorting them into small heaps according to color, and humming a song in a mournful key, but wondering through it all where Sykes, her husband, had gone with her horse and buckboard.

Just then something long, round, limp and black fell upon her back and slithered to the floor beside her. A great terror took hold of her. It softened her knees and dried her mouth so that it was a full minute before she could cry out or move. Then she saw that it was the big bull whip her husband liked to carry when he drove.

She lifted her eyes to the door and saw him standing there bent over with laughter at her fright. She screamed at him.

"Sykes, what you throw dat whip on me like dat? You know it would skeer me—looks just like a snake, an' you knows how skeered Ah is of snakes."

"Course Ah knowed it! That's how come Ah done it." He slapped his leg with his hand and almost rolled on the ground in his mirth. "If you such a big fool dat you got to have a fit over a earth worm or a string, Ah don't keer how bad Ah skeer you."

"You ain't got no business doing it, Gawd knows it's a sin. Some day Ah'm gointuh drop dead from some of yo' foolishness. 'Nother thing, where you been wid mah rig? Ah feeds dat pony. He ain't fuh you to be drivin' wid no bull whip."

"You sho' is one aggravatin' nigger woman!" he declared and stepped into the room. She resumed her work and did not answer him at once. "Ah done tole you time and again to keep them white folks' clothes outa dis house."

He picked up the whip and glared at her. Delia went on with her work. She went out into the yard and returned with a galvanized tub and set it on the washbench. She saw that Sykes had kicked all of the clothes together again, and now stood in her way truculently, his whole manner hoping, *praying*, for an argument. But she walked calmly around him and commenced to re-sort the things.

"Next time, Ah'm gointer kick 'em outdoors," he threatened as he struck a match along the leg of his corduroy breeches.

Delia never looked up from her work, and her thin, stooped shoulders sagged further.

"Ah ain't for no fuss t'night Sykes. Ah just come from taking sacrament at the church house."

He snorted scornfully. "Yeah, you just come from de church house on a Sunday night, but heah you is gone to work on them clothes. You ain't nothing but a hypocrite. One of them amen-corner Christians—sing, whoop, and shout, then come home and wash white folks' clothes on the Sabbath."

He stepped roughly upon the whitest pile of things, kicking them helter-skelter as he crossed the room. His wife gave a little scream of dismay, and quickly gathered them together again.

"Sykes, you quit grindin' dirt into these clothes! How can Ah git through by Sat'day if Ah don't start on Sunday?"

"Ah don't keer if you never git through. Anyhow, Ah done promised Gawd and a couple of other men, Ah ain't gointer have it in mah house. Don't gimme no lip neither, else Ah'll throw 'em out and put mah fist up side yo' head to boot."

Delia's habitual meekness seemed to slip from her shoulders like a blown scarf. She was on her feet; her poor little body, her bare knuckly hands bravely defying the strapping hulk before her.

"Looka heah, Sykes, you done gone too fur. Ah been married to you fur fifteen years, and Ah been takin' in washin' fur fifteen years. Sweat, sweat, sweat! Work and sweat, cry and sweat, pray and sweat!"

"What's that got to do with me?" he asked brutally.

"What's it got to do with you, Sykes? Mah tub of suds is filled yo' belly with vittles more times than yo' hands is filled it. Mah sweat is done paid for this house and Ah reckon Ah kin keep on sweatin' in it."

She seized the iron skillet from the stove and struck a defensive pose, which act surprised him greatly, coming from her. It cowed him and he did not strike her as he usually did.

"Naw you won't," she panted, "that ole snaggle-toothed black woman you runnin' with ain't comin' heah to pile up on *mah* sweat and blood. You ain't paid for nothin' on this place, and Ah'm gointer stay right heah till Ah'm toted out foot foremost."

"Well, you better quit gittin' me riled up, else they'll be totin' you out sooner than you expect. Ah'm so tired of you Ah don't know whut to do. Gawd! How Ah hates skinny wimmen!"

A little awed by this new Delia, he sidled out of the door and slammed the back gate after him. He did not say where he had gone, but she knew too well. She knew very well that he would not return until nearly daybreak also. Her work over, she went on to bed but not to sleep at once. Things had come to a pretty pass!

She lay awake, gazing upon the debris that cluttered their matrimonial trail. Not an image left standing along the way. Anything like flowers had long ago been drowned in the salty stream that had been pressed from her heart. Her tears, her sweat, her blood. She had brought love to the union and he had brought a longing after the flesh. Two months after the wedding, he had given her the first brutal beating. She had the memory of his numerous trips to Orlando with all of his wages when he had returned to her penniless, even before the first year had passed. She was young and soft then, but now she thought of her knotty, muscled limbs, her harsh knuckly hands and drew herself up into an unhappy little ball in the middle of the big feather bed. Too late now to hope for love, even if it were not Bertha it would be someone else. This case differed from the others only in that she was bolder than the others. Too late for everything except her little home. She had built it for her old days, and planted one by one the trees and flowers there. It was lovely to her, lovely.

Somehow, before sleep came, she found herself saying aloud: "Oh well, whatever goes over the Devil's back, is got to come under his belly. Sometime or ruther, Sykes, like everybody else, is gointer reap his sowing." After that she was able to build a spiritual earthworks against her husband. His shells could no longer reach her. AMEN. She went to sleep and slept until he announced his presence in bed by kicking her feet and rudely snatching the covers away.

"Gimme some kivah heah, an' git yo' damn foots over on yo' own side! Ah oughter mash you in you' mouf fuh drawing dat skillet on me."

Delia went clear to the rail without answering him. A triumphant indifference to all that he was or did.

II.

The week was as full of work for Delia as all other weeks, and Saturday found her behind her little pony, collecting and delivering clothes.

It was a hot, hot day near the end of July. The village men on Joe Clarke's porch even chewed cane listlessly. They did not hurl the cane-knots as usual. They let them dribble over the edge of the porch. Even conversation had collapsed under the heat.

"Heah come Delia Jones," Jim Merchant said, as the shaggy pony came 'round the bend of the road toward them. The rusty buckboard was heaped with baskets of crisp, clean laundry.

"Yep," Joe Lindsay agreed. "Hot or col', rain or shine, jes'ez reg'lar ez de weeks roll roun' Delia carries 'em an' fetches 'em on Sat'day."

"She better if she wanter eat," said Moss. "Syke Jones ain't wuth de shot an' powder hit would tek tuh kill 'em. Not to huh he ain't."

"He sho' ain't," Walter Thomas chimed in. "It's too bad, too, cause she wuz a right pretty li'l trick when he got huh. Ah'd uh mah'ied huh mahself if he hadnter beat me to it."

Delia nodded briefly at the men as she drove past.

"Too much knockin' will ruin *any* 'oman. He done beat huh 'nough tuh kill three women, let 'lone change they looks," said Elijah Moseley. "How Syke kin stommuck dat big black greasy Mogul he's layin' roun' wid, gits me. Ah swear dat eight-rock couldn't kiss a sardine can Ah done thowed out de back do' 'way las' yeah."

"Aw, she's fat, thass how come. He's allus been crazy 'bout fat women," put in Merchant. "He'd a' been tied up wid one long time ago if he could a' found one tuh have him. Did Ah tell you 'bout him come sidlin' roun' *mah* wife— bringin' her a basket uh peecans outa his yard fuh a present? Yessir, mah wife! She tol' him tuh take 'em right straight back home, 'cause Delia works so hard ovah dat washtub she reckon everything on de place taste lak sweat an' soapsuds. Ah jus' wisht Ah'd a' caught 'im 'roun' dere! Ah'd a' made his hips ketch on fiah down dat shell road."

"Ah know he done it, too. Ah sees 'im grinnin' at every 'oman dat passes," Walter Thomas said. "But even so, he useter eat some mighty big hunks uh humble pie tuh git dat li'l 'oman he got. She wuz ez pretty ez a speckled pup! Dat wuz fifteen years ago. He useter be so skeered uh losin' huh, she could make him do some parts of a husband's duty. Dey never wuz de same in de mind."

"There oughter be a law about him," said Lindsay. "He ai't fit tuh carry guts tuh a bear."

Clarke spoke for the first time. "Tain't no law on earth dat kin make a man be decent if it ain't in 'im. There's plenty men dat takes a wife lak dey do a joint uh sugar-cane. It's round, juicy an' sweet when dey gits it. But dey squeeze an' grind, squeeze an' grind an' wring tell dey wring every drop uh pleasure dat's in 'em out. When dey's satisfied dat dey is wrung dry, dey treats 'em jes' lak dey do a cane-chew. Dew thows 'em away. Dey knows what dey is doin' while dey is at it, an' hates theirselves fuh it but they keeps on hangin' after huh tell she's empty. Den dey hates huh fuh bein' a cane-chew an' in de way."

"We oughter take Syke an' dat stray 'oman uh his 'n down in Lake Howell swamp an' lay on de rawhide till they cain't say Lawd a'mussy. He allus wuz uh ovahbearin niggah, but since dat white 'oman from up north done teached 'im how to run a automobile, he done got too beggety to live—an' we oughter kill 'im," Old Man Anderson advised.

A grunt of approval went around the porch. But the heat was melting their civic virtue and Elijah Moseley began to bait Joe Clarke.

"Come on, Joe, git a melon outa dere an' slice it up for yo' customers. We'se all sufferin' wid de heat. De bear's done got *me*!"

"Thass right, Joe, a watermelon is jes' whut Ah needs tuh cure de eppizudicks," Walter Thomas joined forces with Moseley. "Come on dere, Joe. We all is steady customers an' you ain't set us up in a long time. Ah chooses dat long, bowlegged Floridy favorite."

"A god, an' be dough. You all gimme twenty cents and slice away," Clarke retorted. "Ah needs a col' slice m'self. Heah, everybody chip in. Ah'll lend y'all mah meat knife."

The money was all quickly subscribed and the huge melon brought forth. At that moment, Sykes and Bertha arrived. A determined silence fell on the porch and the melon was put away again.

Merchant snapped down the blade of his jackknife and moved toward the store door.

"Come on in, Joe, an' gimme a slab uh sow belly an' uh pound uh coffee— almost fuhgot 'twas Sat'day. Got to git on home." Most of the men left also.

Just then Delia drove past on her way home, as Sykes was ordering magnificently for Bertha. It pleased him for Delia to see.

"Git whutsoever yo' heart desires, Honey. Wait a minute, Joe. Give huh two bottles uh strawberry soda-water, uh quart parched ground-peas, an' a block uh chewin' gum."

With all this they left the store, with Sykes reminding Bertha that this was his town and she could have it if she wanted it.

The men returned soon after they left, and held their watermelon feast.

"Where did Syke Jones git da 'oman from nohow?" Lindsay asked.

"Ovah Apopka. Guess dey musta been cleanin' out de town when she lef'. She don't look lak a thing but a hunk uh liver wid hair on it."

Well, she sho' kin squall," Dave Carter contributed. "When she gits ready tuh laff, she jes' opens huh mouf an' latches it back tuh de las' notch. No ole granpa alligator down in Lake Bell ain't got nothin' on huh."

III.

Bertha had been in town three months now. Sykes was still paying her room-rent at Della Lewis'— the only house in town that would have taken her in. Sykes took her frequently to Winter Park to "stomps." He still assured her that he was the swellest man in the state.

"Sho' you kin have dat l'l ole house soon's Ah git dat 'oman outa dere. Everything b'longs tuh me an' you sho' kin have it. Ah sho' 'bominates uh skinny 'oman. Lawdy, you sho' is got one portly shape on you! You kin git *anything* you wants. Dis is *mah* town an' you sho' kin have it."

Delia's work-worn knees crawled over the earth in Gethsemane and up the rocks of Calvary many, many times during these months. She avoided the villagers and meeting places in her efforts to be blind and deaf. But Bertha nullified this to a degree, by coming to Delia's house to call Sykes out to her at the gate.

Delia and Sykes fought all the time now with no peaceful interludes. They slept and ate in silence. Two or three times Delia had attempted a timid friendliness, but she was repulsed each time. It was plain that the breaches must remain agape.

The sun had burned July to August. The heat streamed down like a million hot arrows, smiting all things living upon the earth. Grass withered, leaves browned, snakes went blind in shedding and men and dogs went mad. Dog days!

Delia came home one day and found Sykes there before her. She wondered, but started to go on into the house without speaking, even though he was standing in the kitchen door and she must either stoop under his arm or ask him to move. He made no room for her. She noticed a soap box beside the steps, but paid no particular attention to it, knowing that he must have brought it there. As she was stooping to pass under his outstretched arm, he suddenly pushed her backward, laughingly.

"Look in de box dere Delia, Ah done brung yuh somethin'!"

She nearly fell upon the box in her stumbling, and when she saw what it held, she all but fainted outright.

"Syke! Syke, mah Gawd! You take dat rattlesnake 'way from heah! You *gottah*. Oh Jesus, have mussy!"

"Ah ain't got tuh do nothin' uh de kin'—fact is Ah ain't got tuh do nothin' but die. Tain't no use uh you puttin' on airs makin' out lak you skeered uh dat snake— he's gointer stay right heah tell he die. He wouldn't bite me cause Ah knows how tuh handle 'im. Nohow he wouldn't risk breakin' out his fangs 'gin *yo* skinny laigs."

"Naw, now Syke, don't keep dat thing 'round tryin' tuh skeer me tuh death. You knows Ah'm even feared uh earth worms. Thass de biggest snake Ah evah did see. Kill 'im Syke, please.'

"Doan ast me tuh do nothin' fuh yuh. Goin' 'round tryin' tuh be so damn asterperious. Naw, Ah ain't gonna kill it. Ah think uh damn sight mo' uh him dan you! Dat's a nice snake an' anybody doan lak 'im kin jes' hit de grit."

The village soon heard that Sykes had the snake, and came to see and ask questions.

How de hen-fire did you ketch dat six-foot rattler, Syke?" Thomas asked.

"He's full uh frogs so he cain't hardly move, thass how Ah eased up on 'm. But Ah'm a snake charmer an' knows how tuh handle 'em. Shux, dat ain't nothin'. Ah could ketch one eve'y day if Ah so wanted tuh."

"Whut he needs is a heavy hick'ry club leaned real heavy on his head. Dat's de bes' way tuh charm a rattlesnake."

"Naw, Walt, y'all jes' don't understand dese diamon' backs lak Ah do," said Sykes in a superior tone of voice.

The village agreed with Walter, but the snake stayed on. His box remained by the kitchen door with its screen wire covering. Two or three days later it had digested its meal of frogs and literally came to life. It rattled at any movement in the kitchen or the yard. One day as Delia came down the kitchen steps she saw his chalky-white fangs curved like scimitars hung in the wire meshes. This time she did not run away with averted eyes as usual. She stood for a long time in the doorway in a red fury that grew bloodier for every second that she regarded the creature that was her torment.

That night she broached the subject as soon as Sykes sat down to the table.

"Syke, Ah wants you tuh take dat snake 'way fum heah. You done starved me an' Ah put up widcher, you done beat me an Ah took dat, but you done kilt all mah insides bringin' dat varmint heah."

Sykes poured out a saucer full of coffee and drank it deliberately before he answered her.

"A whole lot Ah keer 'bout how you feels inside uh out. Dat snake ain't goin' no damn wheah till Ah gits ready fuh 'im tuh go. So fur as beatin' is concerned, yuh ain't took near all dat you gointer take ef yuh stay 'round me."

Delia pushed back her plate and got up from the table. "Ah hates you, Sykes," she said calmly. "Ah hates you tuh de same degree dat Ah useter love yuh. Ah done took an' took till mah belly is full up tuh mah neck. Dat's de reason Ah got mah letter fum de church an' moved mah membership tuh Woodbridge— so Ah don't haftuh take no sacrament wid yuh. Ah don't wantuh see yuh 'round me atall. Lay 'round wid dat 'oman all yuh wants tuh, but gwan 'way fum me an' mah house. Ah hates yuh lak uh suck-egg dog."

Sykes almost let the huge wad of corn bread and collard greens he was chewing fall out of his mouth in amazement. He had a hard time whipping himself up to the proper fury to try to answer Delia.

"Well, Ah'm glad you does hate me. Ah'm sho' tiahed uh you hangin' ontuh me. Ah don't want yuh. Look at yuh stringey ole neck! Yo' rawbony laigs an' arms is enough tuh cut uh man to death. You looks jes' lak de devvul's doll-baby tuh *me*. You cain't hate me no worse dan Ah hates you. Ah been hatin' *you* fuh years."

"Yo' ole black hide don't look lak nothin' tuh me, but uh passle uh wrinkled up rubber, wid yo' big ole yeahs flappin' on each side lak up paih uh buzzard wings. Don't think Ah'm gointuh be run 'way fum mah house neither. Ah'm goin' tuh de white folks 'bout y*ou*, mah young man, de very nex' time you lay yo' han's on me. Mah cup is done run ovah." Delia said this with no signs of fear and Sykes departed from the house, threatening her, but made not the slightest move to carry out any of them.

That night he did not return at all, and the next day being Sunday, Delia was glad she did not have to quarrel before she hitched up her pony and drove the four miles to Woodbridge.

She stayed to the night service—"love feast"—which was very warm and full of spirit. In the emotional winds her domestic trials were borne far and wide so that she sang as she drove homeward,

> Jurden water, black an' col
> Chills de body, not de soul
> An' Ah wantah cross Jurden in uh calm time.

She came from the barn to the kitchen door and stopped.

"What's de mattah, ol' Satan, you ain't kickin' up yo' racket?" She addressed the snake's box. Complete silence. She went into the house with new hope in its birth struggles. Perhaps her threat to go to the white folks had frightened Sykes! Perhaps he was sorry! Fifteen years of misery and suppression had brought Delia to the place where she would hope *anything* that looked towards a way over or through her wall of inhibitions.

She felt in the match-safe behind the stove at once for a match. There was only one there.

"Dat niggah wouldn't fetch nothin' heah tuh save his rotten neck, but he kin run thew whut Ah brings quick enough. Now he done toted off nigh on tuh haff uh box uh matches. He done had dat 'oman heah in mah house, too."

Nobody but a woman could tell how she knew this even before she struck the match. But she did and it put her into a new fury.

Presently she brought in the tubs to put the white things to soak. This time she decided she need not bring the hamper out of the bedroom: she would go in there and do the sorting. She picked up the pot-bellied lamp and went in. The room was small and the hamper stood hard by the foot of the white-iron bed. She could sit and reach through the bedposts—resting as she worked.

"*Ah wantah cross Jurden in uh calm time.*" She was singing again. The mood of the "love feast" had returned. She threw back the lid of the basket almost gaily. Then, moved by both horror and terror, she sprang back toward the door. There lay *the snake in the basket!* He moved sluggishly at first but even as she turned round and round, jumped up and down in an insanity of fear, he began to stir vigorously. She saw him pouring his awful beauty from the basket upon the bed, then she seized the lamp and ran as fast as she could to the kitchen. The wind from the open door blew out the light and the darkness added to her terror. She sped to the darkness of the yard, slamming the door after her before she thought to set down the lamp. She did not feel safe even on the ground, so she climbed up in the hay barn.

There for an hour or more she lay sprawled upon the hay a gibbering wreck.

Finally she grew quiet, and after that came coherent thought. With this stalked through her a cold, bloody rage. Hours of this. A period of introspection, a space of retrospection, then a mixture of both. Out of this an awful calm.

"Well, Ah done de bes' Ah could. If things ain't right, Gawd knows tain't mah fault."

She went to sleep—a twitch sleep—and woke up to a faint gray sky. There was a loud hollow sound below. She peered out. Sykes was at the wood-pile, demolishing a wire-covered box.

He hurried to the kitchen door, but hung outside there some minutes before he entered, and stood some minutes more inside before he closed it after him.

The gray in the sky was spreading. Delia descended without fear now, and crouched beneath the low bedroom window. The drawn shade shut out the dawn, shut in the night. But the thin walls held back no sound.

"Dat ol' scratch is woke up now!" She mused at the tremendous whirr inside, which every woodsman knows, is one of the sound illusions. The rattler is a ventriloquist. His whirr sounds to the right, to the left, straight ahead, behind, close under foot—everywhere but where it is. Woe to him who guesses wrong unless he is prepared to hold up his end of the argument! Sometimes he strikes without rattling at all.

Inside, Sykes heard nothing until he knocked a pot lid off the stove while trying to reach the match-safe in the dark. He had emptied his pockets at Bertha's.

The snake seemed to wake up under the stove and Sykes made a quick leap into the bedroom. In spite of the gin he had had, his head was clearing now.

"May Gawd!" he chattered, "ef Ah could on'y strack uh light!"

The rattling ceased for a moment as he stood paralyzed. He waited. It seemed that the snake waited also.

"Oh, fuh de light! Ah thought he'd be too sick"—Sykes was muttering to himself when the whirr began again, closer, right underfoot this time. Long before this, Sykes ability to think had been flattened down to primitive instinct and he leaped—onto the bed.

Outside Delia heard a cry that might have come from a maddened chimpanzee, a stricken gorilla. All the terror, all the horror, all the rage that man possibly could express, without a recognizable human sound.

A tremendous stir inside there, another series of animal screams, the intermittent whirr of the reptile. The shade torn violently down from the window, letting in the red dawn, a huge brown hand seizing the window stick, great dull blows upon the wooden floor punctuating the gibberish of sound long after the rattle of the snake had abruptly subsided. All this Delia could see and hear from her place beneath the window, and it made her ill. She crept over to the four-o'clocks and stretched herself on the cool earth to recover.

She lay there. "Delia, Delia!" She could hear Sykes calling in a most despairing tone as one who expected no answer. The sun crept on up, and he called. Delia could not move—her legs had gone flabby. She never moved, he called, and the sun kept rising.

"Mah Gawd!" She heard him moan, "Mah Gawd fum Heben!" She heard him stumbling about and got up from her flower-bed. The sun was growing warm. As she approached the door she heard him call out hopefully, "Delia, is dat you Ah heah?"

She saw him on his hands and knees as soon as she reached the door. He crept an inch or two toward her—all that he was able, and she saw his horribly swollen neck and one open eye shining with hope. A surge of pity too strong to support bore her away from that eye that must, could not, fail to see the tubs. He would see the lamp. Orlando with its doctors was too far. She could scarcely reach the chinaberry tree, where she waited in the growing heat while inside she knew the cold river was creeping up and up to extinguish that eye which must know by now that she knew.

Jean Toomer

(1894–1967)

Jean Toomer is perhaps as difficult to categorize as the highly influential, complex novel, **Cane**, *upon which his literary reputation largely rests. Of mixed heritage, Toomer preferred to reject racial divisions, choosing instead to define himself as "an American, neither white nor black." Deserted by his father when he was only a year old, Toomer was raised in Washington, D.C., by his mother and grandfather. He graduated from high school and then drifted from one city and university to the next, never staying long enough to earn a degree. After supporting himself with a series of odd jobs in Chicago, New York, Massachusetts, and Wisconsin, Toomer got a teaching position at a small segregated school in Sparta, Georgia, in 1921. There, inspired by the beauty of the land and the haunting melodies of the Black folktales that he heard, Toomer began writing about racial oppression, poverty, and the corrupting materialism of urban life—eventually spinning all of these themes into the experimental composite of fiction, poetry, and drama that would become* **Cane**. *Although the novel was immediately hailed as a masterpiece upon its 1923 publication, Toomer was not pleased by its critical success; nor was he happy with the public's subsequent classification of him as a "Negro" writer. Choosing to drop from public view, Toomer became an avid follower of the Russian mystic Gurdjieff and concentrated on advancing his political and spiritual beliefs. Although he continued to write, much of Toomer's later work went unpublished, and he died a forgotten man in 1967, the same year that* **Cane** *was reprinted for the first time.*

Esther

I
Nine.

Esther's hair falls in soft curls about her high-cheekboned chalk-white face. Esther's hair would be beautiful if there were more gloss to it. And if her face were not prematurely serious, one would call it pretty. Her cheeks are too flat and dead for a girl of nine. Esther looks like a little white child, starched, frilled, as she walks slowly from her home towards her father's grocery store. She is about to turn on Broad from Maple Street. White and black men loafing on the corner hold no interest for her. Then a strange thing happens. A clean-muscled, magnificent, black-skinned Negro, whom she had heard her father mention as King Barlo, suddenly drops to his knees on a spot called the Spittoon. White men, unaware of him, continue squirting tobacco juice in his direction. The saffron fluid splashes on his face. His smooth black face begins to glisten and to shine. Soon, people notice him, and gather round. His eyes are rapturous upon the heavens. Lips and nostrils quiver. Barlo is in a religious trance.

Town folks know it. They are not startled. They are not afraid. They gather round. Some beg boxes from the grocery stores. From old McGregor's notion shop. A coffin case is pressed into use. Folks line the curbstones. Businessmen close shop. And Banker Warply parks his car close by. Silently, all await the prophet's voice. The sheriff, a great florid fellow whose leggings never meet around his bulging calves, swears in three deputies. "Wall, y cant never tell what a nigger like King Barlo might be up t." Soda bottles, five fingers full of shine, are passed to those who want them. A couple of stray dogs start a fight. Old Goodlow's cow comes flopping up the street. Barlo, still as an Indian fakir, has not moved. The town bell strikes six. The sun slips in behind a heavy mass of horizon cloud. The crowd is hushed and expectant. Barlo's under jaw relaxes, and his lips begin to move.

"Jesus has been awhisperin strange words deep down, O way down deep, deep in my ears."

Hums of awe and of excitement.

"He called me to His side an said, 'Git down on your knees beside me, son, Ise gwine t whisper in your ears.'"

An old sister cries, "Ah, Lord."

" 'Ise agwine t whisper in your ears,' He said, and I replied, 'Thy will be done on earth as it is in heaven.' "

"Ah, Lord. Amen. Amen."

"An Lord Jesus whispered strange good words deep down, O way down deep, deep in my ears. An He said, 'Tell em till you feel your throat on fire.' I saw a vision. I saw a man arise, an he was big an black an powerful—"

Someone yells, "Preach it, preacher, preach it!"

"—but his head was caught up in th clouds. An while he was agazin at th heavens, heart filled up with th Lord, some little white ant biddies came and tied his feet to chains. They led him t th coast, they led him t th sea, they led him across th ocean an they didnt set him free. The old coast didnt miss him, an th new coast wasnt free, he left the old-coast brothers, t give birth t you an me. O Lord, great God Almighty, t give birth t you an me."

Barlo pauses. Old gray mothers are in tears. Fragments of melodies are being hummed. White folks are touched and curiously awed. Off to themselves, white and black preachers confer as to how best to rid themselves of the vagrant, usurping fellow. Barlo looks as though he is struggling to continue. People are hushed. One can hear weevils work. Dusk is falling rapidly, and the customary store lights fail to throw their feeble glow across the gray dust and flagging of the Georgia town. Barlo rises to his full height. He is immense. To the people he assumes the outlines of his visioned African. In a mighty voice he bellows:

"Brothers an sisters, turn your faces t th sweet face of the Lord, an fill your hearts with glory! Open your eyes an see th dawnin of th mornin light! Open your ears—"

Years afterwards Esther was told that at that very moment a great, heavy, rumbling voice actually was heard. That hosts of angels and of demons paraded up and down the streets all night. That King Barlo rode out of town astride a pitch-black bull that had a glowing gold ring in its nose. And that old Limp Underwood, who hated niggers, woke up next morning to find that he held a black man in his arms. This much is certain: an inspired Negress, of wide reputation for being sanctified, drew a portrait of a black madonna on the courthouse wall. And King Barlo left town. He left his image indelibly upon the mind of Esther. He became the starting point of the only living patterns that her mind was to know.

II
Sixteen.

Esther begins to dream. The low evening sun sets the windows of McGregor's notion shop aflame. Esther makes believe that they really are aflame. The town fire department rushes madly down the road. It ruthlessly shoves black and white idlers to one side. It whoops. It clangs. It rescues from the second-story window a dimpled infant which she claims for her own. How had she come by it? She thinks of it immaculately. It is a sin to think of it immaculately. She must dream no more. She must repent her sin. Another dream comes. There is no fire department. There are no heroic men. The fire starts. The loafers on the corner form a circle, chew their tobacco faster, and squirt juice just as fast as they can chew. Gallons on top of gallons they squirt upon the flames. The air reeks with the stench of scorched tobacco juice. Women, fat chunky Negro women, lean scrawny white women, pull their skirts up above their heads and display the most ludicrous underclothes. The women scoot in all directions from the danger zone. She alone is left to take the baby in her arms. But what a baby! Black, singed, woolly, tobacco-juice baby—ugly as sin. Once held to her breast, miraculous thing: its breath is sweet and its lips can nibble. She loves it frantically. Her joy in it changes the town folks' jeers to harmless jealousy, and she is left alone.

Twenty-two.

Esther's schooling is over. She works behind the counter of her father's grocery store. "To keep the money in the family," so he said. She is learning to make distinctions between the business and the social worlds. "Good business comes from remembering that the white folks dont divide the niggers, Esther. Be just as black as any man who has a silver dollar." Esther listlessly forgets that she is near white, and that her father is the richest colored man in town. Black folk who drift in to buy lard and snuff and flour of her call her a sweet-natured, accommodating girl. She learns their names. She forgets them. She thinks about men. "I dont appeal to them. I wonder why." She recalls an affair she had with a little fair boy while still in school. It had ended in her shame when he as much as told her that for sweetness he preferred a lollipop. She remembers the salesman from the North who wanted to take her to the movies that first night he was in town. She refused, of course. And he never came back, having found out who she was. She thinks of Barlo. Barlo's image gives her a slightly stale thrill. She spices it by telling herself his glories. Black. Magnetically so. Best cotton picker in the county, in the state, in the whole world for that matter. Best man with his fists, best man with dice, with a razor. Promoter of church benefits. Of colored fairs. Vagrant preacher. Lover of all the women for miles and miles around. Esther decides that she loves him. And with a vague sense of life slipping by, she resolves that she will tell him so, whatever people say, the next time he comes to town. After the making of this resolution, which becomes a sort of wedding cake for her to tuck beneath her pillow and go to sleep upon, she sees nothing of Barlo for five years. Her hair thins. It looks like the dull silk on puny corn ears. Her face pales until it is the color of the gray dust that dances with dead cotton leaves.

III
Esther is twenty-seven.

Esther sells lard and snuff and flour to vague black faces that drift in her store to ask for them. Her eyes hardly see the people to whom she gives change. Her body is lean and beaten. She rests listlessly against the counter, too weary to sit down. From the street someone shouts, "King Barlo has come back to town." He passes her window, driving a large new car. Cut-out open. He veers to the curb and steps out. Barlo has made money on cotton during the war. He is as rich as anyone. Esther suddenly is animate. She goes to her door. She sees him at a distance, the center of a group of credulous men. She hears the deep-bass rumble of his talk. The sun swings low. McGregor's windows are aflame again. Pale flame. A sharply dressed white girl passes by. For a moment Esther wishes that she might be like her. Not white; she has no need for being that. But sharp, sporty, with get-up about her. Barlo is connected with that wish. She mustnt wish. Wishes only make you restless. Emptiness is a thing that grows by being moved. "I'll not think. Not wish. Just set my mind against it." Then the thought comes to her that those purposeless, easygoing men will possess him, if she doesnt. Purpose is not dead in her, now that she comes to think of it. That loose women will have their arms around him at Nat Bowle's place tonight. As if her veins are full of fired sun-bleached southern shanties, a swift heat sweeps them. Dead dreams, and a forgotten resolution are carried upward by the flames. Pale flames. "They shant have him. Oh, they shall not. Not if it kills me they shant have him." Jerky, aflutter, she closes the store and starts home. Folks lazing on store windowsills wonder what on earth can be the matter with Jim Crane's gal, as she passes them. "Come to remember, she always was a little off, a little crazy, I reckon." Esther seeks her own room and locks the door. Her mind is a pink mesh bag filled with baby toes.

Using the noise of the town clock striking twelve to cover the creaks of her departure, Esther slips into the quiet road. The town, her parents, most everyone is sound asleep. This fact is a stable thing that comforts her. After sundown a chill wind came up from the west. It is still blowing, but to her it is a steady, settled thing like the cold. She wants her mind to be like that. Solid, contained, and blank as a sheet of darkened ice. She will not permit herself to notice the peculiar phosphorescent glitter of the sweet-gum leaves. Their movement would excite her. Exciting, too, the recession of the dull familiar homes she knows so well. She doesnt know them at all. She closes her eyes, and holds them tightly. Wont do. Her being aware that they are closed recalls her purpose. She does not want to think of it. She opens them. She turns now into the deserted business street. The corrugated iron canopies and mule- and horse-gnawed hitching posts bring her a strange composure. Ghosts of the commonplaces of her daily life take stride with her and become her companions. And the echoes of her heels upon the flagging are rhythmically monotonous and soothing. Crossing the street at the corner of McGregor's notion shop, she thinks that the windows are a dull flame. Only a fancy. She walks faster. Then runs. A turn into a side street brings her abruptly to Nat Bowle's place. The house is squat and dark. It is always dark. Barlo is within. Quietly she opens the outside door and steps in. She passes through a small room. Pauses before a flight of stairs down which people's voices, muffled, come. The air is heavy with fresh tobacco smoke. It makes her sick. She wants to turn back. She goes up the steps. As if she were mounting to some great height, her head spins. She is violently dizzy. Blackness rushes to her eyes. And then she finds that she is in a large room. Barlo is before her.

"Well, I'm sholy damned—skuse me, but what, what brought you here, lil milk-white gal?"

"You." Her voice sounds like a frightened child's that calls homeward from some point miles away.

"Me?"

"Yes, you Barlo."

"This aint th place fer y. This aint th place fer y."

"I know. I know. But I've come for you."

"For me for what?"

She manages to look deep and straight into his eyes. He is slow at understanding. Guffaws and giggles break out from all around the room. A coarse woman's voice remarks, "So thats how th dictie niggers does it." Laughs. "Mus give em credit fo their gall."

Esther doesn't hear. Barlo does. His faculties are jogged. She sees a smile, ugly and repulsive to her, working upward through thick licker fumes. Barlo seems hideous. The thought comes suddenly that conception with a drunken man must be a mighty sin. She draws away, frozen. Like a somnambulist she wheels around and walks stiffly to the stairs. Down them. Jeers and hoots pelter bluntly upon her back. She steps out. There is no air, no street, and the town has completely disappeared.

Richard Wright

(1908–1960)

Like most authors, Richard Wright based his writing on personal experience, which in his case included extreme poverty, a turbulent childhood, and racial prejudice. Born in Mississippi to impoverished cotton sharecroppers, Wright spent time with his harshly moralistic grandmother and other relatives whenever his partially paralyzed mother could not care for him. At the age of nineteen he moved to Chicago where he became a Communist and worked at several menial jobs while writing poetry, articles, and reviews for radical journals. Shortly after another move to New York, Wright began writing in earnest. In 1937 he finished his first novel and a year later published **Uncle Tom's Children**, *a collection of short stories which brought him a five-hundred-dollar prize from the Federal Writers' Project. While on a Guggenheim Fellowship in 1940, Wright completed* **Native Son**. *Based on an actual murder case, this best-selling naturalistic novel brought him international acclaim. He then wrote* **Twelve Million Black Voices** *(1941) and another best-seller, the autobiographical* **Black Boy** *(1945), which describes the brutal conditions of his childhood. In 1947, after Gertrude Stein had invited him to Paris for a visit, Wright decided to move there permanently. Not only had he expatriated himself, he had by this point become thoroughly disenchanted with Marxist ideology and was beginning to favor Sartre's brand of existentialism. His later novels,* **Savage Holiday** *(1954),* **The Outsiders** *(1953), and* **The Long Dream** *(1958), reflect this change of intellectual direction. Although Wright also published a collection of speeches,* **White Man, Listen** *(1957), and several travel books, including* **Pagan Spain** *(1956), his solid status as one of the world's best-selling African American writers rests on his early novels and memoirs.*

Almos' A Man

Dave struck out across the fields, looking homeward through paling light. Whut's the usa talkin wid em niggers in the field? Anyhow, his mother was putting supper on the table. Them niggers can't understan nothing. One of these days he was going to get a gun and practice shooting, then they couldn't talk to him as though he were a little boy. He slowed, looking at the ground. Shucks, Ah ain scareda them even ef they are biggern me! Aw, Ah know whut Ahma do. Ahm going by ol Joe's sto n git that Sears Roebuck catlog n look at them guns. Mebbe Ma will lemme buy one when she gits mah pay from ol man Hawkins. Ahma beg her t gimme some money. Ahm ol ernough to hava gun. Ahm seventeen. Almos a man. He strode, feeling his long loose-jointed limbs. Shucks, a man oughta have a little gun aftah he done worked hard all day.

He came in sight of Joe's store. A yellow lantern glowed on the front porch. He mounted steps and went through the screen door, hearing it bang behind him. There was a strong smell of coal oil and mackerel fish. He felt very confident until he saw fat Joe walk in through the rear door, then his courage began to ooze.

"Howdy, Dave! Whutcha want?"

"How yuh, Mistah Joe? Aw, Ah don wanna buy nothing. Ah jus wanted t see ef yuhd lemme look at tha catlog erwhile."

"Sure! You wanna see it here?"

"Nawsuh. Ah wans t take it home wid me. Ah'll bring it back termorrow when Ah come in from the fiels."

"You plannin on buying something?"

"Yessuh."

"Your ma lettin you have your own money now?"

"Shucks. Mistah Joe, Ahm gittin t be a man like anybody else!"

Joe laughed and wiped his greasy white face with a red bandanna.

"Whut you plannin on buyin?"

Dave looked at the floor, scratched his head, scratched his thigh, and smiled. Then he looked up shyly.

"Ah'll tell yuh, Mistah Joe, ef yuh promise yuh won't tell."

"I promise."

"Waal, Ahma buy a gun."

"A gun? Whut you want with a gun?"

"Ah wanna keep it."

"You ain't nothing but a boy. You don't need a gun."

"Aw, lemme have the catlog, Mistah Joe. Ah'll bring it back."

Joe walked through the rear door. Dave was elated. He looked around at barrels of sugar and flour. He heard Joe coming back. He craned his neck to see if he was bringing the book. Yeah, he's got it. Gawddog, he's got it!

"Here, but be sure you bring it back. It's the only one I got."

"Sho, Mistah Joe."

"Say, if you wanna buy a gun, why don't you buy one from me? I gotta gun to sell."

"Will it shoot?"

"Sure it'll shoot."

"Whut kind is it?"

"Oh, it's kinda old . . . a left-hand Wheeler. A pistol. A big one."

"Is it got bullets in it?"

"It's loaded."

"Kin Ah see it?"

"Where's your money?"

"Whut yuh wan fer it?"

"I'll let you have it for two dollars."

"Just two dollahs? Shucks, Ah could buy tha when Ah git mah pay."

"I'll have it here when you want it."

"Awright, suh. Ah be in fer it."

He went through the door, hearing it slam again behind him. Ahma git some money from Ma n buy me a gun! Only two dollahs! He tucked the thick catalogue under his arm and hurried.

"Where yuh been, boy?" His mother held a steaming dish of black-eyed peas.

"Aw, Ma, Ah jus stopped down the road t talk wid the boys."

"Yuh know bettah than t keep suppah waitin."

He sat down, resting the catalogue on the edge of the table.

"Yuh git up from there and git to the well n wash yosef! Ah ain feedin no hogs in mah house!"

She grabbed his shoulder and pushed him. He stumbled out of the room, then came back to get the catalogue.

"Whut this?"

"Aw, Ma, it's jusa catlog."

"Who yuh git it from?"

"From Joe, down at the sto."

"Waal, thas good. We kin use it in the outhouse."

"Naw, Ma." He grabbed for it. "Gimme ma catlog, Ma."

She held onto it and glared at him.

"Quit hollerin at me! Whut's wrong wid yuh? Yuh crazy?"

"But Ma, please. It ain mine! It's Joe's! He tol me t bring it back t im termorrow."

She gave up the book. He stumbled down the back steps, hugging the thick book under his arm. When he had splashed water on his face and hands, he groped back to the kitchen and fumbled in a corner for the towel. He bumped into a chair; it clattered to the floor. The catalogue sprawled at his feet. When he had dried his eyes he snatched up the book and held it again under his arm. His mother stood watching him.

"Now, ef yuh gonna act a fool over that ol book, Ah'll take it n burn it up."

"Naw, Ma, please."

"Waal, set down n be still!"

He sat down and drew the oil lamp close. He thumbed page after page, unaware of the food his mother set on the table. His father came in. Then his small brother.

"Whutcha got there, Dave?" his father asked.

"Jusa catlog," he answered, not looking up.

"Yeah, here they is!" His eyes glowed at blue-and-black revolvers. He glanced up, feeling sudden guilt. His father was watching him. He eased the book under the table and rested it on his knees. After the blessing was asked, he ate. He scooped up peas and swallowed fat meat without chewing. Buttermilk helped to wash it down. He did not want to mention money before his father. He would do much better by cornering his mother when she was alone. He looked at his father uneasily out of the edge of his eye.

"Boy, how come yuh don quit foolin wid tha book n eat yo suppah?"

"Yessuh."

"How you n old man Hawkins gitten erlong?"

"Suh?"

"Can't yuh hear? Why don yuh lissen? Ah ast yuh how wuz yuh n ol man Hawkins gittin erlong?"

"Oh, swell, Pa. Ah plows mo lan than anybody over there."

"Waal, yuh oughta keep yo mind on whut yuh doin."

"Yessuh."

He poured his plate full of molasses and sopped it up slowly with a chunk of cornbread. When his father and brother had left the kitchen, he still sat and looked again at the guns in the catalogue, longing to muster courage enough to present his case to his mother. Lawd, ef Ah only had tha pretty one! He could almost feel the slickness of the weapon with his fingers. If he had a gun like that he would polish it and keep it shining so it would never rust. N Ah'd keep it loaded, by Gawd!

"Ma?" His voice was hesitant.

"Hunh?"

"Ol man Hawkins give yuh mah money yit?"

"Yeah, but ain no usa yuh thinking bout throwin nona it erway. Ahm keepin tha money sos yuh kin have cloes t go to school this winter."

He rose and went to her side with the open catalogue in his palms. She was washing dishes, her head bent low over a pan. Shyly he raised the book. When he spoke, his voice was husky, faint.

"Ma, Gawd knows Ah wans one of these."

"One of whut?" she asked, not raising her eyes.

"One of these," he said again, not daring even to point. She glanced up at the page, then at him with wide eyes.

"Nigger, is yuh gone plumb crazy?"

"Aw, Ma—"

"Git outta here! Don yuh talk t me bout no gun! Yuh a fool!"

"Ma, Ah kin buy one fer two dollahs."

"Not ef Ah knows it, yuh ain!"

"But yuh promised me one—"

"Ah don care whut Ah promised! Yuh ain nothing but a boy yit!"

"Ma, ef yuh lemme buy one Ah'll *never* ast yuh fer nothing no mo."

"Ah to yuh t git outta here! Yuh ain gonna toucha penny of tha money fer no gun! Thas how come Ah has Mistah Hawkins t pay yo wages t me, cause Ah knows yuh ain got no sense."

"But, Ma, we needa gun. Pa ain got no gun. We needa gun in the house. Yuh kin never tell whut might happen."

"Now don yuh try to maka fool outta me, boy! Ef we did hava gun, yuh wouldn't have it!"

He laid the catalogue down and slipped his arm around her waist.

"Aw, Ma, Ah done worked hard alla summer n ain ast yuh fer nothin, is Ah, now?"

"Thas whut yuh spose t do!"

"But Ma, Ah wans a gun. Yuh kin lemme have two dollahs outta mah money. Please, Ma. I kin give it to Pa ... Please, Ma! Ah loves yuh, Ma."

When she spoke her voice came soft and low.

"Whut yuh wan wida gun, Dave? Yuh don need no gun. Yuh'll git in trouble. N ef yo pa jus thought Ah let yuh have money t buy a gun he'd hava fit."

"Ah'll hide it, Ma. It ain but two dollahs."

"Lawd, chil, whut's wrong wid yuh?"

"Ain nothin wrong, Ma. Ahm almos a man now. Ah wans a gun."

"Who gonna sell yuh a gun?"

"Ol Joe at the sto."

"N it don cos but two dollahs?"

"Thas all, Ma. Jus two dollahs. Please, Ma."

She was stacking the plates away; her hands moved slowly, reflectively. Dave kept an anxious silence. Finally, she turned to him.

"Ah'll let yuh git tha gun ef yuh promise me one thing."

"Whut's tha, Ma?"

"Yuh bring it straight back t me, yuh hear? It be fer Pa."

"Yessum! Lemme go now, Ma."

She stooped, turned slightly to one side, raised the hem of her dress, rolled down the top of her stocking, and came up with a slender wad of bills.

"Here," she said. "Lawd knows yuh don need no gun. But yer pa does. Yuh bring it right back t me, yuh hear? Ahma put it up. Now ef yuh don, Ahma have yuh pa lick yuh so hard yuh won fergit it."

"Yessum."

He took the money, ran down the steps, and across the yard.

"Dave! Yuuuuh Daaaaave!"

He heard, but he was not going to stop now. "Naw, Lawd!"

The first movement he made the following morning was to reach under his pillow for the gun. In the gray light of dawn he held it loosely, feeling a sense of power. Could kill a man with a gun like this. Kill anybody, black or white. And if he were holding his gun in his hand, nobody could run over him; they would have to respect him. It was a big gun, with a long barrel and a heavy handle. He raised and lowered it in his hand, marveling at its weight.

He had not come straight home with it as his mother had asked; instead he had stayed out in the fields, holding the weapon in his hand, aiming it now and then at some imaginary foe. But he had not fired it; he had been afraid that his father might hear. Also he was not sure he knew how to fire it.

To avoid surrendering the pistol he had not come into the house until he knew that they were all asleep. When his mother had tiptoed to his bedside late that night and demanded the gun, he had first played possum; then he had told her that the gun was hidden outdoors, that he would bring it to her in the morning. Now he lay turning it slowly in his hands. He broke it, took out the cartridges, felt them, and then put them back.

He slid out of bed, got a long strip of old flannel from a trunk, wrapped the gun in it, and tied it to his naked thigh while it was still loaded. He did not go in to breakfast. Even though it was not yet daylight, he started for Jim Hawkins' plantation. Just as the sun was rising he reached the barns where the mules and plows were kept.

"Hey! That you, Dave?"

He turned. Jim Hawkins stood eying him suspiciously.

"What're yuh doing here so early?"

"Ah didn't know Ah wuz gittin up so early, Mistah Hawkins. Ah wuz fixin t hitch up ol Jenny n take her t the fiels."

"Good. Since you're so early, how about plowing that stretch down by the woods?"

"Suits me, Mistah Hawkins."

"O.K. Go to it!"

He hitched Jenny to a plow and started across the fields. Hot dog! This was just what he wanted. If he could get down by the woods, he could shoot his gun and nobody would hear. He walked behind the plow, hearing the traces creaking, feeling the gun tied tight to his thigh.

When he reached the woods, he plowed two whole rows before he decided to take out the gun. Finally, he stopped, looked in all directions, then untied the gun and held it in his hand. He turned to the mule and smiled.

"Know whut this is, Jenny? Naw, yuh wouldn know! Yuhs jusa ol mule! Anyhow, this is a gun, n it kin shoot, by Gawd!"

He held the gun at arm's length. Whut t hell, Ahma shoot this thing! He looked at Jenny again.

"Lissen here, Jenny! When Ah pull this ol trigger, Ah don wan yuh t run n acka fool now!"

Jenny stood with head down, her short ears pricked straight. Dave walked off about twenty feet, held the gun far out from him at arm's length, and turned his head. Hell, he told himself, Ah ain afraid. The gun felt loose in his fingers; he waved it wildly for a moment. Then he shut his eyes and tightened his forefinger. Bloom! The report half deafened him and he thought his right hand was torn from his arm. He heard Jenny whinnying and galloping over the field, and he found himself on his knees, squeezing his fingers hard between his legs. His hand was numb; he jammed it into his mouth, trying to warm it, trying to stop the pain. The gun lay at his feet. He did not quite know what had happened. He stood up and stared at the gun as though it were a living thing. He gritted his teeth and kicked the gun. Yuh almos broke mah arm! He turned to look for Jenny; she was far over the fields, tossing her head and kicking wildly.

"Hol on there, ol mule!"

When he caught up with her she stood trembling, walling her big white eyes at him. The plow was far away; the traces had broken. Then Dave stopped short, looking, not believing. Jenny was bleeding. Her left side was red and wet with blood. He went closer. Lawd, have mercy! Wondah did Ah shoot this mule? He grabbed for Jenny's mane. She flinched, snorted, whirled, tossing her head.

"Hol on now! Hol on."

Then he saw the hole in Jenny's side, right between the ribs. It was round, wet, red. A crimson stream streaked down the front leg, flowing fast. Good Gawd! Ah wuzn't shootin at tha mule. He felt panic. He knew he had to stop that blood, or Jenny would bleed to death. He had never seen so much blood in all his life. He chased the mule for half a mile, trying to catch her. Finally she stopped, breathing hard, stumpy tail half arched. He caught her mane and led her back to where the plow and gun lay. Then he stooped and grabbed handfuls of damp black earth and tried to plug the bullet hole. Jenny shuddered, whinnied, and broke from him.

"Hol on! Hol on now!"

He tried to plug it again, but blood came anyhow. His fingers were hot and sticky. He rubbed dirt into his palms, trying to dry them. Then again he attempted to plug the bullet hole, but Jenny shied away, kicking her heels high. He stood helpless. He had to do something. He ran at Jenny; she dodged him. He watched a red stream of blood flow down Jenny's leg and form a bright pool at her feet.

"Jenny ... Jenny," he called weakly.

His lips trembled. She's bleeding t death! He looked in the direction of home, wanting to go back, wanting to get help. But he saw the pistol lying in the damp black clay. He had a queer feeling that if he only did something, this would not be; Jenny would not be there bleeding to death.

When he went to her this time, she did not move. She stood with sleepy, dreamy eyes; and when he touched her she gave a low-pitched whinny and knelt to the ground, her front knees slopping in blood.

"Jenny ... Jenny ... " he whispered.

For a long time she held her neck erect; then her head sank, slowly. Her ribs swelled with a mighty heave and she went over.

Dave's stomach felt empty, very empty. He picked up the gun and held it gingerly between his thumb and forefinger. He buried it at the foot of a tree. He took a stick and tried to cover the pool of blood with dirt—but what was the use? There was Jenny lying with her mouth open and her eyes walled and glassy. He could not tell Jim Hawkins he had shot his mule. But he had to tell him something. Yeah, Ah'll tell em Jenny started gittin wil n fell on the joint of the plow .... But that would hardly happen to a mule. He walked across the field slowly, head down.

It was sunset. Two of Jim Hawkins' men were over near the edge of the woods digging a hole in which to bury Jenny. Dave was surrounded by a knot of people, all of whom were looking down at the dead mule.

"I don't see how in the world it happened," said Jim Hawkins for the tenth time.

The crowd parted and Dave's mother, father, and small brother pushed into the center.

"Where Dave?" his mother called.

"There he is," said Jim Hawkins.

His mother grabbed him.

"Whut happened, Dave? Whut yuh done?"

"Nothin."

"C mon, boy, talk," his father said.

Dave took a deep breath and told the story he knew nobody believed.

"Waal," he drawled. "Ah brung ol Jenny down here sos Ah could do mah plowin. Ah plowed bout two rows, just like yuh see." He stopped and pointed at the long rows of upturned earth. "Then somethin musta been wrong wid ol Jenny. She wouldn ack right a-tall. She started snortin n kickin her heels. Ah tried t hol her, but she pulled erway, rearin n goin on. Then when the point of the plow was stickin up in the air, she swung erroun n twisted herself back on it ... She stuck herself n started t bleed. N fo Ah could do anything, she wuz dead."

"Did you ever hear of anything like that in all your life?" asked Jim Hawkins.

There were white and black standing in the crowd. They murmured. Dave's mother came close to him and looked hard into his face. "Tell the truth, Dave," she said.

"Looks like a bullet hole to me," said one man.

"Dave, whut yuh do wid the gun?" his mother asked.

The crowd surged in, looking at him. He jammed his hands into his pockets, shook his head slowly from left to right, and backed away. His eyes were wide and painful.

"Did he hava a gun?" asked Jim Hawkins.

"By Gawd, Ah tol yuh that wuz a gun wound," said a man, slapping his thigh.

His father caught his shoulders and shook him till his teeth rattled.

"Tell whut happened, yuh rascal! Tell whut ... "

Dave looked at Jenny's stiff legs and began to cry.

"Whut yuh do wid tha gun?" his mother asked.

"Whut wuz he doin wida gun?" his father asked.

"Come on and tell the truth," said Hawkins. "Ain't nobody going to hurt you ... "

His mother crowded close to him.

"Did yuh shoot tha mule, Dave?"

Dave cried, seeing blurred white and black faces.

"Ahh ddinn gggo tt sshooot hher ... Ah ssswear ffo Gawd Ahh ddin ... .Ah wuz a-tryin t sssee ef the old gggun would sshoot—"

"Where yuh git the gun from?" his father asked.

"Ah got it from Joe, at the sto."

"Where yuh git the money?"

"Ma give it t me."

"He kept worryin me, Bob. Ah had t. Ah tol im t bring the gun right back t me ... It was fer yuh, the gun."

"But how yuh happen to shoot that mule?" asked Jim Hawkins.

"Ah wuzn shootin at the mule, Mistah Hawkins. The gun jumped when Ah pulled the trigger ... N fo Ah knowed anythin Jenny was there a-bleedin."

Somebody in the crowd laughed. Jim Hawkins walked close to Dave and looked into his face.

"Well, looks like you have bought you a mule, Dave."

"Ah swear fo Gawd, Ah didn go t kill the mule, Mistah Hawkins!"

"But you killed her!"

All the crowd was laughing now. They stood on tiptoe and poked heads over one another's shoulders.

"Well, boy, looks like yuh done bought a dead mule! Hahaha!"

"Ain tha ershame."

"Hohohohoho."

Dave stood, head down, twisting his feet in the dirt.

"Well, you needn't worry about it, Bob," said Jim Hawkins to Dave's father. "Just let the boy keep on working and pay me two dollars a month."

"Whut yuh wan fer yo mule, Mistah Hawkins?"

Jim Hawkins screwed up his eyes.

"Fifty dollars."

"Whut yuh do wid tha gun?" Dave's father demanded.

Dave said nothing.

"Yuh wan me t take a tree lim n beat yuh till yuh talk!"

"Nawsuh!"

"Whut yuh do wid it?"

"Ah throwed it erway."

"Where?"

"Ah ... Ah throwed it in the creek."

"Waal, c mon home. N firs thing in the mawnin git to tha creek n fin tha gun."

"Yessuh."

"What yuh pay fer it?"

"Two dollahs."

"Take tha gun n git yo money back n carry it t Mistah Hawkins, yuh hear? N don forgit Ahma lam you black bottom good fer this! Now march yoself on home, suh!"

Dave turned and walked slowly. He heard people laughing. Dave glared, his eyes welling with tears. Hot anger bubbled in him. Then he swallowed and stumbled on.

That night Dave did not sleep. He was glad that he had gotten out of killing the mule so easily, but he was hurt. Something hot seemed to turn over inside him each time he remembered how they had laughed. He tossed on his bed, feeling his hard pillow. N Pa says he's gonna beat me ... He remembered other beatings, and his back quivered. Naw, naw, Ah sho don wan im t beat me tha way no mo. Dam em all! Nobody ever gave him anything. All he did was work. They treat me like a mule, n then they beat me. He gritted his teeth. N Ma had t tell on me.

Well, if he had to, he would take old man Hawkins that two dollars. But that meant selling the gun. And he wanted to keep that gun. Fifty dollars for a dead mule.

He turned over, thinking how he had fired the gun. He had an itch to fire it again. Ef other men kin shoota gun, by Gawd, Ah kin! He was still, listening. Mebbe they all sleepin now. The house was still. He heard the soft breathing of his brother. Yes, now! He would go down and get that gun and see if he could fire it! He eased out of bed and slipped into overalls.

The moon was bright. He ran almost all the way to the edge of the woods. He stumbled over the ground, looking for the spot where he had buried the gun. Yeah, here it is. Like a hungry dog scratching for a bone, he pawed it up. He puffed his black cheeks and blew dirt from the trigger and barrel. He broke it and found four cartridges unshot. He looked around; the fields were filled with silence and moonlight. He clutched the gun stiff and hard in his fingers. But, as soon as he wanted to pull the trigger, he shut his eyes and turned his head. Naw, Ah can't shoot wid mah eyes closed n mah head turned. With effort he held his eyes open; then he squeezed. *Blooooom!* He was stiff, not breathing. The gun was still in his hands. Dammit, he'd done it. He fired again. *Bloooooom!* He smiled. *Bloooooom! Bloooooom! Click, click.* There! It was empty. If anybody could shoot a gun, he could. He put the gun into his hip pocket and started across the fields.

When he reached the top of a ridge he stood straight and proud in the moonlight, looking at Jim Hawkins' big white house, feeling the gun sagging in his pocket. Lawd, ef Ah had just one mo bullet Ah'd taka shot at tha house. Ah'd like t scare ol man Hawkins jusa little ... Jusa enough t let im know Dave Glover is a man.

To his left the road curved, running to the tracks of the Illinois Central. He jerked his head, listening. From far off came a faint hoooof-hoooof; boooof-hoooof; boooof-hoooof .... That's number eight. He took a swift look at Jim Hawkins' house, he thought of Pa, of Ma, of his little brother, and the boys. He thought of the dead mule and heard hoooof-hoooof; hoooof-hoooof; hoooof-hoooof ... .He stood rigid. Two dollahs a mont. Les see now ... Tha means it'll take bout two years. Shucks! Ah'll be dam!

He started down the road, toward the tracks. Yeah, here she comes! He stood beside the track and held himself stiffly. Here she comes, erroun the ben ... C mon, yuh slow poke! C mon! He had his hand on his gun; something quivered in his stomach. Then the train thundered past, the gray and brown box cars rumbling and clinking. He gripped the gun tightly; then he jerked his hand out of his pocket. Ah betcha Bill wouldn't do it! Ah betcha ... The cars slid past, steel grinding upon steel. Ahm ridin yuh ternight, so hep me Gawd! He was hot all over. He hesitated just a moment; then he grabbed, pulled atop of a car, and lay flat. He felt his pocket; the gun was still there. Ahead the long rails were glinting in the moonlight, stretching away, away to somewhere, somewhere where he could be a man ...

Chester Himes

(1909–1984)

Born in Jefferson City, Missouri, Chester Himes spent his childhood in various places in the South and Midwest. After graduating from high school in Cleveland, Ohio, he entered Ohio State University. Expelled for disciplinary reasons, Himes then drifted into a life of crime. His literary career began in the Ohio State Penitentiary, where he served a sentence for armed robbery from 1929 to 1936. After witnessing riots, beatings, and a deadly fire, he began to publish stories based on his prison experience, which would later inspire what many readers consider a classic prison novel, the autobiographical **Cast the First Stone** *(1952). When he was released on parole, Himes worked for the Federal Writers' Project and then moved to the west coast, where he hoped to find government work in a California shipyard. His frustration with discriminatory employment practices inspired his first two novels,* **If He Hollers, Let Him Go** *(1945) and* **Lonely Crusade** *(1947). Himes, however, was unable to support himself in America by writing, so in 1953 he moved to Paris and then to Spain, where he lived as an expatriate.*

Although Himes also wrote a comprehensive two-volume autobiography, **The Quality of Hurt** *(1972) and* **My Life as Absurdity** *(1976), many readers know him best as the author of the "Harlem Domestic" series, the New York–based detective novels that the impoverished writer began writing for a French publisher:* **Cotton Comes to Harlem**, **The Real Cool Killers**, *and* **A Rage in Harlem**. *Often violent and pessimistic in their portrayals of inner-city life, these popular, best-selling novels relate the episodic adventures of two black detectives, "Coffin" Ed Johnson and "Grave Digger" Jones. While some readers have objected to the brutality of these stories, others regard them as some of Himes' best work, seeing in their sensationalism the same unveiled anger toward social oppression and injustice that characterizes such earlier works as* **Third Generation** *(1954) and* **The Primitive** *(1955). He died of Parkinson's disease at his home in Spain.*

Headwaiter

When headwaiter Dick Small pushed through the service hall into the main dining room, he ran smack into an early dinner rush. The creased, careful smile adorning his brown face knotted slightly in self-reproach. He should have been there sooner.

For a brief instant he paused just inside the doorway, head cocked to one side as if deferentially listening. A hum of cultured voices engaged in leisurely conversation, the gentle clatter of silver on fine china, the slight scrape of a chair, the tinkle of ice in glasses, the aroma of hot coffee and savory, well-cooked food, the sight of unhurried dining and hurried service blended into an atmosphere ineffably dear to his heart; for directing the services of this dining room in a commendable manner was the ultimate aim of his life, and as much a part of him as the thin spot in his meticulously brushed hair or the habitual immaculateness of the tuxedo which draped his slight, spright frame.

But he could sense a hint of exasperation in the general mood with that surety of feeling which twenty years as headwaiter at the Park Manor Hotel had bestowed upon him, and his roving gaze searched quickly for flaws in the service inspiring it.

There was fat Mr. McLaughlin knuckling the table impatiently as he awaited— Dick was quite sure that it was broiled lobster that Mr. McLaughlin was so impatiently awaiting. And Mrs. Shipley was frowning with displeasure at the dirty dishes which claimed her elbow room as she endeavored to lean closer to her boon companion, Mrs. Hamilton, and impart in a theatrical whisper a choice morsel of spicy gossip— Dick had no doubt that it was both choice and spicy. When Mr. Lyons lifted his glass to take another sip of iced water, he found to his extreme annoyance that there was no more iced water to be sipped, and even from where he stood, Dick could see Mr. Lyons' forbearance abruptly desert him.

The white-jacketed, black-bowed waiters showed a passable alacrity, he observed without censure, but they were accomplishing very little. Direction was lacking. The captain, black and slow, plodded hither and yon in a stew of indecision.

Dick clapped his hands. "Fill those glasses for that deuce over there," he directed the busboy who had sprung to his side. "Take an ashstand to the party at that center table. Clear up those ladies." He left the busboy spinning in his tracks, turned to the captain who came rushing over. "I'll take it over now, son. You slip into a white jacket and bring in Mr. McLaughlin's lobster."

His presence was established and the wrinkles of exasperation ironed smoothly out.

The captain nodded and flashed white teeth, relieved. He turned away, turned back. "Mr. Erskine has a party of six for seven-thirty. I gave it to Pat. Here's the bill of fare." He gave Dick a scrawled slip of paper.

Dick pocketed the order, aware that this party was something in the way of an event, for Mr. Erskine had been the very first of the older residents who had sworn they would never set food within the dining room again until the "obnoxious"—Mr. Erskine himself had employed the term—syncopatings of "Sonny" Jenkins and his body-rocking "Cotton Pickers" had been everlastingly removed. His glance strayed involuntarily to the band dais at the rear where until just the day before Sonny and his black, foot-stomping troubadours had held forth; but deprived of their colorful appearance and cannonading rhythms it had a skeletoned, abandoned look.

Well, after all it was the older residents like Mr. Erskine who comprised the firm foundation upon which the hotel so staunchly rested, he reflected, agreeing with them (although he would not have admitted it) that the noticeable absence of Sonny and his boys was more to be desired than their somewhat jarring presence.

But he quickly pigeonholed the thought, the press of duty making no allowances for idle reflection. He went straight to the setup and scanned it quickly, his head to one side. After a moment's careful study, he leaned across the table and aligned a fork, smoothed an infinitesimal wrinkle from the linen, shifted the near candlestick just a wee bit to the left; then he rocked back on his heels and allowed his eyes to smile. He was pleased.

Flawless service for discriminating guests evoked in him a complete satisfaction. And who among the many to whom he had catered during his twenty years at the Park Manor had ever showed a finer sense of discrimination than Mr. Erskine, he thought, or a broader sense of appreciation, he added with a glow.

He nodded commendation to Pat, tan and lanky, who was spooning ice cubes into the upturned glasses with slim, deft fingers; and Pat acknowledged it with his roguish smile.

"Here's the bill of fare, Pat," he said in his quick, crisp voice. "Put your cocktails on ice and have everything prepared by a quarter after seven." He glanced at the wall clock and noticed that it was forty-seven minutes after six.

He stepped away, circled an unoccupied table, and came back, frowning slightly. "This is Mrs. Van Denter's table, Pat. Did the captain select it?"

"Cap called the desk, chief," Pat explained. "They said Mrs. Van Denter had gone into the country to spend a week with her sister."

His breath oozed slowly out. "You know how stubborn she is. Been that way for twenty years to my knowledge, ever since her husband died and left her—" he caught himself and stopped abruptly. Gossiping with a waiter. Chagrin bit him lightly, putting snap into his voice. "Put your reserved card on, Pat. Always put your reserved card on first, then—"

The sight of Mrs. Van Denter coming through the entrance archway choked him. She made straight for her table, plowing aside everyone who got in her way. Tonight she looked slightly forbidding, her grayish, stoutish, sixtyish appearance rockier than ever and the tight seam of her mouth carrying an overload of obstinacy. At first glance he thought that she had had a martini too many, but as she lumbered closer with her elephantine directness, he decided that it came from her heart, not her stomach.

Perhaps she and her sister had had a rift, he was thinking as he bowed with more than his customary deference and inquired as to her health. "And how are you this evening, Mrs. Van Denter?" After a pause in which she did not reply he began his apology. "I am very sorry, Mrs. Van Denter, but the captain was under the impression that you were in the country—"

She brushed him aside and aimed her solid body for her table, on which Pat was just placing the reserved card. Dick turned quickly behind her, his mouth hanging slack. There was the hint of a race. But she won.

And for all of the iced glasses and party silver and crimped napkins and bowl of roses and engraved name cards at each plate; for all of the big black-lettered card which read RESERVED, staring up into her face, she reached for the nearest chair, pulled it out, planted her plump body into it with sickening finality, and reached for an iced glass.

Dick dropped a menu card before her and signaled Pat to take her order, his actions registering no more than a natural concern. He picked up the bowl of flowers and the reserved card and placed them on another table, then moved casually away. It was an era of change, he told himself. It made the old more stubborn and the young more reckless—he didn't know which were the more difficult to please. But here were Mrs. Hughes and her guest right beside him, who seemed to be pleased enough even if no one else was, he noted, with obvious enjoyment of the fact.

"How do you do, Mrs. Hughes," he addressed the stately, white-haired lady. "And this is your sister, Mrs. Walpole, of Boston, I am sure. We're delighted to have you with us again, Mrs. Walpole. I remember quite well when you visited us before."

Mrs. Hughes smiled cordially and Mrs. Walpole said, "I've been here several times before."

"But I was referring to your last visit; it was in August three years ago."

"What a remarkable memory," Mrs. Hughes murmured.

Dick was gratified; he prided himself upon his memory and when someone took notice of it he felt rewarded. Turning away he caught his tuxedoed reflection in a paneled mirror and the slightly disturbing thought came to him that the blue and gold decorations of this dining room were too ornate for the casual informality which now existed. A vague regret threaded his thoughts as he recalled the bygone age when dressing for dinner had been the rigid rule. It took a slight effort to banish such recollections and when he spoke again his voice was brusque.

"Clear that table," he ordered a busboy as if the busboy alone was to blame for the change of things.

Then a party of seven at a center table demanded his personal attention. "Good evening, Mr. and Mrs. Seedle," he greeted the elderly hosts, knowing that they considered the service lacking until he made his appearance. "And how is this young gentleman?" he inquired of their seven-year-old grandson.

"I'm all right, Dick," the boy replied, "but I ain't no gentleman 'cause Gramma just said so—"

"Arnold!" Mrs. Seedle rebuked.

"Why does Grandpa eat onions, Dick?" the boy asked, not to be repressed, but Dick bowed a smiling departure without replying.

"So Gramma can find him in the dark," he heard Mr. Seedle elucidate, feeling that "Gramma" could very likely find him right then in the dark without the aid of onions, as lit as he was.

"Fill these glasses," he directed a busy waiter to hide his growing smile, then filled them himself before the waiter had a chance to protest.

"Pst, pst." He called a busboy, received no reply. He hurried across the floor, light lumping slightly on the irritation in his face, shook the boy's shoulder. "What's the matter with you, are you deaf?" he demanded.

"No sir, I—I—er—"

"Go get the salad tray," he snapped and hurried away in his loping walk to greet Mrs. Collar, eighty and cross, who hesitated undecidedly under the entrance archway.

"It's a rather nasty night, Mrs. Collar," he remarked by way of greeting, seating her in a corner nook. "It doesn't seem to be able to make up its mind whether to rain or sleet, but I feel that it will clear up by tomorrow."

Mrs. Collar looked up at him over the rim of her ancient spectacles. "That isn't any encouragement to me," she replied in her harsh, unconciliatory voice.

Confusion took the smoothness out of Dick's speech. "I am not really sure, er—er, I wouldn't be surprised if it continued, er, being indefinite."

"You're indefinite enough yourself," she snapped, scanning the menu card.

He laughed deprecatingly, signaled to a youth less than a year out of prison to take her order. "I'd make a poor gambler," he confessed ruefully.

Her head jerked quickly up again. "You don't gamble, do you, Dick?" she asked sharply.

"No, Mrs. Collar, I do not gamble," said headwaiter Dick Small, gambling then his job at five hundred a month to give an ex-con another chance. "Nor do I employ any man who does."

"You couldn't tell if they did," she pointed out matter-of-factly. "Not unless you had every one of them shadowed night and day."

The indelibleness abandoned his smile. He turned away from her, annoyance tight in his throat, and greeted a sudden influx of diners. But before he had finished seating them the indulgence came back to him. Mrs. Collar was really a very nice old lady, he admitted to himself, and he liked her. She was like olives; you had to acquire a taste for her. And he sincerely hoped that she was pleased with the service.

But after all, Mrs. Collar was just one diner, and he had neither the time nor the inclination to analyze her disposition, for the dining room was rapidly filling with younger and more demanding guests.

It was an unusual weekday crowd, and search his mind as he would, he could not think of one reason for it. There were no conventions in town as he knew of, and there were no more than the usual dinner "specials." And then he had it, and he wondered why he had not thought of it before. It was no more or less than the return of the dissenters, recalled by the serene and comfortable knowledge that "Sonny" Jenkins and his "Cotton Pickers" had no longer to be endured.

A repressed snort of laughter pushed air through his nose. But this was no laughing time, really, he censored himself. It was a time for smooth, fast service. His reputation as a headwaiter and even the prestige of the hotel itself were dependent upon the guests being served with the least possible delay.

He started kitchenward to recruit more waiters from the room service department, he just simply must have more waiters, when something about a busboy halted him. He glanced down, looked up again.

"What kind of shoe polish do you use, son?" he inquired disarmingly.

"Paste," the boy replied, unthinking.

He let his gaze drop meaningfully to the boy's unshined shoes. "Try liquid next time, son," he suggested.

The boy jumped with sudden guilt. Dick stepped quickly around him and passed from the dining room before the boy had a chance to reply.

In the service hall Dick bumped into a waiter gobbling a leftover steak, said pleasantly enough, "Food is like drink, son, it's a habit. There's no place in service for the glutton or the drunkard."

The waiter strangled, blew steak all over the floor, but Dick passed on without a backward glance.

Over by the elevator where the room service was stationed, a waiter lounged indolently by a service table and yelled at the closed elevator doors, "Knock knock!"

Dick drew up quietly behind him, heard the slightly muffled reply from within the elevator: "Who's there?"

"Mr. Small, the headwaiter," he said crisply.

The waiter who had been leaning so indolently by the service table jumped. His hand flew up and knocked over a glass of water on the clean linen. The elevator doors popped open, emitting two more waiters in an impressive hurry.

"If you fellows don't care to work—" Dick began, exceedingly unimpressed.

The first waiter hoisted the room service table on his shoulder and started into the elevator without a word. The other two stammered in unison, "Yes sir, no sir, er—rer—"

"Put down that table," Dick grated at the first waiter.

The waiter let it drop as if it was hot.

"All three of you go into the dining room and report to the captain," Dick ordered. They scampered quickly off.

"Here, serve this dinner," Dick directed a busboy who had performed a magical appearance.

"But I don't, er, know, er—"

"Find out," Dick snapped, at the end of his patience.

When he returned to the dining room he noticed that patrons were still entering. He greeted an incoming couple, seated them, and took their order on note paper, being unable to locate an idle waiter.

A bellboy passed through from the kitchen. Dick stopped him. "Give this order to Howard," he directed.

"But I'm a bellboy," the boy objected.

Dick stood stock still and looked at him. "All stages of existence have their drawbacks, son," he began in a lazy, philosophical vein.

But the boy was not to be fooled. Dick had such a smooth way of telling a servant that he was fired. He took the note and hurried away in search of Howard.

Dick's quick sight scanned the side stand before he turned away, exploring for negligence, but the pitchers were filled and the butter was iced and the silver was neatly arranged in the drawers. He allowed a slight expression of commendation to come into his smile. The busboys whose duty it was to keep the side stands in order had earned stars in their crowns, although they would never know it if they waited for Dick Small, headwaiter, to tell them.

Dick turned back to his guests, feeling a benign omnipotence in caring for their needs. He was as the captain of a ship, he reflected, the master of this dining room and solely responsible for its service. He seemed to derive a becoming dignity from this responsibility.

These people were his passengers; he must feed and serve and humor them with an impartial respect. They were his life; they took up his time, his thoughts, his energy. He was interested in them, interested in their private lives and their individual prosperity. He knew them, knew about them. His most vital emotions absorbed their coloring from the emotions of these dining room patrons: when they were pleased, he was pleased; when they were hurt, he was hurt; when they failed or prospered in their respective endeavors, it had a personal bearing on the course of his life.

Each day when he stood looking over them, as now, he received some feeling which added to his life, although it seldom showed in the imperturbableness of his smile.

Now his gaze drifted slowly from face to face, reading the feelings and emotions of each with an uncanny perception.

There were Tommy and Jackie Rightmire, the polo-playing twins. And did they have healthy appetites? And several tables distant he noticed their sister dining with a Spanish nobleman whom he had never been quite able to admire.

And there were Mr. Andrews and Mrs. Winnings, engaged as was their custom of late in animated chatter as they dined in the dubious seclusion of a rear column. Crowding forty, both of them, he was quite sure, and as obviously in love with each other as a pair of doves. But if the slightest censure threaded his thoughts as his gaze moved slowly on, it did not show in the bland smoothness of his expression.

He wondered what would happen if Mrs. Andrews, forty-two and showing it, and reputedly very jealous of Mr. Andrews' affections, should choose this dining room in which to dine some evening and inadvertently bump into their tête-à-tête.

And coincidentally, as it happens even in masterpieces, Mrs. Andrews did. She came through the entrance archway at the front and beat a hard-heeled, determined path straight toward her spouse's table.

Dick's compelling thought was to deter catastrophe, for catastrophe indeed it would be, he sincerely felt, should Mrs. Andrews encounter Mr. Andrews in such an inexplicable predicament. He headed her off just in time.

"Right this way, Mrs. Andrews," he began, pulling a chair for a conspicuously placed center table.

"No, no, not that." She discarded with a gesture. "I want something—remote, quiet. I'm expecting a friend." Her eyes dared him to think no more than that which she had explicitly stated.

"Then this will be just the ticket for you," he purred smoothly, seating her across the dining room from her husband with her back toward him and the column between them.

"Thank you, this will be just fine." She smiled, pleased, and he had the feeling of a golfer who has just scored a hole in one.

The voice of a waiter halted his casual strolling as he moved away from her. "Chief, see that old man over there at the window? The one with the white goatee?"

Dick did not look at the old man "with the white goatee," he looked very pointedly at the waiter slouching with propped elbows on the side stand and lacking in a proper respect for the hotel's patrons, not to mention the hotel's headwaiter.

"He says all a nigger needs is something to eat and someplace to sleep," the waiter continued, unaware of the pointedness of Dick's frown. "He says he knows 'cause he's got a plantation of them—"

"Do *you* see that table over there from which Mrs. Van Denter is now arising?" he cut in, a forced restraint blunting his voice.

"Yes sir," the waiter replied quickly, sensing his mistake.

"Well, service it for six," he directed, the displeasure breaking through his restraint.

"Yes *sir*." The waiter was glad to be off.

Dick followed him over to Mrs. Van Denter's table and bowed to her again with that slightly exaggerated deference. "Was you dinner enjoyable, madam?" he inquired.

But dinner, enjoyable or not, had not softened the stone of Mrs. Van Denter's face. "Dick," she snapped, "I find your obsequiousness a bit repugnant." Then she plodded smilelessly away.

Dick admitted to himself with a sense of reproach that it had been a *faux pas* but he couldn't take time to explore into it further for he noticed that the table of two women needed clearing and he went in search of a busboy to clear it.

The boy, a greenhorn, approached timidly from the rear of the thin, reedy lady with the lashing voice and reached around her for her plate, taking great care not to disturb her. The lady saw the stealthily reaching hand, "the clutching hand" she might have said had she said it. Her sharp mouth went slack like a fish's. "Oh!" she gasped.

The boy grew panicky. He grabbed the plate as if to dash away with it, as indeed he did. The thin lady clutched the other rim and held on for dear life. There was a moment's tug of war. A chicken bone fell to the table. Then anger jerked the thin lady around in her chair.

"Let loose!" she shrilled.

And "let loose" the now thoroughly frightened boy most certainly did. He not only let loose but he jumped a full yard backward, his nostrils flaring like a winded horse's and his eyes white-rimmed in his black face.

"Always taking my plate before I'm finished," the thin lady added caustically.

But she had no further need to fear that particular boy taking her plate ever again, finished or not finished, for he didn't stop running until he was downstairs in the locker room changing into his street clothes. Dick sent the captain down to bring him back, but the boy had definitely resigned.

"Well, he wouldn't have made a waiter, anyway," he remarked. "He has an innate fear of white people which he couldn't overcome. It makes him nervous and panicky around them." But he was annoyed just the same.

A stag party of four in the rear offered a brief respite from peevish old ladies and frightened busboys. He noticed that a raised window beside them slashed wind across their table and hastened quickly in their direction, concern prodding him.

"Is there too much draft for you, gentlemen?" he inquired solicitously, pausing in a half bow. But on closer observation he saw that they were all strangers to him and slightly drunk and not gentlemen, after all.

They all stopped eating and ogled him. "That's a good-looking tux, boy," one remarked. "Where'd you get it? Steal it?"

"No sir, I purchased it—" he began restrainedly.

"What makes you black?" another cut in. A laugh spurted.

Anger broke loose in him then. It shook him like a squall. But his smile weathered it. When the breath had softened in his lungs he said politely, "God did, gentlemen," and moved away.

At a center table a high-pressure voice was saying, "Just talked to the governor at the capitol. He said—" It sounded unreal to Dick. He turned his glance obliquely, saw the latecomer sit opposite his comely, young wife. It was the wife who signed the checks, he recalled; and who was the woman he had seen him with the other day and had intended to remember?

But the sight of old Mr. Woodford standing in the entrance archway snapped his line of thought before Mnemosyne could come to his aid. He rushed to meet him. "And how are you this evening, Mr. Woodford, sir?" he asked, and then added without awaiting a reply, knowing there would be none, "Right this way, sir. I reserved your table for you." He had already noted that Mr. Woodford's table was unoccupied.

He received Mr. Woodford's grudging nod, led the way rearward, head cocked, arms swinging, recalling reluctantly the time when Mr. Woodford was genial and talkative and worth many millions—broke now since the stock market crash and glum, with slightly bloodshot eyes from drinking a little too much, he suspected.

When he turned away he caught the beckoning finger of old Mrs. Miller, a resident for many years at the Park Manor and a special friend of the Rumanian countess who resided there on her visits to America. He moved quickly toward her, his smile becoming more genuine, less careful.

"And when have you heard from our good friend, her highness, Mrs. Miller?" he inquired with assured familiarity.

"I was just going to tell you, Dick," she replied in a reedy, year-thinned voice. "I had a cablegram from her daughter just this afternoon."

"And when is she going to pay us another visit? Soon, I hope."

"Never, Dick," she quavered. "She died last week."

Dick went rigid. The brown of his face tinged ashily. Then he noticed that Mrs. Miller's eyes were red and swollen from crying and he upbraided himself for not having noticed immediately.

He could find no suitable words for the moment. He pitied her in a sincere, personal way, for he knew that the countess was the one person in all the world whom she considered as a friend. But he could not express his pity. He was only a headwaiter. He thought there was something sublime in her gallantry which would not let her grief prostrate her; and he knew the countess would have wished it so.

Oddly, for a fleeting instant he was a young black waiter in Atlantic City, thirty-six years ago. It was his afternoon off and he had seven dollars. The pretty brown girl beside him was saying, "I want the five-dollar one." It was a wedding ring, and she was to be his bride. Seven dollars—and now he was headwaiter at five hundred a month, had bought a seven-thousand-dollar home, had a few thousand in the bank. That afternoon seemed a long way behind.

He said aloud, a sincere depth of feeling in his voice, "We shall miss her so much, Mrs. Miller. The world can little spare the loss of one so fine."

And by that sincere tribute to one who was dead he earned for himself five thousand dollars in Mrs. Miller's will.

"Indeed we shall miss her, Dick," Mrs. Miller replied, barely able to stem the flow of tears.

When he moved away from her his actions were slowed, groggy, as if he had taken a severe beating. In a very short time he would pass the sixty mark. Sixty was old for a waiter in a busy hotel. He shook himself as if he were awaking from a bad dream, stepped forward with renewed pounce.

Perhaps he wasn't looking, perhaps he couldn't see. He bumped into a busboy with a loaded tray. China crashed on the tiled floor, silver rang. The sudden shatter shook the room. He patted the stooping boy on the shoulder, the unusual show of feeling leaving the boy slightly flustered, turned quickly away, head held high, refusing to notice the shattered crockery. And by his refusal to notice it he averted attention.

The ringing of the telephone in the corner brought relief to his thoughts. He hurried over, picked up the receiver. "Dining room, the headwaiter speaking," he said. Faint traces of emotion still lingered in his eyes.

Behind him a woman's husky voice was saying, "But Mildred is selfish. No matter what you give in material things, my dear, unless you give something of yourself—" He recognized the voice as Mrs. Porter's, of Porter Paints and Varnish…. The telephone began speaking and drew his attention.

He hooked the receiver, stuck a reserved sign on a table, started kitchenward to get a glass of water when the question jerked him up short like the snap of a noose.

"Boy, didn't you get a pardon from the penitentiary about a year back?"

The voices of the other three men and four women at the table stopped and hung rigidly suspended in an all-enveloping gasp. Motion froze as solid as the ice cubes tinkling in the glasses. Silence came in a tight clamp, restricting the breath.

But the waiter to whom the question had been addressed remained placid. "Yes sir," he replied.

Dick turned toward the party, brushing the apprehension from before him with a widespread gesture.

"First degree?" the voice persisted.

A woman said, "Oh!"

"Yes sir," the waiter repeated.

Dick entered the conversation then. "I engaged him, sir." He addressed the genial-faced man who had put the questions. "Turned out to be one of my best boys, too."

"Why?" the man wanted to know, more from curiosity than reprobation. "I imagine that the residents of the hotel here would resent it if they knew. I might myself."

"I felt that he was a good boy and that all he needed was another chance," Dick explained.

The man's eyes lingered a moment appraisingly upon Dick's face, then switched to the waiter's. "Let's give it to him," he decided, closing the incident. Ease came back into the diners and the dinner moved serenely on.

But the genial-faced man had earned Dick's everlasting gratefulness, although he would perhaps never know it.

Dick had forgotten that he was thirsty, drawn again into the maelstrom of duties confronting a headwaiter.

The rush gradually subsided. Dick was made aware of it by the actions of his waiters. They had begun to move about with that Negroid languor which bespoke liberal tips. He was reminded of the Negro of Mark Twain legend who said he didn't want to make a dime 'cause he had a dime. His smile was indulgent. He knew his boys.

His rapid sight counted twenty-one remaining diners. So he released the first shift of waiters with the ironic suggestion: "Don't disappoint your money, boys. Give it a break and spend it."

He watched their happy departure for a moment, knowing full well that they would be hanging over their favorite bars before the hour was passed; then his attention was drawn to a drunken party at a center table, overflow from the bar no doubt. The coarseness of their speech and actions spread a personal humiliation within him. He wanted to feel that his guests deserved the respect which he bestowed upon them.

Someone of the party made a risqué remark and everyone laughed. Everyone except one woman. She was looking at the lobster in front of her with mouth-twitching nausea. Then horror came into her face. "It moved! It moved!" she cried, voice rising hysterically. "It moved!" She backed away from the table, crying over and over again, "It moved!"

Dick stepped quickly forward, his careful smile forced, and whisked the platter of lobster from the table. "Is there something else you desire, madam?" he asked politely, presenting her with a menu.

A man swung leisurely from his seat and winked at him. "She desires a bit of air, that's all," he said.

A waiter smothered a laugh in a napkin.

"Take that napkin from your face!" Dick chastened with severe voice. "Get some side towels and use them, and don't ever let me catch you using a napkin in such a manner." His harshness was an outlet.

He moved toward the side windows, trying to stifle the buildup of emotion in the smoothness of his mind. The guests were always right and a waiter was always impersonal, in action and in thought, no matter what occurred: that was the one rigid tenet in the waiter's code. But platitudes helped him very little. He decided that he must be tired.

George, tall and sepia, passed him. He noticed that George needed new tuxedo trousers. But he didn't say anything because he knew that George had a high-yellow woman who took most of his money. And George knew what a waiter needed, anyway. He'd give him enough rope—

He was surprised to see that it was Mr. Upshaw whom George was serving. Mr. Upshaw had once said he didn't like "yellah niggers," as if they could help being yellow. Maybe Mr. Upshaw didn't consider George as being yellow....

He thought no more about it for he had just noticed Mr. Spivat, half owner of the hotel, dining alone at a window table. He went over and spoke to him. "Nasty weather we're having, Mr. Spivat."

"Yes, it is Dick," Mr. Spivat replied absently, scanning the stocks final.

The window behind Mr. Spivat drew Dick's gaze. He raised his sight into the dark night. Park foliage across the street was a thick blackness, looking slightly gummy in the wet sleet and rain. On a distant summit the museum was a chiseled stone block in white light, hanging from the starless night by invisible strings. Streetlights in the foreground showed a stone wall bordering the park, a strip of sidewalk, slushy pavement.

A car turned the corner, its headlights stabbing into the darkness. Motor purr sounded faintly as it passed, the red taillight bobbed lingeringly into the bog of distant darkness. Dick stared into the void after it, feeling very tired. He thought of a chicken farm in the country, where he could get off his feet. But he knew that he would never be satisfied away from a dining room.

When he turned back traces of weariness showed in the edges of his smile, making it ragged. But his eyes were as sharp as ever. They lingered a moment on the slightly hobbling figure of Bishop. A little stooped, Bishop was, a little paunched, a little gray, with a moon face and soiled eyes and rough skin of midnight blue. A good name, Bishop, a descriptive name, he thought with a half smile.

He noticed Bishop lurch once, so he followed him into the kitchen, overtook him at the pastry room, and spun him about, sniffing his breath. He caught the scent of mints and a very faint odor of alcohol.

"You haven't been drinking again, have you, Bishop?" he asked sharply. He liked Bishop, but Bishop would drink, and a drinking waiter could not be tolerated.

Bishop rolled his eyes and laughed to dispel such a horrid idea. "Nawsuh, chief. Been rubbin' my leg with rubbin' alcawl. Thass what you smell. My n'ritis is terrible bad, suh."

Dick nodded sympathetically. "You need to watch your diet, Bishop," he advised. "Go home when you serve that dessert."

Bishop bobbed, rubbing his hands together involuntarily. "Thank you, suh, Mistah Small."

Dick turned back into the dining room, followed by Bishop with coffee and cream. He stopped just inside the doorway, his gaze lingering on Bishop's limp.

But his frown was inspired by thoughts of his own wife more than by Bishop's limp. She was using an exceeding amount of money lately. He didn't want to start thinking unfair thoughts of her, that was the way so many marriages were broken up.

He caught himself and brought his mind back to the dining room. He tried to recall whether he had assigned Bishop to wait on Mr. Spivat. He certainly wouldn't have, he knew, had he known that Bishop was limping so badly, for Mr. Spivat was convinced, anyway, that all Negro waiters were drunkards; and Bishop did appear drunk.

It all happened so quickly that the picture was telescoped in his mind and his body started moving before thought directed its motions.

Bishop's right leg buckled as he placed the tiny pitcher of cream. He jackknifed forward on his knee. Cream flew in a thin sheet over the front of Mr. Spivat's dark blue suit.

Mr. Spivat blanched, then ripened like a russet apple. Insensate fury jerked him erect. His foot began motion as if to kick the kneeling figure, froze in knotted restraint.

Dick was there in three swift strides, applying a cold, damp towel to Mr. Spivat's suit. "Clean up, George," he directed the other waiter, trying to avert the drama which he felt engulfing them. "Sorry, Mr. Spivat, sir. The boy's got neuritis, it's very bad during this nasty weather. I'll lay him off until it gets better."

But neither could cold, damp towels help Mr. Spivat's suit, nor could expressions of sorrow allay the fury in his mind.

He mashed the words out between his clenched teeth. "Dick, see that this man gets his money, and if I ever see him in this hotel again I'll fire the whole bunch of you!" He wheeled and started walking jerkily from the room, his body moving as if it were being snatched along with slack strings. "Drunk!" he ground out.

Dick motioned Bishop from the dining room and followed behind. He had the checker make out a requisition for Bishop's pay, an even thirteen dollars. He couldn't meet the doglike plea of Bishop's eyes.

Bishop stood at a respectful distance, his shoulders drooping, his whole body sagging; very black, very wordless. Bishop had always liked Mr. Spivat, had liked serving him. He and Mr. Spivat used to discuss baseball during the summer months.

After a time he said irrelevantly, a slight protest in his voice, "I got seven kids."

Dick looked down at his feet, big feet they were, with broken arches from shouldering heavy trays on adamant concrete, big and flat and knotty. He felt in his pockets, discovered a twenty-dollar banknote. He pressed it into Bishop's hand.

Bishop said, "I wasn't drunk, chief," as if Dick might think he was.

Dick wanted to believe that, but he couldn't. Bishop as a rule did not eat mints; he didn't like sweets of any kind. But mints would help kill the odor of whiskey on his breath. Dick sighed. He knew that Bishop liked serving Mr. Spivat. There was very little of the likes and dislikes of all his waiters, of their family affairs and personal lives, that Dick did not know. But of them all, he sympathized most with Bishop.

But what could he do? Bishop would drink.

He said, "Accidents will happen, son. Yours just cost you your job. If there's anything I can ever do for you, anything in reason, let me know. And even if it isn't in reason, come and let me say so." He stood quite still for a moment. His face showed extreme weariness.

Then he shook it all from his mind. It required a special effort. He blinked his eyes clear of the picture of a dejected black face, donned his creased, careful smile and pushed through the service hall into the dining room. His head was cocked to one side as though he were deferentially listening.

Ann Petry

(b. 1911)

Raised in Old Saybrook, Connecticut, by a pharmacist father and a chiropodist mother, Ann Petry grew up comfortably in a closely knit middle-class family comprised of storytellers whose tales, she says, she had been retelling "over and over again in various ways." Although proof of her writing talents came early when the teenaged Petry wrote a prize-winning slogan for a perfume company, she would not begin writing seriously until 1938, working until then as a pharmacist. Upon marrying mystery writer George D. Petry that same year, Petry moved to New York and started reporting for the **Harlem Weekly** *and the* **People's Voice***. During this time she founded a political advocacy group, Negro Women, Inc., designed special education programs for a Harlem elementary school, acted in American Negro Theater, and taught courses at the Harlem branch of the NAACP. While Petry busied herself with these civic activities, she also continued to hone her talent for fiction, taking creative writing classes at Columbia University and trying to build a career out of short stories. The promise of "On Saturday the Siren Sounds at Noon" resulted in a 1945 Houghton-Mifflin Literary Fellowship, which enabled Petry to complete her first novel,* **The Street** *(1946). Two more novels,* **Country Place** *(1947) and* **The Narrows** *(1953), followed, as well as Petry's short story collection,* **Miss Muriel and Other Stories** *(1971), which includes the Best American Short Stories of 1946 selection "Like a Winding Sheet." Although Petry has devoted the latter part of her career almost exclusively to titles for children, such as* **The Drugstore Cat** *(1949),* **Tituba of Salem Village** *(1964), and* **Legends of Saints** *(1970), Petry's adult fiction remains notable for its focus on the effects of environment and bigotry on individuals. Peopled by small-town characters and urban types that are modeled after people whom she knew in Old Saybrook or met while working in Harlem as a journalist, Petry's stories offer penetrating glimpses into the ways that race, class, and gender can collide, often tragically.*

Like a Winding Sheet

He had planned to get up before Mae did and surprise her by fixing breakfast. Instead he went back to sleep and she got out of bed so quietly he didn't know she wasn't there beside him until he woke up and heard the queer soft gurgle of water running out of the sink in the bathroom.

He knew he ought to get up but instead he put his arms across his forehead to shut the afternoon sunlight out of his eyes, pulled his legs up close to his body, testing them to see if the ache was still in them.

Mae had finished in the bathroom. He could tell because she never closed the door when she was in there and now the sweet smell of talcum powder was drifting down the hall and into the bedroom. Then he heard her coming down the hall.

"Hi, babe," she said affectionately.

"Hum," he grunted, and moved his arms away from his head, opened one eye. "It's a nice morning."

"Yeah," he rolled over and the sheet twisted around him, outlining his thighs, his chest. "You mean afternoon, don't ya?"

Mae looked at the twisted sheet and giggled. "Looks like a winding sheet," she said. "A shroud—" Laughter tangled with her words and she had to pause for a moment before she could continue. "You look like a huckleberry—in a winding sheet—"

"That's no way to talk. Early in the day like this," he protested.

He looked at his arms silhouetted against the white of the sheets. They were inky black by contrast and he had to smile in spite of himself and he lay there smiling and savoring the sweet sound of Mae's giggling.

"Early?" She pointed a finger at the alarm clock on the table near the bed, and giggled again. "It's almost four o'clock. And if you don't spring up out of there you're going to be late again."

"What do you mean 'again'?"

"Twice last week. Three times the week before. And once the week before and—"

"I can't get used to sleeping in the daytime," he said fretfully. He pushed his legs out from under the covers experimentally. Some of the ache had gone out of them but they weren't really rested yet. "It's too light for good sleeping. And all that standing beats the hell out of my legs."

"After two years you oughtta be used to it," Mae said.

He watched her as she fixed her hair, powdered her face, slipping into a pair of blue denim overalls. She moved quickly and yet she didn't seem to hurry.

"You look like you'd had plenty of sleep," he said lazily. He had to get up but he kept putting the moment off, not wanting to move, yet he didn't dare let his legs go completely limp because if he did he'd go back to sleep. It was getting later and later but the thought of putting his weight on his legs kept him lying there.

When he finally got up he had to hurry and he gulped his breakfast so fast that he wondered if his stomach could possibly use food thrown at it at such a rate of speed. He was still wondering about it as he and Mae were putting their coats on in the hall.

Mae paused to look at the calendar. "It's the thirteenth," she said. Then a faint excitement in her voice. "Why it's Friday the thirteenth." She had one arm in her coat sleeve and she held it there while she stared at the calendar. "I oughtta stay home," she said. "I shouldn't go otta the house."

"Aw don't be a fool," he said. "Today's payday. And payday is a good luck day everywhere, any way you look at it." And as she stood hesitating he said, "Aw, come on."

And he was late for work again because they spent fifteen minutes arguing before he could convince her she ought to go to work just the same. He had to talk persuasively, urging her gently and it took time. But he couldn't bring himself to talk to her roughly or threaten to strike her like a lot of men might have done. He wasn't made that way.

So when he reached the plant he was late and he had to wait to punch the time clock because the day shift workers were streaming out in long lines, in groups and bunches that impeded his progress.

Even now just starting his workday his legs ached. He had to force himself to struggle past the outgoing workers, punch the time clock, and get the little cart he pushed around all night because he kept toying with the idea of going home and getting back in bed.

He pushed the cart out on the concrete floor, thinking that if this was his plant he'd make a lot of changes in it. There were too many standing up jobs for one thing. He'd figure out some way most of 'em could be done sitting down and he'd put a lot more benches around. And this job he had—this job that forced him to walk ten hours a night, pushing this little cart, well, he'd turn it into a sittin-down job. One of those little trucks they used around railroad stations would be good for a job like this. Guys sat on a seat and the thing moved easily, taking up little room and turning in hardly any space at all, like on a dime.

He pushed the cart near the foreman. He never could remember to refer to her as the forelady even in his mind. It was funny to have a woman for a boss in a plant like this one.

She was sore about something. He could tell by the way her face was red and her eyes were half shut until they were slits. Probably been out late and didn't get enough sleep. He avoided looking at her and hurried a little, head down, as he passed her though he couldn't resist stealing a glance at her out of the corner of his eyes. He saw the edge of the light colored slacks she wore and the tip end of a big tan shoe.

"Hey, Johnson!" the woman said.

The machines had started full blast. The whirr and the grinding made the building shake, made it impossible to hear conversations. The men and women at the machines talked to each other but looking at them from just a little distance away they appeared to be simply moving their lips because you couldn't hear what they were saying. Yet the woman's voice cut across the machine sounds—harsh, angry.

He turned his head slowly. "Good Evenin', Mrs. Scott," he said and waited.

"You're late again."

"That's right. My legs were bothering me."

The woman's face grew redder, angrier looking. "Half this shift comes in late," she said. "And you're the worst one of all. You're always late. Whatsa matter with ya?"

"It's my legs," he said. "Somehow they don't ever get rested. I don't seem to get used to sleeping days. And I just can't get started."

"Excuses. You guys always got excuses," her anger grew and spread. "Every guy comes in here late always has an excuse. His wife's sick or his grandmother died or somebody in the family had to go to the hospital," she paused, drew a deep breath. "And the niggers are the worse. I don't care what's wrong with your legs. You get in here on time. I'm sick of you niggers—"

"You got the right to get mad," he interrupted softly. "You got the right to cuss me four ways to Sunday but I ain't letting nobody call me a nigger.

He stepped closer to her. His fists were doubled. His lips were drawn back in a thin narrow line. A vein in his forehead stood out swollen, thick.

And the woman backed away from him, not hurriedly but slowly—two, three steps back.

"Aw, forget it," she said. "I didn't mean nothing by it. It slipped out. It was a accident." The red of her face deepened until the small blood vessels in her cheeks were purple. "Go on and get to work," she urged. And she took three more slow backward steps.

He stood motionless for a moment and then turned away from the red lipstick on her mouth that made him remember that the foreman was a woman. And he couldn't bring himself to hit a woman. He felt a curious tingling in his fingers and he looked down at his hands. They were clenched tight, hard, ready to smash some of those purple veins in her face.

He pushed the cart ahead of him, walking slowly. When he turned his head, she was staring in his direction, mopping her forehead with a dark blue handkerchief. Their eyes met and then they both looked away.

He didn't glance in her direction again but moved past the long work benches, carefully collecting the finished parts, going slowly and steadily up and down, back and forth the length of the building and as he walked he forced himself to swallow his anger, get rid of it.

And he succeeded so that he was able to think about what had happened without getting upset about it. An hour went by but the tension stayed in his hands. They were clenched and knotted on the handles of the cart as though ready to aim a blow.

And he thought he should have hit her anyway, smacked her hard in the face, felt the soft flesh of her face give under the hardness of his hands. He tried to make his hands relax by offering them a description of what it would have been like to strike her because he had the queer feeling that his hands were not exactly a part of him any more—they had developed a separate life of their own over which he had no control. So he dwelt on the pleasure his hands would have felt—both of them cracking at her, first one and then the other. If he had done that his hands would have felt good now—relaxed, rested.

And he decided that even if he'd lost his job for it he should have let her have it and it would have been a long time, maybe the rest of her life before she called anybody else a nigger.

The only trouble was he couldn't hit a woman. A woman couldn't hit back the same way a man did. But it would have been a deeply satisfying thing to have cracked her narrow lips wide open with just one blow, beautifully timed and with all his weight in back of it. That way he would have gotten rid of all the energy and tension his anger had created in him. He kept remembering how his heart had started pumping blood so fast he had felt it tingle even in the tips of his fingers.

With the approach of night fatigue nibbled at him. The corners of his mouth dropped, the frown between his eyes deepened, his shoulders sagged; but his hands stayed tight and tense. As the hours dragged by he noticed that the women workers had started to snap and snarl at each other. He couldn't hear what they said because of the sound of machines but he could see the quick lip movements that sent words tumbling from the sides of their mouths. They gestured irritably with their hands and scowled as their mouths moved.

Their violent jerky motions told him that it was getting close on to quitting time but somehow he felt that the night still stretched ahead of him, composed of endless hours of steady walking on his aching legs. When the whistle finally blew he went on pushing the cart, unable to believe that it had sounded. The whirring of the machines died away to a murmur and he knew then that he'd really heard the whistle. He stood still for a moment filled with a relief that made him sigh.

Then he moved briskly, putting the cart in the store room, hurrying to take his place in the line forming before the paymaster. That was another thing he'd change, he thought. He'd have the pay envelopes handed to the people right at their benches so there wouldn't be ten or fifteen minutes lost waiting for the pay. He always got home about fifteen minutes late on payday. They did it better in the plant where Mae worked, brought the money right to them at their benches.

He stuck his pay envelope in his pants' pocket and followed the line of workers heading for the subway in a slow moving stream. He glanced up at the sky. It was a nice night, the sky looked packed full to running over with stars. And he thought if he and Mae would go right to bed when they got home from work they'd catch a few hours of darkness for sleeping. But they never did. They fooled around—cooking and eating and listening to the radio and he always stayed in a big chair in the living room and went almost but not quite to sleep and when they finally got to bed it was five or six in the morning and daylight was already seeping around the edges of the sky.

He walked slowly, putting off the moment when he would have to plunge into the crowd hurrying toward the subway. It was a long ride to Harlem and tonight the thought of it appalled him. He paused outside an all-night restaurant to kill time, so that some of the first rush of workers would be gone when he reached the subway.

The lights in the restaurant were brilliant, enticing. There was life and motion inside. And as he looked through the window he thought that everything within range of his eyes gleamed—the long imitation marble counter, the tall stools, the white porcelain topped tables and especially the big metal coffee urn right near the window. Steam issued from its top and a gas flame flickered under it—a lively, dancing, blue flame.

A lot of the workers from his shift—men and women—were lining up near the coffee urn. He watched them walk to the porcelain topped tables carrying steaming cups of coffee and he saw that just the smell of the coffee lessened the fatigue lines in their faces. After the first sip their faces softened, they smiled, they began to talk and laugh.

On a sudden impulse he shoved the door open and joined the line in front of the coffee urn. The line moved slowly. And as he stood there the smell of the coffee, the sound of the laughter and of the voices, helped dull the sharp ache in his legs.

He didn't pay any attention to the girl who was serving the coffee at the urn. He kept looking at the cups in the hands of the men who had been ahead of him. Each time a man stepped out of the line with one of the thick white cups the fragrant steam got in his nostrils. He saw that they walked carefully so as not to spill a single drop. There was a broth of bubbles at the top of each cup and he thought about how he would let the bubbles break against his lips before he actually took a big deep swallow.

Then it was his turn. "A cup of coffee," he said, just as he had heard the others say.

The girl looked past him, put her hands up to her head and gently lifted her hair away from the back of her neck, tossing her head back a little. " No more coffee for awhile," she said.

He wasn't certain he'd heard her correctly and he said, "What?" blankly.

"No more coffee for awhile," she repeated.

There was silence behind him and then uneasy movement. He thought someone would say something, ask why or protest, but there was only silence and then a faint shuffling sound as though the men standing behind him had simultaneously shifted their weight from one foot to the other.

He looked at her without saying anything. He felt his hands begin to tingle and the tingling went all the way down to his finger tips so that he glanced down at them. They were clenched tight, hard, into fists. Then he looked at the girl again. What he wanted to do was hit her so hard that the scarlet lipstick on her mouth would smear and spread over her nose, her chin, out toward her cheeks; so hard that she would never toss her head again and refuse a man a cup of coffee because he was black.

He estimated the distance across the counter and reached forward, balancing his weight on the balls of his feet, ready to let the blow go. And then his hands fell back down to his sides because he forced himself to lower them, to unclench them and make them dangle loose. The effort took his breath away because his hands fought against him. But he couldn't hit her. He couldn't even now bring himself to hit a woman, not even this one, who had refused him a cup of coffee with a toss of her head. He kept seeing the gesture with which she had lifted the length of her blond hair from the back of her neck as expressive of her contempt for him.

When he went out the door he didn't look back. If he had he would have seen the flickering blue flame under the shiny coffee urn being extinguished. The line of men who had stood behind him lingered a moment to watch the people drinking coffee at the tables and then they left just as he had without having had the coffee they wanted so badly. The girl behind the counter poured water in the urn and swabbed it out and as she waited for the water to run out she lifted her hair gently from the back of her neck and tossed her head before she began making a fresh lot of coffee.

But he walked away without a backward look, his head down, his hands in his pockets, raging at himself and whatever it was inside of him that had forced him to stand quiet and still when he wanted to strike out.

The subway was crowded and he had to stand. He tried grasping an overhead strap and his hands were too tense to grip it. So he moved near the train door and stood there swaying back and forth with the rocking of the train. The roar of the train beat inside his head, making it ache and throb, and the pain in his legs clawed up into his groin so that he seemed to be bursting with pain and he told himself that it was due to all that anger-born energy that had piled up in him and not been used and so it had spread through him like a poison—from his feet and legs all the way up to his head.

Mae was in the house before he was. He knew she was home before he put the key in the door of the apartment. The radio was going. She had it turned up loud and she was singing along with it.

"Hello, Babe," she called out as soon as he opened the door.

He tried to say "hello" and it came out half a grunt and half sigh.

"You sure sound cheerful," she said.

She was in the bedroom and he went and leaned against the door jamb. The denim overalls she wore to work were carefully draped over the back of a chair by the bed. She was standing in front of the dresser, tying the sash of a yellow housecoat around her waist and chewing gum vigorously as she admired her reflection in the mirror over the dresser.

"Whatsa matter?" she said. "You get bawled out by the boss or somep'n?"

"Just tired," he said slowly. "For God's sake do you have to crack that gum like that?"

"You don't have to lissen to me," she said complacently. She patted a curl in place near the side of her head and then lifted her hair away from the back of her neck, ducking her head forward and then back.

He winced away from the gesture. "What you got to be always fooling with your hair for?" he protested.

"Say, what's the matter with you, anyway?" she turned away from the mirror to face him, put her hands on her hips. "You ain't been in the house two minutes and you're picking on me."

He didn't answer her because her eyes were angry and he didn't want to quarrel with her. They'd been married too long and got along too well and so he walked all the way into the room and sat down in the chair by the bed and stretched his legs out in front of him, putting his weight on the heels of his shoes, leaning way back in the chair, not saying anything.

"Lissen," she said sharply. "I've got to wear those overalls again tomorrow. You're going to get them all wrinkled up leaning against them like that."

He didn't move. He was too tired and his legs were throbbing now that he had sat down. Besides the overalls were already wrinkled and dirty, he thought. They couldn't help but be for she'd worn them all week. He leaned further back in the chair.

"Come on, get up," she ordered.

"Oh, what the hell," he said wearily and got up from the chair. "I'd just as soon live in a subway. There'd be just as much place to sit down."

He saw that her sense of humor was struggling with her anger. But her sense of humor won because she giggled.

"Aw, come on and eat," she said. There was a coaxing note in her voice. "You're nothing but a old hungry nigger trying to act tough and—" she paused to giggle and then continued, "You—"

He had always found her giggling pleasant and deliberately said things that might amuse her and then waited, listening for the delicate sound to emerge from her throat. This time he didn't even hear the giggle. He didn't let her finish what she was saying. She was standing close to him and that funny tingling started in his finger tips, went fast up his arms and sent his fist shooting straight for her face.

There was the smacking sound of soft flesh being struck by a hard object and it wasn't until she screamed that he realized he had hit her in the mouth—so hard that the dark red lipstick had blurred and spread over her full lips, reaching up toward the tip of her nose, down toward her chin, out toward her cheeks.

The knowledge that he had struck her seeped through him slowly and he was appalled but he couldn't drag his hands away from her face. He kept striking her and he thought with horror that something inside him was holding him, binding him to this act, wrapping and twisting about him so that he had to continue it. He had lost all control over his hands. And he groped for a phrase, a word, something to describe what this thing was like that was happening to him and he thought it was like being enmeshed in a winding sheet—that was it—like a winding sheet. And even as the thought formed in his mind his hands reached for her face again and yet again.

Frank Yerby

(1916–1991)

Best known in his heyday as a pulp writer of "costume novels," Frank Yerby has written thirty novels that have sold over fifty-five million copies in eighty-two countries and twenty-three languages. He became an overnight celebrity when his first novel, **The Foxes of Harrow,** *was a runaway best-seller in 1946. Not only was the southern romance-adventure turned into a movie starring Rex Harrison and Maureen O'Hara, it would eventually become one of the top-selling books of the decade.*

A native of Georgia, Yerby received his master's degree in English from Fisk University before beginning doctoral studies at the University of Chicago. Forced to drop out because of financial difficulties, Yerby then worked at the Federal Writers' Project in Chicago where he met such authors as Arna Bontemps, Margaret Walker, and Richard Wright. After brief teaching stints in Florida and Louisiana, Yerby got a job at a defense plant in Michigan. During this time he began publishing poetry and short stories in various literary journals and was awarded an O. Henry Memorial Award in 1944 for his short story "Health Card." Following the success of **The Foxes of Harrow,** *Yerby moved to Europe, where he resided in France and Spain before finally settling in Madrid. Perhaps one of the most prolific expatriates America has ever produced, Yerby spent the next thirty years of his literary career writing such historical thrillers and romances as* **A Woman Called Fancy** *(1951),* **Jarrett's Jade** *(1959), and* **A Rose for Anna Maria** *(1976). While some reviewers have commented unfavorably on Yerby's tendency to avoid overtly racial themes in his fiction, they have done so only by ignoring his superbly researched novels about African American history,* **The Dahomean** *(1971) and* **A Darkness at Ingraham's Crest: A Tale of the Slaveholding South** *(1979). In response to his critics, Yerby has insisted that "the novelist hasn't any right to inflict on the public his private ideas on politics, religion or race."*

The Homecoming

The train stretched itself out long and low against the tracks and ran very fast and smooth. The drive rods flashed out of the big pistons like blades of light, and the huge counter-weighted wheels were blurred solid with the speed. Out of the throat of the stack, the white smoke blasted up in stiff, hard pants, straight up for a yard; then the backward rushing mass of air caught it, trailing it out over the cars like a veil.

In the Jim Crow coach, just back of the mail car, Sergeant Willie Jackson pushed the window up a notch higher. The heat came blasting in the window in solid waves, bringing the dust with it, and the cinders. Willie mopped his face with his handkerchief. It came away stained with the dust and sweat.

"Damn," he said without heat, and looked out at the parched fields that were spinning backward past his window. Up on the edge of the skyline, a man stopped his plowing to wave at the passing train.

"How come we always do that?" Willie speculated idly. "Don't know a soul on this train—not a soul—but he got to wave. Oh, well ... "

The train was bending itself around a curve, and the soft, long, lost, lonesome wail of the whistle cried out twice. Willie stirred in his seat, watching the cabins with the whitewash peeling off spinning backward past the train, lost in the immensity of sun-blasted fields under a pale, yellowish white sky, the blue washed out by the sun swath, and no cloud showing.

Up ahead, the water tower was rushing toward the train. Willie grinned. He had played under that tower as a boy. Water was always leaking out of it, enough water to cool a hard, skinny, little black body even in the heat of summer. The creek was off somewhere to the south, green and clear under the willows, making a little laughing sound over the rocks. He could see the trees that hid it now, the lone clump standing up abruptly in the brown and naked expanse of the fields.

Now the houses began to thicken, separated by only a few hundred yards instead of by miles. The train slowed, snorting tiredly into another curve. Across the diagonal of the bend, Willie could see the town, all of it—a few dozen buildings clustered around the Confederate Monument, bisected by a single paved street. The heat was pushing down on it like a gigantic hand, flattening it against the rust-brown earth.

Now the train was grinding to a stop. Willie swung down from the car, carefully keeping his left leg off the ground, taking the weight on his right. Nobody else got off the train.

The heat struck him in the face like a physical blow. The sunlight brought great drops of sweat out on his forehead, making his black face glisten. He stood there in the full glare, the light pointing up the little strips of colored ribbon on his tunic. One of them was purple, with two white ends. Then there was a yellow one with thin red, white, and blue stripes in the middle and red and white stripes near the two ends. Another was red with three white stripes near the ends. Willie wore his collar loose, and his uniform was faded, but he still stood erect, with his chest out and his belly sucked in.

He started across the street toward the Monument, throwing one leg a little stiffly. The white men who always sat around it on the little iron benches looked at him curiously. He came on until he stood in the shadow of the shaft. He looked up at the statue of the Confederate soldier, complete with knapsack and holding the musket with the little needle-type bayonet ready for the charge. At the foot of the shaft there was an inscription carved in stone. Willie spelled out the words:

"No nation rose so white and pure; none fell so free of stain."

He stood there, letting the words sink into his brain.

One of the tall loungers took a sliver of wood out of his mouth and grinned. He nudged his companion.

"What do it say, boy?" he asked.

Willie looked past him at the dusty, unpaved streets straggling out from the Monument.

"I ask you a question, boy." The white man's voice was very quiet.

"You talking to me?" Willie said softly.

"You know Goddamn well I'm talking to you. You got ears, ain't you?"

"You said boy," Willie said. "I didn't know you was talking to me."

"Who the hell else could I been talking to, nigger?" the white man demanded.

"I don't know," Willie said. "I didn't see no boys around."

The two white men got up.

"Ain't you forgetting something, nigger?" one of them asked, walking toward Willie.

"Not that I knows of," Willie declared.

"Ain't nobody ever told you to say sir to a white man?"

"Yes," Willie said. "They told me that."

"Yes what?" the white man prompted.

"Yes nothing." Willie said quietly. "Just plain yes. And I don't think you better come any closer, white man."

"Nigger, do you know where you're at?"

"Yes," Willie said. "Yes, I knows. And I knows you can have me killed. But I don't care about that. Long time now I don't care. So please don't come no closer, white man. I'm asking you kindly."

The two men hesitated. Willie started toward them, walking very slowly. They stood very still, watching him come. Then at the last moment, they stood aside and let him pass. He limped across the street and went into the town's lone Five and Ten Cent Store.

"How come I come in here?" he muttered. "Ain't got nobody to buy nothing for." He stood still a moment, frowning. "Reckon I'll get some post cards to send the boys," he decided. He walked over to the rack and made his selections carefully: the new Post Office Building, the Memorial Bridge, the Confederate Monument. "Make this look like a real town," he said. "Keep that one hoss outa sight." Then he was limping over to the counter, the cards and the quarter in his hand. The salesgirl started toward him, her hand outstretched to take the money. But just before she reached him, a white woman came toward the counter, so the girl went on past Willie, smiling sweetly, saying, "Can I help you?"

"Look a here, girl," Willie said sharply. "I was here first."

The salesgirl and the woman both turned toward him, their mouths dropping open.

"My money the same color as hers," Willie said. He stuffed the cards in his pocket. Then deliberately he tossed the quarter on the counter and walked out the door.

"Well, I never!" the white woman gasped.

When Willie came out on the sidewalk, a little knot of men had gathered around the Monument. Willie could see the two men in the center talking to the others. Then they all stopped talking at once and looked at him. He limped on down the block and turned the corner.

At the next corner he turned again, and again at the next. Then he slowed. Nobody was following him.

The houses thinned out again. There were no trees shading the dirt road, powder-dry under the hammer blows of the sun. Willie limped on, the sweat pouring down his black face, soaking his collar. Then at last he was turning into a flagstone driveway curving toward a large, very old house, set well back from the road in a clump of pine trees. He went up on the broad, sweeping veranda, and rang the bell.

A very old black man opened the door. He looked at Willie with a puzzled expression, squinting his red, mottled old eyes against the light.

"Don't you remember me, Uncle Ben?" Willie said.

"Willie!" the old man said. "The Colonel sure be glad to see you! I go call him— right now!" Then he was off, trotting down the hall. Willie stood still, waiting.

The Colonel came out of the study, his hand outstretched.

"Willie," he said. "You little black scoundrel! Damn! You aren't little any more, are you?"

"No," Willie said. "I done growed."

"So I see! So I see! Come on back in the kitchen, boy. I want to talk to you."

Willie followed the lean, bent figure of the old white man through the house. In the kitchen Martha, the cook, gave a squeal of pleasure.

"Willie! My, my, how fine you's looking! Sit down! Where you find him, Colonel Bob?"

"I just dropped by," Willie said.

"Fix him something to eat, Martha," the Colonel said, "while I pry some military information out of him."

Martha scurried off, her white teeth gleaming in a pleased smile.

"You've got a mighty heap of ribbons, Willie," the Colonel said. "What are they for?"

"This here purple one is the Purple Heart," Willie explained. "That was for my leg."

"Bad?" the Colonel demanded.

"Hand grenade. They had to take it off. This here leg's a fake."

"Well, I'll be damned! I never would have known it."

"They make them good now. And they teaches you before you leaves the hospital."

"What are the others for?"

"The yellow one means Pacific Theater of War," Willie said. "And the red one is the Good Conduct Medal."

"I knew you'd get that one," the Colonel declared. "You always were a good boy, Willie."

"Thank you," Willie said.

Martha was back now with coffee and cake. "Dinner be ready in a little," she said. "You're out for good, aren't you, Willie?"

"Yes."

"Good. I'll give you your old job back. I need an extra man on the place."

"Begging your pardon, Colonel Bob," Willie said, "I ain't staying here. I'm going North."

"What! What the clinking ding dang ever gave you such an idea?"

"I can't stay here, Colonel Bob. I ain't suited for here no more."

"The North is no place for niggers, Willie. Why, those dang-blasted Yankees would let you starve to death. Down here a good boy like you always got a white man to look after him. Any time you get hungry you can always come up to most anybody's back door and they'll feed you."

"Yes," Willie said. "They feed me all right. They say that's Colonel Bob's boy, Willie, and they give me a swell meal. That's how come I got to go."

"Now you're talking riddles, Willie."

"No, Colonel Bob, I ain't talking riddles. I seen men killed. My friends. I done growed inside, too, Colonel Bob."

"What's that got to do with your staying here?"

Martha came over to the table, bearing the steaming food on the tray. She stood there holding the tray, looking at Willie. He looked past her out the doorway where the big pines were shredding the sunlight.

"I done forgot too many things," he said slowly. "I done forgot how to scratch my head and shuffle my feet and grin when I don't feel like grinning."

"Willie!" Martha said. "Don't talk like that! Don't you know you can't talk like that?"

Colonel Bob silenced her with a lifted hand.

"Somebody's been talking to you," he declared, "teaching you the wrong things."

"No. Just had a lot of time for thinking. Thought it up all by myself. I done fought and been most killed and now I'm a man. Can't be a boy no more. Nobody's boy. Not even yours, Colonel Bob."

"Willie!" Martha moaned.

"Got to be a man. My own man. Can't let my kids cut a buck and wing on the sidewalk for pennies. Can't ask for handouts round the back door. Got to come in the front door. Got to git it myself. Can't git it, then I starves proud, Colonel Bob."

Martha's mouth was working, forming the words, but no sound came out of it, no sound at all.

"Do you think it's right," Colonel Bob asked evenly, "for you to talk to a white man like this—any white man—even me?"

"I don't know. All I know is I got to go. I can't even say yessir no more. Ever time I do, it choke up in my throat like black vomit. Ain't coming to no more back doors. And when I gits old, folks going to say Mister Jackson—not no Uncle Willie."

"You're right, Willie," Colonel Bob said. "You better go. In fact, you'd better go right now."

Willie stood up and adjusted his overseas cap.

"Thank you, Colonel Bob," he said. "You been awful good to me. Now I reckon I be going."

Colonel Bob did not answer. Instead he got up and held the screen door open. Willie went past him out the door. On the steps he stopped.

"Good-by, Colonel Bob," he said softly.

The old white man looked at Willie as though he were going to say something, but then he thought better of it and closed his jaw down tight.

Willie turned away to go, but Uncle Ben was scurrying through the kitchen like an ancient rabbit.

"Colonel Bob!" he croaked. "There's trouble up in town. Man want you on the phone right now! Say they's after some colored soldier. Lawdy!"

"Yes," Willie said. "Maybe they after me."

"You stay right there," Colonel Bob growled, "and don't move a muscle! I'll be back in a minute." He turned and walked rapidly toward the front of the house.

Willie stood very still, looking up through a break in the trees at the pale, whitish blue sky. It was very high and empty. And in the trees, no bird sang. But Colonel Bob was coming back now, his face very red, and knotted into hard lines.

"Willie," he said, "did you tell two white men you'd kill them if they came nigh you?"

"Yes. I didn't say that, but that's what I meant."

"And did you have some kind of an argument with a white *woman*?"

"Yes, Colonel Bob."

"My God!"

"He crazy, Colonel Bob," Martha wailed. "He done gone plum outa his mind!"

"You better not go back to town," the Colonel said. "You better stay here until I can get you out after dark."

Willie smiled a little.

"I'm gonna ketch me a train," he said. "Two o'clock today, I'm gonna ketch it."

"You be kilt!" Martha declared. "They kill you sure!"

"We done run too much, Martha," Willie said slowly. "We done run and hid and anyhow we done got caught. And then we goes down on our knees and begs. I ain't running. Done forgot how. Don't know how to run. Don't know how to beg. Just knows how to fight, that's all, Martha."

"Oh, Jesus, he crazy! Told you he crazy, Colonel Bob!"

Colonel Bob was looking at Willie, a slow, thoughtful look.

"Can't sneak off in the dark, Colonel Bob. Can't steal away to Jesus. Got to go marching. And don't a man better touch me." He turned and went down the steps. "Good-by Colonel Bob," he called.

"Crazy," Martha wept. "Out of his mind!"

"Stop your blubbering!" Colonel Bob snapped. "Willie's no more crazy than I am. Maybe it's the world that's crazy. I don't know. I thought I did, but I don't." His blue eyes looked after the retreating figure. "Three hundred years of wounded pride," he mused. "Three centuries of hurt dignity. Going down the road marching. What would happen if we let them—no, it's God-damned impossible ... "

"Looney!" Martha sobbed. "Plum tetched!"

"They'll kill him," Colonel Bob said. "And they'll do it in the meanest damned way they can think of. His leg won't make any difference. Not all the dang blasted ribbons in the world. Crazy thing. Willie, a soldier of the republic—wounded, and this thing to happen. Crazy." He stopped suddenly, his blue eyes widening in his pale, old face. "Crazy!" he roared. "That's it! If I can make them think—That's it, that's it, by God!"

Then he was racing through the house toward the telephone.

Willie had gone on around the house toward the dirt road, where the heat was a visible thing, and turned his face in the direction of town.

When he neared the one paved street, the heat was lessening. He walked very slowly, turning off the old country road into Lee Avenue, the main street of the town. Then he was moving toward the station. There were many people in the street, he noticed, far more than usual. The sidewalk was almost blocked with men with eyes of blue ice, and a long, slow slouch to their walk. He went on quietly, paying no attention to them. He walked in an absolutely straight line, turning neither to the right nor the left, and each time they opened up their ranks to let him pass through. But afterwards came the sound of their footsteps falling in behind him, each man that he passed swelling the number until the sound of them walking was loud in the silent street.

He did not look back. He limped on his artificial leg making a scraping rustle on the sidewalk, and behind him, steadily, beat upon beat, not in perfect time, a little ragged, moving slowly, steadily, no faster nor slower than he was going, the white men came. They went down the street until they had almost reached the station. Then, moving his lips in prayer that had no words, Willie turned and faced them. They swung out into a broad semicircle, without hastening their steps, moving in toward him in the thick hot silence.

Willie opened his mouth to shriek at them, curse them, goad them into haste, but before his voice could rush past his dried and thickened tongue, the stillness was split from top to bottom by the wail of a siren. They all turned then, looking down the road, to where the khaki-colored truck was pounding up a billowing wall of dust, hurling straight toward them.

Then it was upon them, screeching to a stop, the great red crosses gleaming on its sides. The two soldiers were out of it almost before it was still, grabbing Willie by the arms, dragging him toward the ambulance. Then the young officer with the single silver bar on his cap was climbing down, and with him an old man with white hair.

"This the man, Colonel?" the young officer demanded.

Colonel Bob nodded.

"All right," the officer said. "We'll take over now. This man is a combat fatigue case—not responsible for his actions."

"But I got to go!" Willie said. "Got to ketch that train. Got to go North where I can be free, where I can be a man. You hear me, lieutenant, I got to go!"

James Baldwin

(1924–1987)

Born in New York City in 1924, the prolific James Baldwin—writer of essays, novels, short stories, plays, and poems—lived for most of his adult life in France and the suburbs of Istanbul. He attended Harlem's Public School 24, where he composed the school song. With the publication in 1952 of **Go Tell It on the Mountain**, *his critically acclaimed first novel, Baldwin was regarded as a major American writer. He is one of the twentieth century's finest essayists writing in English. Collections such as* **Notes of a Native Son**, **Nobody Knows My Name**, *and* **The Fire Next Time** *made him a best-selling spokesman for the Civil Rights era. His novels* **Giovanni's Room** *and* **Another Country** *have been widely translated; two of his plays,* **Blues for Mister Charlie** *and* **Amen Corner**, *originally written and produced during the 1960s, have been performed successfully ever since. In his fiction and other dramatic works, Baldwin has focused on African American family life—its fragility, its subtleties, and its strength. "Sonny's Blues" is his most popular short story.*

Sonny's Blues

I READ ABOUT IT IN the paper, in the subway, on my way to work. I read it, and I couldn't believe it, and I read it again. Then perhaps I just stared at it, at the newsprint spelling out his name, spelling out the story. I stared at it in the swinging lights of the subway car, and in the faces and bodies of the people, and in my own face, trapped in the darkness which roared outside.

It was not to be believed, and I kept telling myself that as I walked from the subway station to the high school. And at the same time I couldn't doubt it. I was scared, scared for Sonny. He became real to me again. A great block of ice got settled in my belly, and kept melting there slowly all day long, while I taught my classes algebra. It was a special kind of ice. It kept melting, sending trickles of water all up and down my veins, but it never got less. Sometimes it hardened and seemed to expand until I felt my guts were going to come spilling out or that I was going to choke or scream. This would always be at a moment when I was remembering some specific thing Sonny had once said or done.

When he was about as old as the boys in my classes his face had been bright and open, there was a lot of copper in it; and he'd had wonderfully direct brown eyes, and great gentleness and privacy. I wondered what he looked like now. He had been picked up, the evening before, in a raid on an apartment downtown, for peddling and using heroin.

I couldn't believe it: but what I mean by that is that I couldn't find any room for it anywhere inside me. I had kept it outside me for a long time. I hadn't wanted to know. I had had suspicions, but I didn't name them, I kept putting them away. I told myself that Sonny was wild, but he wasn't crazy. And he'd always been a good boy, he hadn't ever turned hard or evil or disrespectful, the way kids can, so quick, so quick, especially in Harlem. I didn't want to believe that I'd ever see my brother going down, coming to nothing, all that light in his face gone out, in the condition I'd already seen so many others. Yet it had happened and here I was, talking about algebra to a lot of boys who might, every one of them for all I knew, be popping off needles every time they went to the head. Maybe it did more for them than algebra could.

I was sure that the first time Sonny had ever had horse, he couldn't have been much older than these boys were now. These boys, now, were living as we'd been living then; they were growing up with a rush and their heads bumped abruptly against the low ceiling of their actual possibilities. They were filled with rage. All they really knew were two darknesses, the darkness of their lives, which was now closing in on them, and the darkness of the movies, which had blinded them to that other darkness, and in which they now, vindictively, dreamed, at once more together than they were at any other time, and more alone.

When the last bell rang, the last class ended. I let out my breath. It seemed I'd been holding it for all that time. My clothes were wet—I may have looked as though I'd been sitting in a steam bath, all dressed up, all afternoon. I sat alone in the classroom a long time. I listened to the boys outside, downstairs, shouting and cursing and laughing. Their laughter struck me for perhaps the first time. It was not the joyous laughter which—God knows why—one associates with children. It was mocking and insular, its intent was to denigrate. It was disenchanted, and in this, also, lay the authority of their curses. Perhaps I was listening to them because I was thinking about my brother and in them I heard my brother. And myself.

One boy was whistling a tune, at once very complicated and very simple, it seemed to be pouring out of him as though he were a bird, and it sounded very cool and moving through all that harsh, bright air, only just holding its own through all those other sounds.

I stood up and walked over to the window and looked down into the courtyard. It was the beginning of the spring and the sap was rising in the boys. A teacher passed through them every now and again, quickly, as though he or she couldn't wait to get out of that courtyard, to get those boys out of their sight and off their minds. I started collecting my stuff. I thought I'd better get home and talk to Isabel.

The courtyard was almost deserted by the time I got downstairs. I saw this boy standing in the shadow of a doorway, looking just like Sonny. I almost called his name. Then I saw that it wasn't Sonny, but somebody we used to know, a boy from around our block. He'd been Sonny's friend. He'd never been mine, having been too young for me, and, anyway, I'd never liked him. And now, even though he was a grown-up man, he still hung around that block, still spent hours on the street corner, was always high and raggy. I used to run into him from time to time and he'd often work around to asking me for a quarter or fifty cents. He always had some real good excuse, too, and I always gave it to him, I don't know why.

But now, abruptly, I hated him. I couldn't stand the way he looked at me, partly like a dog, partly like a cunning child. I wanted to ask him what the hell he was doing in the school courtyard.

He sort of shuffled over to me, and he said, "I see you got the papers. So you already know about it."

"You mean about Sonny? Yes, I already know about it. How come they didn't get you?"

He grinned. It made him repulsive and it also brought to mind what he'd looked like as a kid. "I wasn't there. I stay away from them people."

"Good for you." I offered him a cigarette and I watched him through the smoke. "You come all the way down here just to tell me about Sonny?"

"That's right." He was sort of shaking his head and his eyes looked strange, as though they were about to cross. The bright sun deadened his damp dark-brown skin and it made his eyes look yellow and showed up the dirt in his conked hair. He smelled funky. I moved a little away from him and I said, "Well, thanks, but I already know about it and I got to get home."

"I'll walk you a little ways," he said. We started walking. There were a couple of kids still loitering in the courtyard and one of them said good night to me and looked strangely at the boy beside me.

"What're you going to do?" he asked me. "I mean, about Sonny?"

"Look, I haven't seen Sonny for over a year. I'm not sure I'm going to do anything. Anyway, what the hell can I do?"

"That's right," he said quickly, "ain't nothing you can do. Can't much help old Sonny no more, I guess."

It was what I was thinking and so it seemed to me he had no right to say it.

"I'm surprised at Sonny, though," he went on—he had a funny way of talking, he looked straight ahead as though he were talking to himself—"I thought Sonny was a smart boy, I thought he was too smart to get hung."

"I guess he thought so too," I said sharply, "and that's how he got hung. And how about you? You're pretty goddamn smart, I bet."

Then he looked directly at me, just for a minute. "I ain't smart," he said. "If I was smart, I'd have reached for a pistol a long time ago."

"Look. Don't tell me your sad story, if it was up to me, I'd give you one." Then I felt guilty—guilty, probably, for never having supposed that the poor bastard had a story of his own, much less a sad one, and I asked, quickly, "What's going to happen to him now?"

He didn't answer this. He was off by himself some place. "Funny thing," he said, and from his tone we might have been discussing the quickest way to get to Brooklyn, "when I saw the papers this morning, the first thing I asked myself was if I had anything to do with it. I felt sort of responsible."

I began to listen more carefully. The subway station was on the corner, just before us, and I stopped. He stopped, too. We were in front of a bar and he ducked slightly, peering in, but whoever he was looking for didn't seem to be there. The juke box was blasting away with something black and bouncy and I half watched the barmaid as she danced her way from the juke box to her place behind the bar. And I watched her face as she laughingly responded to something someone said to her, still keeping time to the music. When she smiled one saw the little girl, one sensed the doomed, still-struggling woman beneath the battered face of the semi-whore.

"I never give Sonny nothing," the boy said finally, "but a long time ago I come to school high and Sonny asked me how it felt." He paused, I couldn't bear to watch him; I watched the barmaid, and I listened to the music which seemed to be causing the pavement to shake. "I told him it felt great." The music stopped, the barmaid paused and watched the juke box until the music began again. "It did."

All this was carrying me some place I didn't want to go. I certainly didn't want to know how it felt. It filled everything, the people, the houses, the music, the dark, quicksilver barmaid, with menace; and this menace was their reality.

"What's going to happen to him now?" I asked again.

"They'll send him away some place and they'll try to cure him." He shook his head. "Maybe he'll even think he's kicked the habit. Then they'll let him loose"—he gestured, throwing his cigarette into the gutter. "That's all."

"What do you mean, 'that's all'?"

But I knew what he meant.

"I mean, that's all." He turned his head and looked at me, pulling down the corners of his mouth. "Don't you know what I mean?" he asked, softly.

"How the hell would I know what you mean?" I almost whispered it, I don't know why.

"That's right," he said to the air, "how would he know what I mean?" He turned toward me again, patient and calm, and yet I somehow felt him shaking, shaking as though he were going to fall apart. I felt that ice in my guts again, the dread I'd felt all afternoon; and again I watched the barmaid, moving about the bar, washing glasses, singing. "Listen. They'll let him out and then it'll just start all over again. That's what I mean."

"You mean—they'll let him out. And then he'll just start working his way back in again. You mean he'll never kick the habit? Is that what you mean?"

"That's right," he said cheerfully. "You see what I mean."

"Tell me," I said at last, "why does he want to die? He must want to die, he's killing himself, why does he want to die?"

He looked at me in surprise. He licked his lips. "He don't want to die. He wants to live. Don't nobody want to die, ever."

Then I wanted to ask him—too many things. He could not have answered, or if he had, I could not have borne the answers. I started walking. "Well, I guess it's none of my business."

"It's going to be rough on old Sonny," he said. We reached the subway station. "This is your station?" he asked. I nodded. I took one step down. "Damn!" he said, suddenly. I looked up at him. He grinned again. "Damn, if I didn't leave all my money home. You ain't got a dollar on you, have you? Just for a couple of days, is all."

All at once something inside gave and threatened to come pouring out of me. I didn't hate him anymore. I felt that in another moment I'd start crying like a child.

"Sure," I said. "Don't sweat." I looked in my wallet and didn't have a dollar; I only had a five. "Here," I said. "That hold you?"

He didn't look at it—he didn't want to look at it. A terrible, closed look came over his face, as though he were keeping the number on the bill a secret from him and me. "Thanks," he said, and now he was dying to see me go. "Don't worry about Sonny. Maybe I'll write him or something."

"Sure," I said. "You do that. So long."

"Be seeing you," he said. I went on down the steps.

And I didn't write Sonny or send him anything for a long time. When I finally did, it was just after my little girl died, he wrote me back a letter which made me feel like a bastard.

Here's what he said:

Dear brother,

You don't know how much I needed to hear from you. I wanted to write you many a time but I dug how much I must have hurt you and so I didn't write. But now I feel like a man who's been trying to climb out of some deep, real deep and funky hole and just saw the sun up there, outside. I got to get outside.

I can't tell you much about how I got here. I mean I don't know how to tell you. I guess I was afraid of something or I was trying to escape from something and you know I have never been very strong in the head (smile). I'm glad Mama and Daddy are dead and can't see what's happened to their son and I swear if I'd known what I was doing I would never have hurt you so, you and a lot of other fine people who were nice to me and who believed in me.

I don't want you to think it had anything to do with me being a musician. It's more than that. Or maybe less than that. I can't get anything straight in my head down here and I try not to think about what's going to happen to me when I get outside again. Sometime I think I'm going to flip and never get outside and sometime I think I'll come straight back. I tell you one thing, though, I'd rather blow my brains out than go through this again. But that's what they all say, so they tell me. If I tell you when I'm coming to New York and if you could meet me, I sure would appreciate it. Give my love to Isabel and the kids and I was sure sorry to hear about little Gracie. I wish I could be like Mama and say the Lord's will be done, but I don't know it seems to me that trouble is the one thing that never does get stopped and I don't know what good it does to blame it on the Lord. But maybe it does some good if you believe it.

Your brother, Sonny

Then I kept in constant touch with him and I sent him whatever I could and I went to meet him when he came back to New York. When I saw him many things I thought I had forgotten came flooding back to me. This was because I had begun, finally, to wonder about Sonny, about the life that Sonny lived inside. This life, whatever it was, had made him older and thinner and it had deepened the distant stillness in which he had always moved. He looked very unlike my baby brother. Yet, when he smiled, when we shook hands, the baby brother I'd never known looked out from the depths of his private life, like an animal waiting to be coaxed into the light.

"How you been keeping?" he asked me.

"All right. And you?"

"Just fine." He was smiling all over his face. "It's good to see you again."

"It's good to see you."

The seven years' difference in our ages lay between us like a chasm: I wondered if these years would ever operate between us as a bridge. I was remembering, and it made it hard to catch my breath, that I had been there when he was born; and I had heard the first words he had ever spoken. When he started to walk, he walked from our mother straight to me. I caught him just before he fell when he took the first steps he ever took in this world.

"How's Isabel?"

"Just fine. She's dying to see you."

"And the boys?"

"They're fine, too. They're anxious to see their uncle."

"Oh, come on. You know they don't remember me."

"Are you kidding? Of course they remember you."

He grinned again. We got into a taxi. We had a lot to say to each other, far too much to know how to begin.

As the taxi began to move, I asked, "You still want to go to India?"

He laughed. "You still remember that. Hell, no. This place is Indian enough for me."

"It used to belong to them," I said.

And he laughed again. "They damn sure knew what they were doing when they got rid of it."

Years ago, when he was around fourteen, he'd been all hipped on the idea of going to India. He read books about people sitting on rocks, naked, in all kinds of weather, but mostly bad, naturally, and walking barefoot through hot coals and arriving at wisdom. I used to say that it sounded to me as though they were getting away from wisdom as fast as they could. I think he sort of looked down on me for that.

"Do you mind," he asked, "if we have the driver drive alongside the park? On the West Side—I haven't seen the city in so long."

"Of course not," I said. I was afraid that I might sound as though I were humoring him, but I hoped he wouldn't take it that way.

So we drove along, between the green of the park and the stony, lifeless elegance of hotels and apartment buildings, toward the vivid, killing streets of our childhood. These streets hadn't changed, though housing projects jutted up out of them now like rocks in the middle of a boiling sea. Most of the houses in which we had grown up had vanished, as had the stores from which we had stolen, the basements in which we had first tried sex, the rooftops from which we had hurled tin cans and bricks. But houses exactly like the houses of our past yet dominated the landscape, boys exactly like the boys we once had been found themselves smothering in these houses, came down into the streets for light and air and found themselves encircled by disaster. Some escaped the trap, most didn't. Those who got out always left something of themselves behind, as some animals amputate a leg and leave it in the trap. It might be said, perhaps, that I had escaped; after all, I was a school teacher. Or that Sonny had, he hadn't lived in Harlem for years. Yet, as the cab moved uptown through streets which seemed, with a rush, to darken with dark people, and as I covertly studied Sonny's face, it came to me that what we both were seeking through our separate cab windows was that part of ourselves which had been left behind. It's always at the hour of trouble and confrontation that the missing member aches.

We hit 110th Street and started rolling up Lenox Avenue. And I'd known this avenue all my life, but it seemed to me again, as it had seemed on that day I'd first heard about Sonny's trouble, filled with a hidden menace which was its very breath of life.

"We almost there," said Sonny.

"Almost." We were both too nervous to say anything more.

We live in a housing project. It hasn't been up long. A few days after it was up it seemed uninhabitably new; now, of course, it's already run-down. It looks like a parody of the good, clean, faceless life—God knows the people who live in it do their best to make it a parody. The beat-looking grass lying around isn't enough to make their lives green, the hedges will never hold out the streets, and they know it. The big windows fool no one; they aren't big enough to make space out of no space. They don't bother with the windows, they watch the TV screen instead. The playground is most popular with the children who don't play at jacks, or skip rope, or roller skate, or swing, and they can be found in it after dark. We moved in partly because it's not too far from where I teach, and partly for the kids; but it's really just like the houses in which Sonny and I grew up. The same things happen, they'll have the same things to remember. The moment Sonny and I started into the house I had the feeling that I was simply bringing him back into the danger he had almost died trying to escape.

Sonny had never been talkative. So I don't know why I was sure he'd be dying to talk to me when supper was over the first night. Everything went fine, the oldest boy remembered him, and the youngest boy liked him, and Sonny had remembered to bring something for each of them; and Isabel, who is really much nicer than I am, more open and giving, had gone to a lot of trouble about dinner and was genuinely glad to see him. And she's always been able to tease Sonny in a way that I haven't. It was nice to see her face so vivid again and to hear her laugh and watch her make Sonny laugh. She wasn't, or, anyway, she didn't seem to be, at all uneasy or embarrassed. She chatted as though there were no subject which had to be avoided and she got Sonny past his first faint stiffness. And thank God she was there, for I was filled with that icy dread again. Everything I did seemed awkward to me, and everything I said sounded freighted with hidden meaning. I was trying to remember everything I'd heard about dope addiction and I couldn't help watching Sonny for signs. I wasn't doing it out of malice. I was trying to find out something about my brother. I was dying to hear him tell me he was safe.

"Safe!" my father grunted, whenever Mama suggested trying to move to a neighborhood which might be safer for children. "Safe, hell! Ain't no place safe for kids, nor nobody."

He always went on like this, but he wasn't ever really as bad as he sounded; not even on weekends, when he got drunk. As a matter of fact, he was always on the lookout for "something a little better," but he died before he found it. He died suddenly, during a drunken weekend in the middle of the war, when Sonny was fifteen. He and Sonny hadn't ever got on too well. And this was partly because Sonny was the apple of his father's eye. It was because he loved Sonny so much and was frightened for him that he was always fighting with him. It doesn't do any good to fight with Sonny. Sonny just moves back, inside himself, where he can't be reached. But the principal reason that they never hit it off is that they were so much alike. Daddy was big and rough and loud-talking, just the opposite of Sonny, but they both had—that same privacy.

Mama tried to tell me something about this, just after Daddy died. I was home on leave from the Army.

This was the last time I ever saw my mother alive. Just the same, this picture gets all mixed up in my mind with pictures I had of her when she was younger. The way I always see her is the way she used to be on a Sunday afternoon, say, when the old folks were talking after the big Sunday dinner. I always see her wearing pale blue. She'd be sitting on the sofa. And my father would be sitting in the easy chair, not far from her. And the living room would be full of church folks and relatives. There they sit, in chairs all around the living room, and the night is creeping up outside, but nobody knows it yet. You can see the darkness growing against the windowpanes and you hear the street noises every now and again, or maybe the jangling beat of a tambourine from one of the churches close by, but it's real quiet in the room. For a moment nobody's talking, but every face looks darkening, like the sky outside. And my mother rocks a little from the waist, and my father's eyes are closed. Everyone is looking at something a child can't see. For a minute they've forgotten the children. Maybe a kid is lying on the rug, half asleep. Maybe somebody's got a kid in his lap and is absent-mindedly stroking the kid's head. Maybe there's a kid, quiet and big-eyed, curled up in a big chair in the corner. The silence, the darkness coming, and the darkness in the faces frightens the child obscurely. He hopes that the hand which strokes his forehead will never stop—will never die. He hopes that there will never come a time when the old folks won't be sitting around the living room, talking about where they've come from, and what they've seen, and what's happened to them and their kinfolk.

But something deep and watchful in the child knows that this is bound to end, is already ending. In a moment someone will get up and turn on the light. Then the old folks will remember the children and they won't talk any more that day. And when light fills the room, the child is filled with darkness. He knows that every time this happens he's moved just a little closer to that darkness outside. The darkness outside is what the old folks have been talking about. It's what they've come from. It's what they endure. The child knows that they won't talk any more because if he knows too much about what's happened to them, he'll know too much too soon, about what's going to happen to him.

The last time I talked to my mother, I remember I was restless. I wanted to get out and see Isabel. We weren't married then and we had a lot to straighten out between us.

There Mama sat, in black, by the window. She was humming an old church song—Lord, you brought me from a long ways off. Sonny was out somewhere. Mama kept watching the streets.

"I don't know," she said, "if I'll ever see you again, after you go off from here. But I hope you'll remember the things I tried to teach you."

"Don't talk like that," I said, and smiled. "You'll be here a long time yet."

She smiled, too, but she said nothing. She was quiet for a long time. And I said, "Mama, don't you worry about nothing. I'll be writing all the time, and you be getting the checks ... "

"I want to talk to you about your brother," she said, suddenly. "If anything happens to me he ain't going to have nobody to look out for him."

"Mama," I said, "ain't nothing going to happen to you or Sonny. Sonny's all right. He's a good boy and he's got good sense."

"It ain't a question of his being a good boy," Mama said, "nor of his having good sense. It ain't only the bad ones, nor yet the dumb ones that gets sucked under." She stopped, looking at me. "Your Daddy once had a brother," she said, and she smiled in a way that made me feel she was in pain. "You didn't never know that, did you?"

"No," I said, "I never knew that," and I watched her face.

"Oh, yes," she said, "your Daddy had a brother." She looked out of the window again. "I know you never saw your Daddy cry. But I did—many a time, through all these years."

I asked her, "What happened to his brother? How come nobody's ever talked about him?"

This was the first time I ever saw my mother look old.

"His brother got killed," she said, "when he was just a little younger than you are now. I knew him. He was a fine boy. He was maybe a little full of the devil, but he didn't mean nobody no harm."

Then she stopped and the room was silent, exactly as it had sometimes been on those Sunday afternoons. Mama kept looking out into the streets.

"He used to have a job in the mill," she said, "and, like all young folks, he just liked to perform on Saturday nights. Saturday nights, him and your father would drift around to different places, go to dances and things like that, or just sit around with people they knew, and your father's brother would sing, he had a fine voice, and play along with himself on his guitar. Well, this particular Saturday night, him and your father was coming home from some place, and they were both a little drunk and there was a moon that night, it was bright like day. Your father's brother was feeling kind of good, and he was whistling to himself, and he had his guitar slung over his shoulder. They was coming down a hill and beneath them was a road that turned off from the highway. Well, your father's brother, being always kind of frisky, decided to run down this hill, and he did, with that guitar banging and clanging behind him, and he ran across the road, and he was making water behind a tree. And your father was sort of amused at him and he was still coming down the hill, kind of slow. Then he heard a car motor and that same minute his brother stepped from behind the tree, into the road, in the moonlight. And he started to cross the road. And your father started to run down the hill, he says he don't know why. This car was full of white men. They was all drunk, and when they seen your father's brother they let out a great whoop and holler and they aimed the car straight at him. They was having fun, they just wanted to scare him, the way they do sometimes, you know. But they was drunk. And I guess the boy, being drunk, too, and scared, kind of lost his head. By the time he jumped it was too late. Your father says he heard his brother scream when the car rolled over him, and he heard the wood of that guitar when it give, and he heard them strings go flying, and he heard them white men shouting, and the car kept on a-going and it ain't stopped till this day. And, time your father got down the hill, his brother weren't nothing but blood and pulp."

Tears were gleaming on my mother's face. There wasn't anything I could say.

"He never mentioned it," she said, "because I never let him mention it before you children. Your Daddy was like a crazy man that night and for many a night thereafter. He says he never in his life seen anything as dark as that road after the lights of the car had gone away. Weren't nothing, weren't nobody on that road, just your Daddy and his brother and that busted guitar. Oh, yes. Your Daddy never did really get right again. Till the day he died he weren't sure but that every white man he saw was the man that killed his brother."

She stopped and took out her handkerchief and dried her eyes and looked at me.

"I ain't telling you all this," she said, "to make you scared or bitter or to make you hate nobody. I'm telling you this because you got a brother. And the world ain't changed."

I guess I didn't want to believe this. I guess she saw this in my face. She turned away from me, toward the window again, searching those streets.

"But I praise my Redeemer," she said at last, "that He called your Daddy home before me. I ain't saying it to throw no flowers at myself, but, I declare, it keeps me from feeling too cast down to know I helped your father get safely through this world. Your father always acted like he was the roughest, strongest man on earth. And everybody took him to be like that. But if he hadn't had me there—to see his tears!"

She was crying again. Still, I couldn't move. I said, "Lord, Lord, Mama, I didn't know it was like that."

"Oh, honey," she said, "there's a lot that you don't know. But you are going to find it out." She stood up from the window and came over to me. "You got to hold on to your brother," she said, "and don't let him fall, no matter what it looks like is happening to him and no matter how evil you gets with him. You going to be evil with him many a time. But don't you forget what I told you, you hear?"

"I won't forget," I said. "Don't worry, I won't forget. I won't let nothing happen to Sonny."

My mother smiled as though she were amused at something she saw in my face. Then, "You may not be able to stop nothing from happening. But you got to let him know you's there."

Two days later I was married, and then I was gone. And I had a lot of things on my mind and I pretty well forgot my promise to Mama until I got shipped home on a special furlough for her funeral.

And, after the funeral, with just Sonny and me alone in the empty kitchen, I tried to find out something about him.

"What do you want to do?" I asked him.

"I'm going to be a musician," he said.

For he had graduated, in the time I had been away, from dancing to the juke box to finding out who was playing what, and what they were doing with it, and he had bought himself a set of drums.

"You mean, you want to be a drummer?" I somehow had the feeling that being a drummer might be all right for other people but not for my brother Sonny.

"I don't think," he said, looking at me very gravely, "that I'll ever be a good drummer. But I think I can play a piano."

I frowned. I'd never played the role of the older brother quite so seriously before, had scarcely ever, in fact, asked Sonny a damn thing. I sensed myself in the presence of something I didn't really know how to handle, didn't understand. So I made my frown a little deeper as I asked: "What kind of musician do you want to be?"

He grinned. "How many kinds do you think there are?"

"Be serious," I said.

He laughed, throwing his head back, and then looked at me. "I am serious."

"Well, then, for Christ's sake, stop kidding around and answer a serious question. I mean, do you want to be a concert pianist, you want to play classical music and all that, or—or what?" Long before I finished he was laughing again. "For Christ's sake, Sonny!"

He sobered, but with difficulty. "I'm sorry. But you sound so—scared!" and he was off again.

"Well, you may think it's funny now, baby, but it's not going to be so funny when you have to make your living at it, let me tell you that." I was furious because I knew he was laughing at me and I didn't know why.

"No," he said, very sober now, and afraid, perhaps, that he'd hurt me, "I don't want to be a classical pianist. That isn't what interests me. I mean"—he paused, looking hard at me, as though his eyes would help me to understand, and then gestured helplessly, as though perhaps his hand would help— "I mean, I'll have a lot of studying to do, and I'll have to study everything, but, I mean, I want to play with—jazz musicians." He stopped. "I want to play jazz," he said.

Well, the word had never before sounded as heavy, as real, as it sounded that afternoon in Sonny's mouth. I just looked at him and I was probably frowning a real frown by this time. I simply couldn't see why on earth he'd want to spend his time hanging around nightclubs, clowning around on bandstands, while people pushed each other around a dance floor. It seemed—beneath him, somehow. I had never thought about it before, had never been forced to, but I suppose I had always put jazz musicians in a class with what Daddy called "good-time people."

"Are you serious?"

"Hell, yes, I'm serious."

He looked more helpless than ever, and annoyed, and deeply hurt.

I suggested, helpfully: "You mean—like Louis Armstrong?"

His face closed as though I'd struck him. "No. I'm not talking about none of that old-time, down home crap."

"Well, look, Sonny, I'm sorry, don't get mad. I just don't altogether get it, that's all. Name somebody—you know, a jazz musician you admire."

"Bird."

"Who?"

"Bird! Charlie Parker! Don't they teach you nothing in the goddamn Army?"

I lit a cigarette. I was surprised and then a little amused to discover that I was trembling. "I've been out of touch," I said. "You'll have to be patient with me. Now. Who's this Parker character?"

"He's just one of the greatest jazz musicians alive," said Sonny, sullenly, his hands in his pockets, his back to me. "Maybe the greatest," he added bitterly, "that's probably why you never heard of him."

"All right," I said, "I'm ignorant. I'm sorry. I'll go out and buy all the cat's records right away, all right?"

"It don't," said Sonny, with dignity, "make any difference to me. I don't care what you listen to. Don't do me no favors."

I was beginning to realize that I'd never seen him so upset before. With another part of my mind I was thinking that this would probably turn out to be one of those things kids go through and that I shouldn't make it seem important by pushing it too hard. Still, I didn't think it would do any harm to ask: "Doesn't all this take a lot of time? Can you make a living at it?"

He turned back to me and half leaned, half sat, on the kitchen table. "Everything takes time," he said, "and—well, yes, sure, I can make a living at it. But what I don't seem to be able to make you understand is that it's the only thing I want to do."

"Well, Sonny," I said gently, "you know people can't always do exactly what they want to do—"

"No, I don't know that," said Sonny, surprising me, "I think people ought to do what they want to do, what else are they alive for?"

"You getting to be a big boy," I said desperately, "it's time you started thinking about your future."

"I'm thinking about my future," said Sonny, grimly. "I think about it all the time."

I gave up. I decided, if he didn't change his mind, that we could always talk about it later. "In the meantime," I said, "you got to finish school." We had already decided that he'd have to move in with Isabel and her folks. I knew this wasn't the ideal arrangement, because Isabel's folks are inclined to be dicty and they hadn't especially wanted Isabel to marry me. But I didn't know what else to do. "And we have to get you fixed up at Isabel's."

There was a long silence. He moved from the kitchen table to the window. "That's a terrible idea. You know it yourself."

"Do you have a better idea?"

He just walked up and down the kitchen for a minute. He was as tall as I was. He had started to shave. I suddenly had the feeling that I didn't know him at all.

He stopped at the kitchen table and picked up my cigarettes. Looking at me with a kind of mocking, amused defiance, he put one between his lips. "You mind?"

"You smoking already?"

He lit the cigarette and nodded, watching me through the smoke. "I just wanted to see if I'd have the courage to smoke in front of you." He grinned and blew a great cloud of smoke to the ceiling. "It was easy." He looked at my face. "Come on, now. I bet you was smoking at my age, tell the truth."

I didn't say anything but the truth was on my face, and he laughed. But now there was something very strained in his laugh. "Sure. And I bet that ain't all you was doing."

He was frightening me a little. "Cut the crap," I said. "We already decided that you was going to go and live at Isabel's. Now what's got into you all of a sudden?"

"You decided it," he pointed out. "I didn't decide nothing." He stopped in front of me, leaning against the stove, arms loosely folded. "Look, brother. I don't want to stay in Harlem no more, I really don't." He was very earnest. He looked at me, then over toward the kitchen window. There was something in his eyes I'd never seen before, some thoughtfulness, some worry all his own. He rubbed the muscle of one arm. "It's time I was getting out of here."

"Where do you want to go, Sonny?"

"I want to join the Army. Or the Navy, I don't care. If I say I'm old enough, they'll believe me."

Then I got mad. It was because I was so scared. "You must be crazy. You goddamn fool, what the hell do you want to go and join the Army for?"

"I just told you. To get out of Harlem."

"Sonny, you haven't even finished school. And if you really want to be a musician, how do you expect to study if you're in the Army?"

He looked at me, trapped, and in anguish. "There's ways. I might be able to work out some kind of deal. Anyway, I'll have the G.I. Bill when I come out."

"If you come out." We stared at each other. "Sonny, please. Be reasonable. I know the setup is far from perfect. But we got to do the best we can."

"I ain't learning nothing in school," he said. "Even when I go." He turned away from me and opened the window and threw his cigarette out into the narrow alley. I watched his back. "At least, I ain't learning nothing you'd want me to learn." He slammed the window so hard I thought the glass would fly out, and turned back to me. "And I'm sick of the stink of these garbage cans!"

"Sonny," I said, "I know how you feel. But if you don't finish school now, you're going to be sorry later that you didn't." I grabbed him by the shoulders. "And you only got another year. It ain't so bad. And I'll come back and I swear I'll help you do whatever you want to do. Just try to put up with it till I come back. Will you please do that? For me?"

He didn't answer and he wouldn't look at me.

"Sonny. You hear me?"

He pulled away. "I hear you. But you never hear anything I say."

I didn't know what to say to that. He looked out of the window and then back at me. "O.K.," he said, and sighed. "I'll try."

Then I said, trying to cheer him up a little, "They got a piano at Isabel's. You can practice on it."

And as a matter of fact, it did cheer him up for a minute. "That's right," he said to himself. "I forgot that." His face relaxed a little. But the worry, the thoughtfulness, played on it still, the way shadows play on a face which is staring into the fire.

But I thought I'd never hear the end of that piano. At first, Isabel would write me, saying how nice it was that Sonny was so serious about his music and how, as soon as he came in from school, or wherever he had been when he was supposed to be at school, he went straight to that piano and stayed there until suppertime. And after supper, he went back to that piano and stayed there until everybody went to bed. He was at that piano all day Saturday and all day Sunday. Then he bought a record player and started playing records. He'd play one record over and over again, all day long sometimes, and he'd improvise along with it on the piano. Or he'd play one section of the record, one chord, one change, one progression, then he'd do it on the piano. Then back to the record. Then back to the piano.

Well, I really don't know how they stood it. Isabel finally confessed that it wasn't like living with a person at all, it was like living with sound. And the sound didn't make any sense to her, didn't make any sense to any of them—naturally. They began, in a way, to be afflicted by this presence that was living in their home. It was as though Sonny were some sort of god, or monster. He moved in an atmosphere which wasn't like theirs at all. They fed him and he ate, he washed himself, he walked in and out of their door; he certainly wasn't nasty or unpleasant or rude. Sonny isn't any of those things; but it was as though he were all wrapped up in some cloud, some fire, some vision all his own; and there wasn't any way to reach him.

At the same time, he wasn't really a man yet, he was still a child, and they had to watch out for him in all kinds of ways. They certainly couldn't throw him out. Neither did they dare to make a great scene about that piano because even they dimly sensed, as I sensed, from so many thousands of miles away, that Sonny was at that piano playing for his life.

But he hadn't been going to school. One day a letter came from the school board and Isabel's mother got it—there had, apparently, been other letters, but Sonny had torn them up. This day when Sonny came in, Isabel's mother showed him the letter and asked where he'd been spending his time. And she finally got it out of him that he'd been down in Greenwich Village, with musicians and other characters, in a white girl's apartment. And this scared her and she started to scream at him, and what came up, once she began—though she denies it to this day—was what sacrifices they were making to give Sonny a decent home and how little he appreciated it.

Sonny didn't play the piano that day. By evening, Isabel's mother had calmed down but then there was the old man to deal with, and Isabel herself. Isabel says she did her best to be calm, but she broke down and started crying. She says she just watched Sonny's face. She could tell, by watching him, what was happening with him. And what was happening was that they penetrated his cloud, they had reached him. Even if their fingers had been a thousand times more gentle than human fingers ever are, he could hardly help feeling that they had stripped him naked and were spitting on that nakedness. For he also had to see that his presence, that music, which was life or death to him, had been torture for them and that they had endured it, not at all for his sake, but only for mine. And Sonny couldn't take that. He can take it a little better today than he could then, but he's still not very good at it and, frankly, I don't know anybody who is.

The silence of the next few days must have been louder than the sound of all the music ever played since time began. One morning, before she went to work, Isabel was in his room for something and she suddenly realized that all of his records were gone. And she knew for certain that he was gone. And he was. He went as far as the Navy would carry him. He finally sent me a postcard from some place in Greece, and that was the first I knew that Sonny was still alive. I didn't see him any more until we were both back in New York and the war had long been over.

He was a man by then, of course, but I wasn't willing to see it. He came by the house from time to time, but we fought almost every time we met. I didn't like the way he carried himself, loose and dreamlike all the time, and I didn't like his friends, and his music seemed to be merely an excuse for the life he led. It sounded just that weird and disordered.

Then we had a fight, a pretty awful fight, and I didn't see him for months. By and by I looked him up, where he was living, in a furnished room in the Village, and I tried to make it up. But there were lots of other people in the room and Sonny just lay on his bed, and he wouldn't come downstairs with me, and he treated these other people as though they were his family and I weren't. So I got mad and then he got mad, and then I told him that he might just as well be dead as live the way he was living. Then he stood up and told me not to worry about him anymore in life, that he was dead as far as I was concerned. Then he pushed me to the door and the other people looked on as though nothing were happening, and he slammed the door behind me. I stood in the hallway, staring at the door. I heard somebody laugh in the room and then the tears came to my eyes. I started down the steps, whistling to keep from crying, I kept whistling to myself, You going to need me, baby, one of these cold, rainy days.

I read about Sonny's trouble in the spring. Little Grace died in the fall. She was a beautiful little girl. But she only lived a little over two years. She died of polio and she suffered. She had a slight fever for a couple of days, but it didn't seem like anything and we just kept her in bed. And we would certainly have called the doctor, but the fever dropped, she seemed to be all right. So we thought it had just been a cold. Then, one day, she was up, playing, Isabel was in the kitchen fixing lunch for the two boys when they'd come in from school, and she heard Grace fall down in the living room. When you have a lot of children you don't always start running when one of them falls, unless they start screaming or something. And, this time, Grace was quiet. Yet Isabel says that when she heard the thump and then that silence, something happened in her to make her afraid. And she ran to the living room and there was little Grace on the floor, all twisted up, and the reason she hadn't screamed was that she couldn't get her breath. And when she did scream, it was the worst sound, Isabel says, that she'd ever heard in all her life, and she still hears it sometimes in her dreams. Isabel will sometimes wake me up with a low, moaning, strangled sound, and I have to be quick to awaken her and hold her to me, and where Isabel is weeping against me seems a mortal wound.

I think I may have written Sonny the very day that little Grace was buried. I was sitting in the living room in the dark, by myself, and I suddenly thought of Sonny. My trouble made his real.

One Saturday afternoon, when Sonny had been living with us, or, anyway, been in our house, for nearly two weeks, I found myself wandering aimlessly about the living room, drinking from a can of beer, and trying to work up the courage to search Sonny's room. He was out, he was usually out whenever I was home, and Isabel had taken the children to see their grandparents. Suddenly I was standing still in front of the living room window, watching Seventh Avenue. The idea of searching Sonny's room made me still. I scarcely dared to admit to myself what I'd be searching for. I didn't know what I'd do if I found it. Or if I didn't.

On the sidewalk across from me, near the entrance to a barbecue joint, some people were holding an old-fashioned revival meeting. The barbecue cook, wearing a dirty white apron, his conked hair reddish and metallic in the pale sun, and a cigarette between his lips, stood in the doorway, watching them. Kids and older people paused in their errands and stood there, along with some older men and a couple of very tough-looking women who watched everything that happened on the avenue, as though they owned it, or were maybe owned by it. Well, they were watching this, too. The revival was being carried on by three sisters in black, and a brother. All they had were their voices and their Bibles and a tambourine. The brother was testifying, and while he testified two of the sisters stood together, seeming to say, Amen, and the third sister walked around with the tambourine outstretched and a couple of people dropped coins into it. Then the brother's testimony ended and the sister who had been taking up the collection dumped the coins into her palm and transferred them to the pocket of her long black robe. Then she raised both hands, striking the tambourine against the air, and then against one hand, and she started to sing. And the two other sisters and the brother joined in.

It was strange, suddenly, to watch, though I had been seeing these street meetings all my life. So, of course, had everybody else down there. Yet, they paused and watched and listened and I stood still at the window. "'Tis the old ship of Zion," they sang, and the sister with the tambourine kept a steady, jangling beat, "it has rescued many a thousand!" Not a soul under the sound of their voices was hearing this song for the first time, not one of them had been rescued. Nor had they seen much in the way of rescue work being done around them. Neither did they especially believe in the holiness of the three sisters and the brother, they knew too much about them, knew where they lived, and how. The woman with the tambourine, whose voice dominated the air, whose face was bright with joy, was divided by very little from the woman who stood watching her, a cigarette between her heavy, chapped lips, her hair a cuckoo's nest, her face scarred and swollen from many beatings, and her black eyes glittering like coal. Perhaps they both knew this, which was why, when, at the rare times they addressed each other, they addressed each other as "sister." As the singing filled the air, the watching, listening faces underwent a change, the eyes focusing on something within; the music seemed to soothe a poison out of them; and time seemed, nearly, to fall away from the sullen, belligerent, battered faces, as though they were fleeing back to their first condition, while dreaming of their last. The barbecue cook half shook his head and smiled, and dropped his cigarette and disappeared into his joint. A man fumbled in his pockets for change and stood holding it in his hand impatiently, as though he had just remembered a pressing appointment further up the avenue. He looked furious. Then I saw Sonny, standing on the edge of the crowd. He was carrying a wide, flat notebook with a green cover, and it made him look, from where I was standing, almost like a schoolboy. The coppery sun brought out the copper in his skin; he was very faintly smiling, standing very still. Then the singing stopped, the tambourine turned into a collection plate again. The furious man dropped in his coins and vanished; so did a couple of the women, and Sonny dropped some change in the plate, looking directly at the woman with a little smile. He started across the avenue, toward the house. He has a slow, loping walk, something like the way Harlem hipsters walk, only he's imposed on this his own half-beat. I had never really noticed it before.

I stayed at the window, both relieved and apprehensive. As Sonny disappeared from my sight, they began singing again. And they were still singing when his key turned in the lock.

"Hey," he said.

"Hey, yourself. You want some beer?"

"No. Well, maybe." But he came up to the window and stood beside me, looking out. "What a warm voice," he said.

They were singing, "If I Could Only Hear My Mother Pray Again!"

"Yes," I said, "and she can sure beat that tambourine."

"But what a terrible song," he said, and laughed. He dropped his notebook on the sofa and disappeared into the kitchen. "Where's Isabel and the kids?"

"I think they went to see their grandparents. You hungry?"

"No." He came back into the living room with his can of beer. "You want to come some place with me tonight?"

I sensed, I don't know how, that I couldn't possibly say no. "Sure. Where?"

He sat down on the sofa and picked up his notebook and started leafing through it. "I'm going to sit in with some fellows in a joint in the Village."

"You mean, you're going to play, tonight?"

"That's right." He took a swallow of his beer and moved back to the window. He gave me a sidelong look. "If you can stand it."

"I'll try," I said.

He smiled to himself and we both watched as the meeting across the way broke up. The three sisters and the brother, heads bowed, were singing, "God be with you 'till we meet again." The faces around them were very quiet. Then the song ended. The small crowd dispersed. We watched the three women and the lone man walk slowly up the avenue.

"When she was singing before," said Sonny, abruptly, "her voice reminded me for a minute of what heroin feels like sometimes—when it's in your veins. It makes you feel sort of warm and cool at the same time. And distant. And—and sure." He sipped his beer, very deliberately not looking at me. I watched his face. "It makes you feel—in control. Sometimes you've got to have that feeling."

"Do you?" I sat down slowly in the easy chair.

"Sometimes." He went to the sofa and picked up his notebook again. "Some people do."

"In order," I asked, "to play?" And my voice was very ugly, full of contempt and anger.

"Well"—he looked at me with great, troubled eyes, as though, in fact, he hoped his eyes would tell me things he could never otherwise say—"they think so. And if they think so ... !"

"And what do you think?" I asked.

He sat on the sofa and put his can of beer on the floor. "I don't know," he said, and I couldn't be sure if he were answering my question or pursuing his thoughts. His face didn't tell me. "It's not so much to play. It's to stand it, to be able to make it at all. On any level." He frowned and smiled: "In order to keep from shaking to pieces."

"But these friends of yours," I said, "they seem to shake themselves to pieces pretty goddamn fast."

"Maybe." He played with the notebook. And something told me that I should curb my tongue, that Sonny was doing his best to talk, that I should listen. "But of course you only know the ones that've gone to pieces. Some don't—or at least they haven't yet, and that's just about all any of us can say." He paused. "And then there are some who just live, really, in hell, and they know it and they see what's happening and they go right on. I don't know." He sighed, dropped the notebook, folded his arms. "Some guys, you can tell from the way they play, they on something all the time. And you can see that, well, it makes something real for them. But of course," he picked up his beer from the floor and sipped it and put the can down again, "they want to, too, you've got to see that. Even some of them that say they don't— some, not all."

"And what about you?" I asked—I couldn't help it. "What about you? Do you want to?"

He stood up and walked to the window and remained silent for a long time. Then he sighed. "Me," he said. Then: "While I was downstairs before, on my way here, listening to that woman sing, it struck me all of a sudden how much suffering she must have had to go through—to sing like that. It's repulsive to think you have to suffer that much."

I said: "But there's no way not to suffer—is there, Sonny?"

"I believe not," he said, and smiled, "but that's never stopped anyone from trying." He looked at me. "Has it?" I realized, with this mocking look, that there stood between us, forever, beyond the power of time or forgiveness, the fact that I had held silence— so long! when he had needed human speech to help him. He turned back to the window. "No, there's no way not to suffer. But you try all kinds of ways to keep from drowning in it, to keep on top of it, and to make it seem—well, like you. Like you did something, all right, and now you're suffering for it. You know?" I said nothing. "Well, you know," he said, impatiently, "why do people suffer? Maybe it's better to do something, to give it a reason, any reason."

"But we just agreed," I said, "that there's no way not to suffer. Isn't it better, then, just to—take it?"

"But nobody just takes it," Sonny cried, "that's what I'm telling you! Everybody tries not to. You're just hung up on the way some people try—it's not your way!"

The hair on my face began to itch, my face felt wet. "That's not true," I said, "that's not true. I don't give a damn what other people do, I don't even care how they suffer. I just care how you suffer." And he looked at me. "Please believe me," I said, "I don't want to see you—die—trying not to suffer."

"I won't," he said, flatly, "die trying not to suffer. At least, not any faster than anybody else."

"But there's no need," I said, trying to laugh, "is there? in killing yourself."

I wanted to say more, but I couldn't. I wanted to talk about will power and how life could be—well, beautiful. I wanted to say that it was all within; but was it? or, rather, wasn't that exactly the trouble? And I wanted to promise that I would never fail him again. But it would all have sounded—empty words and lies.

So I made the promise to myself and prayed that I would keep it.

"It's terrible sometimes, inside," he said, "that's what's the trouble. You walk these streets, black and funky and cold, and there's not really a living ass to talk to, and there's nothing shaking, and there's no way of getting it out—that storm inside. You can't talk it and you can't make love with it, and when you finally try to get with it and play it, you realize nobody's listening. So you've got to listen. You got to find a way to listen."

And then he walked away from the window and sat on the sofa again, as though all the wind had suddenly been knocked out of him. "Sometimes you'll do anything to play, even cut your mother's throat." He laughed and looked at me. "Or your brother's." Then he sobered. "Or your own." Then: "Don't worry. I'm all right now and I think I'll be all right. But I can't forget—where I've been. I don't mean just the physical place I've been, I mean where I've been. And, what I've been."

"What have you been, Sonny?" I asked.

He smiled—but sat sideways on the sofa, his elbow resting on the back, his fingers playing with his mouth and chin, not looking at me. "I've been something I didn't recognize, didn't know I could be. Didn't know anybody could be." He stopped, looking inward, looking helplessly young, looking old. "I'm not talking about it now because I feel guilty or anything like that—maybe it would be better if I did. I don't know. Anyway, I can't really talk about it. Not to you, not to anybody." And now he turned and faced me. "Sometimes, you know, and it was actually when I was most out of the world, I felt that I was in it, that I was with it, really, and I could play or I didn't really have to play, it just came out of me, it was there. And I don't know how I played, thinking about it now, but I know that I did awful things, those times, sometimes, to people. Or it wasn't that I did anything to them—it was that they weren't real." He picked up the beer can; it was empty; he rolled it between his palms: "And other times—well, I needed a fix. I needed to find a place to lean, I needed to clear a space to listen—and I couldn't find it, and I—went crazy, I did terrible things to me, I was terrible for me." He began pressing the beer can between his hands; I watched the metal begin to give. It glittered, as he played with it, like a knife, and I was afraid he would cut himself, but I said nothing. "Oh, well. I can never tell you. I was all by myself at the bottom of something, stinking and sweating and crying and shaking, and I smelled it, you know? my stink, and I thought I'd die if I couldn't get away from it and yet, all the same, I knew that everything I was doing was just locking me in with it. And I didn't know," he paused, still flattening the beer can. "I didn't know, I still don't know, something kept telling me that maybe it was good to smell your own stink, but I didn't think that that was what I'd been trying to do—and—who can stand it?" and he abruptly dropped the ruined beer can, looking at me with a small, still smile, and then rose, walking to the window as though it were a lodestone. I watched his face, he watched the avenue. "I couldn't tell you when Mama died—but the reason I wanted to leave Harlem so bad was to get away from drugs. And then, when I ran away, that's what I was running from—really. When I came back, nothing had changed, I hadn't changed, I was just—older." And he stopped, drumming with his fingers on the windowpane. The sun had vanished, soon darkness would fall. I watched his face. "It can come again," he said, almost as though speaking to himself. Then he turned to me. "It can come again," he repeated. "I just want you to know that."

"All right," I said, at last. "So it can come again. All right."

He smiled, but the smile was sorrowful. "I had to try to tell you," he said.

"Yes," I said. "I understand that."

"You're my brother," he said, looking straight at me, and not smiling at all.

"Yes," I repeated, "yes, I understand that."

He turned back to the window, looking out. "All that hatred down there," he said, "all that hatred and misery and love. It's a wonder it doesn't blow the avenue apart."

We went to the only nightclub on a short, dark street, downtown. We squeezed through the narrow, chattering, jam-packed bar to the entrance of the big room, where the bandstand was. And we stood there for a moment, for the lights were very dim in this room and we couldn't see. Then, "Hello, boy," said a voice, and an enormous black man, much older than Sonny or myself, erupted out of all that atmospheric lighting and put an arm around Sonny's shoulder. "I been sitting right here," he said, "waiting for you."

He had a big voice, too, and heads in the darkness turned toward us.

Sonny grinned and pulled a little away, and said, "Creole, this is my brother. I told you about him."

Creole shook my hand. "I'm glad to meet you, son," he said, and it was clear that he was glad to meet me there, for Sonny's sake. And he smiled, "You got a real musician in your family," and he took his arm from Sonny's shoulder and slapped him, lightly, affectionately, with the back of his hand.

"Well. Now I've heard it all," said a voice behind us. This was another musician, and a friend of Sonny's, a coal-black, cheerful-looking man, built close to the ground. He immediately began confiding to me, at the top of his lungs, the most terrible things about Sonny, his teeth gleaming like a lighthouse and his laugh coming up out of him like the beginning of an earthquake. And it turned out that everyone at the bar knew Sonny, or almost everyone; some were musicians, working there, or nearby, or not working, some were simply hangers-on, and some were there to hear Sonny play. I was introduced to all of them and they were all very polite to me. Yet, it was clear that, for them, I was only Sonny's brother. Here, I was in Sonny's world. Or, rather: his kingdom. Here, it was not even a question that his veins bore royal blood.

They were going to play soon and Creole installed me, by myself, at a table in a dark corner. Then I watched them, Creole, and the little black man, and Sonny, and the others, while they horsed around, standing just below the bandstand. The light from the bandstand spilled just a little short of them and, watching them laughing and gesturing and moving about, I had the feeling that they, nevertheless, were being most careful not to step into that circle of light too suddenly: that if they moved into the light too suddenly, without thinking, they would perish in flame. Then, while I watched, one of them, the small, black man, moved into the light and crossed the bandstand and started fooling around with his drums. Then—being funny and being, also, extremely ceremonious—Creole took Sonny by the arm and led him to the piano. A woman's voice called Sonny's name and a few hands started clapping. And Sonny, also being funny and ceremonious, and so touched, I think, that he could have cried, but neither hiding it nor showing it, riding it like a man, grinned, and put both hands to his heart and bowed from the waist.

Creole then went to the bass fiddle, and a lean, very bright-skinned brown man jumped up on the bandstand and picked up his horn. So there they were, and the atmosphere on the bandstand and in the room began to change and tighten. Someone stepped up to the microphone and announced them. Then there were all kinds of murmurs. Some people at the bar shushed others. The waitress ran around, frantically getting in the last orders, guys and chicks got closer to each other, and the lights on the bandstand, on the quartet, turned to a kind of indigo. Then they all looked different there. Creole looked about him for the last time, as though he were making certain that all his chickens were in the coop, and then he—jumped and struck the fiddle. And there they were.

All I know about music is that not many people ever really hear it. And even then, on the rare occasions when something opens within, and the music enters, what we mainly hear, or hear corroborated, are personal, private, vanishing evocations. But the man who creates the music is hearing something else, is dealing with the roar rising from the void and imposing order on it as it hits the air. What is evoked in him, then, is of another order, more terrible because it has no words, and triumphant, too, for that same reason. And his triumph, when he triumphs, is ours. I just watched Sonny's face. His face was troubled, he was working hard, but he wasn't with it. And I had the feeling that, in a way, everyone on the bandstand was waiting for him, both waiting for him and pushing him along. But as I began to watch Creole, I realized that it was Creole who held them all back. He had them on a short rein. Up there, keeping the beat with his whole body, wailing on the fiddle, with his eyes half closed, he was listening to everything, but he was listening to Sonny. He was having a dialogue with Sonny. He wanted Sonny to leave the shoreline and strike out for the deep water. He was Sonny's witness that deep water and drowning were not the same thing—he had been there, and he knew. And he wanted Sonny to know. He was waiting for Sonny to do the things on the keys which would let Creole know that Sonny was in the water.

And, while Creole listened, Sonny moved deep within, exactly like someone in torment. I had never before thought of how awful the relationship must be between the musician and his instrument. He has to fill it, this instrument, with the breath of life, his own. He has to make it do what he wants it to do. And a piano is just a piano. It's made out of so much wood and wires and little hammers and big ones, and ivory. While there's only so much you can do with it, the only way to find this out is to try to make it do everything.

And Sonny hadn't been near a piano for over a year. And he wasn't on much better terms with his life, not the life that stretched before him now. He and the piano stammered, started one way, got scared, stopped; started another way, panicked, marked time, started again; then seemed to have found a direction, panicked again, got stuck. And the face I saw on Sonny I'd never seen before. Everything had been burned out of it, and, at the same time, things usually hidden were being burned in, by the fire and fury of the battle which was occurring in him up there.

Yet, watching Creole's face as they neared the end of the first set, I had the feeling that something had happened, something I hadn't heard. Then they finished, there was scattered applause, and then, without an instant's warning, Creole started into something else; it was almost sardonic, it was "Am I Blue." And, as though he commanded, Sonny began to play. Something began to happen. And Creole let out the reins. The dry, low, black man said something awful on the drums; Creole answered, and the drums talked back. Then the horn insisted, sweet and high, slightly detached perhaps, and Creole listened, commenting now and then, dry, and driving, beautiful and calm and old. Then they all came together again, and Sonny was part of the family again. I could tell this from his face. He seemed to have found, right there beneath his fingers, a damn brand-new piano. It seemed that he couldn't get over it. Then, for awhile, just being happy with Sonny, they seemed to be agreeing with him that brand-new pianos certainly were a gas.

Then Creole stepped forward to remind them that what they were playing was the blues. He hit something in all of them, he hit something in me, myself, and the music tightened and deepened, apprehension began to beat the air. Creole began to tell us what the blues were all about. They were not about anything very new. He and his boys up there were keeping it new, at the risk of ruin, destruction, madness, and death, in order to find new ways to make us listen. For, while the tale of how we suffer, and how we are delighted, and how we may triumph is never new, it always must be heard. There isn't any other tale to tell, it's the only light we've got in all this darkness.

And this tale, according to that face, that body, those strong hands on those strings, has another aspect in every country, and a new depth in every generation. Listen, Creole seemed to be saying, listen. Now these are Sonny's blues. He made the little black man on the drums know it, and the bright, brown man on the horn, Creole wasn't trying any longer to get Sonny in the water. He was wishing him Godspeed.

Then he stepped back, very slowly, filling the air with the immense suggestion that Sonny speak for himself.

Then they all gathered around Sonny and Sonny played. Every now and again one of them seemed to say, Amen. Sonny's fingers filled the air with life, his life. But that life contained so many others. And Sonny went all the way back, he really began with the spare, flat statement of the opening phrase of the song. Then he began to make it his. It was very beautiful because it wasn't hurried and it was no longer a lament. I seemed to hear with what burning he had made it his, with what burning we had yet to make it ours, how we could cease lamenting. Freedom lurked around us and I understood, at last, that he could help us to be free if we would listen, that he would never be free until we did. Yet, there was no battle in his face now. I heard what he had gone through, and would continue to go through until he came to rest in earth. He had made it his; that long line, of which we knew only Mama and Daddy. And he was giving it back, as everything must be given back, so that, passing through death, it can live forever. I saw my mother's face again, and felt, for the first time, how the stones of the road she had walked on must have bruised her feet. I saw the moonlit road where my father's brother died. And it brought something else back to me, and carried me past it; I saw my little girl again and felt Isabel's tears again, and I felt my own tears begin to rise. And I was yet aware that this was only a moment, that the world waited outside, as hungry as a tiger, and that trouble stretched above us, longer than the sky.

Then it was over. Creole and Sonny let out their breath, both soaking wet, and grinning. There was a lot of applause and some of it was real. In the dark, the girl came by and I asked her to take drinks to the bandstand. There was a long pause, while they talked up there in the indigo light, and after awhile, I saw the girl put a Scotch and milk on top of the piano for Sonny. He didn't seem to notice it, but just before they started playing again, he sipped from it and looked toward me, and nodded. Then he put it back on top of the piano. For me, then, as they began to play again, it glowed and shook above my brother's head like the very cup of trembling.

John A. Williams

(b. 1925)

*"I like to switch-hit from fiction to nonfiction," says the prolific John Alfred Williams. The author of more than twenty novels, biographies, monographs, and dramas, the Mississippi-born Williams began writing when he was a pharmacist's mate in the Navy during World War II. He did not regard his efforts seriously, however, until he returned to school at Syracuse University where he began studying for a degree in journalism and English. Upon graduation Williams worked as a special correspondent for several magazines, including **Ebony** and **Jet**, and served as an announcer for several radio and television stations before taking a job in publishing. During his spare time he worked on his first novel, **One for New York.** This story about Greenwich Village and its jazz musicians was eventually published in 1960 as* **The Angry Ones***.*

A writer who often tackles the ways in which racism affects individual identity and pride, Williams has received international acclaim for his novels **The Man Who Cried I Am** *(1967) and* **!Click Song** *(1982). In addition to publishing widely in various periodicals, he has also edited an anthology,* **The Angry Black** *(1962), and written biographies of Martin Luther King, Jr., Richard Wright, and Richard Pryor. "What I try to do," Williams has said of his writing, "is to deal in forms that are not standard, to improvise as jazz musicians do with their music, so that a standard theme comes out looking brand new." Appointed the Paul Robeson Professor of English at Rutgers University in 1990, Williams taught there until 1993.*

Son in the Afternoon

IT WAS HOT. I tend to be a bitch when it's hot. I goosed the little Ford over Sepulveda Boulevard toward Santa Monica until I got stuck in the traffic that pours from L.A. into the surrounding towns. I'd had a very lousy day at the studio.

I was—still am—a writer and this studio had hired me to check scripts and films with Negroes in them to make sure the Negro moviegoer wouldn't be offended. The signs were already clear one day the whole of American industry would be racing pell-mell to get Negro, showcase a spade. I was kind of a pioneer. I'm a *Negro* writer, you see. The day had been tough because of a couple of verbs—slink and walk. One of those Hollywood hippies had done a script calling for a Negro waiter to slink away from the table where a dinner party was glaring at him. I said the waiter should walk, not slink, because later on he becomes a hero. The Hollywood hippie, who understood it all because he had some colored friends, said that it was essential to the plot that the waiter slink. I said you don't slink one minute and become a hero the next; there has to be some consistency. The Negro actor I was standing up for said nothing either way. He had played Uncle Tom roles so long that he had become Uncle Tom. But the director agreed with me.

Anyway ... hear me out now. I was on my way to Santa Monica to pick up my mother, Nora. It was a long haul for such a hot day. I had planned a quiet evening: a nice shower, fresh clothes, and then I would have dinner at the Watkins and talk with some of the musicians on the scene for a quick taste before they cut to their gigs. After, I was going to the Pigalle down on Figueroa and catch Earl Grant at the organ, and still later, if nothing exciting happened, I'd pick up Scottie and make it to the Lighthouse on the Beach or to the Strollers and listen to some of the white boys play. I liked the long drive, especially while listening to Sleepy Stein's show on the radio. Later, much later of course, it would be home, back to Watts.

So you see, this picking up Nora was a little inconvenient. My mother was a maid for the Couchmans. Ronald Couchman was an architect, a good one I understood from Nora who has a fine sense for this sort of thing; you don't work in some hundred-odd houses during your life without getting some idea of the way a house should be laid out. Couchman's wife, Kay, was a playgirl who drove a white Jaguar from one party to another. My mother didn't like her too much; she didn't seem to care much for her son, Ronald, junior. There's something wrong with a parent who can't really love her own child, Nora thought. The Couchmans lived in a real fine residential section, of course. A number of actors lived nearby, character actors, not really big stars.

Somehow it is very funny. I mean that the maids and butlers knew everything about these people, and these people knew nothing at all about the help. Through Nora and her friends I knew who was laying whose wife; who had money and who *really* had money; I knew about the wild parties hours before the police, and who smoked marijuana, when, and where they got it.

To get to Couchman's driveway I had to go three blocks up one side of a palm-planted center strip and back down the other. The driveway bent gently, then swept back out of sight of the main road. The house, sheltered by slim palms, looked like a transplanted New England Colonial. I parked and walked to the kitchen door, skirting the growling Great Dane who was tied to a tree. That was the route to the kitchen door.

I don't like kitchen doors. Entering people's houses by them, I mean. I'd done this thing most of my life when I called at places where Nora worked to pick up the patched or worn sheets or the half-eaten roasts, the battered, tarnished silver—the fringe benefits of a housemaid. As a teen-ager I'd told Nora I was through with that crap; I was not going through anyone's kitchen door. She only laughed and said I'd learn. One day soon after, I called for her and without knocking walked right through the front door of this house and right on through the living room. I was almost out of the room when I saw feet behind the couch. I leaned over and there was Mr. Jorgensen and his wife making out like crazy. I guess they thought Nora had gone and it must have hit them sort of suddenly and they went at it like the hell-bomb was due to drop any minute. I've been that way too, mostly in the spring. Of course, when Mr. Jorgensen looked over his shoulder and saw me, you know what happened. I was thrown out and Nora right behind me. It was the middle of winter, the old man was sick and the coal bill three months overdue. Nora was right about those kitchen doors: I learned.

My mother saw me before I could ring the bell. She opened the door. "Hello," she said. She was breathing hard, like she'd been running or something. "Come in and sit down. I don't know w*here* that Kay is. Little Ronald is sick and she's probably out gettin' drunk again." She left me then and trotted back through the house, I guess to be with Ronnie. I hated the combination of her white nylon uniform, her dark brown face and the wide streaks of gray in her hair. Nora had married this guy from Texas a few years after the old man had died. He was all right. He made out okay. Nora didn't have to work, but she just couldn't be still; she always had to be doing something. I suggested she quit work, but I had as much luck as her husband. I used to tease her about liking to be around those white folks. It would have been good for her to take an extended trip around the country visiting my brothers and sisters. Once she got to Philadelphia, she could go right out to the cemetery and sit awhile with the old man.

I walked through the Couchman home. I liked the library. I thought if I knew Couchman I'd like him. The room made me feel like that. I left it and went into the big living room. You could tell that Couchman had let his wife do that. Everything in it was fast, dart-like, with no sense of ease. But on the walls were several of Couchman's conceptions of buildings and homes. I guess he was a disciple of Wright. My mother walked rapidly through the room without looking at me and said, "Just be patient, Wendell. She should be here real soon."

"Yeah," I said, "with a snootful." I had turned back to the drawings when Ronnie scampered into the room, his face twisted with rage.

"Nora!" he tried to roar, perhaps the way he'd seen the parents of some of his friends roar at their maids. I'm quite sure Kay didn't shout at Nora, and I don't think Couchman would. But then no one shouts at Nora. "Nora, you come right back here this minute!" the little bastard shouted and stamped and pointed to a spot on the floor where Nora was supposed to come to roost. I have a nasty temper. Sometimes it lies dormant for ages and at other times, like when the weather is hot and nothing seems to be going right, it's bubbling and ready to explode. "Don't talk to *my* mother like that, you little—!" I said sharply, breaking off just before I cursed. I wanted him to be large enough for me to strike. "How'd you like for me to talk to *your* mother like that?"

The nine-year-old looked up at me in surprise and confusion. He hadn't expected me to say anything. I was just another piece of furniture. Tears rose in his eyes and spilled out onto his pale cheeks. He put his hands behind him, twisted them. He moved backwards, away from me. He looked at my mother with a "Nora, come help me" look. And sure enough, there was Nora, speeding back across the room, gathering the kid in her arms, tucking his robe together. I was too angry to feel hatred for myself.

Ronnie was the Couchman's only kid. Nora loved him. I suppose that was the trouble. Couchman was gone ten, twelve hours a day. Kay didn't stay around the house any longer than she had to. So Ronnie had only my mother. I think kids should have someone to love, and Nora wasn't a bad sort. But somehow when the six of us, her own children, were growing up we never had her. She was gone, out scuffling to get those crumbs to put into our mouths and shoes for our feet and praying for something to happen so that all the space in between would be taken care of. Nora's affection for us took the form of rushing out into the morning's five o'clock blackness to wake some silly bitch and get her coffee; took form in her trudging five miles home every night instead of taking the streetcar to save money to buy tablets for us, to use at school, we said. But the truth was that all of us liked to draw and we went through a writing tablet in a couple of hours every day. Can you imagine? There's not a goddamn artist among us. We never had the physical affection, the pat on the head, the quick, smiling kiss, the "gimmee a hug" routine. All of this Ronnie was getting.

Now he buried his little blond head in Nora's breast and sobbed. "There, there now," Nora said. "Don't you cry, Ronnie. Ol' Wendell is just jealous, and he hasn't much sense either. He didn't mean nuthin'."

I left the room. Nora had hit it of course, hit it and passed on. I looked back. It didn't look so incongruous, the white and black together, I mean. Ronnie was still sobbing. His head bobbed gently on Nora's shoulder. The only time I ever got that close to her was when she trapped me with a bearhug so she could whale the daylights out of me after I put a snowball through Mrs. Grant's window. I walked outside and lit a cigarette. When Ronnie was in the hospital the month before, Nora got me to run her way over to Hollywood every night to see him. I didn't like that worth a damn. All right, I'll admit it: it did upset me. All that affection I didn't get nor my brothers and sisters going to that little white boy who, without a doubt, when away from her called her the names he'd learned from adults. Can you imagine a nine-year-old kid calling Nora a "girl," "our girl?" I spat at the Great Dane. He snarled and then I bounced a rock off his fanny. "Lay down, you bastard," I muttered. It was a good thing he was tied up.

I heard the low cough of the Jaguar slapping against the road. The car was throttled down, and with a muted roar it swung into the driveway. The woman aimed it for me. I was evil enough not to move. I was tired of playing with these people. At the last moment, grinning, she swung the wheel over and braked. She bounded out of the car like a tennis player vaulting over a net.

"Hi," she said, tugging at her shorts.

"Hello."

"You're Nora's boy?"

"I'm Nora's son." Hell, I was as old as she was; besides, I can't stand "boy."

"Nora tells us you're working in Hollywood. Like it?"

"It's all right."

"You must be pretty talented."

We stood looking at each other while the dog whined for her attention. Kay had a nice body and it was well tanned. She was high, boy, was she high. Looking at her, I could feel myself going into my sexy bastard routine; sometimes I can swing it great. Maybe it all had to do with the business inside. Kay took off her sunglasses and took a good look at me. "Do you have a cigarette?"

I gave her one and lit it. "Nice tan," I said. Most white people I know think it's a great big deal if a Negro compliments them on their tans. It's a large laugh. You have all this volleyball about color and come summer you can't hold the white folks back from the beaches, anyplace where they can get some sun. And of course the blacker they get, the more pleased they are. Crazy. If there is ever a Negro revolt, it will come during the summer and Negroes will descend upon the beaches around the nation and paralyze the country. You can't conceal cattle prods and bombs and pistols and police dogs when you're showing your birthday suit to the sun.

"You like it?" she asked. She was pleased. She placed her arm next to mine. "Almost the same color," she said.

"Ronnie isn't feeling well," I said.

"Oh, the poor kid. I'm so glad we have Nora. She's such a charm. I'll run right in and look at him. Do have a drink in the bar. Fix me one too, will you?" Kay skipped inside and I went to the bar and poured out two strong drinks. I made hers stronger than mine. She was back soon. "Nora was trying to put him to sleep and she made me stay out." She giggled. She quickly tossed off her drink. "Another, please?" While I was fixing her drink she was saying how amazing it was for Nora to have such a talented son. What she was really saying was that it was amazing for a servant to have a son who was not also a servant. "Anything can happen in a democracy," I said. "Servants' sons drink with madames and so on."

"Oh, Nora isn't a servant," Kay said. "She's part of the family."

Yeah, I thought. Where and how many times had I heard *that* before?

In the ensuing silence, she started to admire her tan again. "You think it's pretty good, do you? You don't know how hard I worked to get it." I moved close to her and held her arm. I placed my other arm around her. She pretended not to see or feel it, but she wasn't trying to get away either. In fact she was pressing closer and the register in my brain that tells me at the precise moment when I'm in, went off. Kay was very high. I put both arms around her and she put both hers around me. When I kissed her, she responded completely.

"Mom!"

"Ronnie, come back to bed," I heard Nora shout from the other room. We could hear Ronnie running over the rug in the outer room. Kay tried to get away from me, push me to one side, because we could tell that Ronnie knew where to look for his Mom: he was running right for the bar, where we were. "Oh, please," she said, "don't let him see us." I wouldn't let her push me away. "Stop!" she hissed. "He'll *see* us!" We stopped struggling just for an instant, and we listened to the echoes of the word *see*. She gritted her teeth and renewed her efforts to get away.

Me? I had the scene laid right out. The kid breaks into the room, see, and sees his mother in this real wriggly clinch with this colored guy who's just shouted at him, see, and no matter how his mother explains it away, the kid has the image—the colored guy and his mother—for the rest of his life, see?

That's the way it happened. The kid's mother hissed under her breath, *"You're crazy!"* and she looked at me as though she were seeing me or something about me for the very first time. I'd released her as soon as Ronnie, romping into the bar, saw us and came to a full open-mouthed halt. Kay went to him. He looked first at me, then at his mother. Kay turned to me, but she couldn't speak.

Outside in the living room my mother called, "Wendell, where are you? We can go now."

I started to move past Kay and Ronnie. I felt many things, but I made myself think mostly, *There you little bastard, there.*

My mother thrust her face inside the door and said, " Good-bye, Mrs. Couchman. See you tomorrow. 'Bye, Ronnie."

"Yes," Kay said, sort of stunned. "Tomorrow." She was reaching for Ronnie's hand as we left, but the kid was slapping her hand away. I hurried quickly after Nora, hating the long drive back to Watts.

Paule Marshall

(b. 1929)

Born to émigrés from Barbados who settled in Brooklyn, New York, Paule Marshall grew up keenly aware of how her Caribbean heritage intermingled with the urban American environment in which she was raised. Translated into writing, these diverse cultural influences would bring to Marshall's fiction a sense of ritual and of the importance of history. Her first novel, **Brown Girl, Brownstone** *(1959), was written while she was a journalist for* **Our World***, an African American magazine that she worked for after graduating Phi Beta Kappa from Brooklyn College in 1953. Although Marshall's subsequent books did not thrive commercially, she nonetheless published steadily throughout the sixties, producing such well-received books as* **Soul Clap Hands and Sing** *(1961) and* **The Chosen Place, The Timeless People** *(1969). Marshall also continued to explore her favorite topic, African American women and their relationship to culture, as a university lecturer and as contributor to the* **New York Times Book Review***. With the publication of* **Praisesong for the Widow** *(1983) and* **Daughters** *(1991), Marshall began to enjoy commercial success as well as critical acclaim. A recipient of a Guggenheim Fellowship (1960), a Rosenthal Award from the National Institute of Arts and Letters (1962), a Before Columbus Foundation American Book Award (1984), and various grants from the Ford Foundation and the National Endowment for the Arts, Marshall was honored with a prestigious MacArthur Fellowship in 1992.*

To Da-duh In Memoriam

" ... Oh Nana! all of you is not involved in this evil business
   Death,
Nor all of us in life."
                    —From "At My Grandmother's Grave," by Lebert Bethune

I did not see her at first I remember. For not only was it dark inside the crowded disembarkation shed in spite of the daylight flooding in from outside, but standing there waiting for her with my mother and sister I was still somewhat blinded from the sheen of tropical sunlight on the water of the bay which we had just crossed in the landing boat, leaving behind us the ship that had brought us from New York lying in the offing. Besides, being only nine years of age at the time and knowing nothing of islands I was busy attending to the alien sights and sounds of Barbados, the unfamiliar smells.

I did not see her, but I was alerted to her approach by my mother's hand which suddenly tightened around mine, and looking up I traced her gaze through the gloom in the shed until I finally made out the small, purposeful, painfully erect figure of the old woman headed our way.

Her face was drowned in the shadow of an ugly rolled-brim brown felt hat, but the details of her slight body and of the struggle taking place within it were clear enough—an intense, unrelenting struggle between her back which was beginning to bend ever so slightly under the weight of her eighty-odd years and the rest of her which sought to deny those years and hold that back straight, keep it in line. Moving swiftly toward us (so swiftly it seemed she did not intend stopping when she reached us but would sweep past us out the doorway which opened onto the sea and like Christ walk upon the water!), she was caught between the sunlight at her end of the building and the darkness inside—and for a moment she appeared to contain them both: the light in the long severe old-fashioned white dress she wore which brought the sense of a past that was still alive into our bustling present and in the snatch of white at her eye; the darkness in her black high-top shoes and in her face which was visible now that she was closer.

It was as stark and fleshless as a death mask, that face. The maggots might have already done their work, leaving only the framework of bone beneath the ruined skin and deep wells at the temple and jaw. But her eyes were alive, unnervingly so for one so old, with a sharp light that flicked out of the dim clouded depths like a lizard's tongue to snap up all in her view. Those eyes betrayed a child's curiosity about the world, and I wondered vaguely seeing them, and seeing the way the bodice of her ancient dress had collapsed in on her flat chest (what had happened to her breasts?), whether she might not be some kind of child at the same time that she was a woman, with fourteen children, my mother included to prove it. Perhaps she was both, both child and woman, darkness and light, past and present, life and death—all the opposites contained and reconciled in her.

"My Da-duh," my mother said formally and stepped forward. The name sounded like thunder fading softly in the distance.

"Child," Da-duh said, and her tone, her quick scrutiny of my mother, the brief embrace in which they appeared to shy from each other rather than touch, wiped out the fifteen years my mother had been away and restored the old relationship. My mother, who was such a formidable figure in my eyes, had suddenly with a word been reduced to my status.

"Yes, God is good," Da-duh said with a nod that was like a tic. "He has spared me to see my child again."

We were led forward then, apologetically because not only did Da-duh prefer boys but she also liked her grandchildren to be "white," that is, fair-skinned, and we had, I was to discover, a number of cousins, the outside children of white estate managers and the like, who qualified. We, though, were as black as she.

My sister being the oldest was presented first. "This one takes after the father," my mother said and waited to be reproved.

Frowning, Da-duh tilted my sister's face toward the light. But her frown soon gave way to a grudging smile, for my sister with her large mild eyes and little broad winged nose, with our father's high-cheeked Barbadian cast to her face, was pretty.

"She's goin' be lucky," Da-duh said and patted her once on the cheek. "Any girl child that takes after the father does be lucky."

She turned then to me. But oddly enough she did not touch me. Instead learning close, she peered hard at me, and then quickly drew back. I thought I saw her hand start up as though to shield her eyes. It was almost as if she saw not only me, a thin truculent child who it was said took after no one but myself, but something in me which for some reason she found disturbing, even threatening. We looked silently at each other for a long time in the noisy shed, our gaze locked. She was the first to look away.

"But Adry," she said to my mother and her laugh was cracked, thin, apprehensive. "Where did you get this one here with this fierce look?"

"We don't know where she came out of, my Da-duh," my mother said, laughing also. Even I smiled to myself. After all I had won the encounter. Da-duh had recognized my small strength—and this was all I ever asked of the adults in my life then.

"Come, soul," Da-duh said and took my hand. "You must be one of those New York terrors you hear so much about."

She led us, me at her side and my sister and mother behind, out of the shed into the sunlight that was like a bright driving summer rain and over to a group of people clustered beside a decrepit lorry. They were our relatives, most of them from St. Andrews although Da-duh herself lived in St. Thomas, the women wearing bright print dresses, the colors vivid against their darkness, the men rusty black suits that encased them like straightjackets. Da-duh, holding fast to my hand, became my anchor as they circled round us like a nervous sea, exclaiming, touching us with their calloused hands, embracing us shyly. They laughed in awed bursts, "But look Adry got big-big children!" /"And see the nice things they wearing, wrist watch and all!" / "I tell you. Adry has done all right for sheself in New York …."

Da-duh, ashamed at their wonder, embarrassed for them, admonished them the while. "But oh Christ," she said, "why you all got to get on like you never saw people from 'Away' before? You would think New York is the only place in the world to hear wunna. That's why I don't like to go anyplace with you St. Andrews people, you know. You all ain't been colonized."

We were in the back of the lorry finally, packed in among the barrels of ham, flour, cornmeal, and rice and the trunks of clothes that my mother had brought as gifts. We made our way slowly through Bridgetown's clogged streets, part of a funeral procession of cars and open-sided buses, bicycles and donkey carts. The dim little limestone shops and offices along the way marched with us, at the same mournful pace, toward the same grave ceremony—as did the people, the women balancing huge baskets on top their heads as if they were no more than hats they wore to shade them from the sun. Looking over the edge of the lorry I watched as their feet slurred the dust. I listened, and their voices, raw and loud and dissonant in the heat, seemed to be grappling with each other high overhead.

Da-duh sat on a trunk in our midst, a monarch amid her court. She still held my hand, but it was different now. I had suddenly become her anchor, for I felt her fear of the lorry with its asthmatic motor (a fear and distrust, I later learned, she held of all machines) beating like a pulse in her rough palm.

As soon as we left Bridgetown behind though, she relaxed, and while the others around us talked she gazed at the canes standing tall on either side of the winding marl road. "C'dear," she said softly to herself after a time. "The canes this side are pretty enough."

They were too much for me. I thought of them as giant weeds that had overrun the island, leaving scarcely any room for the small tottering houses of sunbleached pine we passed or the people, dark streaks as our lorry hurtled by. I suddenly feared that we were journeying, unaware that we were, toward some dangerous place where the canes, grown as high and thick as a forest, would close in on us and run us through with their stiletto blades. I longed then for the familiar; for the street in Brooklyn where I lived, for my father who had refused to accompany us ("Blowing out good money on foolishness," he had said of the trip), for a game of tag with my friends under the chestnut tree outside our aging brownstone house.

"Yes, but wait till you see St. Thomas canes," Da-duh was saying to me. "They's canes father, bo," she gave a proud arrogant nod. "Tomorrow, God willing, I goin' take you out in the ground and show them to you."

True to her word, Da-duh took me with her the following day out into the ground. It was a fairly large plot adjoining her weathered board and shingle house and consisting of a small orchard, a good-sized canepiece and behind the canes, where the land sloped abruptly down, a gully. She had purchased it with Panama money sent her by her eldest son, my uncle Joseph, who had died working on the canal. We entered the ground along a trail no wider than her body and as devious and complex as her reasons for showing me her land. Da-duh strode briskly ahead, her slight form filled out this morning by the layers of sacking petticoats she wore under her working dress to protect her against the damp. A fresh white cloth, elaborately arranged around her head, added to her height, and lent her a vain, almost roguish air.

Her pace slowed once we reached the orchard, and glancing back at me occasionally over her shoulder, she pointed out the various trees.

"This here is a breadfruit," she said. "That one yonder is a papaw. Here's a guava. This is a mango. I know you don't have anything like these in New York.

Here's a sugar apple." (The fruit looked more like artichokes than apples to me.) "This one bears limes ... " She went on for some time, intoning the names of the trees as though they were those of her gods. Finally, turning to me, she said, "I know you don't have anything this nice where you come from." Then, as I hesitated: "I said I know you don't have anything this nice where you come from ...."

"No," I said, and my world did seem suddenly lacking.

Da-duh nodded and passed on. The orchard ended and we were on the narrow cart road that led through the canepiece, the canes clashing like swords above my cowering head. Again she turned and her thin muscular arms spread wide, her dim gaze embracing the small field of canes, she said—and her voice almost broke under the weight of her pride—"Tell me, have you got anything like these in that place where you were born?"

"No."

"I din' think so. I bet you don't even know that these canes here and the sugar you eat is one and the same thing. That they does throw the canes into some damn machine at the factory and squeeze out all the little life in them to make sugar for you in New York to eat. I bet you don't know that."

"I've got two cavities and I'm not allowed to eat a lot of sugar."

But Da-duh didn't hear me. She had turned with an inexplicably angry motion and was making her way rapidly out of the canes and down the slope at the edge of the field which led to the gully below. Following her apprehensively down the incline amid a stand of banana plants whose leaves flapped like elephants ears in the wind, I found myself in the middle of a small tropical wood—a place dense and damp and gloomy and tremulous with the fitful play of light and shadow as the leaves high above moved against the sun that was almost hidden from view. It was a violent place, the tangled foliage fighting each other for a chance at the sunlight, the branches of the trees locked in what seemed an immemorial struggle, one both necessary and inevitable. But despite the violence, it was pleasant, almost peaceful in the gully, and beneath the thick undergrowth the earth smelled like spring.

This time Da-duh didn't even bother to ask her usual question, but simply turned and waited for me to speak.

"No," I said, my head bowed. "We don't have anything like this in New York."

"Ah," she cried, her triumph complete. "I din' think so. Why, I've heard that's a place where you can walk till you drop and never see a tree."

"We've got a chestnut tree in front of our house," I said.

"Does it bear?" She waited. "I ask you, does it bear?"

"Not anymore," I muttered. "It used to, but not anymore."

She gave the nod that was like a nervous twitch. "You see," she said. "Nothing can bear there." Then, secure behind her scorn, she added, "But tell me, what's this snow like that you hear so much about?"

Looking up, I studied her closely, sensing my chance, and then I told her, describing at length and with as much drama as I could summon not only what snow in the city was like, but what it would be like here, in her perennial summer kingdom.

" ... And you see all these trees you got here," I said. "Well, they'd be bare. No leaves, no fruit, nothing. They'd be covered in snow. You see your canes. They'd be buried under tons of snow. The snow would be higher than your head, higher than your house, and you wouldn't be able to come down into this here gully because it would be snowed under ... "

She searched my face for the lie, still scornful but intrigued. "What a thing, huh?" she said finally, whispering it softly to herself.

"And when it snows you couldn't dress like you are now," I said. "Oh no, you'd freeze to death. You'd have to wear a hat and gloves and galoshes and ear muffs so your ears wouldn't freeze and drop off, and a heavy coat. I've got a Shirley Temple coat with fur on the collar. I can dance. You wanna see?"

Before she could answer I began, with a dance called the Truck which was popular back in the 1930s. My right forefinger waving, I trucked around the nearby trees and around Da-duh's awed and rigid form. After the Truck I did the Suzy-Q, my lean hips swishing, my sneakers sliding zigzag over the ground. "I can sing," I said and did so, starting with "I'm Gonna Sit Right Down and Write Myself a Letter," then without pausing, "Tea for Two," and ending with "I Found a Million Dollar Baby in a Five and Ten Cent Store."

For long moments afterwards Da-duh stared at me as if I were a creature from Mars, an emissary from some world she did not know but which intrigued her and whose power she both felt and feared. Yet something about my performance must have pleased her, because bending down she slowly lifted her long skirt and then, one by one, the layers of petticoats until she came to a drawstring purse dangling at the end of a long strip of cloth tied round her waist. Opening the purse she handed me a penny. "Here," she said half-smiling against her will. "Take this to buy yourself a sweet at the shop up the road. There's nothing to be done with you, soul."

From then on, whenever I wasn't taken to visit relatives, I accompanied Da-duh out into the ground, and alone with her amid the canes or down in the gully I told her about New York. It always began with some slighting remark on her part: "I know they don't have anything this nice where you come from," or "Tell me, I hear those foolish people in New York does do such and such...." But as I answered, re-creating my towering world of steel and concrete and machines for her, building the city out of words, I would feel her give way. I came to know the signs of her surrender: the total stillness that would come over her little hard dry form, the probing gaze that like a surgeon's knife sought to cut through my skull to get at the images there, to see if I were lying, above all, her fear, a fear nameless and profound, the same one I had felt beating in the palm of her hand that day in the lorry.

Over the weeks I told her about refrigerators, radios, gas stoves, elevators, trolley cars, wringer washing machines, movies, airplanes, the cyclone at Coney Island, subways, toasters, electric lights: "At night, see, all you have to do is flip this little switch on the wall and all the lights in the house go on just like that. Like magic. It's like turning on the sun at night."

"But tell me," she said to me once with a faint mocking smile, "do the white people have all these things too or it's only the people looking like us?"

I laughed. "What d'ya mean," I said. "The white people have even better." Then: "I beat up a white girl in my class last term."

"Beating up white people!" Her tone was incredulous.

"How you mean!" I said, using an expression of hers. "She called me a name."

For some reason Da-duh could not quite get over this and repeated in the same hushed, shocked voice, "Beating up white people now! Oh, the lord, the world's changing up so I can scarce recognize it anymore."

One morning toward the end of our stay, Da-duh led me into a part of the gully that we had never visited before, an area darker and more thickly overgrown than the rest, almost impenetrable. There in a small clearing amid the dense bush, she stopped before an incredibly tall royal palm which rose cleanly out of the ground, and drawing the eye up with it, soared high above the trees around it into the sky. It appeared to be touching the blue dome of sky, to be flaunting its dark crown of fronds right in the blinding white face of the late morning sun.

Da-duh watched me a long time before she spoke, and then she said very quietly, "All right, now, tell me if you've got anything this tall in that place you're from."

I almost wished, seeing her face, that I could have said no. "Yes," I said. "We've got buildings hundreds of times this tall in New York. There's one called the Empire State Building that's the tallest in the world. My class visited it last year and I went all the way to the top. It's got over a hundred floors. I can't describe how tall it is. Wait a minute. What's the name of that hill I went to visit the other day, where they have the police station?"

"You mean Bissex?"

"Yes, Bissex. Well, the Empire State Building is way taller than that."

"You're lying now!" she shouted, trembling with rage. Her hand lifted to strike me.

"No, I'm not," I said. "It really is, if you don't believe me I'll send you a picture postcard of it as soon as I get back home so you can see for yourself. But it's way taller than Bissex."

All the fight went out of her at that. The hand poised to strike me fell limp to her side, and as she stared at me, seeing not me but the building that was taller than the highest hill she knew, the small stubborn light in her eyes (it was the same amber as the flame in the kerosene lamp she lit at dusk) began to fail. Finally, with a vague gesture that even in the midst of her defeat still tried to dismiss me and my world, she turned and started back through the gully, walking slowly, her steps groping and uncertain, as if she were suddenly no longer sure of the way, while I followed triumphant yet strangely saddened behind.

The next morning I found her dressed for our morning walk but stretched out on the Berbice chair in the tiny drawing room where she sometimes napped during the afternoon heat, her face turned to the window beside her. She appeared thinner and suddenly indescribably old.

"My Da-duh," I said.

"Yes, nuh," she said. Her voice was listless and the face she slowly turned my way was, now that I think back on it, like a Benin mask, the features drawn and almost distorted by an ancient abstract sorrow.

"Don't you feel well?" I asked.

"Girl, I don't know."

"My Da-duh, I goin' boil you some bush tea," my aunt, Da-duh's youngest child, who lived with her, called from the shed roof kitchen.

"Who tell you I need bush tea?" she cried, her voice assuming for a moment its old authority. "You can't even rest nowadays without some malicious person looking for you to be dead. Come girl," she motioned to me to a place beside her on the old-fashioned lounge chair, "give us a tune."

I sang for her until breakfast at eleven, all my brash irreverent Tin Pan Alley songs, and then just before noon we went out into the ground. But it was a short, dispirited walk. Da-duh didn't even notice that the mangoes were beginning to ripen and would have to be picked before the village boys got to them. And when she paused occasionally and looked out across the canes or up at her trees it wasn't as if she were seeing them but something else. Some huge, monolithic shape had imposed itself, it seemed, between her and the land, obstructing her vision. Returning to the house she slept the entire afternoon on the Berbice chair.

She remained like this until we left, languishing away the mornings on the chair at the window gazing out at the land as if it were already doomed; then, at noon, taking the brief stroll with me through the ground during which she seldom spoke, and afterwards returning home to sleep till almost dusk sometimes.

On the day of our departure she put on the austere, ankle-length white dress, the black shoes and brown felt hat (her town clothes she called them), but she did not go with us to town. She saw us off on the road outside her house and in the midst of my mother's tearful protracted farewell, she leaned down and whispered in my ear, "Girl, you're not to forget now to send me the picture of that building, you hear."

By the time I mailed her the large colored picture postcard of the Empire State Building she was dead. She died during the famous '37 strike which began shortly after we left. On the day of her death England sent planes flying low over the island in a show of force—so low, according to my aunt's letter, that the downdraft from them shook the ripened mangoes from the trees in Da-duh's orchard. Frightened, everyone in the village fled into the canes. Except Da-duh. She remained in the house at the window so my aunt said, watching as the planes came swooping and screaming like monstrous birds down over the village, over her house, rattling her trees and flattening the young canes in her field. It must have seemed to her lying there that they did not intend pulling out of their dive, but like the hardback beetles which hurled themselves with suicidal force against the walls of the house at night, those menacing silver shapes would hurl themselves in an ecstasy of self-immolation on the land, destroying it utterly.

When the planes finally left and the villagers returned they found her dead on the Berbice chair at the window.

She died and I lived, but always, to this day even, within the shadow of her death. For a brief period after I was grown I went to live alone, like one doing penance, in a loft above a noisy factory in downtown New York and there painted seas of sugarcane and huge swirling Van Gogh suns and palm trees striding like brightly-plumed Tutsi warriors across a tropical landscape, while the thunderous tread of the machines downstairs jarred the floor beneath my easel, mocking my efforts.

Kristin Hunter

(b. 1931)

A native Philadelphian who began writing features for the Pittsburgh **Courier** *when she was only fourteen, Kristin Hunter is the only child of two educators who encouraged her to become a teacher. However, shortly after graduating with a bachelor's degree in education from the University of Pennsylvania, Hunter decided to drop her job as a third-grade teacher and pursue a career in writing. She became a copywriter for the Lavenson Bureau of Advertising where she eventually wrote and produced a television documentary,* **Minority of One**, *which won a CBS Fund for the Republic Prize. While juggling freelance writing assignments with various other jobs, Hunter wrote her first novel,* **God Bless the Child**. *Published to wide critical acclaim in 1964, this tragic story about a woman who tries to escape the slums was followed by a novel about a white ghetto landlord,* **The Landlord** *(1966). Hunter also wrote the screenplay for the 1970 film adaptation of* **The Landlord**.*

Praised for her realistic and optimistic treatment of Black city life, Hunter has also been recognized for her contributions to young adult literature. Her best-selling young adult novel about young musicians, **The Soul Brothers and Sister Lou** *(1968), won the Council on Interracial Books Children's Award, the Mass Media Brotherhood Award, and the Lewis Carroll Shelf Award. In addition, her highly acclaimed story collection,* **Guests in the Promised Land**, *was nominated for the National Book Award and received the Chicago* **Tribune** *Book World Prize in 1973. A regular contributor to such publications as* **Nation**, **Essence**, *and* **Good Housekeeping**, *Hunter has been anthologized in Langston Hughes's* **The Best Short Stories by Negro Writers** *(1967). She has been teaching creative writing at the University of Pennsylvania since 1972.*

The Jewel in the Lotus

Doc Earl Eisey was one of the Eisey brothers but not the ones famous for soul singing. He was known more for soul seeing. And maybe not beyond his immediate neighborhood of Little South Point but that was fame enough for Doc, who lived alone in the Father-Son-and-Holy-Ghost house he had been born in and where seekers of all kinds tried to visit him. Those he didn't want to see never found the house. Those he did, whether they came from around the corner or from Tanzania, always found the door unlocked and Doc home.

Numbers had predestined Doc for greatness from birth. He was born on the 22nd of September, 1921, just before the sun rolled out of Virgo and into The Balance. He weighed 9 pounds and 2 ounces at birth and vibrated to a high number 9. Address of the Father-Son-and-Holy-Ghost was 922 South 19th Street, located in the Ninth Precinct, Twenty-second Ward. He was not the seventh son, but the third after a pair of twins. Doc Earl Eisey had been a twin himself, but his brother Eric died in the womb they shared.

Doc told me so, late one night after the last client had been sent home whole and glorious and we were polishing off a bottle of his Dom Perignon and a pot of my peas and rice. Doc told me he always felt that, being such a big baby, he'd crowded his twin Eric out of the world. Also that he had to be the 4th son because $2 + 2 = 4$. Which is as simple and as deep as $E = Mc^2$ if you have Doc Eisey's kind of vision. If you don't, no eyeglasses will help you see my point, but later for that part.

When he was seven Doc was tested and found to have 20/20 vision and an I.Q. of over 200, which means way above the limits of the testing scale, 100 being what testing types consider normal. Doc decided he had inherited his twin's intelligence along with his own.

That thought troubled him even as he noticed with satisfaction that at age 9 he weighed 72 pounds; at age 12, a scrawny 99; and that at age 21 he was exactly 72 inches tall. That was the year he returned home from Fort Benning on compassionate leave to look after his failing parents while his older brothers Judson and Perry marched off to their respective deaths in the Pacific and European theaters. The next year saw Doc's entire family buried, his parents in Southwark Cemetery, and his brothers in France and on an atoll somewhere in the South Pacific.

Doc returned to duty with the 372nd Infantry and asked the C.O. to be assigned to the chaplain corps. Request denied because he had no seminary diploma or certificates to support his contention that he was a priest. Then he asked to be assigned to the medical corps as a healer. Request denied for the above reasons. He was assigned to the kitchen corps, where he was frequently observed peeling whole onions, removing each spherical layer intact, saying the onion was the holy lotus and there was a jewel at its center. He would get down to the jewel, the innermost bud, and then ask anyone who happened to be present, "But what is at the center of the jewel?"

His medical discharge came through in six weeks, with a recommendation that he be placed in a "low-stress" civilian job.

On his 22nd birthday, September 22, 1943, Doc re-arranged the little three-room house to suit himself. Son, the first floor, remained his cooking and eating and visiting/consulting room. Father, the second-story room where his parents had slept, became Doc's bedroom and bath. Holy Ghost, the top floor, once the boys' bedroom, received the most attention because it was to be his study. Bookcases, tables, a desk, and such objects as wands, charts, prisms and pyramids were carefully chosen and arranged there. Its door was kept locked and Doc wore the key around his neck.

Doc began to study The Secrets relentlessly and systematically. He believed his intellectual gifts had to be put to some better use than sorting mail at the South Branch Post Office because he bore the weight of at least two unfulfilled lies, maybe four.

Doc trained himself to live on four hours of sleep in Father plus an occasional fifteen-minute nap on the floor of Holy Ghost. The rest of the time, day or night, and there was no telling the difference in that house with its heavy curtains, he pored over the Rosicrucian books, the Bible, the Kaballah, the Koran and the Masonic texts which had come his way magically, left for him on park and bus station benches, without his ever joining any lodge. He moved from Zen and Confucian writings to the I Ching and Karl Jung's commentaries. From Swedenborg and Mary Baker Eddy to Simone Weil and Kierkegaard and even more subtle philosophers. When he was grappling with an especially difficult concept such as Being is All-One-Ness and Non-Being is All-Nothingness, Embrace Both, the neighbors thought a dog chained up in one of the tiny yards was howling at the moon.

Doc continued to study. He read books on yoga, spiritualism and ESP. Learned to put himself into trance states in which he attempted to contact his brothers on the astral plane. But they remained silent and remote, Judson in France, Perry on his atoll, Eric in whatever container they had flung the wastes of the womb they shared.

One morning or afternoon, Doc never could tell the difference, he was studying a chapter on live stones and talismans when he began to have eye trouble. Jasper and jade changed places; amethyst shimmered in purple waves across the page; opals and amber danced in blue, green, and yellow spots before his vision. He continued to read until the print began to grow living spikes and spurs and his mind seemed like a large clouded crystal.

Doc Eisey descended to Son, where he had to put his face close to his father's wind-up Westclox to discover it was three o'clock. He suspected it was P.M., not A.M., but he had to look through the curtains and see daylight to make sure. He was right; in two hours he had to be at the P.O. to pull his 5 P.M. to 1 A.M. shift.

Maybe it was the unfamiliar sunlight that made Doc Eisey fear blindness coming on. But he managed to make it through the golden shimmer up 19th Street and around the corner to Main Point Avenue. His destination, The Gold Vision Centre, Walk In, No One Refused, was too big a target to miss. It had a gigantic pair of eyeglasses hanging above the sidewalk. The lenses were usually blank but today Doc Eisey thought he saw three golden eyes staring at him, two inside the lenses, one between. This apparition, especially the larger eye in the center, helped him move faster.

Business was not brisk in Doc Gold's. There was no Medicaid in those days and therefore no waiting.

"You haven't been reading a lot lately, have you, Earl?" the optometrist asked after he discovered Doc couldn't read even the big E at the top of the chart.

"Sure have, Dave," replied Doc Eisey, never one to go along with first-naming on first-time business contacts or fourth-time ones for that matter. If they wanted his money they would have to give him his respect. And even if he couldn't read the chart he could read this white man. Who thought Doc was illiterate. Who wanted to be called Doctor Gold in return for Earl. Who, on getting his first name back instead, almost dropped the lens he was putting into the examining apparatus.

"Better, Mister Easy?" he asked cautiously.

'E, W K L D, M R Z V L U E T, b x e d c z r v," Doc recited, and so on down to the bottom of the chart. "My name is Eisey."

"I see."

"No you don't, but that's close. And *I* see, which is more to the point, since it is what I came here for. It will be a girl."

"What?" exclaimed the doctor, dropping his pen.

"That baby your wife is pregnant with will be a girl. Born May thirteenth of this year, 1945."

Doc Gold tried to ignore this. "Your eyes are 20/200. That means you can only see—"

"—at twenty feet what I ought to see at two hundred," Doc concluded. "Good."

"Not good."

"I know but I like the numbers. She will finish college, marry a doctor, have two children, get divorced, take her divorce settlement and run off to Mexico with a migrant farm laborer. But this year, at least, she will make you happy. And for the next 25 years as well."

"Have you ever worn glasses before, Mr. Icy?"

"No."

"Too much reading in insufficient light can cause myopia."

"I know. I need glasses and you are going to prescribe them. You are going to charge me enough to take care of three months' payments on your new DeSoto. Better have the steering column checked, it's defective."

"You saw it parked out front!" Doc Gold screamed.

"Calm down, please. How could I? Your wife has it today. You didn't want her driving around in her seventh month, but she won the argument. She usually does. Don't worry, driving won't cause her to abort, but someday you'll wish it had."

"That will be nine dollars for the examination," Doc Gold said, trying very hard to sound professional and restore the reversed doctor-patient roles. "Let me recommend these frames. A new compound imported from France. Heavy duty, rugged and masculine. Do you like them?"

Doc Eisey tried to see himself in the trembling mirror but had to take it from the optometrist's hands for a steady look. The square black frames matched his crisp hair and mustache and complemented his high brown cheekbones. For the first time Doc Eisey realized he was handsome. He handed the mirror back. "Yes, I do. But it doesn't matter. You'll charge me the same price no matter what frames I select.

That's a valuable ruby but you shouldn't wear it. You're a fish, born March 16th, 1920. Give the stone to your rammy wife, keep the setting and put an aquamarine in it."

"It's all I have." Doc Gold said pathetically. "She's already loaded with diamonds."

"I know. She should be. Save your strength for the big arguments and let her win the little ones. Otherwise you'll have to contend with your bullheaded no-neck mother-in-law. And three bossy women will be too overbearing for your son."

"What son? I don't have any son."

"He will be born on your birthday, March 16th, three years from now. He will be sensitive, emotional and easily overwhelmed, like you. Name him Samuel if you want him to excel you, Saul if you don't. A 6 beats a 5 any day, and a 5 beats a 4. Buy that house in Florida and put your mother-in-law in it as soon as possible."

"Everyone thinks I'm a rich man," Doc Gold complained.

"You will be. And you will thank me for my advice in the future. The house in Florida will be a fine place to get rid of your mother-in-law now, and to send your wife and daughter and son-in-law later when they get on your nerves. You should never go there under any circumstances even though you will have to pay for it.

"The glasses will be ninety dollars. Plus nine for the examination."

"Too much, but I like the numbers," Doc Eisey said. "Don't let your son go to Florida after his sixth birthday, if you can help it. Certainly not after his bar mitzvah."

"You certainly know a lot of interesting things," Doc Gold complimented him excitedly. "You know, you are an extremely well educated man. Very different from the usual class of customer I get in here."

"I don't want to hear that 'special Negro' hockey," Doc told him. "And don't waste time telling me to cut down on my reading, either, because I won't."

"Then rest your eyes ten minutes out of every hour."

Doc considered this but made no promises. "When will my glasses be ready?"

"Sometime next week. I'll call you. In the meantime, I'll need a deposit."

"You can get them in three days and you know it. Two if you really push the lab but I'll give you three. This is Tuesday. I'll be back on Friday. I'll pay you your ninety-nine dollars then in cash and not one cent before. I know you're overcharging me but I'll pay because I like the numbers."

And Doc Eisey strolled out of that office with the tall cool lopsided glide like a skater's, leaning to keep balance on the curves, that had everybody calling him Doc Icy. That plus his seemingly aloof manner. He was cold to strangers, cool to casuals, warm to friends, of which he soon had plenty.

Don Eisey sorted mail by intuition for three nights, picked up his eyeglasses on Friday, warned Doc Gold again about that steering column, came home and resumed reading his text on gems. He was already seeing with the third eye and had lenses to correct the other two, but he thought a talisman might help all three vision centers.

After several hours of studying in Holy Ghost, he decided a tiger's eye would serve him best. He ran down to Father and rummaged in bureau drawers for his father's wedding-anniversary cuff links. In his haste he dropped his new glasses. The new, rugged, heavy-duty compound split cleanly in half at the bridge, leaving the lenses intact but separate. Doc lay down with half an eyeglass in each hand and some choice curses for Doc Gold on his lips.

But before sleep took him completely, there was a light floaty interval in which his brothers spoke to him for the first time. "Heal," said Eric, his own twin, who said he would have become a doctor at Meharry had he lived. "Preach," said Judson, the eldest, who had planned to use his G.I. bill to attend Morris Brown Theological Seminary. "Teach," said Perry, who had intended to major in education at North Carolina Central. "But," he added, "only teach the deserving ones. Doc Gold for instance is not worthy of your anger, let alone your gifts."

"But these eyeglasses are shoddy goods," Doc answered in his inner voice. "He cheated me."

"Mend," said his twin Eric when Doc woke in the same trance state several hours later. "Mend, then heal."

Doc's eyes were sharp enough now to find some Magic Mend glue at the back of the kitchen cabinet in Son. He carefully mended the glasses with it and left them on the kitchen table. Went out strolling in the sunny humming Saturday neighborhood, feeling and looking fine and noticing that people moved away from him or drew closer to him as he chose. When he came home he brought with him his first pupil, 14-year-old Boothby Carruthers, a mathematical genius who had been flunked by teachers too stupid to understand him. They spent an hour on quantum theory, information theory, logarithms and relativity, communicating rapidly with thoughts spilling over words. Before Boothby left Doc had him set up for his G.E.D. on Monday, his S.A.T. on Saturday, and M.I.T. in the fall.

His first patient was 92-year-old Mary Gathers, who'd broken her hip while carrying a great-great grandchild down some do-funny landlord's rickety stairs. Doc held his hand a couple of inches over her hip, jolted her with about 20 volts of magnetism, and told her to get up and boogie. She did. Then he asked her how long she wanted to live. Long enough to see the youngest great-great reach 18, she said, on account of the great who was his mother was doing so poorly. Mary Gathers, a practical nurse who'd never thought of retiring, lamented some about each generation getting weaker and more wayward and all. Doc promised her she'd live to 108, and reminded her that exceptional anything tends to skip generations. His own parents had been supremely ordinary but his grandfather come to think of it had been a root doctor who could cure anything. Mary admitted on reflection that her grands were doing better than her immediates and was consoled by the idea that the greats might not amount to much but the great-greats ought to move mountains. Cheered immensely, she got up and boogied home.

Doc was just about to start rummaging for his grandfather's herb books and journals when his first disciple walked in. A tall leggy beauty with an oval indentation in her forehead between wide-set hazel eyes. She called herself Tallulah because her parents had named her Sapphire and that was not a righteous name, meaning a brassy, bossy, hands-on-wide-hips auntie stereo type with an amplified bass voice. "Tallulah's the same thing in whiteface," Doc Eisey informed her. "And you do not have a white face. Of course you could call yourself Lula; that's a 4 and so are you."

"Lula sounds kind of countrified to me," she responded. "And I'm strictly a city kiddie."

"How about Jade?" he suggested. "Jade's a 4 and it's also a good talisman for you. Get an oval piece and wear it in that concave spot there."

Her eyes on either side of the dent turned black. "The name's O.K., but I don't like to call attention to the hole in my head. I don't appreciate you mentioning it, either. That's where the doctors took out the brain tumor."

"And opened the path for you to see beyond material barriers. The gemstone would strengthen your inner vision and also keep outsiders from looking in. Look here, at this passage about the stones and their affinities."

But Jade had to read the passage out loud to him because he still needed the glasses, though not as much as before.

"Excuse me," Doc said, and went to get them. The Magic Mend had worked but there was an ugly crust of it at the seam. He started to curse Doc Gold again but Judson warned him against wasting his energy in destructive channels. So Doc turned it positive and creative and glued the square-set tiger's eye from his father's cuff link over the unsightly join.

He showed the results to Jade. "Now, since I don't have an indentation at the inner-vision site, I'm going to wear this. It's a good invention."

"Some white man will steal it off you and get rich," she told him.

Doc acknowledged she was probably right. "But," he said, "even if they steal it they won't know how to use it."

Doc Eisey wore the glasses from then on, attributing to them the increase in his powers to read and move people from a distance. First he could read them from a block away, and then ten blocks, and then miles. As his vision lengthened his powers strengthened, helping him send the hustlers and pseudos packing while he attracted more worthy pupils, patients and disciples.

Jade, the first disciple, became his apprentice and then his assistant. She also cooked and did a few other things for him around the house. Often she wanted to sleep over too, but Judson had admonished him, "Work and pray," and Doc took that to mean no time out for pleasure.

Jade pouted over this for awhile, but finally accepted it and became very brisk and businesslike. She was very good at starting pupils at their right levels of development and coaxing them soft-voiced to move on at their proper rate of progress, and she looked very good with that green gem between her large tawny eyes that flashed a matching green at intense moments. Often those green beacons beckoned so brightly Doc had to look away.

Jade was very accurate about worldly matters, too. Strolling past the Gold Vision Centre one morning, Doc Eisey saw a new window display: "Our Latest 'Gold Originals'! Genuine or Simulated Birthstones in Flattering Frames."

Business was brisk, the people along Main Point Avenue loving flash. Coming out of there in stumbling streams with their inner vision warped by wrong stones or blocked by dead ones. Some of them so messed up they were walking backwards from helping Doc Gold pay for the Florida house.

"I see," said Doc Eisey sadly, and went around the corner and put $100 on 999 and hit for fifty thousand.

With it he opened his first Inner Vision Centre for which Jade wrote the proposals for enough feasibility study, seed, research, demonstration, development, planning and training grants to keep the Centre and its spinoffs going for a couple of centuries.

But by now even the dime stores were selling Simulated Simulated Gold Originals and the people were bumping into each other all over the place because their headlights were so badly misaligned.

"What we gonna do, Doc?" a worried Jade asked. "The ones who come here are OK but the masses are more messed up than ever. They can't even walk without stumbling all over their own feet, let alone dance. When things were at their worse we never used to have that kind of problem."

"I don't know," Doc Eisey replied. "All we can do is go on teaching the worthy and hope there will eventually be enough of them to straighten out the masses and their mixed-up glasses."

"Don't you think we ought to get married?"

"Not yet," he told her. "I'm too young to settle down."

"You're 36. How long do I have to wait?"

"I have a life expectancy of 72 times 4, which is to say 288 years. I guess I'll get married sometime in mid-life, say around the year 2150."

Jade, who had taken to wearing drapey dresses in her name shade, brushed silkily against him. Doc felt like the door of a blast furnace had been opened in front of him, and stiffened.

"They sure don't call you Doc Icy for nothin'," Jade grumbled. "And here I be hanging around here working for you day and night, teaching The Secrets to the Beginners, Advanced, Apprentice and Adept groups, plus shopping and cooking and cleaning house and—"

"Wait a minute," Doc said with a finger upraised for silence. A strong flash was coming through from all three of his brothers. The message was, "Work and *Play*."

"I didn't hear it right the first time," he said. "Come here, girl."

A pile of green silk slithered to the floor and they fell on top of it. With all that pent-up passion to let loose, Doc didn't pay attention to much else for awhile. But then he groped around the floor for his glasses and found they had split in two again.

"I should have followed the first advice," he said. "Look what happened. This proves it. Fooling around dissipates the Higher Energy."

"Wait a minute, fool," Jade said. "You think your higher power is controlled by some plastic artifact or somepin'? Can you see me? What do you see?"

"I see a fine brown mama who is so turned off the black tips on her titties have stopped sticking out and are inverted. Who is so mad her eyes are flashing from brown to green to black and *back*."

"Pupil enlargement. I can do it whenever I want to."

"I taught you."

"Of course. What else? Can you see *into* the pupils? Can you read me?"

"Of course. You're thinking, 'With all his studying, this fool has over-educated himself. He been dealing too much with Augustinian writers and all their born-evil, bad-body messages. Result is he thinks his powers can't work along with his nature. Error is thinking they're distinct and separate. Also he thinks he needs a pair of fancy decorated glasses to see with, when all the time . . .I *see!*'"

"Yes. You're 20/20 on all counts, all over."

Their eyes locked in a long meaningful look. Two small candle flames flared up in Jade's, but she extinguished them. "No, you don't see it all yet. You still don't think you can use your nature without losing your power. You don't see the only way to use it is *not* to use it. There's no end to the power because it comes from a bottomless well, long as you keep steady dipping. You may see someday but by that time, even if you ain't dried up, I'll be too old. And I'm a hot-natured woman so I best be on my way soon as I finish up a few things we started around here."

Jade told me all this after I moved from Apprentice to Adept class and starting preparing to take over her job. The fad for Simulated Gold Originals peaked and died down after Doc stopped wearing his glasses, except for the mirrored ones he uses for disguise. The masses have begun to walk straight again and have stopped having so many pedestrian accidents. Our teachers are beginning to get some of their minds back on center too.

Jade went out to the West Coast to open Doc's first spin-off school and train managers for the other Inner Vision Centres in 22 Third World countries.

Doc Gold's daughter got admitted to the one in Chihuahua on account of her Mexican second husband and is starting to get herself straightened out.

Doc Eisey is 59 and taking good care of himself, looking maybe a distinguished 42, far from being near the end of the first of his four lives. But he's speeded up his life plan a little, about to take on a steady mate. Name of Amber (a 5 beats a 4 anytime). Age over 40 but I look 30 thanks to the studies and treatments and I switch a mean switch in the kitchen, the classroom and the bedroom. Which is to say I'm tight with the Father, the Son and Holy Ghost. As any woman Doc picks for his first-lifetime mate and partner has to be.

Toni Morrison

(b. 1931)

*One of the most accomplished prose stylists of the twentieth century, Toni Morrison writes to "transfigure the complexity and wealth of Afro-American culture into a language worthy of the culture." Her efforts have resulted in six richly allusive and precisely crafted novels about "how people behave ... when their backs are up against the wall": **The Bluest Eye** (1969), **Sula** (1973), **Song of Solomon** (1977), **Tar Baby** (1981), **Beloved** (1987), and **Jazz** (1992). While all of her novels have inspired the lush praise of academics, critics, and general readers alike, Morrison's best-known work is the Pulitzer Prize–winning **Beloved**, a powerful, often harrowing ghost story about a Black fugitive slave who kills her baby to spare it from a life of slavery.*

Born Chloe Anthony Wofford in Ohio, Morrison grew up in an atmosphere steeped in black folklore, music, ritual, myth, and storytelling. An avid reader who favored Jane Austen and Gustave Flaubert when she was "a little black girl in Lorraine, Ohio," Morrison was influenced by her early exposure to the classics of American and European literature. In 1953, she graduated from Howard University, where she majored in English and minored in Classics. Morrison then earned her master's degree in English from Cornell University in 1955. After briefly teaching at Texas Southern University, she returned to Howard University as a professor. In 1964, without giving up her teaching responsibilities, Morrison became a senior editor at Random House. During her twenty years in that position she championed such writers as Toni Cade Bambara, Angela Davis, and Henry Dumas, while publishing her own four novels. She left Random House in 1984 when she was appointed to the Albert Schweitzer Chair of the Humanities at the State University of New York at Albany. At present, Morrison is the Robert F. Goheen Professor of the Council of the Humanities at Princeton University, where she teaches Afro-American Studies and creative writing.

*Morrison has also written a play, **Dreaming Emmett** (1986), numerous essays and short stories, and two volumes of criticism, **Playing in the Dark: Whiteness and the Literary Imagination** (1993) and **Race-ing Justice, En-gendering Power** (1992). Perhaps her own best critic, she has graciously acknowledged that her literary success is due in part to the efforts of her readers, whose "ruminations" and "knowingness" must "fill in" the spaces she leaves open in her stories, and to the work of those critics "for whom the study of Afro-American literature is not a crash course in neighborliness and tolerance ... but the serious study of art forms that have much work to do."*

Recitatif

My mother danced all night and Roberta's was sick. That's why we were taken to St. Bonny's. People want to put their arms around you when you tell them you were in a shelter, but it really wasn't bad. No big long room with one hundred beds like Bellevue. There were four to a room, and when Roberta and me came, there was a shortage of state kids, so we were the only ones assigned to 406 and could go from bed to bed if we wanted to. And we wanted to, too. We changed beds every night and for the whole four months we were there we never picked one out as our own permanent bed.

It didn't start out that way. The minute I walked in and the Big Bozo introduced us, I got sick to my stomach. It was one thing to be taken out of your own bed early in the morning—it was something else to be stuck in a strange place with a girl from a whole other race. And Mary, that's my mother, she was right. Every now and then she would stop dancing long enough to tell me something important and one of the things she said was that they never washed their hair and they smelled funny. Roberta sure did. Smell funny, I mean. So when the Big Bozo (nobody ever called her Mrs. Itkin, just like nobody ever said St. Bonaventure)—when she said, "Twyla, this is Roberta. Roberta, this is Twyla. Make each other welcome," I said, "My mother won't like you putting me in here."

"Good," said Bozo. "Maybe then she'll come and take you home."

How's that for mean? If Roberta had laughed I would have killed her, but she didn't. She just walked over to the window and stood with her back to us.

"Turn around," said the Bozo. "Don't be rude. Now Twyla. Roberta. When you hear a loud buzzer, that's the call for dinner. Come down to the first floor. Any fights and no movie." And then, just to make sure we knew what we would be missing, "*The Wizard of Oz.*"

Roberta must have thought I meant that my mother would be mad about my being put in the shelter. Not about rooming with her, because as soon as Bozo left she came over to me and said, "Is your mother sick too?"

"No," I said. "She just likes to dance all night."

"Oh." She nodded her head and I liked the way she understood things so fast. So for the moment it didn't matter that we looked like salt and pepper standing there and that's what the other kids called us sometimes. We were eight years old and got F's all the time. Me because I couldn't remember what I read or what the teacher said. And Roberta because she couldn't read at all and didn't even listen to the teacher. She wasn't good at anything except jacks, at which she was a killer: pow scoop pow scoop pow scoop.

We didn't like each other all that much at first, but nobody else wanted to play with us because we weren't real orphans with beautiful dead parents in the sky. We were dumped. Even the New York City Puerto Ricans and the upstate Indians ignored us. All kinds of kids were in there, black ones, white ones, even two Koreans. The food was good, though. At least I thought so. Roberta hated it and left whole pieces of things on her plate: Spam, Salisbury steak—even Jell-O with fruit cocktail in it, and she didn't care if I ate what she wouldn't. Mary's idea of supper was popcorn and a can of Yoo-Hoo. Hot mashed potatoes and two weenies was like Thanksgiving for me.

It really wasn't bad, St. Bonny's. The big girls on the second floor pushed us around now and then. But that was all. They wore lipstick and eyebrow pencil and wobbled their knees while they watched TV. Fifteen, sixteen, even, some of them were. They were put-out girls, scared runaways most of them. Poor little girls who fought their uncles off but looked tough to us, and mean. God, did they look mean. The staff tried to keep them separate from the younger children, but sometimes they caught us watching them in the orchard where they played radios and danced with each other. They'd light out after us and pull our hair or twist our arms. We were scared of them, Roberta and me, but neither of us wanted the other one to know it. So we got a good list of dirty names we could shout back when we ran from them through the orchard. I used to dream a lot and almost always the orchard was there. Two acres, four maybe, of these little apple trees. Hundreds of them. Empty and crooked like beggar women when I first came to St. Bonny's but fat with flowers when I left. I don't know why I dreamt about that orchard so much. Nothing really happened there. Nothing all that important, I mean. Just the big girls dancing and playing the radio. Roberta and me watching. Maggie fell down there once. The kitchen woman with legs like parentheses. And the big girls laughed at her. We should have helped her up, I know, but we were scared of those girls with lipstick and eyebrow pencil. Maggie couldn't talk. The kids said she had her tongue cut out, but I think she was just born that way: mute. She was old and sandy-colored and she worked in the kitchen. I don't know if she was nice or not. I just remember her legs like parentheses and how she rocked when she walked. She worked from early in the morning till two o'clock, and if she was late, if she had too much cleaning and didn't get out till two-fifteen or so, she'd cut through the orchard so she wouldn't miss her bus and have to wait another hour. She wore this really stupid little hat—a kid's hat with ear flaps—and she wasn't much taller than we were. A really awful little hat. Even for a mute, it was dumb—dressing like a kid and never saying anything at all.

"But what about if somebody tries to kill her?" I used to wonder about that. "Or what if she wants to cry? Can she cry?"

"Sure," Roberta said. "But just tears. No sounds come out."

"She can't scream?"

"Nope. Nothing."

"Can she hear?"

"I guess."

"Let's call her," I said. And we did.

"Dummy! Dummy!" She never turned her head.

"Bow legs! Bow legs!" Nothing. She just rocked on, the chin straps of her baby-boy hat swaying from side to side. I think we were wrong. I think she could hear and didn't let on. And it shames me even now to think there was somebody in there after all who heard us call her those names and couldn't tell on us.

We got along all right, Roberta and me. Changed beds every night, got F's in civics and communication skills and gym. The Bozo was disappointed in us, she said. Out of 130 of us state cases, 90 were under twelve. Almost all were real orphans with beautiful dead parents in the sky. We were the only ones dumped and the only ones with F's in three classes including gym. So we got along—what with her leaving whole pieces of things on her plate and being nice about not asking questions.

I think it was the day before Maggie fell down that we found out our mothers were coming to visit us on the same Sunday. We had been at the shelter twenty-eight days (Roberta twenty-eight and a half) and this was their first visit with us. Our mothers would come at ten o'clock in time for chapel, then lunch with us in the teacher's lounge. I thought if my dancing mother met her sick mother it might be good for her. And Roberta thought her sick mother would get a big bang out of a dancing one. We got excited about it and curled each other's hair. After breakfast we sat on the bed watching the road from the window. Roberta's socks were still wet. She washed them the night before and put them on the radiator to dry. They hadn't, but she put them on anyway because their tops were so pretty—scalloped in pink. Each of us had a purple construction-paper basket that we had made in craft class. Mine had a yellow crayon rabbit on it. Roberta's had eggs with wiggly lines of color. Inside were cellophane grass and just the jelly beans because I'd eaten the two marshmallow eggs they gave us. The Big Bozo came herself to get us. Smiling she told us we looked very nice and to come downstairs. We were so surprised by the smile we'd never seen before, neither of us moved.

"Don't you want to see your mommies?"

I stood up first and spilled the jelly beans all over the floor. Bozo's smile disappeared while we scrambled to get the candy up off the floor and put it back in the grass.

She escorted us downstairs to the first floor, where the other girls were lining up to file into the chapel. A bunch of grown-ups stood to one side. Viewers mostly. The old biddies who wanted servants and the fags who wanted company looking for children they might want to adopt. Once in a while a grandmother. Almost never anybody young or anybody whose face wouldn't scare you in the night. Because if any of the real orphans had young relatives they wouldn't be real orphans. I saw Mary right away. She had on those green slacks I hated and hated even more now because didn't she know we were going to chapel? And that fur jacket with the pocket linings so ripped she had to pull to get her hands out of them. But her face was pretty—like always—and she smiled and waved like she was the little girl looking for her mother, not me.

I walked slowly, trying not to drop the jelly beans and hoping the paper handle would hold. I had to use my last Chiclet because by the time I finished cutting everything out, all the Elmer's was gone. I am left-handed and the scissors never worked for me. It didn't matter, though; I might just as well have chewed the gum. Mary dropped to her knees and grabbed me, mashing the basket, the jelly beans, and the grass into her ratty fur jacket.

"Twyla, baby. Twyla, baby!"

I could have killed her. Already I heard the big girls in the orchard the next time saying, "Twyyyyyla, baby!" But I couldn't stay mad at Mary while she was smiling and hugging me and smelling of Lady Esther dusting powder. I wanted to stay buried in her fur all day.

To tell the truth I forgot about Roberta. Mary and I got in line for the traipse into chapel and I was feeling proud because she looked so beautiful even in those ugly green slacks that made her behind stick out. A pretty mother on earth is better than a beautiful dead one in the sky even if she did leave you all alone to go dancing.

I felt a tap on my shoulder, turned, and saw Roberta smiling. I smiled back, but not too much lest somebody think this visit was the biggest thing that ever happened in my life. Then Roberta said, "Mother, I want you to meet my roommate, Twyla. And that's Twyla's mother."

I looked up it seemed for miles. She was big. Bigger than any man and on her chest was the biggest cross I'd ever seen. I swear it was six inches long each way. And in the crook of her arm was the biggest Bible ever made.

Mary, simpleminded as ever, grinned and tried to yank her hand out of the pocket with the raggedy lining—to shake hands, I guess. Roberta's mother looked down at me and then looked down at Mary too. She didn't say anything, just grabbed Roberta with her Bible-free hand and stepped out of line, walking quickly to the rear of it. Mary was still grinning because she's not too swift when it comes to what's really going on. Then this light bulb goes off in her head and she says "That bitch!" really loud and us almost in the chapel now. Organ music whining; the Bonny Angels singing sweetly. Everybody in the world turned around to look. And Mary would have kept it up—kept calling names if I hadn't squeezed her hands as hard as I could. That helped a little, but she still twitched and crossed and uncrossed her legs all through service. Even groaned a couple of times. Why did I think she would come there and act right? Slacks. No hat like the grandmothers and viewers, and groaning all the while. When we stood for hymns she kept her mouth shut. Wouldn't even look at the words on the page. She actually reached in her purse for a mirror to check her lipstick. All I could think of was that she really needed to be killed. The sermon lasted a year, and I knew the real orphans were looking smug again.

We were supposed to have lunch in the teacher's lounge, but Mary didn't bring anything, so we picked fur and cellophane grass off the mashed jelly beans and ate them. I could have killed her. I sneaked a look at Roberta. Her mother had brought chicken legs and ham sandwiches and oranges and a whole box of chocolate-covered grahams. Roberta drank milk from a thermos while her mother read the Bible to her.

Things are not right. The wrong food is always with the wrong people. Maybe that's why I got into waitress work later—to match up the right people with the right food. Roberta just let those chicken legs sit there, but she did bring a stack of grahams up to me later when the visit was over. I think she was sorry that her mother would not shake my mother's hand. And I liked that and I liked the fact that she didn't say a word about Mary groaning all the way through the service and not bringing any lunch.

Roberta left in May when the apple trees were heavy and white. On her last day we went to the orchard to watch the big girls smoke and dance by the radio. It didn't matter that they said, "Twyyyyyla, baby." We sat on the ground and breathed. Lady Esther. Apple blossoms. I still go soft when I smell one or the other. Roberta was going home. The big cross and the big Bible was coming to get her and she seemed sort of glad and sort of not. I thought I would die in that room of four beds without her and I knew Bozo had plans to move some other dumped kid in there with me. Roberta promised to write every day, which was really sweet of her because she couldn't read a lick so how could she write anybody? I would have drawn pictures and sent them to her but she never gave me her address. Little by little she faded. Her wet socks with the pink scalloped tops and her big serious-looking eyes—that's all I could catch when I tried to bring her to mind.

I was working behind the counter at the Howard Johnson's on the Thruway just before the Kingston exit. Not a bad job. Kind of a long ride from Newburgh, but okay once I got there. Mine was the second night shift, eleven to seven. Very light until a Greyhound checked in for breakfast around six-thirty. At that hour the sun was all the way clear of the hills behind the restaurant. The place looked better at night—more like shelter—but I loved it when the sun broke in, even if it did show all the cracks in the vinyl and the speckled floor looked dirty no matter what the mop boy did.

It was August and a bus crowd was just unloading. They would stand around a long while: going to the john, and looking at gifts and junk-for-sale machines, reluctant to sit down so soon. Even to eat. I was trying to fill the coffeepots and get them all situated on the electric burners when I saw her. She was sitting in a booth smoking a cigarette with two guys smothered in head and facial hair. Her own hair was so big and wild I could hardly see her face. But the eyes. I would know them anywhere. She had on a powder-blue halter and shorts outfit and earrings the size of bracelets. Talk about lipstick and eyebrow pencil. She made the big girls look like nuns. I couldn't get off the counter until seven o'clock, but I kept watching the booth in case they got up to leave before that. My replacement was on time for a change, so I counted and stacked my receipts as fast as I could and signed off. I walked over to the booth, smiling and wondering if she would remember me. Or even if she wanted to remember me. Maybe she didn't want to be reminded of St. Bonny's or to have anybody know she was ever there. I know I never talked about it to anybody.

I put my hands in my apron pockets and leaned against the back of the booth facing them.

"Roberta? Roberta Fisk?"

She looked up. "Yeah?"

"Twyla."

She squinted for a second and then said, "Wow."

"Remember me?"

"Sure. Hey. Wow."

"It's been awhile," I said, and gave a smile to the two hairy guys.

"Yeah. Wow. You work here?"

"Yeah," I said. "I live in Newburgh."

"Newburgh? No kidding?" She laughed then, a private laugh that included the guys but only the guys, and they laughed with her. What could I do but laugh too and wonder why I was standing there with my knees showing out from under that uniform. Without looking I could see the blue-and-white triangle on my head, my hair shapeless in a net, my ankles thick in white oxfords. Nothing could have been less sheer than my stockings. There was this silence that came down right after I laughed. A silence it was her turn to fill up. With introductions, maybe, to her boyfriends or an invitation to sit down and have a Coke. Instead she lit a cigarette off the one she'd just finished and said, "We're on our way to the Coast. He's got an appointment with Hendrix." She gestured casually toward the boy next to her.

"Hendrix? Fantastic," I said. "Really fantastic. What's she doing now?"

Roberta coughed on her cigarette and the two guys rolled their eyes up at the ceiling.

"Hendrix. Jimi Hendrix, asshole. He's only the biggest—Oh, wow. Forget it."

I was dismissed without anyone saying good-bye, so I thought I would do it for her.

"How's your mother?" I asked. Her grin cracked her whole face. She swallowed. "Fine," she said. "How's yours?"

"Pretty as a picture," I said and turned away. The backs of my knees were damp. Howard Johnson's really was a dump in the sunlight.

James is as comfortable as a house slipper. He liked my cooking and I liked his big loud family. They have lived in Newburgh all of their lives and talk about it the way people do who have always known a home. His grandmother has a porch swing older than his father and when they talk about streets and avenues and buildings they call them names they no longer have. They still call the A&P Rico's because it stands on property once a mom-and-pop store owned by Mr. Rico. And they call the new community college Town Hall because it once was. My mother-in-law puts up jelly and cucumbers and buys butter wrapped in cloth from a dairy. James and his father talk about fishing and baseball and I can see them all together on the Hudson in a raggedy skiff. Half the population of Newburgh is on welfare now, but to my husband's family it was still some upstate paradise of a time long past. A time of ice houses and vegetable wagons, coal furnaces and children weeding gardens. When our son was born my mother-in-law gave me the crib blanket that had been hers.

But the town they remembered had changed. Something quick was in the air. Magnificent old houses, so ruined they had become shelter for squatters and rent risks, were bought and renovated. Smart IBM people moved out of their suburbs back into the city and put shutters up and herb gardens in their backyards. A brochure came in the mail announcing the opening of a Food Emporium. Gourmet food, it said—and listed items the rich IBM crowd would want. It was located in a new mall at the edge of town and I drove out to shop there one day—just to see. It was late in June. After the tulips were gone and the Queen Elizabeth roses were open everywhere. I trailed my cart along the aisle tossing in smoked oysters and Robert's sauce and things I knew would sit in my cupboard for years. Only when I found some Klondike ice cream bars did I feel less guilty about spending James's fireman's salary so foolishly. My father-in-law ate them with the same gusto little Joseph did.

Waiting in the checkout line I heard a voice say, "Twyla!"

The classical music piped over the aisles had affected me and the woman leaning toward me was dressed to kill. Diamonds on her hand, a smart white summer dress. "I'm Mrs. Benson," I said.

"Ho. Ho. The Big Bozo," she sang.

For a split second I didn't know what she was talking about. She had a bunch of asparagus and two cartons of fancy water.

"Roberta!"

"Right."

"For heaven's sake. Roberta."

"You look great," she said.

"So do you. Where are you? Here? In Newburgh?"

"Yes. Over in Annandale."

I was opening my mouth to say more when the cashier called my attention to her empty counter.

"Meet you outside." Roberta pointed her finger and went into the express line.

I placed the groceries and kept myself from glancing around to check Roberta's progress. I remembered Howard Johnson's and looking for a chance to speak only to be greeted with a stingy "wow." But she was waiting for me and her huge hair was sleek now, smooth around a small, nicely shaped head. Shoes, dress, everything lovely and summery and rich. I was dying to know what happened to her, how she got from Jimi Hendrix to Annandale, a neighborhood full of doctors and IBM executives. Easy, I thought. Everything is so easy for them. They think they own the world.

"How long," I asked her. "How long have you been here?"

"A year. I got married to a man who lives here. And you, you're married too, right? Benson, you said."

"Yeah. James Benson."

"And is he nice?"

"Oh, is he nice?"

"Well, is he?" Roberta's eyes were steady as though she really meant the question and wanted an answer.

"He's wonderful, Roberta. Wonderful."

"So you're happy."

"Very."

"That's good," she said and nodded her head. "I always hoped you'd be happy. Any kids? I know you have kids."

"One. A boy. How about you?"

"Four."

"Four?"

She laughed. "Step kids. He's a widower."

"Oh."

"Got a minute? Let's have a coffee."

I thought about the Klondikes melting and the inconvenience of going all the way to my car and putting the bags in the trunk. Served me right for buying all that stuff I didn't need. Roberta was ahead of me.

"Put them in my car. It's right here."

And then I saw the dark blue limousine.

"You married a Chinaman?"

"No." She laughed. "He's the driver."

"Oh, my. If the Big Bozo could see you now."

We both giggled. Really giggled. Suddenly, in just a pulse beat, twenty years disappeared and all of it came rushing back. The big girls (whom we called gar girls—Roberta's misheard word for the evil stone faces described in a civics class) there dancing in the orchard, the ploppy mashed potatoes, the double weenies, the Spam with pineapple. We went into the coffee shop holding on to one another and I tried to think why we were glad to see each other this time and not before. Once, twelve years ago, we passed like strangers. A black girl and a white girl meeting in a Howard Johnson's on the road and having nothing to say. One in a blue-and-white triangle waitress hat, the other on her way to see Hendrix. Now we were behaving like sisters separated for much too long. Those four short months were nothing in time. Maybe it was the thing itself. Just being there, together. Two little girls who knew what nobody else in the world knew—how not to ask questions. How to believe what had to be believed. There was politeness in that reluctance and generosity as well. Is your mother sick too? No, she dances all night. Oh—and an understanding nod.

We sat in a booth by the window and fell into recollection like veterans.

"Did you ever learn to read?"

"Watch." She picked up the menu. "Special of the day. Cream of corn soup. Entrées. Two dots and a wriggly line. Quiche. Chef salad, scallops…"

I was laughing and applauding when the waitress came up.

"Remember the Easter baskets?"

"And how we tried to *introduce* them?"

"Your mother with that cross like two telephone poles."

"And yours with those tight slacks."

We laughed so loudly heads turned and made the laughter hard to suppress.

"What happened to the Jimi Hendrix date?"

Roberta made a blow-out sound with her lips.

"When he died I thought about you."

"Oh, you heard about him finally?"

"Finally. Come on, I was a small-town country waitress."

"And I was a small-town country dropout. God, were we wild. I still don't know how I got out of there alive."

"But you did."

"I did. I really did. Now I'm Mrs. Kenneth Norton."

"Sounds like a mouthful."

"It is."

"Servants and all?"

Roberta held up two fingers.

"Ow! What does he do?"

"Computers and stuff. What do I know?"

"I don't remember a hell of a lot from those days, but Lord, St. Bonny's is as clear as daylight. Remember Maggie? The day she fell down and those gar girls laughed at her?"

Roberta looked up from her salad and stared at me. "Maggie didn't fall," she said.

"Yes, she did. You remember."

"No, Twyla. They knocked her down. Those girls pushed her down and tore her clothes. In the orchard."

"I don't—that's not what happened."

"Sure it is. In the orchard. Remember how scared we were?"

"Wait a minute. I don't remember any of that."

"And Bozo was fired."

"You're crazy. She was there when I left. You left before me."

"I went back. You weren't there when they fired Bozo."

"What?"

"Twice. Once for a year when I was about ten, another for two months when I was fourteen. That's when I ran away."

"You ran away from St. Bonny's?"

"I had to. What do you want? Me dancing in that orchard?"

"Are you sure about Maggie?"

"Of course I'm sure. You've blocked it, Twyla. It happened. Those girls had behavior problems, you know."

"Didn't they, though. But why can't I remember the Maggie thing?"

"Believe me. It happened. And we were there."

"Who did you room with when you went back?" I asked her as if I would know her. The Maggie thing was troubling me.

"Creeps. They tickled themselves in the night."

My ears were itching and I wanted to go home suddenly. This was all very well but she couldn't just comb her hair, wash her face, and pretend everything was hunky-dory. After the Howard Johnson's snub. And no apology. Nothing.

"Were you on dope or what that time at Howard Johnson's?" I tried to make my voice sound friendlier than I felt.

"Maybe, a little. I never did drugs much. Why?"

"I don't know, you acted sort of like you didn't want to know me then."

"Oh, Twyla, you know how it was in those days: black—white. You know how everything was."

But I didn't know. I thought it was just the opposite. Busloads of blacks and whites came into Howard Johnson's together. They roamed together then: students, musicians, lovers, protesters. You got to see everything at Howard Johnson's, and blacks were very friendly with whites in those days. But sitting there with nothing on my plate but two hard tomato wedges wondering about the melting Klondikes it seemed childish remembering the slight. We went to her car and, with the help of the driver, got my stuff into my station wagon.

"We'll keep in touch this time," she said.

"Sure," I said. "Sure. Give me a call."

"I will," she said, and then, just as I was sliding behind the wheel, she leaned into the window. "By the way. Your mother. Did she ever stop dancing?"

I shook my head. "No. Never."

Roberta nodded.

"And yours? Did she ever get well?"

She smiled a tiny sad smile. "No. She never did. Look, call me, okay?"

"Okay," I said, but I knew I wouldn't. Roberta had messed up my past somehow with that business about Maggie. I wouldn't forget a thing like that. Would I?

Strife came to us that fall. At least that's what the paper called it. Strife. Racial strife. The word made me think of a bird—a big shrieking bird out of 1,000,000,000 B.C. Flapping its wings and cawing. Its eye with no lid always bearing down on you. All day it screeched and at night it slept on the rooftops. It woke you in the morning, and from the *Today* show to the eleven o'clock news it kept you an awful company. I couldn't figure it out from one day to the next. I knew I was supposed to feel something strong, but I didn't know what, and James wasn't any help. Joseph was on the list of kids to be transferred from the junior high school to another one at some far-out-of-the-way place and I thought it was a good thing until I heard it was a bad thing. I mean I didn't know. All the schools seemed dumps to me, and the fact that one was nicer looking didn't hold much weight. But the papers were full of it and then the kids began to get jumpy. In August, mind you. Schools weren't even open yet. I thought Joseph might be frightened to go over there, but he didn't seem scared so I forgot about it, until I found myself driving along Hudson Street out there by the school they were trying to integrate and saw a line of women marching. And who do you suppose was in line, big as life, holding a sign in front of her bigger than her mother's cross? MOTHERS HAVE RIGHTS TOO! it said.

I drove on and then changed my mind. I circled the block, slowed down, and honked my horn.

Roberta looked over and when she saw me she waved. I didn't wave back, but I didn't move either. She handed her sign to another woman and came over to where I was parked.

"Hi."

"What are you doing?"

"Picketing. What's it look like?"

"What for?"

"What do you mean, 'What for?' They want to take my kids and send them out of the neighborhood. They don't want to go."

"So what if they go to another school? My boy's being bussed too, and I don't mind. Why should you?"

"It's not about us, Twyla. Me and you. It's about our kids."

"What's more *us* than that?"

"Well, it is a free country."

"Not yet, but it will be."

"What the heck does that mean? I'm not doing anything to you."

"You really think that?"

"I know it."

"I wonder what made me think you were different."

"I wonder what made me think you were different."

"Look at them," I said. "Just look. Who do they think they are? Swarming all over the place like they own it. And now they think they can decide where my child goes to school. Look at them, Roberta. They're Bozos."

Roberta turned around and looked at the women. Almost all of them were standing still now, waiting. Some were even edging toward us. Roberta looked at me out of some refrigerator behind her eyes. "No, they're not. They're just mothers."

"And what am I? Swiss cheese?"

"I used to curl your hair."

"I hated your hands in my hair."

The women were moving. Our faces looked mean to them of course and they looked as though they could not wait to throw themselves in front of a police car or, better yet, into my car and drag me away by my ankles. Now they surrounded my car and gently, gently began to rock it. I swayed back and forth like a sideways yo-yo. Automatically I reached for Roberta, like the old days in the orchard when they saw us watching them and we had to get out of there, and if one of us fell the other pulled her up and if one of us was caught the other stayed to kick and scratch, and neither would leave the other behind. My arm shot out of the car window but no receiving hand was there. Roberta was looking at me sway from side to side in the car and her face was still. My purse slid from the car seat down under the dashboard. The four policemen who had been drinking Tab in their car finally got the message and strolled over, forcing their way through the women. Quietly, firmly they spoke. "Okay, ladies. Back in line or off the streets."

Some of them went away willingly; others had to be urged away from the car doors and the hood. Roberta didn't move. She was looking steadily at me. I was fumbling to turn on the ignition, which wouldn't catch because the gearshift was still in drive. The seats of the car were a mess because the swaying had thrown my grocery coupons all over and my purse was sprawled on the floor.

"Maybe I am different now, Twyla. But you're not. You're the same little state kid who kicked a poor old black lady when she was down on the ground. You kicked a black lady and you have the nerve to call me a bigot."

The coupons were everywhere and the guts of my purse were bunched under the dashboard. What was she saying? Black? Maggie wasn't black.

"She wasn't black," I said.

"Like hell she wasn't, and you kicked her. We both did. You kicked a black lady who couldn't even scream."

"Liar!"

"You're the liar! Why don't you just go on home and leave us alone, huh?"

She turned away and I skidded away from the curb.

The next morning I went into the garage and cut the side out of the carton our portable TV had come in. It wasn't nearly big enough, but after a while I had a decent sign: red spray-painted letters on a white background—AND SO DO CHILDREN****. I meant just to go down to the school and tack it up somewhere so those cows on the picket line across the street could see it, but when I got there, some ten or so others had already assembled—protesting the cows across the street. Police permits and everything. I got in line and we strutted in time on our side while Roberta's group strutted on theirs. That first day we were all dignified, pretending the other side didn't exist. The second day there was name calling and finger gestures. But that was about all. People changed signs from time to time, but Roberta never did and neither did I. Actually my sign didn't make sense without Roberta's. "And so do children what?" one of the women on my side asked me. Have rights, I said, as though it was obvious.

Roberta didn't acknowledge my presence in any way, and I got to thinking maybe she didn't know I was there. I began to pace myself in the line, jostling people one minute and lagging behind the next, so Roberta and I could reach the end of our respective lines at the same time and there would be a moment in our turn when we would face each other. Still, I couldn't tell whether she saw me and knew my sign was for her. The next day I went early before we were scheduled to assemble. I waited until she got there before I exposed my new creation. As soon as she hoisted her MOTHERS HAVE RIGHTS TOO I began to wave my new one, which said, HOW WOULD YOU KNOW? I know she saw that one, but I had gotten addicted now. My signs got crazier each day, and the women on my side decided that I was a kook. They couldn't make heads or tails out of my brilliant screaming posters.

I brought a painted sign in queenly red with huge black letters that said, IS YOUR MOTHER WELL? Roberta took her lunch break and didn't come back for the rest of the day or any day after. Two days later I stopped going too and couldn't have been missed because nobody understood my signs anyway.

It was a nasty six weeks. Classes were suspended and Joseph didn't go to anybody's school until October. The children—everybody's children—soon got bored with that extended vacation they thought was going to be so great. They looked at TV until their eyes flattened. I spent a couple of mornings tutoring my son, as the other mothers said we should. Twice I opened a text from last year that he had never turned in. Twice he yawned in my face. Other mothers organized living room sessions so the kids would keep up. None of the kids could concentrate, so they drifted back to *The Price Is Right* and *The Brady Bunch*. When the school finally opened there were fights once or twice and some sirens roared through the streets every once in a while. There were a lot of photographers from Albany. And just when ABC was about to send up a news crew, the kids settled down like nothing in the world had happened. Joseph hung my HOW WOULD YOU KNOW? sign in his bedroom. I don't know what became of AND SO DO CHILDREN****. I think my father-in-law cleaned some fish on it. He was always puttering around in our garage. Each of his five children lived in Newburgh, and he acted as though he had five extra homes.

I couldn't help looking for Roberta when Joseph graduated from high school, but I didn't see her. It didn't trouble me much what she had said to me in the car. I mean the kicking part. I know I didn't do that, I couldn't do that. But I was puzzled by her telling me Maggie was black. When I thought about it I actually couldn't be certain. She wasn't pitch-black, I knew, or I would have remembered that. What I remember was the kiddie hat and the semicircle legs. I tried to reassure myself about the race thing for a long time until it dawned on me that the truth was already there, and Roberta knew it. I didn't kick her, I didn't join in with the gar girls and kick that lady, but I sure did want to. We watched and never tried to help her and never called for help. Maggie was my dancing mother. Deaf, I thought, and dumb. Nobody inside. Nobody who would hear you if you cried in the night. Nobody who could tell you anything important that you could use. Rocking, dancing, swaying as she walked. And when the gar girls pushed her down and started roughhousing, I knew she wouldn't scream, couldn't—just like me—and I was glad about that.

We decided not to have a tree, because Christmas would be at my mother-in-law's house, so why have a tree at both places? Joseph was at SUNY New Paltz and we had to economize, we said. But at the last minute, I changed my mind. Nothing could be that bad. So I rushed around town looking for a tree, something small but wide. By the time I found a place, it was snowing and very late. I dawdled like it was the most important purchase in the world and the tree man was fed up with me. Finally I chose one and had it tied onto the trunk of the car. I drove away slowly because the sand trucks were not out yet and the streets could be murder at the beginning of a snowfall. Downtown the streets were wide and rather empty except for a cluster of people coming out of the Newburgh Hotel. The one hotel in town that wasn't built out of cardboard and Plexiglas. A party, probably. The men huddled in the snow were dressed in tails and the women had on furs. Shiny things glittered from underneath their coats. It made me tired to look at them. Tired, tired, tired. On the next corner was a small diner with loops and loops of paper bells in the window. I stopped the car and went in. Just for a cup of coffee and twenty minutes of peace before I went home and tried to finish everything before Christmas Eve.

"Twyla?"

There she was. In a silvery evening gown and dark fur coat. A man and another woman were with her, the man fumbling for change to put in the cigarette machine. The woman was humming and tapping on the counter with her fingernails. They all looked a little bit drunk.

"Well. It's you."

"How are you?"

I shrugged. "Pretty good. Frazzled. Christmas and all."

"Regular?" called the woman from the counter.

"Fine," Roberta called back and then, "Wait for me in the car."

She slipped into the booth beside me. "I have to tell you something, Twyla. I made up my mind if I ever saw you again, I'd tell you."

"I'd just as soon not hear anything, Roberta. It doesn't matter now, anyway."

"No," she said. "Not about that."

"Don't be long," said the woman. She carried two regulars to go and the man peeled his cigarette pack as they left.

"It's about St. Bonny's and Maggie."

"Oh, please."

"Listen to me. I really did think she was black. I didn't make that up. I really thought so. But now I can't be sure. I just remember her as old, so old. And because she couldn't talk—well, you know, I thought she was crazy. She'd been brought up in an institution like my mother was and like I thought I would be too. And you were right. We didn't kick her. It was the gar girls. Only them. But, well, I wanted to. I really wanted them to hurt her. I said we did it, too. You and me, but that's not true. And I don't want you to carry that around. It was just that I wanted to do it so bad that day—wanting to is doing it."

Her eyes were watery from the drinks she'd had, I guess. I know it's that way with me. One glass of wine and I start bawling over the littlest thing.

"We were kids, Roberta."

"Yeah. Yeah. I know, just kids."

"Eight."

"Eight."

"And lonely."

"Scared, too."

She wiped her cheeks with the heel of her hand and smiled. "Well, that's all I wanted to say."

I nodded and couldn't think of any way to fill the silence that went from the diner past the paper bells on out into the snow. It was heavy now. I thought I'd better wait for the sand trucks before starting home.

"Thanks, Roberta."

"Sure."

"Did I tell you? My mother, she never did stop dancing."

"Yes. You told me. And mine, she never got well." Roberta lifted her hands from the tabletop and covered her face with her palms. When she took them away she really was crying. "Oh, shit, Twyla. Shit, shit, shit. What the hell happened to Maggie?"

Ernest J. Gaines

(b. 1933)

Ernest J. Gaines was born on a Louisiana plantation; no doubt the historical irony of this setting has not been lost on the author of **The Autobiography of Miss Jane Pittman** *(1971), the popular novel whose 1974 television adaptation garnered nine Emmy awards. Although Gaines moved to northern California in his early teens, he would constantly return to his native state both in his fiction and in his life. After being drafted in 1953, Gaines left the Army after two years and was able to resume his interrupted studies at California State University, San Francisco. In 1958 he went to Stanford University under the auspices of the prestigious Wallace Stegner Creative Writing Fellowship and was honored with the Joseph Henry Jackson Literary Award. Although his first two novels, both love stories, were published to favorable critical notice,* **Catherine Carmier** *(1964) and* **Of Love and Dust** *(1967), Gaines feels that the best of his early writing is found in his short story collections,* **Bloodlines** *(1968) and* **A Long Day in November** *(1971). The subsequent success of* **Miss Jane Pittman**, *a historical narrative of a former slave who lives to see the beginning of the Civil Rights movement of the sixties, would allow Gaines to devote his life entirely to his writing, and he has since published* **In My Father's House** *(1978) and* **A Gathering of Old Men** *(1983). In commenting on his gentle, reminiscent treatment of his Louisiana characters, Alice Walker has written of Gaines that he "is mellow with historical reflection, supple with wit, relaxed and expansive because he does not equate his people with failure."*

The Sky Is Gray

Go'n be coming in a few minutes. Coming round that bend down there full speed. And I'm go'n get out my handkerchief and wave it down, and we go'n get on it and go.

I keep on looking for it, but Mama don't look that way no more. She's looking down the road where we just come from. It's a long old road, and far's you can see you don't see nothing but gravel. You got dry weeds on both sides, and you got trees on both sides, and fences on both sides, too. And you got cows in the pastures and they standing close together. And when we was coming out here to catch the bus I seen the smoke coming out of the cow's noses.

I look at my mama and I know what she's thinking. I been with Mama so much, just me and her, I know what she's thinking all the time. Right now it's home—Auntie and them. She's thinking if they got enough wood—if she left enough there to keep them warm till we get back. She's thinking if it go'n rain and if any of them go'n have to go out in the rain. She's thinking 'bout the hog—if he go'n get out, and if Ty and Val be able to get him back in. She always worry like that when she leaves the house. She don't worry too much if she leave me there with the smaller ones, 'cause she know I'm go'n look after them and look after Auntie and everything else. I'm the oldest and she say I'm the man.

I look at my mama and I love my mama. She's wearing that black coat and that black hat and she's looking sad. I love my mama and I want put my arm round her and tell her. But I'm not supposed to do that. She say that's weakness and that's crybaby stuff, and she don't want no crybaby round her. She don't want you to be scared, either. 'Cause Ty's scared of ghosts and she's always whipping him. I'm scared of the dark, too, but I make 'tend I ain't. I make 'tend I ain't cause I'm the oldest, and I got to set a good example for the rest. I can't ever be scared and I can't ever cry. And that's why I never said nothing 'bout my teeth. It's been hurting me and hurting me close to a month now, but I never said it. I didn't say it 'cause I didn't want act like a crybaby, and 'cause I know we didn't have enough money to go have it pulled. But, Lord, it been hurting me. And look like it wouldn't start till at night when you was trying to get yourself little sleep. Then soon's you shut your eyes—ummmummm, Lord, look like it go right down to your heartstring.

"Hurting, hanh?" Ty'd say.

I'd shake my head, but I wouldn't open my mouth for nothing. You open your mouth and let that wind in, and it almost kill you.

I'd just lay there and listen to them snore. Ty there, right 'side me, and Auntie and Val over by the fireplace. Val younger than me and Ty, and he sleeps with Auntie. Mama sleeps round the other side with Louis and Walker.

I'd just lay there and listen to them, and listen to that wind out there, and listen to that fire in the fireplace. Sometimes it'd stop long enough to let me get little rest. Sometimes it just hurt, hurt, hurt. Lord, have mercy.

Auntie knowed it was hurting me. I didn't tell nobody but Ty, 'cause we buddies and he ain't go'n tell nobody. But some kind of way Auntie found out. When she asked me, I told her no, nothing was wrong. But she knowed it all the time. She told me to mash up a piece of aspirin and wrap it in some cotton and jugg it down in that hole. I did it, but it didn't do no good. It stopped for a little while, and started right back again. Auntie wanted to tell Mama, but I told her, "Uh-uh." 'Cause I knowed we didn't have any money, and it just was go'n make her mad again. So Auntie told Monsieur Bayonne, and Monsieur Bayonne came over to the house and told me to kneel down 'side him on the fireplace. He put his finger in his mouth and made the Sign of the Cross on my jaw. The tip of Monsieur Bayonne's finger is some hard, 'cause he's always playing on that guitar. If we sit outside at night we can always hear Monsieur Bayonne playing on his guitar. Sometimes we leave him out there playing on the guitar.

Monsieur Bayonne made the Sign of the Cross over and over on my jaw, but that didn't do no good. Even when he prayed and told me to pray some, too, that tooth still hurt me.

"How you feeling?" he say.

"Same," I say.

He kept on praying and make the Sign of the Cross and I kept on praying, too.

"Still hurting?" he say.

"Yes, sir."

Monsieur Bayonne mashed harder and harder on my jaw. He mashed so hard he almost pushed me over on Ty. But then he stopped.

"What kind of prayers you praying, boy?" he say.

"Baptist," I say.

"Well, I'll be—no wonder that tooth still killing him. I'm going one way and he pulling the other. Boy, don't you know any Catholic prayers?"

"I know 'Hail Mary,' " I say.

"Then you better start saying it."

"Yes, sir."

He started mashing on my jaw again, and I could hear him praying at the same time. And, sure enough, after while it stopped hurting me.

Me and Ty went outside where Monsieur Bayonne's two hounds was and we started playing with them. "Let's go hunting," Ty say. "All right," I say; and we went on back in the pasture. Soon the hounds got on a trail, and me and Ty followed them all 'cross the pasture and then back in the woods, too. And then they cornered this little old rabbit and killed him, and me and Ty made them get back, and we picked up the rabbit and started on back home. But my tooth had started hurting me again. It was hurting me plenty now, but I wouldn't tell Monsieur Bayonne. That night I didn't sleep a bit, and first thing in the morning Auntie told me to go back and let Monsieur Bayonne pray over me some more. Monsieur Bayonne was in his kitchen making coffee when I got there. Soon 's he seen me he knowed what was wrong.

"All right, kneel down there 'side that stove," he say. "And this time make sure you pray Catholic. I don't know nothing 'bout that Baptist, and I don't want know nothing 'bout him."

Last night Mama said, "Tomorrow we going to town."

"It ain't hurting me no more," I say. "I can eat anything on it."

"Tomorrow we going to town," she say.

And after she finished eating, she got up and went to bed. She always go to bed early now. 'Fore Daddy went in the Army, she used to stay up late. All of us sitting out on the gallery or round the fire. But now, look like soon 's she finish eating she go to bed.

This morning when I woke up, her and Auntie was standing 'fore the fireplace. She say: "Enough to get there and get back. Dollar and a half to have it pulled. Twenty-five for me to go, twenty-five for him. Twenty-five for me to come back, twenty-five for him. Fifty cents left. Guess I get little piece of salt meat with that."

"Sure can use it," Auntie say. "White beans and no salt meat ain't white beans."

"I do the best I can," Mama say.

They was quiet after that, and I made 'tend I was still asleep.

"James, hit the floor," Auntie say.

I still made 'tend I was asleep. I didn't want them to know I was listening.

"All right," Auntie say, shaking me by the shoulder. "Come on. Today's the day."

I pushed the cover down to get out, and Ty grabbed it and pulled it back.

"You, too, Ty," Auntie say.

"I ain't getting no teef pulled," Ty say.

"Don't mean it ain't time to get up," Auntie say.

"Hit it, Ty."

Ty got up grumbling.

"James, you hurry up and get in your clothes and eat your food," Auntie say. "What time y'all coming back?" she say to Mama.

"That 'leven o'clock bus," Mama say. "Got to get back in that field this evening."

"Get a move on you, James," Auntie say.

I went in the kitchen and washed my face, then I ate my breakfast. I was having bread and syrup. The bread was warm and hard and tasted good. And I tried to make it last a long time.

Ty came back there grumbling and mad at me.

"Got to get up," he say. "I ain't having no teefes pulled. What I got to be getting up for?"

Ty poured some syrup in his pan and got a piece of bread. He didn't wash his hands, neither his face, and I could see that white stuff in his eyes.

"You the one getting your teef pulled," he say. "What I go to get up for. I bet if I was getting a teef pulled, you wouldn't be getting up. Shucks; syrup again. I'm getting tired of this old syrup. Syrup, syrup, syrup. I'm go'n take with the sugar diabetes. I want me some bacon sometime."

"Go out in the field and work and you can have your bacon," Auntie say. She stood in the middle door looking at Ty. "You better be glad you got syrup. Some people ain't got that—hard 's time is."

"Shucks," Ty say. "How can I be strong."

"I don't know too much 'bout your strength," Auntie say; "but I know where you go'n be hot at, you keep that grumbling up. James, get a move on you; your mama waiting."

I ate my last piece of bread and went in the front room. Mama was standing 'fore the fireplace warming her hands. I put on my coat and my cap, and we left the house.

I look down there again, but it still ain't coming. I almost say, "It ain't coming yet," but I keep my mouth shut. 'Cause that's something else she don't like. She don't like for you to say something just for nothing. She can see it ain't coming, I can see it ain't coming, so why say it ain't coming. I don't say it, I turn and look at the river that's back of us. It's so cold the smoke's just raising up from the water. I see a bunch of pool-doos not too far out—just on the other side the lilies. I'm wondering if you can eat pool-doos. I ain't too sure, 'cause I ain't never ate none. But I done ate owls and blackbirds, and I done ate redbirds, too. I didn't want kill the redbirds, but she made me kill them. They had two of them back there. One in my trap, one in Ty's trap. Me and Ty was go'n play with them and let them go, but she made me kill them 'cause we needed the food.

"I can't," I say. "I can't."

"Here," she say. "Take it."

"I can't," I say. "I can't. I can't kill him, Mama, please."

"Here," she say. "Take this fork, James."

"Please, Mama, I can't kill him," I say.

I could tell she was go'n hit me. I jerked back, but I didn't jerk back soon enough. "Take it," she say.

I took it and reached in for him, but he kept on hopping to the back.

"I can't, Mama," I say. The water just kept on running down my face. "I can't," I say.

"Get him out of there," she say.

I reached in for him and he kept on hopping to the back. Then I reached in farther, and he pecked me on the hand.

"I can't, Mama," I say.

She slapped me again.

I reached in again, but he kept on hopping out my way. Then he hopped to one side and I reached there. The fork got him on the leg and I heard his leg pop. I pulled my hand out 'cause I had hurt him.

"Give it here," she say, and jerked the fork out my hand.

She reached in and got the little bird right in the neck. I heard the fork go in his neck, and I heard it go in the ground. She brought him out and helt him right in front of me.

"That's one," she say. She shook him off and gived me the fork. "Get the other one."

"I can't, Mama," I say. "I'll do anything, but don't make me do that."

She went to the corner of the fence and broke the biggest switch over there she could find. I knelt 'side the trap, crying.

"Get him out of there," she say.

"I can't, Mama."

She started hitting me 'cross the back. I went down on the ground, crying.

"Get him," she say.

"Octavia?" Auntie say.

'Cause she had come out of the house and she was standing by the tree looking at us.

"Get him out of there," Mama say.

"Octavia," Auntie say, "explain to him. Explain to him. Just don't beat him. Explain to him."

But she hit me and hit me and hit me.

I'm still young—I ain't no more than eight; but I know now; I know why I had to do it. (They was so little, though. They was so little. I 'member how I picked the feathers off them and cleaned them and helt them over the fire. Then we all ate them. Ain't had but a little bitty piece each, but we all had a little bitty piece, and everybody just looked at me 'cause they was so proud.) Suppose she had to go away? That's why I had to do it. Suppose she had to go away like Daddy went away? Then who was go'n look after us? They had to be somebody left to carry on. I didn't know it then, but I know it now. Auntie and Monsieur Bayonne talked to me and made me see.

Time I see it I get out my handkerchief and start waving. It's still 'way down there, but I keep waving anyhow. Then it come up and stop and me and Mama get on. Mama tell me go sit in the back while she pay. I do like she say, and the people look at me. When I pass the little sign that say "White" and "Colored," I start looking for a seat. I just see one of them back there, but I don't take it, 'cause I want my mama to sit down herself. She comes in the back and sit down, and I lean on the seat. They got seats in the front, but I know I can't sit there, 'cause I have to sit back of the sign. Anyhow, I don't want sit there if my mama go'n sit back here.

They got a lady sitting 'side my mama and she looks at me and smiles little bit. I smile back, but I don't open my mouth, 'cause the wind'll get in and make that tooth ache. The lady take out a pack of gum and reach me a slice, but I shake my head. The lady just can't understand why a little boy'll turn down gum, and she reach me a slice again. This time I point to my jaw. The lady understands and smiles little bit, and I smile little bit, but I don't open my mouth, though.

They got a girl sitting 'cross from me. She got on a red overcoat and her hair's plaited in one big plait. First, I make 'tend I don't see her over there, but then I start looking at her little bit. She make 'tend she don't see me, either, but I catch her looking that way. She got a cold, and every now and then she h'ist that little handkerchief to her nose. She ought to blow it, but she don't. Must think she's too much a lady or something.

Every time she h'ist that little handkerchief, the lady 'side her say something in her ear. She shakes her head and lays her hand in her lap again. Then I catch her kind of looking where I'm at. I smile at her little bit. But think she'll smile back? Uh-uh. She just turn up her little old nose and turn her head. Well, I show her both of us can turn us head. I turn mine too and look out at the river.

The river is gray. The sky is gray. They have pool-doos on the water. The water is wavy, and the pool-doos go up and down. The bus go round a turn, and you got plenty trees hiding the river. Then the bus go round another turn, and I can see the river again.

I look toward the front where all the white people sitting. Then I look at that little old gal again. I don't look right at her, 'cause I don't want all them people to know I love her. I just look at her little bit, like I'm looking out that window over there. But she knows I'm looking that way, and she kind of look at me, too. The lady sitting 'side her catch her this time, and she leans over and says something in her ear.

"I don't love him nothing," that little old gal says out loud.

Everybody back there hear her mouth, and all of them look at us and laugh.

"I don't love you, either," I say. "So you don't have to turn up your nose, miss."

"You the one looking," she say.

"I wasn't looking at you," I say. "I was looking out that window, there."

"Out that window, my foot," she say. "I seen you. Everytime I turned round you was looking at me."

"You must of been looking yourself if you seen me all them times," I say.

"Shucks," she say, "I got me all kind of boyfriends."

"I got girlfriends, too," I say.

"Well, I just don't want you getting your hopes up," she say.

I don't say no more to that little old gal 'cause I don't want to have to bust her in the mouth. I lean on the seat where Mama sitting, and I don't even look that way no more. When we get to Bayonne, she jugg her little old tongue out at me. I made 'tend I'm go'n hit her, and she duck down 'side her mama. And all the people laugh at us again.

Me and Mama get off and start walking in town. Bayonne is a little bitty town. Baton Rouge is a hundred times bigger than Bayonne. I went to Baton Rouge once—me, Ty, Mama, and Daddy. But that was 'way back yonder, 'fore Daddy went in the Army. I wonder when we go'n see him again. I wonder when. Look like he ain't ever coming back home.... Even the pavement all cracked in Bayonne. Got grass shooting right out the sidewalk. Got weeds in the ditch, too; just like they got at home.

It's some cold in Bayonne. Look like it's colder than it is home. The wind blows in my face, and I feel that stuff running down my nose. I sniff. Mama says use that handkerchief. I blow my nose and put it back.

We pass a school and I see them white children playing in the yard. Big old red school, and them children just running and playing. Then we pass a café, and I see a bunch of people in there eating. I wish I was in there 'cause I'm cold. Mama tells me keep my eyes in front where they belong.

We pass stores that's got dummies, and we pass another café, and then we pass a shoe shop, and that bald-head man in there fixing on a shoe. I look at him and I butt into that white lady, and Mama jerks me in front and tells me stay there.

We come up to the courthouse, and I see the flag waving there. This flag ain't like the one we got at school. This one here ain't got but a handful of stars. One at school got a big pile of stars—one for every state. We pass it and we turn and there it is—the dentist office. Me and Mama go in, and they got people sitting everywhere you look. They even got a little boy in there younger than me.

Me and Mama sit on that bench, and a white lady come in there and ask me what my name is. Mama tells her and the white lady goes on back. Then I hear somebody hollering in there. Soon 's that little boy hear him hollering, he starts hollering, too. His mama pats him and pats him, trying to make him hush up, but he ain't thinking 'bout his mama.

The man that was hollering in there comes out holding his jaw. He is a big old man and he's wearing overalls and a jumper.

"Got it, hanh?" another man asks him.

The man shakes his head—don't want open his mouth.

"Man, I thought they was killing you in there," the other man says. "Hollering like a pig under a gate."

The man don't say nothing. He just heads for the door, and the other man follows him.

"John Lee," the white lady says. "John Lee Williams."

The little boy juggs his head down in his mama's lap and holler more now. His mama tells him go with the nurse, but he ain't thinking 'bout his mama. His mama tells him again, but he don't even hear her. His mama picks him up and takes him in there, and even when the white lady shuts the door I can still hear little old John Lee.

"I often wonder why the Lord let a child like that suffer," a lady says to my mama. The lady's sitting right in front of us on another bench. She's got on a white dress and a black sweater. She must be a nurse or something herself, I reckon.

"Not us to question," a man says.

"Sometimes I don't know if we shouldn't," the lady says.

"I know definitely we shouldn't," the man says. The man looks like a preacher. He's big and fat and he's got on a black suit. He's got a gold chain, too.

"Why?" the lady says.

"Why anything?" the preacher says.

"Yes," the lady says. "Why anything?"

"Not us to question," the preacher says.

The lady looks at the preacher a little while and looks at Mama again.

"And look like it's the poor who suffers the most," she says. "I don't understand it."

"Best not to even try," the preacher says. "He works in mysterious ways—wonders to perform."

Right then little John Lee bust out hollering, and everybody turn they head to listen.

"He's not a good dentist," the lady says. "Dr. Robillard is much better. But more expensive. That's why most of the colored people come here. The white people go to Dr. Robillard. Y'all from Bayonne?"

"Down the river," my mama says. And that's all she go'n say, 'cause she don't talk much. But the lady keeps on looking at her, and so she says, "Near Morgan."

"I see," the lady says.

"That's the trouble with the black people in this country today," somebody else says. This one here's sitting on the same side me and Mama's sitting, and he is kind of sitting in front of that preacher. He looks like a teacher or somebody that goes to college. He's got on a suit, and he's got a book that he's been reading. "We don't question is exactly our problem," he says. "We should question and question and question—question everything."

The preacher just looks at him a long time. He done put a toothpick or something in his mouth, and he just keeps on turning it and turning it. You can see he don't like that boy with that book.

"Maybe you can explain what you mean," he says.

"I said what I meant," the boys says. "Question everything. Every stripe, every star, every word spoken. Everything."

"It 'pears to me that this young lady and I was talking 'bout God, young man," the preacher says.

"Question Him too," the boys says.

"Wait," the preacher says. "Wait now."

"You heard me right," the boy says. "His existence as well as everything else. Everything."

The preacher just looks across the room at the boy. You can see he's getting madder and madder. But mad or no mad, the boy ain't thinking 'bout him. He looks at that preacher just s' hard 's the preacher looks at him.

"Is this what they coming to?" the preacher says. "Is this what we educating them for?"

"You're not educating me," the boys says. "I wash dishes at night so that I can go to school in the day. So even the words you spoke need questioning."

The preacher just looks at him and shakes his head.

"When I come in this room and seen you there with your book, I said to myself, 'There's an intelligent man.' How wrong a person can be."

"Show me one reason to believe in the existence of a God," the boy says.

"My heart tells me," the preacher says.

" 'My heart tells me,' " the boy says. " 'My heart tells me.' Sure, 'My heart tells me.' And as long as you listen to what your heart tells you, you will have only what the white man gives you and nothing more. Me, I don't listen to my heart. The purpose of the heart is to pump blood throughout the body, and nothing else."

"Who's your paw, boy?" the preacher says.

"Why?"

"Who is he?"

"He's dead."

"And your mom?"

"She's in Charity Hospital with pneumonia. Half killed herself, working for nothing."

"And 'cause he's dead and she's sick, you mad at the world?"

"I'm not mad at the world. I'm questioning the world. I'm questioning it with cold logic, sir. What do words like Freedom, Liberty, God, White, Colored mean? I want to know. That's why *you* are send us to school, to read and to ask questions. And because we ask these questions, you call us mad. No sir, it is not us who are mad."

"You keep saying 'us'?"

" 'Us.' Yes—us. I'm not alone."

The preacher just shakes his head. Then he looks at everybody in the room—everybody. Some of the people look down at the floor, keep from looking at him. I kind of look 'way myself, but soon 's I know he done turn his head, I look that way again.

"I'm sorry for you," he says to the boy.

"Why?" the boy says. "Why not be sorry for yourself? Why are you so much better off than I am? Why aren't you sorry for these other people in here? Why not be sorry for the lady who had to drag her child into the dentist office? Why not be sorry for the lady sitting on that bench over there? Be sorry for them. Not for me. Some way or the other I'm going to make it."

"No, I'm sorry for you," the preacher says.

"Of course, of course," the boy says, nodding his head. "You're sorry for me because I rock that pillar you're leaning on."

"You can't ever rock the pillar I'm leaning on, young man. It's stronger than anything man can ever do."

"You believe in God because a man told you to believe in God," the boy says. "A white man told you to believe in God. And why? To keep you ignorant so he can keep his feet on your neck."

"So now we the ignorant?" the preacher says.

"Yes," the boy says. "Yes." And he opens his book again.

The preacher just looks at him sitting there. The boy done forgot all about him. Everybody else make 'tend they done forgot the squabble, too.

Then I see that preacher getting up real slow. Preacher's a great big old man and he got to brace himself to get up. He comes over where the boy is sitting. He just stands there a little while looking down at him, but the boy don't raise his head.

"Get up, boy," preacher says.

The boy looks up at him, then he shuts his book real slow and stands up. Preacher just hauls back and hit him in the face. The boy falls back 'gainst the wall, but he straightens himself up and looks right back at that preacher.

"You forgot the other cheek," he says.

The preacher hauls back and hit him again on the other side. But this time the boy braces himself and don't fall.

"That hasn't changed a thing," he says.

The preacher just looks at the boy. The preacher's breathing real hard like he just run up a big hill. The boy sits down and opens his book again.

"I feel sorry for you," the preacher says. "I never felt so sorry for a man before."

The boy makes 'tend he don't even hear that preacher. He keeps on reading his book. The preacher goes back and gets his hat off the chair.

"Excuse me," he says to us. "I'll come back some other time. Y'all, please excuse me."

And he looks at the boy and goes out the room. The boy h'ist his hand up to his mouth one time to wipe 'way some blood. All the rest of the time he keeps on reading. And nobody else in there say a word.

Little John Lee and his mama come out the dentist office, and the nurse calls somebody else in. Then little bit later they come out, and the nurse calls another name. But fast 's she calls somebody in there, somebody else comes in the place where we sitting, and the room stays full.

The people coming in now, all of them wearing big coats. One of them says something 'bout sleeting, another one says he hope not. Another one says he think it ain't nothing but rain. 'Cause, he says, rain can get awful cold this time of year.

All round the room they talking. Some of them talking to people right by them, some of them talking to people clear 'cross the room, some of them talking to anybody'll listen. It's a little bitty room, no bigger than us kitchen, and I can see everybody in there. The little old room's full of smoke, 'cause you got two old men smoking pipes over by that side door. I think I feel my tooth thumping me some, and I hold my breath and wait. I wait and wait, but it don't thump me no more. Thank God for that.

I feel like going to sleep, and I lean back 'gainst the wall. But I'm scared to go to sleep. Scared 'cause the nurse might call my name and I won't hear her. And Mama might go to sleep, too, and she'll be mad if neither one of us heard the nurse.

I look up at Mama. I love my mama. I love my mama. And when cotton come I'm go'n get her a new coat. And I ain't go'n get a black one, either. I think I'm go'n get her a red one.

"They got some books over there," I say. "Want read one of them?"

Mama looks at the books, but she don't answer me.

"You got yourself a little man there," the lady says.

Mama don't say nothing to the lady, but she must've smiled, 'cause I seen the lady smiling back. The lady looks at me a little while, like she's feeling sorry for me.

"You sure got that preacher out here in a hurry," she says to that boy.

The boy looks up at her and looks in his book again. When I grow up I want be just like him. I want clothes like that and I want keep a book with me, too.

"You really don't believe in God?" the lady says.

"No," he says.

"But why?" the lady says.

"Because the wind is pink," he says.

"What?" the lady says.

The boy don't answer her no more. He just reads in his book.

"Talking 'bout the wind is pink," that old lady says. She's sitting on the same bench with the boy and she's trying to look in his face. The boy makes 'tend the old lady ain't even there. He just keeps on reading. "Wind is pink," she says again. "Eh, Lord, what children go'n be saying next?"

The lady 'cross from us bust out laughing.

"That's a good one," she says. "The wind is pink. Yes sir, that's a good one."

"Don't you believe the wind is pink?" the boy says. He keeps his head down in the book.

"Course I believe it, honey," the lady says. "Course I do." She looks at us and winks her eye. "And what color is grass, honey?"

"Grass? Grass is black."

She bust out laughing again. The boy looks at her.

"Don't you believe grass is black?" he says.

The lady quits her laughing and looks at him. Everybody else looking at him, too. The place quiet, quiet.

"Grass is green, honey," the lady says. "It was green yesterday, it's green today, and it's go'n be green tomorrow."

"How do you know it's green?"

"I know because I know."

"You don't know it's green," the boy says. "You believe it's green because someone told you it was green. If someone had told you it was black you'd believe it was black."

"It's green," the lady says. "I know green when I see green."

"Prove it's green," the boy says.

"Sure, now," the lady says. "Don't tell me it's coming to that."

"It's coming to just that," the boy says. "Words mean nothing. One means no more than the other."

"That's what it all coming to?" that old lady says. That old lady got on a turban and she got on two sweaters. She got a green sweater under a black sweater. I can see the green sweater 'cause some of the buttons on the other sweater's missing.

"Yes ma'am," the boy says. "Words mean nothing. Action is the only thing. Doing. That's the only thing."

"Other words, you want the Lord to come down here and show Hisself to you?" she says.

"Exactly, ma'am" he says.

"You don't mean that, I'm sure?" she says.

"I do, ma'am," he says.

"Done, Jesus," the old lady says, shaking her head.

"I didn't go 'long with that preacher at first," the other lady says; "but now—I don't know. When a person say the grass is black, he's either a lunatic or something's wrong."

"Prove to me that it's green," the boy says.

"It's green because the people say it's green."

"Those same people say we're citizens of these United States," the boy says.

"I think I'm a citizen," the lady says.

"Citizens have certain rights," the boy says. "Name me one right that you have. One right, granted by the Constitution, that you can exercise in Bayonne."

The lady don't answer him. She just looks at him like she don't know what he's talking 'bout. I know I don't.

"Things changing," she says.

"Things are changing because some black men have begun to think with their brains and not their hearts," the boy says.

"You trying to say these people don't believe in God?"

"I'm sure some of them do. Maybe most of them do. But they don't believe that God is going to touch these white people's hearts and change things tomorrow. Things change through action. By no other way."

Everybody sit quiet and look at the boy. Nobody says a thing. Then the lady 'cross the room from me and Mama just shakes her head.

"Let's hope that not all your generation feel the same way you do," she says.

"Think what you please, it doesn't matter," the boy says. "But it will be men who listen to their heads and not their hearts who will see that your children have a better chance than you had."

"Let's hope they ain't all like you, though," the old lady says. "Done forgot the heart absolutely."

"Yes ma'am, I hope they aren't all like me," the boy says. "Unfortunately, I was born too late to believe in your God. Let's hope that the ones who come after will have your faith—if not in your God, then in something else, something definitely that they can lean on. I haven't anything. For me, the wind is pink, the grass is black."

The nurse comes in the room where we all sitting and waiting and says the doctor won't take no more patients till one o'clock this evening. My mama jumps up off the bench and goes up to the white lady.

"Nurse, I have to go back in the field this evening," she says.

"The doctor is treating his last patient now," the nurse says. "One o'clock this evening."

"Can I at least speak to the doctor?" my mama asks.

"I'm his nurse," the lady says.

"My little boy's sick," my mama says. "Right now his tooth almost killing him."

The nurse looks at me. She's trying to make up her mind if to let me come in. I look at her real pitiful. The tooth ain't hurting me at all, but Mama say it is, so I make 'tend for her sake.

"This evening," the nurse says, and goes on back in the office.

"Don't feel 'jected, honey," the lady says to Mama. "I been round them a long time—they take you when they want to. If you was white, that's something else; but we the wrong color."

Mama don't say nothing to the lady, and me and her go outside and stand 'gainst the wall. It's cold out there. I can feel that wind going through my coat. Some of the other people come out of the room and go up the street. Me and Mama stand there a little while and we start walking. I don't know where we going. When we come to the other street we just stand there.

"You don't have to make water, do you?" Mama says.

"No, ma'am," I say.

We go on up the street. Walking real slow. I can tell Mama don't know where she's going. When we come to a store we stand there and look at the dummies. I look at a little boy wearing a brown overcoat. He's got on brown shoes, too. I look at my old shoes and look at his'n again. You wait till summer, I say.

Me and Mama walk away. We come up to another store and we stop and look at them dummies, too. Then we go on again. We pass a café where the white people in there eating. Mama tells me keep my eyes in front where they belong, but I can't help from seeing them people eat. My stomach starts to growling 'cause I'm hungry. When I see people eating, I get hungry; when I see a coat, I get cold.

A man whistles at my mama when we go by a filling station. She makes 'tend she don't even see him. I look back and I feel like hitting him in the mouth. If I was bigger, I say; if I was bigger, you'd see.

We keep on going. I'm getting colder and colder, but I don't say nothing. I feel that stuff running down my nose and I sniff.

"That rag," Mama says.

I get it out and wipe my nose. I'm getting cold all over now—my face, my hands, my feet, everything. We pass another little café, but this'n for white people, too, and we can't go in there, either. So we just walk. I'm so cold now I'm 'bout ready to say it. If I knowed where we was going I wouldn't be so cold, but I don't know where we going. We go, we go, we go. We walk clean out of Bayonne. Then we cross the street and we come back. Same thing I seen when I got off the bus this morning. Same old trees, same old walk, same old weeds, same old cracked pave—same old everything.

I sniff again.

"That rag," Mama says.

I wipe my nose real fast and jugg that handkerchief back in my pocket 'fore my hand gets too cold. I raise my head and I can see David's hardware store. When we come up to it, we go in. I don't know why, but I'm glad.

It's warm in there. It's so warm in there you don't ever want to leave. I look for the heater, and I see it over by them barrels. Three white men standing round the heater talking in Creole. One of them comes over to see what my mama want.

"Got any axe handles?" she says.

Me, Mama and the white man start to the back, but Mama stops me when we come up to the heater. She and the white man go on. I hold my hands over the heater and look at them. They go all the way to the back, and I see the white man pointing to the axe handles 'gainst the wall. Mama takes one of them and shakes it like she's trying to figure how much it weighs. Then she rubs her hand over it from one end to the other end. She turns it over and looks at the other side, then she shakes it again, and shakes her head and puts it back. She gets another one and she does it just like she did the first one, then she shakes her head. Then she gets a brown one and do it that, too. But she don't like this one, either. Then she gets another one, but 'fore she shakes it or anything, she looks at me. Look like she's trying to say something to me, but I don't know what it is. All I know is I done got warm now and I'm feeling right smart better. Mama shakes this axe handle just like she did the others, and shakes her head and says something to the white man. The white man just looks at his pile of axe handles, and when Mama pass him to come to the front, the white man just scratch his head and follows her. She tells me come on and we go on out and start walking again.

We walk and walk, and no time at all I'm cold again. Look like I'm colder now 'cause I can still remember how good it was back there. My stomach growls and I suck it in to keep Mama from hearing it. She's walking right 'side me, and it growls so loud you can hear it a mile. But Mama don't say a word.

When we come up to the courthouse, I look at the clock. It's got quarter to twelve. Mean we got another hour and a quarter to be out here in the cold. We go and stand 'side a building. Something hits my cap and I look up at the sky. Sleet's falling.

I look at Mama standing there. I want stand close 'side her, but she don't like that. She say that's crybaby stuff. She say you got to stand for yourself, by yourself.

"Let's go back to that office," she says.

We cross the street. When we get to the dentist office I try to open the door, but I can't. I twist and twist, but I can't. Mama pushes me to the side and she twist the knob, but she can't open the door, either. She turns 'way from the door. I look at her, but I don't move and I don't say nothing. I done seen her like this before and I'm scared of her.

"You hungry?" she says. She says it like she's mad at me, like I'm the cause of everything.

"No, ma'am," I say.

"You want eat and walk back, or you rather don't eat and ride?"

"I ain't hungry," I say.

I ain't just hungry, but I'm cold, too. I'm so hungry and cold I want to cry. And look like I'm getting colder and colder. My feet done got numb. I try to work my toes, but I don't even feel them. Look like I'm go'n die. Look like I'm go'n stand right here and freeze to death. I think 'bout home. I think 'bout Val and Auntie and Ty and Louis and Walker. It's 'bout twelve o'clock and I know they eating dinner now. I can hear Ty making jokes. He done forgot 'bout getting up early this morning and right now he's probably making jokes. Always trying to make somebody laugh. I wish I was right there listening to him. Give anything in the world if I was home round the fire.

"Come on," Mama says.

We start walking again. My feet so numb I can't hardly feel them. We turn the corner and go on back up the street. The clock on the courthouse starts hitting for twelve.

The sleet's coming down plenty now. They hit the pave and bounce like rice. Oh, Lord; oh, Lord, I pray. Don't let me die, don't let me die, don't let me die, Lord.

Now I know where we going. We going back of town where the colored people eat. I don't care if I don't eat. I been hungry before. I can stand it. But I can't stand the cold.

I can see we go'n have a long walk. It's 'bout a mile down there. But I don't mind. I know when I get there I'm go'n warm myself. I think I can hold out. My hands numb in my pockets and my feet numb, too, but if I keep moving I can hold out. Just don't stop no more, that's all.

The sky's gray. The sleet keeps on falling. Falling like rain now—plenty, plenty. You can hear it hitting the pave. You can see it bouncing. Sometimes it bounces two times 'fore it settles.

We keep on going. We don't say nothing. We just keep on going, keep on going.

I wonder what Mama's thinking. I hope she ain't mad at me. When summer come I'm go'n pick plenty cotton and get her a coat. I'm go'n get her a red one.

I hope they'd make it summer all the time. I'd be glad if it was summer all the time—but it ain't. We got to have winter, too. Lord, I hate the winter. I guess everybody hate the winter.

I don't sniff this time. I get out my handkerchief and wipe my nose. My hand's so cold I can hardly hold the handkerchief.

I think we getting close, but we ain't there yet. I wonder where everybody is. Can't see a soul but us. Look like we the only two people moving round today. Must be too cold for the rest of the people to move round in.

I can hear my teeth. I hope they don't knock together too hard and make that bad one hurt. Lord, that's all I need, for that bad one to start off.

I hear a church bell somewhere. But today ain't Sunday. They must be ringing for a funeral or something.

I wonder what they doing at home. They must be eating. Monsieur Bayonne might be there with his guitar. One day Ty played with Monsieur Bayonne's guitar and broke one of the strings. Monsieur Bayonne was some mad with Ty. He say Ty wasn't go'n ever 'mount to nothing. Ty can go just like Monsieur Bayonne when he ain't there. Ty can make everybody laugh when he starts to mocking Monsieur Bayonne.

I used to like to be with Mama and Daddy. We used to be happy. But they took him in the Army. Now, nobody happy no more.... I be glad when Daddy comes home.

Monsieur Bayonne say it wasn't fair for them to take Daddy and give Mama nothing and give us nothing. Auntie say, "Shhh, Etienne. Don't let them hear you talk like that." Monsieur Bayonne say, "It's God truth. What they giving his children? They have to walk three and a half miles to school hot or cold. That's anything to give for a paw? She's got to work in the field rain or shine just to make ends meet. That's anything to give for a husband?" Auntie say, "Shhh, Etienne, shhh." "Yes, you right," Monsieur Bayonne say. "Best don't say it in front of them now. But one day they go'n find out. One day." "Yes, I suppose so," Auntie say. "Then what, Rose Mary?" Monsieur Bayonne say. "I don't know, Etienne," Auntie say. "All we can do is us job, and leave everything else in His hand...."

We getting closer, now. We getting closer. I can even see the railroad tracks.

We cross the tracks, and now I see the cafe'. Just to get in there, I say. Just to get in there. Already I'm starting to feel little better.

We go in. Ahh, it's good. I look for the heater; there 'gainst the wall. One of them little brown ones. I just stand there and hold my hands over it. I can't open my hands too wide 'cause they almost froze.

Mama's standing right 'side me. She done unbuttoned her coat. Smoke rises out of the coat, and the coat smells like a wet dog.

I move to the side so Mama can have more room. She opens out her hands and rubs them together. I rub mine together, too, 'cause this keep them from hurting. If you let them warm too fast, they hurt you sure. But if you let them warm just little bit at a time, and you keep rubbing them, they be all right every time.

They got just two more people in the café. A lady back of the counter, and a man on this side the counter. They been watching us ever since we come in.

Mama gets out the handkerchief and count up the money. Both of us know how much money she's got there. Three dollars. No, she ain't got three dollars, 'cause she had to pay us way up here. She ain't got but two dollars and a half left. Dollar and a half to get my tooth pulled, and fifty cents for us to go back on, and fifty cents worth of salt meat.

She stirs the money round with her finger. Most of the money is change 'cause I can hear it rubbing together. She stirs it and stirs it. Then she looks at the door. It's still sleeting. I can hear it hitting 'gainst the wall like rice.

"I ain't hungry, Mama," I say.

"Got to pay them something for they heat," she says.

She takes a quarter out of the handkerchief and ties the handkerchief up again. She looks over her shoulder at the people, but she still don't move. I hope she don't spend the money. I don't want her spending it on me. I'm hungry, I'm almost starving I'm so hungry, but I don't want her spending the money on me.

She flips the quarter over like she's thinking. She's must be thinking 'bout us walking back home. Lord, I sure don't want walk home. If I thought it'd do any good to say something, I'd say it. But Mama makes up her own mind 'bout things.

She turns 'way from the heater right fast, like she better hurry up and spend the quarter 'fore she change her mind. I watch her go toward the counter. The man and the lady look at her, too. She tells the lady something and the lady walks away. The man keeps on looking at her. Her back's turned to the man, and she don't even know he's standing there.

The lady puts some cakes and a glass of milk on the counter. Then she pours up a cup of coffee and sets it 'side the other stuff. Mama pays her for the things and comes on back where I'm standing. She tells me sit down at the table 'gainst the wall.

The milk and the cake's for me; the coffee's for Mama. I eat slow and I look at her. She's looking outside at the sleet. She's looking real sad. I say to myself, I'm go'n make all this up one day. You see, one day, I'm go'n make all this up. I want say it now; I want tell her how I feel right now; but Mama don't like for us to talk like that.

"I can't eat all this," I say.

They ain't got but just three little old cakes there. I'm so hungry right now, the Lord knows I can eat a hundred times three, but I want my mama to have one.

Mama don't even look my way. She knows I'm hungry, she knows I want it. I let it stay there a little while, then I get it and eat it. I eat just on my front teeth, though, 'cause if cake touch that back tooth I know what'll happen. Thank God it ain't hurt me at all today.

After I finish eating I see the man go to the juke box. He drops a nickel in it, then he just stand there a little while looking at the record. Mama tells me keep my eyes in front where they belong. I turn my head like she say, but then I hear the man coming toward us.

"Dance, pretty?" he says.

Mama gets up to dance with him. But 'fore you know it, she done grabbed the little man in the collar and done heaved him 'side the wall. He hit the wall so hard he stop the juke box from playing.

"Some pimp," the lady back of the counter says. "Some pimp."

The little man jumps up off the floor and starts toward my mama. 'Fore you know it, Mama done sprung open her knife and she's waiting for him.

"Come on," she says. "Come on. I'll gut you from your neighbo to your throat. Come on."

I go up to the little man to hit him, but Mama makes me come and stand 'side her. The little man looks at me and Mama and goes on back to the counter.

"Some pimp," the lady back of the counter says. "Some pimp." She starts laughing and pointing at the little man. "Yes sir, you a pimp, all right. Yes sir-ree."

"Fasten that coat, let's go," Mama says.

"You don't have to leave," the lady says.

Mama don't answer the lady, and we right out in the cold again. I'm warm right now—my hands, my ears, my feet—but I know this ain't go'n last too long. It done sleet so much now you got ice everywhere you look.

We cross the railroad tracks, and soon 's we do, I get cold. That wind goes through this little old coat like it ain't even there. I got on a shirt and a sweater under the coat, but that wind don't pay them no mind. I look up and I can see we got a long way to go. I wonder if we go'n make it 'fore I get too cold.

We cross over to walk on the sidewalk. They got just one sidewalk back here, and it's over there.

After we go just a little piece, I smell bread cooking. I look, then I see a baker shop. When we get closer, I can smell it more better. I shut my eyes and make 'tend I'm eating. But I keep them shut too long and I butt up 'gainst a telephone post. Mama grabs me and see if I'm hurt. I ain't bleeding or nothing and she turns me loose.

I can feel I'm getting colder and colder, and I look up to see how far we still got to go. Uptown is 'way up yonder. A half mile more, I reckon. I try to think of something. They say think and you won't get cold. I think of that poem, "Annabel Lee." I ain't been to school in so long—this bad weather—I reckon they done passed "Annabel Lee" by now. But passed it or not, I'm sure Miss Walker go'n make me recite it when I get there. That woman don't never forget nothing. I ain't never seen nobody like that in my life.

I'm still getting cold. "Annabel Lee" or no "Annabel Lee," I'm still getting cold. But I can see we getting closer. We getting there gradually.

Soon's we turn the corner, I see a little old white lady up in front of us. She's the only lady on the street. She's all in black and she's got a long black rag over her head.

"Stop," she says.

Me and Mama stop and look at her. She must be crazy to be out in all this bad weather. Ain't got but a few other people out there, and all of them's men.

"Y'all done ate?" she says.

"Just finish," Mama says.

"Y'all must be cold then?" she says.

"We headed for the dentist," Mama says. "We'll warm up when we get there."

"What dentist?" the old lady says. "Mr. Bassett?"

"Yes, ma'am," Mama says.

"Come on in," the old lady says. "I'll telephone him and tell him y'all coming."

Me and Mama follow the old lady in the store. It's a little bitty store, and it don't have much in there. The old lady takes off her head rag and folds it up.

"Helena?" somebody calls from the back.

"Yes, Alnest?" the old lady says.

"Did you see them?"

"They're here. Standing beside me."

"Good. Now you can stay inside."

The old lady looks at Mama. Mama's waiting to hear what she brought us in here for. I'm waiting for that, too.

"I saw y'all each time you went by," she says. "I came out to catch you, but you were gone."

"We went back of town," Mama says.

"Did you eat?"

"Yes, ma'am."

The old lady looks at Mama a long time, like she's thinking Mama might be just saying that. Mama looks right back at her. The old lady looks at me to see what I have to say. I don't say nothing. I sure ain't going 'gainst my mama.

"There's food in the kitchen," she says to Mama. "I've been keeping it warm."

Mama turns right around and starts for the door.

"Just a minute," the old lady says. Mama stops. "The boy'll have to work for it. It isn't free."

"We don't take no handout," Mama says.

"I'm not handing out anything," the old lady says. "I need my garbage moved to the front. Ernest has a bad cold and can't go out there."

"James'll move it for you," Mama says.

"Not unless you eat," the old lady says. "I'm old, but I have my pride, too, you know."

Mama can see she ain't go'n beat this old lady down, so she just shakes her head.

"All right," the old lady says. "Come into the kitchen."

She leads the way with that rag in her hand. The kitchen is a little bitty little old thing, too. The table and the stove just 'bout fill it up. They got a little room to the side. Somebody in there laying 'cross the bed—'cause I can see one of his feet. Must be the person she was talking to: Ernest or Alnest—something like that.

"Sit down," the old lady says to Mama. "Not you," she says to me. "You have to move the cans."

"Helena?" the man says in the other room.

"Yes, Alnest?" the old lady says.

"Are you going out there again?"

"I must show the boy where the garbage is, Alnest," the old lady says.

"Keep that shawl over your head," the old man says.

"You don't have to remind me, Alnest. Come, boy," the old lady says.

We got out in the yard. Little old back yard ain't no bigger than the store or the kitchen. But it can sleet here just like it can sleet in any big back yard. And 'fore you know it, I'm trembling.

"There," the old lady says, pointing to the cans. I pick up one of the cans and set it right back down. The can's so light, I'm go'n see what's inside of it.

"Here," the old lady says. "Leave that can alone."

I look back at her standing there in the door. She's got that black rag wrapped round her shoulders, and she's pointing one of her little old fingers at me.

"Pick it up and carry it to the front," she says. I go by her with the can, and she's looking at me all the time. I'm sure the can's empty. I'm sure she could've carried it herself—maybe both of them at the same time. "Set it on the sidewalk by the door and come back for the other one," she says.

I go and come back, and Mama looks at me when I pass her. I get the other can and take it to the front. It don't feel a bit heavier than that first one. I tell myself I ain't go'n be nobody's fool, and I'm go'n look inside this can to see just what I been hauling. First, I look up the street, then down the street. Nobody coming. Then I look over my shoulder toward the door. That little old lady done slipped up there quiet 's mouse, watching me again. Look like she knowed what I was go'n do.

"Ehh, Lord," she says. "Children, children. Come in here, boy, and go wash your hands."

I follow her in the kitchen. She points toward the bathroom, and I go in there and wash up. Little bitty old bathrooom, but it's clean, clean. I don't use any of her towels; I wipe my hands on my pants legs.

When I come back in the kitchen the old lady done dished up the food. Rice, gravy, meat—and she even got some lettuce and tomato in a saucer. She even got a glass of milk and a piece of cake there, too. It looks so good, I almost start eating 'fore I say my blessing.

"Helena?" the old man says.

"Yes, Alnest?"

"Are they eating?"

"Yes," she says.

"Good," he says. "Now you'll stay inside."

The old lady goes in there where he is and I can hear them talking. I look at Mama. She's eating slow like she's thinking. I wonder what's the matter now. I reckon she's thinking 'bout home.

The old lady comes back in the kitchen.

"I talked to Dr. Bassett's nurse," she says. "Dr. Bassett will take you as soon as you get there."

"Thank you, ma'am," Mama says.

"Perfectly all right," the old lady says. "Which one is it?"

Mama nods toward me. The old lady looks at me real sad. I look sad, too.

"You're not afraid, are you?" she says.

"No ma'am," I say.

"That's a good boy," the old lady says. "Nothing to be afraid of. Dr. Bassett will not hurt you."

When me and Mama get through eating, we thank the old lady again.

"Helena, are they leaving?" the old man says.

"Yes, Alnest."

"Tell them I say good-bye."

"They can hear you, Alnest."

"Good-bye both mother and son," the old man says. "And may God be with you."

Me and Mama tell the old man good-bye, and we follow the old lady in the front room. Mama opens the door to go out, but she stops and comes back in the store.

"You sell salt meat?" she says.

"Yes."

"Give me two bits worth."

"That isn't very much salt meat," the old lady says.

"That's all I have," Mama says.

The old lady goes back to the counter and cuts a big piece off the chunk. Then she wraps it up and puts it in a paper bag.

"Two bits," she says.

"That looks like awful lot of meat for a quarter," Mama says.

"Two bits," the old lady says. "I've been selling salt meat behind this counter twenty-five years. I think I know what I'm doing."

"You got a scale there," Mama says.

"What?" the old lady says.

"Weigh it," Mama says.

"What?" the old lady says. "Are you telling me how to run my business?"

"Thanks very much for the food," Mama says.

"Just a minute," the old lady says.

"James," Mama says to me. I move toward the door.

"Just one minute, I said," the old lady says.

Me and Mama stop again and look at her. The old lady takes the meat out of the bag and unwraps it and cuts 'bout half of it off. Then she wraps it up again and juggs it back in the bag and gives the bag to Mama. Mama lays the quarter on the counter.

"Your kindness will never be forgotten," she says. "James," she says to me.

We go out, and the old lady comes to the door to look at us. After we go a little piece I look back, and she's still there watching us.

The sleet's coming down heavy, heavy now, and I turn up my coat collar to keep my neck warm. My mama tells me turn it right back down.

"You not a bum," she says. "You a man."

Amiri Baraka

(b. 1934)

Like many former sixties radicals, Amiri Baraka has reinvented himself several times in the past few decades, and his literary works have always mirrored those changes. Born Everett LeRoi Jones in Newark, New Jersey, Baraka grew up in a comfortable middle-class environment, received his bachelor's degree from Howard University (1954), and studied philosophy and German literature at Columbia and the New School. In the fifties, after being dishonorably discharged from the Air Force, Baraka lived in New York's Greenwich Village, where he wrote jazz criticism and mingled with such prominent Beat poets as Allen Ginsberg and Charles Olson. Baraka published his first volume of poetry, **Preface to a Twenty Volume Suicide Note** (1961), to general acclaim. An invitation to Cuba in 1960, however, shattered his bohemian complacency. After being ridiculed for his lack of political commitment by various Cuban artists and intellectuals, Baraka forsook the Village and moved to Harlem, where he became a fervent Black nationalist. While in spiritual transition, he published his second volume of poetry, **The Dead Lecturer** (1964), and several violent one-act plays, including the highly successful Obie-winning **Dutchman** (1964). As Baraka's political beliefs grew more radical, he began rejecting White culture altogether, a shift that was symbolized by his name change from LeRoi Jones to the Muslim title, Imamu Amiri Baraka, or "blessed spiritual leader." The first two volumes of poetry to be published under this new name include **Black Magic...** (1969) and **In Our Terribleness** (1971). During this prolific period Baraka also wrote several sociopolitical plays, two volumes of jazz criticism, an episodic novel, **The System of Dante's Hell** (1965), a collection of short stories, **Tales** (1967), and a sociological tract, **Raise Race Rays Raze** (1971).

By the mid-seventies, Baraka had begun to espouse Marxist-Leninist thought in response to what he perceived as the limitations of Black nationalism as an instrument of Black liberation. There were, as he explained, "certain dead ends theoretically and ideologically, as far as Nationalism was concerned." Publications from Baraka's socialist phase include a volume of poetry, **Hard Facts** (1975), and several plays. At this time he also began teaching creative writing at the University of New York at StonyBrook. Baraka published his autobiography, **The Autobiography of LeRoi Jones—Amiri Baraka,** in 1984, and his works have been collected in **Selected Plays and Prose** and **Selected Poetry,** both published in 1979.

Answers in Progress

Can you die in air-raid jiggle
torn arms flung through candystores
Touch the edge of answer. The waves of nausea
as change sweeps the frame of breath and meat.

> *"Stick a knife through his throat,"*
> *he slid*
> *in the blood*
> *got up running toward*
> *the blind newsdealer. He screamed*
> *about "Cassius Clay," and slain there in the*
> *street, the whipped figure of jesus, head opened*
> *eyes flailing against his nose. They beat him to*
> *pulpy answers. We wrote Muhammad Ali across his*
> *face and chest, like a newspaper of bleeding meat.*

The next day the spaceships landed. Art Blakey records was what they were looking for. We gave them Buttercorn Lady and they threw it back at us. They wanted to know what happened to The Jazz Messengers. And right in the middle, playing the Sun Ra tape, the blanks staggered out of the department store. Omar had missed finishing the job, and they staggered out, falling in the snow, red all over the face, chest, the stab wounds in one in the top of a Adam hat.

The space men thought that's what was really happening. One beeped (Ali mentioned this in the newspapers) that this was evolution. Could we dig it? Shit, yeh. We were laughing. Some blanks rounded one corner, Yaa and Dodua were behind them, to take them to the Center. Nationalized on the spot.

The space men could dig everything. They wanted to take one of us to a spot and lay for a minute, to dig what they were in to. Their culture and shit. Whistles Newark was broke up in one section. The dead mayor and other wops carried by in black trucks. Wingo, Rodney and them waving at us. They stopped the first truck and Cyril wanted to know about them thin cats hopping around us. He's always very fast finger.

Space men wanted to know what happened after Blakey. They'd watched but couldn't get close enough to dig exactly what was happening. Albert Ayler they dug immediately from Russell's mouth imitation. That's later. Red spam cans in their throats with the voices, and one of them started to scat. It wigged me. Bamberger's burning down, dead blancos all over and a cat from Sigma Veda, and his brothers, hopping up and down asking us what was happening.

We left Rachel and Lefty there to keep explaining. Me and Pinball had to go back to headquarters, and report Market Street Broad Street rundown. But we told them we'd talk to them. I swear one of those cats had a hip walk. Even thought they was hoppin and bopadoppin up and down, like they had to pee. Still this one cat had a stiff tentacle, when he walked. Yeh; long blue winggly cats, with soft liquid sounds out of their throats for voices. Like, "You know where Art Blakey, Buhainia, is working?" We fell out.

***

Walk through life
beautiful more than anything
stand in the sunlight
walk through life
love all the things
that make you strong, be lovers, be anything
for all the people of
earth.

You have brothers
you love each other, change up
and look at the world
now, it's
ours, take it slow
we've long time, a long way
to go,

we have
each other, and the
world,
don't be sorry
walk on out through sunlight life, and know
we're on the go
for love
to open
our lives
to walk
tasting the sunshine
of life.

Boulevards played songs like that and we rounded up blanks where we had to. Space men were on the south side laying in some of the open houses. Some brothers came in from the west, Chicago, they had a bad thing going out there. Fires were still high as the buildings, but Ram sent a couple of them out to us, to dig what was happening. One of them we sent to the blue cats, to take that message back. Could we dig what was happening with them? We sent our own evaluation back, and when I finished the report me and Pinball started weaving through the dead cars and furniture. Waving at the brothers, listening to the sounds, we had piped through the streets.

Smokey Robinson was on now. But straight up fast and winging. No more unrequited love. Damn Smokey got his thing together too. No more tracks or mirages. Just the beauty of the whole. I hope they play Sun Ra for them blue cats, so they can dig where we at.

Magic City played later. By time we got to the courthouse. The whole top of that was out. Like you could look inside from fourth or fifth floor of the Hall of Records. Cats were all over that joint. Ogun wanted the records intact.

Past the playgrounds and all them blanks in the cold standing out there or laying on the ground crying. The rich ones really were funny. This ol cat me and Pinball recognized still had a fag thing going for him. In a fur coat, he was some kind of magistrate. Bobby and Moosie were questioning him about some silver he was supposed to have stashed. He was a silver freak. The dude was actually weeping. Crying big sobs; the women crowded away from him. I guess they really couldn't feel sorry for him because he was crying about money.

By the time we got to Weequahic Avenue where the space men and out-of-town brothers were laying I was tired as a dog. We went in there and wanted to smoke some bush, but these blue dudes had something better. Taste like carrots. It was a cool that took you. You thought something was mildly amusing and everything seemed interesting.

I talked with Pinball and the blue leader about Ben Caldwell's paintings ... the one where the guy is smoking the reefer. We thought about the changing reference, of our new world. As it stood already in the old ruins. And we all felt like Bird. The old altosaxophonist ... but the limits opened out into the pure lyric tone of powerful beings. But when the Sun Ra tape came on this blue dude really opened up. He dug the hell out of it. Perfect harmony these cats had too. Boooooo-liiiiiiiiioooooooooooooo ... daaaaaah hhhhhh aaaaahhhhhh ... booooooooooooooooooooooooooooo aaaaaaaaoooaaaaa

Claude McKay I started quoting. Four o'clock in the morning to a blue dude gettin cooled out on carrots. We didn't have no duty until ten o'clock the next day, and me and Lorenzo and Ish had to question a bunch of prisoners and stuff for the TV news. Chazee had a play to put on that next afternoon about the Chicago stuff. Ray talked to him. And the name of the play was Big Fat Fire.

Man I was tired. We had taped the Sigma. They were already infested with Buddhas there, and we spoke very quietly about how we knew it was our turn. I had burned my hand somewhere and this blue cat looked at it hard and cooled it out. White came in with the design for a flag he'd been working on. Black heads, black hearts, and blue fiery space in the background. Love was heavy in the atmosphere. Ball wanted to know what the blue chicks looked like. But I didn't. Cause I knew after tomorrow's duty, I had a day off, and I knew somebody waitin for me at my house, and some kids, and some fried fish, and those carrots, and wow.

That's the way the fifth day ended.

Clarence Major

(b. 1936)

Hailed as a pioneer in the realm of experimental fiction, Clarence Major is a literary innovator who uses unreliable narrators, montage, and chronological distortion in his self-conscious, postmodern stories. Not content with simply probing the relations between author, text, and reader, Major further complicates the boundary between fiction and reality by bringing into his work various politically charged themes relating to Black experience and identity. While he is best known for his novels, such as **All-Night Visitors** *(1969),* **Reflex and Bone Structure** *(1975), and* **Emergency Exit** *(1979), Major launched his literary career with a collection of poetry published in 1954 when he was only eighteen. A year later he joined the Air Force. After serving for two years, Major returned to Chicago, where he had been raised, when he was offered a painting scholarship at the Art Institute there. "The physical world of lines, color, and composition," he would later say, "definitely influenced my writing." Major's poetry has been collected in* **Love Poems of a Black Man** *(1965),* **The Syncopated Cakewalk** *(1974),* **Inside Diameter** *(1985), and* **Some Observations of a Stranger at Zuni in the Latter Part of the Century** *(1989). His other works include* **Juba to Five: A Dictionary of African-American Slang** *(1994), a volume of literary criticism entitled* **The Dark and Feeling: Black American Writers and Their Work** *(1974), and two short-story collections,* **Fun and Games** *(1989) and* **Calling the Wind** *(1993). Major has said of writing, "The only thing you really have is words. You begin with words, and you end with words." He is currently Chairman of Creative Writing at the University of California, Davis, where he has been teaching since 1989.*

Five Years Ago

It was Labor Day, September 2, a Monday, five years ago, and I was twenty-seven years old and about to bring my forty-four-year-old mother and my forty-four-year-old father together for the first time in my adult life. All my life I had daydreamed about this moment, wondered if it would ever happen, and now that it was about to happen, I was so emotional, I was almost out of control. The night before, my father had flown into Chicago from Boston, where he worked as a real estate broker. He was staying, like the last time, at his mother's house. I drove down to his mother's on Fifty-fifth and Indiana Avenue to pick him up. Mother Zoe—that's what I call his mother, my grandmother—was sitting at the kitchen table with her cup of coffee when I knocked on the back door and there was my father—whom I hadn't seen but once before—two years earlier when he came back to Chicago, that time, I think, because a brokers convention was being held in Chicago. He was slender and brown and handsome and wore a beard and was smiling at me as I came in. Apparently ready to go, he was already holding a tan summer jacket across his arm. I blushed and felt something like a current of electricity shoot through my body as I simply lowered my head, hiding my joy, and walked straight over to him and slid my arms under his and around his body—which fitted mine nicely—and hugged him for all I was worth. I knew I was going to cry. Tears were already rimming my eyes. All it would take was a blink. And I wanted my face over his shoulder, so I'd be looking out the kitchen window, my back to Mother Zoe, when the tears came. But it didn't help and finally it didn't matter. I not only cried but I sobbed, sobbed with joy and pain and love for this man I'd dreamed of and fearfully wondered about all my life. And here he was. Two years before, I had expected him to appear suddenly bigger than life, but when I came into Mother Zoe's house that time and saw him sitting at the dining room table with his mother, with his elbows on the table, he seemed so small, so fragile, so frail, compared to the giant I'd imagined. He was just a flesh and blood human being, a man, and one not especially imposing, just an ordinary man. But that time I didn't rush to him and hug him. I was too confused, too scared. He stood up and came to me and hugged me, put his arms around me and kissed my forehead. And, yes, that time, too, I cried. I cried but I pulled away in embarrassment, pulled back and went and sat down beside Mother Zoe, who patted me on my thigh. I was wearing jeans. I remember. Jeans and a blouse. And my curly hair was pulled back. I hadn't known how to dress for him. Before going down to Mother Zoe's, I'd tried on four different dresses and six pairs of shoes and finally rejected all of them and pulled on a pair of jeans and told my husband, Austin, "If my father can't accept me in jeans then, then—" but I couldn't finish the sentence. And I remember my husband—who, by the way, is ten years older than my father—saying, "Don't worry. He'll be happy to see you." But, you know, I was never quite sure that he was. Something about him seemed guarded. I'm still talking about that first time two years before. Sure, he hugged me but it was a stiff hug. Maybe he was nervous, too. Maybe it was simply that he didn't know what to expect and was maybe even a little bit scared of me. Yes, that's what I felt. Felt that he was scared of me. After all, he hadn't seen me since, since … Well, actually, I don't think he ever saw me after two or three. And I don't remember him at all. I know from what Mother told me. They took him to court, you know. Tried to force him to marry or support her. But my mother, Pandora, was only sixteen. And my father, Barry Stanton, was exactly sixteen, too. Both of them still in high school. Messing around, they got me. And got themselves in a world of trouble. In fact, Mother got thrown out of school and Father joined the Army. Mother's family said he ran away from his responsibility. That's the way they saw it. But I was talking about that first time seeing him and comparing it to seeing him this time. And this time I just walked right over to him and put my arms around him and he didn't feel like a stranger anymore. And I had gotten this fantasy version of him, this giant of a man, down to size. I was just hugging my father, just a normal human being, a man, a handsome man with a face like mine. I could see myself in his face. Looking into his eyes, in a wonderfully strange way, gave me myself in a new way for the first time. I felt so close to him it was almost terrifying. When I hugged him I felt his heart beating against my breast and I held him close just to continue feeling his rhythm. Tears running down my cheeks, sobbing, I held him long and hard. But I started shaking and I pulled back and said, "I'm sorry, I'm sorry—" but I couldn't bring myself to call him Daddy or Father. I also couldn't call him Barry, just plain Barry. I didn't know what to call him. Anyway, the plan was he'd have breakfast, no, brunch, with Pandora—his old high school girlfriend—and my husband, Austin, and my sister, Yvette, and my six-year-old daughter, Octavia, and me. Mother Zoe was still in her bathrobe, with her gray hair kind of standing out every whichaway. And just as we were leaving Winona came down the hall into the kitchen and said, "Now, Ophelia, when are you bringing Barry back? You know we got plans for this afternoon?" And something in Winona's tone offended me but I held back and refused to lash out although I wanted to. He was *my* father. I had spent twenty-seven years without him and here was his sister—who grew up with him, who had visited him more than once in Boston—telling me to cut my time with him short, bring him back, don't hog his time. I got so pissed I could have screamed but I didn't. I just looked at Winona standing there in her bathrobe with the corners of her big pretty mouth turned up like she was expecting me to give her trouble. And Mother Zoe jumped in and said, "That's right. And I sure hope you ain't planning to have your mother over there. I told you not to invite her. Didn't I?" And I couldn't remember Mother Zoe making such a request or demand till she said, "Remember, I said, just you and Barry, quiet brunch together with you and your husband and your daughter. Just to get to know your father." Then I remembered but I hadn't taken her words to imply that Mother wasn't to be invited. And anyway, what was this thing about, anyway? Mother Zoe hated my mother from the beginning, from the time she came home from work unexpectedly and caught Mother and her son making love on the couch. Mother told me all about it. Mother Zoe drove her out, shouting at her, calling her a whore, a tramp, a cheap little bitch. No woman, Mother said, was ever good enough for Mother Zoe's son. Mother said she thought he would turn into a faggot—her word—the situation was so bad. But why now all these years later did I have to be the victim of this shit, the victim of these ill feelings that existed between Mother Zoe and sixteen-year-old Pandora Lowell years ago? Why did the mess present itself just when I wanted more than anything in the world to bring my mother and father together and feel, for the first time, like I had a real family? So, I didn't say anything. I just nodded. I assured Winona I'd get her brother back before noon. And my father and I left. Octavia was waiting in the car in the back seat. And while we drove south—I live at Ninety-fifth and Yates—I had the warmest feeling listening to my father talking with my daughter. He was asking her about her school, about what she liked to do, and being the smart kid she was, she kept telling him about a spelling contest she'd just won, and about her winning in the girl's footrace, and about her great math scores. They seemed to hit it off better this time than they had the first time when she was four. Back then she wasn't really that interested in him. But now she had a great curiosity because she had been made to feel his importance. Some kids had grandfathers, others didn't. In a way, it had become very important to her in the last year or so to have a grandfather. Having one—at least at her school, Martin R. Delany School, the best private school on the South Side—was a status symbol, especially since so many kids there don't. In fact, I had encouraged her to write to him in Boston and she did send him three or four letters but he answered only once, and only with a postcard. I had to reassure her that her grandfather loved her—though I didn't believe it, didn't even believe he loved me, his own daughter—and that he was simply too busy to spare time to write often. Anyway, when we got to the house my sister, Yvette, was in the kitchen working on the muffins. She makes great blueberry muffins. We could smell them the minute I turned off the motor and the smell got stronger as we walked up the back walkway from the garage, and while crossing the patio, I slid my arm around my father's waist and hugged him to me. My father, I thought, my father, here with me. And I quickly kissed his cheek. And the minute we stepped up onto the back porch there was Mother sitting in one of the straw chairs waiting. And I thought of Mother Zoe and her warning and all I could hope was that my father would not tell. This was the moment. I had brought these two together for the first time since they were teenagers. I think the last time they saw each other was in a courtroom when they both were eighteen, and Mother was trying to get some money out of him, just before he joined the Army and disappeared. But this was the big moment now. The one I had waited for. This was my moment. The three of us stood there. Octavia walked between us into the house and into the kitchen, following the smell of blueberry muffins. I watched my father and Mother just looking at each other, looking fearfully. There was a distance of about five feet between them. He was trying to smile. God only knows what he was thinking. He didn't look happy to see her. In fact, he seemed a bit irritated. And she was giving him this cynical sideways look she can get. It's a half sneer. I've seen it all my life. Then she did something she no doubt thought was a smile but it really didn't come out right. It was more a grimace. But she sort of slung her string bean of a body over to him and for a split second I thought she was going to hug him, thought he was going to respond by hugging her, but that's not what happened. She grabbed his beard and tugged at it forcefully, yanked it back and forth, and her mouth was twisted in an agonizing grin and her eyes were blazing with contempt, though she was trying to laugh and to be playful. I'm sure she meant the gesture to be playful but it didn't come off that way at all. She yanked him too hard and he frowned and stepped back a couple of paces, pulling away from her. And she was saying, "What is this crap on your face?" And he was beginning to sneer. I saw just the edge of his canine. An almost imperceptible shudder moved through his face—his cheeks and his chin especially, and his eyes, like her own, blazed. And I wondered why I myself was feeling so elated, so up, so complete—for the first time—and why at the same time everything was obviously going wrong. These two people, I could see, should never have been brought together. Not only did they not like each other, they held contempt for each other. And though I had known that to be the case I hadn't wanted to know it. And it gave me for the first time in my life a clear sense of the emotional foundation of my life. But even then, sensing this then, I didn't want to face it, didn't want the full sense of it to reach my conscience. So I ignored it, pretended the hostility between them was not serious, not important, that, in fact, there was something deeper that held them together and that something was me, my presence in the world. Like it or not, I was their link. And I wanted them to like it. Oh, I so desperately wanted them to like it. So, grabbing Mother by the sleeve and my father by his elbow, I pulled them toward the kitchen, saying, "Come on, let's see what's cooking." And in the kitchen there was my sister and my husband and my daughter. My sister turned around from the stove as I introduced her to my father, Barry Stanton, and she reached out, smiling, and shook his hand. Yvette is a very pretty girl, with bright red full lips, yellowish green eyes, tall and slender with naturally reddish hair, a hair color unusual for a colored girl. (People say we look alike. It's because we both look like Mother, whose hair is also red.) My sister was twenty-three then. And men were after her like crazy. In fact, she said, "I invited Robert over for brunch. Hope you guys don't mind." And though I resented the liberty she'd taken, I held back saying anything. Then my husband, Austin, standing in the doorway watching my father meet my sister, was smiling. Austin is such an elegant gentleman. He was nearing retirement, early retirement at that time. He was fifty-five and had been head of his own law firm, Tate, Jones and Bedford, on Seventy-third and Cottage Grove, for the last fifteen years. He was now financially secure and wanted to stop work so he could go fishing when he felt like it, so he could be with his young daughter more and with me, too. Although he and I hadn't been getting along all that well lately, I still respected and liked him. He was like a father to me. In fact, it's true, he had raised me, in a way. Taught me a lot. As he put it, he had made a "lady" out of me, sent me to law school and given me a comfortable middle-class life in a good South Side neighborhood. I now had a position in his firm and I was holding my own. And after passing the bar last year I defended my first client in a civil case, a woman fighting for child support. I was saying, "Austin Tate, my husband, meet Barry Stanton, my father," and I sounded awkward but the moment seemed grand to me and I felt that a certain formality was needed. Now, my husband and my father were shaking hands and gazing into each other's eyes with tentative kindness. And at least their meeting was going well. Then Austin said, "Welcome to our home. How does it feel to be back in Chicago?" and my father was saying something but I was no longer listening to him because Yvette was having an emergency with the omelettes she was making, breaking eggs into a big enamel bowl, she'd come across a bad egg, and she'd cried out as though bitten by a snake or as though she'd burned her hand on the hot stove, and I turned to her to help. And Mother all this time stood in the doorway between the kitchen and the back porch watching, I sensed, with a lingering though slight expression of contempt. And Octavia ran her finger around in the blueberry batter bowl, then, with her eyes closed in bliss, licked the finger. And I said, "By the way, we're eating out on the patio. It's nice out there this time of morning. You guys go on out," I said with a wave of the hand, "and get started, I want to get my camera, and show my father my office." And I took him by the hand and pulled him up the hall, then up the narrow stair to the second floor where Austin's and my and Octavia's bedrooms were. And I led him into my little study at the back of the house. A place I was proud of. My law diploma was framed on the wall over my desk and I wanted him to see it. But I wasn't planning to point his nose in that direction. But I did stand with my back to my desk—my camera was there on the desk—and took my father by both of his hands and pulled him to me, so that he would be facing—over my shoulders— the vivid evidence of my accomplishment. Three things I was proud of, this degree, my career, and my daughter. And I wanted my father to admire me for those three accomplishments. So I pulled him against my belly and put my arms around him and held him close so that our bodies were breathing together. Thinking back on that moment I know it was a strange thing to do, but I felt so close to him, needed to be so close to him, and wanted him to feel what I was feeling. Touching him this way was the only way I knew how to reach him. Then I kissed him, fully on the mouth and forced my tongue into his mouth, kissed him the way I kissed my husband, kissed him deeply, so deeply he would have to feel how passionately I loved him, how deeply I felt for him, how much he meant to me. I held his head with one hand and held his back with the other and I lifted my stomach toward him and pressed harder and harder, and I felt him respond, felt his whole body come alive in my arms. Then I slowly let him go and nodded toward my diploma, and said, "See? I learned that all by myself." And he took his glasses out of his jacket pocket and put them on and read the words, actually read the words, read them slowly, then he said, "I'm very proud of you, Ophelia." And I squeezed his hand. Then he said, "We have so much to talk about. I wish there was time—" and I said, "Now that we've found each other, there will be endless time. I want to know everything, everything you've ever felt and done, *everything*." And while he looked a little embarrassed by my passion I picked up my camera and pulled him by the hand and we went downstairs and out to the patio where the others had gathered. Robert, Yvette's boyfriend, had arrived. Robert was tall like Yvette, and good-looking with curly hair. He was standing there by Yvette at the table as she set out the plates. Mother and Octavia were helping at the other end. After I introduced Robert and my father, Yvette and I brought out the various platters of eggs and bacon and muffins and, following us, Octavia brought out the jam tray and other miscellaneous condiments. Then Mother went in and got the pitcher of orange juice. Now Austin was in his natural place, at the head of the table. I sat down to his right, my usual place, and when I saw my father beginning to sit between Robert and Octavia, I said, "Oh, no you don't." And I patted the seat next to me. "You're sitting right here next to me." And everybody laughed and he came over and sat down beside me. Then I said, "Let's all hold hands." I took my father's hand and my husband's hand. We all held hands and closed our eyes. Then Austin said grace, a short, to-the-point prayer of gratitude. I glanced at Mother down the table and she was looking cheerier than before as she reached for the muffins and held them in front of Octavia, saying, "Just take one at a time, now. Don't let your eyes be bigger than your stomach." And I remembered her saying those same words to me when I was a child and I had to choke back resentment. One thing I dreaded was her influence on Octavia. I felt that in many ways she had given me an unnecessarily hard time, had often struck me in rage for minor things, and had nagged me constantly when I was growing up. I felt in myself a tendency to treat Octavia this way and I was on guard all the time against the tendency. I meant to break the cycle. All the more reason why I was leery of Mother's presence around Octavia. Anyway, this was a happy moment and I wasn't going to let anything spoil it. I had put the camera down at the end of the table. Just before we started to eat, I looked down the table and said, "Robert, do me a favor. Please take a picture of my father and me together here like this at the table?" And I could see everybody glancing at me, understanding my eagerness, and sympathizing with me. I was acting frantic, acting like I'd thought he was going to suddenly disappear and I'd never see him again. And the fear wasn't unfounded. So Robert, a sweetie, got the camera and stood up and went into a crouch and snapped the picture as I leaned closer to my father, my face cheek-to-cheek with his. Later, after brunch, we took more pictures. And before I knew it, it was eleven-thirty and I shouted, "Oh, Winona's going to *kill* me! We've got to get you back!" So I ran inside, grabbed my purse and car keys while my father shook hands with Austin and Mother and Robert and kissed my sister on the cheek. Octavia hopped in the back seat and we drove back down to Fifty-fifth and Indiana Avenue. Octavia waited in the car. And we walked into Mother Zoe's kitchen exactly at five minutes to twelve. Both Mother Zoe and Winona were dressed now and both were sitting at the kitchen table smoking cigarettes and drinking instant coffee. Giving me this severe look, her crazy look, the first thing Mother Zoe said to her son was "You have a nice time?" and he said, "Yes, very nice." And she wanted to know who else was there. And my heart stopped. I tell you, my heart literally stopped because I had forgotten her concern. I started to say something but couldn't. Then my father said, "Oh, just Ophelia's sister and her boyfriend." And the relief I felt was obvious, maybe too obvious. I'd been holding my breath, then I let it go. And it was then, for the first time, that I thought to ask my father how long he was planning to stay, and he said, "I'm leaving in the morning, Ophelia. Gotta get back. An important transaction coming up. I'm representing both the buyer and the seller this time and it's a very sensitive situation. But I'm coming back when I can stay longer. Okay?" But all I heard was him saying he had to leave and it caused something in me to cave in and I couldn't hide my feelings. With all my might I tried not to start crying and shaking. Somehow I'd thought he would be around at least a week. At *least*. I sighed and said, "Can I take you to the airport?" But Winona answered for him, saying, "That's all right, Ophelia. I've already asked for the morning off so I can drive him out to O'Hare." And I said, "Oh, I see. Then I guess this is the last time I'll see you, at least for a while. Huh?" I could feel the tears coming up again and I didn't want Winona and Mother Zoe to see me cry again so I said, "Come out to the car with me and say goodbye to Octavia. Okay?" And he followed me back out the back door, down through the backyard, out the gate, to the curb where Octavia was sitting at the wheel pretending to drive. By now I was shaking all over and tears were running down my cheeks and I didn't give a damn who knew it. I was miserable. He squatted down by the car door and spoke softly to Octavia for a minute or so, then stood up and I grabbed him and hugged him. I know I was being dramatic, too melodramatic. But I couldn't help it. It was how I felt. I didn't know how to feel or be any other way. I held him like it was the last time I would ever see him. And, like I said, that was five years ago.

William Melvin Kelley

(b. 1937)

A born and bred New Yorker, William Melvin Kelley attended a private preparatory school before entering Harvard University in 1956, where his teachers John Hawkes and Archibald MacLeish inspired him to write. His fiction, which is often varied in technique and style, often probes into race relations and the effect of the environment upon individual identity. Kelley's first novel, **A Different Drummer** *(1962), presents the tale of a Black sharecropper whose experiences reflect the effects of the Black exodus from the South. His second novel,* **A Drop of Patience** *(1965), details the life of a fictional blind musician by describing how the protagonist relies on his other senses. After publishing his short story collection,* **Dancers on the Shore** *(1964), Kelley wrote two more novels,* **dem** *(1967), a remarkable send-up of white suburban life and mores, and the Joyceanesque* **Dunfords Travels Everywheres** *(1970). Both works satirize contemporary attitudes toward race and social class. Honored with awards from the John Hay Whitney Foundation and the National Institute of Arts and Letters, Kelley has taught at the New School for Social Research and the State University of New York at Genesee. After traveling widely in Europe and the West Indies, he has since returned to New York.*

The Only Man on Liberty Street

She was squatting in the front yard, digging with an old brass spoon in the dirt, which was an ocean to the islands of short yellow grass. She wore a red-and-white checkered dress, which hung loosely from her shoulders and obscured her legs. It was early spring and she was barefoot. Her toes stuck out from under the skirt. She could not see the man yet, riding down Liberty Street, his shoulders square, the duster he wore spread back over the horse's rump, a carpetbag tied with a leather strap to his saddle horn and knocking against his leg. She could not see him until he had dismounted and tied his horse to a small black iron Negro jockey and unstrapped the bag. She watched now as he opened the wooden gate, came into the yard, and stood, looking down at her, his face stern, almost gray beneath the brim of his wide hat.

She knew him. Her mother called him Mister Herder and had told Jennie that he was Jennie's father. He was one of the men who came riding down Liberty Street in their fine black suits and starched shirts and large dark ties. Each of these had a house to go to, into which, in the evening usually, he would disappear. Only women and children lived on Liberty Street. All of them were Negroes. Some of the women were quite dark, but most were coffee color. They were all very beautiful. Her mother was light. She was tall, had black eyes, and black hair so long she could sit on it.

The man standing over her was the one who came to her house once or twice a week. He was never there in the morning when Jennie got up. He was tall, and thin, and blond. He had a short beard that looked as coarse as the grass beneath her feet. His eyes were blue, like Jennie's. He did not speak English very well. Jennie's mother had told her he came from across the sea, and Jennie often wondered if he went there between visits to their house.

"Jennie? Your mother tells me that you ask why I do not stay at night. Is so?"

She looked up at him. "Yes, Mister Herder." The hair under his jaw was darker than the hair on his cheeks.

He nodded. "I stay now. Go bring your mother."

She left the spoon in the dirt and ran into the house, down the long hall, dark now because she had been sitting in the sun. She found her mother standing over the stove, a great black lid in her left hand, a wooden spoon in her right. There were beads of sweat on her forehead. She wore a full black skirt and a white blouse. Her one waist-length braid hung straight between her shoulder blades. She turned to Jennie's running steps.

"Mama? That man? My father? He in the yard. He brung a carpetbag."

First her mother smiled, then frowned, then looked puzzled. "A carpetbag, darling?"

"Yes, Mama."

She followed her mother through the house, pausing with her at the hall mirror, where the woman ran her hand up the back of her neck to smooth stray black hair. Then they went onto the porch, where the man was now seated, surveying the tiny yard and the dark green hedge that enclosed it. The carpetbag rested beside his chair. Her mother stood with her hands beneath her apron, staring at the bag. "Mister Herder?"

He turned to them. "I will not go back this time. No matter what. Why should I live in that house when I must come here to know what home is?" He nodded sharply as if in answer to a question. "So! I stay, I give her that house. I will send her money, but I stay here."

Her mother stood silently for an instant, then turned to the door. "Dinner'll be on the table in a half hour." She opened the screen door. The spring whined and cracked. "Oh." She let go the door and picked up the carpetbag. "I'll take this on up." She went inside. As she passed, Jennie could see she was smiling again.

After that, Jennie's mother became a celebrity on Liberty Street. The other women would stop her to ask about the man. "And he staying for good, Josie?"

"Yes."

"You have any trouble yet?"

"Not yet."

"Well, child, you make him put that there house in your name. You don't want to be no Sissie Markham. That white woman come down the same day he died and moved Sissie and her children right into the gutter. You get that house put in your name. You hear?"

"Yes."

"How is it? It different?"

Her mother would look dazed. "Yes, it different. He told me to call him Maynard."

The other women were always very surprised.

At first, Jennie too was surprised. The man was always there in the morning and sometimes even woke her up. Her mother no longer called him Mister Herder, and at odd times, though still quite seldom, said, No. She had never before heard her mother say no to anything the man ever said. It was not long before Jennie was convinced that he actually was her father. She began to call him Papa.

Daily now a white woman had been driving by their house. Jennie did not know who she was or what she wanted but, playing in the yard, would see the white woman's gray buggy turn the corner and come slowly down the block, pulled by a speckled horse that trudged in the dry dust. A Negro driver sat erect in his black uniform, a whip in his fist. The white woman would peer at the house as if looking for an address or something special. She would look at the curtained windows, looking for someone, and sometimes even at Jennie. The look was not kind or tender, but hard and angry as if she knew something bad about the child.

Then one day the buggy stopped, the Negro pulling gently on the reins. The white woman leaned forward, spoke to the driver, and handed him a small pink envelope. He jumped down, opened the gate, and without looking at Jennie, his face dark and shining, advanced on the porch, up the three steps, which knocked hollow beneath his boots, opened the screen door, and twisted the polished brass bell key in the center of the open winter door.

Her mother came, drying her hands. The Negro reached out the envelope and her mother took it, looking beyond him for an instant at the buggy and the white woman, who returned her look coldly. As the Negro turned, her mother opened the letter and read it, moving her lips slightly. Then Jennie could see the twinkling at the corners of her eyes. Her mother stood framed in the black square of doorway, tall, fair, the black hair swept to hide her ears, her eyes glistening.

Jennie turned back to the white woman now and saw her lean deeper into her seat. Then she pulled forward. "Do you understand what I will have them do?" She was shouting shrilly and spoke like Jennie's father. "You tell him he has got one wife! You are something different!" She leaned back again, waved her gloved hand, and the buggy lurched down the street, gained speed, and jangled out of sight around the corner.

Jennie was on her feet and pounding up the stairs. "Mama?"

"Go play, Jennie. Go on now, *play*!" Still her mother stared straight ahead, as if the buggy and the white woman remained in front of the house. She still held the letter as if to read it. The corners of her eyes were wet. Then she turned and went into the house. The screen door clacked behind her.

At nights now Jennie waited by the gate in the yard for her father to turn the corner, walking. In the beginning she had been waiting too for the day he would not turn the corner. But each night he came, that day seemed less likely to come. Even so, she was always surprised to see him. When she did, she would wave, timidly, raising her hand only to her shoulder, wiggling only her fingers as if to wave too wildly would somehow cause the entire picture of his advancing to collapse as only a slight wind would be enough to disarrange a design of feathers.

That night too she waved and saw him raise his hand high over his head, greeting her. She backed away when he reached the gate so he might open it, her head thrown way back, looking up at him.

"Well, my Jennie, what kind of day did you have?"

She only smiled, then remembered the white woman. "A woman come to visit Mama. She come in a buggy and give her a letter too. She made Mama cry."

His smile fled. He sucked his tongue, angry now. "We go see what is wrong. Come." He reached for her hand.

Her mother was in the kitchen. She looked as if she did not really care what she was doing or how, walking from pump to stove, stove to cupboard in a deep trance. The pink envelope was on the table.

She turned to them. Her eyes were red. Several strands of hair stuck to her temples. She cleared her nose and pointed to the letter. "She come today."

Her father let go Jennie's hand, picked up the letter, and read it. When he was finished he took it to the stove and dropped it into the flame. There was a puff of smoke before he replaced the lid. He shook his head. "She cannot make me go back, Josephine."

Her mother fell heavily into a wooden chair, beginning to cry again. "But she's white, Maynard."

He raised his eyebrows like a priest or a displeased schoolteacher. "Your skin is whiter."

"My mother was a slave."

He threw up his hands, making fists. "Your mother did not ask to be a slave!" Then he went to her, crouched on his hunches before her, speaking quietly. "No one can make me go back."

"But she can get them to do what she say." She turned her gaze on Jennie, but looked away quickly. "You wasn't here after the war. But I seen things. I seen things happen to field niggers that ... I was up in the house; they didn't bother me. My own father, General Dewey Willson, he stood on a platform in the center of town and promised to keep the niggers down. I was close by." She took his face in her hands. "Maynard, maybe you better go back, leastways—"

"I go back—dead! You hear? Dead. These children, these cowardly children in their masks will not move me! I go back dead. That is all. We do not discuss it." And he was gone. Jennie heard him thundering down the hall, knocking against the table near the stairs, going up to the second floor.

Her mother was looking at her now, her eyes even more red than before, her lips trembling, her hands active in her lap. "Jennie?"

"Yes, Mama." She took a step toward her, staring into the woman's eyes.

"Jennie, I want you to promise me something and not forget it."

"Yes, Mama." She was between her mother's knees, felt the woman's hands clutching her shoulders.

"Jennie, you'll be right pretty when you get grown. Did you know that? Promise me you'll go up north. Promise me if I'm not here when you get eighteen, you'll go north and get married. You understand?"

Jennie was not sure she did. She could not picture the North, except that she had heard once it was cold and white things fell from the sky. She could not picture being eighteen and her mother not being there. But she knew her mother wanted her to understand and she lied. "Yes, Mama."

"Repeat what I just said."

She did. Her mother kissed her mouth, the first time ever.

From the kitchen below came their voices. Her father's voice sounded hard, cut short; Jennie knew he had made a decision and was sticking to it. Her mother was pleading, trying to change his mind. It was July the Fourth, the day of the shooting match.

She dressed in her Sunday clothes and, coming downstairs, heard her mother. "Maynard, please don't take her." She was frantic now. "I'm begging you. Don't take that child with you today."

"I take her. We do not discuss it. I take her. Those sneaking cowards in their masks ... " Jennie knew now what they were talking about. Her father had promised to take her to the shooting match. For some reason, her mother feared there would be trouble if Jennie went downtown. She did not know why her mother felt that way, except that it might have something to do with the white woman, who continued to ride by their house each morning, after her father had left for the day. Perhaps her mother did not want to be alone in the house when the white woman drove by in her gray buggy, even though she had not stopped the buggy since the day, two months ago, when the Negro had given her mother the pink envelope.

But other strange things had happened after that. In the beginning she and her mother, as always before, had gone downtown to the market, to shop amid the bright stalls brimming with green and yellow vegetables and brick-red meats, tended by dark country Negroes in shabby clothes and large straw hats. It would get very quiet when they passed, and Jennie would see the Negroes look away, fear in their eyes, and knots of white men watching, sometimes giggling. But the white women in fine clothes were the most frightening; sitting on the verandas or passing in carriages, some even coming to their windows, they would stare angrily as if her mother had done something terrible to each one personally, as if all these white women could be the one who drove by each morning. Her mother would walk through it all, her back straight, very like her father's, the bun into which she wove her waist-length braid on market days gleaming dark.

In the beginning they had gone to the suddenly quiet market. But now her mother hardly set foot from the house, and the food was brought to them in a carton by a crippled Negro boy, who was coming just as Jennie and her father left the house that morning.

Balancing the carton on his left arm, he removed his ragged hat and smiled. "Morning, Mister Herder. Good luck at the shooting match, sir." His left leg was short and he seemed to tilt.

Her father nodded. "Thank you, Felix. I do my best."

"Then you a sure thing, Mister Herder." He replaced his hat and went on around the house.

Walking, her hand in her father's, Jennie could see some of the women of Liberty Street peering out at them through their curtains.

Downtown was not the same. Flags and banners draped the verandas; people wore their best clothes. The square had been roped off, a platform set up to one side, and New Marsails Avenue, which ran into the square, had been cleared for two blocks. Far away down the avenue stood a row of cotton bales onto which had been pinned oilcloth targets. From where they stood, the bull's-eyes looked no bigger than red jawbreakers.

Many men slapped her father on the back and, furtively, looked at her with a kind of clinical interest. But mostly they ignored her. The celebrity of the day was her father, and unlike her mother he was very popular. Everyone felt sure he would win the match; he was the best shot in the state.

After everyone shot, the judge came running down from the targets, waving his arms. "Maynard Herder. Six shots, and you can cover them all with a good gob of spit!" He grabbed her father's elbow and pulled him toward the platform, where an old man with white hair and beard, wearing a gray uniform trimmed with yellow, waited. She followed them to the platform steps, but was afraid to go any farther because now some women had begun to look at her as they had at her mother.

The old man made a short speech, his voice deep but coarse, grainy-sounding, and gave her father a silver medal in a blue velvet box. Her father turned and smiled at her. She started up the steps toward him, but just then the old man put his hand on her father's shoulder.

People had begun to walk away from the streets leading out of the square. There was less noise now, but she could not hear the first words the old man said to her father.

Her father's face tightened into the same look she had seen the day the letter came, the same as this morning in the kitchen. She went halfway up the stairs, stopped.

The old man went on. "You know I'm no meddler. Everybody knows about Liberty Street. I had a woman down there myself ... before the war."

"I know that." The words came out of her father's face, though his lips did not move.

The old man nodded. "But, Maynard, what you're doing is different."

"She's your own daughter."

"Maybe that's why ... " The old man looked down the street, toward the cotton bales and the targets. "But she's a nigger. And now the talking is taking an ugly turn, and the folks talking are the ones I can't hold."

Her father spoke in an angry whisper. "You see what I do to that target? You tell those children in their masks I do that to the forehead of any man ... or woman ... that comes near her or my house. You tell them."

"Maynard, that wouldn't do any real good *after* they'd done something to her." He stopped, looked at Jennie, and smiled. "That's my only granddaughter, you know." His eyes clicked off her. "You're a man who knows firearms. You're a gunsmith. I know firearms too. Pistols and rifles can do lots of things, but they don't make very good doctors. Nobody's asking you to give her up. Just go back home. That's all. Go back to your wife."

Her father turned away, walking fast, came down the stairs, and grabbed her hand. His face was red as blood between the white of his collar and the straw yellow of his hair.

They slowed after a block, paused in a small park with green trees shading several benches and a statue of a stern-faced young man in uniform, carrying pack and rifle. "We will sit."

She squirmed up onto the bench beside him. The warm wind smelled of salt from the Gulf of Mexico. The leaves were a dull, low tambourine. Her father was quiet for a long while.

Jennie watched birds bobbing for worms in the grass near them, then looked at the young stone soldier. Far off but, from where she viewed it, just over the soldier's hat, a gliding sea gull dived suddenly behind the rooftops. That was when she saw the white man, standing across the street from the park, smiling at her. There were other white men with him, some looking at her, others at the man, all laughing. He waved to her. She smiled at him, though he was the kind of man her mother told her always to stay away from. He was dressed as poorly as any Negro. From behind his back, he produced a brown rag doll, looked at her again, then grabbed the doll by its legs and tore it part way up the middle. Then he jammed his finger into the rip between the doll's legs. The other men laughed uproariously.

Jennie pulled her father's sleeve. "Papa? What he doing?"

"Who?" Her father turned. The man repeated the show and her father bolted to his feet, yelling, "I will kill you! You hear? I will kill you for that!"

The men only snickered and ambled away.

Her father was red again. He had clenched his fists; now his hands were white like the bottoms of fishes. He sighed, shook his head, and sat down. "I cannot kill everybody." He shook his head again, then leaned forward to get up. But first he thrust the blue velvet medal box into her hand. It was warm from his hand, wet and prickly. "When you grow up, you go to the North like your mother tells you. And you take this with you. It is yours. Always remember I gave it to you." He stood. "Now you must go home alone. Tell your mother I come later."

That night, Jennie tried to stay awake until he came home, until he was there to kiss her good night, his whiskers scratching her cheek. But all at once there was sun at her window and the sound of carts and wagons grating outside in the dirt street. Her mother was quiet while the two of them ate. After breakfast, Jennie went into the yard to wait for the gray buggy to turn the corner, but for the first morning in many months, the white woman did not jounce by, peering at the house, searching for someone or something special.

Toni Cade Bambara

(b. 1939)

A New Yorker who grew up in Harlem, Brooklyn, and Jersey City, Toni Cade Bambara studied theater arts and English at Queens College before receiving her master's degree from the City College of New York. Her surname, which she took from a sketchbook found in her great-grandmother's trunk, is also the name of a northwest African tribe famous for their delicate wood carvings—and an analogy can be drawn between those creations and her own intricately crafted stories. Praised for its musicality and its evocative dialogue, Bambara's literary fiction is represented by two short story collections, **Gorilla, My Love** *(1972) and* **The Sea Birds Are Still Alive** *(1977), and a novel,* **The Salt Eaters** *(1980), which won an American Book Award.*

A member of the Screenwriters' Guild of America since 1980, Bambara now writes primarily for television and film, admitting "quite frankly" that she is "a film person." Nevertheless, her importance to African American letters is unquestionable. Even before she had begun publishing her own works, Bambara had championed black writers by editing two anthologies, **The Black Woman** *(1970) and* **Tales and Stories for Black Folks** *(1971). The first volume, which grew out of her sympathies with black liberation and feminism, showcased together for the first time the emerging talents of such women writers as Nikki Giovanni, Audre Lorde, Alice Walker, and Paule Marshall. The second anthology of short stories was produced in homage to the great African American tradition of storytelling—what Bambara has dubbed "Our Great Kitchen Tradition." Widely admired by such peers as Toni Morrison and Lucille Clifton, Bambara is an artist of great compassion whose writing, as one critic has observed, "sustains black Americans."*

The Lesson

Back in the days when everyone was old and stupid or young and foolish and me and Sugar were the only ones just right, this lady moved on our block with nappy hair and proper speech and no makeup. And quite naturally we laughed at her, laughed the way we did at the junk man who went about his business like he was some big-time president and his sorry-ass horse his secretary. And we kinda hated her too, hated the way we did the winos who cluttered up our parks and pissed on our handball walls and stank up our hallways and stairs so you couldn't halfway play hide-and-seek without a goddamn gas mask. Miss Moore was her name. The only woman on the block with no first name. And she was black as hell, cept for her feet, which were fish-white and spooky. And she was always planning these boring-ass things for us to do, us being my cousin, mostly, who lived on the block cause we all moved north the same time and to the same apartment then spread out gradual to breathe. And our parents would yank our heads into some kinda shape and crisp up our clothes so we'd be presentable for travel with Miss Moore, who always looked like she was going to church, though she never did. Which is just one of the things the grown-ups talked about when they talked behind her back like a dog. But when she came calling with some sachet she'd sewed up or some gingerbread she'd made or some book, why then they'd all be too embarrassed to turn her down and we'd get handed over all spruced up. She'd been to college and said it was only right that she should take responsibility for the young ones' education, and she not even related by marriage or blood. So they'd go for it. Specially Aunt Gretchen. She was the main gofer in the family. You got some ole dumb shit foolishness you want somebody to go for, you send for Aunt Gretchen. She been screwed into the go-along for so long, it's a blood-deep natural thing with her. Which is how she got saddled with me and Sugar and Junior in the first place while our mothers were in a la-de-da apartment up the block having a good ole time.

So this one day Miss Moore rounds us all up at the mailbox and it's puredee hot and she's knockin herself out about arithmetic. And school suppose to let up in summer, I heard, but she don't never let up. And the starch in my pinafore scratching the shit outa me and I'm really hating this nappy-head bitch and her goddamn college degree. I'd much rather go to the pool or to the show where it's cool. So me and Sugar leaning on the mailbox being surly, which is a Miss Moore word. And Flyboy checking out what everybody brought for lunch. And Fat Butt already wasting his peanut-butter-and-jelly sandwich like the pig he is. And Junebug punchin on Q.T.'s arm for potato chips. And Rosie Giraffe shifting from one hip to the other waiting for somebody to step on her foot or ask her if she from Georgia so she can kick ass, preferably Mercedes'. And Miss Moore asking us do we know what money is, like we a bunch of retards. I mean real money, she say, like it's only poker chips or monopoly papers we lay on the grocer. So right away I'm tired of this and say so. And would much rather snatch Sugar and go to the Sunset and terrorize the West Indian kids and take their hair ribbons and their money too. And Miss Moore files that remark away for next week's lesson on brotherhood, I can tell. And finally I saw we oughta get to the subway cause it's cooler and besides we might meet some cute boys. Sugar done swiped her mama's lipstick, so we ready.

So we heading down the street and she's boring us silly about what things cost and what our parents make and how much goes for rent and how money ain't divided up right in this country. And then she gets to the part about we all poor and live in the slums, which I don't feature. And I'm ready to speak on that, but she steps out in the street and hails two cabs just like that. Then she hustles half the crew in with her and hands me a five-dollar bill and tells me to calculate ten-percent tip for the driver. And we're off. Me and Sugar and Junebug and Flyboy hangin out the window and hollering to everybody, putting lipstick on each other cause Flyboy a faggot anyway, and making farts with our sweaty armpits. But I'm mostly trying to figure how to spend this money. But they all fascinated with the meter ticking and Junebug starts laying bets as to how much it'll read when Flyboy can't hold his breath no more. Then Sugar lays bets as to how much it'll be when we get there. So I'm stuck. Don't nobody want to go for my plan, which is to jump out at the next light and run off to the first bar-b-que we can find. Then the driver tells us to get the hell out cause we there already. And the meter reads eighty-five cents. And I'm stalling to figure out the tip and Sugar say give him a dime. And I decide he don't need it bad as I do, so later for him. But then he tries to take off with Junebug foot still in the door so we talk about his mama something ferocious. Then we check out that we on Fifth Avenue and everybody dressed up in stockings. One lady in a fur coat, hot as it is. White folks crazy.

"This is the place," Miss Moore say, presenting it to us in the voice she uses at the museum. "Let's look in the windows before we go in."

"Can we steal?" Sugar asks very serious like she's getting the ground rules squared away before she plays.

"I beg your pardon," say Miss Moore, and we fall out. So she leads us around the windows of the toy store and me and Sugar screamin, "This is mine, that's mine, I gotta have that, that was made for me, I was born for that," till Big Butt drowns us out.

"Hey, I'm goin to buy that there."

"That there? You don't even know what it is, stupid."

"I do so," he say, punchin on Rosie Giraffe. "It's a microscope."

"Whatcha gonna do with a microscope, fool?"

"Look at things."

"Like what, Donald?" ask Miss Moore. And Big Butt ain't got the first notion. So here go Miss Moore gabbing about the thousands of bacteria in a drop of water and the somethin or other in a speck of blood and the million and one living things in the air around us is invisible to the naked eye. And what she say that for? Junebug go to town on that "naked" and we rolling. Then Miss Moore ask what it cost. So we all jam into the window smudgin it up and the price tag say $300. So then she ask how long'd take for Big Butt and Junebug to save up their allowances. "Too long," I say. "Yeah," adds Sugar, "outgrown it by that time." And Miss Moore says no, you never outgrow learning instruments. "Why, even medical students and interns and—" blah, blah, blah. And we ready to choke Big Butt for bringing it up in the first damn place.

"This here costs four hundred eighty dollars," say Rosie Giraffe. So we pile up all over her to see what she pointin out. My eyes tell me it's a chunk of glass cracked with something heavy, and different-color inks dripped into the splits, then the whole thing put into a oven or something. But for $480 it don't make sense.

"That's a paperweight made of semiprecious stones fused together under tremendous pressure," Miss Moore explains slowly, with her hands doing the mining and all the factory work.

"So what's a paperweight?" asks Rosie Giraffe.

"To weigh paper with, dumbbell," say Flyboy, the wise man from the East.

"Not exactly," say Miss Moore, which is what she say when you warm or way off too. "It's to weigh paper down so it won't scatter and make your desk untidy." So right away me and Sugar curtsy to each other and then to Mercedes, who is more the tidy type.

"We don't keep paper on top of the desk in my class," say Junebug, figuring Miss Moore crazy or lyin, one.

"At home, then," she say. "Don't you have a calendar and a pencil case and a blotter and a letter opener on your desk at home where you do your homework?" And she know damn well what our homes look like 'cause she noseys around in them every chance she gets.

"I don't even have a desk," say Junebug. "Do we?"

"No. And I don't get no homework neither," says Big Butt.

"And I don't even have a home," say Flyboy, like he do at school to keep the white folks off his back and sorry for him. Send-this-poor-kid-to-camp posters is his specialty.

"I do," says Mercedes. "I have a box of stationery on my desk and a picture of my cat. My godmother bought the stationery and the desk. There's a big rose on each sheet and the envelopes smell like roses."

"Who wants to know about your smelly-ass stationery," say Rosie Giraffe fore I can get my two cents in.

"It's important to have a work area all your own so that—"

"Will you look at this sailboat, please," say Flyboy, cuttin her off and pointin to the thing like it was his. So once again we tumble all over each other to gaze at this magnificent thing in the toy store which is just big enough to maybe sail two kittens across the pond if you strap them to the posts tight. We all start reciting the price tag like we in assembly. "Handcrafted sailboat of fiberglass at one thousand one hundred ninety-five dollars."

"Unbelievable," I hear myself say and am really stunned. I read it again for myself just in case the group recitation put me in a trance. Same thing. For some reason this pisses me off. We look at Miss Moore and she lookin at us, waiting for I dunno what.

"Who'd pay all that when you can buy a sailboat set for a quarter at Pop's, a tube of glue for a dime, and a ball of string for eight cents? It must have a motor and a whole lot else besides," I say. "My sailboat cost me about fifty cents."

"But will it take water?" say Mercedes with her smart ass.

"Took mine to Alley Pond Park once," say Flyboy. "String broke. Lost it. Pity."

"Sailed mine in Central Park and it keeled over and sank. Had to ask my father for another dollar."

"And you got the strap," laugh Big Butt. "The jerk didn't even have a string on it. My old man wailed on his behind."

Little Q.T. was staring hard at the sailboat and you could see he wanted it bad. But he too little and somebody'd just take it from him. So what the hell. "This boat for kids, Miss Moore?"

"Parents silly to buy something like that just to get all broke up," say Rosie Giraffe.

"That much money it should last forever," I figure.

"My father'd buy it for me if I wanted it."

"Your father, my ass," say Rosie Giraffe, getting a chance to finally push Mercedes.

"Must be rich people shop here," say Q.T.

"You are a very bright boy," say Flyboy. "What was your first clue?" And he rap him on the head with the back of his knuckles, since Q.T. the only one he could get away with. Though Q.T. liable to come up behind you years later and get his licks in when you half expect it.

"What I want to know is," I says to Miss Moore, though I never talk to her, I wouldn't give the bitch that satisfaction, "is how much a real boat costs? I figure a thousand'd get you a yacht any day."

"Why don't you check that out," she says, "and report back to the group?" Which really pains my ass. If you gonna mess up a perfectly good swim day least you could do is have some answers. "Let's go in," she say like she got something up her sleeve. Only she don't lead the way. So me and Sugar turn the corner to where the entrance is, but when we get there I kinda hang back. Not that I'm scared, what's there to be afraid of, just a toy store. But I feel funny, shame. But what I got to be shamed about? Got as much right to go in as anybody. But somehow I can't seem to get hold of the door, so I step away from Sugar to lead. But she hangs back too. And I look at her and she looks at me and this is ridiculous. I mean, damn, I have never ever been shy about doing nothing or going nowhere. But then Mercedes steps up and then Rosie Giraffe and Big Butt crowd in behind and shove, and next thing we all stuffed into the doorway with only Mercedes squeezing past us, smoothing out her jumper and walking right down the aisle. Then the rest of us tumble in like a glued-together jigsaw done all wrong. And people lookin at us. And it's like the time me and Sugar crashed into the Catholic church on a dare. But once we got in there and everything so hushed and holy and the candles and the bowin and the handkerchiefs on all the drooping heads, I just couldn't go through with the plan. Which was for me to run up to the altar and do a tap dance while Sugar played the nose flute and messed around in the holy water. And Sugar kept givin me the elbow. Then later teased me so bad I tied her up in the shower and turned it on and locked her in. And she'd be there till this day if Aunt Gretchen hadn't finally figured I was lyin about the boarder takin a shower.

Same thing in the store. We all walkin on tiptoe and hardly touchin the games and puzzles and things. And I watched Miss Moore who is steady watchin us like she waitin for a sign. Like Mama Drewery watches the sky and sniffs the air and takes note of just how much slant is in the bird formation. Then me and Sugar bump smack into each other, so busy gazing at the toys, 'specially the sailboat. But we don't laugh and go into our fat-lady bump-stomach routine. We just stare at that price tag. Then Sugar run a finger over the whole boat. And I'm jealous and want to hit her. Maybe not her, but I sure want to punch somebody in the mouth.

"Watcha bring us here for, Miss Moore?"

"You sound angry, Sylvia. Are you mad about something?" Givin me one of them grins like she tellin a grown-up joke that never turns out to be funny. And she's lookin very closely at me like maybe she plannin' to do my portrait from memory. I'm mad, but I won't give her that satisfaction. So I slouch around the store bein very bored and say, "Let's go."

Me and Sugar at the back of the train watchin the tracks whizzin by, large then small then gettin gobbled up in the dark. I'm thinkin about this tricky toy I saw in the store. A clown that somersaults on a bar then does chin-ups just cause you yank lightly at his leg. Cost $35. I could see me askin my mother for a $35 birthday clown. "You wanna who that costs what?" she'd say, cocking her head to the side to get a better view of the hole in my head. Thirty-five dollars could buy new bunk beds for Junior and Gretchen's boy. Thirty-five dollars and the whole household could go visit Granddaddy Nelson in the country. Thirty-five dollars would pay for the rent and the piano bill too. Who are these people that spend that much for performing clowns and a thousand dollars for toy sailboats? What kinda work they do and how they live and how come we ain't in on it? Where we are is who we are, Miss Moore always pointin out. But it don't necessarily have to be that way, she always adds, then waits for somebody to say that poor people have to wake up and demand their share of the pie and don't none of us know what kind of pie she talking about in the first damn place. But she ain't so smart 'cause I still got her four dollars from the taxi and she sure ain't gettin it. Messin up my day with this shit. Sugar nudges me in my pocket and winks.

Miss Moore lines us up in front of the mailbox where we started from, seem like years ago, and I got a headache for thinkin so hard. And we lean all over each other so we can hold up under the draggy-ass lecture she always finishes us off with at the end before we thank her for borin us to tears. But she just looks at us like she readin tea leaves. Finally she say, "Well, what did you think of F.A.O. Schwarz?"

Rosie Giraffe mumbles, "White folks crazy."

"I'd like to go there again when I get my birthday money," says Mercedes, and we shove her out the pack so she has to lean on the mailbox by herself.

"I'd like a shower. Tiring day," say Flyboy.

Then Sugar surprises me by saying, "You know, Miss Moore, I don't think all of us here put together eat in a year what that sailboat costs." And Miss Moore lights up like somebody goosed her. "And?" she say, urging Sugar on. Only I'm standin on her foot so she don't continue.

"Imagine for a minute what kind of society it is in which some people can spend on a toy what it would cost to feed a family of six or seven. What do you think?"

"I think," say Sugar, pushing me off her feet like she never done before, 'cause I whip her ass in a minute, "that this is not much of a democracy if you ask me. Equal chance to pursue happiness means an equal crack at the dough, don't it?" Miss Moore is besides herself and I am disgusted with Sugar's treachery. So I stand on her foot one more time to see if she'll shove me. She shuts up, and Miss Moore looks at me, sorrowfully I'm thinkin. And somethin weird is goin on, I can feel it in my chest.

"Anybody else learn anything today?" Lookin dead at me. I walk away and Sugar has to run to catch up and don't even seem to notice when I shrug her arm off my shoulder.

"Well, we got four dollars anyway," she says.

"Uh hunh."

"We could go to Hascombs and get half a chocolate layer and then go to the Sunset and still have plenty money for potato chips and ice cream sodas."

"Uh hunh."

"Race you to Hascombs," she say.

We start down the block and she gets ahead, which is O.K. by me cause I'm going to the West End and then over to the Drive to think this day through. She can run if she want to and even run faster. But ain't nobody gonna beat me at nuthin.

John Edgar Wideman

(b. 1941)

Brought out of a Pittsburgh ghetto by a basketball scholarship to the University of Pennsylvania, John Edgar Wideman has since returned to his childhood neighborhood, Homewood, through his fiction. His critically acclaimed "Homewood Trilogy," which is comprised of the short story collection **Damballah** *(1981) and two novels,* **Hiding Place** *(1981) and* **Sent for You Yesterday** *(1983), has been compared to the work of William Faulkner, whose characters, like Wideman's, are often haunted by their pasts.*

Although Wideman earned a place in the Philadelphia Big Five Basketball Hall of Fame, he stopped playing after college, realizing that he "wasn't going to be able to get into the NBA." Instead he went to Oxford as a Rhodes Scholar, where he earned a degree in philosophy in 1966. His subsequent stint as a Kent Fellow at the University of Iowa's prestigious writing workshop led directly to the publication of his first novel, **A Glance Away** *(1967), a story about a drug addict who tries to stay sober. Two more novels,* **Hurry Home** *(1969) and* **The Lynchers** *(1973), followed, both garnering enthusiastic reviews from critics. A highly literary writer whose formal training is apparent in his narrative skill and fluent prose, Wideman easily blends European influences with Black literary traditions. His work has been recognized by two PEN/ Faulkner Awards, a National Book Award nomination, and an American Book Award. Wideman's other works include his memoirs,* **Brothers and Keepers** *(1984), and the semi-autobiographical novel* **Philadelphia Fire** *(1990), both of which deal with his personal anguish over the brother and son who are serving life sentences for murder. Previously a professor at the University of Pennsylvania and the University of Wyoming, Wideman has been a professor of English at the University of Massachusetts, Amherst, since 1986. His most recent publications are* **The Stories of John Edgar Wideman** *(1992),* **All Stories Are True** *(1993), and* **Fatheralong: A Meditation on Fathers and Sons, Race and Society** *(1994).*

everybody knew bubba riff

Voices are a river you step in once and again never the same Bubba here you are dead boy dead dead dead nigger with spooky Boris Karloff powder caked on your face boy skin lightener skin brightener and who did it to you I'm talking to you boy don't roll your eyes at me don't suckee teeth and cutee eye look how that boy's grown come here baby gimme some sugar baby look at the feet on him they you know the size of the dog by the puppy's feet his long feet this one be a giant some day I swear some man's long feet and his Mama's curly eyes Mama's baby Daddy's maybe I wonder if Bubba's feet bare if his big ass and gorilla thighs and donkey dick are naked down inside the coffin under the snow white satin naked as the day he was born a big bouncy boy on his mama's knee touch him touch him he won't bite he's yours now too man boy your daddy brought you into this world but I can take you out the man wags a finger in the boy's face the boy sees the yellowed long john top three undone buttons at the chewed neck and bagged about the man's middle he's scared them funky pants slide down the man's hips man be standing there fussing at him in his long johns his behind hanging out the holes his knees bagged out like the baggy middle what he wants to do is put his thumbs in the suspenders and hike them back on the trifling runty little man's narrow shoulders here you are that's better ain't it little fellow you was about the lose your britches now go play sit back on down where you was sitting drinking your wine before you got all up in my face about nothing cause you ain't my real daddy and you can wave your finger and holler all you want but if you ever lay a hand on me again I'ma break you in half old man don't care how much my mama need the shit you bring around here no more whipping on me you touch me or put a hand on her ever again it's rumble time mano a mano motherfucker me and you on the green and if you can't stand the heat get out of the kitchen this ain't no Papa Bear Mama Bear and li'l Sugar Baby Bear jam no more I'm grown now ain't taking your whiskeyhead shit no more hit my mama hit me Im'a bust you up my sweet Bubba how I loved that boy seem like he came out smiling like he arrived here know something that made him the grinningest baby you ever seen he was easy easy girl my first and the only easy one I ever had I didn't know better I thought pain and blood and walking the floor all night the way it spozed to be you know stuff you spozed to learn growing up to be a woman so you mize well go ahead and get on with what you got to do no way round it like falling off roller skates when you little learning to skate and scuffed up knees bloody elbow you climb back up off the ground ain't nothing the matter with you girl you sneak back up on your feet and look around hope nobody saw you down on the pavement wipe the tears out your eyes make sure your clothes ain't ripped and go ahead about your business you know you learning a lesson you know how it is dues you got to pay Mama Mama look at you boy look what a mess you made out the side of your face it always hurt you worse than it hurts them you bound to fall once twice three times falling falling and tear up your ass as many falls as you need to learn your lesson then you starts understanding you know better you know ain't no lesson and ain't no learning you just keep on falling your babies keep falling you pick yourself up pick up that boy put him down he's big enough to be carrying you around woman look at where he bit me little devil he's too young to start him on a bottle the falling ain't teaching nobody nothing you keep on falling because falling down's what you born to do all the days of your life amen till one time thank you Father amen you can't stand back up no more little devil knows when he's biting me he look up all cutie-pie wide-eyed and I'm seeing stars think the bloods trickling down my chest boy oh boy next time Im'a smack you balder headed than you already is you know good and well you ain't spozed to be biting your Mama like that got the nerve to have teeth little bitty nubs pushing up I rub his gums help his teeth come in rub a ice cube on his

gums when he frets please don't lose your little smile now ain't no time to take back
my titty let him nibble if he needs to nibble he needs me now I rock him and rub his
tummy he grin up at me I lifts him and wiggle him he shakes like a bowl of jelly my
little old man him diaper droopy and creases in him thighs him knees wobble shake
him bake him paddy cake him sing him froggy went a courtin and he did ride this
room uh huh these walls uh huh she lifts the dumpling baby uh huh uh huh tastes its
rubbery flesh she is dressed in black beside the coffin her face veiled her gloved hands
somewhere out of sight the music winds on she must not stand too long the others
behind her prop her ease her along the line fed from rows of benches into the center
aisle Amazing Grace you would think they'd get their fill of young black men's bodies
but no no end to it she must not hover too long over the crib because the others are
lined up for their turn passing passing down the rows of benches onto the carpeted
aisle then down towards the flower-decked altar flowers flowers everywhere who pays
for so many flowers pays for the dope nobody around here has nothing not one red
cent so he stands there in them yellow past patching long johns trembling like a rattle
snake he would break the boy apart if he could but Bubba too big for that bullshit now
I can't do nothing with him find me a stick break a board upside his big hard nappy
head maybe he start to listening to someone no no no that's not the way Bubba's a
good boy just needs a man to talk to him tell him wildness not the only way to be a
man please help me I try try I talk till I'm blue in the face snapped a broom handle
over his back he laughed and ran out the kitchen big old boy like that he should be
carrying you around put him down woman you got a muscle in your arm big as mine
it ain't nothing it's a pimple look big cause my arm's skinny put that boy down on his
own two feet feets big as mine already his shoes cost as much as mine already put that
boy down boy you got teeth in them feet boy chewing out the toes of your shoes they
ain't a week old look like dogshit already I ain't made of money smack some sense
he's just a boy don't mean no harm let him be Bubba Bubba too late for crying he's
gone gone gone the others push out their hard wooden seats the rows empty one by
one Amazing Grace how sweet the sound his cold cold eye on the sparrow the mourners
shuffle they squeeze past ancient knees the ones too tired too old who keep their
places on the benches too weary to move they sit alone left behind while the others
are a river flowing to the altar and the waters part and rise again two streams returning
up the side aisles to the rear of Homewood African Methodist Episcopal Zion Church
where the ushers stand in white and once upon a time one of them my first love
dimple-cheeked almost old as my mama she smiled at me and melted every hard leg
dusty butt knucklehead I don't want to be here in church in the first place anger fear
and awkwardness of being a boy force-marched Sunday morning every Sunday morning
to this woman-haunted place their cries and prayers and wet-eyed singing and hats
and moans and veils and bosoms Jesus help me legs Jesus in love and the loneliness

beneath those closets of noisy clothes they packed their bodies in Jesus help me the organ when church finally had one when we chased out the white people and moved into their big church on Homewood Avenue first thing you hear the organ when you come in think it some old sister humming in the amen corner as you tiptoe you always tiptoed you always stumbled or shuffled or slid like on ice because your feet would tattle on you how much didn't want to be in church how much you wanted to fly back out the door and you'd be long gone if it wasn't for your mama dragging you in dragging you away from Bubba and them and what they into Sunday morning you set down one foot after the other careful as rain pitta patta look at the dogs on that boy Bubba you gonna be a big man pardner when you grows into them dogs must cost a pretty penny just keeping you in shoes I'd rather clothe him than feed him on his stoop we ate two dozen hot dogs and drank a gallon of grape Kool-Aid Bubba'd wait till his mama watching then cram a whole hot dog bun wiener and mustard in his mouth shove the end till it disappeared like a train in a tunnel you do that again boy Im'a smack you bald-headed but she smiled when he tricked her into catching him in the act same smile on my first love's face greeting me as I crossed the threshold of A.M.E. Zion but her skin shades lighter and not as old and blemishless and warm to the touch of my eyes and her smile sliced me melted me undressed us both her smile crackling like her swift white uniform so white I could see her brownskin sealskin underneath and her smooth cheeks and dark lips part swelling the rustle of wings of power of furled wings behind her back as she handed me a Sunday program and I tripped onto the purple carpet falling head over heels in love with everything I'd set my jaw against Sunday mornings being gathered being plucked from where I was happily minding my own business dreaming of Bubba and them free as birds somewhere they shouldn't be I'm back again in line pushing forward in stiff new shoes the soles still slick I'm slipping I glide feel static electricity charging my body the green worm of flame that will spit if my fingers touch the metal-edged fountain in the church lobby who's in such a hurry this morning why do I feel the push the rush can't stop for a drink of water somebody's breath on my neck she peers down at Bubba is he sleeping is he dead babies die sometimes just lay there dead a cat suckee breath steal breath a fat white cat in her dream in his crib a green-eyed Chessy cat grin too late too late cat got his tongue all his sweet breath sweet smile got it and gone gone don't you hear me talking to you boy Sunday morning the bells stroll up and down Homewood Avenue black hands ring them our bells now telling time for all Homewood the biggest church on the block on the corner ours now the pretty stained-glass windows till some junky steals them an organ high-domed ceiling we must wash white as snow again tall scaffolds and ladders for the men to climb Bubba won't be there it's Wednesday your mother promised you'd help the men Wednesday evening old deacons and ushers and trustees ancient monkeys in the web of pipe and board rising to the arched ceiling jack be

monkey quick angels they are lighter and faster than you've ever seen them in these
work clothes they never wear to church I climb one foot after the other into heaven
through the door she guards in white welcoming me each finger in white and I love
every one her touch veiled but warmer washed white as snow in white glove softness
the white that sighs and stretches and must abide her brown body within its shape
her fullness her secret scents and white teeth perched within the blackness of her lips
her heavy lashes bowing as if she's been waiting shy and puzzled too as the smile sinks
back into her entering and warming the ebb returning as sure as the outward flow if
you were a spider high up in the tit of swelling vault you would see the pattern how
rows empty one by one and the mourners file towards the coffin and the line breaks
on the rock of the flower-draped altar returning them in two streams to the source
the rear aisle and street door narrow and straight where she nods and smiles at you
and touches your cheek once once more gentle scratch than touch more of a tracing
her pointy nail inside the glove some bright winged humming insect testing the field
of your cheek faint brush of its breathy legs a path with no destination just there an
instant then gone back to wildness as if your face is a flower as if your whole life has
been nothing till now nothing before nothing after just this quick brush this kiss you
wish now as you remember it you wish the world would go away again as it did when
she lifted her white winged hand touched her lips teeth breath on your cheek Bubba
how long how long behind me beyond me over yonder on the bank one of the old
ones too stiff and ridden to shuffle down the aisle shouts like that rock did crying out
no hiding place don't leave me this morning weak and desperate as Old Charley
Rackett's voice in that down home story I told you Bubba about my people you said
you never had no people your Mama found you in the trash you said you liked that
Charley Rackett story tell it again man that tough old nigger got some Bubba in him
weak and feeble and old but they knew he'd push hisself out his chair and crawl after
them to the fields how old was he then my great-great-Bubba grandfather maybe a
hundred maybe more they called him the African because when he first landed in this
wilderness he spoke a bubba dubba language no one understood not one word of
English and even after he *could* speak most days he *wouldn't* speak Charley Rackett
whipped till he'd answer to that Charley Charley Charley shit a language of blows and
animal noises as if he was the beast not them in those old time slavery days then it was
Freedom and my people working our own briar patch of land in South Carolina and
Charley he's too old go to the fields every morning we sit him in his chair by the door
so's he can look out and little Bubba one the gran kids his job to mind the old man
from can to cain't from sunup to sundown in that chair by the door then one morning
old rusty black Charley Rackett said him say don't leave me behind this morning I
gwine wit youall this godblasted morning and up he stood and bram down he tumble
out his chair and Oh my God Oh my Blessed Savior they's running around hollering

and pull bag of bones Charley off the floor and stuff him back in the chair but he flies right out again quick as a grasshopper and bram hits the floor again his nose bleeding lip cut ain't nobody seen him rise out that chair for years he's hollering and nobody don't know what to do help me Jesus Charley Rackett's mind made up he'll drag behind them on his bloody elbows bloody knees so they gathers him up and ties him on the mule and that's what happens every day till he dies one night after supper in his bed Charley Bubba Rackett riding on the mule with them to the fields he worked a hundred hundred years slavery days and the slaving days after and they couldn't keep him down I was Bubba the boy left behind with him I follow Charley Rackett's stare through the open doorway across the scraped-clean place our cabin sits on like a turned-over bucket study rolling hills and broccoli tops of trees that rise from a crease where the creek runs to a river and river to delta fanning draining to the dark sea where her teeth flash like waves at night my job to fetch him coolish water shoo flies and plow his dinner from the skillet I left too long on the stove fasten scraps of button at the neck of his long johns tend his knobby hands the color of turned earth wipe the corner of his mouth always the silvery web the slobber the grunts groans wheezes of words he can't twist his mouth around he grinds them on the stumps of his teeth chews and spits them at me I sit much of the time as far away as I'm able in the space we occupy him in his pew me scattered in a corner on the floor sucking a tit of cane worrying a hard kernel of something anything caught in my teeth playing funny little tunes in my brain bird cries train thunder lightning crickets the women washing snap beans crack crack drumming in a tin bowl he coughs the walls shake I wipe sweat from his brow wet from his chin it's broad daylight flies buzz I tuck him in pull up his suspenders he calls my name a word a sound nobody else in the whole world knows Bubba and next morning he tries to stand hits the floor and steals from me the long peace of day after day alone with him listening learning my name because next morning they take him and I trail the mule's mulish stink mulish swish of its shitty tail its pitta pat clomp to the fields that morning lost to me unremembered until Bubba lying up there like you sleeping like you ain't got a care in the world boy and you say tell it one more time the old timey story I like and your mama looking down at you her little brown bouncing baby broken boy Bubba I hear one of those stones behind me send up your name in a prayer like Charley Rackett hollered Take me goddammit take me this godblasted morning saying Bubba to myself the sound before the sense of it Bubba Bubba Bubba everybody knew Bubba how old was he was he was he was the sound of it before the sense Big Bubba that's the way we talk we say it make the sound the sense of what we're talking about when I return home I walk up Susquehanna Street the people if people had been outside on their porches would have been close enough to touch their voices loud in my ear if I'd have stopped and squatted on one of these stoops we would rap about Bubba you know Big Bubba yeah oh yeah that was some sorry shit man you know how they did him some evil cold blood shit sure enough man you know I must be getting old because it don't bother me that much anymore I mean you know for a minute or two I want to wring a million motherfuckers' necks but then I let it go got to let it go got to chill out I seen too much be crazy if I don't chill out brothers cut down every day shit it don't mean a thing everybody got to go one day you know like a shooting gallery or some motherfucking evil ass lottery we all got a number just a matter of sooner or later today or tomorrow all the brothers got a chain round they necks and a number on the chain and somebody pulling numbers daily bang bang down you go it's just a matter of time bloods be extinct you know like them endangered species and shit don't laugh it's true we ought to fire up a campaign shit they got one for elephants and whales and ring-tailed sap-sucking woody woodpeckers why not posters and TV ads and buttons and T-shirts S.O.N. *Save Our Niggers* go on man you crazy man I pass by on the sidewalk listening but nobody on their stoops maybe everybody knew I was coming up Susquehanna Street with my sad self and ran inside shut their windows shut their doors hiding till I pass with my mournful lost-my-best-friend self I wish for voices hear empty porches hear my own feet on the pavement hear a car pass at the intersection of Braddock half a block away the oldest Homewood streets Albion Tioga Finance these streets where Bubba's known there they say his names *Junior June Juney Junebug JB J Bub Bub Bubby Bubba* all the silent names hidden behind curtains and blinds the darkness of old walls and tight corners and lids and hoods and secrets you can't tell without giving their power up Bubba Big Bubba I thought when I returned home one time it would be different I didn't know exactly how but maybe better somehow things supposed to change I'm older and heavier and slower now can't disappear down an alley streak like a panther part of black night when I need to rendezvous with my kind who once ruled here talking trash knocking heads the fly arch rulers and kings of pussy and bullshit and smoke Bubba June-Boy Sonny Bo sitting high up on the wall of our pretty where nothing no one could touch us one time it will surely be different these empty porches and empty footsteps and lights of empty cars whizzing by on Braddock but the only difference now Bubba Big Bubba gone they say the junkies tired of him dealers tired of him cops tired of him stealing and muscling people carried a baseball bat and you know Bubba never could play no baseball what he look like carrying around a bat he wouldn't listen that hard head still hard as brick man couldn't nobody never tell Bubba nothing he'd bogart and stomp people take their shit and walk off like dudes don't be remembering like you can do shit to people today and just walk on away and like it's over like all you got to do is get yours today and turn your back and walk away like ain't nothing happened like tomorrow ain't another day yeah he was stone crazy Bubba leave me alone now I'm not for no play today Bubba say fuck you punk and your mama too and snatch people's shit like he's Superman or Br'er Bear with that tree slung over his shoulder that was Big Bubba man big as he was ain't never growed up your boy your old time boon coon and cruising cut-buddy main man yeah we go back don't we bro way back to the olden days you me Bubba the Golden Knights and badass Laredos those banging gangs we runned wit runned from we was bad in our day but it's a new day out here cats ain't seeking glory punching some bad dude's lights out no way see everybody carries these days mess wit my shit I blow you away in a minute see Bubba living in the past Bubba a throwback man like them old time big hat eldorado Iceberg Slim pimps beat they women with coathangers and shit it's all business today dude making it on the street today got to have computers and beepers no time for cowboys and indins and gorillaing people's dope that two-bit King Kong gangster jive ain't what's happening out here today it's business business build yourself an organization man power to the people good product good distribution good vibes spread a little change round keep the boy off your back everybody gets what they want plenty to go round if your shits tight it's these free-lance Rambo motherfuckers fucking things up just a matter of time before somebody waste Bubba don't care how big he is how many bad brothers he busted up with his bare hands his big bat Bubba go down just like anybody else you bust a cap in his chest no man the word on the set is nobody knows who did it but nobody in business don't care neither cause he was way out of line overdue for getting done man cause everyody knows the way it goes moving west mister moving on out bro up and out to star time don't fuck with the product product won't fuck wit you you got to remember today's today and yesterday shit yesterday's long gone we was kids back then you and me and Bubba playing kid games then time runs out it's spozed to run out things spozed to change and we sure ain't babies no more Big Bubba a dinosaur man wasn't even in the right century man living by the wrong clock man he was Bubba all right your man Bubba Bubba Bubba everybody knew Bubba.

Alice Walker

(b. 1944)

When Alice Walker was awarded the Pulitzer Prize and the American Book Award for her second novel, **The Color Purple** (1982), her reputation as one of America's most important contemporary writers was assured. The Georgia-born Walker launched her remarkable literary career with a volume of poetry, **Once**, which was published three years after she graduated from Sarah Lawrence College in 1965. That book was followed by **Good Night, Willie Lee, I'll See You in the Morning** (1979), and several other volumes of short stories, poetry, and fiction, the most recent of which are her novels, **Temple of My Familiar** (1989) and **Possessing the Secret of Joy** (1992). Praised for its compassionate portrayals of women who have survived extreme forms of emotional and physical adversity, Walker's creative writing constitutes only part of her work. In addition to writing numerous critical essays, which have been collected in a volume entitled **In Search of Our Mother's Gardens** (1983), Walker has edited the works of Zora Neale Hurston and written a biography of Langston Hughes. Her other honors include a Rosenthal Award from the American Academy of Arts and Letters for her short story collection **In Love and Trouble** (1973), a Lillian Smith Award for her volume of poetry **Revolutionary Petunias** (1973), and a Guggenheim Fellowship. Once a Civil Rights activist and an editor at **Ms.**, Walker is a self-styled "womanist" who has taught at numerous universities, including Wellesley, Yale, and the University of California at Berkeley. Currently she runs a publishing company, Wild Tree Press, and lives on a ranch in northern California.

Nineteen Fifty-Five

1955

The car is a brandnew red Thunderbird convertible, and it's passed the house more than once. It slows down real slow now, and stops at the curb. An older gentleman dressed like a Baptist deacon gets out on the side near the house, and a young fellow who looks about sixteen gets out on the driver's side. They are white, and I wonder what in the world they doing in this neighborhood.

Well, I say to J. T., put your shirt on, anyway, and let me clean these glasses offa the table.

We had been watching the ballgame on T.V. I wasn't actually watching, I was sort of daydreaming, with my foots up in J. T.'s lap.

I seen 'em coming on up the walk, brisk, like they coming to sell something, and then they rung the bell, and J. T. declined to put on a shirt but instead disappeared into the bedroom where the other television is. I turned down the one in the living room; I figured I'd be rid of these two double quick and J. T. could come back out again.

Are you Gracie Mae Still? asked the old guy, when I opened the door and put my hand on the lock inside the screen.

And I don't need to buy a thing, said I.

What makes you think we're sellin'? he asks, in that hearty Southern way that makes my eyeballs ache.

Well, one way or another and they're inside the house and the first thing the young fellow does is raise the TV a couple of decibels. He's about five feet nine, sort of womanish looking, with real dark white skin and a red pouting mouth. His hair is black and curly and he looks like a Loosianna creole.

About one of your songs, says the deacon. He is maybe sixty, with white hair and beard, white silk shirt, black linen suit, black tie and black shoes. His cold gray eyes look like they're sweating.

One of my songs?

Traynor here just *loves* your songs. Don't you, Traynor?

He nudges Traynor with his elbow. Traynor blinks, says something I can't catch in a pitch I don't register.

The boy learned to sing and dance livin' round you people out in the country. Practically cut his teeth on you.

Traynor looks up at me and bites his thumbnail.

I laugh.

Well, one way or another they leave with my agreement that they can record one of my songs. The deacon writes me a check for five hundred dollars, the boy grunts his awareness of the transaction, and I am laughing all over myself by the time I rejoin J. T.

Just as I am snuggling down beside him though I hear the front door bell going off again.

Forgit his hat? asks J. T.

I hope not, I say.

The deacon stands there leaning on the door frame and once again I'm thinking of those sweaty-looking eyeballs of his. I wonder if sweat makes your eyeballs pink because his are sure pink. Pink and gray and it strikes me that nobody I'd care to know is behind them.

I forgot one little thing, he says pleasantly. I forgot to tell you Traynor and I would like to buy up all of those records you made of the song. I tell you we sure do love it.

Well, love it or not, I'm not so stupid as to let them do that without making 'em pay. So I says, Well, that's gonna cost you. Because, really, that song never did sell all that good, so I was glad they was going to buy it up. But on the other hand, them two listening to my song by themselves, and nobody else getting to hear me sing it, give me a pause.

Well, one way or another the deacon showed me where I would come out ahead on any deal he had proposed so far. Didn't I give you five hundred dollars? he asked. What white man—and don't even need to mention colored—would give you more? We buy up all your records of that particular song: first, you git royalties. Let me ask you, how much you sell that song for in the first place? Fifty dollars? A hundred, I say. And no royalties from it yet, right? Right. Well, when we buy up all of them records you gonna git royalties. And that's gonna make all of them race record shops sit up and take notice of Gracie Mae Still. And they gonna push all them other records of yourn they got. And you no doubt will become one of the big name colored recording artists. And then we can offer you another five hundred dollars for letting us do all this for you. And by God you'll be sittin' pretty! You can go out and buy you the kind of outfit a star should have. Plenty sequins and yards of red satin.

I had done unlocked the screen when I saw I could get some more money out of him. Now I held it wide open while he squeezed through the opening between me and the door. He whipped out another piece of paper and I signed it.

He sort of trotted out to the car and slid in beside Traynor, whose head was back against the seat. They swung around in a u-turn in front of the house and then they was gone.

J. T. was putting his shirt on when I got back to the bedroom. Yankees beat the Orioles 10—6, he said. I believe I'll drive out to Paschal's pond and go fishing. Wanta go?

While I was putting on my pants J. T. was holding the two checks.

I'm real proud of a woman that can make cash money without leavin' home, he said. And I said *Umph*. Because we met on the road with me singing in first one little low-life jook after another, making ten dollars a night for myself if I was lucky, and sometimes bringin' home nothing but my life. And J. T. just loved them times. The way I was fast and flashy and always on the go from one town to another. He loved the way my singin' made the dirt farmers cry like babies and the womens shout Honey, hush! But that's mens. They loves any style to which you can get 'em accustomed.

1956

My little grandbaby called me one night on the phone: Little Mama, Little Mama, there's a white man on the television singing one of your songs! Turn on channel 5.

Lord, if it wasn't Traynor. Still looking half asleep from the neck up, but kind of awake in a nasty way from the waist down. He wasn't doing too bad with my song either, but it wasn't just the song the people in the audience was screeching and screaming over, it was that nasty little jerk he was doing from the waist down.

Well, Lord have mercy, I said, listening to him. If I'da closed my eyes, it could have been me. He had followed every turning of my voice, side streets, avenues, red lights, train crossings and all. It give me a chill.

Everywhere I went I heard Traynor singing my song, and all the little white girls just eating it up. I never had so many ponytails switched across my line of vision in my life. They was so *proud*. He was a *genius*.

Well, all that year I was trying to lose weight anyway and that and high blood pressure and sugar kept me pretty well occupied. Traynor had made a smash from a song of mine, I still had seven hundred dollars of the original one thousand dollars in the bank, and I felt if I could just bring my weight down, life would be sweet.

1957

I lost ten pounds in 1956. That's what I give myself for Christmas. And J. T. and me and the children and their friends and grandkids of all description had just finished dinner—over which I had put on nine and a half of my lost ten—when who should appear at the front door but Traynor. Little Mama, Little Mama! It's that white man who sings———— ———— ————. The children didn't call it my song anymore. Nobody did. It was funny how that happened. Traynor and the deacon had bought up all my records, true, but on his record he had put "written by Gracie Mae Still." But that was just another name on the label, like "produced by Apex Records."

On the TV he was inclined to dress like the deacon told him. But now he looked presentable.

Merry Christmas, said he.

And same to you, Son.

I don't know why I called him Son. Well, one way or another they're all our sons. The only requirement is that they be younger than us. But then again, Traynor seemed to be aging by the minute.

You looks tired, I said. Come on in and have a glass of Christmas cheer.

J. T. ain't never in his life been able to act decent to a white man he wasn't working for, but he poured Traynor a glass of bourbon and water, then he took all the children and grandkids and friends and whatnot out to the den. After while I heard Traynor's voice singing the song, coming from the stereo console. It was just the kind of Christmas present my kids would consider cute.

I looked at Traynor, complicit. But he looked like it was the last thing in the world he wanted to hear. His head was pitched forward over his lap, his hands holding his glass and his elbows on his knees.

I done sung that song seem like a million times this year, he said. I sung it on the Grand Ole Opry, I sung it on the Ed Sullivan show. I sung it on Mike Douglas, I sung it at the Cotton Bowl, the Orange Bowl. I sung it at Festivals. I sung it at Fairs. I sung it overseas in Rome, Italy, and once in submarine *underseas.* I've sung it and sung it, and I'm making forty thousand dollars a day offa it, and you know what, I don't have the faintest notion what that song means.

Whatchumean, what do it mean? It mean what it says. All I could think was: These suckers is making forty thousand a *day* offa my song and now they gonna come back and try to swindle me out of the original thousand.

It's just a song, I said. Cagey. When you fool around with a lot of no count mens you sing a bunch of 'em. I shrugged.

Oh, he said. Well. He started brightening up. I just come by to tell you I think you are a great singer.

He didn't blush, saying that. Just said it straight out.

And I brought you a little Christmas present too. Now you take this little box and you hold it until I drive off. Then you take it outside under that first streetlight back up the street aways in front of that green house. Then you open the box and see Well, just *see.*

What had come over this boy, I wondered, holding the box. I looked out the window in time to see another white man come up and get in the car with him and then two more cars full of white mens start out behind him. They was all in long black cars that looked like a funeral procession.

Little Mama, Little Mama, what it is? One of my grandkids come running up and started pulling at the box. It was wrapped in gay Christmas paper—the thick, rich kind that it's hard to picture folks making just to throw away.

J. T. and the rest of the crowd followed me out the house, up the street to the streetlight and in front of the green house. Nothing was there but somebody's gold-grilled white Cadillac. Brandnew and most distracting. We got to looking at it so till I almost forgot the little box in my hand. While the others were busy making 'miration I carefully took off the paper and ribbon and folded them up and put them in my pants pocket. What should I see but a pair of genuine solid gold caddy keys.

Dangling the keys in front of everybody's nose, I unlocked the caddy, motioned for J. T. to git in on the other side, and us didn't come back home for two days.

1960
Well, the boy was sure nuff famous by now. He was still a mite shy of twenty but already they was calling him the Emperor of Rock and Roll.

Then what should happen but the draft.

Well, says J. T. There goes all this Emperor of Rock and Roll business.

But even in the army the womens was on him like white on rice. We watched it on the News.

Dear Gracie Mae[he wrote from Germany],

How you? Fine I hope as this leaves me doing real well. Before I come in the army I was gaining a lot of weight and gitting jittery from making all them dumb movies. But now I exercise and eat right and get plenty of rest. I'm more awake than I been in ten years.

I wonder if you are writing any more songs?

Sincerely,
Traynor

I wrote him back:

Dear Son,

We is all fine in the Lord's good grace and hope this finds you the same. J. T. and me be out all times of the day and night in that car you give me—which you know you didn't have to do. Oh, and I do appreciate the mink and the new self-cleaning oven. But if you send anymore stuff to eat from Germany I'm going to have to open up a store in the neighborhood just to get rid of it. Really, we have more than enough of everything. The Lord is good to us and we don't know Want.

Glad to hear you is well and gitting your right rest. There ain't nothing like exercising to help that along. J. T. and me work some part of every day that we don't go fishing in the garden.

Well, so long Soldier.

Sincerely,
Gracie Mae

He wrote:

Dear Gracie Mae,

I hope you and J. T. like that automatic power tiller I had one of the stores back home send you. I went through a mountain of catalogs looking for it—I wanted something that even a woman could use.

I've been thinking about writing some songs of my own but every time I finish one it don't seem to be about nothing I've actually lived myself. My agent keeps sending me other people's songs but they just sound mooney. I can hardly git through 'em without gagging.

Everybody still loves that song of yours. They ask me all the time what do I think it means, really. I mean, they want to know just what I want to know. Where out of your life did it come from?

Sincerely,
Traynor

1968
I didn't see the boy for seven years. No. Eight. Because just about everybody was dead when I saw him again. Malcolm X, King, the president and his brother, and even J. T. J. T. died of a head cold. It just settled in his head like a block of ice, he said, and nothing we did moved it until one day he just leaned out the bed and died.

His good friend Horace helped me put him away, and then about a year later Horace and me started going together. We was sitting out on the front porch swing one summer night, dusk–dark, and I saw this great procession of lights winding to a stop.

Holy Toledo! said Horace. (He's got a real sexy voice like Ray Charles.) Look *at* it. He meant the long line of flashy cars and the white men in white summer suits jumping out on the drivers' sides and standing at attention. With wings they could pass for angels, with hoods they could be the Klan.

Traynor comes waddling up the walk.

And suddenly I know what it is he could pass for. An Arab like the ones you see in storybooks. Plump and soft and with never a care about weight. Because with so much money, who cares? Traynor is almost dressed like someone from a storybook too. He has on, I swear, about ten necklaces. Two sets of bracelets on his arms, at least one ring on every finger, and some kind of shining buckles on his shoes, so that when he walks you get quite a few twinkling lights.

Gracie Mae, he says, coming up to give me a hug. J. T.

I explain that J. T. passed. That this is Horace.

Horace, he says, puzzled but polite, sort of rocking back on his heels, Horace. That's it for Horace. He goes in the house and don't come back.

Looks like you and me is gained a few, I say.

He laughs. The first time I ever heard him laugh. It don't sound much like a laugh and I can't swear that it's better than no laugh a'tall.

He's gitting fat for sure, but he's still slim compared to me. I'll never see three hundred pounds again and I've just about said (excuse me) fuck it. I got to thinking about it one day an' I thought: aside from the fact that they say it's unhealthy, my fat ain't never been no trouble. Mens always have loved me. My kids ain't never complained. Plus they's fat. And fat like I is I looks distinguished. You see me coming and know somebody's *there.*

Gracie Mae, he says, I've come with a personal invitation to you to my house tomorrow for dinner. He laughed. What did it sound like? I couldn't place it. See them men out there? he asked me. I'm sick and tired of eating with them. They don't never have nothing to talk about. That's why I eat so much. But if you come to dinner tomorrow we can talk about the old days. You can tell me about that farm I bought you.

I sold it, I said.

You did?

Yeah, I said, I did. Just cause I said I liked to exercise by working in a garden didn't mean I wanted five hundred acres! Anyhow, I'm a city girl now. Raised in the country it's true. Dirt poor—the whole bit—but that's all behind me now.

Oh well, he said, I didn't mean to offend you.

We sat a few minutes listening to the crickets.

Then he said: You wrote that song while you was still on the farm, didn't you, or was it right after you left?

You had somebody spying on me? I asked.

You and Bessie Smith got into a fight over it once, he said.

You *is* been spying on me!

But I don't know what the fight was about, he said. Just like I don't know what happened to your second husband. Your first one died in the Texas electric chair. Did you know that? Your third one beat you up, stole your touring costumes and your car and retired with a chorine to Tuskegee. He laughed. He's still there.

I had been mad, but suddenly I calmed down. Traynor was talking very dreamily. It was dark but seems like I could tell his eyes weren't right. It was like some*thing* was sitting there talking to me but not necessarily with a person behind it.

You gave up on marrying and seem happier for it. He laughed again. I married but it never went like it was supposed to. I never could squeeze any of my own life either into it or out of it. It was like singing somebody else's record. I copied the way it was sposed to be *exactly* but I never had a clue what marriage meant.

I bought her a diamond ring big as your fist. I bought her clothes. I built her a mansion. But right away she didn't want the boys to stay there. Said they smoked up the bottom floor. Hell, there were *five* floors.

No need to grieve, I said. No need to. Plenty more where she come from.

He perked up. That's part of what that song means, ain't it? No need to grieve. Whatever it is, there's plenty more down the line.

I never really believed that way back when I wrote that song, I said. It was all bluffing then. The trick is to live long enough to put your young bluffs to use. Now if I was to sing that song today I'd tear it up. 'Cause I done lived long enough to know it's *true*. Them words could hold me up.

I ain't lived that long, he said.

Look like you on your way, I said. I don't know why, but the boy seemed to need some encouraging. And I don't know, seem like one way or another you talk to rich white folks and you end up reassuring *them*. But what the hell, by now I feel something for the boy. I wouldn't be in his bed all alone in the middle of the night for nothing. Couldn't be nothing worse than being famous the world over for something you don't even understand. That's what I tried to tell Bessie. She wanted that same song. Overheard me practicing it one day, said, with her hands on her hips: Gracie Mae, I'ma sing your song tonight. I *likes* it.

Your lips be too swole to sing, I said. She was mean and she was strong, but I trounced her.

Ain't you famous enough with your own stuff? I said. Leave mine alone. Later on, she thanked me. By then she was Miss Bessie Smith to the World, and I was still Miss Gracie Mae Nobody from Notasulga.

The next day all these limousines arrived to pick me up. Five cars and twelve bodyguards. Horace picked that morning to start painting the kitchen.

Don't paint the kitchen, fool, I said. The only reason that dumb boy of ours is going to show me his mansion is because he intends to present us with a new house.

What you gonna do with it? he asked me, standing there in his shirtsleeves stirring the paint.

Sell it. Give it to the children. Live in it on weekends. It don't matter what I do. He sure don't care.

Horace just stood there shaking his head. Mama you sure looks *good*, he says. Wake me up when you git back.

Fool, I say, and pat my wig in front of the mirror.

The boy's house is something else. First you come to this mountain, and then you commence to drive and drive up this road that's lined with magnolias. Do magnolias grow on mountains? I was wondering. And you come to lakes and you come to ponds and you come to deer and you come up on some sheep. And I figure these two is sposed to represent England and Wales. Or something out of Europe. And you just keep on coming to stuff. And it's all pretty. Only the man driving my car don't look at nothing but the road. Fool. And then *finally*, after all this time, you begin to go up the driveway. And there's more magnolias—only they're not in such good shape. It's sort of cool up this high and I don't think they're gonna make it. And then I see this building that looks like if it had a name it would be The Tara Hotel. Columns and steps and outdoor chandeliers and rocking chairs. Rocking chairs? Well, and there's the boy on the steps dressed in a dark green satin jacket like you see folks wearing on TV late at night, and he looks sort of like a fat dracula with all that house rising behind him, and standing beside him there's this little white vision of loveliness that he introduces as his wife.

He's nervous when he introduces us and he says to her: This is Gracie Mae Still, I want you to know me. I mean. . . and she gives him a look that would fry meat.

Won't you come in, Gracie Mae, she says, and that's the last I see of her.

He fished around for something to say or do and decides to escort me to the kitchen. We go through the entry and the parlor and the breakfast room and the dining room and the servants' passage and finally get there. The first thing I notice is that, altogether, there are five stoves. He looks about to introduce me to one.

Wait a minute, I say. Kitchens don't do nothing for me. Let's go sit on the front porch.

Well, we hike back and we sit in the rocking chairs rocking until dinner.

Gracie Mae, he says down the table, taking a piece of fried chicken from the woman standing over him, I got a little surprise for you.

It's a house, ain't it? I ask, spearing a chitlin.

You're getting *spoiled*, he says. And the way he says *spoiled* sounds funny. He slurs it. It sounds like his tongue is too thick for his mouth. Just that quick he's finished the chicken and is now eating chitlins *and* a pork chop. *Me* spoiled, I'm thinking.

I already got a house. Horace is right this minute painting the kitchen. I bought that house. My kids feel comfortable in that house.

But this one I bought you is just like mine. Only a little smaller.

I still don't need no house. And anyway who would clean it?

He looks surprised.

Really, I think, some peoples advance *so* slowly.

I hadn't thought of that. But what the hell, I'll get you somebody to live in.

I don't want other folks living 'round me. Makes me nervous.

You *don't*? It *do*?

What I want to wake up and see folks I don't even know for?

He just sits there downtable staring at me. Some of that feeling is in the song, ain't it? Not the words, the *feeling*. What I want to wake up and see folks I don't even know for? But I see twenty folks a day I don't even know, including my wife.

This food wouldn't be bad to wake up to though, I said. The boy had found the genius of corn bread.

He looked at me real hard. He laughed. Short. They want what you got but they don't want you. They want what I got only it ain't mine. That's what makes 'em so hungry for me when I sing. They getting the flavor of something but they ain't getting the thing itself. They like a pack of hound dogs trying to gobble up a scent.

You talking 'bout your fans?

Right. Right. He says.

Don't worry 'bout your fans, I say. They don't know their asses from a hole in the ground. I doubt there's a honest one in the bunch.

That's the point. Dammit, that's the point! He hits the table with his fist. It's so solid it don't even quiver. You need a honest audience! You can't have folks that's just gonna lie right back to you.

Yeah, I say, it was small compared to yours, but I had one. It would have been worth my life to try to sing 'em somebody else's stuff that I didn't know nothing about.

He must have pressed a buzzer under the table. One of his flunkies zombies up.

Git Johnny Carson, he says.

On the phone? asks the zombie.

On the phone, says Traynor, what you think I mean, git him offa the front porch? Move your ass.

So two weeks later we's on the Johnny Carson show.

Traynor is all corseted down nice and looks a little bit fat but mostly good. And all the women that grew up on him and my song squeal and squeal. Traynor says: The lady who wrote my first hit record is here with us tonight, and she's agreed to sing it for all of us, just like she sung it forty-five years ago. Ladies and Gentlemen, the great Gracie Mae Still!

Well, I had tried to lose a couple of pounds my own self, but failing that I had me a very big dress made. So I sort of rolls over next to Traynor, who is dwarfed by me, so that when he puts his arm around back of me to try to hug me it looks funny to the audience and they laugh.

I can see this pisses him off. But I smile out there at 'em. Imagine squealing for twenty years and not knowing why you're squealing? No more sense of endings and beginnings than hogs.

It don't matter, Son, I say. Don't fret none over me.

I commence to sing. And I sound——wonderful. Being able to sing good ain't all about having a good singing voice a'tall. A good singing voice helps. But when you come up in the Hard Shell Baptist church like I did you understand early that the fellow that sings is the singer. Them that waits for programs and arrangements and letters from home is just good voices occupying body space.

So there I am singing my own song, my own way. And I give it all I got and enjoy every minute of it. When I finish Traynor is standing up clapping and clapping and beaming at first me and then the audience like I'm his mama for true. The audience claps politely for about two seconds.

Traynor looks disgusted.

He comes over and tries to hug me again. The audience laughs.

Johnny Carson looks at us like we both weird.

Traynor is mad as hell. He's supposed to sing something called a love ballad. But instead he takes the mike, turns to me and says: Now see if my imitation still holds up. He goes into the same song, *our* song, I think, looking out at his flaky audience. And he sings it just the way he always did. My voice, my tone, my inflection, everything. But he forgets a couple of lines. Even before he's finished the matronly squeals begin.

He sits down next to me looking whipped.

It don't matter, Son, I say, patting his hand. You don't even know those people. Try to make the people you know happy.

Is that in the song? he asks.

Maybe. I say.

1977

For a few years I hear from him, then nothing. But trying to lose weight takes all the attention I got to spare. I finally faced up to the fact that my fat is the hurt I don't admit, not even to myself, and that I been trying to bury it from the day I was born. But also when you git real old, to tell the truth, it ain't as pleasant. It gits lumpy and slack. Yuck. So one day I said to Horace, I'ma git this shit offa me.

And he fell in with the program like he always try to do and Lord such a procession of salads and cottage cheese and fruit juice!

One night I dreamed Traynor had split up with his fifteenth wife. He said: *You meet 'em for no reason. You date 'em for no reason. You marry 'em for no reason. I do it all but I swear it's just like somebody else doing it. I feel like I can't remember Life.*

The boy's in trouble, I said to Horace.

You've always said that, he said.

I have?

Yeah. You always said he looked asleep. You can't sleep through life if you wants to live it.

You not such a fool after all, I said, pushing myself up with my cane and hobbling over to where he was. Let me sit down on your lap, I said, while this salad I ate takes effect.

In the morning we heard Traynor was dead. Some said fat, some said heart, some said alcohol, some said drugs. One of the children called from Detroit. Them dumb fans of his is on a crying rampage, she said. You just ought to turn on the T.V.

But I didn't want to see 'em. They was crying and crying and didn't even know what they was crying for. One day this is going to be a pitiful country, I thought.

Brenda Flanagan

(b. 1944)

*Almost thirty years ago Brenda Flanagan left her birthplace of Trinidad, West Indies, to move to the United States. She earned her master's and doctorate degrees at the University of Michigan and is currently a professor of English at Eastern Michigan University. Flanagan is also a novelist, playwright, poet, and critic. She has won three Avery and Julie Hopwood Awards from the University of Michigan for her plays and fiction, and her first novel, **You Alone Are Dancing**, was published in 1990. Flanagan's stories and essays, which have won favorable critical reviews, have appeared in such journals as **Callaloo**, **Caribbean Review**, **Witness**, **Caliban**, and **City Arts Quarterly**. The recipient of a James Michener Fellowship for Creative Writing, Flanagan has also been awarded grants from the National Endowment for the Humanities, the Mellon Foundation, and the Lily Foundation.*

To Die of Old Age in a Foreign Country

They think I can't remember things because I'm getting old and I can't see so good. I have two cataracts. But I am eighty-four years old this September. A Virgo. And I does read my horoscope book every day as God send. They think I going down. Huh. What they know? I live my four score already and I'm still here. I'm luckier than most. Look how Miss Ivy dead. And Valto. He thought he would outlive me but God outsmarted him. I am still going strong. And I'm not forgetting ONE damn thing.

My birthday is sixth of September, 1906. I live a long time. You don't think so? I am the last of my brothers and sisters. My mother make twelve of us. Poor Vivian, my last sister, died five years ago this month. Twenty-fifth of March, 1985. I was over here, but you know what? They didn't tell me she died until they had put my one last sister in the ground and throw dirt on top of her. You could imagine that? My one last sister. She was two years older than me. We grow up together. Jenna and the rest of them say I wouldn't be able to take the news. I might have dropped down. You could imagine that? I was so damn vexed with them for keeping that news from me. My one last sister. These young people always think they know best what to do for old people, but I still have a lot of cross to bear. I could handle death.

If I was home, I would have washed my sister myself and put white powder on her face and sing Amazing Grace before they put her in the hole. But I'm in this foreign country getting old day by day and all my life passing me by. Vivian had two thick-thick gold bracelets. You can't get gold like that these days. Jenna take them.

That's why she didn't want me to come home for the funeral. She wanted to take my sister's gold bracelets. But I tell you, one day one day congotay. Those gold bracelets was to go to me. My Ta'ar Mille gave them to Vivian in 1913, and she told Vivian to pass them on to me. But that thiefing Jenna, she's my daughter back home, she take them. Cobeaux will pick out her eyes for that.

God forgive me, I shouldn't curse my daughter. Jenna is a Godsend. She had a bad-bad husband. He give her a lot of children, seven boys and nine girls and I remember all their birthdays. You know how many grandchildren I have? Seventy-eight. Count them. Seventy-eight grandchildren. Fifty of them is girls. And I have forty-nine greatgrand. All Jenna's daughters have children. And bad-bad husbands. Poor she. She has her hands full day in and day out since Leroy dead. I'm glad she keep the gold bracelets. Ta'ar Mille get those gold bracelets from down the Main when Agard come back from working in the oilfields on July seventh, 1913. You can't get gold like that these days. Better Jenna have them to pawn. She has sixteen children in the house to feed, ten of them my greatgrand.

All those children breaking down my poor little house. Is my house they're living in, you know, because they lost theirs years ago. I remember the day. Ninth of June, 1962. Leroy gamble the house away. Jenna cried once and she never cry again. She's strong like me. And she is quiet, God rest the dead. She is Mother Theresa. Everybody comes to her and say, "Miss Jenna, I can't take care of my child. You could help me?" Jenna taking the child. My poor house is an orphanage. Valto and I pour the first cement for the foundation on May eleventh, 1943. I'm not going to have any house to live in when I go back home. I want to go back home, you know. I don't want to die in this country. It's too cold. But what house I will have, eh? Tell me that. Jenna's taking everybody's children, and the people don't give her a cent to mind them. But somehow she does manage. She should have been a nun. She has pictures of the Pope stick up all over my house like wallpaper and I'm Nazarene. She's high up in the church, you know. They're always calling on her to go and tend to somebody sick. And she herself have so much troubles. Yes.

She had troubles with Leroy when he was alive, and she had troubles when he died. On the day she was burying him, some Indian woman come to the burial ground making a big come-mess for them to pass her child over Leroy's grave. The woman say the child belong to Leroy. You could tell me what a young-young girl like that was doing with a grown man who had nine children with his wife? Young people too worthless these days, oui. She come making big bacchanal in the cemetery. But look my crosses, nuh. If I was there, I would have hit that woman one slap in her face! But I was up here. It's a sad-sad thing to be living in this foreign country when your family die at home. My whole life passing me by.

All my sons dying out.

Kenneth died last year. Heart attack. He just drop down. He was my oldest son. It's bad luck for a mother to see her son dead, old people say.

Right after that, Noel die. He was my third son. Laundryman. Cancer. He had nice gold teeth in the front. He died in Tobago.

And then my darling son Nate. He died third of February. This year. In Toronto. He was my fourth son. I make seven of them, you know. And seven girl children too. They said it was bad luck for me to go, but I went to bury him. And I overhear them shoo-shooing that he died from AIDS. I ask them why. Why they didn't tell me? They said they didn't think I could take it. I couldn't take it? ME? I who take so much already? I who bring fourteen children into this world? I who live to see so much beyond my time and more. My back is a cement block.

I went and kissed my son. They tried to hold me back, but I went and kissed my son. And I brush his hair back from his forehead, and I pat his face with white powder and I sing Amazing Grace. And I didn't let them hold me back.

I want to go home. I stay too long up here. Since August seventeenth, 1973. That's when I first come. Too long now. I tell Jenna to send for me. I don't want to end my days in this foreign country with all my life passing me by. I tell her to pick out a spot near my sons so when I stretch out my arms, I could hold them. I hope she remember.

Charles Johnson

(b. 1948)

Charles Johnson gained national prominence when his novel **Middle Passage** *won the National Book Award in 1990. It was not, however, his first critical success. Ever since the publication of his first novel in 1974, Johnson had been steadily attracting attention as a deeply philosophical but readable writer concerned with examining metaphysical issues in the context of Black American life. As he has said of his fiction, "there is a progression from ignorance to knowledge, or from a lack of understanding to some greater understanding."*

Educated at Southern Illinois University where he was intrigued by the moral aesthetic of novelist John Gardner, Johnson continued his studies at the State University of New York. There, while studying phenomenology and aesthetics as a Ph.D. student, he wrote **Faith and the Good Thing,** *the first novel he published after six previous attempts. This story about a southern Black girl's quest for the meaning of life was followed by* **Oxherding Tale** *(1982), a fictional "slave narrative," and* **Middle Passage,** *his prize-winning 1990 novel about a freedman who mistakenly boards a slave ship bound for Africa. Johnson has also published a lavishly praised short story collection,* **The Sorcerer's Apprentice: Tales and Conjurations** *(1986), and a volume of critical essays,* **Being and Race** *(1988).*

A professor of English at the University of Washington, Seattle, since 1976, Johnson has also been fiction editor for the **Seattle Review** *since 1978. Multi-talented as well as productive, Johnson finds additional creative outlets in drawing and screenwriting. He has published two collections of satirical political cartoons,* **Black Humor** *(1970) and* **Half-Past Nation-Time** *(1972). His screenplay credits include* **Charlie Smith and the Fritter Tree** *(1978), a dramatization of the life of a 135-year-old African American for the PBS Vision series, and* **Booker** *(1988), a program about the childhood of Booker T. Washington for the Walt Disney channel. He has recently completed a screenplay adaptation of* **Middle Passage.** *To Johnson, writing is "a long conversation, and the writer does not come into this discussion* ex nihilo, *born with nothing behind him." He also believes "that art should be socially responsible ... Where social responsibility comes into play is in the simple fact that whatever the work is, whatever the book is, whatever the product is, it's something that we interject into the public space. It's a public act. It's our human expression, and we are responsible for all our forms of human expression, all our deeds and actions, of which art is one. The artist has a tremendous degree of responsibility."*

Menagerie

Among watchdogs in Seattle, Berkeley was known generally as one of the best. Not the smartest, but steady. A pious German shepherd (Black Forest origins, probably), with big shoulders, black gums, and weighing more than some men, he sat guard inside the glass door of Tilford's Pet Shoppe, watching the pedestrians scurry along First Avenue, wondering at the derelicts who slept ever so often inside the foyer at night, and sometimes he nodded when things were quiet in the cages behind him, lulled by the bubbling of the fishtanks, dreaming of an especially fine meal he'd once had, or the little female poodle, a real flirt, owned by the aerobic dance teacher (who was no saint herself) a few doors down the street; but Berkeley was, for all his woolgathering, never asleep at the switch. He took his work seriously. Moreover, he knew exactly where he was at every moment, what he was doing, and why he was doing it, which was more than can be said for most people, like Mr. Tilford, a real gumboil, whose ways were mysterious to Berkeley. Sometimes he treated the animals cruelly, or taunted them; he saw them not as pets but profit. Nevertheless, no vandals, or thieves, had ever brought trouble through the doors or windows of Tilford's Pet Shoppe, and Berkeley, confident of his power but never flaunting it, faithful to his master though he didn't deserve it, was certain that none ever would.

At closing time, Mr. Tilford, who lived alone, as most cruel men do, always checked the cages, left a beggarly pinch of food for the animals, and a single biscuit for Berkeley. The watchdog always hoped for a pat on his head, or for Tilford to play with him, some sign of approval to let him know he was appreciated, but such as this never came. Mr. Tilford had thick glasses and a thin voice, was stubborn, hot-tempered, a drunkard and a loner who, sliding toward senility, sometimes put his shoes in the refrigerator, and once—Berkeley winced at the memory—put a Persian he couldn't sell in the Mix Master during one of his binges. Mainly, the owner drank and watched television, which was something else Berkeley couldn't understand. More than once he'd mistaken gunfire on screen for the real thing (a natural error, since no one told him violence was entertainment for some), howled loud enough to bring down the house, and Tilford booted him outside. Soon enough, Berkeley stopped looking for approval; he didn't bother to get up from biting fleas behind the counter when he heard the door slam.

But it seemed one night too early for closing time. His instincts on this had never been wrong before. He trotted back to the darkened storeroom; then his mouth snapped shut. His feeding bowl was as empty as he'd last left it.

"Say, Berkeley," said Monkey, whose cage was near the storeroom. "What's goin' on? Tilford didn't put out the food."

Berkeley didn't care a whole lot for Monkey, and usually he ignored him. He was downright wicked, a comedian always grabbing his groin to get a laugh, throwing feces, or fooling with the other animals, a clown who'd do anything to crack up the iguana, Frog, Parrot, and the Siamese, even if it meant aping Mr. Tilford, which he did well, though Berkeley found this parody frightening, like playing with fire, or literally biting the hand that fed you. But he, too, was puzzled by Tilford's abrupt departure.

"I don't know," said Berkeley. "He'll be back, I guess."

Monkey, his head through his cage, held onto the bars like a movie inmate. "Wanna bet?"

"What're you talking about?"

"Wake *up*," said Monkey. "Tilford's sick. I seen better faces on dead guppies in the fishtank. You ever see a pulmonary embolus?" Monkey ballooned his cheeks, then started breathing hard enough to hyperventilate, rolled up both red-webbed eyes, then crashed back into his cage, howling.

Not thinking this funny at all, Berkeley padded over to the front door, gave Monkey a grim look, then curled up against the bottom rail, waiting for Tilford's car to appear. Cars of many kinds, and cars of different sizes, came and went, but that Saturday night the owner did not show. Nor the next morning, or the following night, and on the second day it was not only Monkey but every beast, bird, and fowl in the Shoppe that shook its cage or tank and howled at Berkeley for an explanation—an ear-shattering babble of tongues, squawks, trills, howls, mewling, bellows, hoots, blorting, and belly growls because Tilford had collected everything from baby alligators to zebra-striped fish, an entire federation of cultures, with each animal having its own distinct, inviolable nature (so they said), the rows and rows of counters screaming with a plurality of so many backgrounds, needs, and viewpoints that Berkeley, his head splitting, could hardly hear his own voice above the din.

"Be patient!" he said. "Believe me, he's comin' back!"

"Come *off* it," said one of three snakes. "Monkey says Tilford's *dead*. Question is, what're we gonna *do* about it?"

Berkeley looked, witheringly, toward the front door. His empty stomach gurgled like a sewer. It took a tremendous effort to untangle his thoughts. "If we can just hold on a—"

"We're *hungry*!" shouted Frog. "We'll starve before old Tilford comes back!"

Throughout this turmoil, the shouting, beating of wings, which blew feathers everywhere like confetti, and an angry slapping of fins that splashed water to the floor, Monkey simply sat quietly, taking it all in, stroking his chin as a scholar might. He waited for a space in the shouting, then pushed his head through the cage again. His voice was calm, studied, like an old-time barrister before the bar. "Berkeley? Don't get mad now, but I think it's obvious that there's only one solution."

"What?"

"Let us out," said Monkey. "Open the cages."

"No!"

"We've got a crisis situation here." Monkey sighed like one of the elderly, tired lizards, as if his solution bothered even him. "It calls for courage, radical decisions. You're in charge until Tilford gets back. That means you gotta feed us, but you can't do that, can you? Only one here with hands is *me*. See, we all have different talents, unique gifts. If you let us out, we can pool our resources. I can *open* the feed bags!"

"You can?" The watchdog swallowed.

"Uh-huh." He wiggled his fingers dexterously, then the digits on his feet. "But somebody's gotta throw the switch on this cage. I can't reach it. Dog, I'm asking you to be democratic! Keeping us locked up is fascist!"

The animals clamored for release; they took up Monkey's cry, "Self-determination!" But everything within Berkeley resisted this idea, the possibility of chaos it promised, so many different, quarrelsome creatures uncaged, set loose in a low-ceilinged Shoppe where even he had trouble finding room to turn around between the counters, pens, displays of paraphernalia, and heavy, bubbling fishtanks. The chances for mischief were incalculable, no question of that, but slow starvation was certain if he didn't let them in the storeroom. Furthermore, he didn't want to be called a fascist. It didn't seem fair, Monkey saying that, making him look bad in front of the others. It was the one charge you couldn't defend yourself against. Against his better judgement, the watchdog rose on his hindlegs and, praying this was the right thing, forced open the cage with his teeth. For a moment Monkey did not move. He drew breath loudly and stared at the open door. Cautiously, he stepped out, stood up to his full height, rubbed his bony hands together, then did a little dance and began throwing open the other cages one by one.

Berkeley cringed. "The tarantula, too?"

Monkey gave him a cold glance over one shoulder. "You should get to know him, Berkeley. Don't be a bigot."

Berkeley shrank back as Tarantula, an item ordered by a Hell's Angel who never claimed him, shambled out—not so much an insect, it seemed to Berkeley, as Pestilence on legs. ("Be fair!" he scolded himself. "He's okay, I'm okay, we're all okay.") He watched helplessly as Monkey smashed the ant farm, freed the birds, and then the entire troupe, united by the spirit of a bright, common future, slithered, hopped, crawled, bounded, flew, and clawed its way into the storeroom to feed. All except crankled, old Tortoise, whom Monkey hadn't freed, who, in fact, didn't want to be released and snapped at Monkey's fingers when he tried to open his cage. No one questioned it. Tortoise had escaped the year before, remaining at large for a week, and then he returned mysteriously on his own, his eyes strangely unfocused, as if he'd seen the end of the world, or a vision of the world to come. He hadn't spoken in a year. Hunched inside his shell, hardly eating at all, Tortoise lived in the Shoppe, but you could hardly say he was part of it, and even the watchdog was a little leery of him.

Berkeley, for his part, had lost his hunger. He dragged himself, wearily, to the front door, barked frantically when a woman walked by, hoping she would stop, but after seeing the window sign, which read—DESOLC—from his side, she stepped briskly on. His tail between his legs, he went slowly back to the storeroom, hoping for the best, but what he found there was no sight for a peace-loving watchdog.

True to his word, Monkey had broken open the feed bags and boxes of food, but the animals, who had always been kept apart by Tilford, discovered as they crowded into the tiny storeroom and fell to eating that sitting down to table with creatures so different in their gastronomic inclinations took the edge off their appetites. The birds found the eating habits of the reptiles, who thought eggs were a delicacy, disgusting and drew away in horror; the reptiles, who were proud of being cold-blooded, and had an elaborate theory of beauty based on the aesthetics of scales, thought the body heat of the mammals cloying and nauseating, and refused to feed beside them, and this was fine for the mammals, who, led by Monkey, distrusted anyone odd enough to be born in an egg, and dismissed them as lowlifes on the evolutionary scale; they were shoveling down everything—bird food, dog biscuits, and even the thin wafers reserved for the fish.

"Don't touch that!" said Berkeley. "The fish have to eat, too! They can't leave the tanks!"

Monkey, startled by the watchdog, looked at the wafers in his fist thoughtfully for a second, then crammed them into his mouth. "That's their problem."

Deep inside, Berkeley began a rumbling bark, let it build slowly, and by the time it hit the air it was a full-throated growl so frightening that Monkey jumped four, maybe five feet into the air. He threw the wafers at Berkeley. "Okay—okay, give it to 'em! But remember one thing, dog: You're a mammal, too. It's unnatural to take sides against your own kind."

Scornfully, the watchdog turned away, trembling with fury. He snuffled up the wafers in his mouth, carried them to the huge, man-sized tanks, and dropped them in amongst the sea horses, guppies, and jellyfish throbbing like hearts. Goldfish floated toward him, his voice and fins fluttering. He kept a slightly startled expression. "What the hell is going on? Where's Mr. Tilford?"

Berkeley strained to keep his voice steady. "Gone."

"For good?" asked Goldfish. "Berkeley, we heard what the others said. They'll let us starve—"

"No," he said. "I'll protect you."

Goldfish bubbled relief, then looked panicky again. "What if Tilford doesn't come back ever?"

The watchdog let his head hang. The thought seemed too terrible to consider. He said, more to console himself than Goldfish, "It's his Shoppe. He has to come back."

"But suppose he *is* dead, like Monkey says." Goldfish's unblinking, lidless eyes grabbed at Berkeley and refused to release his gaze. "Then it's our Shoppe, right?"

"Eat your dinner."

Goldfish called, "Berkeley, wait—"

But the watchdog was deeply worried now. He returned miserably to the front door. He let fly a long, plaintive howl, his head tilted back like a mountaintop wolf silhouetted by the moon in a Warner Brothers cartoon—he did look like that—his insides hurting with the thought that if Tilford was dead, or indifferent to their problems, that if no one came to rescue them, then they were dead, too. True, there was a great deal of Tilford inside Berkeley, what he remembered from his training as a pup, but this faint sense of procedure and fair play hardly seemed enough to keep order in the Shoppe, maintain the peace, and more important provide for them as the old man had. He'd never looked upon himself as a leader, preferring to attribute his distaste for decision to a rare ability to see all sides. He was no hero like Old Yeller, or the legendary Gellert, and testing his ribs with his teeth, he wondered how much weight he'd lost from worry. Ten pounds? Twenty pounds? He covered both eyes with his black paws, whimpered a little, feeling a failure of nerve, a soft white core of fear like a slug in his stomach. Then he drew breath and, with it, new determination. The owner couldn't be dead. Monkey would never convince him of that. He simply had business elsewhere. And when he returned, he would expect to find the Shoppe as he left it. Maybe even running more smoothly, like an old Swiss watch that he had wound and left ticking. When the watchdog tightened his jaws, they creaked at the hinges, but he tightened them all the same. His eyes narrowed. No evil had visited the Shoppe from outside. He'd seen to that. None, he vowed, would destroy it from within.

But he could not be everywhere at once. The corrosion grew day by day. Cracks, then fissures began to appear, it seemed to Berkeley, everywhere, and in places where he least expected them. Puddles and pyramidal plops were scattered underfoot like traps. Bacterial flies were everywhere. Then came maggots. Hamsters gnawed at electrical cords in the storeroom. Frog fell sick with a genital infection. The fish, though the gentlest of creatures, caused undertow by demanding day-and-night protection, claiming they were handicapped in the competition for food, confined to their tanks, and besides, they were from the most ancient tree; all life came from the sea, they argued, the others owed *them*.

Old blood feuds between beasts erupted, too, grudges so tired you'd have thought them long buried, but not so. The Siamese began to give Berkeley funny looks, and left the room whenever he entered. Berkeley let him be, thinking he'd come to his senses. Instead, he jumped Rabbit when Berkeley wasn't looking, the product of this assault promising a new creature—a cabbit—with jackrabbit legs and long feline whiskers never seen in the Pet Shoppe before. Rabbit took this badly. In the beginning she sniffed a great deal, and with good reason—rape was a vicious thing—

but her grief and pain got out of hand, and soon she was lost in it with no way out, like a child in a dark forest, and began organizing the females of every species to stop cohabiting with the males. Berkeley stood back, afraid to butt in because Rabbit said that it was none of his damned business and he was as bad as all the rest. He pleaded reason, his eyes burnt-out from sleeplessness, with puffy bags beneath them, and when that did no good, he pleaded restraint.

"The storeroom's half-empty," he told Monkey on the fifth day. "If we don't start rationing the food, we'll starve."

"There's always food."

Berkeley didn't like the sound of that. "Where?"

Smiling, Monkey swung his eyes to the fishtanks.

"Don't you go near those goldfish!"

Monkey stood at bay, his eyes tacked hatefully on Berkeley, who ground his teeth, possessed by the sudden, wild desire to bite him, but knowing, finally, that he had the upper hand in the Pet Shoppe, the power. In other words, bigger teeth. As much as he hated to admit it, his only advantage, if he hoped to hold the line, his only trump, if he truly wanted to keep them afloat, was the fact that he outweighed them all. They were afraid of him. Oddly enough, the real validity of his values and viewpoint rested, he realized, on his having the biggest paw. The thought fretted him. For all his idealism, truth was decided in the end by those who could be bloodiest in fang and claw. Yet and still, Monkey had an arrogance that made Berkeley weak in the knees.

"Dog," he said, scratching under one arm, "you got to sleep *sometime.*"

And so Berkeley did. After hours of standing guard in the storeroom, or trying to console Rabbit, who was now talking of aborting the cabbit, begging her to reconsider, or reassuring the birds, who crowded together in one corner against, they said, threatening moves by the reptiles, or splashing various medicines on Frog, whose sickness had now spread to the iguana—after all this, Berkeley did drop fitfully to sleep by the front door. He slept greedily, dreaming of better days. He twitched and woofed in his sleep, seeing himself schtupping the little French poodle down the street, and it was good, like making love to lightning, she moved so well with him; and then of his puppyhood, when his worst problems were remembering where he'd buried food from Tilford's table, or figuring out how to sneak away from his mother, who told him all dogs had cold noses because they were late coming to the Ark and had to ride next to the rail. His dream cycled on, as all dreams do, with greater and greater clarity from one chamber of vision to the next until he saw, just before waking, the final drawer of dream-work spill open on the owner's return. Splendidly dressed, wearing a bowler hat and carrying a walking stick, sober, with a gentle smile for Berkeley (Berkeley was sure), Tilford threw open the Pet Shoppe door in a blast of wind and burst of preternatural brilliance that rayed the whole room, evaporated every shadow, and brought the squabbling, the conflict of interpretations, mutations, and internecine battles to a halt. No one dared move. They stood frozen like fish in ice, or a bird caught in the crosswinds, the colorless light behind the owner so blinding it obliterated their outlines, blurred their precious differences, as if each were a rill of the same ancient light somehow imprisoned in form, with being—formed itself the most preposterous of conditions, outrageous, when you thought it through, because it occasioned suffering, meant separation from other forms, and the illusion of identity, but even this ended like a dream within the watchdog's dream, and only he and the owner remained. Reaching down, he stroked Berkeley's head. And at last he said, like God whispering to Samuel: *Well done*. It was all Berkeley had ever wanted. He woofed again, snoring like a sow, and scratched in his sleep; he heard the owner whisper *begun*, which was a pretty strange thing for him to say, even for Tilford, even in a dream. His ears strained forward; *begun,* Tilford said again. And for an instant Berkeley thought he had the tense wrong, intending to say, "Now we can begin," or something prophetically appropriate like that, but suddenly he was awake, and Parrot was flapping his wings and shouting into Berkeley's ear.

"The gun," said Parrot. "Monkey has it."

Berkeley's eyes, still phlegmed by sleep, blearily panned the counter. The room was swimming, full of smoke from a fire in the storeroom. He was short of wind. And, worse, he'd forgotten about the gun, a Smith and Wesson, that Tilford had bought after pet shop owners in Seattle were struck by thieves who specialized in stealing exotic birds. Monkey had it now. Berkeley's water ran down his legs. He'd propped the pistol between the cash register and a display of plastic dog collars, and his wide, yellow grin was frighteningly like that of a general Congress had just given the go-ahead to on a scorched-earth policy.

"Get it!" said Parrot. "You promised to protect us, Berkeley!"

For a few fibrous seconds he stood trembling paw-deep in dung, the odor of decay burning his lungs, but he couldn't come full awake, and still he felt himself to be on the fringe of a dream, his hair moist because dreaming of the French poodle had made him sweat. But the pistol ... There was no power balance now. He'd been outplayed. No hope unless he took it away. Circling the counter, head low and growling, or trying to work up a decent growl, Berkeley crept to the cash register, his chest pounding, bunched his legs to leap, then sprang, pretending the black explosion of flame and smoke was like television gunfire, though it ripped skin right off his ribs, sent teeth flying down his throat, and blew him back like an empty pelt against Tortoise's cage. He lay still. Now he felt nothing in his legs. Purple blood like that deepest in the body cascaded to the floor from his side, rushing out with each heartbeat, and he lay twitching a little, only seeing now that he'd slept too long. Flames licked along the floor. Fish floated belly up in a dark, unplugged fishtank. The females had torn Siamese to pieces. Spackled lizards were busy sucking baby canaries from their eggs. And in the holy ruin of the Pet Shoppe the tarantula roamed free over the corpses of Frog and Iguana. Beneath him, Berkeley heard the ancient Tortoise stir, clearing a rusty throat clogged from disuse. Only he would survive the spreading fire, given his armor. His eyes burning from the smoke, the watchdog tried to explain his dream before the blaze reached them. "We could have endured, we had enough in common—for Christ's sake, we're *all* animals."

"Indeed," said Tortoise grimly, his eyes like headlights in a shell that echoed cavernously. "Indeed."

Jamaica Kincaid

(b. 1949)

Born Elaine Potter Richardson in Saint John, Antigua, Jamaica Kincaid left for the United States when she was sixteen to become an au pair *girl. Although she had intended to go to nursing school, she studied photography instead. She fell into writing when she was asked to contribute commentary on Caribbean and Black American culture to the* **New Yorker**'s *"Talk of the Town" column. Kincaid eventually joined the magazine in 1976 as a staff writer. Explaining that her name change in 1973 was not "really anything meaningful," Kincaid says simply that she changed her name because she had always hated it. An unabashedly autobiographical writer, Kincaid often sets her stories in the Caribbean and writes about mother-daughter relationships, a theme that prevails in her short story collection,* **At the Bottom of the River** *(1983), which won the Morton Dauwen Zabel Award from the American Academy and Institute of Arts and Letters. "Girl," her most frequently anthologized piece and one of ten stories in that collection, is a hypnotic series of commands from a mother to her daughter.*

Kincaid has also published two semi-autobiographical novels set in the West Indies, **Annie John** *(1985) and* **Lucy** *(1990), and an angry polemic against colonialism,* **A Small Place** *(1988). Critic Diane Simmons has written of Kincaid's work that it is "about loss, an all but unbearable fall from a paradise partially remembered, partially dreamed, a state of wholeness in which things are unchangeably themselves and division is unknown. This paradise has been displaced by a constantly shifting reality, which is revealed to the reader through the rhythms and repetitions of Kincaid's prose. In the long, seemingly artless, list-like sentences, the reader is mesmerized into Kincaid's world, a world in which one reality constantly slides into another under cover of the ordinary rhythms of life."*

Girl

Wash the white clothes on Monday and put them on the stone heap; wash the color clothes on Tuesday and put them on the clothesline to dry; don't walk barehead in the hot sun; cook pumpkin fritters in very hot sweet oil; soak your little cloths right after you take them off; when buying cotton to make yourself a nice blouse, be sure that it doesn't have gum on it, because that way it won't hold up well after a wash; soak salt fish overnight before you cook it; is it true that you sing benna in Sunday school?; always eat your food in such a way that it won't turn someone else's stomach; on Sundays try to walk like a lady and not like the slut you are so bent on becoming; don't sing benna in Sunday school; you mustn't speak to wharf-rat boys, not even to give directions; don't eat fruits on the street—flies will follow you; *but I don't sing benna on Sundays at all and never in Sunday school*; this is how to sew on a button;

on a button; this is how to make a buttonhole for the button you have just sewed on; this is how to hem a dress when you see the hem coming down and so to prevent yourself from looking like the slut I know you are bent on becoming; this is how you iron your father's khaki shirt so that it doesn't have a crease; this is how you iron your father's khaki pants so that they don't have a crease; this is how you grow okra—far from the house, because okra tree harbors red ants; when you are growing dasheen, make sure it gets plenty of water or else it makes your throat itch when you are eating it; this is how you sweep a corner; this is how you sweep a whole house; this is how you sweep a yard; this is how you smile to someone you don't like too much; this is how you smile to someone you don't like at all; this is how you smile to someone you like completely; this is how you set a table for tea; this is how you set a table for dinner; this is how you set a table for dinner with an important guest; this is how you set a table for lunch; this is how you set a table for breakfast; this is how to behave in the presence of men who don't know you very well, and this way they won't recognize immediately the slut I have warned you against becoming; be sure to wash every day, even if it is with your own spit; don't squat down to play marbles—you are not a boy, you know; don't pick people's flowers—you might catch something; don't throw stones at blackbirds, because it might not be a blackbird at all; this is how to make a bread pudding; this is how to make doukona; this is how to make pepper pot; this is how to make a good medicine for a cold; this is how to make a good medicine to throw away a child before it even becomes a child; this is how to catch a fish; this is how to throw back a fish you don't like, and that way something bad won't fall on you; this is how to bully a man; this is how a man bullies you; this is how to love a man, and if this doesn't work there are other ways, and if they don't work don't feel too bad about giving up; this is how to spit up in the air if you feel like it, and this is how to move quick so that it doesn't fall on you; this is how to make ends meet; always squeeze bread to make sure it's fresh; *but what if the baker won't let me feel the bread?*; you mean to say that after all you are really going to be the kind of woman who the baker won't let near the bread?

Gloria Naylor

(b. 1950)

Written to "immortalize the spirit" she saw in her grandmother, great aunt, and mother, **The Women of Brewster Place** *(1982) is Gloria Naylor's first and best-known novel. About seven Black women who live in an urban housing project, it met with tremendous critical success and was praised for its stark portrayal of sexism and ghetto life. After winning an American Book Award in 1983, the novel was turned into a 1989 television movie starring Oprah Winfrey and Cicely Tyson. Naylor's most recent novel,* **Bailey's Cafe** *(1992), was published to rave reviews and is also being made into a movie.*

Naylor, who graduated from Brooklyn College in 1981, began writing **The Women of Brewster Place** *while she attended classes and worked as a hotel switchboard operator. She then earned a master's degree (1983) in African-American Studies from Yale University before writing the next two novels in her fictional "series."* **Linden Hills** *(1985), an allegorical adaptation of Dante's* **Inferno**, *is an ambitious novel about economic mobility and the divisive effects of materialism within the Black community. The folkloric* **Mama Day** *(1988), on the other hand, alludes to Shakespeare's* **Tempest** *while spinning an absorbing tale about hoodoo, history, and human love. The recipient of an NEA Fellowship, a Guggenheim Fellowship, and a Lillian Smith Award, Naylor has taught at various colleges and universities, including NYU, Princeton, Boston University, and Cornell. She is currently the president of a film production company, One Way Productions.*

Kiswana Browne

From the window of her sixth-floor studio apartment, Kiswana could see over the wall at the end of the street to the busy avenue that lay just north of Brewster Place. The late-afternoon shoppers looked like brightly clad marionettes as they moved between the congested traffic, clutching their packages against their bodies to guard them from sudden bursts of the cold autumn wind. A portly mailman had abandoned his cart and was bumping into indignant window shoppers as he puffed behind the cap that the wind had snatched from his head. Kiswana leaned over to see if he was going to be successful, but the edge of the building cut him off from her view.

A pigeon swept across her window, and she marveled at its liquid movements in the air waves. She placed her dreams on the back of the bird and fantasized that it would glide forever in transparent silver circles until it ascended to the center of the universe and was swallowed up. But the wind died down, and she watched with a sigh as the bird beat its wings in awkward, frantic movements to land on the corroded top of a fire escape on the opposite building. This brought her back to earth.

Humph, it's probably sitting over there crapping on those folks' fire escape, she thought. Now, that's a safety hazard … And her mind was busy again, creating flames and smoke and frustrated tenants whose escape was being hindered because they were slipping and sliding in pigeon shit. She watched their cussing, haphazard descent on the fire escapes until they had all reached the bottom. They were milling around, oblivious to their burning apartments, angrily planning to march on the mayor's office about the pigeons. She materialized placards and banners for them, and they had just reached the corner, boldly sidestepping fire hoses and broken glass, when they all vanished.

A tall copper-skinned woman had met this phantom parade at the corner, and they had dissolved in front of her long, confident strides. She plowed through the remains of their faded mists, unconscious of the lingering wisps of their presence on her leather bag and black fur-trimmed coat. It took a few seconds for this transfer from one realm to another to reach Kiswana, but then suddenly she recognized the woman.

"Oh, God, it's Mama!" She looked down guiltily at the forgotten newspaper in her lap and hurriedly circled random job advertisements.

By this time Mrs. Browne had reached the front of Kiswana's building and was checking the house number against a piece of paper in her hand. Before she went into the building she stood at the bottom of the stoop and carefully inspected the condition of the street and the adjoining property. Kiswana watched this meticulous inventory with growing annoyance but she involuntarily followed her mother's slowly rotating head, forcing herself to see her new neighborhood through the older woman's eyes. The brightness of the unclouded sky seemed to join forces with her mother as it highlighted every broken stoop railing and missing brick. The afternoon sun glittered and cascaded across even the tiniest fragments of broken bottle, and at that very moment the wind chose to rise up again, sending unswept grime flying into the air, as a stray tin can left by careless garbage collectors went rolling noisily down the center of the street.

Kiswana noticed with relief that at least Ben wasn't sitting in his usual place on the old garbage can pushed against the far wall. He was just a harmless old wino, but Kiswana knew her mother only needed one wino or one teenager with a reefer within a twenty-block radius to decide that her daughter was living in a building seething with dope factories and hangouts for derelicts. If she had seen Ben, nothing would have made her believe that practically every apartment contained a family, a Bible, and a dream that one day enough could be scraped from those meager Friday night paychecks to make Brewster Place a distant memory.

As she watched her mother's head disappear into the building, Kiswana gave silent thanks that the elevator was broken. That would give her at least five minutes' grace to straighten up the apartment. She rushed to the sofa bed and hastily closed it without smoothing the rumpled sheets and blanket or removing her nightgown. She felt that somehow the tangled bedcovers would give away the fact that she had not slept alone last night. She silently apologized to Abshu's memory as she heartlessly crushed his spirit between the steel springs of the couch. Lord, that man was sweet. Her toes curled involuntarily at the passing thought of his full lips moving slowly over her instep. Abshu was a foot man, and he always started his lovemaking from the bottom up. For that reason Kiswana changed the color of the polish on her toenails every week. During the course of their relationship she had gone from shades of red to brown and was now into the purples. I'm gonna have to start mixing them soon, she thought aloud as she turned from the couch and raced into the bathroom to remove any traces of Abshu from there. She took up his shaving cream and razor and threw them into the bottom drawer of her dresser beside her diaphragm. Mama wouldn't dare pry into my drawers right in front of me, she thought, as she slammed the drawer shut. Well, at least not the *bottom* drawer. She may come up with some sham excuse for opening the top drawer, but never the bottom one.

When she heard the first two short raps on the door, her eyes took a final flight over the small apartment, desperately seeking out any slight misdemeanor that might have to be defended. Well, there was nothing she could do about the crack in the wall over that table. She had been after the landlord to fix it for two months now. And there had been no time to sweep the rug, and everyone knew that off-gray always looked dirtier than it really was. And it was just too damn bad about the kitchen. How was she expected to be out job-hunting every day and still have time to keep a kitchen that looked like her mother's, who didn't even work and still had someone come in twice a month for general cleaning. And besides—

Her imaginary argument was abruptly interrupted by a second series of knocks, accompanied by a penetrating, "Melanie, Melanie, are you there?"

Kiswana strode toward the door. She's starting before she even gets in here. She knows that's not my name anymore.

She swung the door open to face her slightly flushed mother. "Oh, hi, Mama. You know, I thought I heard a knock, but I figured it was for the people next door, since no one hardly ever calls me Melanie." Score one for me, she thought.

"Well, it's awfully strange you can forget a name you answered to for twenty-three years," Mrs. Browne said, as she moved past Kiswana into the apartment. "My, that was a long climb. How long has your elevator been out? Honey, how do you manage with your laundry and groceries up all those steps? But I guess you're young, and it wouldn't bother you as much as it does me."

This long string of questions told Kiswana that her mother had no intentions of beginning her visit with another argument about her new African name.

"You know I would have called before I came, but you don't have a phone yet. I didn't want you to feel that I was snooping. As a matter of fact, I didn't expect to find you home at all. I thought you'd be out looking for a job." Mrs. Browne had mentally covered the entire apartment while she was talking and taking off her coat.

"Well, I got up late this morning. I thought I'd buy the afternoon paper and start early tomorrow."

"That sounds like a good idea." Her mother moved toward the window and picked up the discarded paper and glanced over the hurriedly circled ads. "Since when do you have experience as a fork-lift operator?"

Kiswana caught her breath and silently cursed herself for her stupidity. "Oh, my hand slipped—I meant to circle file clerk." She quickly took the paper before her mother could see that she had also marked cutlery salesman and chauffeur.

"You're sure you weren't sitting here moping and daydreaming again?" Amber specks of laughter flashed in the corner of Mrs. Browne's eyes.

Kiswana threw her shoulders back and unsuccessfully tried to disguise her embarrassment with indignation.

"Oh, God, Mama! I haven't done that in years—it's for kids. When are you going to realize that I'm a woman now?"

She sought desperately for some womanly thing to do and settled for throwing herself on the couch and crossing her legs in what she hoped looked like a nonchalant arc.

"Please, have a seat," she said, attempting the same tones and gestures she'd seen Bette Davis use on the late movies.

Mrs. Browne, lowering her eyes to hide her amusement, accepted the invitation and sat at the window, also crossing her legs. Kiswana saw immediately how it should have been done. Her celluloid poise clashed loudly against her mother's quiet dignity, and she quickly uncrossed her legs. Mrs. Browne turned her head toward the window and pretended not to notice.

"At least you have a halfway decent view from here. I was wondering what lay beyond that dreadful wall—it's the boulevard. Honey, did you know that you can see the trees in Linden Hills from here?"

Kiswana knew that very well, because there were many lonely days that she would sit in her gray apartment and stare at those trees and think of home, but she would rather have choked than admit that to her mother.

"Oh, really? I never noticed. So how is Daddy and things at home?"

"Just fine. We're thinking of redoing one of the extra bedrooms since you children have moved out, but Wilson insists that he can manage all that work alone. I told him that he doesn't really have the proper time or energy for all that. As it is, when he gets home from the office, he's so tired he can hardly move. But you know you can't tell your father anything. Whenever he starts complaining about how stubborn you are, I tell him the child came by it honestly. Oh, and your brother was by yesterday," she added, as if it had just occurred to her.

So that's it, thought Kiswana. That's why she's here.

Kiswana's brother, Wilson, had been to visit her two days ago, and she had borrowed twenty dollars from him to get her winter coat out of layaway. That son-of-a-bitch probably ran straight to Mama—and after he swore he wouldn't say anything. I should have known, he was always a snotty-nosed sneak, she thought.

"Was he?" she said aloud. "He came by to see me, too, earlier this week. And I borrowed some money from him because my unemployment checks hadn't cleared in the bank, but now they have and everything's just fine." There, I'll beat you to that one.

"Oh, I didn't know that," Mrs. Browne lied. "He never mentioned you. He had just heard that Beverly was expecting again, and he rushed over to tell us."

Damn. Kiswana could have strangled herself.

"So she's knocked up again, huh?" she said irritably.

Her mother started. "Why do you always have to be so crude?"

"Personally, I don't see how she can sleep with Willie. He's such a dishrag."

Kiswana still resented the stance her brother had taken in college. When everyone at school was discovering their blackness and protesting on campus, Wilson never took part; he had even refused to wear an Afro. This had outraged Kiswana because, unlike her, he was dark-skinned and had the type of hair that was thick and kinky enough for a good "Fro." Kiswana had still insisted on cutting her own hair, but it was so thin and fine-textured, it refused to thicken even after she washed it. So she had to brush it up and spray it with lacquer to keep it from lying flat. She never forgave Wilson for telling her that she didn't look African, she looked like an electrocuted chicken.

"Now that's some way to talk. I don't know why you have an attitude against your brother. He never gave me a restless night's sleep, and now he's settled with a family and a good job."

"He's an assistant to an assistant junior partner in a law firm. What's the big deal about that?"

"The job has a future, Melanie. And at least he finished school and went on for his law degree."

"In other words, not like me, huh?"

"Don't put words into my mouth, young lady. I'm perfectly capable of saying what I mean."

Amen, thought Kiswana.

"And I don't know why you've been trying to start up with me from the moment I walked in. I didn't come here to fight with you. This is your first place away from home, and I just wanted to see how you were living and if you're doing all right. And I must say, you've fixed this apartment up very nicely."

"Really, Mama?" She found herself softening in the light of her mother's approval.

"Well, considering what you had to work with." This time she scanned the apartment openly.

"Look, I know it's not Linden Hills, but a lot can be done with it. As soon as they come and paint, I'm going to hang my Ashanti print over the couch. And I thought a big Boston fern would go well in that corner, what do you think?"

"That would be fine, baby. You always had a good eye for balance."

Kiswana was beginning to relax. There was little she did that attracted her mother's approval. It was like a rare bird, and she had to tread carefully around it lest it fly away.

"Are you going to leave that statue out like that?"

"Why, what's wrong with it? Would it look better somewhere else?"

There was a small wooden reproduction of a Yoruba goddess with large protruding breasts on the coffee table.

"Well"—Mrs. Browne was beginning to blush—"it's just that it's a bit suggestive, don't you think? Since you live alone now, and I know you'll be having male friends stop by, you wouldn't want to be giving them any ideas. I mean, uh, you know, there's no point in putting yourself in any unpleasant situations because they may get the wrong impression and uh, you know, I mean, well ... " Mrs. Browne stammered on miserably.

Kiswana loved it when her mother tried to talk about sex. It was the only time she was at a loss for words.

"Don't worry, Mama." Kiswana smiled. "That wouldn't bother the type of men I date. Now maybe if it had big feet—" And she got hysterical, thinking of Abshu.

Her mother looked at her sharply. "What sort of gibberish is that about feet? I'm being serious, Melanie."

"I'm sorry, Mama." She sobered up. "I'll put it away in the closet," she said, knowing that she wouldn't.

"Good," Mrs. Browne said, knowing that she wouldn't either. "I guess you think I'm too picky, but we worry about you over here. And you refuse to put in a phone so we can call and see about you."

"I haven't refused, Mama. They want seventy-five dollars for a deposit, and I can't swing that right now."

"Melanie, I can give you the money."

"I don't want you to be giving me money—I've told you that before. Please, let me make it by myself."

"Well, let me lend it to you, then."

"No!"

"Oh, so you can borrow money from your brother, but not from me."

Kiswana turned her head from the hurt in her mother's eyes. "Mama, when I borrow from Willie, he makes me pay him back. You never let me pay you back," she said into her hands.

"I don't care. I still think it's downright selfish of you to be sitting over here with no phone, and sometimes we don't hear from you in two weeks—anything could happen—especially living among these people."

Kiswana snapped her head up. "What do you mean, *these people*? They're my people and yours, too, Mama—we're all black. But maybe you've forgotten that over in Linden Hills."

"That's not what I'm talking about, and you know it. These streets—this building—it's so shabby and rundown. Honey, you don't have to live like this."

"Well, this is how poor people live."

"Melanie, you're not poor."

"No, Mama, *you're* not poor. And what you have and I have are two totally different things. I don't have a husband in real estate with a five-figure income and a home in Linden Hills—*you* do. What I have is a weekly unemployment check and an overdrawn checking account at United Federal. So this studio on Brewster is all I can afford."

"Well, you could afford a lot better," Mrs. Browne snapped, "if you hadn't dropped out of college and had to resort to these dead-end clerical jobs."

"Uh-huh, I knew you'd get around to that before long." Kiswana could feel the rings of anger begin to tighten around her lower backbone, and they sent her forward onto the couch. "You'll never understand, will you? Those bourgie schools were counterrevolutionary. My place was in the streets with my people, fighting for equality and a better community."

"Counterrevolutionary!" Mrs. Browne was raising her voice. "Where's your revolution now, Melanie? Where are all those black revolutionaries who were shouting and demonstrating and kicking up a lot of dust with you on that campus? Huh? They're sitting in wood-paneled offices with their degrees in mahogany frames, and they won't even drive their cars past this street because the city doesn't fix potholes in this part of town."

"Mama," she said, shaking her head slowly in disbelief, "how can you—a black woman—sit there and tell me that what we fought for during the Movement wasn't important just because some people sold out?"

"Melanie, I'm not saying it wasn't important. It was damned important to stand up and say that you were proud of what you were and to get the vote and other social opportunities for every person in this country who had it due. But you kids thought you were going to turn the world upside down, and it just wasn't so. When all the smoke had cleared, you found yourself with a fistful of new federal laws and a country still full of obstacles for black people to fight their way over—just because they're black. There was no revolution, Melanie, and there will be no revolution."

"So what am I supposed to do, huh? Just throw up my hands and not care about what happens to my people? I'm not supposed to keep fighting to make things better?"

"Of course you can. But you're going to have to fight within the system, because it and these so-called 'bourgie' schools are going to be here for a long time. And that means that you get smart like a lot of your old friends and get an important job where you can have some influence. You don't have to sell out, as you say, and work for some corporation, but you could become an assembly-woman or a civil liberties lawyer or open a freedom school in this very neighborhood. That way you could really help the community. But what help are you going to be to these people on Brewster while you're living hand-to-mouth on file-clerk jobs waiting for a revolution? You're wasting your talents, child."

"Well, I don't think they're being wasted. At least I'm here in day-to-day contact with the problems of my people. What good would I be after four or five years of a lot of white brainwashing in some phony prestige institution, huh? I'd be like you and Daddy and those other educated blacks sitting over there in Linden Hills with a terminal case of middle-class amnesia."

"You don't have to live in a slum to be concerned about social conditions, Melanie. Your father and I have been charter members of the NAACP for the last twenty-five years."

"Oh, God!" Kiswana threw her head back in exaggerated disgust. "That's being concerned? That middle-of-the-road Uncle Tom dumping ground for black Republicans!"

"You can sneer all you want, young lady, but that organization has been working for black people since the turn of the century, and it's still working for them. Where are all those radical groups of yours that were going to put a Cadillac in every garage and Dick Gregory in the White House? I'll tell you where."

I knew you would, Kiswana thought angrily.

"They burned themselves out because they wanted too much too fast. Their goals weren't grounded in reality. And that's always been your problem."

"What do you mean, my problem? I know exactly what I'm about."

"No, you don't. You constantly live in a fantasy world—always going to extremes— turning butterflies into eagles, and life isn't about that. It's accepting what is and working from that. Lord, I remember how worried you had me, putting all that lacquered hair spray on your head. I thought you were going to get lung cancer—trying to be what you're not."

Kiswana jumped up from the couch. "Oh, God, I can't take this anymore. Trying to be something I'm not—trying to be something I'm not, Mama? Trying to be proud of my heritage and the fact that I was of African descent. If that's being what I'm not, then I say fine. But I'd rather be dead than be like you—a white man's nigger who's ashamed of being black!"

Kiswana saw streaks of gold and ebony light follow her mother's flying body out of the chair. She was swung around by the shoulders and made to face the deadly stillness in the angry woman's eyes. She was too stunned to cry out from the pain of the long fingernails that dug into her shoulders, and she was brought so close to her mother's face that she saw her reflection, distorted and wavering, in the tears that stood in the older woman's eyes. And she listened in that stillness to a story she had heard as a child.

"My grandmother," Mrs. Browne began slowly in a whisper, "was a full-blooded Iroquois, and my grandfather a free black from a long line of journeymen who had lived in Connecticut since the establishment of the colonies. And my father was a Bajan who came to this country as a cabin boy on a merchant mariner."

"I know all that," Kiswana said, trying to keep her lips from trembling.

"Then know this." And the nails dug deeper into her flesh. "I am alive because of the blood of proud people who never scraped or begged or apologized for what they were. They lived asking only one thing of this world—to be allowed to be. And I learned through the blood of these people that black isn't beautiful and it isn't ugly—black is! It's not kinky hair and it's not straight hair—it just is."

"It broke my heart when you changed your name. I gave you my grandmother's name, a woman who bore nine children and educated them all, who held off six white men with a shotgun when they tried to drag one of her sons to jail for 'not knowing his place.' Yet you needed to reach into an African dictionary to find a name to make you proud."

"When I brought my babies home from the hospital, my ebony son and my golden daughter, I swore before whatever gods would listen—those of my mother's people or those of my father's people—that I would use everything I had and could ever get to see that my children were prepared to meet this world on its own terms, so that no one could sell them short and make them ashamed of what they were or how they looked—whatever they were or however they looked. And Melanie, that's not being white or red or black—that's being a mother."

Kiswana followed her reflection in the two single tears that moved down her mother's cheeks until it blended with them into the woman's copper skin. There was nothing and then so much that she wanted to say, but her throat kept closing up every time she tried to speak. She kept her head down and her eyes closed, and thought, Oh, God, just let me die. How can I face her now?

Mrs. Browne lifted Kiswana's chin gently. "And the one lesson I wanted you to learn is not to be afraid to face anyone, not even a crafty old lady like me who can outtalk you." And she smiled and winked.

"Oh, Mama, I..." and she hugged the woman tightly.

"Yeah, baby." Mrs. Browne patted her back. "I know." She kissed Kiswana on the forehead and cleared her throat. "Well, now, I better be moving on. It's getting late, there's dinner to be made, and I have to get off my feet—these new shoes are killing me."

Kiswana looked down at the beige leather pumps. "Those are really classy. They're English, aren't they?"

"Yes, but, Lord, do they cut me right across the instep." She removed the shoe and sat on the couch to massage her foot.

Bright red nail polish glared at Kiswana through the stockings. "Since when do you polish your toenails?" she gasped. "You never did that before."

"Well"—Mrs. Browne shrugged her shoulders—"your father sort of talked me into it, and, uh, you know, he likes it and all, so I thought, uh, you know, why not, so..." And she gave Kiswana an embarrassed smile.

I'll be damned, the young woman thought, feeling her whole face tingle. Daddy's into feet! And she looked at the blushing woman on her couch and suddenly realized that her mother had trod through the same universe that she herself was now traveling. Kiswana was breaking no new trails and would eventually end up just two feet away on that couch. She stared at the woman she had been and was to become.

"But I'll never be a Republican," she caught herself saying aloud.

"What are you mumbling about, Melanie?" Mrs. Browne slipped on her shoe and got up from the couch.

She went to get her mother's coat. "Nothing, Mama. It's really nice of you to come by. You should do it more often."

"Well, since it's not Sunday, I guess you're allowed at least one lie."

They both laughed.

After Kiswana had closed the door and turned around, she spotted an envelope sticking between the cushions of her couch. She went over and opened it up; there was seventy-five dollars in it.

"Oh, Mama, darn it!" She rushed to the window and started to call to the woman, who had just emerged from the building, but she suddenly changed her mind and sat down in the chair with a long sigh that caught in the upward draft of the autumn wind and disappeared over the top of the building.

Terry McMillan

(b. 1951)

Like the feisty and gritty heroines in her novels, Terry McMillan is witty, outspoken, and fiercely independent. "I grew up and became," she has said, "what my mama prayed out loud I'd become: educated, strong, smart, independent, and reliable." Born in Michigan, McMillan began writing when she was a journalism major at the University of California, Berkeley. She published her first story, "The End," when she was only 25. While in New York, where she had gone to earn an MFA in film from Columbia University, McMillan joined the Harlem Writers' Guild. Encouraged by her colleagues there, she expanded one of her short stories into a novel. The successful result was **Mama** *(1983), a funny and poignant tale about a single mother with five children. Not content simply to see her book debut on its own, McMillan actively participated in its marketing by writing thousands of letters to bookstores, universities, and Black organizations. The novel went into its third printing only six weeks after its release. Her third book,* **Waiting to Exhale** *(1992), tells the stories of four Black women who "have it all"—except love. Right after this runaway best-seller was optioned for a film, its paperback rights were sold in a record-breaking deal that made publishing history. By this point, however, McMillan was no stranger to celebrity; in 1990 a former lover sued her for defamation of character, claiming that the protagonist in her second novel,* **Disappearing Acts** *(1989), was modeled on himself. The highly publicized case, settled ruled in McMillan's favor. Currently a professor at the University of Arizona in Tucson, McMillan has also edited an anthology of contemporary African American fiction,* **Breaking Ice** *(1990), and written a book of film criticism,* **Five for Five: The Films of Spike Lee** *(1991).*

The End

It is seven a.m., Monday morning. Detroit's lower east side is still. Pobre Blackstone turns off the alarm and lets his head drop back deep into his pillow. Another day another dollar. Ford Motor Company's assembly line is waiting for him to show up, punch the clock and do his time for the day. Dammit, better get up. He has felt the same way each morning for the past twelve years.

Forgetting to brush his teeth or comb his hair thoroughly, Pobre runs out into the brisk morning air and waits for his 1973 Cadillac to warm up. Pobre's legs aren't as long as he'd like them to be so he has to pull the seat up as far as it will go. He doesn't look like the Cadillac type with his short dumpy frame, but he handles the car with grace. He looks more like a Mustang Man, you'd think. He's handsome enough to get away with a Cadillac because when he takes his Sunday Afternoon drives, all the women on the street turn in wonder at this handsome creature in the gold Coupe de Ville.

He turns on the soulful f.m. station for some music to heat his body, but the news is on instead. Let me see what's up today, Pobre says out loud. Nixon's dead!? Hallelujah, the sorry muthafucka shoulda been dead, long time ago. People are in mourning but are going to work anyway. What was it they said he had? Phlebitis or some shit? Turns out he committed suicide and no one can understand why for the life of them. Turn the station. This is too morbid and funny at the same time. AM. That's more like it, and one of his favorite tunes accompanies him towards the freeway.

Every dull ass morning I drive the same dull ass way, wear the same dull ass uniform and feel the same dull ass way going to this lousy job. And look at that old bitch over there. Got enough hairspray in her hair to starch a laundry of clothes. She can afford to bleach her hair to lightening frightening blond and tease it so everybody can see it cause she's rich. In her Mercedes Benz, bitch. All them honkies is rich, including the women. This must be her neighbor behind her. Seems like rich people don't mind tailgating each other. But if it was me behind em, they'd change lanes. I'd like to run into one of em and get me some insurance, something ugly. I bet that dude is in Ford's office from 8 to 5, and I bet he has clean fingernails, and I bet he loves his job. I bet he doesn't mind getting up in the morning. He can drink coffee and eat doughnuts all day and have lunch with the fellas. Probably drinks wine with his lunch and eats his steaks rare. That's about how often some of us get em too. And look at me, driving this damn Cadillac and don't even have a savings account for my daughter's college education. Ain't had a vacation since we visited Salina's folks in Norfolk six years ago, and that was a drag anyway. I bet that sucker was in Europe last summer. I work my nuts loose six days a week to make money to survive, and can't say I liked one day, not one damn day.

He parks the car in the lot filled with thousands of automobiles. He tries to count the Fords but hardly any are visible. Good. At least all of us aren't as stupid and dedicated as they think we are. Here comes Gus, smiling his ass off, and I wonder what makes this man so damn cheerful every morning coming to this Giant Machine.

"Hey, what's happening Gus? Why don't you wipe that smirky smile off your face and be serious? I can't smile when I get up: can't think of one good reason to. One day I'm gonna wake up and say fuck Ford Motor Company, you know what I mean, man? Doesn't this job, this place, just make you want to vomit sometimes?"

"Here we go again, you know darn well it's alright here, man. The pay is good, benefits are excellent, overtime is great, and, besides, where will you ever get a three-week vacation after working two years in a place? You niggers are all alike. Never satisfied with anything but sex. What's wrong, didn't you get any last night?"

Gus Nixon, a 29 year-old country boy, looks down at Pobre and taps him on the shoulder. Gus doesn't complain about his job. After eight years in the Navy he sees Ford's assembly line as somewhat of a relaxing atmosphere. He doesn't have to exert any mental energy like he did then. He just collects his check every Friday, gets drunk on the weekends and smiles. These are his plans for the next thirty years. Ford has a family plan that Gus is crazy about because it has fit his needs perfectly. What's to complain about?

Pobre follows him, smiling with his eyes at this fool, but with a serious look on his face bolts out, "Man, if you weren't my only white friend I'd kick your ass for saying that shit. I can never be satisfied with a dull ass job like this, and, if you are, then you're not as intelligent as the rest of your race, you're a stupid man. Can't you do anything else? You shouldn't be here noway. If it wasn't for your Godfather I probably wouldn't be here now. All the rest of your people got every damn thing. What's your problem? I know you didn't dream of growing up to be a Ford's play toy or did you? This job is enough to drain all your guts dry. No. Hell no! I'm not satisfied with this job. As long as I have to get up every morning when I don't want to, as long as my paycheck keeps getting bigger and buying less, man, I can't be satisfied. If I was, then I'd be just like you. Now we can't let that happen, can we?"

The two men laugh it off and go their separate ways. Pobre walks past rows and rows of grey and black machines until he gets to his own personal spot. It is already in operating order because the man on the night shift has just gone home. Swissh. Shzzz. Swisssh. Shzzzz. All the machines are holding their daily arguments, each seeing who can be the loudest. Pobre has gotten used to the noise, but he hears nothing as he puts the first steel wedge into its socket. This wedge is the embryo of a car door. I hope all the doors fall off before it leaves the plant. But they won't. They never do, never have, and if they did, he wouldn't be there today.

If this were the pickle factory, I could just spit in the jars or something, but here there isn't much I could get away with without getting jammed. I used to crack up when Salina told me how they used to flick cigarette ashes in the jars, put buggers in em and anything else they could find. They hated that job. I guess everybody hates their job.

As Pobre begins his daily ritual, his mind goes blank. This happens every morning. This is when he can get his thoughts out of his system because he doesn't have to use his brain to run a stupid machine. Pobre's mind begins to drift to last night's dream or nightmare, and he goes over it again in his head.

It was worse than the 30s. It had to be. The country was in a big bind, and everybody was freaking scared, almost to the point of leaving. But, there was nowhere to go. Everybody was having internal and external problems with other nations. They were all fighting for the same thing. Power. Control. Money. They couldn't see how impossible it was to sustain all three without the likelihood of war. But that was another thing that had been conspired by all the nations. War was the safest and most undetectable form of genocide.

Even on the domestic front things were taking on the shape of total societal perversion. Men no longer screwed women. Everyone smoked packs of cigarettes a day and bought valiums in supermarkets for their nerves. Women and men had begun negotiations for a civil war for the same reasons that the nations were battling over. Power. Religious fanatics were all making concessions and preparations for the day the whole world would end because they said it would be any day now. They had foreseen it long ago. It was true though. Every traumatic incident had taken place and shape in the past five years, and it was just one big scene after another.

The government had initiated a new program called Project Search. It was geared towards capturing all Black people under 30 who were not educated and making them slaves to the government. They all had guaranteed jobs, a place to stay and good pensions. It created more jobs that people didn't like but did anyway. All for the same reasons. They didn't understand what was going on at all. No one did. They just did what they were told and asked no questions. Had a good time.

Things were bad. It seemed as if the Bible was telling the truth after all. Universal Studios recently had gotten a federal grant to turn it into a movie so that in case it was finished before the world ended, everyone would be able to understand why. The movie would be free. Who cared?

On the six, seven, and eight o'clock news, a nervous voice stated the following: "Well, folks, this will be the last newscast for all eternity. Today's the day. The founders of this land, this world, have given up. Each nation has become so overwhelmed with problems they have exhausted their resources for solutions. They candidly state that the problems are too complex to solve and that each of them are so interrelated it would take forever to straighten things out. At this point in time, they don't rightly know themselves what could straighten things out, and, if it could, they don't know how they would be able to tell if things *were* straightened out. They all had a conference at the United Nations last night and came to a general consensus; Fuck it, just fuck it. Therefore, at 11 o'clock, say your last prayers and spend these last precious days or hours reminiscing about your lives. Think about what it has meant to you and what you have accomplished in it. Many of us will have to agree that it was not all in vain. We have learned to cope with pain so this shouldn't be any worse. Personally, I wish to extend my sincere hopes that all of you folks out there will find some peace somewhere after this is over. And for those of you who have learned your lesson well by what those in power have done to our world, perhaps next time you can help avoid this kind of mess again. Good luck, Goodbye and Goodnight."

It was lunch time and Pobre's brow was sweating ferociously. Damn, that's why I'm so irritable today, huh? Hell, it was only a stupid dream. But what about life? Is it really that absurd? It feels just like reality. Nothin surprises me anymore. The people in power are capable of doing anything, especially things that do more harm for us than good. People like me. I better start paying closer attention to the news to see what is going to happen next.

Pobre lived in a fine brick home that cost him $8,500 when he bought it twelve years ago. It's now worth $22,000. It is filled with the finest furniture his paycheck could buy. Salina has just finished looking at the 4:30 movie. "Hi, honey. The food is on the stove, and Nostalgia is in the basement playing. You tired? Want me to rub you neck and ankles for you? You look beat, or worried. Something wrong?"

"No honey," as he caresses her behind. "I just got some serious thinking to do. I gotta start thinking about the future, our future, everybody's future. I had this crazy ass dream last night about the world coming to an end, and, shit, it's been bugging me all day."

"Pobre, don't let no silly dream start messing up your head now. Dreams don't mean nothing. The world's gotta end one day anyway, so let it happen on its own course. Nostalgia kid's kid's kid's will probably be around, maybe more than that. We gonna be here a long time, less you worries all of us to death bout some crazy dream. I got something to ease the tension for you, why don't you lie down, and I'll be in in a minute."

He slipped off his work boots in the middle of the living room floor, dropped his overcoat on the chair and sat down. He didn't really feel like making love, not right now. "Honey, would you get me a beer, please? That'll be enough for my nerves right now, okay? Nothing personal, honey, just one of them days."

Salina was a 32-year-old Southern beauty. She had the roundest ass Pobre had ever seen, and he used to pour ice water on it just to see it roll off and watch her nipples rise. After five years of marriage, Nostalgia was born and had the same chocolate skin as her father, and the same bone structure as her mother.

Nostalgia came running into the living room and stood beside her father. "Hi, Daddy. Wanna see what I wrote today?" Before he could answer, she pulled out a neatly folded piece of notebook paper. Pobre opened it and read out loud:

"Dear God: My mama cries when daddy goes to hard work. She is scared
for Daddy. Mama says everything be worse and we might go to the
poorhouse. Please, God, don't let everything be worse. Mama, Daddy
and me don't want to go nowhere. Love Nostalgia"

Pobre's heart was beating too fast. He felt his puffy face flush and flutter. The blood seemed to fall from his head to his feet, and he just looked at Nostalgia with a mixture of strength and pity. Who had told her God could solve all the problems, and Lord, this child was smart enough to think about writing God for help. Pobre didn't know what to say. He didn't know Salina had been tripping on the same things his dream had conveyed. It may have been a little exaggerated version of reality, but it wasn't far off.

"Honey, daddy ain't going nowhere, none of us are. And I'll work until ain't no such thing as work. If God gets this letter in time, maybe everything will get better. Now go tell your mama to come here so we can help love her a little more so she won't be crying when I go the hard work, okay?"

"Okay, daddy." Nostalgia runs into the kitchen to get her mother and found her leaning against the refrigerator in tears. "Mama, daddy said come here so he can love you." She hugged her mama around the thighs and Salina held her hand as they walked into the living room.

Pobre heard tears before he could turn to see them. He pulled her to him and held her as if it were the last day on earth. They all cried until they couldn't cry anymore. They both knew then that no matter what was to come into their lives, there was nothing they could do but love each other and keep on loving each other. They would do just that.

The news that evening resembled statements one would normally associate with science fiction movies. Out of this world.

... At Vladivostok summit, it was the intention of President Rockefeller and Chairman Brezhnev to lay plans to work hard for an agreement on the further limitation of nuclear strategic weapons.

... Mideast ... torn by new rounds of terrorism and reprisal between Arab and Israeli. Both sides must decide on new moves toward peace or more war.

... Mideast ... If pushed too far, the U.S. will be forced to choose between economic ruin and armed action if Arab oil supplies are not secured in time to eliminate an international disaster. Could be early as 1976.

... Western Europe: As Russia encourages its Communist parties, the U.S. is watching its allies trying to deal with inflation, strikes, the energy crisis and the gradual decline of the quality of human life.

... Italy ... is in desperate straits, awaiting action by its 37th government in 31 years. Inflation rate is 25 percent annually. Vital imports take a billion dollars a month more than Italy earns. A million Italians are jobless: Many only work part-time. The West's biggest Communist party is waiting.

... Britain ... also is running a billion-dollar deficit abroad each month. Prime Minister Wilson says Britain faces its greatest crisis since World War II.

... France ... is plunging into economic recession and social strife. A wave of strikes by workers in state-run industries deprived the French of mail for six weeks and garbage collections for a week.

... Just ahead ... not only in France, but elsewhere in Western Europe, you can expect a three-way struggle. Part of Western Europe wants to work closely with the U.S. as an essential ally. Part wants to keep the U.S. at arm's length while trying to make Western Europe the "third superpower," united and equal to U.S. and Russia. A relative few want Western Europe to line up with Russia.

The telephone interrupts the news report, and Pobre goes to answer it. It is Gus. "Hello Pobre?"

"Yeah, Gus, how you doing, what's happening, man?"

"Man, you won't believe this. Those sons of bitches laid me off today. Would you believe that? I knew I should've stayed in the Navy. At least they treated me like a human being. Man, I don't know what I'm gonna do now, not the slightest idea. Unemployment won't pay my rent, and the car note and food and hell, man, I got two kids. What is a guy suppose to do when shit like this happens, just what kind of alternatives does a guy have? If I saw that Ford character I'd piss in his eyeballs and shit in his face and see how he likes it. Pobre, you were right, man. Ford is so fucked up it's pitiful.

"I just wanted to let you know you won't be seeing me in the parking lot tomorrow man. Take it easy, and I'll keep in touch, man."

Pobre said his good-byes and hung up the phone. Too bad it happens like this. I never thought I'd live to see a day when everything was so mixed up like a big crossword puzzle and none of the pieces seem to fit. I wonder what the world will be like for Nostalgia.

It is seven a.m., Monday morning, and Pobre Blackstone turns off the alarm. He decides to go back to sleep. He's tired.

Fatima Shaik

(b. 1952)

New Yorker Fatima Shaik is the author of a collection of novellas entitled **The Mayor of New Orleans: Just Talking Jazz** *(1987). Her work has appeared in the anthology* **Breaking Ice** *(1990) and in such periodicals as* **Tribes, Callaloo, The Southern Review,** *and* **The Review of Contemporary Fiction**. *A former reporter for the* **Miami News** *and the* **New Orleans Times-Picayune***, Shaik has also served as a correspondent for* **McGraw-Hill World News***. She has most recently completed two children's books,* **On Mardi Gras Day** *and* **The Jazz of Our Street**. *Shaik received her bachelor's degree from Boston University in 1974 and her master's degree from New York University in 1978. She was awarded a National Endowment of the Arts Fellowship in 1981.*

The One That Did Not Get Away

I

My boyfriend refuses to tell me where he got the scar on his face.

"It's from fishing," he says.

"It's from some war," I suggest.

His profile is charming like one of those men who would stand calmly in the midst of burning rockets and order attack.

"It's from casting too far out," he says. "A hook getting caught in my neck."

"It's from a night in the moat trying to save a damsel in distress," I joke. I try to jolly him. Maybe if he's caught unaware, he will blurt it out. It's such a fine scar traveling from below the chin to the front of his ear like a slow passionate kiss. At various points, the scar makes little snags and bursts.

It is keloid. Tissue never healed over the cut so now it appears shiny and reflective against the mat of his face.

"It looks like lightning against the black of the sky," I tell him.

He bows his head, smiles and kisses my hand. He says he admires my sense of poetry.

I think that's what brought us together—my poetic spirit and his mystery to me.

He is very handsome and kind in the way of Southern gentlemen. He is also very humble and noble. "Simple," is how he calls himself.

"No," I tell him, "you are too fast for the average person to recognize, much, much too adventurous. By the way, where did you get that scar?"

"In a sinking boat," he answers.

Maybe this is a clue.

Men are like that in New Orleans and possibly the world. From what I've seen they will not tell you the truth. They couch themselves in our overwrought lives—women's that is. On our brocade couches, men languor and bathe silently, handsomely and romantically while we must figure them out. "What to do with the man," we concentrate.

In my girlhood and my womanhood, I look for a mate. I must find him from his disguises of masculinity. It is the Southern tradition. They chase. We pray.

In the cathedral, I sit with my girlfriend. In the diffracted, prismatic, stained-glass light, under our veils, in their shadows, we whisper our hopes.

"He is dangerous," my friend says.

We live in the small parts of New Orleans. In the Catholic, feminine and familial territories where all is known. We tell stories. We sit on porches and near sickbeds. We gather in churches and bingo parlors. We make our own entertainment.

There is a big tree down by the river where we picnic with distant cousins and men from our past like uncles and fathers. They talk big and brag. We laugh lightly. We flirt. We practice our feminine wiles and hone our traditions of desire. We pray for the right men to come along.

In my young life, everything was so plain. Up too early in the morning for school. Come home to find Mama cooking. Papa on his way out to get drunk.

My boyfriend is the first man I met who has mystery. He has excitement, a past I don't know and a scar as proof of his difference.

"Looks like your Papa when he was a boy," Mama likes to relate everything. She wants all the same from past to present to the times beyond.

But it is my life ahead. I am old enough to see what has gone before me was wasted. Sixteen years I already spent without harpooning romance, without waltzing desire, without fulfillment. I have never been fought over under the Dueling Oaks. I have never kissed on the levee and then held hands in suicidal duet and plunged into the river. I have never lived in a bordello or run with pirates even though this is New Orleans. This is my history.

It is my privilege now to have finally met a man with a scar. Not a deep scar, a fine scar. One that gives character to him and excitement to me — the plain, the sheltered and the unadventured.

I will change. We are going to change my life. I will rise from my knees, throw off my veil, pierce my ears. I will marry a man with a scar.

"Should I really worry about where you got it?" I tease.

"Back of Lake Borgne."

I laugh.

Lake Borgne is a little rural fork in the water between high mosquito grass where shrimpers and other lonely men go. They start out early in the morning when the only light they see is from their own kerosene lamps. They come home smelling like swamp, and fall tired and drunk into their beds at night.

"Lake Borgne," I laugh. "That sounds like an old man's fish tale."

The nights will be unimportant to me until he and I see them together, beginning the evening we are married. "We will elope. We will ride in a horse-drawn carriage through the jasmine streets. We will pass the cathedral to make the sign of the cross," I place one finger on the side of his neck when I tell him. I trace the line of his scar, our scar, following it right up to the ear, then independently, I go around.

"Are you listening?" I moisten my finger with a kiss so it will feel sweet and soft, "if you will not tell me where you got this scar, about your past, I will not tell you about our future. Don't you want to know?"

He nods.

"We will live in a little white house," I tell him.

"Near Lake Borgne," he says.

"We will sleep on a bed of down and moss. We will not get home until dawn on the night of our elopement from drinking champagne and dancing the waltz. We will arrive at our door when the peach of the rising sun tints the morning onto our wedding white clothes. And only then will we make passionate love. And only then will we sleep," I take his hand.

He studies the lines of my palms, first the left and then the right before he places them together and closed. Then he envelopes my hands with his own.

"We will get home at dawn," he repeats, "Dawn? What month?"

"June, of course."

"Good. Then they ought to be running trout."

II

Sometimes I feel like he is not listening to me. But men make such pretenses. They claim their muscles are a sign of their strength. They brag their eyes are not the windows to their souls. They tell each other that together they could win such things as wars, when wars are won by ideas and deals, no matter the number of dead.

We will be married in wedding white, whether he hears it or not.

The dress I plan for elopement is sheer and pure, cut from the mid-bolt of the cloth. It has no dirty ends or flaws running lightning-like, first one wrong direction then another. The holes of the weave are very small and sturdier than mosquito net and the fabric glows new and white like a lantern guiding a skiff in the dark. It will be a beacon for the beginning of my life, a last reflection on all of us.

My girlfriend and I, we maidens, demonstrate our breeding through such simplicity. Our knees never show far below the bottom of our dresses. The shoulders of our boat collars never quite slide off. Our hair obeys nights of meticulous training to stay on our necks or behind the ear. Just about the place where my boyfriend's scar begins, on me a wiry branch from my scalp threatens to jump out. I will let it go, once I am wed. I will start to be dangerous.

"The sizzors," my girlfriend hands me the implement for making my entrance. The elopement dress has been sewn askew. I rip open a seam. The front and back fly open easily and silently like skin willing to part.

"Catch it."

My girlfriend lays out her arms for the pieces of shroud while I rethink the construction. It should be straight. The stitches should not show to anyone else. Only I will know how they got there.

"That scar," I asked him once, "has anyone told you about it? Do they ask why it never went away?"

"It's in my blood, I guess." He has inherited the factors of clotting and unclotting himself, the skin that heals, but does not bind over, the genes for keeping infection at bay.

This scar is a sign of his health, his fighting spirit, his eternal resistance. It will be mine when we are married, this wound against even the body's conventions.

My girlfriend puts the needle back into the seam. She memorizes for me the last night I will be among them. She promises to tell everyone.

"I will say that you reached the cathedral at midnight," she takes a ricochet stitch, "And that he looked only into your eyes."

"Tell them that he wanted to take me then. But I refused."

She blushes.

"Tell them that I said first when and where we made love," I remind.

Back of Lake Borgne it has already happened. But it was not sin, is hardly remembered. It was more like a miracle, the saint descending onto the flowers and blessing them, changing their colors from white to red, in abundance, profoundness and silence. Then gone. Nothing remained but the swaying reeds flattened, the roses, an overripe smell tainting the air.

Nobody knows but me, not even him. He claims I was not there.

"Still a virgin," he tells everybody.

Once I saw him unhook a fish. He had to take the metal prongs out through the same holes that they entered. He held it still, his hands firm against the open jaws. There was a kindness in his making it immobile. The fish swung and shivered from its tail to its chest. Finally it submitted about the same time he got through. The hook came out with a slight bit of flesh on it and even the bait came out again. Then he tossed the fish into the ice chest. There was one sound of flop, then writhing, then grating, then stillness.

I swim not far from Lake Borgne, in the Intercoastal Canal where there is sometimes dangerous water. You can see whirlpools if you stand in the rocking boat. But you cannot when they are level with your head. You only feel little tugs at your arms, legs and hair as if you were caught but not yet drowning. Or it can be exciting and pleasant like getting caught in a school of mullet.

"Men enter marriage with their eyes closed," my Mama said. Is it true? They come in from the blind, dark side of the church. They wait with lips dry and mind suspended, swimming into the unknown. Sometimes I wonder, "Do I."

I wriggled the hook at my boyfriend, the day he took off the fish. "With this," I said, "I'm going to get you."

He took it out of my hand, stuck on a worm and dropped it back into the water, "Don't play." I fear he meant it.

It was a sullen afternoon when we came home. It was smelly and cloudy and dark. We dropped the bait and the ice in the side of the grass at the shore to feed the fish we had not caught, to proliferate the species. Then we pulled up the boat.

His arms turning the crank assured me. His body was something into which I could merge. The muscles could be taken apart bit by bit, dived through, fileted. Then in the open, bare bones of himself, he would know he would really want me.

"Do I put words in your mouth," once I asked him.

"Nothing much else goes in there."

He was eating a sandwich, drinking a beer, and tossing the pickle up in the air to catch it like a fish snapping a fly. Full, open mouth, he grinned.

I felt like slicing him just at the moment. Taking the knife from the table and running it, serrated and all, just above the line of his scar. "Take me seriously," I wanted to say. But I didn't. I was still unsure then whether he would take me at all.

That night it happened. The first love on the banks. The moonlight, the moored rocking boat, the reeds, the sounds of insects and splashing. The saint descending just for me. We were for each other, were we not, in our virginal pre-nuptial pairing?

Each of my uncles and brothers and cousins, each of them fathers has said, "Never." Then one by one, I heard from the girlfriends, mothers and wives that they were the lovers. They were the lovers, the women, long before marriage. Love alone made them do it.

"Love is a powerful thing," they hand me this secret like they would give me the dust or the candle. They cup my palm with theirs, make a pocket that is empty and they said the invisible word, "Love."

"It is love," they nod over my boyfriend's glazed eyes and they see the line caught from his mind to his heart, "You are safe." These are powerful women.

We all picnic by the river. Women and men. We spread the blankets, toss the balls, babble to babies, cuddle the children. We break into our separate domains, women near the food and the tables, men by the cars, parked up on the grass, talking loudly and drinking.

It is not by force that we get together. It is not by accident. It is not by aberration. It is not only bait, prayer, flirtation, aphrodisiac, mojo, root. It is love, I have been well trained.

"What will you do on our wedding night," I ask my boyfriend. "The night after we are married? Will we honeymoon well? Will we stay in the chambers?"

"I'm thinking of going out to fish. That's how I make my living."

His head is turned and his profile is straight, a flat, dark shadow from his lowered temple to his high chest. He is almost invisible with the night all around him, around us. I feel I must turn this corner, get to the other side of his face, where the scar sits in all its contentedness.

"I don't think you love me. I don't think you want me. I'm just something else that you caught," I suggest.

A thought splashes above his brow for a moment before he responds, "Do you want to be an old fisherman's wife, to be the wife of a scarfaced, sometimes drunk?"

I recognize a proposal when I hear one at last, "Yes." I answer, "Yes. Yes."

III

I have looked for this wedding all of my life, at least the part I can remember. Before that, I tumbled aimlessly, playing the rolling games of babies, winding in my mother's stomach, floating like a piece of dry bark on water.

Before dresses and boyfriends, and smiles for uncles and Papa, before I knew up and down, north and south, when there was only me, I seem to remember there was nothing at all. There was nothing asked and nothing given. There was no want or fear or even love. There was no destiny.

The destination began with my girlhood and a need to make everything right in the world. Before generations had leftover chores for me. There was a sin in the original tale told on Eve. Mother whispered, it was men who from the beginning of time to this day ate all the forbidden fruit. But this gave women meaning.

To understand and forgive, to carry the secrets, to accept spirits: women bore these as love, heavy and clumsy, and sometimes hurtful and weak to illuminate the dark path from Eden.

To walk up the altar was passage too, against the dangerous male freedom. I was already enslaved because of my fault, my fissure, my actual femininity that increasingly had to be covered over, hidden and prided, laced and decorated, paraded and used.

I told my boyfriend once that I have a scar but it bleeds every month, just like the stigmata or the weeping heart of Jesus.

"Don't make blasphemy," he said and he did not touch me for a long, long time after that.

I went fishing once alone. I pressed myself into the morning darkness between endless lake and sky where stepping off shore was an act of sound rather than sight. Like the young men, the old men and the old women who sometimes grow beards and wear hats tacked down to their heads with leftover scarves, I sat in a barely rocking boat. "Is this," I wondered to the barren patter of waves upon wood, "the feeling of just being?"

"How often do you look in the mirror?" I asked my boyfriend once when I was examining my eyes for the lashes that sometimes turn downward and tear my vision, obscure sight without me ever knowing why.

"I find my reflection when I brush my teeth over the lake in the morning," he answered.

I imagine his face stretches with the rise of each wave. The sun comes over his back.

"Don't you ever see yourself plainly?"

"Sometimes fast in the bar mirror. But then I've been drinking, so it doesn't hold much interest." He'd rather see me sleeping, he said, or waking with him in the bed, or smiling to him with the dinner plate.

I did not leave the hand mirror. But sometimes I wonder if I made the only possible choice.

My girlfriend and I covered our foreheads in church for many years before the invention of the chapel veil. It looked like a lace pie plate or the kind of scrap you might put under a vase over the wooden sideboard to protect it from bruising.

The invention of the chapel veil was that it could be carried in the pocketbook, along with the rain bonnet. It could be secured by the metal bob pin. It could be recognized by the church as covering the head without compromising the hair.

We wore the chapel veil for a while. But it always seemed odd. Our problem was that we prayed in the cathedral. We knelt in the elegant half-light, under the ornate, iron-encased glass, amid the gold furnishings, before the silk vestments. The chapel veil did not fit. We returned to the mantilla.

I am excited to elope. So much that already I feel a strain on my heart. My body feels full as if it is beating for two.

"Do you know what you're doing?" my boyfriend asks me. "Be careful when you put your fingernail to your eye. You could get hurt from a scratch you don't even see, blindness from a scrape the size of a hairline.

"I know. I know," I point slowly toward my face. There were so many eyes ahead. Big and small eyes reflect back into themselves as far as I could perceive and I had to be careful with each.

IV

The baby inside me grows like a minnow. I dream of fish, reeling them close, throwing them back. I tell no one, especially him, of my condition. He may not want to get married. Perhaps, he will find me distastefully large, too importantly fat.

"Let us retreat to abandon," I suggest to him. "Be wed without vestments, run off without the trappings of romance."

"Do you want to get shotgun married? Make back seat magic? Jump a broom? Buy a six pack?"

I give in.

He relents.

V

The wedding pictures that were not taken, no one is surprised not to see.

"Look at my album," the women in the family call, for the first time pulling out books with torn and blank pages. "Here is when I was a girl. There is where I was wed. This is childbirth." They look at me.

I blame no one for my mistakes, I explain. I look at the ground. I do not see my feet.

Now, I am the biggest of all of us. I am their potential explosion of dreams. Future and past to burst forth in blood, bones and gore.

"The pain," the mothers exclaim. "Why do it?" They grow large and eternally hopeful, "What is it for?"

Then gathering the unease of men, they repeat assurances. My nourishment will be in my child. "Your future is yet coming," they cannot explain enough about motherhood, the same, given history, and, so different, as they still believe possible.

My girlfriend puts the elopement dress against my shoulders. "Still fits," she says.

I won't disagree. Only if we travel the seams past the arms will we notice that the fabric won't stretch, that my shape is more woman, that I have grown emphatically.

She will save the dress for my daughter, my girlfriend says. "Perhaps she will have what you can't."

"It's no longer important. It's far too tame an end. It's not even scary, much less the measure of danger," I want to lie. Instead, I say, "Please don't."

When I lay in bed, I convince my husband that I see not one difference between marrying him under the guise of romantic attachment or under the guidance of rush. Partly, it's true that the end is the same while only the means are deflowered. Isn't that reason enough?

That night, a dream brings my husband to the side of my hospital bed. I have just given birth.

"Where is my child?" I ask.

"She is swimming in the Intercoastal Canal. She is boarding a trawl in Lake Pontchatrain at the corner of Elysian Fields Avenue. She is too small, too weak, too skimpy, too female," he says, "I threw her back."

A woman behind my bed says, "You have been wishing aloud."

I scream.

"You have been crying while not half awake," says a female voice from the other side.

"Look, the baby is not yet lost," they remind. "She is surrounded under your breasts, close to your heart, caught in your arms."

I wake only to cling to myself wearing a gown too thin for comfort with hands that will not reach around.

I turn to my husband, "How can I allow my daughter the dreams of a girl without making her hate a woman's hard life?"

"That's not a question," he goes back to sleep.

"What do you know?" I respond. "As a man, you have been visibly scarred. Now stay safe," I curse. "Keep your small aspirations."

He breathes shallow and soft, like swimming on course. He has been, he once said, since he met me.

VI

I pray in the alcove that shelters the Virgin. Mothers here rise up from the kneelers brushing down trails of electricity that have risen and traveled the center aisle of their skirts. They lift flimsy material from big, sweaty legs, sit to rub the red impressions of bones that come through to their skin before walking outside to the street. This is the only clue they give sometimes that it hurts.

The Virgin, for us much more than plaster, stands patient and placid as symbol, untouched by our pain. She shares only one heartache, the loss of the child within the unfairness of the world. In greatest measure, she is our ideal, knowing God before man, having a secret self far above earthly conditions.

As we stand, woman and girls, or sit in prayer or in loathing outside of the church, we have so many doubts. But there is no place for our fear. No saint is the patron of mistake, of stupidity, of idleness, weakness, of loss. We must pray to a heaven that is perfectly clear.

Along cathedral corridors, laid chipped stone by rough hand, past fountains of blessed water and statues whose bare feet we touch lightly with whispered petition, there is no niche for confusion, misinformation, mispurpose. There is no creche for a rest.

When my husband comes into my bed in the evenings, he stays moving in ways I know not for their blessedness, nor for their freeing. The scar on his face shines like my road map.

When my infant daughter nests in the half circle that is my right arm, she nudges and suckles, and does not recognize and does not speak. She does not wish, consider herself or fail. Now, she is very like me.

Trey Ellis

(b. 1962)

A native of Washington, D.C., Ellis attended Phillips Academy and Stanford University. An experienced world traveler, he has spent time abroad in Italy, where he worked as a journalist and translator, Central America, Africa, and Greece, where he lived for awhile. His debut novel, **Platitudes** *(1988), is the account of a young writer who is struggling to achieve literary recognition. Praised by critics for its portrayal of the African American middle class and for its insightful commentary on the position of the young artist in America today,* **Platitudes** *combines parody with classical literary traditions to recreate what critic J. Martin Favor has called "our sprawling American culture." Ellis's second novel,* **Home Repairs** *(1993), tells the comic, often poignant story of a young privileged Black man who is always in love but never successfully. In his 1989 critical manifesto,* **The New Black Aesthetic***, Ellis has said that African American artists "no longer need to deny or suppress any part of our complicated and sometimes contradictory cultural baggage to please either white people or black." He currently lives in Venice, California.*

Guess Who's Coming to Seder

What?

Shhhhh.

So now you, my son, my only son, shush me? The one who took all your vicious kicks? Like a Nazi bastard you goose-stepped in my belly and now with the shush?

Buba.

So now with the Yiddish? I thought you'd forgotten in front of your pretty shiksa wife and your goyim friends, call me Mammy or something?

Mrs. Cohen's son, Alan, explodes his eyes overwide at his mother's bifocal lenses. Hidden absolutely are her eyes; instead, the weighty glasses only televise the two candle flames next to the two platefuls of matzoh in front of her.

It's getting late, Alan, Megan. Donnel Washington eyes first his wife, Carlene, then Vietta, his little girl. Their six palms push on the tablecloth, raising their asses off the cane geometry of the Cohens' chairs' seat bottoms simultaneously.

Donnel, please. My mother's from New York and she's lost almost all her hearing and her mind too. She doesn't mean anything by it. Carlene, I'm sorry.

You call *this* wine? Does *she* think French is kosher now that she's an expert on our religion or something?

Heather, *please* pass your grandmother the Mogen David. Megan Cohen, Heather's mother, starts to throw her hands at her mother-in-law's trachea but snatches them back to wring her own blond bun.

Heather slides the now wet curl of brown hair from the soft crack between her lips, latches it behind an ear. Pouring, her right nipple, through her bra and her blouse, jostles a liver spot on her grandmother's bare triceps. The noise of a car's wheels rolling, its engine screwing through missed gears to stop near the house, pulls Heather's eyes, her head, to the door.

Such large, firm roses. I had such firm roses when I was young and sweet too, back when grandfather was alive ... but what use are they to anyone now that they hang over the fat of my belly like dead things. Heatherchick, if you go a day in your life without wearing a brassiere, so help me God I'll chop yours off.

Drink the first cup of wine, and fill Elijah's cup. Pass around a basin to wash the hands. Take parsley or spring onion, dip them in vinegar or salt water, pass them around the table, and say:

"Blessed are you YHWH our God, Ruler of the Universe who create the fruit of the earth."

"Barukh atay YHWH elohenu melekh ha-olam boray p'ri ha a-da-mah."

It's a shame Derrick isn't here for this part of the ceremony. I think he would have liked it. Heather, you're sure you told him eight o'clock?

Yes, Dad. I told you already he has a big paper due. But I don't know where he is *all* the time. You *could* ask Mister and Miz Washington.

Carlene and Donnel Washington smile with Alan and Megan Cohen at the new pink on Heather's face.

We must apologize for him. I left a note on the kitchen table, but that boy's so willful no telling what mess he's into now. As she speaks about her son, Carlene reties the bow that her daughter has again untied in the burnt offering of her hot-combed hair.

Mah nishtanah ha-lai-lah? Mah nishtanah ha-lai-lah? Who's going to say it already? Billy, you're the baby, so tell me what is it that holds you so quiet?

Billy Cohen slurps the dangling lunger of saliva back through his lips but not before the last inch and three-quarters detaches, dives through the red surface of his Paschal wine, floats back white bubbles.

Actually, Buba, Vietta Washington is the youngest. Vietta, could you please read from the top of page 72. Where it says, Why is this night ... ?

Vietta looks hard at her mother. Ma, can't I just eat the crackers? I feel stupid.

Go on, baby. Don't be bashful. Carlene pets her neck.

Let Derrick do it, if he ever makes it. This is all his fault anyway.

Don't make me tell you twice.

[Huff] "Whyisthisnightdifferentfromallothernights? On all, other, nights we may—"

What? I'm sure she's not speaking Hebrew. Then let me help for God's sake: She-b'khol ha-le-lot a-nu okh-lin sh'ar y'ra-kot, ha-lai-lah ha-zeh ma-ror. She-b'khol ha-le-lot eyn anu mat-bilin a-fi-lu p-am a-chat, ha-lai-lah ha-zeh sh-tay f' a-mim. She-b'khol ha-le-lot a-nu okh-lin beyn yosh-vin u-veyn m'su-bin, ha-lai-lah ha-zeh ku-la-nu m'su-bin.

Thank you, Buba. Continue reading, Vietta, please?

The teaching invites us to meet and to teach four children: one wise and one wicked, one innocent and one who does not relate by asking.

What does the wise one say? "What are the testimonies, and the statutes, and the rules which...?"

... which, Y-H-W ...?

Yahweh, Vietta. It's a sin for Jews to pronounce the real name of Him or Her.

You mean you can't say *God-God-God-God!*

I'll slap the black off you, girl, when we get home. Apologize.

That's okay, Carlene, my mother started it. Alan's eyes flick to their corners to watch his mother.

So now with the killer looks? At your own mother even? I wish I could've heard what terrible things you've all been spitting at me now that I'm deaf, more dead than alive, my last seder in all probability.

Invite and wait for discussion on these questions. Who are the four children? Are they among us? Are they within each of us? Are these good answers?

It must be time to talk about the four children now and of course they are still with us, especially the wicked one who's lost the language, doesn't even get bat mitzvahed like my beautiful granddaughter next to me, or who marries out of the religion like my only son, so technically my two grandchildren here aren't even really Jewish. Back in olden times these would have been the ones saying, Freedom, shmeedom, I'd rather stay here with this bunch of greasy Arabs as their dirty slave... no offense.

Carlene crinkles the skin around her eyes, raising weakly her cheeks and upper lip from her teeth.

Why should anyone be offended, Buba? All of us, blacks and Jews, have been enslaved, there's no hiding from it, right?

Come on, Alan, *our* emancipation was a tad more recent, don't you think? Were your great-grandparents born slaves? Hmmm? The knife in Donnel's left hand, coated in haroseth (ritualized mortar made of diced apples and nuts, wine and raisins), disintegrates the matzoh (representing the brick), in his right hand. Haroseth and matzoh flakes stucco his palm, then the napkin.

Yes, but … Heather, honey, what's your take on all this?

I don't know.

Come one now, sweetie, is tonight really that bad?

Heather handles the bottle of kosher French by its neck, jams its nose into the bottom of her glass until the rising choppy waves of wine redden her knuckles, then overflow and wound the white tablecloth.

Heatherchick! You know that it's not yet that we toast. I swear before your grandfather's ghost you even *sip* before the right time and *ping!* there again goes my blood clot and half of my face will die like your Aunt Estelle's in the home.

Lifting the glass to her mouth, Heather looks at no one. Noisily, gulp after gulp of wine bubbles back around her mouth's corners.

Young lady, that wasn't too nice. Megan turns a bit from her daughter, tilts her face into her hand, milks her rising smile from her cheeks into her palm.

Mrs. Cohen whistles "Dai Dai Enu" at the Hockney lithograph on the wall.

Buba, we're still trying to discuss the four children as the B'nai B'rak rabbi's instructed.

Now it's getting very late, Megan, Alan; and Vietta has school tomorrow.

So they're leaving in the middle of seder? They hate Jewish so that they want calamity to strike us all down?

Uh, Donnel, I'm so sorry. My mother thinks if anyone leaves, gets up from their chair before the last cup of wine is drunk, all the Jews in the house will be slain. See, in 1583, there was this thing in Istanbul.

Maybe they're Farrakhan Mooslims.

I'll have you know that the Washingtons' son, Derrick, and our Megan have been seeing each other all through U of M, so they might very soon be "family."

Ma!

After discussion, all sing.

> Go tell it on the mountain,
> over the hills and everywhere.
> Go tell it on the mountain—
> Let my people go!

Who are the people dressed in white?
Let my people go!
Must be the children of the Israelite—
Let my people go!

Where did you get this hippie seder from anyhow?
Cousin Naomi found it at the Rainbow Reformed Temple in New York.

[A moment of silence. Then a reader says:]
"But let us also question the plagues: Can the winning of freedom be bloodless? It was not bloodless when Nat Turner proclaimed, 'I had a vision, and I saw white spirits and black spirits engaged in battle, and the sun was darkened—the thunder rolled in the heavens and blood flowed in streams—and I heard a voice saying, Such is your luck, such you are called to see, and let it come rough or smooth, you must surely bear it.' "

I-lu i-lu ho-tzi-a-nu ho-tzi-a-nu mi-mitz-ra-yim, ho-tzi-a-nu mi-mitz-ra-yim dai-ye-nu. DAI-DAI-YE-NU, DAI-DAI-YE-NU, DAI-DAI-YE-NU, dayenu, dayenu!
[All drink the third cup. Refill glasses, but not to the top.]
[The door is opened.]

Alan returns Vietta's bow from the floor to her lap, slouches down to her as she confetties her paper napkin. It's almost over, sweetheart, then Billy can show you his Nintendo. He just got Donkey Kong. We're just waiting a little bit for the ghost of Elijah to come down and drink his cup of wine. If you leave milk and cookies out for Santa Claus, it's sort of like that. Alan stretches to pat Vietta's shoulder, but she flinches.
Miss Thing, I raised you better than acting up like this outside the house.
Dingdingding-dong.
Billy's curtains of matzoh-flaked lips pull back, reveal teeth behind braces. Heather's back straightens, red reclaims her face.
Did I hear the doorbell go off? At least this you did right, my little Alan. Mrs. Cohen laughs. The messiah rings the doorbell! My uncle's half-brother, Arkady, the Shostakovich of indoor plumbing, used to rig a pump to Elijah's cup to make it look like the spirit was drinking it. Oh how I always fell for that as a girl.
Dingdingding-dong.
Heather, get the door, it's okay.

Jerome Wilson

(b. 1969)

Jerome Wilson has lived in Memphis, Tennessee, his entire life. Currently a student in English at the University of Memphis, he began writing after meeting Toni Cade Bambara. Wanting "to be like her," he published his first short story when he was only nineteen. He has said that he models his writing "after John Steinbeck and Toni Cade Bambara," adding ruefully, "if you can imagine that." The "real common everyday things" in Wilson's fictional world, however, are not so very different from what is found in the work of the writers that he so admires. Having just completed a collection of short stories, Wilson is currently trying to finish a novel. The widely anthologized "Paper Garden" first appeared in **Ploughshares** *in 1993.*

Paper Garden

Back in the days when life was easy and you could walk down the street at night and not worry about anybody knocking you over the head with some blunt object and taking all of your pocket change, Miss Mamie Jamison, the neighborhood kids' godmother who gave us money and candy and let us hide in her parlor when the big boys chased us from the playground, took seriously ill one summer and had to be put to bed. Her daughter, the one all the way from New York, moved in with her, dressed in nothing but what looked like black bodysuits and tall fruit-basket hats like that Chiquita woman wears on banana peels. If it wasn't black bodysuits, she was wearing a pair of men's trousers and shirt along with a mighty fine pair of work boots. But despite her icky clothes, she looked like a movie star from the silent screens: deep, dark black hair, thin red lips, and that pale, powdery skin color, like she was waiting for some invisible director to yell "Action!" and give her the go-ahead to say her lines like that was the only thing God created her for.

Of course, the only reason the Chiquita woman, Miss Marion, wasn't talked about like a dog too much by the other ladies in the neighborhood was because she *was* from New York. Meaning, Miss Marion obviously knew what the latest fashions were, and knew much more about fads and styles than these country women, including my own mama, would ever know in their whole lifetime. Which was also why she was called "Miss" Marion, even by the old folks—the way she spoke, calling everybody "darling" and "sweetie" and always saying how much she loved somebody, even complete strangers she met walking down the street. You would have thought they were blood relatives.

My mama was the main gofer over Miss Marion; she would come home just about every other day with some catchy word or phrase that she had heard Miss Marion say, or what someone else had heard her say. Once, while leaving out the door to go to a Daughters of the Confederate Army meeting, Mama said to Papa and me, "I'll be back in about an hour. Chow." And when she closed the door, Papa, with a puzzled look on his face, looked up from his evening paper and asked me, "What dog?"

Something was happening to the town of Harper. All the women wanted to be Miss Marion, ordering just about every dress and hat and scarf and shoe that the Sears, Roebuck catalog had to offer. Even the men, down to the youngest and up to the oldest, watched Miss Marion out of the corner of their eyes. We watched how she swished her way through town knowing full well everybody was looking at her in a skirt that was at least ten inches too short and ten years ahead of Harper's time. Eddie T., who claimed he was blind, sat on that old tree stump at the end of the main street playing his harmonica, wrote and sang a song about her that teetered on the edge of vulgarity, sometimes drawing a good crowd if it was a Saturday and a nice pile of spending money in his ragged hat that he kept between his feet.

Even Papa, whenever he saw Miss Marion coming up on our side of the sidewalk, all of a sudden had to go check the oil in the car, or he had to go clip the hedges, or the grass was too tall and he had to go cut it. I think Mama knew what Papa was up to, but it was summer and it was hot and the price of ground beef had dropped and life was just too wonderful so Mama didn't say anything. "At least he's away from that paper," she said. It was true: Papa had about three weeks' worth of *Harper's Sentinels* piled up on the coffee table. Most times now, he spent looking out the big picture window.

It wasn't long before Miss Marion had announced that she would start giving acting lessons down at the community center, since she had some acting degree from NYU and saw that it was not only a good deed but "an absolute duty"—another one of her catchy phrases that she almost wore out—that she bring some of her "expertise" back home to those who weren't as fortunate as her.

So, to be honest, I wasn't in the least bit surprised when I came home from playing kickball with Terry and Kicky, and Mama asked me if I was planning to take any acting lessons from Miss Marion—as if we had already discussed it before.

"I thought you were going to play football this summer, Sonny Buck?" Papa asked me, not even giving my head the chance to let the first question sink in good.

"And what's wrong with acting lessons?" Mama asked Papa in that tone of voice that said you best watch what you say.

And Papa caught the hint, so he shuffled around in his favorite chair, the one that sits in front of the television set, then he lowered his newspaper just enough so we could see his eyes. "There's nothing wrong with taking acting lessons if that's what Sonny Buck wants to do. I just thought maybe he wanted to play football since he's been playing for the last three summers."

"Well, missing football this year is not going to kill him none. I think it will do you some good to expand your culture, Sonny Buck. I'll give you ten dollars." Then she gave Papa that look that told him that he had better not bid against her. And when he didn't, she said, "Good. Now that's settled. The class starts Monday."

I looked over at Papa, but he was already behind his paper again. So there I was.

But it wasn't bad. Come to find out, all the mothers in the neighborhood—except for Kicky's mama—made their kids go see Miss Marion for acting lessons, which consisted mainly of remembering some line from a Shakespeare play and reciting it while she shouted how you should be standing, or lecturing you on the proper facial expression, or having fits on when you should be breathing. And if you weren't doing it just right, she would just get all undone: flapping her arms, twisting her face, then sometimes dropping to her knees and saying: "Lord, please help me educate these ignorant people." That ignorant part was something we didn't feature too well and Debra Ann told her so, being since Debra Ann was brought up that way; that is, brought up to cuss grown folks out and not think twice about it.

But Miss Marion took an interest in me. She didn't yell when I read, but watched me with her mouth hanging open, telling everybody to knock off the noise back there—mainly Terry and another boy we called Scootie who could make funny noises with his armpits. Miss Marion said that I was talented.

What she say that for? I recited Shakespeare for Mama and Papa almost every evening before, during, and after dinner. Papa said that I was real good. Mama said I was a born actor. A genius was the word Miss Robbins—the school's English teacher who doubled as the drama coach in the springtime—used one night when she came over just to hear me read a few lines from *A Midsummer Night's Dream*. I was good. No lie. I imagined myself going to Hollywood, or to New York like Miss Marion, and becoming a real actor like James Cagney or Humphrey Bogart and star in films where I get to shoot the bad guy and run off with his dame because he's nothing but a big gorilla and she had been giving me the eye all along at the bar between sippings of tequilas and straight shots of brandy. I was Othello hanging upside down from a big tree in our front yard; I was Romeo on the football field. At the groceries: Puck. At the gas station with Papa: Macbeth. Then Henry VIII, then Hamlet, then King Lear, and I couldn't stop. Terry and Kicky couldn't keep up and came close to hating me, something I couldn't blame them for. I was crazy. I figured if I didn't make it in pro football, at least I had my acting talents to fall back on.

But the gist of this story really didn't kick in until about a month later, a July evening. Terry and Kicky were over my house for dinner: Terry was fat and would eat anything that couldn't get up and run; but Mama was always inviting Kicky over because she said Kicky was from a dysfunctioning family on account of his daddy been to jail about ten times and his mama was always hooking up with somebody who was going to Memphis for a couple of days. So, sometimes, if Kicky didn't eat with us, he didn't eat.

"So, how's the acting coming along?" Papa asked Terry and me.

Terry, between mouthfuls of some hot meatball dish—a recipe Mama got from Miss Marion: "It's okay. We studying *Romeo and Juliet.* Can I have some water?"

"Oh, that's nice," Mama said. "I remember in the springtime the senior class would always put on *Romeo and Juliet* out on the front lawn of the school. That's how we paid for the prom every year. I was Juliet. We decorated the whole stage with honeysuckles and white clovers and I wore a crown of white roses." Mama smiled. "I was beautiful then."

Papa said, "What do you mean? You're still beautiful."

Mama looked up at Papa, just like everybody else at the table did. I remember one time he was telling everybody down at the lodge how his boy was going to make the football team and go on to play for some Ivy League school. But I remember getting cut the first week of tryouts, so I hid out over Kicky's house all day long. It didn't do any good, Papa knew exactly where I was because Debra Ann told him out of spite on account of me not wanting to carry her books after school. When he found me, he said, "Let's go home, Sonny Buck," and the way he said it I knew I had let him down. At home Papa got on the phone and called an emergency meeting being since he was sort of like the vice-president of the lodge. He told me to come with him. When we got there all the men were fussing and wondering what was so important. Then Papa said, "This is my son, William 'Sonny Buck' Jackson, and he didn't make the Little League football team. If he never makes any other team in his life, he's still my boy and I love him. And if any of you say anything out of pocket I'll bust your damn noses." Then we went down to Olive Branch and he bought me a beer at Tang's. Papa said not to say anything about the nose busting or the beer drinking, being since he was sort of like a deacon at the church. That was the only time I ever remember Papa saying or doing something profound and not being behind his paper.

At the table, Mama put her napkin up to her face and dabbed at the corner of her eyes. "Frank, you're so kind. I love you. I love you all." Then she got up and went around the table kissing everybody. Just like Miss Marion, except Mama wasn't performing. Even Kicky probably wanted to cry; I don't think he had ever been kissed by his mother.

And right then and there I made a vow that if ever the moon and the sun and all the constellations ever decided to twist, switch up, collide, or explode in the heavens and cause me to lose my mind and want to run away from home, I was going to take these two beloved people with me.

After dinner, Mama told me to take a plate of rum muffins over to Miss Marion. She told Kicky and Terry to go with me, but they suddenly claimed to hear their mothers calling them. So I had to go by myself. I picked up the plate and said "Chow" to everybody.

When I got to the house, I was standing in an open doorway. "Miss Marion?" I peeped in, looking into a dark living room full of bulky antique furniture, the stench of Vick's Vapor Rub and the confined, wet, musty smell, like after a long, hot summer rain—and it crept out on the porch with me and tingled my nose. "Miss Marion?" I repeated.

"William, is that you?"

I peeped farther into the room and saw a figure move in a chair over there in a corner. "Yes, this is me."

"Well, why you out there? Come in here."

I walked in, bumped into something, and she clicked on a table lamp.

She had been drinking. She wasn't wearing a hat. Her hair was down and she was more white than usual except for her eyes: bloodshot and veiny red-like.

"You okay, Miss Marion?"

"I couldn't be better," she said slowly, then she brought a glass up to her mouth and sipped.

I stood there watching, not knowing what to do, but then I remembered why I had come. "My mama sent you these." I held the plate out in front of me. "She made rum muffins."

She laughed. "That's all I need." She downed the rest of her drink. Then she frowned up at me like I was something awful. "Do you know how evil the world is?"

"Excuse me?" I asked, steady holding onto the plate of muffins because I was too nervous to do anything else.

"The world is full of evil. You knew that, didn't you?"

"Ahh ... yes, I knew that."

"But you know, I don't think anybody else knows about this world but me and you." She burped. "I don't think most folks know they're mean. If they don't know any better, how do you expect them to act good? You see what I'm saying, William?"

"Yes, I think so."

"You know what bad thing I did one time? I made this fat girl cry. When I was up in New York, I went to this restaurant with this friend of mine and he brought his girlfriend with him. She was as big as a house. I don't know what Judd saw in her. She must've pissed Jack Daniels. I don't know. Anyway, I think I was drinking, I can't remember, but I remember telling this girl that I bet she eats a lot. Then Judd tells me that she's a vegetarian. A vegetarian. Can you believe that, William? A three-hundred-pound vegetarian?"

I shook my head no.

"I couldn't believe it either. So I ask him what in the hell has his vegetarian been snacking on? A damn California redwood? I thought it was funny but she started crying and Judd was trying to hush her up because everybody was looking at us. The more she cried, the louder I got, until they put all of us out of the restaurant. They didn't have good food anyway. But now I feel so bad about what I said. I got to tell everybody what I've done. That's my punishment." She grabbed some tissues from a roll of toilet paper and dabbed at her eyes and blew her nose. "You know, I think this world would be a lot better place to live if everyone would just do as I say. Know what I'm talking about, William?"

"Miss Marion," I hesitated, "are you drunk?"

"Not yet, but I have the potential of becoming an outstanding alcoholic. You just give me time."

I didn't say a word. I picked up the roll of toilet paper and tore some off, and out of nervousness started playing with it as Miss Marion was steady talking—mainly about how much money her mama had spent on her education and now she can't even find an acting job off-Broadway. I twisted the paper—tucking it here, pulling it there, twisting the bottom—until finally, I had created a little flower, something between a carnation or a rose, but a nice-looking flower just the same. We both looked down at the object in my hand; I think I was more surprised.

She took the flower from me and started crying. "You know what this is, William?"

"A paper flower?"

"No," between sobs, "this is beauty. Painful beauty. You're just like me. You can look right through pain and see the beauty of it. This is painful beauty. Thank you, William."

I was ready to go home. I tried to throw a hint by moving closer to the door and shuffling my feet like I suddenly heard someone calling my name.

"Sit down, William," she said, handing me the roll of paper. She refilled her glass, then leaned back on the couch. "You got it, William."

"Got what, Miss Marion?" I asked, steady making the paper flowers.

"It! You got that third eye right here"—she tapped her forehead—"and you can see right down that narrow line. I can't see that line as clearly as I want to. I never seen anybody read Shakespeare like you can. How do you do it? You ain't got to answer that. Most folks who are good at something usually don't know how they do it."

Since it wasn't a big roll, I had quickly made about twenty flowers and they were on the floor around my feet.

Miss Marion dropped to her knees and ran her fingers through the flowers like they were gold coins. "These are beautiful." Then, like a sudden afterthought: "I'll be back. I got to go check on Mama."

She disappeared down the dark hallway, leaving me alone in the parlor. I was trying to decide whether to leave, figuring that she was too drunk to remember whether I was here or not, but that wouldn't be a proper thing to do. By the time I had made up my mind to make a break for the door, Miss Marion came back with a flashlight and two new rolls of toilet paper.

"Mama's doing just fine. Let's go."

"Where we going?"

Miss Marion looked at me like I had a hole in my head. "Outside. We're going to plant these beautiful flowers in the garden. You don't actually think that I'm going to let all these flowers just multiply inside my house, do you?"

Though it was late, about eight or nine, it was still hot. Miss Marion started digging small holes in the empty garden with her fingers. She placed a flower in the hole and then she mashed the soft dirt around the paper stem. She was quiet, working quickly, stopping every once in a while to take a sip from the bottle that she had brought out here, or to grab some more paper flowers from me, or to tell me where to shine the flashlight. This went on for about an hour until we had the whole flower bed in the front yard covered in paper flowers.

Miss Marion started crying again. "This is just damn lovely!"

We stood there in the night looking at the paper garden. It really did look nice.

"You know, William, some things are just too good for this world." Then she looked up at me like she was expecting me to add to what she had just said. But I kept my eyes on the garden.

Fortunately, I heard Papa calling me and I told Miss Marion that I had to go. I started running down the street, pushing what she had said off to the side somewhere.

She yelled, "Goodbye, William! Come back in the morning and we can see how beautiful this garden looks in the daylight!"

"Okay," I yelled, running wildly in the middle of the street like I had just been set free out of a cage, looking back only once just in time to see her wave at me and take another sip.

But the next day it rained, a thunderstorm so terrible that even Mama said, "Maybe you shouldn't go to class today, Sonny Buck. Miss Marion will understand." I sat in the house all day until the rain stopped about early evening.

Later I walked down to Miss Marion's house and stood in front of the paper garden. The rain had melted the flowers and the only thing that was left was soggy toilet paper all over the yard. I stared at the garden for a long time.

I knocked on the door, but there wasn't an answer. I peeped through the windows into the parlor, but I didn't see anything. Once, I thought I saw Miss Marion ducking down the dark hallway, but I wasn't sure. I knocked on the door and yelled her name, but there was no answer. I went home.

Suddenly, everything changed. Not a change back, not a change forward, but a change like the closing scene of a play when the curtain comes down and you wonder were you really there. Like the melting of the paper garden was an omen of what was to happen next: Miss Mamie Jamison died toward the end of the summer. She was buried the next day, then the next day after that Miss Marion packed up everything in the middle of the night and left, and not too long after that the house was boarded up. Just like that. Then slowly Harper went back to the way it was: boring. Like a rubberband, Harper had stretched to accommodate one of its own, then quickly snapped back into place—nothing different, but the same. My mother went back to her meatloaf on Mondays, spaghetti on Tuesdays, and pork chops, chicken, roast, noodles, and stew on the other days. I went back to my football practices, and Papa slipped back behind his paper.

Once, I wondered if Miss Marion was a real person, or if she was one of those fallen angels who comes to earth to earn her wings. You would wonder about anybody who steps into your life and charms and dazzles you, forces your imagination to soar higher than the heavens, then for no reason, quietly disappears, never realizing that someone has been left behind whose love for life is now running on an uncontrollable high. Though it didn't last long, but for one brief moment in my life, I wasn't William "Sonny Buck" Jackson, the junior varsity football player. Instead, I was William "Sonny Buck" Jackson, the Broadway star, the Hollywood actor—the whole town not the town, but a stage; the townspeople not the townspeople, but the audience. Maybe Miss Marion knew what she was doing and was just giving me a taste of what could be, letting me know that there's a different world outside the four walls of Harper.

I wondered what had become of Miss Marion. I imagined myself traveling from town to town, city to city, looking for a Miss Marion. Stories would spring up about me, about some kid looking for a friend that he met one summer. Toothless old men with guitars will be moaning some sad song about lost friendship and loneliness and how cruel the world can get without a good friend or a faithful dog. I will become a legend. Of course, some folks will say I never existed, but just somebody's crazy imagination gone wild. But that wouldn't get me down, since worrying about that kind of stuff doesn't bother me none anyway.

POETRY

Jupiter Hammon

(1720?–1806?)

*In his **Address to the Negroes of the State of New York** (1786), Jupiter Hammon would write that he is "now upwards of seventy years old." Although he appeared resigned to his own slavery in that document, Hammon nonetheless urged younger Blacks to fight for freedom. Like many colonial slaves, he left no record of himself and the best estimate of his active years has been offered by biographer Oscar Wegelin. A devout Methodist and an obedient servant, Hammon was owned by the influential Lloyds of Long Island. Historians have speculated that he could have been a minister. "An Evening Thought. Salvation by Christ, with Penetential (sic) Cries" is believed by scholars to be the first poem ever published by an African American. It is signed: "Composed by Jupiter Hammon, a Negro belonging to Mr. Lloyd of Queen's Village, on Long Island, the 25th of December, 1760."*

An Evening Thought

Salvation by Christ, With Penitential Cries

Salvation comes by Christ alone,
The only Son of God;
Redemption now to every one,
That love his holy Word.
Dear Jesus we would fly to Thee,
And leave off every Sin,
Thy tender Mercy well agree;
Salvation from our King;
Salvation comes now from the Lord,
Our victorious King.
His holy Name be well ador'd,
Salvation surely bring.
Dear Jesus give thy Spirit now,
Thy Grace to every Nation,
That han't the Lord to whom we bow,
The Author of Salvation.
Dear Jesus unto Thee we cry,
Give us the Preparation;
Turn not away thy tender Eye;
We see thy true Salvation.

Salvation comes from God we know,
The true and only One;
It's well agreed and certain true,
He gave his only Son.
Lord hear our penitential Cry:
Salvation from above;
It is the Lord that doth supply,
With his Redeeming Love.
Dear Jesus by thy precious Blood,
The World Redemption have:
Salvation now comes from the Lord,
He being thy captive slave.
Dear Jesus let the Nations cry,
And all the People say,
Salvation comes from Christ on high,
Haste on Tribunal Day.
We cry as Sinners to the Lord,
Salvation to obtain;
It is firmly fixt his holy Word,
Ye shall not cry in vain.
Dear Jesus unto Thee we cry,
And make our Lamentation:
O let our Prayers ascend on high;
We felt thy Salvation.
Lord turn our dark benighted Souls;
Give us a true Motion,
And let the Hearts of all the World,
Make Christ their Salvation.
Ten Thousand Angels cry to Thee,
Yea louder than the Ocean.
Thou art the Lord, we plainly see;
Thou art the true Salvation.
Now is the Day, excepted Time;
The Day of Salvation;
Increase your Faith, do not repine:
Awake ye every Nation.
Lord unto whom now shall we go,
Or see a safe Abode;
Thou hast the Word Salvation too

The only Son of God.
Ho! every one that hunger hath,
Or pineth after me,
Salvation be thy leading Staff,
To set the Sinner free.
Dear Jesus unto Thee we fly;
Depart, depart from Sin,
Salvation doth at length supply,
The Glory of our King.
Come ye Blessed of the Lord,
Salvation greatly given;
O turn your Hearts, accept the Word,
Your souls are fit for Heaven.
Dear Jesus we now turn to Thee,
Salvation to obtain;
Our Hearts and Souls do meet again,
To magnify thy Name.
Come holy Spirit, Heavenly Dove,
The Object of our Care;
Salvation doth increase our Love;
Our Hearts hath felt thy fear.
Now Glory be to God on High,
Salvation high and low;
And thus the Soul on Christ rely,
To Heaven surely go.
Come Blessed Jesus, Heavenly Dove,
Accept Repentance here;
Salvation give, with tender Love;
Let us with Angels share. Finis.

Lucy Terry

(1730–1821)

Kidnapped as a child in Africa and then brought to Rhode Island, Lucy Terry was purchased by Ebenezer Wells of Deerfield, Massachusetts. She married the free Abijah Prince in 1756 and they had six children: Cesar, Duroxa, Drucilla, Festus, Tatnai, and Abijah, Jr. A shrewd businessman, Prince amassed a fortune in real estate in several New England towns, including Sunderland, Vermont, where he is named in the town charter as one of its founders. Together, Lucy and Abijah were a courageous couple; they memorably fought a land encroachment claim filed against them by their famous neighbor, Colonel Ethan Allen. Eventually the case reached the Federal Supreme Court, where the couple argued—and won—their own case against future Supreme Court judge Royall Tyler. Terry would later try to convince the authorities of William College to admit her son by arguing her case in front of them,, she was refused, despite her impressive references to Scripture and the law. Her only known poem, "Bars Fight," qualifies her as the first African American poet. Originally composed in 1746, this verse retelling of an actual Indian raid on Deerfield was not published until 1893. Although simple in its execution, the poem is regarded by historians to be the most accurate record of that event.

Bars Fight

August 'twas the twenty fifth
Seventeen hundred forty-six
The Indians did in ambush lay
Some very valiant men to slay
The names of whom I'll not leave out
Samuel Allen like a hero fout
And though he was so brave and bold
His face no more shall we behold.
Eleazer Hawks was killed outright
Before he had time to fight
Before he did the Indians see
Was shot and killed immediately.
Oliver Amsden he was slain
Which caused his friends much grief and pain.
Samuel Amsden they found dead
Not many rods off from his head.
Adonijah Gillet we do hear
Did lose his life which was so dear.

John Saddler fled across the water
And so escaped the dreadful slaughter.
Eunice Allen see the Indians comeing
And hoped to save herself by running
And had not her petticoats stopt her
The awful creatures had not cotched her
And tommyhawked her on the head
And left her on the ground for dead.
Young Samuel Allen, Oh! lack a–day
Was taken and carried to Canada.

Phillis Wheatley

(1753–1784)

Phillis Wheatley is believed to have been born in West Africa (presumably in either present-day Gambia or Senegal). After her arrival in Boston in 1761 on a slave ship, Mr. John Wheatley purchased the eight-year-old girl at an auction as a gift for his aging wife. The Wheatleys oversaw the frail, studious servant-child's classical education, an education to which few women in colonial times had access. Reading first the Bible, then Homer, Alexander Pope and John Milton, the child rapidly acquired proficiency and fluency in grammar, rhetoric, and literary style. As a captive poet whose immediate audience would be White, Phillis Wheatley chose as her model the celebrated seventeenth-century poet John Milton. And, like Milton, Wheatley expressed in all of her poems profound religious convictions. In 1772 Wheatley sailed to London, where her first book, **Poems on Various subjects, Religious and Moral, Negro Servant to Mr. John Wheatley of Boston**, *was being published. There she made the acquaintance of Benjamin Franklin. One year later, in 1773, the Wheatleys set her free. By the mid-1770s, all the Wheatleys had died.*

After he read her pre–Revolutionary War poem, "To His Excellency General Washington," Washington himself wrote to Wheatley and invited her to visit him at the Continental Army Camp. John Peters, a free Black Bostonian, married Phillis Wheatley in 1778. After losing all three of their children, Wheatley herself, barely thirty, became ill and died in 1784. Centuries later, Wheatley's eloquent poems, rich in Biblical allusion and composed largely in heroic couplets, still provoke controversy. Critics and readers variously view her as a brilliant prodigy—or as an unfortunate, even pitiable, "Uncle Tom."

On Imagination

Thy various works, imperial queen, we see,
How bright their forms! how deck'd with pomp by thee!
Thy wond'rous acts in beauteous order stand,
And all attest how potent is thine hand.
      From *Helicon's* refulgent heights attend
Ye sacred choir, and my attempts befriend:
To tell her glories with a faithful tongue,
Ye blooming graces, triumph in my song.
      Now here, now there, the roving *Fancy* flies,
Till some lov'd object strikes her wand'ring eyes
Whose silken fetters all the senses bind,
And soft captivity involves the mind.
      Imagination! who can sing thy force?
Or who describe the swiftness of thy course?

Soaring through air to find the bright abode?
Th' empyreal palace of the thund'ring God,
We on thy pinions can surpass the wind,
And leave the rolling universe behind:
From star to star the mental optics rove,
Measure the skies, and range the realms above;
There in one view we grasp the mighty whole,
Or with the new world amaze th' unbounded soul.

        Though *Winter* frowns to *Fancy's* raptur'd eyes
The fields may flourish, and gay scenes arise;
The frozen deeps may break their iron bands,
And bid their waters murmur o'er the sands.
Fair *Flora* may resume her fragrant reign.
And with her flow'ry riches deck the plain;
Sylvanus may diffuse his honors round,
And all the forest may with leaves be crown'd:
Show'rs may descend, and dews their gems disclose,
And nectar sparkle on the blooming rose.

        Such is thy pow'r, nor are thine orders vain,
O thou the leader of the mental train:
In full perfection all thy works are wrought,
And thine the sceptre o'er the realms of thought.
Before thy throne the subject-passions bow,
Of subject-passions sov'reign ruler thou:
At thy command joy rushes on the heart,
And through the glowing veins the spirits dart.
Fancy might now her silken pinions try
To rise from earth, and sweep th' expanse on high;
From *Tithon's* bed now might *Aurora* rise,
Her cheeks all glowing with celestial dyes,
While a pure stream of light o'erflows the skies.
The monarch of the day I might behold,
And all the mountains tipt with radiant gold,
Bit I reluctant leave the pleasing views,
Which *Fancy* dresses to delight the *Muse;*
Winter austere forbids me to aspire,
And northern tempests damp the rising fire;
They chill the tides of *Fancy's* flowing sea,
Cease then, my song, cease the unequal lay.

George Moses Horton

(1797–1883)

America's first full-time Black poet, George Moses Horton published three volumes of poetry, **Hope of Liberty** *(1829; reprinted as* **Poems by a Slave**, *1837, 1838),* **Poetical Works of George M. Horton, the Colored Bard of North Carolina** *(1845), and* **Naked Genius** *(1865). Scholars believe that a manuscript for another volume, entitled "The Black Poet," may yet exist. Horton began his literary career by dictating flowery, sentimental love poems to students at the University of North Carolina, Chapel Hill, who paid him from twenty-five to seventy-five cents per poem. After arranging permission from his master, he moved to the campus and supported himself in this fashion until he had learned how to read and write. In these efforts he received help from students and from the University president, Joseph D. Caldwell, as well. Horton's most supportive mentor, however, was Caroline Lee Hentz, a poet and novelist who helped him publish his first book. Horton's poem "On Liberty and Slavery" was first published in Hentz's hometown newspaper, the* **Lancaster Gazette**, *and was later reprinted in William Lloyd Garrison's* **Liberator** *in 1834. Although he continually hoped to sell enough books to purchase his freedom, Horton was not freed until Union forces occupied North Carolina. He then moved to Philadelphia where he worked as a hack writer until his death in 1883.*

On Liberty and Slavery

Alas! and am I born for this,
    To wear this slavish chain?
Deprived of all created bliss,
    Through hardship, toil and pain!

How long have I in bondage lain,
    And languished to be free!
Alas! and must I still complain—
    Deprived of liberty.

Oh, Heaven! and is there no relief
    This side the silent grave—
To soothe the pain—to quell the grief
    And anguish of a slave?

Come, Liberty, thou cheerful sound,
    Roll through my ravished ears!

Come, let my grief in joys be drowned,
    And drive away my fears.

Say unto foul oppression, Cease:
    Ye tyrants rage no more,
And let the joyful trump of peace,
    Now bid the vassal soar.

Soar on the pinions of that dove
    Which long has cooed for thee,
And breathed her notes from Afric's grove,
    The sound of Liberty.

Oh, Liberty! thou golden prize,
    So often sought by blood—
We crave thy sacred sun to rise,
    The gift of nature's God!

Bid Slavery hide her haggard face,
    And barbarism fly:
I scorn to see the sad disgrace
    In which enslaved I lie.

Dear Liberty! upon thy breast,
    I languish to respire;
And like the Swan unto her nest,
    I'd to thy smiles retire.

Oh, blest asylum—heavenly balm!
    Unto thy boughs I flee—
And in thy shades the storm shall calm,
    With songs of Liberty!

Frances E. W. Harper

(1825–1911)

One of the most popular and mesmerizing speakers on the nineteenth-century lecture circuit, Frances E. W. Harper tirelessly crusaded for such contemporary reforms as women's rights, temperance, and abolition. Although she was often heckled at the podium, she doggedly persisted in her public crusades. By the end of her career she had lectured in almost every state in the South with the exception of Texas and Arkansas. Born Frances E. Watkins in Baltimore, Maryland, to free parents, Harper was raised by her abolitionist uncle and aunt after her mother died. She moved to Ohio where she married Fenton Harper in 1860 and gave birth to a daughter. When her husband died four years later, Harper devoted herself exclusively to reform work. A best-selling writer who contributed portions of her earnings to the abolitionist cause, Harper published several volumes of poetry and a novel, **Iola Leroy** (1892). Her collection of verse, **Poems of Miscellaneous Subjects** (1854), reached twenty editions by 1870, and two other books, **Poems** (1871) and **Sketches of Southern Life** (1872), were reprinted at least twice. Her essays and articles appeared in numerous literary and religious periodicals of the day, and some of her letters have been reprinted in **The Underground Railroad** (1972), edited by William Still. Filled with religious and moral fervor, Harper's poetry transcends its technical awkwardness.

The Slave Auction

The sale began—young girls were there,
    Defenceless in their wretchedness,
Whose stifled sobs of deep despair
    Revealed their anguish and distress.

And mothers stood with streaming eyes,
    And saw their dearest children sold;
Unheeded rose their bitter cries,
    While tyrants bartered them for gold.

And woman, with her love and truth—
    For these in sable forms may dwell—
Gaz'd on the husband of her youth,
    With anguish none may paint or tell.

And men, whose sole crime was their hue,

The impress of their Maker's hand,
And frail and shrinking children, too,
Were gathered in that mournful band.

Ye who have laid your love to rest,
And wept above their lifeless clay,
Know not the anguish of that breast,
Whose lov'd are rudely torn away.

Ye may not know how desolate
Are bosoms rudely forced to part,
And how a dull and heavy weight
Will press the life-drops from the heart

W. E. B. Du Bois

(1868–1963)

*A renowned scholar as well as a passionate advocate of civil rights for African Americans, William Edward Burghardt Du Bois was one of the founding leaders of Black protest in the United States. Raised in Great Barrington, Massachusetts, Du Bois was inspired by his Dutch African mother to excel academically. He attended Fisk University in Tennessee and then went to Harvard, where he became the first African American to receive a doctorate in American History. Believing that the problems of African Americans could not be understood without systematic investigation, Du Bois wrote his 1896 dissertation on the slave trade (***The Suppression of the African Slave-Trade to the United States of America, 1638–1870***) and then, in 1899, published ***The Philadelphia Negro: A Social Study*** *(1899), the first sociological analysis ever done on an urban population of African Americans.*

Although Du Bois lectured on economics and history for several years at Wilberforce University, the University of Pennsylvania, and Atlanta University, he gradually gave up his teaching responsibilities so that he could devote more time to political activism. Horrified by the racial violence at the turn of the century and frustrated with the conservative solutions proposed by such fellow reformers as Booker T. Washington, Du Bois brought to the cause of Black Civil Rights formidable intellectual resources, polished rhetorical skills, and the belief, then quite radical, that racial equality could not be compromised. After organizing young Black intellectuals in the Niagara Movement, Du Bois helped to found the National Association for the Advancement of Colored People, whose journal, **The Crisis***, he edited (1910–34) until ideological differences made him disavow the organization.*

During the last three years of his life, Du Bois—skeptical about American government and disappointed with the stalling Civil Rights movement of the early sixties—joined the Communist Party and moved to Ghana. While his historical and sociological studies, such as **The Gift of Black Folk: The Negroes in the Making of America** *(1924) and* **Dusk of Dawn: An Essay Toward an Autobiography of a Race Concept** *(1940), would have secured Du Bois's reputation as a significant writer, his place in African American literature was doubly assured with* **The Souls of Black Folk** *(1903), his poignant collection of original essays, sketches, and verse.*

The Song of the Smoke

     I am the Smoke King
     I am black!
I am swinging in the sky,
I am wringing worlds awry;
I am the thought of the throbbing mills,
I am the soul of the soul—toil kills,
Wraith of the ripple of trading rills;

Up I'm curling from the sod,
I am whirling home to God;
  I am the Smoke King
  I am black.

  I am the Smoke King,
  I am black!
I am wreathing broken hearts,
I am sheathing love's light darts;
  Inspiration of iron times
  Wedding the toil of toiling climes,
  Shedding the blood of bloodless crimes—
Lurid lowering 'mid the blue,
Torrid towering toward the true,
  I am the Smoke King,
  I am black.

  I am the Smoke King
  I am black!
I am darkening with song,
I am hearkening to wrong!
  I will be black as blackness can—
  The blacker the mantle, the mightier the man!
  For blackness was ancient ere whiteness began.
I am daubing God in night,
I am swabbing Hell in white:
  I am the Smoke King
  I am black.

  I am the Smoke King
  I am black!
I am cursing ruddy morn,
I am hearsing hearts unborn:
  Souls unto me are as stars in a night,
  I whiten my black men—I blacken my white!
  What's the hue of a hide to a man in his might?
Hail! great, gritty, grimy hands—
Sweet Christ, pity toiling lands!
  I am the Smoke King
  I am black.

James Weldon Johnson

(1871–1938)

A native of Florida, James Weldon Johnson attended Atlanta University and became the first African American to be admitted to the Florida bar. He left the South, however, to join his brother John in New York City where the brothers wrote stage music together, composing such popular songs as "Under the Bamboo Tree" and "Lift Every Voice and Sing." At the same time, Johnson was an active Republican; he served as U.S. consul in Nicaragua and Venezuela and investigated the brutalization of Haiti by occupying American forces. Considered by his contemporaries to be the quintessential "Renaissance man," Johnson enjoyed various successes as a U.S. diplomat, educator, Civil Rights activist, and musician—all the while receiving steady acclaim for his prose and poetry.

His critically acclaimed novel about the absurdity of racial injustice from the perspective of a man who can pass as White, **The Autobiography of an Ex-Colored Man** *(1912), was followed by Johnson's first collection of poetry,* **Fifty Years and Other Poems** *(1917). Both works established Johnson as a key figure in the Harlem Renaissance. Not only did he contribute substantially to its creative legacy with his writing, he worked on behalf of its political goal, serving as the executive secretary of the NAACP from 1920 to 1930. Johnson published two more volumes of poetry;* **God's Trombones or Seven Negro Sermons and Verse** *(1927) and* **St. Peter Relates an Incident of the Resurrection Day** *(1935). He also produced a historical study,* **Black Manhattan** *(1930), edited an influential anthology,* **The Book of American Negro Poetry** *(1922, 1931), and with his brother's assistance published two collections of spirituals (1925, 1926). After publishing his autobiography,* **Along this Way***, in 1933, Johnson collected his Fisk University lectures in the volume,* **Negro American, What Now?** *(1934). His literary achievements and social commitment to the African American community were honored in 1925 with a Spingarn Medal.*

Lift Every Voice and Sing

Lift every voice and sing
Till earth and heaven ring,
Ring with the harmonies of Liberty;
Let our rejoicing rise
High as the listening skies,
Let it resound loud as the rolling sea.
Sing a song full of the faith that the dark past has taught us,
Sing a song full of the hope that the present has brought us,
Facing the rising sun of our new day begun
Let us march on till victory is won.

Stony the road we trod,
Bitter the chastening rod,
Felt in the days when hope unborn had died;
Yet with a steady beat,
Have not our weary feet
Come to the place for which our fathers sighed?
We have come over a way that with tears has been watered,
We have come, treading our path through the blood of the slaughtered,
Out from the gloomy past,
Till now we stand at last
Where the white gleam of our bright star is cast.

God of our weary years,
God of our silent tears,
Thou who has brought us thus far on the way;
Thou who has by Thy might
Led us into the light,
Keep us forever in the path, we pray.
Lest our feet stray from the places, our God, where we met Thee;
Lest, our hearts drunk with the wine of the world, we forget Thee;
Shadowed beneath Thy hand,
May we forever stand.
True to our God,
True to our native Land.

The Creation

A Negro Sermon

And God stepped out on space,
And he looked around and said,
"I'm lonely—
I'll make a world."

And far as the eye of God could see.
Darkness covered everything,
Blacker than a hundred midnights
Down in a cypress swamp.

Then God smiled,
And the light broke,
And the darkness rolled up on one side,
And the light stood shining on the other,
And God said, *"That's good!"*

Then God reached out and took the light in His hands,
And God rolled the light around in His Hands
Until He made the sun;
And He set that sun a-blazing in the heavens.
And the light that was left from making the sun
God gathered it up in a shining ball
And flung it against the darkness,
Spangling the night with the moon and stars.
Then down between
The darkness and the light
He hurled the world;
And God said, *"That's good!"*

Then God himself stepped down—
And the sun was on His right hand,
And the moon was on His left;
And the stars were clustered about His head,
And the earth was under His feet.
And God walked, and where He trod
His footsteps hollowed the valleys out
And bulged the mountains up.

Then He stopped and looked and saw
And the earth was hot and barren.
So God stepped over to the edge of the world
And He spat out the seven seas;
He batted His eyes, and the lightning flashed;
He clapped His hands, and the thunders rolled,
And the waters above the earth came down,
The cooling waters came down.

Then the green grass sprouted,
And the little red flowers blossomed,
The pinetree pointed his finger to the sky,
And the oak spread out his arms,
The lakes cuddled down in the hollows of the ground,
And the rivers ran down to the sea;
And God smiled again,
And the rainbow appeared.
And curled itself around His shoulder.

Then God raised His arm and He waved His hand
Over the sea and over the land,
And He said, *"Bring forth! Bring forth!"*
And quicker than God could drop His hand,
Fishes and fowls
And beasts and birds
Swam the rivers and the seas,
Roamed the forests and the woods,
And split the air with their wings.
And God said, *"That's good!"*

Then God walked around,
And God looked around
On all that He had made.
He looked at His sun,
And He looked at His moon,
And He looked at His little stars;
He looked on His world
With all its living things,
And God said, *"I'm lonely still."*

Then God sat down
On the side of a hill where he could think;
By a deep, wide river He sat down;
With His head in His hands,
God thought and thought,
Till He thought, *"I'll make me a man!"*

Up from the bed of the river
God scooped the clay;
And by the bank of the river
He kneeled Him down;
And there the great God Almighty
Who lit the sun and fixed it in the sky,
Who flung the stars to the most far corners of the night,
Who rounded the earth in the middle of His hand;
This great God,
Like a mammy bending over her baby,
Kneeled down in the dust
Toiling over a lump of clay
Till He shaped it in His own image;
Then into it He blew the breath of life,
And man became a living soul.
Amen. Amen.

Paul Laurence Dunbar

(1872–1906)

It is all too tempting to wonder what Paul Laurence Dunbar might have accomplished as a writer had he lived longer than his thirty-four years. Fortunately, he embarked upon his literary career early. The Ohio-born son of former slaves, Dunbar started writing verse as a youth, and in high school served as editor-in-chief of the school newspaper, president of the literary society, and class poet. In 1893, Dunbar published his first book of poems, **Oak and Ivy**, *which was then followed by* **Majors and Minors** *(1894), a collection of poems written in standard English ("major") and in dialect ("minor"). When the influential editor of the* **Atlantic Monthly**, *William Dean Howells, favorably endorsed the second book in a long and enthusiastic article, Dodd, Meade, and Company, a major publishing house, printed* **Lyrics of the Lowly Life** *(1893). This collection of poetry became an instant bestseller and enabled Dunbar to earn his living entirely from his writing and from his enormously popular readings on the lecture circuit. Dunbar also wrote a musical, four sentimental novels, and numerous stories.*

In such volumes of poetry as **Lyrics of the Hearthside** *(1899),* **Lyrics of Love and Laughter** *(1903), and* **Lyrics of Sunshine and Shadow** *(1905), Dunbar depicts scenes of plantation life using folk songs and tales. Although he resorted to the vernacular only in order to attract the notice of publishers, the popularity of such "minor"-infected pieces with his contemporary White audience had the unfortunate effect of reinforcing negative stereotypes about African Americans. Today, Dunbar is best known for his "majors."*

Sympathy

I know what the caged bird feels, alas!
When the sun is bright on the upland slopes;
When the wind stirs soft through the springing grass,
And the river flows like a stream of glass;
When the first bird sings and the first bud opens,
And the faint perfume from its chalice steals—
I know what the caged bird feels!

I know why the caged bird beats his wing
Till its blood is red on the cruel bars;
For he must fly back to his perch and cling
When he fain would be on the bough a-swing;
And a pain still throbs in the old, old scars
And they pulse again with a keener sting—
I know why he beats his wing!

I know why the caged bird sings, ah me,
When his wing is bruised and his bosom sore—
When he beats his bars and he would be free;
It is not a carol of joy or glee,
But a prayer that he sends from his heart's deep core,
But a plea, that upward to Heaven he flings—
I know why the caged bird sings!

When Malindy Sings

G'way an' quit dat noise, Miss Lucy—
    Put dat music book away;
What's de use to keep on tryin'?
    Ef you practice twell you're gray,
You cain't sta't no notes a-flyin'
    Lak de ones dat rants and rings
F'om the kitchen to de big woods
    When Malindy sings.

You ain't got de nachel o'gans
    Fu' to make de soun' come right,
You ain't got de tu'ns an' twistin's
    Fu' to make it sweet an' light.

Tell you one thing now, Miss Lucy,
    An' I'm tellin' you fu' true,
When hit comes to raal right singin',
    Tain't no easy thing to do.

Easy 'nough fu' folks to hollah,
    Lookin' at de lines an' dots,
When dey ain't no one kin sense it',
    An' de chune comes in, in spots;
But fu' real melojous music,
    Dat jes' strikes yo' hea't and clings,
Jes' you stan' an' listen wif me
    When Malindy sings.

Ain't you nevah hyeahd Malindy?
      Blessed soul, tek up de cross!
Look hyeah, ain't you jokin', honey?
      Well, you don't know whut you los'.
Y' ought to hyeah dat gal a-wa'blin',
      Robins, la'ks, an' all dem things,
Heish dey moufs an' hides dey faces
      When Malindy sings.

Fiddlin' man jes' stop his fiddlin',
      Lay his fiddle on de she'f;
Mockin'-bird quit try'n' to whistle,
      'Cause he jes' so shamed hisse'f.
Folks a-playin' on de banjo
      Draps dey fingahs on de strings—
Bless yo' soul—fu'gits to move 'em,
      When Malindy sings.

She jes' spreads huh mouf and hollahs,
      "Come to Jesus," twell you hyeah
Sinnahs' tremblin' steps and voices,
      Timid-lak a-drawin' neah;

Den she tu'ns to "Rock of Ages,"
      Simply to de cross she clings,
An' you fin' yo' teahs a-drappin'
      When Malindy sings.

Who dat says dat humble praises
      Wif de Master nevah counts?
Heish yo' mouf, I hyeah dat music,
      Ez hit rises up an' mounts—
Floatin' by de hills an' valleys,
      Way above dis buryin' sod,
Ez hit makes its way in glory
      To de very gates of God!

Oh, hit's sweetah dan de music
      Of an edicated band;
An' hit's dearah dan de battle's
      Song o' triumph in de lan'.
It seems holier dan evenin'
      When de solemn chu'ch bell rings,
Ez I sit an' ca'mly listen
      While Malindy sings.

Towsah, stop dat ba'kin', hyeah me!
      Mandy, mek dat chile keep still;
Don't you hyeah de echoes callin'
      F'om de valley to de hill?
Let me listen, I can hyeah it,
      Th'oo de bresh of angels' wings,
Sof' an' sweet, "Swing low, Sweet Chariot,"
      Ez Malindy sings.

We Wear the Mask

We wear the mask that grins and lies,
It hides our cheeks and shades our eyes,—
This debt we pay to human guile;
With torn and bleeding hearts we smile,
And mouth with myriad subtleties.

Why should the world be over-wise,
In counting all our tears and sighs?
Nay, let them only see us, while
      We wear the mask.

We smile, but, O great Christ, our cries
To thee from tortured souls arise.
We sing, but oh the clay is vile
Beneath our feet, and long the mile;
But let the world dream otherwise,
      We wear the mask.

Claude McKay

(1889–1948)

*Jamaican-born Claude McKay wrote fondly of the folk tales that his father, Francis McKay, a peasant farmer descended from West Africa's Ashanti culture, told him in childhood. It would be easy to speculate that this early identification with Africa might explain McKay's flamboyant radicalism, so pronounced in his work and his politics that, by the 1920s, he often found himself excluded from African American magazines and journals. After winning a prize in Jamaica for two volumes of verse published in 1912 (***Songs of Jamaica*** and ***Constab Ballads***), McKay immigrated to the United States, where he briefly attended Tuskegee Institute before transferring to Kansas State College. Five years after his move in 1914 to Manhattan, where he worked odd jobs to support his writing habit, McKay's poems began appearing regularly in such magazines as* **The Liberator** *and* **Pearson's***.*

In 1919 he journeyed to Europe, settled in the Soviet Union for a fiery, colorful stay, and did not return to the United States until 1934. Ten years later, he was teaching in Chicago.

McKay is generally regarded as a radical's radical; that is, his idealism would not permit him to tolerate any political, religious, or social doctrine that threatened or placed limits on human freedom. His other books of poems are **Spring in New Hampshire** *(1920) and* **Harlem Shadows** *(1922). His four works of fiction are the novels* **Home to Harlem** *(1928),* **Banjo, A Story Without a Plot** *(1929), and* **Banana Bottom** *(1933), along with* **Ginger Town** *(1932), a collection of short stories.* **A Long Way from Home***, Claude McKay's autobiography, was published in 1937.*

The Tropics in New York

Bananas ripe and green, and ginger-root,
    Cocoa in pods and alligator pears,
And tangerines and mangoes and grapefruit,
    Fit for the highest prize at parish fairs.

Set in the window, bringing memories
    Of fruit-trees laden by low-singing rills,
And dewy dawns, and mystical blue skies
    In benediction over nun-like hills.

My eyes grew dim, and I could no more gaze;
    A wave of longing through my body swept,
And, hungry for the old, familiar ways,
    I turned aside and bowed my head and wept.

The Lynching

His spirit in smoke ascended to high heaven.
His father, by the cruelest way of pain,
Had bidden him to his bosom once again;
The awful sin remained still unforgiven.
All night a bright and solitary star
(Perchance the one that ever guided him,
Yet gave him up at last to Fate's wild whim),
Hung pitifully o'er the swinging char.
Day dawned, and soon the mixed crowds came to view
The ghostly body swaying in the sun:
The women thronged to look, but never a one
Showed sorrow in her eyes of steely blue;
And little lads, lynchers that were to be,
Danced round the dreadful thing in fiendish glee.

If We Must Die

If we must die, let it not be like hogs
Hunted and penned in an inglorious spot,
While round us bark the mad and hungry dogs,
Making their mock at our accursed lot.
If we must die, O let us nobly die,
So that our precious blood may not be shed
In vain; then even the monsters we defy
Shall be constrained to honor us though dead!
O kinsmen! we must meet the common foe!
Though far outnumbered let us show us brave,
And for their thousand blows deal one deathblow!
What though before us lies the open grave?
Like men we'll face the murderous, cowardly pack,
Pressed to the wall, dying, but fighting back!

Melvin B. Tolson

(1898–1966)

A poet who would not receive critical appreciation until after his death, Melvin B. Tolson was nonetheless respected by such distinguished peers as Sterling Brown, Arna Bontemps, and Langston Hughes. Born Melvin Beaunorus Tolson in Moberly, Missouri, he was the son of a Methodist minister. He attended Fisk University and then Lincoln University, where he would cultivate his legendary public speaking and debating skills. His time as a graduate student at Columbia University exposed Tolson to the Harlem Renaissance, an experience which inspired his first poetry collection, **A Gallery of Harlem Portraits**. *A vast complex of over three hundred poems, the structure of* **Portraits** *was inspired by Edgar Lee Masters'* **Spoon River Anthology** *(1915). The manuscript, however, could not find a publisher, and it was shelved for forty years until it was published posthumously in 1979. Tolson was undaunted, and continued to write while devoting himself to numerous other activities. A popular and committed teacher of English and American literature at Wiley College in Texas, he also coached the junior varsity football team, directed the college theater program, and trained a championship debate team. From 1937 to 1944 Tolson wrote a weekly column, "Caviar and Cabbage" for the* **Washington Tribune**; *selected columns were published in a 1982 collection under the same title. Tolson also served as the mayor of Langston, Oklahoma. Elected when he was fifty-four, he held the office for four terms.*

Tolson was nationally recognized as a poet of considerable talent when his poem "Dark Symphony" was awarded first prize in the 1940 American Negro Exposition by judges Frank Marshall Davis, Arna Bontemps, and Langston Hughes. His debut volume of poetry, **Rendezvous with America**, *subsequently appeared in 1944. It was followed by* **Libretto for the Republic of Liberia** *(1953), which was written while Tolson was Poet Laureate of Liberia, and* **Harlem Gallery: Book I, The Curator** *(1965). Noted for its technical mastery and intellectual rigor, Tolson's poetry does not shy away from difficult subjects, tackling both literary aesthetics and social analysis with a formidable precision that requires the reader's careful and concentrated attention.*

Lamda

From the mouth of the Harlem Gallery
    came a voice like a
      ferry horn in a river of fog:

    King Oliver of New Orleans
has kicked the bucket, but he left behind
    old Satchmo with his red-hot horn

to syncopate the heart and mind.
The honky-tonks in Storyville
have turned to ashes, have turned to dust,
        but old Satchmo is still around
like Uncle Sam's IN GOD WE TRUST.

        Where, oh, where is Bessie Smith
with her heart as big as the blues of truth?
        Where, oh, where is Mister Jelly Roll
        with his Cadillac and diamond tooth?
        Where, oh, where is Papa Handy
with his blue notes a-dragging from bar to bar?
        Where, oh, where is bulletproof Leadbelly
        with his tall tales and 12-string guitar?

        Old Hip Cats,
when you sang and played the blues
        the night Satchmo was born,
did you know hypodermic needles in Rome
couldn't hoodoo him away from his horn?
Wyatt Earp's legend, John Henry's too,
        is a dare and a bet to old Satchmo
when his groovy blues put headlines in the news
        from the Gold Coast to cold Moscow.

        Old Satchmo's
gravelly voice and tapping foot and crazy notes
        set my soul on fire
                If I climbed
        the seventy-seven steps of the Seventh
Heaven, Satchmo's high C would carry me higher!
        Are you hip to this, Harlem? Are you hip?
        On Judgment Day, Gabriel will say
                after he blows his horn:
"I'd be the greatest trumpeter in the Universe,
        if old Satchmo had never been born!"

African China

1
A connoisseur of pearl
necklace phrases,
Wu Shang disdains
his laundry, lazes
among his bric-a-brac
metaphysical;
and yet dark customers,
on Harlem's rack
quizzical,
sweat and pack
the forked caldera of
his Stygian shop:
some worship God,
and some Be-Bop.

Wu Shang discovers
the diademed word to be,
on the sly,
a masterkey
to Harlem pocketbooks,
outjockeyed by
policy
and brimstone
theology
alone!

2
As bust and hips
her corset burst,
An Amazonian fantasy,
A Witness of Jehovah
by job and husband curst,
lumbers in.

A yellow mummy in a mummery
a tip-toe,
Wu Shang unsheathes a grin,
and then, his fingers sleeved,
gulps an ugh and eats his crow,
disarmed by ugliness disbelieved!

At last he takes his wits
from balls of moth,
salaams. "Dear Lady, I, for you,
wear goats' sackcloth
to mark this hour and place;
cursed be the shadow of delay
that for a trice conceals a trace
of beauty in thy face!"

Her jug of anger emptied, now he sighs:
"Her kind cannot play euchre.
The master trick belongs to him
who holds the joker."
His mind's eyes see a black hand drop
a red white poker.

3
The gingered gigolo,
vexed by the harrow of a date
and vanity torn,
goddamns the yellow sage,
four million yellow born,
and yellow fate!

The gigolo
a wayward bronco
seen but unheard,
Wu Shang applies the curb-bit word:
"Wise lovers know
that in their lottery success
belongs to him who plays a woman
with titbits of a guess."

The sweet man's sportive whack
paralyzes Wu Shang's back.
"Say, Yellah Boy, I call yo' stuff
the hottest dope in town!
That red hot mama'll never know
she got her daddy down."

4
Sometimes the living dead
stalk in and sue for grace,
the tragic uncommon
in the comic commonplace,
the evil that the good
begets in love's embrace,
a Harlem melodrama
like that in Big John's face

as Wu Shang peers at him
and cudgels a theorem.

The sage says in a voice ilang-ilang,
"Do you direct the weathercock?"
And then his lash, a rackarock,
descends with a bang,
"Show me the man who has not thrown
a boomerang!"

...words, no longer pearls,
but drops of Gilead's balm.
Later, later, Wu Shang remarks,
"Siroccos mar the toughest palm."
The bigger thing, as always, goes unsaid:
the look behind the door of Big John's eyes,
awareness of the steps of *Is,*
the freedom of the wise.

5
When Dixie Dixon breaks a leg
on arctic Lenox Avenue

and Wu Shang homes her, pays her fees,
old kismet knots the two
unraveled destinies.
The unperfumed
wag foot, forefinger, head;
and belly laughter waifs ghost rats
foxed by the smells of meat and bread;
and black walls blab, "Good Gawd,
China and Africa gits wed!"

6
Wu Shang, whom nothing sears,
says Dixie is a dusky passion flower
unsoiled by envious years.

And Dixie says
her Wu Shang is a Mandarin
with seven times seven ways of love,
her very own oasis in
the desert
of Harlem men.

In dignity, Wu Shang and Dixie walk
the gauntlet, Lenox Avenue;
their son has Wu Shang's cast
and Dixie's hue.

The dusky children roll
their oyster eyes
at Wu Shang, Junior, flash
a premature surmise,
as if afraid:
in accents Carolina
on the streets they never made,
the dusky children tease,
"African China!"

Sterling A. Brown

(1901–1989)

Throughout his long career as a poet, critic, editor, and teacher, Sterling Allen Brown dedicated himself to the study of African American folk language and literature. One of the first writers to treat the vernacular with literary respect, Brown fell in love with the rhythms and the colors of everyday speech after he began teaching in the rural South. There, among semiliterate farmers and migrant workers, the privileged young man from Washington, D.C., found what would be his greatest artistic discovery: "something to write about … a people's poetry."

Brown graduated phi beta kappa from Williams College in 1918 and then received his master's degree in English from Harvard University before teaching in various places in the South. As he traveled through Virginia, Missouri, and Tennessee, Brown began gathering the fragments of ballads, spirituals, and blues that would eventually coalesce into his first volume of poems, **Southern Road** *(1932). Although the work was highly praised by such influential readers as James Weldon Johnson, Brown was unable to publish his second collection,* **No Hiding Place***. He would not receive the recognition he deserved until the late 60s, when college students whom he had taught drew attention to his work during the Black Arts movement. By that point, Brown had been teaching at Howard University for over thirty years, and, during this time, he had written criticism and edited* **The Negro Caravan** *(1941), the first comprehensive anthology of African American literature. A reissued edition of* **Southern Road***, a new volume of poetry,* **The Last Ride of Wild Bill** *and* **Eleven Narratives** *(1975), and a retrospective collection,* **The Collected Poems of Sterling A. Brown** *(1980), began the process of serious scholarly reappraisal that is still ongoing today.*

After Winter

He snuggles his fingers
In the blacker loam
The lean months are done with,
The fat to come.

> His eyes are set
> On a brushwood-fire
> But his heart is soaring
> Higher and higher.

Though he stands ragged
An old scarecrow,

This is the way
His swift thoughts go,

> *"Butter beans fo' Clara*
> *Sugar corn fo' Grace*
> *An' fo' de little feller*
> *Runnin' space.*

"Radishes and lettuce
Eggplants and beets
Turnips fo' de winter
An' candied sweets.

> *"Homespun tobacco*
> *Apples in de bin*
> *Fo' smokin' an' fo' cider*
> *When de folks draps in."*

He thinks with the winter
His troubles are gone;
Ten acres unplanted
To raise dreams on.

> The lean months are done with,
> The fat to come.
> His hopes, winter wanderers,
> Hasten home.

"Butterbeans fo' Clara
Sugar corn fo' Grace
An' fo' de little feller
Runnin' space...."

Foreclosure

Father Missouri takes his own.
These are the fields he loaned them,
Out of hearts' fullness; gratuitously;
Here are the banks he built up for his children—
Here are the fields; rich, fertile silt.

Father Missouri, in his dotage
Whimsical and drunkenly turbulent,
Cuts away the banks; steals away the loam;
Washes the ground from under wire fences,
Leaves fenceposts grotesquely dangling in the air;
And with doddering steps approaches the shanties.

Father Missouri; far too old to be so evil.

Uncle Dan, seeing his garden lopped away,
Seeing his manured earth topple slowly in the stream,
Seeing his cows knee-deep in yellow water,
His pig-sties flooded, his flower beds drowned,
Seeing his white leghorns swept down the stream—

Curses Father Missouri, impotently shakes
His fist at the forecloser, the treacherous skinflint;
Who takes what was loaned so very long ago,
And leaves puddles in his parlor, and useless lakes
In his fine pasture land.

Sees years of work turned to nothing—
Curses, and shouts in his hoarse old voice,
"Ain't got no right to act dat way at all"
And the old river rolls on, slowly to the gulf.

Langston Hughes

(1902–1967)

Langston Hughes was running track for his Cleveland, Ohio, high school when he wrote "The Negro Speaks of Rivers," which has since become one of his most widely anthologized poems. Raised by his maternal grandmother after his parents separated and his father moved to Mexico, the teenaged Hughes made honor roll and edited the school yearbook while submitting his poetry to the influential publication of the NAACP, **The Crisis**. In 1921, upon his father's condition that he study engineering, Hughes entered Columbia University—only to leave, dissatisfied and yearning to be a writer, a year later. He then joined the Merchant Marines and traveled to Italy, Africa, and France as a cook's helper. Eventually Hughes received his bachelor's degree (1929) from Lincoln University in Pennsylvania.

After returning to the states in 1925, Hughes worked as a busboy in a Washington, D.C., hotel restaurant, where, as the famous story goes, he noticed the poet Vachel Lindsay and conveniently left several poems in prominent view by his dinner plate. The next day, Hughes read newspaper headlines about the discovery of a "busboy poet," and later that year, eleven of his poems appeared in **The New Negro**, Alain Locke's seminal anthology of African American literature. Two books of poetry followed quickly, **The Weary Blues** (1926), and **Fine Clothes to the Jew** (1927). More than a talented writer had been born: one of the most influential figures of the Harlem Renaissance and of American modernism had launched his richly varied life and productive career.

With his writing career at full steam, Hughes traveled widely to such places as Cuba, Russia, China, and Japan, and at one point covered the Spanish War as a correspondent for the Baltimore **Afro American**. When he was not abroad, he actively encouraged the development of other artists. Offering his valuable support to such writers as Gwendolyn Brooks and James Weldon Johnson, Hughes also collaborated on projects with Zora Neale Hurston and Arna Bontemps. And, in the interest of furthering the creation working relationships between poetry and the other arts, Hughes founded several theatrical groups in New York, Chicago, and Los Angeles. Meanwhile, his enormous body of published work steadily accumulated; eventually it would total ten volumes of poetry, including the famous **Montage of a Dream Deferred** (1951), nine books of fiction, five of which are based on his Jesse B. Semple character, nine plays, and two autobiographies—not to mention several scholarly studies, film scripts, children's books, translations, librettos, newspaper articles, and the numerous anthologies that he edited.

Despite his impressive versatility, poetry remained Hughes's literary priority, and his innovations in that realm would influence subsequent generations of American poets. By capturing in verses the way that average folks spoke and sang about the dark ironies and quiet glories of everyday living, Langston Hughes demonstrated how writers could, like the jazz musicians and blues singers he so admired, rearrange the hidden rhythms and cadences of colloquial idioms into the highest of literary forms.

Harlem

What happens to a dream deferred?

   Does it dry up
   like a raisin in the sun?
Or fester like a sore—
And then run?
   Does it stink like rotten meat?
Or crust and sugar over
   like a syrupy sweet?

   Maybe it just sags
like a heavy load.

Or does it explode?

The Weary Blues

Droning a drowsy syncopated tune,
Rocking back and forth to a mellow croon,
        I heard a Negro play.
Down on Lenox Avenue the other night
By the pale dull pallor of an old gas light
        He did a lazy sway. . . .
        He did a lazy sway. . . .
To the tune o' those Weary Blues.
With his ebony hands on each ivory key
He made that poor piano moan with melody.
        O Blues!
Swaying to and fro on his rickety stool
He played that sad raggy tune like a musical fool.
        Sweet Blues!
Coming from a black man's soul.
        O Blues!
In a deep song voice with a melancholy tone
I heard that Negro sing, that old piano moan—
        "Ain't got nobody in all this world,

> Ain't got nobody but ma self.
> I's gwine to quit ma frownin'
> And put ma troubles on the shelf."
Thump, thump, thump, went his foot on the floor.
He played a few chords then he sang some more—
> "I got the Weary Blues
> And I can't be satisfied.
> Got the Weary Blues
> And can't be satisfied—
> I ain't happy no mo'
> And I wish that I had died."
And far into the night he crooned that tune.
The stars went out and so did the moon.
The singer stopped playing and went to bed
While the Weary Blues echoed through his head.
He slept like a rock or a man that's dead.

The Negro Speaks of Rivers

I've known rivers:
I've known rivers ancient as the world and older than the flow
    of human blood in human veins.

My soul has grown deep like the rivers.

I bathed in the Euphrates when dawns were young.
I built my hut near the Congo and it lulled me to sleep.
I looked upon the Nile and raised the pyramids above it.
I heard the singing of the Mississippi when Abe Lincoln went
    down to New Orleans, and I've seen its muddy bosom turn
    all golden in the sunset.

I've known rivers:
Ancient, dusky rivers.

My soul has grown deep like the rivers.

I, Too, Sing America

I, too, sing America.

I am the darker brother.
They send me to eat in the kitchen
When company comes,
But I laugh,
And eat well,
And grow strong.

Tomorrow,
I'll sit at the table
When company comes.
Nobody'll dare
Say to me,
"Eat in the kitchen,"
Then.

Besides,
They'll see how beautiful I am
And be ashamed—

I, too, am America.

Mother to Son

Well, son, I'll tell you:
Life for me ain't been no crystal stair.
It's had tacks in it,
And splinters,
And boards torn up,
And places with no carpet on the floor—
Bare.
But all the time
I'se been a-climbin' on,
And reachin' landin's,

And turnin' corners,
And sometimes goin' in the dark
Where there ain't been no light.
So, boy, don't you turn back.
Don't you set down on the steps
'Cause you finds it's kinder hard.
Don't you fall now—
For I'se still goin', honey,
I'se still climbin',
And life for me ain't been no crystal stair.

Havana Dreams

The dream is a cocktail at Sloppy Joe's—
(Maybe—nobody knows.)

The dream is the road to Batabano.
(But nobody knows if that is so.)

Perhaps the dream is only her face—
Perhaps it's a fan of silver lace—
Or maybe the dream's a Vedado rose—
(*Quien sabe?* Who really knows?)

Birmingham Sunday

(September 15, 1963)

Four little girls
Who went to Sunday School that day
And never came back home at all—
But left instead
Their blood upon the wall
With spattered flesh
And bloodied Sunday dresses
Scorched by dynamite that
China made aeons ago

Did not know what China made
Before China was ever Red at all
Would redden with their blood
This Birmingham-on-Sunday wall.
Four tiny girls
Who left their blood upon that wall,
In little graves today await
    The dynamite that might ignite
    The ancient fuse of Dragon Kings
    Whose tomorrow sings a hymn
    The missionaries never taught
    In Christian Sunday School
    To implement the Golden Rule.

    Four little girls
    Might be awakened someday soon
    By songs upon the breeze
        As yet unfelt among
        Magnolia trees.

Robert Hayden

(1913–1980)

Robert Hayden, a native of Detroit, Michigan, earned his bachelor's degree from Wayne State University, and a master's degree from the University of Michigan. He taught at Fisk University in Nashville for twenty-two years (1946–1968), then at the University of Michigan for the rest of his life (1969–1980). Though erudite and scholarly, Hayden was not unfamiliar with vernacular life and culture. His work strikes an elegant balance between formal and informal diction just as Hayden proved himself comfortable and formidable whether working in traditional fixed forms or in open forms. During the Great Depression in the 1930s he worked—along with Ralph Ellison, Richard Wright, and other American writers—as a field researcher of African American history, oral and written for the Federal Writers' Project. Hayden's award-winning poems celebrating heroes of Black history—Harriet Tubman, Nat Turner, Frederick Douglass, Bessie Smith, and Malcolm X—rank among his finest.

As a religious devotee, Robert Hayden was poetry editor for the **Baha'i World Faith Magazine. Kaleidoscope: Poems by American Negro Poets**, *his 1967 anthology, continues to be highly regarded. Twenty-five years following publication of his first poetry collection,* **Heart-Shape in the Dust**, *an international panel of judges awarded Hayden's* **A Ballad of Remembrance** *(1962) the grand prize for poetry at the 1965 World Festival of African Arts in Dakar, Senegal. Hayden's other books include* **The Lion and the Archer**, *written in collaboration with Myron O'Higgins (1948);* **Figure of Time: Poems** *(1955);* **Selected Poems** *(1966);* **Words in the Mourning Time** *(1970);* **The Night-Blooming Cereus** *(1972);* **Angle of Ascent: New and Selected Poems** *(1979); and the posthumously edited* **Robert Hayden: Selected Poems** *(1985). His honors include the University of Michigan's Avery Hopwood Award, a Rosenwald Literary Fellowship, and a Ford Foundation grant. The first Black American to serve as poetry consultant to the Library of Congress, Hayden carried out his appointment with dignity and dedication.*

Frederick Douglass

When it is finally ours, this freedom, this liberty, this beautiful
and terrible thing, needful to man as air,
usable as earth; when it belongs at last to all,
when it is truly instinct, brain matter, diastole, systole,
reflex action; when it is finally won; when it is more
than the gaudy mumbo jumbo of politicians:
this man, this Douglass, this former slave, this Negro
beaten to his knees, exiled, visioning a world
where none is lonely, none hunted, alien,
this man, superb in love and logic, this man

shall be remembered. Oh, not with statues' rhetoric,
not with legends and poems and wreaths of bronze alone,
but with the lives grown out of his life, the lives
fleshing his dream of the beautiful, needful thing.

The Whipping

The old woman across the way
　　　　is whipping the boy again
and shouting to the neighborhood
　　　　her goodness and his wrongs.

Wildly he crashes through elephant ears,
　　　　pleads in dusty zinnias,
while she in spite of crippling fat
　　　　pursues and corners him.

She strikes and strikes the shrilly circling
　　　　boy till the stick breaks
in her hand. His tears are rainy weather
　　　　to woundlike memories:

My head gripped in bony vise
　　　　of knees, the writhing struggle
to wrench free, the blows, the fear
　　　　worse than blows that hateful

Words could bring, the face that I
　　　　no longer knew or loved. ...
Well, it is over now, it is over,
　　　　and the boy sobs in his room,

And the woman leans muttering against
　　　　a tree, exhausted, purged—
avenged in part for lifelong hidings
　　　　she has had to bear.

Homage to the Empress of the Blues

Because there was a man somewhere in a candystripe silk shirt,
gracile and dangerous as a jaguar and because a woman moaned
for him in sixty-watt gloom and mourned him Faithless Love
Twotiming Love Oh Love Oh Careless Aggravating Love,

> She came out on the stage in yards of pearls, emerging like
> a favorite scenic view, flashed her golden smile and sang.

Because grey laths began somewhere to show from underneath
torn hurdygurdy lithographs of dollfaced heaven;
and because there were those who feared alarming fists of snow
on the door and those who feared the riot-squad of statistics,

> She came out on the stage in ostrich feathers, beaded satin,
> and shone that smile on us and sang.

Countee Cullen

(1903—1946)

Born to a single mother in Louisville, Kentucky, Countee Cullen was informally adopted in his mid-teens by Reverend and Mrs. Frederick Asbury Cullen of the Salem Methodist Episcopal Church in Harlan, Kentucky. Educated at Manhattan's public but prestigious DeWitt Clinton High School, New York University, and Harvard University, where he received his master's degree, Cullen had established himself while still an undergraduate as a gifted, prize-winning poet. At twenty-three he began editorial work at the **History Opportunity** *magazine as Charles S. Johnson's assistant. He moved in the highest intellectual and literary circles, and in 1928 married W. E. B. Du Bois's daughter Nina Yolanda Du Bois, a marriage that lasted two years.*

The concluding lines of "From the Dark Tower" encapsulate Countee Cullen's abiding concern for social justice and human dignity that permeate his poetry: "So in the dark we hide the heart that bleeds, /And wait, and tend our agonizing seeds." Reflecting his captivation with African retentions in African American culture, his works include: **Color** *(1925),* **The Ballad of the Brown Girl: An Old Ballad Retold** *(1927);* **Copper Sun** *(1927); the novel* **One Way to Heaven** *(1932); and the play, co-authored with Arna Bontemps,* **St. Louis Women** *(1946). He is also the author of the children's books* **The Lost Zoo (A Rhyme for the Young, But Not Too Young)** *(1940), and* **My Lives and How I Lost Them** *(1942).*

The Wise

Dead men are wisest, for they know
How far the roots of flowers go,
How long a seed must rot to grow.

Dead men alone bear frost and rain
On throbless heart and heartless brain,
And feel no stir of joy or pain.

Dead men alone are satiate;
They sleep and dream and have no weight,
To curb their rest, of love or hate.

Strange, men should flee their company,
Or think me strange who long to be
Wrapped in their cool immunity.

Incident

(For Eric Walrond)

Once riding in old Baltimore,
    Heart-filled, head-filled with glee,
I saw a Baltimorean
    Keep looking straight at me.

Now I was eight and very small,
    And he was no whit bigger,
And so I smiled, but he poked out
    His tongue, and called me, "Nigger."

I saw the whole of Baltimore
    From May until December;
Of all the things that happened there
    That's all that I remember.

Dudley Randall

(b. 1914)

An esteemed poet and editor, Dudley Randall was also the founder of Broadside Press, one of the crucial forces behind the emergence of Black poetry in the sixties. Randall was not only a visionary publisher, but a beloved mentor who inspired the loyalty of such poets as Gwendolyn Brooks, Haki Madhubuti, Toni Cade Bambara, Audre Lorde, Robert Hayden, Sonia Sanchez, and Etheridge Knight—all of whom continued to publish with Broadside even after they had achieved mainstream success.

Born in Washington, D.C., to a minister and teacher, Randall wrote his first poem when he was four and published his verse in the **Detroit Free Press** *when he was thirteen. After graduating he served in the Army signal corps before returning to school to earn a degree in library science at the University of Michigan. While working as a reference librarian for various institutions, Randall founded the Broadside Press in 1963. Beginning with the publication of Randall's "The Ballad of Birmingham," the young press would go on to publish over one hundred leaflets by 1982. Its first book-length publication would be a volume of poems about Malcom X,* **For Malcolm: Poems on the Life and Death of Malcolm X** *(1967).*

A distinguished poet in his own right, Randall is regarded by literary scholars to be a bridge between the poets of the Harlem Renaissance, whom he had read as a child, and the militant Black poets of the 1960s, whom he mentored. His volumes of poetry include: **Poem, Counterpoem** *(1966),* **Cities Burning** *(1968),* **Love You** *(1970),* **After the Killing** *(1973), and* **Homage to Hoyt Fuller** *(1984). Selected poetry has been collected in* **More to Remember: Poems of Four Decades** *(1971) and* **A Litany of Friends: New and Selected Poems** *(1981). "Booker T. and W.E.B" is Randall's most frequently anthologized piece. A dramatic dialogue between the two distinguished Black leaders, this poem contrasts Washington's conservative practicality with   Du Bois's vision of equal opportunity and universal justice.*

Booker T. and W.E.B.

"It seems to me," said Booker T.,
"It shows a mighty lot of cheek
To study chemistry and Greek
When Mister Charlie needs a hand
To hoe the cotton on his land,
And when Miss Ann looks for a cook,
Why stick your nose inside a book?"

"I don't agree," said W.E.B.,
"If I should have the drive to seek

Knowledge of chemistry or Greek,
I'll do it. Charles and Miss can look
Another place for hand or cook.
Some men rejoice in skill of hand,
And some in cultivating land,
But there are others who maintain
The right to cultivate the brain."

"It seems to me," said Booker T.,
"That all you folks have missed the boat
Who shout about the right to vote,
And spend vain days and sleepless nights
In uproar over civil rights.
Just keep your mouths shut, do not grouse,
But work, and save, and buy a house."

"I don't agree," said W.E.B.,
"For what can property avail
If dignity and justice fail.
Unless you help to make the laws,
They'll steal your house with trumped-up clause.
A rope's as tight, a fire as hot,
No matter how much cash you've got.
Speak soft, and try your little plan,
But as for me, I'll be a man."

"It seems to me," said Booker T.—

"I don't agree,"
Said W.E.B.

An Answer To Lerone Bennett's Questionnaire on a Name for Black Americans

Discarding the Spanish word for black
and taking the Anglo-Saxon word for Negro,
discarding the names of English slavemasters
and taking the names of Arabian slave-traders
won't put a single
bean in your belly
or an inch of steel
in your spine.

Call a skunk a rose,
and he'll still stink,
and make the name stink too.

Call a rose a skunk,
and it'll still smell sweet,
and even sweeten the name.

The spirit informs the name,
not the name the spirit.

If the white man took the name Negro,
and you took the name Caucasian,
he'd still kick your ass,
as long as you let him.

If you're so insecure
that a word makes you quake,
another word
won't cure you.

Change your mind,
not your name.

Change your life,
not your clothes.

Margaret Walker

(b. 1915)

*The daughter of a Methodist minister and music teacher, Margaret Walker was born in Birmingham, Alabama. Encouraged in her early efforts at writing poetry by W. E. B. Du Bois, Langston Hughes, and Richard Wright, Walker has in turn influenced such younger writers as Nikki Giovanni, Alice Walker, and Sonia Sanchez. She received her bachelor's degree from Northwestern University in 1935, and while in Chicago became associated with the Federal Writers' Project and the South Side Writers' Group. After receiving her master's degree from the University of Iowa in 1940, she published her collection of poetry, **For My People** (1942, 1969). Walker was honored with a Yale Series of Younger Poets Award (1942) for that volume; its title piece is one of her most frequently anthologized poems. Subsequent volumes of poetry include **Ballad of the Free** (1966) and **Prophets for a New Day** (1970), both of which reflect on issues of faith and civil rights, and **October Journey** (1973), which contains biographical portraits of such historical figures as Paul Laurence Dunbar and Phillis Wheatley. In her two-volume collection of new and selected poems, **This Is My Century** (1988), Walker declares that all of her poems "come out of [her] living" as "a woman and a black person." The best proof of this statement is the historical saga **Jubilee** (1965), which Walker wrote while raising four children and earning her doctorate from the University of Iowa (1965).*

*Her other works include **A Poetic Equation: Conversations Between Nikki Giovanni and Margaret Walker** (1974) and a controversial biography of Richard Wright, **The Daemonic Genius of Richard Wright: A Portrait of the Man** (1987). A recipient of a Rosenwald Fellowship, a Houghton Mifflin Literary Fellowship, a Fulbright Fellowship, and a Senior Fellowship from the National Endowment for the Humanities, Walker has taught at various colleges and universities and has been awarded numerous honorary degrees. She is currently working on her autobiography.*

Miss Molly Means

Old Molly Means was a hag and a witch;
Chile of the devil, the dark, and sitch.
Her heavy hair hung thick in ropes
And her blazing eyes was black as pitch.
Imp at three and wench at 'leben
She counted her husbands to the number seben.
    O Molly, Molly, Molly Means
    There goes the ghost of Molly Means.

Some say she was born with a veil on her face
So she could look through unnatchal space
Through the future and through the past
And charm a body or an evil place
And every man could well despise
The evil look in her coal black eyes.
        Old Molly, Molly, Molly Means
        Dark is the ghost of Molly Means.

And when the tale begun to spread
Of evil and of holy dread:
Her black-hand arts and her evil powers
How she cast her spells and called the dead,
The younguns was afraid at night
And the farmers feared their crops would blight.
        Old Molly, Molly, Molly Means
        Cold is the ghost of Molly Means.

Then one dark day she put a spell
On a young gal-bride just come to dwell
In the lane just down from Molly's shack
And when her husband come riding back
His wife was barking like a dog
And on all fours like a common hog.
        O Molly, Molly, Molly Means
        Where is the ghost of Molly Means?

The neighbors come and they went away
And said she'd die before break of day
But her husband held her in his arms
And swore he'd break the wicked charms;
He'd search all up and down the land
And turn the spell on Molly's hand.
        O Molly, Molly, Molly Means
        Sharp is the ghost of Molly Means.

So he rode all day and he rode all night
And at the dawn he come in sight
Of a man who said he could move the spell

And cause the awful thing to dwell
On Molly Means, to bark and bleed
Till she died at the hands of her evil deed.
      Old Molly, Molly, Molly Means
      This is the ghost of Molly Means.

Sometimes at night through the shadowy trees
She rides along on a winter breeze.
You can hear her holler and whine and cry.
Her voice is thin and her moan is high,
And her cackling laugh or her barking cold
Bring terror to the young and old.
      O Molly, Molly, Molly Means
      Lean is the ghost of Molly Means.

October Journey

Traveller take heed for journeys undertaken in the dark of the
      year.
Go in the bright blaze of Autumn's equinox.
Carry protection against ravages of a sun-robber, a vandal, and a
      thief.
Cross no bright expanse of water in the full of the moon.
Choose no dangerous summer nights;
no heady tempting hours of spring;
October journeys are safest, brightest, and best.

I want to tell you what hills are like in October
when colors gush down mountainsides
and little streams are freighted with a caravan of leaves.
I want to tell you how they blush and turn in fiery shame and
      joy,
how their love burns with flames consuming and terrible
until we wake one morning and woods are like a smoldering
      plain—
a glowing caldron full of jewelled fire:
the emerald earth a dragon's eye
the poplars drenched with yellow light
and dogwoods blazing bloody red.

Traveling southward earth changes from gray rock to green
        velvet.
Earth changes to red clay
with green grass growing brightly
with saffron skies of evening setting dully
with muddy rivers moving sluggishly.

In the early spring when the peach tree blooms
wearing a veil like a lavender haze
and the pear and plum in their bridal hair
gently snow their petals on earth's grassy bosom below
then the soughing breeze is soothing
and the world seems bathed in tenderness,
but in October
blossoms have long since fallen.
A few red apples hang on leafless boughs;
wind whips bushes briskly.
And where a blue stream sings cautiously
a barren land feeds hungrily.
An evil moon bleeds drops of death.
The earth burns brown.
Grass shrivels and dries to a yellowish mass.
Earth wears a dun-colored dress
like an old woman wooing the sun to be her lover,
be her sweetheart and her husband bound in one.
Farmers heap hay in stacks and bind corn in shocks
against the biting breath of frost.

The train wheels hum, "I am going home, I am going home,
I am moving toward the South."
Soon cypress swamps and muskrat marshes
and black fields touched with cotton will appear.
I dream again of my childhood land
of a neighbor's yard with a redbud tree
the smell of pine for turpentine
an Easter dress, a Christmas eve
and winding roads from the top of a hill.
A music sings within my flesh
I feel the pulse within my throat

my heart fills up with hungry fear
while hills and flatlands stark and staring
before my dark eyes sad and haunting
appear and disappear.

Then when I touch this land again
the promise of a sun-lit hour dies.
The greenness of an apple seems
to dry and rot before my eyes.
The sullen winter rains
are tears of grief I cannot shed.
The windless days are static lives.
The clock runs down
timeless and still.
The days and nights turn hours to years
and water in a gutter makes the circle of another world
hating, resentful, and afraid
stagnant, and green, and full of slimy things.

Gwendolyn Brooks

(b. 1917)

Born in Topeka, Kansas, and raised on Chicago's South Side, Gwendolyn Brooks began writing in elementary school to shield herself from the taunting of classmates who ridiculed her darkness and her clumsiness. Encouraged by her parents who assured the girl that she "would one day be a writer," Brooks published her first poem in a popular children's magazine, **American Childhood,** *when she was thirteen. By the time she was seventeen, she was writing regularly for* **Chicago Defender** *and corresponding with James Weldon Johnson and Langston Hughes. Both men, who also wrote for the Chicago weekly, recognized the teenager's considerable promise and encouraged her literary efforts.*

Her first volume of poetry, **A Street in Bronzeville** *(1945), which Brooks hoped would show "that Negroes are just like other people," brought to her career the considerable acclaim that has since distinguished it. After receiving a Guggenheim Fellowship and a prize from the American Academy of Arts and Letters for her first book, Brooks was awarded the Pulitzer Prize in 1950 for* **Annie Allen** *(1949). This three-part verse-narrative about a young Black girl showcases Brooks's sensitivity to psychological nuance and her technical mastery of language, especially her ability to interweave traditional verse forms with contemporary Black vernacular. In the 60s, Brooks began to direct these finely tuned sensibilities to the subjects of race, gender, and class, resulting in the urgent and angry poems of* **In the Mecca** *(1968),* **Riot** *(1969),* **Beckonings** *(1975),* **Primer for Black** *(1980), and* **The Near-Johannesburg Boy and Other Poems** *(1986). Critics regard these volumes as the literary link between the conservative verse of the late 40s and the militant lyrics of the late 60s.*

Brooks has also published a collection of essays, **Report from Port One** *(1972), and a novel,* **Maud Martha** *(1953). A holder of several honorary degrees, she was named Poet Laureate of Illinois in 1968 and was appointed Poetry Consultant to the Library of Congress in 1985.*

First Fight. Then Fiddle

First fight. Then fiddle. Ply the slipping string
With feathery sorcery; muzzle the note
With hurting love; the music that they wrote
Bewitch, bewilder. Qualify to sing
Threadwise. Devise no salt, no hempen thing
For the dear instrument to bear. Devote
The bow to silks and honey. Be remote
A while from malice and from murdering.
But first to arms, to armor. Carry hate
In front of you and harmony behind.

Be deaf to music and to beauty blind.
Win war. Rise bloody, maybe not too late
For having first to civilize a space
Wherein to play your violin with grace.

On De Witt Williams
on His Way to Lincoln Cemetery

He was born in Alabama.
He was bred in Illinois.
He was nothing but a
Plain black boy.

Swing low swing low sweet sweet chariot.
Nothing but a plain black boy.

Drive him past the Pool Hall.
Drive him past the Show.
Blind within his casket,
But maybe he will know.

Down through Forty-seventh Street:
Underneath the L,
And—Northwest Corner, Prairie,
That he loved so well.

Don't forget the Dance Halls—
Warwick and Savoy,
Where he picked his women, where
He drank his liquid joy.

Born in Alabama.
Bred in Illinois.
He was nothing but a
Plain black boy.

Swing low swing low sweet sweet chariot.
Nothing but a plain black boy.

The Birth in a Narrow Room

Weeps out of Kansas country something new.
Blurred and stupendous. Wanted and unplanned.
Winks. Twines, and weakly winks
Upon the milk-glass fruit bowl, iron pot,
The bashful china child tipping forever
Yellow apron and spilling pretty cherries.

Now, weeks and years will go before she thinks
"How pinchy is my room! how can I breathe!
I am not anything and I have got
Not anything, or anything to do!"—
But prances nevertheless with gods and fairies
Blithely about the pump and then beneath
The elms and grapevines, then in darling endeavor
By privy foyer, where the screenings stand
And where the bugs buzz by in private cars
Across old peach cans and old jelly jars.

We Real Cool

The Pool Players.
Seven At The Golden Shovel.

We real cool. We
Left school. We

Lurk late. We
Strike straight. We

Sing sin. We
Think gin. We

Jazz June. We
Die soon.

James A. Emanuel

(b. 1921)

Born in Nebraska, James A. Emanuel came to his love of language while listening to his mother read the Bible to him and his six siblings. He was educated at Howard University, where he graduated summa cum laude, and at Northwestern University and Columbia University, where he received his master's and doctorate degrees. While a professor of English at the City College of New York (CCNY) in the sixties, Emanuel published two scholarly books, a study of Langston Hughes entitled **Langston Hughes** *(1967) and an anthology,* **Dark Symphony** *(1968). He also published his first volume of poetry,* **The Treehouse and Other Poems** *(1968), a collection of quiet, introspective poems. Emanuel's voice, however, grew more strident as his involvement in racial politics intensified. His second volume of poetry,* **Panther Man** *(1970), reflects his feelings of frustration with the prejudices so deeply engrained in American society. Although Emanuel traveled abroad widely as a visiting scholar and Fulbright Fellow to France and Poland during the seventies, he nontheless published steadily. His other books of poetry include* **Black Man Abroad** *(1978),* **A Chisel in the Dark** *(1980),* **A Poet's Mind** *(1983), and* **The Broken Bowl** *(1993). In 1983 Emanuel retired from his teaching duties at CCNY and moved to France.*

Black Muslim Boy in a Hospital

Are you hot there too?
(Down in the grates of you,
Banked for long burning,
Some cindered yearning,
Looked in despair,
Kindles your glare.)

Does it hurt? (Something cries
When I gently press your eyes.
A tiny light in you goes out,
Blinking in a stream of doubt,
When this white though healing hand
Trespasses and takes command.)

(Hate for friends and hate for foes
Who have not endured hate's blows
Digested with the crumbs of years.
What can stop these ancient tears
Burning in a little face
So captive in a starched embrace?)

Son

Cross-legged on his bed,
The President is twelve,
Signalling to order all his crew:
Himself as Treasurer, Chief Spy,
Keeper of the Chemicals,
And only member, too.

The minutes of Club Fantastic
tell it all:
The Indianheads his paper route
turned up for dues,
The four-way-grid code messages
he found in shoes,
The fingerprints and buttons
marked in basement hush,
The friends he filed away in
"Sent by Thrush"

Barefoot at the desk no one
disturbs,
The President nods over geometry
and German verbs
And Orwell's *1984*, all done,
What can a President do—

Or Treasurer, Chief Spy, Keeper
of the Chemicals too—
When all of his fantastic crew,
Despite all signals, doze as one?

Founder of the Club, mystery of
twelve,
How signal to you? How softly
delve
Into your lonely sleep, that even
there, even you
Might close hands with this
crew?

Bob Kaufman

(1925–1986)

"My ambition is to be completely forgotten," Bob Kaufman would confide to the editor of his last volume of poetry, **The Ancient Rain** *(1981). No doubt the wishes of this intriguing personality will be frustrated, so compelling is the poetry of this man who cofounded the Beat movement. Born in New Orleans to an Orthodox Jew and a Black Catholic from Martinique, Kaufman ran away from home and joined the Merchant Marine when he was thirteen. He began reading avidly while at sea, and when he left the Merchant Marine in the 1940s after twenty years of service, he moved to New York to study literature at the New School for Social Research. There, he met Allen Ginsberg and William S. Burroughs, with whom he traveled to San Francisco. Inspired by the blues and bebop jazz musicians of North Beach, Kaufman began improvising spontaneous, rhythmic poems in jazz bars and coffeehouses, eventually becoming known as "The Original BeBop Man."*

    Indifferent to his literary career, Kaufman did not write down many of his poems; most of his publications were transcripts sent to publishers by friends and admirers. **Does the Secret Mind Whisper**, **Second April**, *and* **Abomunist Manifesto**, *were published in 1959, and they were eventually collected into a 1965 volume,* **Solitudes Crowded with Loneliness**. *Barely noticed in the United States,* **Solitudes** *became a critical success in Europe, where it was translated into eight languages. In 1961 Kaufman was nominated along with T. S. Eliot for Britain's prestigious Guinness Poetry Award. Eliot won the prize, and Kaufman returned to the United States. Disenchanted with society, he took a Buddhist vow of silence in 1963 and did not speak again until 1975, on the day the Vietnam War ended. During the last few years of his life, the reclusive Kaufman seldom spoke, eventually dying of emphysema in 1986.*

Walking Parker Home

Sweet beats of jazz impaled on slivers of wind
Kansas Black Morning/First Horn Eyes/
Historical sound pictures on New Bird wings
People shouts/boy alto dreams/Tomorrow's
Gold belled pipe of stops and future Blues Times
Lurking Hawkins/shadows of Lester/realization
Bronze fingers—brain extensions seeking trapped sounds
Ghetto thoughts/bandstand courage/solo flight
Nerve-wracked suspicions of newer songs and doubts
New York altar city/black tears/secret disciples
Hammer horn pounding soul marks on unswinging gates
Culture gods/mob sounds/visions of spikes

Panic excursions to tribal Jazz wombs and transfusions
Heroin nights of birth/and soaring/over boppy new ground.
Smothered rage covering pyramids of notes spontaneously
        exploding
Cool revelations/shrill hopes/beauty speared into
        greedy ears
Birdland nights on bop mountains, windy saxophone
        revolutions
Dayrooms of junk/and melting walls and circling vultures/
Money cancer/remembered pain/terror flights/
Death and indestructible existence

In that Jazz corner of life
Wrapped in a mist of sound
His legacy, our Jazz-tinted dawn
Wailing his triumphs of oddly begotten dreams
Inviting the nerveless to feel once more
That fierce dying of humans consumed
In raging fires of Love.

Battle Report

One thousand saxophones infiltrate the city,
Each with a man inside,
Hidden in ordinary cases,
Labeled FRAGILE.

A fleet of trumpets drops their hooks,
Inside at the outside.

Ten waves of trombones approach the city
Under blue cover
Of late autumn's neoclassical clouds.

Five hundred bassmen, all string feet tall,
Beating it back to the bass.

One hundred drummers, each a stick in each hand,
The delicate rumble of pianos, moving in.

The secret agent, an innocent bystander,
Drops a note in the wail box.

Five generals, gathered in the gallery,
Blowing plans.

At last, the secret code is flashed:
Now is the time, now is the time.

Attack: The sound of jazz.

The city falls.

Maya Angelou

(b. 1928)

   *By turning the astonishing trials of her life—a childhood rape, homelessness, drug addiction—into the frank and poignant continuous autobiography that she is best known for, Maya Angelou has challenged the boundary between life and art in a way that very few writers have been able to do well or even honestly. Born Marguerite Johnson in St. Louis, Missouri, Angelou was shuttled between Stampe, Arkansas, where her maternal grandmother ran a general store, and the cities where her itinerant mother lived. These early childhood experiences are described in the critically acclaimed first installment, **I Know Why the Caged Bird Sings** (1970), which was eventually turned into a television movie. The subsequent volumes—**Gather Together in My Name** (1974), **Singin' and Swingin' and Gettin' Merry like Christmas** (1976), **The Heart of a Woman** (1981), and **All God's Children Need Traveling Shoes** (1986)—describe a thirty-year period in which Angelou danced on stage, worked for civil rights, acted in movies, lived in Ghana, and produced screenplays. During this time she was also nominated for an Emmy for her performance in Alex Haley's **Roots** (1977) and was appointed to the Bicentennial Commission and the Commission of the International Woman's Year by Presidents Gerald Ford and Jimmy Carter.*

   *In addition to her well-known prose, Angelou has written several volumes of lyrical and jazzy poetry, including the Pulitzer-nominated **Just Give Me a Cool Drink of Water 'fore I Diiie** (1971) and the more recent **I Shall Not Be Moved** (1990). A recipient of numerous honorary degrees from such institutions as Smith College, Mills College, and Lawrence University, Angelou has been a professor of American Studies at Wake Forest University in North Carolina since 1974. In 1993 Angelou wrote the Inauguration Day poem "On the Pulse of the Morning," which she read during President Bill Clinton's swearing-in ceremony.*

Willie

Willie was a man without fame
Hardly anybody knew his name.
Crippled and limping, always walking lame,
He said, "I keep on movin'
Movin' just the same."

Solitude was the climate in his head
Emptiness was the partner in his bed,
Pain echoed in the steps of his tread,
He said, "I keep on followin'
Where the leaders led."

I may cry and I will die,
But my spirit is the soul of every spring.
Watch for me and you will see
That I'm present in the songs that children sing.

People called him "Uncle," "Boy" and "Hey,"
Said, "You can't live through this another day."
Then, they waited to hear what he would say.
He said, "I'm living
In the games that children play."

"You may enter my sleep, people my dreams,
Threaten my early morning's ease,
But I keep comin' followin' laughin' cryin',
Sure as a summer breeze.

"Wait for me, watch for me.
My spirit is the surge of open seas.
Look for me, ask for me.
I'm the rustle in the autumn leaves."

"When the sun rises
I am the time.
When the children sing
I am the Rhyme."

Derek Walcott

(b. 1930)

One of the most critically esteemed poets of the twentieth century, 1992 Nobel Laureate Derek Walcott interweaves Caribbean history, folklore, and patois with European literary traditions and forms, producing a structurally sophisticated verse that has been described as "oceanic," "tidal," and "overwhelming." He was born in St. Lucia and raised by his mother, a widowed schoolteacher who read Shakespeare aloud to her twin sons and daughter. Intrigued by the paintings and poetry that his deceased father left behind, Walcott resolved to become a painter. He nonetheless began writing poetry, and by the time he finished his studies at St. Mary's College and the University of West Indies in Jamaica, he had published three volumes of verse. Walcott's best-known books include **Another Life** *(1973),* **The Star-Apple Kingdom** *(1979), and* **Omeros** *(1990), and his vast work has been collected in* **Selected Verse** *(1976),* **Selected Poetry** *(1981), and* **Collected Poems: 1948–1984** *(1986). A prolific dramatist as well as a poet, Walcott studied drama in the United States as a Rockefeller Fellow and has written over fifteen plays, the best known being* **Dream on Monkey Mountain** *(1967), winner of the 1971 Obie Award. His Nobel Lecture,* **The Antilles: Fragments of Epic Memory**, *was published in 1993. Since the 1970s Walcott has divided his time between Boston, where he currently teaches poetry and play-writing at Boston University, and Trinidad.*

Based on Homer's **Odyssey**, *the critically acclaimed* **Omeros** *is a West Indies sea epic with a Caribbean fisherman and a prostitute standing in for Achilles and Helen. More than an adaptation of the* **Odyssey**, *however,* **Omeros** *is a meditation on several recurring themes in Walcott's poetry: the pain of exile, the weight of a colonial past, and the role of the artist in dealing with these matters. The earlier "A Far Cry from Africa" was written when Walcott was only eighteen. Stylistically accomplished, this poem analyzes the moral complexities of the bloody Mau Mau rebellion and closes with the famous line: "How choose / Between this Africa and the English tongue I Love?" Of Walcott's poetry esteemed critic–writer Joseph Brodsky has said: "His throbbing and relentless lines have kept arriving on the English language like tidal waves, coagulating into an archipelago of poems.... [H]e gives us a sense of infinity embodied in the language as well as in the ocean, which is always present in his poems...."*

A Far Cry From Africa

A wind is ruffling the tawny pelt
Of Africa. Kikuyu, quick as flies,
Batten upon the bloodstreams of the veldt.
Corpses are scattered through a paradise.
Only the worm, colonel of carrion, cries:
"Waste no compassion on these separate dead!"

Statistics justify and scholars seize
The salients of colonial policy.
What is that to the white child hacked in bed?
To savages, expendable as Jews?

Threshed out by beaters, the long rushes break
In a white dust of ibises whose cries
Have wheeled since civilization's dawn
From the parched river or beast-teeming plain.
The violence of beast on beast is read
As natural law, but upright man
Seeks his divinity by inflicting pain.
Delirious as these worried beasts, his wars
Dance to the tightened carcass of a drum,
While he calls courage still that native dread
Of the white peace contracted by the dead.

Again brutish necessity wipes its hands
Upon the napkin of a dirty cause, again
A waste of our compassion, as with Spain,
The gorilla wrestles with the superman.
I who am poisoned with the blood of both,
Where shall I turn, divided to the vein?
I who have cursed
The drunken officer of British rule, how choose
Between this Africa and the English tongue I love?
Betray them both, or give back what they give?
How can I face such slaughter and be cool?
How can I turn from Africa and live?

Omeros

Now he heard the griot muttering his prophetic song of sorrow that would be the past. It was a note, long-drawn and endless in its winding like the brown river's tongue:

"We were the colour of shadows when we came down with tinkling leg-irons to join the chains of the sea, for the silver coins multiplying on the sold horizon,

and these shadows are reprinted now on the white sand of antipodal coasts, your
ashen ancestors from the Bight of Benin, from the margin of Guinea.

There were seeds in our stomachs, in the cracking pods of our skulls on the
scorching decks, the tubers withered in no time. We watched as the river-gods

changed from snakes into currents. When inspected, our eyes showed dried fronds
in their brown irises, and from our curved spines, the rib-cages radiated

like fronds from a palm-branch. Then, when the dead palms were heaved overside,
the ribbed corpses floated, riding, to the white sand they remembered,

to the Bight of Benin, to the margin of Guinea. So, when you see burnt branches
riding the swell, trying to reclaim the surf through crooked fingers,

after a night of rough wind by some stone-white hotel, past the bright triangular
passage of the windsurfers, remember us to the black waiter bringing the bill."

But they crossed, they survived. There is the epical splendour. Multiply the rain's
lances, multiply their ruin, the grace born from subtraction as the hold's iron door

rolled over their eyes like pots left out in the rain, and the bolt rammed home its
echo, the way that thunderclaps perpetuate their reverberation.

So there went the Ashanti one way, the Mandingo another, the Ibo another, the
Guinea. Now each man was a nation in himself, without mother, father, brother.

Etheridge Knight

(1931–1991)

Mississippi-born Etheridge Knight began writing poetry while he was serving a prison term for robbery, and his poems reveal their maker's view of society from its margins. A master of "toasts" or verbal jousts, Knight brought his love of rhyme, rhythm, and street slang into his poems, which often meditate on the nature of time and the significance of freedom—but always in a lyrical and slyly humorous way. Unsure of his talents at first, Knight was gradually convinced by the encouragement of Dudley Randall, the influential editor of Broadside Press who visited him regularly during his eight-year incarceration at the Indiana State Prison. In 1968, the year he was paroled, Knight published his first collection of verse, **Poems from Prison***, which included a preface by Gwendolyn Brooks. For the next three years he was writer-in-residence at the University of Pittsburgh, University of Hartford, and Lincoln University. Knight's second volume,* **Belly Song and Other Poems** *(1973), was nominated for both the Pulitzer Prize and the National Book Award. Admired by such accomplished poets as Robert Bly, Galway Kinnell, and Gwendolyn Brooks, Knight has long been considered one of the best "blues" poets to date. His other publications include* **Born of a Woman: New and Selected Poems** *(1980) and* **The Essential Etheridge Knight** *(1986). Knight was also honored with grants from the National Endowment for the Arts and a Guggenheim fellowship.*

Hard Rock Returns to Prison from the Hospital for the Criminal Insane

Hard Rock/ was / "known not to take no shit
From nobody," and he had the scars to prove it:
Split purple lips, lumbed ears, welts above
His yellow eyes, and one long scar that cut
Across his temple and plowed through a thick
Canopy of kinky hair.

The WORD / was / that Hard Rock wasn't a mean nigger
Anymore, that the doctors had bored a hole in his head,
Cut out part of his brain, and shot electricity
Through the rest. When they brought Hard Rock back,
Handcuffed and chained, he was turned loose,
Like a freshly gelded stallion, to try his new status.
And we all waited and watched, like a herd of sheep,
To see if the WORD was true.

As we waited we wrapped ourselves in the cloak
Of his exploits: "Man, the last time, it took eight
Screws to put him in the Hole." "Yeah, remember when he
Smacked the captain with his dinner tray?" "He set
The record for time in the Hole—67 straight days!"
"Ol Hard Rock! Man, that's one crazy nigger."
And then the jewel of a myth that Hard Rock had once bit
A screw on the thumb and poisoned him with syphilitic spit.

The testing came, to see if Hard Rock was really tame.
A hillbilly called him a black son of a bitch
And didn't lose his teeth, a screw who knew Hard Rock
from before shook him down and barked in his face.
And Hard Rock did *nothing*. Just grinned and looked silly,
His eyes empty like knot holes in a fence.

And even after we discovered that it took Hard Rock
Exactly 3 minutes to tell you his first name,
We told ourselves that he had just wised up,
Was being cool; but we could not fool ourselves for long,
And we turned away, our eyes on the ground. Crushed.

He had been our Destroyer, the doer of things
We dreamed of doing but could not bring ourselves to do,
The fears of years, like a biting whip,
Had cut deep bloody grooves
Across our backs.

The Idea of Ancestry

I
Taped to the wall of my cell are 47 pictures: 47 black faces: my father, mother,
grandmothers (1 dead), grandfathers (both dead), brothers, sisters, uncles, aunts,
cousins (1st & 2nd), nieces, and nephews. They stare across the space at me
sprawling on my bunk. I know their dark eyes, they know mine. I know their style,
they know mine. I am all of them, they are all of me; they are farmers, I am a thief, I
am me, they are thee.

I have at one time or another been in love with my mother, 1 grandmother, 2 sisters, 2 aunts (1 went to the asylum), and 5 cousins. I am now in love with a 7 yr old niece (she sends me letters written in large block print, and her picture is the only one that smiles at me).

I have the same name as 1 grandfather, 3 cousins, 3 nephews, and 1 uncle. The uncle disappeared when he was 15, just took off and caught a freight (they say). He's discussed each year when the family has a reunion, he causes uneasiness in the clan, he is an empty space. My father's mother, who is 93 and who keeps the Family Bible with everybody's birth dates (and death dates) in it, always mentions him. There is no place in her Bible for "whereabouts unknown."

II
Each Fall the graves of my grandfathers call me, the brown hills and red gullies of Mississippi send out their electric messages, galvanizing my genes. Last yr/like a salmon quitting the cold ocean—leaping and bucking up his birthstream/I hitchhiked my way from L.A. with 16 caps in my pocket and a monkey on my back, and I almost kicked it with the kinfolks.

I walked barefoot in my grandmother's backyard/I smelled the old land and the woods/I sipped cornwhiskey from fruit jars with the men/ I flirted with the women/I had a ball till the caps ran out and my habit came down. That night I looked at my grandmother and split/my guts were screaming for junk/but I was almost contented/I had almost caught up with me.
The next day in Memphis I cracked a croaker's crib for a fix.

This yr there is a gray stone wall damming my stream, and when the falling leaves stir my genes, I pace my cell or flop on my bunk and stare at 47 black faces across the space. I am all of them, they are all of me, I am me, they are thee, and I have no sons to float in the space between.

Haiku

1.
Eastern guard tower
glints in sunset; convicts rest
like lizards on rocks.

2

The piano man
is stingy at 3 A.M.
his songs drop like plum.

3

Morning sun slants cell.
Drunks stagger like cripple flies
On jailhouse floor.

4

To write a blues song
is to regiment riots
and pluck gems from graves.

5

A bare pecan tree
slips a pencil shadow down
a moonlit snow slope.

6

The falling snow flakes
Cannot blunt the hard aches nor
Match the steel stillness.

7

Under moon shadows
A tall boy flashes knife and
Slices star bright ice.

8

In the August grass
Struck by the last rays of sun
The cracked teacup screams.

9

Making jazz swing in
Seventeen syllables AIN'T
No square poet's job.

Amiri Baraka

(b. 1934)

(See Amiri Baraka headnote in the Fiction section)

Preface to a
Twenty Volume Suicide Note

(For Kellie Jones, born 16 May 1959)

Lately, I've become accustomed to the way
The ground opens up and envelops me
Each time I go out to walk the dog.
Or the broad edged silly music the wind
Makes when I run for a bus ...

Things have come to that.

And now, each night I count the stars,
And each night I get the same number.
And when they will not come to be counted,
I count the holes they leave.

Nobody sings anymore.

And then last night, I tiptoed up
To my daughter's room and heard her
Talking to someone, and when I opened
The door, there was no one there ...
Only she on her knees, peeking into

Her own clasped hands.

Audre Lorde

(1934–1992)

The passionately outspoken Audre Lorde has been described by colleague Adrienne Rich as a poet who writes very much aware of her identity "as a Black woman, a mother, a daughter, a Lesbian, a feminist, a visionary...." A native of Harlem, Lorde was the daughter of Caribbean immigrants; painfully shy, she did not speak until she was five years old. It is perhaps because of this childhood experience that she has always championed "the oppressed, the disenfranchised silent people" in her writing.

*Lorde earned her bachelor's degree at Hunter College and obtained her master's in library science from Columbia University in 1961. She subsequently married and had two children. While working as head librarian at Town School Library in New York City, she began writing the poems for her first book, **The First Cities**, which was published in 1968 and which revealed her lesbianism openly. After her divorce in 1970, sixteen other publications followed, including the National Book Award nominee **From a Land Where Other People Live** (1973), **Coal** (1976), and the critically acclaimed **The Black Unicorn** (1978). The recipient of honorary doctorates from Hunter, Oberlin, and Haverford, Lorde was also known by her African name, Gamba Adisa, and her pseudonym, Rey Domini. In addition to her poetry, she published a "biomythography," **Zami: A New Spelling of My Name** (1983), and a collection of essays and speeches, **Sister Outsider** (1984). Perhaps her best-known work is the account of her triumph over breast cancer, **The Cancer Journals** (1980), the hopefulness of which was tragically countered by **A Burst of Light** (1988), the quietly despairing series of meditations on her relapse, this time with liver cancer. Three years after **A Burst of Light** won the National Book Award in 1989, Lorde died in Christiansted, St. Croix. Her last collection of poems, **The Marvellous Arithmetics of Distance**, was published posthumously in 1993. Lorde's most important legacy is her courageous transformation of personal pain into poetry, a project which would inspire the present generation of female poets to write with greater urgency and openness of expression.*

125th Street and Abomey

Head bent, walking through snow
I see you Seboulisa
printed inside the back of my head
like marks of the newly-wrapped akai
that kept my sleep fruitful in Dahomey
and I poured on the red earth in your honor
those ancient parts of me
most precious and least needed
my well-guarded past

the energy-eating secrets
I surrender to you as libation
mother, illuminate my offering
of old victories
over men over women over my selves
who has never before dared
to whistle into the night
take my fear of being alone
like my warrior sisters
who rode in defense of your queendom
disguised and apart
give me the woman strength
of tongue in this cold season.

Half earth and time splits us apart

Sonia Sanchez

(b. 1934)

"I write," says Sonia Sanchez, "to tell the truth about the black condition as I see it." In doing so, Sanchez brings to poetry her unerring ear for the rhythm, the musicality, and the raw emotion of the word spoken or sung out loud. Born Wilsonia Benita Driver in Birmingham, Alabama, Sanchez was the daughter of a musician who moved with her to Harlem in 1943. While Sanchez attended Hunter College, she was encouraged by the poet Louise Bogan to write. Her poetic voice was first heard as a member of the politically vocal Broadside Quarter of poets, whose other associates included Haki R. R. Madhubuti and Nikki Giovanni. In her first two volumes of poetry, **Homecoming** *(1969) and* **We a BaddDDD People** *(1970), Sanchez wrote about the harsh realism of urban life and about such inspirational figures as John Coltrane and Malcolm X. While a member of the Nation of Islam from 1972 to 1975, Sanchez published* **A Blue Book for Blue Black Magical Women** *(1973) and* **Love Poems** *(1973), the latter of which displays her talent for the haiku form.*

The author of more than twelve books, Sanchez was awarded the American Book Award from the Before Columbus Foundation for her poetry volume **homegirls & handgrenades** *(1984). In addition to garnering lush praise for her verse, Sanchez has also published numerous plays, edited two anthologies, and produced recordings of her poetry readings. True to her belief that "the poet is a creator of social values," Sanchez affirms the value of familial relationships and urges her readers to reject all forms of racism, sexism, classism, and ignorance.*

A Letter to Dr. Martin Luther King

DEAR Martin,

Great God, what a morning, Martin!

The sun is rolling in from faraway places. I watch it reaching out, circling these bare trees like some reverent lover. I have been standing still listening to the morning, and I hear your voice crouched near hills, rising from the mountain tops, breaking the circle of dawn.

You would have been 54 today.

As I point my face toward a new decade, Martin, I want you to know that the country still crowds the spirit. I want you to know that we still hear your footsteps setting out on a road cemented with black bones. I want you to know that the stuttering of guns could not stop your light from crashing against cathedrals chanting piety while hustling the world.

Great God, what a country, Martin!

The decade after your death docked like a spaceship on a new planet. Voyagers all we were. We were the aliens walking up the '70s, a holocaust people on the move looking out from dark eyes. A thirsty generation, circling the peaks of our country for more than a Pepsi taste. We were youngbloods, spinning hip syllables while saluting death in a country neutral with pain.

And our children saw the mirage of plenty spilling from capitalistic sands.

And they ran toward the desert.

And the gods of sand made them immune to words that strengthen the breast.

And they became scavengers walking on the earth.

And you can see them playing. Hide-and-go-seek robbers.

Native sons. Running on their knees. Reinventing slavery on

asphalt. Peeling their umbilical cords for a gold chain.

And you can see them on Times Square, in N.Y.C., Martin, selling 11-, 12-year-old, 13-, 14-year-old bodies to suburban forefathers.

And you can see them on Market Street in Philadelphia bobbing up bellywise, young fishes for old sharks.

And no cocks are crowing on those mean streets.

Great God, what a morning it'll be someday, Martin!

That decade fell like a stone on our eyes. Our movements. Rhythms. Loves. Books. Delivered us from the night, drove out the fears keeping some of us hoarse. New births knocking at the womb kept us walking.

We crossed the cities while a backlash of judges tried to turn us into moles with blackrobed words of reverse racism. But we knew. And our knowing was like a sister's embrace. We crossed the land where famine was fed in public. Where black stomachs exploded on the world's dais while men embalmed their eyes and tongues in gold. But we knew. And our knowing squatted from memory.

Sitting on our past, we watch the new decade dawning. These are strange days, Martin, when the color of freedom becomes disco fever; when soap operas populate our Zulu braids; as the world turns to the conservative right and general hospitals are closing in Black neighborhoods and the young and the restless are drugged by early morning reefer butts. And houses tremble.

There are dangerous days, Martin, when cowboy-riding presidents corral Blacks (and others) in a common crown of thorns; when nuclear-toting generals recite an alphabet of blood; when multinational corporations assassinate ancient cultures while inaugurating new civilizations. Comeout comeout wherever you are. Black country. Waiting to be born ...

But, Martin, on this, your 54th birthday—with all the reversals—we have learned that black is the beginning of everything.

it was black in the universe before the sun;

it was black in the mind before we opened our eyes;

it was black in the womb of our mother;

black is the beginning,
and if we are the beginning we will be forever.

Martin, I have learned too that fear is not a Black man or woman. Fear cannot disturb the length of those who struggle against material gains for self-aggrandizement. Fear cannot disturb the good of people who have moved to a meeting place where the pulse pounds out freedom and justice for the universe.

Now is the changing of the tides, Martin. You forecast it where leaves dance on the wings of man. Martin. Listen. On this your 54th year, listen and you will hear the earth delivering up curfews to the missionaries and assassins. Listen. And you will hear the tribal songs:

Ayeeee	*Ayooooo*	*Ayeee*	
Ayeeee	*Ayooooo*	*Ayeee*	
Malcolm ...			*Ke wa rona*
Robeson ...			*Ke wa rona*
Lumumba ...			*Ke wa rona*
Fannie Lou ...			*Ke wa rona*
Garvey ...			*Ke wa rona*
Johnbrown ...			*Ke wa rona*
Tubman ...			*Ke wa rona*
Mandela ...			*Ke wa rona*
(free Mandela,			
(free Mandela)			
Assata ...			*Ke wa rona*

As we go with you to the sun,
as we walk in the dawn, turn
our eyes
Eastward and let the prophecy
come true
and let the prophecy come true.
    Great God, Martin, what a
morning it will be!

Colleen J. McElroy

(b. 1936)

Colleen McElroy is a speech therapist, writer, and teacher of creative writing and third-world women's literature. Her six volumes of poetry include **Queen of the Ebony Isles**, *which was awarded the Before Columbus American Book Award in 1985,* **Bone Flames** *(1987), and* **What Madness Brought Me Here: New and Selected Poemes, 1968–1988** *(1990). She has also written numerous short stories which have been collected in* **Jesus and Fat Tuesday and Other Short Stories** *(1987) and in* **Driving Under the Cardboard Pines and Other Stories** *(1990). The recipient of grants from the National Endowment for the Arts, the Fulbright Foundation, and the Rockefeller Foundation, McElroy was designated a Jessie DuPont Distinguished Black Scholar in 1992, and she was awarded the Washington State Governor's Award for Fiction and Poetry in 1988. Her first book,* **Music from Home: Selected Poems** *(1976), won a Pushcart Prize in 1976. McElroy earned her bachelor's and master's degrees at Kansas State University and received her doctorate from the University of Washington, Seattle, where she is currently a professor of English.*

My Father's Wars

Once he followed simple rules
of casual strength,
summoned violence with the flick
of combat ribbon or hash mark;
now he forces a pulse into treasonous muscles
and commands soap opera villains.
He is camped in a world regimented
by glowing tubes,
his olive-black skin begging for the fire
of unlimited color.
In towns where he can follow
the orders of silence,
gunfights are replayed
in thirty-minute intervals
familiar as his stiff right arm
or the steel brace scaffolding his leg.

By midday the room is filled
with game shows and private eyes hurling
questions against all those who swear

their innocence;
his wife is in full retreat
and jumps when he answers in half-formed words
of single grunts deadly as shrapnel.
He need not remind her
he is always the hero;
the palms of his hands
are muddy with old battle lines.
He has fallen
heir to brutal days where he moves
battalions of enemies;
his mornings are shattered with harsh echoes
of their electronic voices.

Here he is on neutral ground
and need not struggle to capture words
he can no longer force his brain to master;
he plans his roster
and does not attend to his wife's
rapid-fire review of the neighbor's behavior.
He recalls too clearly the demarcation of blacks,
of Buffalo Soldier and 93rd Division.
By late afternoon he is seen rigidly
polishing his car in broad one-arm swipes,
its side windows and bumpers emblazoned
with stickers: US ARMY RETIRED REGULAR

Queen of the Ebony Isles

this old woman follows me from room to room
screams like my mother   angers like my child
teases me   rolling her tattooed hips forward
and out   steals my food   my name   my smile
when you call her I come running

when we were young and perfect
we danced together and oh we loved well
all the husbands and lovers   children and books

the sunshine and long walks on lonely nights
now she sucks me thin with her affairs

weaves romantic shadows over the windows
and curses my sober moods   kisses everyone
and insists on wearing red shoes
she hums the same songs over and over
something about love and centuries turning upon us

each time she changes the verse
shifting the words like cards in a game
of solitaire   the hot patent-leather colors
her mercurial moods as she flies about
her red heels glittering and clicking out of tune

she has seen too many comic strips
believes she's as deadly lovely
as Dragon Lady and Leopard Girl   I resist
but her limbs are daring   oiled for movement

without me who are you she asks   I am heavy
with silence   my hands are maps of broken lines
without her all sounds are hollow   I am numbed
cold and cannot read the cycles of the moon
even the sun   the sun cannot warm me

aloneness is a bad fiddle I play against my own
burning   bet your kinky muff she cackles knowing
the symptoms   then draped in feather boas
she drags me toward yet another lover   beckoning
with her brash reds pulsing like haunting violins

on midnight-blue nights she screams
into the eyes of the moon   twirling her war machine
like some Kamikaze pilot   her heat bakes my skin
even blacker   she's never happy unless we're falling
in love or hate   she grows younger while I

age and age   bandage wounds and tire too easily
she says   play the game   play the game she says
when I complain she says I'm hearing voices
she's hacked my rocking chair into firewood
I am the clown in all her dreams

when she looks into the mirror from my eyes
I want to float away unscathed
drift like patches of early morning fog
she thinks I stay because I love her
one day soon I'll move while she's sleeping

Lucille Clifton

(b. 1936)

"I grew up a well-loved child in a loving family," Lucille Clifton has written of her childhood in DePew, New York. Although the household was modest, Clifton's parents infused their love of literature into their children: Clifton's mother would read poetry to her four children, and her father would dramatically describe how his grandmother, who had been seized as a child and brought to America as a slave, walked eight hundred miles from New Orleans to Virginia—when she was only eight years old. This story, which Clifton relates in her autobiography, **Generations** *(1976), symbolizes for her the enduring quality of womanly love and compassion in times of adversity.*

A drama major at Howard University who began her studies in 1953, Clifton eventually finished her degree at Fredonia State Teachers' College. In 1969 she sent some of her work to the poet Robert Hayden, who encouraged her to publish. Clifton's first book, **Good Times** *(1969)—from which a popular seventies television series took its name—was received with wide critical acclaim. A poet noted for her technical prowess and her ability to evoke powerfully realistic urban images using simple language, Clifton often writes about the ways in which individuals react to their environment and deal with issues of faith. Twice nominated for the Pulitzer Prize, Clifton is also prolific: she has conceived and nurtured six children, twenty-one books of juvenile fiction, and seven volumes, including* **Good News About the Earth** *(1972),* **An Ordinary Woman** *(1974),* **Two-Headed Woman** *(1980),* **Next** *(1987), and* **Quilting** *(1991).*

Good Times

My Daddy has paid the rent
and the insurance man is gone
and the lights is back on
and my uncle Brud has hit
for one dollar straight
and they is good times
good times
good times

My mama has made bread
and Grampaw has come
and everybody is drunk
and dancing in the kitchen
and singing in the kitchen

oh these is good times
good times
good times

oh children think about the
good times

Homage to My Hips

these hips are big hips.
they need space to
move around in.
they don't fit into little
petty places. these hips
are free hips.
they don't like to be held back.
these hips have never been enslaved,
they go where they want to go
they do what they want to do.
these hips are mighty hips.
i have known them
to put a spell on a man and
spin him like a top!

Quilting

somewhere in the unknown world
a yellow eyed woman
sits with her daughter
quilting.

some other where
alchemists mumble over pots.
their chemistry stirs
into science. their science
freezes into stone.

in the unknown world
the woman
threading together her need
and her needle
nods toward the smiling girl
remember
this will keep us warm.

how does this poem end?
      do the daughters' daughters quilt?
      do the alchemists practice their tables?
      do the worlds continue spinning
      away from each other forever?

Ishmael Reed

(b. 1938)

   Assessing Ishmael Reed's prodigious literary output is no easy feat: he has written nine novels, including the highly praised **Mumbo Jumbo** *(1972), six books of poetry, one of which,* **Conjure: Selected Poems, 1963–1970** *(1972), was nominated for both the National Book Award and the Pulitzer Prize, and four collections of essays—not to mention the numerous publications and anthologies that he has edited and published. In addition, he has taught at such institutions as Columbia, Dartmouth, Harvard, the University of California Berkeley, and Yale, chaired numerous arts commissions, and founded several publishing and production companies, the best known being the Before Columbus Foundation. The recipient of numerous awards, Reed has been honored with a John Simon Guggenheim Memorial Foundation Award, an American Civil Liberties Award, a Pushcart Prize, and grants from the National Endowment for the Arts.*

   A prolific author, Reed is a gifted verbal gymnast whose range encompasses both poetry and prose. While his current reputation rests largely on his novels and essays, Reed launched his literary career as a poet, and he was an early participant in the Umbra Workshop, the influential Black writers' group that was one of the forces behind the flowering of Black American poetry. His widely anthologized poetry—most often selected from **Conjure, Chattanooga** *(1973) and* **A Secretary to the Spirits** *(1978)—uses satire and parody to expose the failings of both the victims and perpetrators of economic exploitation, racism, and sexism. Not just directed at social and political themes, Reed's poetic activism often takes issue with literary convention itself. Eschewing the constraints of "sonnets, iambic pentameter, ballads, and every possible Western gentleman's form," Reed is most interested in doing "what has never been done before."*

Railroad Bill, A Conjure Man

A Hoodoo Suite
Railroad Bill, a conjure man
Could change hisself to a tree
He could change hisself to a
Lake, a ram, he could be
What he wanted to be

When a man-hunt came he became
An old slave shouting boss
He went thataway. A toothless
Old slave standing next to a

Hog that laughed as they
Galloped away.
Would laugh as they galloped
Away

Railroad Bill was a conjure man
He could change hisself to a bird
He could change hisself to a brook
A hill he could be what he wanted
To be

One time old Bill changed hisself
To a dog and led a pack on his
Trail. He led the hounds around
And around. And laughed a-wagging
His tail. And laughed
A-wagging his tail

Morris Slater was from Escambia
County, he went to town a-toting
A rifle. When he left that
Day he was bounty.
Morris Slater was Railroad Bill
Morris Slater was Railroad Bill

Railroad Bill was an electrical
Man he could change hisself into
Watts. He could up his voltage
Whenever he pleased
He could, you bet he could
He could, you bet he could

Now look here boy hand over that
Gun, hand over it now not later
I needs my gun said Morris Slater
The man who was Railroad Bill
I'll shoot you dead you SOB
let me be whatever I please

The policeman persisted he just
Wouldn't listen and was buried the
Following eve. Was buried the
Following eve. Many dignitaries
Lots of speech-making.

Railroad Bill was a hunting man
Never had no trouble fetching game
He hid in the forest for those
Few years and lived like a natural
King. Whenever old Bill would
Need a new coat he'd sound out his
Friend the Panther. When Bill got
Tired of living off plants the
Farmers would give him some hens.
In swine-killing time the leavings of
Slaughter. They'd give Bill the
Leavings of slaughter. When he
needed love their fine Corinas
They'd lend old Bill their daughters

Railroad Bill was a conjure man he
Could change hisself to a song. He
Could change hisself to some blues
Some reds he could be what he wanted
To be

E. S. McMillan said he'd get old
Bill or turn in his silver star
Bill told the Sheriff you best
Leave me be said the outlaw from
Tombigbee. Leave me be warned
Bill in 1893

Down in Yellowhammer land
By the humming Chattahoochee
Where the cajun banjo pickers
Strum. In Keego, Volina, and

Astoreth they sing the song of
How come

Bill killed McMillan but wasn't
Willin rather reason than shoot
A villain. Rather reason than
Shoot McMillan

"Railroad Bill was the worst old coon
Killed McMillan by the light of the
Moon
Was looking for Railroad Bill
Was looking for Railroad Bill"

Railroad Bill was a gris-gris man
He could change hisself to a mask
A Ziba, a Zulu
A Zambia mask. A Zaramo
Doll as well
One with a necklace on it
A Zaramo doll made of wood

I'm bad, I'm bad said Leonard
McGowin. He'll be in hell and dead he
          Said in 1896
Shot old Bill at Tidmore's store
This was near Atmore that Bill was
          Killed in 1896.

He was buying candy for some children
Procuring sweets for the farmers' kids

Leonard McGowin and R. C. John as
Cowardly as they come. Sneaked up
On Bill while he wasn't lookin.
Ambushed old Railroad Bill
Ambushed the conjure man. Shot him
In the back. Blew his head off.

Well, lawmen came from miles around
All smiles the lawmen came.
They'd finally got rid of
Railroad Bill who could be what
He wanted to be.

Wasn't so the old folks claimed
From their shacks in the Wawbeek
Wood. That aint our Bill in that
old coffin, that aint our man
You killed. Our Bill is in the
Dogwood flower and in the grain
We eat
See that livestock grazing there
That Bull is Railroad Bill
The mean one over there near the
Fence, that one is Railroad Bill

Now Hollywood they's doing old
Bill they hired a teacher from
Yale. To treat and script and
Strip old Bill, this classics
Professor from Yale.
He'll take old Bill the conjure
Man and give him a-na-ly-sis. He'll
Put old Bill on a leather couch
And find out why he did it.
Why he stole the caboose and
Avoided nooses why Bill raised so
Much sand.

He'll say Bill had a complex
He'll say it was all due to Bill's
Mother. He'll be playing the
Dozens on Bill, this
Professor from Yale

They'll make old Bill a neurotic
Case these tycoons of the silver

Screen. They'll take their cue
From the teacher from Yale they
Gave the pile of green
A bicycle-riding dude from Yale
Who set Bill for the screen
Who set Bill for the screen

They'll shoot Bill zoom Bill and
Pan old Bill until he looks plain
Sick. Just like they did old Nat
The fox and tried to do Malik
Just like they did Jack Johnson
Just like they did Jack Johnson

But it wont work what these hacks
Will do, these manicured hacks from
Malibu cause the people will see
That aint our Bill but a haint of
The silver screen. A disembodied
Wish of a Yalie's dream

Our Bill is where the camellia
Grows and by the waterfalls. He's
Sleeping in a hundred trees and in
A hundred skies. That cumulus
That just went by that's Bill's
Old smiling face. He's having a joke
On Hollywood
He's on the varmint's case.

Railroad Bill was a wizard. And
His final trick was tame. Wasn't
Nothing to become some celluloid
And do in all the frames.

And how did he manage technology
And how did Bill get so modern?
He changed hisself to a production
Assistant and went to work with

The scissors.
While nobody looked he scissored
Old Bill he used the scissors.

Railroad Bill was a conjure man
He could change hisself to the end.
He could outwit the chase and throw
Off the scent he didn't care what
They sent. He didn't give a damn what
They sent.
Railroad Bill was a conjure man
Railroad Bill was a star he could change
Hisself to the sun, the moon
Railroad Bill was free
Railroad Bill was free

The Reactionary Poet

If you are a revolutionary
Then I must be a reactionary
For if you stand for the future
I have no choice but to
Be with the past

Bring back suspenders!
Bring back Mom!
Homemade ice cream
Picnics in the park
Flagpole sitting
Straw hats
Rent parties
Corn liquor
The banjo
Georgia quilts
Krazy Kat
Restock

The syncopation of
Fletcher Henderson
The Kiplingesque lines
of James Weldon Johnson
Black Eagle
Mickey Mouse
the Bach Family
Sunday School
Even Mayor La Guardia
Who read the comics
Is more appealing than
Your version of
What Lies Ahead
In your world of
Tomorrow Humor
Will be locked up and
The key thrown away
The public address system
Will pound out headaches
All day
Everybody will wear the same
Funny caps
And the same funny jackets
Enchantment will be found
Expendable, charm, a
Luxury
Love and kisses
A crime against the state
Duke Ellington will be
Ordered to write more marches
"For the people," naturally

If you are what's coming
I must be what's going

Make it by steamboat
I likes to take it real slow

Lake Bud

Lake Merritt is Bud Powell's piano
The sun tingles its waters
Snuff-jawed pelicans descend
tumbling over each other like
Bud's hands playing Tea For Two
or Two For Tea

Big Mac containers, tortilla chips, Baby Ruth
wrappers, bloated dead cats, milkshake
cups, and automobile tires
float on its surface
Seeing Lake Merritt this way is
like being unable to hear
Bud Powell at Birdland
Because people are talking
Clinking glasses of whiskey and
shouting
"Hey, waiter"

Michael S. Harper

(b. 1938)

A poet who is profoundly and creatively engaged with history, Michael Steven Harper has written on jazz musician John Coltrane, baseball player Jackie Robinson, abolitionist John Brown, and his own family members. Ranging freely over the past without worrying about lines of racial division, Harper draws upon the rhythm and music of the Black aesthetic—while alluding to such poets as Frost, Yeats, Hughes, and Auden—to reveal the unity of the past with the present and to solidify the essential kinship among all kinds of people. Noted for emphasizing that he is "both a Black poet and an American poet," Harper has explained in **Callaloo**, *"Most of my ancestors were black; I'm one of their trustees; the context is America; from an imaginative point of view the country's still up for grabs, in terms of definition. No one has a tight hold on its contours. It's open season on the language; the game is metaphor.... [W]e need some sophisticated truth-telling, and we should be selective. I don't apologize for loving Keats and Frost; I locate myself in their terrain as swiftly as I do in my own family, personal and extended. In literature you have to earn your way into the family archive; you do this by eloquence."*

Born in Brooklyn, Harper received his bachelor's and master's degrees from California State University. He attended the University of Iowa Writers' Workshop, graduating with an M.F.A in 1963. The promise of his critically acclaimed first book, **Dear John, Dear Coltrane** *(1970), was followed by* **History Is Your Own Heartbeat** *(1971), which was awarded the Black Academy of Arts and Letters Award. The recipient of various honors, including awards from the National Institute of Arts and Letters, the Guggenheim Foundation, the American Academy of Poets, and the National Endowment for the Arts, Harper was also nominated for the National Book Award for his collection* **Images of Kin: New and Selected Poems** *(1977). In addtion to his most recent volume of poetry,* **Healing Song for the Inner Ear** *(1985), he has edited the* **Collected Poems of Sterling Brown** *(1980) and an anthology of African American poetry,* **Every Shut Eye Ain't Asleep** *(1994). A contributor to numerous journals and periodicals, he has served on the editorial boards of* **TriQuarterly**, **Obsidian**, *and the* **Georgia Review**. *He has been a professor of English at Brown University since 1970.*

Blue Ruth: America

I am telling you this:
the tubes in your nose,
in the esophagus,
in the stomach;
the small balloon
attached to its end

is your bleeding gullet;
yellow in the canned
sunshine of gauze,
stitching, bedsores,
each tactoe cut
sewn back
is America:
I am telling you this:
history is your own heartbeat.

Time For Tyner: Folksong

The medley goes like this:
We sit in a bar in a draft
from the swinging door as
some patrons leave in wings
which are fleecelined coats
echoing with the ice cream
red of the police pick-up van;
an African instrument is not
the piano; an African village
is not the Both/And; an African
waltz is not in 3/4.

It strikes me in his juice
is the love of melody;
he thumbs the solo piano
in a wickerchair blues
tripping a rung tune in its
scratching black keys
shimmering in the plant light:
we are all covered green.

It is a political evening:
posters of Mingus and Trane,
recordings of Bud Powell,
Bird under false names,
the economy of Miles;
I take it in scratchpad

English in the waxed light
as his liner notes pucker
on our lips in this country
abiding and earless.

   for McCoy Tyner,
   and gone musicians

Primus St. John

(b. 1942)

*Born in New York, Primus St. John was raised by his West Indian grandparents, Balbena and Primus St. Louis. He was educated at the University of Maryland and Lewis and Clark College. His first volume of poetry, **Skins on the Earth**, was published in 1976. His other collections include **Love Is Not a Consolation; It is a Light** (1982) and **Dreamer** (1990). He has also edited an anthology, **Zero Makes Me Hungry**. A frequently anthologized poet, St. John has been awarded several grants from the National Endowment for the Arts, and he won the Oregon Book Award in 1991. At various points a bartender, waiter, gambler, civil servant, and construction worker, he has been teaching at Portland State University since 1973, where he is currently a professor. His most recent publication is **From Here We Speak** (1993), a collection of poetry by Northwest writers, which he edited with Ingrid Wendt.*

Worship

The storm god kneels down
And attends the river.
Men bring their boats in
With the same beat
That pumps their hearts.
When they are finished,
They stand in a huddle
And admire him.
Some think over the years
His hair has grown longer
And so magnificent
For the crowds that provide
The bones, and the blood,
And the breath of his life.

Joyce Carol Thomas

(b. 1942)

*Although she is best known for her prize-winning young adult novel series based on the character Abyssinia Jackson, Joyce Carol Thomas first established her reputation as a poet and dramatist in the San Francisco Bay area of California. In addition to such plays as **Ambrosia** (1978) and **Gospel Roots** (1981), she has written several volumes of poetry, including **Black Child** (1981) and **Poems for Grandmothers** (1990), and several novels, including **Water Girl** (1986) and **The Golden Pasture** (1986). Her work, which has been compared to the writings of Maya Angelou and Alice Walker, has been recognized with awards from the American Library Association, the Association of American Publishers, and the Before Columbus Foundation.*

*The bulk of Thomas's writing has been inspired by her childhood in Ponca City, Oklahoma, which is the setting of her first "Abyssinia" novel, **Marked by Fire** (1982). The fifth child in a family of nine, Thomas grew up in a deeply religious household surrounded by the sound of her father's singing and by the stories spun by her storytelling relatives during harvest time. Acknowledging the influence of her upbringing in her writing, Thomas has said that she uses her pen "to carve voices as technicolored as the voices of [her] father's radio quartet." Her most recent works include an anthology for young readers, **A Gathering of Flowers** (1990), a novel, **When the Nightingale Sings**, and a collection of poetry, **Brown Honey in Broomwheat Tea** (1993), which was selected as a 1994 Coretta Scott King Award Honor Book. The holder of a master's degree in education from Stanford University, Thomas is currently a professor of English at the University of Tennessee, where she has been teaching since 1989.*

Church Poem

The smell of sage
Mingles with burnt hair
And mama prepares Sunday dinner
On Saturday night
Chicken and dressing
Whisper promises
In the ear you hold
      with one hand
So your edges will be straight
As she does your hair

"Bend your head so you
      won't get burnt"

If you bend your head
on Saturday evening
Is it the same God
You bend to on Sunday morning?

Mama, how long do you
        beat the cake
Until your arms get too sore
        to beat some more
But Betty Crocker says 4 minutes
This ain' no white folks cake
        I aim to bake

Now line up with lye soap
and bath towel, pajamas,
Slippers and robes
Sink into the hot tin tub
Scrub off a week's worth
        of dirt
Grease down in cold cream
And warm your backside
By bubbling fire

On the Sabbath morning
The organ begins its descent
Choir comes rocking
Down the aisle
Like so many black notes
Stroking the carpet floor
And rising til rested by
Elsa's wanded finger
Sister Elsa's First Sunday
Sermon in song
Holding a phrase
Kneading it like new dough
        Turning it round
        in her head
Singing it different
        everytime
You can hear her shout

"Take me to the water"
Then adding in a whisper
"I know I got religion"
"I been baptized"

Did you feel the water
Riding over your feet
Sucking up the white garment
Kissing the breath
From your mouth
When she moaned
"I been baptized"

I saw a silent man leap
Straight up in the air
Sit down, then go striding
Across the room
To sit again
Understanding
The Disciplined Notes
in Undisciplined song
The unofficial concert

When does the melody end
And where does it begin?
YPWW, BYU, Bible Drill
In shiny legs
and velvet ribbons

Testimony service
And Brother Jackson shouted
Then danced the pewed benches
Front row to back
Because I held my breath
He never missed a step

It is the same God
You bend to now on Sunday morning
When does the melody end
And where does it begin?

Cecil M. Brown

(b. 1943)

*Born in North Carolina, Cecil Brown was educated at Columbia University and the University of Chicago. He received his Ph.D. in folklore from the University of California, Berkeley. His first novel, **The Life and Loves of Mr. Jiveass Nigger** (1969), relates the misadventures of George Washington as he travels around the world looking for "invisibility," and has inspired comparisons with the work of James Joyce and Ralph Ellison. His next novel, **Days Without Weather** (1982), is a satirical exposé of Hollywood. Based on his experience working as a screenwriter for Warner Brothers and Universal Studios during the seventies, **Days without Weather** won the American Book Award in 1984. Brown, who has taught at the University of Illinois, the University of California, Berkeley, and Merritt College, has also written several plays, including **The African Shades** and **The Gila Monster**. He most recently published **Coming Up Down Home: A Memoir of a Southern Childhood** (1993), and a book-length study of the mythical Stagolee is forthcoming from Harvard University Press.*

Excerpts From Stagolee's Memoirs

a poem (or record of the proceedings)

(1)
Now check this out, Jim
I was about to make love
To this German woman after
Dinner. (Her husband
Disappeared mysteriously after Eduscho coffee.)
Before I make love to a woman
I want to know where her husband is
She said, "Don't worry" and then
I saw him coming in with a noose
Back in the Mississippi world
I would have been afraid
While we watched, he hanged himself.

(2)
I was suddenly in a strange place
with lights and music—a jazz club
Berlin before the war!
The music is so beautiful,

Suddenly I can't remember anything.
The light is so bright! What's this?
What's going on here?
Now I see: the place is full of Nazis
I think I see Billy Lyon among them
The music has stopped, the fun is gone
Quickly, a fight breaks out.
      "How did you turn out after the war, darlin'?
I'm rushing over to the music stand
In the bright lights I read
The music notations engraved in brick gold
My great discovery suddenly we have lights
We have music (I wrote it down)
After the Nazis leave we can
Play jazz again!
      "The Americans are coming! The Americans
      are playing jazz!"

      "So the Americans came and so here we are?"
      "Would you like to dance?"

(3)
One of the musicians, an African friend
Invites me into his home
A German woman fixed us tea.
She was pregnant that I could plainly see
She was pregnant everywhere
Toes, eyes, eyelids, arms, neck
She brought the tea utilizing
A pregnant walk and smiled
A pregnant smile
When Africans get women pregnant
They are pregnant everywhere!
As if some of his fat cheeks
Had been blown through his lips
While they kissed in making love.

It was late at night
And except for a bit of light

The bar was dark
But in this bit of light
Sat the Beautiful One,
The Sibyl of Lübeck
       The freak of the week!

Alone, always alone, in her usual place
In this bit of light, arranging her
Usual things, arranging her personal
Items: her cigarette lighter, her
Cigarettes, her ashtray, the tall
Glass for the campari, her shot glass
For the whiskey, her tequila glass
For her tequila, her sunglasses from
Last year in Cyprus, only in her head now.
       Oh, the freak of the week!
In this bit of light, she is a movie star!
She is Marilyn Monroe, trapped in Berlin
Because the dollar is too high!
       Oh, the freak! The freak of the week!

I, Teriesea, sat in the darker corner
And watched it all, for I had seen it
All before.
I saw the Young MAN when he came in the door
       Oh, Staggerlee! O, tragic boy!

I saw him when he saw her
Sitting in that bit of light
I saw him not believing his eyes
(Cause I've been there before!)
I saw what he saw, He Who Is
Always looking for the Beautiful Ones
       Oh, Staggerlee! O, tragic boy!

She saw him seeing her
She was on to him from the start
       Go back home, Stagger, Don't break
       My heart!

Sibyl moved, rearranged a glass on
The bar, as though she was setting
Destiny into play, and then ceremoniously,
Took out a cigarette! And I saw the
Boy take out his cigarette lighter!
I saw him when he flicked the wick!
Under the large black hat she wore
Which had an extra brim, with this
small light, he saw her eyes, penetrating
Beams, that put him in a trance,
And that did the trick!
          Oh, Staggerlee, Go now, quick!
Then he saw her long white arms
Encased in long black gloves,
Like nylon stockings on long white thighs
          Staggerlee, dont let her take your
          life! Remember your three kids
          And your sickly wife!
(I was not surprised, I been there before)
She didnt ask his name (She never does)
Didnt ask his game (she's only interested in herself)
And she said only this, "Now can we go?"
          Oh, if only I could tell him!
          Oh, if only he would listen!
          Dont waste your money,
          Dont waste your time
          She'll smoke up your smoke
          Tell you an unfunny joke
          and wont give up the honey!
I raised my withered finger in protest
But one look foretold the rest, a look so bold
And out of the door with the beautiful one
Staggerlee began to stroll, singing
"I got the freak, I got the Beautiful one
          Freak of the Week! OH, Staggerlee
          If only I could tell him,
          If only he would listen!
I, too, have sung the bold song

And I, too, have drunk with the
Beautiful One until morn
I, too, have ridden in that saddle
Across the desert of time
And found my pleasure no crime
And have heard such screaming
That would wake up the dead.
(And sometimes the neighbors)
I have let sex go to my head.
I too have smoked cigarettes in bed.
But like all of the Beautiful ones,
She had one bold unforgettable regret
A man she loved had done her wrong
He didnt think she was so fine
She was in love with a man
Who didnt know how to grind
He had something else on his mind
He would give her the world
As soon as he won it. He's sick,
She's sick, and you?

      Oh, Staggerlee! I tried to tell you
      But you wouldnt listen
      Dont waste your time, dont waste
      Your money on the Beautiful one
      She's in love with a man who done
      Her wrong!
      I do not lie, there is no alibi
StaggerLee came in the bar
He asked the bartender for something strong
I think they call it Red Label
The look in his face had begun to sag,
But as soon as he opened his mouth,
He began to brag,
I had the great one, I had the freak
      If only I could tell him
      If only he would listen,
      All I would say, that was not the
      Freak of the Week
      That was the freak of the Day!

Nikki Giovanni

(b. 1943)

The prolific, personal, and passionate Nikki Giovanni was born Yolande Cornelia Giovanni in Knoxville, Tennessee. From her maternal grandmother, with whom she briefly lived as a teenager, Giovanni would inherit a fierce pride about her Black heritage, and this intensity of feeling pervades all of her work. While an undergraduate at Fisk University, Giovanni edited the campus literary magazine and participated in campus politics by founding a Civil Rights organization. After graduating magna cum laude with a degree in history in 1967, she briefly attended graduate school, meanwhile becoming increasingly involved with such writers and political activists as Amiri Baraka and H. Rap Brown. Her first two volumes of poetry, **Black Feeling, Black Talk** *(1967) and* **Black Judgment** *(1968), reflect this era of her life with their strident denunciations of social oppression and their militant demands for change. Not only did these books bring her national attention, they established her, along with Haki Madhubuti (Don L. Lee) and Sonia Sanchez, as one of the three leading figures of Black poetry at the time. After the birth of her son in 1969, however, Giovanni's poetry softened;* **Re: Creation** *(1970),* **My House** *(1972),* **The Women and the Men** *(1975), and* **Cotton Candy on a Rainy Day** *(1978) are generally considered representative of the more personal and introspective quality of her poetry in the seventies. More recently, Giovanni's poetry (***Those Who Ride the Night Winds***, 1983) has taken on a more global perspective as she writes about how humans connect with their environment and the universe through the imagination.*

Giovanni is a popular speaker and reader who has recorded several albums of her poetry readings: **Truth Is on Its Way** *(1972),* **The Way I Feel** *(1974), and* **The Poetry of Nikki Giovanni** *(1976), among others. An editorial board member of* **Artemis***, a widely published essayist, and a regular commentator for National Public Radio, Giovanni has been teaching at Virginia Polytechnic and State University since 1989. In addition to her widely anthologized poetry, she has published her autobiography,* **Gemini** *(1971), a collection of essays,* **Sacred Cows ... and Other Edibles** *(1988), and dialogues with James Baldwin and Margaret Walker. In 1988, two awards were established in her honor: McDonald's Literary Achievement Award and the Nikki Giovanni Award for young African American Storytellers, sponsored by the National Festival of Black Storytelling.*

Nikki-Rosa

Nikki Giovanni
childhood remembrances are always a drag
if you're Black
you always remember things like living in Woodlawn
with no inside toilet

and if you become famous or something
they never talk about how happy you were to have your mother
all to yourself and
how good the water felt when you got your bath from one of those
big tubs that folk in chicago barbecue in
and somehow when you talk about home
it never gets across how much you
understood their feelings
as the whole family attended meetings about Hollydale
and even though you remember
your biographers never understand
your father's pain as he sells his stock
and another dream goes
and though you're poor it isn't poverty that
concerns you
and though they fought a lot
it isn't your father's drinking that makes any difference
but only that everybody is together and you
and your sister have happy birthdays and very good christ-
masses and I really hope no white person ever has cause to
write about me because they never understand Black life
is Black wealth and they'll probably talk about my hard
childhood and never understand that all the while I was
quite happy

David Henderson

(b. 1943)

A self-styled "griot," poet, and storyteller, David Henderson was born in Harlem and educated at Hunter College and the New School for Social Research. One of the founders of **East Village Other***, he began writing as part of the influential "Umbra Poets" writers' group. Although he was strongly influenced by the Black nationalist movement of the sixties, he believes that the cultural diversity in the United States can serve as a source of unity: "There is such a powerful spectrum in Black art and thought that I don't think it should be tied down by racial ideology and politics." Henderson has written several collections of poetry, including* **Felix of the Silent Forest** *(1967),* **De Mayor of Harlem** *(1970), and* **The Low East** *(1980). His other works include the* **Umbra Anthology** *(1967) and a biography,* **Jimi Hendrix: Voodoo Child of the Aquarian Age** *(1978), which was condensed and reissued as* **'Scuse Me While I Kiss the Sky: The Life of Jimi Hendrix** *(1981). A frequently anthologized writer, he has contributed to numerous periodicals, including* **Paris Review**, **Essence**, **Poetry**, **New American Review**, *and the* **New York Times**.

Third Eye World

faces in the street
in the financial district or ghetto red zone
the anonymity of casual citizenry
faces of color recall another land
the mind can hear the music
pentatonic or percussive
and song
the relationship with the official language
everyone can sing

the soul of an egyptian chanteuse
of a bangkok songstress
or a mambo chorale in brazil
the ecological harmonies of the pygmies
or the subterranean hi-life of azania
namibia zimbabwe

third world and american
english speaking with roots in ancestral lands
(like everybody else, just about)
belonging to a new world
yet of an older world
but with the perception of both
keen in the mind
that gives another world
consciousness even cosmic
the third eye
astral base of the third world

Death of the Ice Queen

The Egyptians called what we know as America the 'Land of the Dead'

ICE QUEEN OF ICE
MOTHER OF MEN OF ICE
FROZEN EARTH
HOLLOW CORE

HE THE HOARY ONE
SITTING ATOP THE NORTH POLE
THE GOD OF ICE
SAW IT IN THE STARS
THROWING BOLTS OF LIGHTNING
CHURNING THE ATLANTIC MAD
CAUSING PEACEFUL SHIPS TO SINK AT ONCE
THE GOD OF ICE

MEAN WHILE
IN AMERICA SHE SKATES
ACROSS THE VALLEY OF THE SUN
COVERED WITH ICE
QUEEN OF THE ICE

THE WHITE BEARDED ONE IS THE FATHER OF TIME
HE WATCHES HER SILVER THIGHS
CHURN IN HER SHORT SKIRT

FUHERER/THE ASTROLOGER
HANDLES HIS SLIDE RULE LIKE A PHALLUS
HE WHISPERS IN THE EAR OF THE HOARY ONE
        aint she fine?
        aint she divine?
        she used to trick for Thor
        but they wasn't much trade in the North
        so she went west to hollywood

THE DECREE!
THERE WILL BE ETERNAL ICE ALL OVER THE PLANET/
HERE IN THE WEST SUNBATHING AND AFRO
        RHYTHMS ARE THE GREATEST THREAT
TO OUR WAY OF LIFE

DOCTOR CALIGARI RISES TO SPEAK
Dr. Caligari:
        The patterns of the Nibelingen are resumed
        in Nazi pageantry
APPLAUSE!

search for the hidden treasure
the grail containment of all wisdom
untold riches the Grimm brothers
initiate
the Golem of Rabbi Loew
returns to the womb

MEN OF THE STORM
BLOCKS OF ICE
THRU SNOW
HIGH STEPPING METHREDRINE BOOTS
ACROSS A CONTINENT

        they walked across europe and kicked ass
        they walked into Africa and kicked ass
        They walked into Russia
abandoned by the Ice god thru abundance of rationale
they were frozen to death

between the fires of the burning grain fields
and the american queen of ice

mutant extant
pure white race like ice
all four corners of the earth
requested by/Thor
request thunder
marching men frozen
marching men
frozen marching men
blocks of ice
they who believed in
the dictator of time
those who believed
the center of the earth frozen core
so likewise believed their women frozen and hollow
a super race of legend and lore
held together by frozen water
doctor frankenstein
and his family of golems ghouls and zombies
lost the war
and won the west

THE ICE QUEEN MEETS THE GRAND ORISHA/
SHOWDOWN IN LAND OF THE DEAD

the boogie man of fire
dancing thru dark vectors
jericho jamming upfront blues
woogie boogie

death of the ice queen
queen of ice
skating on top of ice bergs
across the top of the world
thule tide

her silver thighs gleam

twirling across plates of ice of silver
to become
impaled upon the northern most pole

> *island rising out of the torrent sea*
> *white and unscathed*
> *... above the passions of common form*
> *white mountain*
> *stable and superior*
> *moon*
>   *of the Hebrews*

THOSE WHO BELIEVE IN THE ETERNAL ICE
WOULD FREEZE THE WORLD TO PRESERVE HER
THEY BELIEVE THEMSELVES TO BE PERFECTLY
 CORRECT
THEY BELIEVED THEY KNEW WHAT HAD TO BE
THEY BELIEVED THEY KNEW WHAT HAD TO BE
 DONE
WHO BELIEVED THE EARTH COLD AND PRECISE
WHO BELIEVED A GOD COLD AND PRECISE

> *the old man*
> *hoary beard*
> *made his bid*
> *the ice was his friend*
> *would not do him wrong*
> *he checked the blue dog stars*
> *then tried to fuck fire*
> *with a frozen dick*

Quincy Troupe

(b. 1943)

Music, especially the blues, has profoundly influenced Quincy Troupe's writing—so much so that his best-known work is the best-selling autobiography of Miles Davis, **Miles, the Autobiography** (1989), written with the jazz legend himself as collaborator. "The blues," Troupe has said, is "a cultural form of historical importance, which produced jazz, which produced bebop, which produced rhythm and blues, which produced rock and roll." More than a jazz aficionado, however, Troupe is first a poet, one who was schooled by the sights and sounds of growing up in St. Louis the son of Quincy Troupe, Sr., Negro Baseball League great. The next stage of his education took place in Louisiana, where he earned a bachelor's degree in history and political science from Grambling College. Troupe then moved to California and earned a journalism degree at Los Angeles City College. It was while in Los Angeles that Troupe became heavily involved in the arts. Not only did he serve as the editor of a number of literary journals, he also directed several jazz festivals and taught creative writing for the Watts Writers' Movement.

Troupe's first collection of poetry, **Embryo Poems** (1971), was received with lavish praise, as were his subsequent volumes, **Snake-back Solos** (1978), which won the American Book Award in 1980, and the more recent **Weather Reports** (1991). In addition to his widely anthologized poetry, Troupe has edited a critically acclaimed homage to James Baldwin, **James Baldwin: The Legacy** (1989), and written a screenplay about Thelonious Monk. He coauthored with David Wolper **The Inside Story of TV's "Roots,"** and he has also published **Skulls Along the River** (1984). The recipient of grants from the National Endowment for the Arts, among others, Troupe is currently a professor of literature at the University of California in San Diego.

Poem for My Father

For Quincy T. Troupe, Sr.

father, it was an honor to be there, in the dugout
with you, the glory of great black men swinging their lives
as bats, at tiny white balls
burning in at unbelievable speeds, riding up & in & out
a curve breaking down wicked, like a ball falling off a table
moving away, snaking down, screwing its stitched magic
into chitling circuit air, its comma seams spinning
toward breakdown, dipping, like a hipster
bebopping a knee-dip stride, in the charlie parker forties

wrist curling, like a swan's neck
behind a slick black back
cupping an invisible ball of dreams

& you there, father, regal, as an african, obeah man
sculpted out of wood, from a sacred tree, of no name, no place, origin
thick branches branching down, into cherokee & someplace else lost
way back in africa, the sap running dry
crossing from north carolina into georgia, inside grandmother mary's
womb, where your mother had you in the violence of that red soil
ink blotter news, gone now, into blood graves
of american blues, sponging rococo
truth long gone as dinosaurs
the agent-oranged landscape of former names
absent of african polysyllables, dry husk consonants there
now, in their place, names, flat, as polluted rivers
& that guitar string smile always snaking across
some virulent, american, redneck's face
scorching, like atomic heat, mushrooming over nagasaki
& hiroshima, the fever blistered shadows of it all
inked, as etchings, into sizzled concrete

but you, there, father, through it all, a yardbird solo
riffing on bat & ball glory, breaking down the fabricated myths
of white major league legends, of who was better than who
beating them at their own crap game, with killer bats,
as bud powell swung his silence into beauty of a josh
gibson home run, skittering across piano keys of bleachers
shattering all manufactured legends up there in lights
struck out white knights, on the risky edge of amazement
awe, the miraculous truth sluicing through
steeped & disguised in the blues
confluencing, like the point at the cross
when a fastball hides itself up in a slider, curve
breaking down & away in a wicked, sly grin
curved & posed as an ass-scratching uncle tom, who
like old sachel paige delivering his famed hesitation pitch
before coming back with a hard, high, fast one, is slicker
sliding, & quicker than a professional hitman—

the deadliness of it all, the sudden strike
like that of the "brown bomber's" crossing right
of sugar ray robinson's, lightning, cobra bite

& you, there, father, through it all, catching rhythms of *chono
pozo* balls, drumming, like conga beats into your catcher's mitt
hard & fast as "cool papa" bell jumping into bed
before the lights went out

of the old, negro baseball league, a promise, you were
father, a harbinger, of shock waves, soon come

Lorenzo Thomas

(b. 1944)

Lorenzo Thomas, who was born in Panama, immigrated to the United States with his parents when he was four years old, eventually settling in New York City. He received his bachelor's degree from Queens College in 1967 and did graduate work at the Pratt Institute before going to Vietnam as a Naval Reservist. An early participant in the avant-garde literary experimentation of the Umbra Workshop, the Black Arts Theater, and the Poetry Project at Saint Marks, Thomas shaped his aesthetic sensibility in both Harlem and Greenwich Village. The result is an extremely visual poetry that is cinematic in its reference to and use of popular culture. His volumes of poetry include **A Visible Island** *(1967)*, **Fit Music** *(1972)*, **Framing the Sunrise** *(1975)*, and **Chances Are Few** *(1979)*. His selected poems have been published in **The Bathers: Selected Poems** *(1978)*. A devotee of the blues, Thomas has organized several music festivals in Texas and has served on the advisory board of KPFT-FM, Houston, since 1973. "I write poems," he has said, "because I can't sing." His work has been recognized with a National Endowment for the Arts Fellowship and a Poets Foundation Award, among others. Thomas currently lives and teaches in Houston, where he devotes much of his time to improving the quality of bilingual and multicultural education.

Wonders

I know where I belong
But I been away so long,
Sometimes I wonder.
Will I ever hear
Nostalgia In Times Square
Again, in some Avenue B
Break-in 1/2 bath flat
Will I ever sit
In the sun, high
On a Lenox terrace
And watch the Harlem River run
Away from the dope
And the crime
To the gray East
Again? And me
With some Boone's Farm
Meaning no harm

On anybody
Sitting there digging
Eddie Palmieri's
Hip conversations
With Obatala.
Sometimes I wonder
About that.
Or to be freak again
Be in the Bronx
Stoned on the rocks
As Jr Walker strains
His voice and young girls'
Credulity. Again?
Oh girls I can hear
Your radios
Loud at midnight
in Harlem or Elmhurst
And the smog a gangster
To ask proud
Stars to give it up
Girls
Check it out
When you pout and talk bad
Think of me, exiled
Almost a year
From the life
Lord, and don't be so hard
Sometimes I be distracted
When I think how you style.
Hold it. I sound like
The Browning of America!
I feel so simple to be thinking of Harlem
New York, the apple
Where we had our own Adam
And damn near all
The wonders of the world.

Historiography

1

The junkies loved Charles Parker and the sports
And the high living down looking ones
Those who loved music and terror and lames
Who in Bird's end would someday do better

As the Bird spiralled down in disaster
Before the TV set some would come to prefer
Out of the sadness of Mr Parker's absence
Never again hearing the strings of Longines

Symphonette

Without hearing the keening cry of the Bird
Nailed to the wax they adored. In the memories
And warmth of their bodies where our Bird
Stays chilly and gone. Every cat caught with

A white girl wailed Bird Lives! And the dopies
Who loved Charlie Parker made his memory live
Those who loved music made his memory live
And made the young ones never forget Bird

Was a junkie

2

We lost others to pain stardom and
Some starved at vicious banquets
Where they played until the victuals
Was gone. Pretty music. For all that
Pain. Who made the young ones remember the pain
And almost forget the dances? Who did that?
Steal the prints and the master and burn down
The hope of his rage when he raged? It was

Not only pain

There was beauty and longing. And Love run
Down like the cooling waters from heaven
And sweat off the shining black brow. Bird
Was thinking and singing. His only thought

Was a song. He saw the truth. And shout the Truth
Where Indiana was more than the dim streets of Gary
A hothouse of allegedly fruitful plain America
Some will never forgive the brother for that. Bird

Was a junkie

3
According to my records, there was something
More. There was space. Seeking. And mind
Bringing African control on the corny times
Of the tunes he would play. There was Space

And the Sun and the Stars he saw in his head
In the sky on the street and the ceilings
Of nightclubs and lounges as we sought to
Actually lounge trapped in the dull asylum

Of our own enslavements. But Bird *was* a junkie!

O. O. Gabugah

(b. 1945)

Born on Lincoln's birthday "in a taxicab right smack on 125th and Lenox in Harlem," O. O. Gabugah was originally christened Franklin Delano Watson. "O. O.," the outspoken and politically committed poet has said, "stands for Our Own, i.e., we need to do our own thing." Gabugah has published six volumes of poetry, the most popular of which is his **Slaughter the Pig & Git Yo'self Some Chit'lins***. He has also written several prize-winning plays, among which are* **Transistor Willie & Latrine Lil** *and* **Go All the Way Down & Come Up Shakin** *(a revolutionary Black musical). The recipient of a Federal Arts Agency grant as well as a Vanderbilt Fellowship, Gabugah has written a critical piece entitled* **Nothing Niggers Do Will Ever Please Me***, forthcoming later this year. Gabugah's writing,* **The Nation** *has commented, "draws strong folk poetry from the voice of a strident but vital revolutionary...." A militant advocate of the oral tradition, Gabugah never writes his own poems, choosing instead to dictate them to others.*

The Old O. O. Blues

Like right now it's the summertime
      and I'm so all alone
I gots to blow some fonky rhyme
      on my mental saxophone

Brother Trane done did his thang
      and so have Wes Montgomery,
both heavyweights in the music rang,
      now I'mo play my summary

It's lotsa yall that thank yall white
      (ought I say European?)
who thank Mozart and Bach's all right,
      denyin your Black bein

Well, honkyphiles, yall's day done come,
      I mean we gon clean house
and rid the earth of Oreo scum
      that put down Fats for Faust

This here's one for-real revolution
    where aint nobody playin
We intends to stop this cultural pollution
    Can yall git to what I'm sayin?

Sittin up there in your Dior gown
    and Pierre Cardin suit
downtown where all them devil clowns
    hang out and they aint poot!

We take the white man's bread and grants
    but do our own thang with it
while yall bees itchin to git in they pants
    and taint the true Black spirit

I'm blowin for Bird and Dinah and Billie,
    for Satch, Sam Cooke, and Otis,
for Clifford, Eric, and Trane outta Philly
    who split on moment's notice

Chump, you aint gon never change,
    your narrow ass is sankin
Like Watergate, your shit is strange
    You drownin while we thankin

My simple song might not have class
    but you cant listen with impunity
We ought to smash your bourgeois ass
    and by *we* I mean the Community!

A Poem for Players

Yes, theyll let you play,
let you play third base or fender bass,
let you play Harrah's Club or Shea Stadium

Theyll let you play
in a play anyway: Shakespeare,

Ionesco, Bullins, Baraka, or Genet,
only dont get down *too* much
& dont go gettin too uppity

Theyll let you play,
oh yes, on the radio, stereo,
even on the video, Ojays,
O.J. Simpson, only please dont stray
too far from your ghetto rodeo

Theyll let you be Satchmo,
theyll let you be Diz,
theyll let you be Romeo,
        or star in *The Wiz*
but you gots to remember that
        that's all there is

Oh, you can be a lawyer or a medico,
a well-briefcased executive with Texaco;
you can even get yourself hired, man,
to go teach *Ulysses* in Dublin, Ireland

Theyll let you play
so long as you dont play around,
so long as you play it hot or cool,
so long as you dont play down the blues
        theyll let you play in *Playboy, Playgirl,*
        or the *Amsterdam News*

Finally theyll let you play
politics if you dont get in the way
the way some of us did and had to be
iced by conspiracy, international mystery

Theyll let you play anybody but you,
that's pretty much what they will do

Nathaniel Mackey

(b. 1947)

Experimental writer Nathaniel Mackey has published two volumes of poetry,
Eroding Witness *(1985) and* **School of Udhra** *(1993), in addition to four chapbooks
of verse,* **Four for Trane** *(1978),* **Septet for the End of Time** *(1983),* **Outlandish**
(1992), and **Song of the Andoumboulou: 18-20** *(1994). He has been working on a
continuous epistolary novel,* **From a Broken Bottle Traces of Perfume Still
Emanate**, *since the early 1980s. The first volume,* **Bedouin Hornbook**, *appeared in
the* **Callaloo** *Fiction Series in 1986, and the second,* **Djbot Baghostus's Run**, *was
published in 1993. Based on the experiences of a composer/musician named N.,
these stories reveal the spiritual significance of music, especially jazz, to Mackey's
work. As he has said, "I'm post bebop. I come after Bud Powell and Bird and Monk
and so forth ... " In his writing, Mackey hopes to "go beyond schism" and "to come up
against the limitations of the self" so that he can "better understand the self."*

The co-editor of the literary magazine **Hambone**, *Mackey has also published an
anthology,* **Moment's Notice: Jazz in Poetry and Prose** *(co-edited with Art Lange,
1993) and a volume of critical essays,* **Discrepant Engagement: Dissonance, Cross-
Culturality, and Experimental Writing** *(1993). The Miami-born Mackey grew up in
California. He received his bachelor's degree from Princeton in 1969 and his
doctorate from Stanford University in 1975. Formerly a professor at the University of
Wisconsin-Madison and the University of Southern California, he has been a professor
of Literature at the University of California, Santa Cruz, since 1979.*

New and Old Gospel

The pillows wet our faces with
the sweat of soft
leaves. And ragmen pick
the city like
sores. The gummed
hush of watered
grasses fondles our
unrest, and as
outside the approach
of autumn whispers all our
unkept secrets
random winds unkink what hints your
hair lets fall. And
bits of rainbow wet the
floor and voices

punish what was silence.
As stars walk the
backs of our
heads our heads
turn waking.

while
we press for what at last
will be our lives
to be so,
soon.

George Barlow

(b. 1948)

A California native who was raised in Richmond, Virginia, George Barlow grew up enchanted by the rhythm and blues of James Brown and by the lyrics of such Motown greats as Smokey Robinson. He developed "a real excitement about language, about Black speech" while playing with his friends in the closely knit, all-Black community of Parkchester Village. Influenced by such colleagues as Michael Harper and Robert Hayden, and "especially by the inspirational poetry and life of Etheridge Knight," Barlow began writing poetry during the early 1970s. After graduating from California State University, Hayward, in 1970 with a bachelor's degree in English, Barlow attended the Writers' Workshop at the University of Iowa. He graduated with two degrees—a master's in fine arts and a master's in American studies.

Barlow's first book of poetry, Gabriel, was published in 1974, and his second collection, Gumbo, was selected by the Before Columbus Foundation for its 1981 National Poetry Series. He has been widely featured in several anthologies, including Every Shut Eye Ain't Asleep and In Search of Color Everywhere. He is currently an associate professor of American Studies and English at Grinnell College.

American Plethora: MacCorporate MacDream

come come come
to the mustard & the ketchup
the pickles & the lettuce
come together spares come to us
for macmiracles & maclife
we will macknowledge you
come   believe

follow our clown through
the great golden arches
he'll do it all for you
the world is a filet-o-fish
a quarter pounder with cheese
a raspberry shake with fries
believe believe

we'll mince the idea
with the onions

spread the notion
on the egg macmuffins
spike the coke with the vision

believe believe
that when you sleep
you'll macdream
when you wake
you'll macstretch
macbrush your teeth
& come come come
to us for coffee

james brown

kate smith
the carpenters
& fleetwood mac
will macsing our macsong

come come & sing
our rare destiny
look to the macfuture citizens
macsteak & maclobster
salt & pepper
for your souls
cream & sugar
for your bodies
come come come

we're the biggest macs
on earth
machustling the world
from the back seats
of our long black maccaddilacs

all all
all we macwant is maceverything

Ntozake Shange

(b. 1948)

Personally introduced to such greats as Charlie Parker, Miles Davis, W. E. B. Du Bois, and Josephine Baker—all friends of her prominent, highly cultured parents—Ntozake Shange was immersed in great African American art at a very young age. Born Paulette Williams in Trenton, New Jersey, to a surgeon and a psychiatric social worker/educator, Shange took her African names, Ntozake, "she who comes with her own things," and Shange, "she who walks with lion," in 1971.

After graduating from Barnard College in 1970 with honors in American Studies, Shange moved to Los Angeles, where she received her master's degree from the University of Southern California. She then moved to northern California where she became passionately involved with the feminist press and worked on developing an "Afrocentric" aesthetic for the stage and in her writing. All of these interests coalesced in her Broadway-produced **"choreopoem," for colored girls who have considered suicide/when the rainbow is enuf** *(1976). Originally published as a book of twenty poems in 1975, this dramatic and controversial staging of poetry, music, and dance won an Obie and an Outer Circle Critics Award and was also nominated for Tony, Emmy, and Grammy awards.*

An accomplished dancer, actress, and educator, Shange is also a poet-mother whose writing celebrates the strength of African American women. She writes, as she has said, "to make her daughter's dreams as real as her menses." Her other works include: **Nappy Edges** *(1978),* **Sassafrass** *(1976),* **Three Pieces** *(1981),* **Cypress and Indigo** *(1983),* **A Daughter's Geography** *(1983),* **See No Evil** *(1984), and* **Ridin' the Moon in Texas** *(1987).*

Rite-ing

for Oliver Lake, Anthony Davis, Michael Gregory Jackson, Paul Maddox, Leonard Jones and Buster Williams

hold til there is not a breath to
    take
and i take the moment
imagine how you would sing
    song
if you had a right to gold with
    wings & sing
i can be every whenever in a
    while
real melody is unpredictable

see yellow unicorn with blue
       horn
red unicorn with yellow mane
a great while gallopin stallion
       of a unicorn
braised in a sea of orange
3 emerald women rolling shells
       in aqua waves
nineteen quartermoons dance/
       the sea is orange
the sky is orange

a chinese lady fans
with the wings of a scarlet
       butterfly
two lovers hold the fantasy
two lovers undone
two lovers in paradise with a gun
a woman laughing from a redwood tree
eight faces smiling from the
       idol's secret space

an arched man with a
       saxophone
misted
the disappointing thing about
       artists is that they die

wednesday is the favored day
for blk people to kill themselves
not monday/not friday/not
       sunday
a holy day
but wednesday in the middle of
       so much
we have not paced it

my shawls are not bones i wrap
          myself in
not bones i throw to the dogs
my shawls are not bones to bury
          in palm roots
they are shrouds—my shawls
commemorate the old one
when she was young

hold til there is not a breath to
          take
and i take the moment
imagine how you would sing
          song
if you had a right to gold with
          wings & sing
i can be every whenever in a
          while
real melody is unpredictable
with spells to shed
if touched
with the manners of a witch the
          ivory unicorn watches
the sunrise/a sorrel
wades by the waterfall
a felon writes his poems
an ebony woman her arms filled
          with flowers
lays memory in the soil
that we might dig out
our beginnings

Kofi Natambu

(b. 1950)

   Kofi Natambu is a writer who also teaches cultural criticism, music history, film studies, political science, literary theory and criticism, and creative writing. He is currently a professor of Fine Arts and Social Sciences at the University of California, Irvine. The author of two books, **Intervals** *(1983) and* **The Melody Never Stops** *(1991), Natambu has two forthcoming volumes of critical essays entitled* **What Is an Aesthetic?** *and* **Rap & the Hiphop Aesthetic in the United States**. *His essays, criticism, and poetry have been featured in such anthologies as* **Cultures in Contention** *(1985),* **Black Popular Culture** *(1992),* **Moment's Notice: Jazz Poetry and Prose in America** *(1993), and* **Rap & Hip Hop Voices** *(1995). The founder and editor of a literary magazine,* **Solid Ground**, *Natambu has served as a curator for the Museum of African History in Detroit and is currently the president of the Miles Davis Society, a nonprofit cultural organization. He has lectured and taught at numerous colleges and universities including the California Institute of the Arts, Wayne State University, Empire State College (SUNY), the University of California, Santa Cruz, and Brooklyn College. A native of Detroit, Michigan, Natambu did his undergraduate and graduate work at Oakland University and the Massachusetts Institute of Technology.*

For Billie Holiday

Deep within her voice
there is a bird
& inside that bird is a song
& inside that song is a Light
& inside that light is a Joy
& inside that Joy is a Monster
& inside that Monster is a memory
& inside that memory is a celebration
& inside that celebration is a hunger
& inside that hunger is a dance
& inside that dance is a moan
& inside that moan is a majesty
& inside that majesty is a longing
& inside that longing is a history
& inside that history is a mystery
& inside that mystery is a fear
& inside that fear is a truth
& inside that truth is a passion

& inside that passion is a whisper
& inside that whisper is a wolf
& inside that wolf is a howl
& inside that howl is a lover
& inside that lover is an escape
& inside that escape is a regret
& inside that regret is a fantasy
& inside that fantasy is a death
& inside that death is a life
& inside that life is a woman
& inside that woman is a scream
& inside that scream is a release
& inside that release is a power
& inside that power is a voice
& inside that voice is a song
& inside that song is a singer
& inside that singer is a Holiday
& inside that Holiday is Billie

The History of Faces

(For Chuleenan)

Every Crevice speaks what cannot be spoken
Every eyelash remembers what you struggle to forget
Every crease in your forehead burns with desire
Every sullen smile smolders
Every aspect of your eyes enlightens & disturbs me
Every magnificent sadness reminds me
of the beauty no one else can see
Every dent in your jawline entices me
Every joy in your lips gives me a thrill
The history of faces
The evidence of truth
The map of reality

Rita Dove

(b. 1952)

1987 Pulitzer Prize recipient Rita Dove was born in Akron, Ohio, to Elvira and Ray Dove, who was a chemist. Revealing her considerable intellectual gifts early, Dove was named a 1970 Presidential Scholar as a high school senior. In 1973 she graduated summa cum laude *from Miami University and then went to Germany to study European literature as a Fulbright Fellow. Three years after receiving her M.F.A. from the prestigious Iowa Writers' Workshop in 1977, Dove published her first book of poetry,* **The Yellow House on the Corner**. *This book, along with her work in numerous anthologies and magazines, garnered for Dove a considerable amount of early critical acclaim that was soon justified by the award-winning* **Thomas and Beulah** *(1986), a collection of lyrical narratives based on her grandmother's and grandfather's migration from the South to the North. Her other works of poetry include* **Museum** *(1983) and* **Grace Notes** *(1989).*

*The youngest American writer ever to be appointed Poet Laureate (1993), Dove is also the first African American to receive that honor. Former professor at Arizona State University, Dove now teaches at the University of Virginia and serves as poetry consultant to the Library of Congress. While she has written short stories—***Fifth Sunday** *(1985) and* **Through the Ivory Gate** *(1992)—and a novel,* **The Darker Face of Earth** *(1993), Dove's literary abilities are best represented by her poems. Snatches of sound and bright bits of imagery are arranged with such precision that the poetic relationships she constructs—between consciousness and language, between objects and their environment—flicker in and out of probability, implausible in one moment, entirely believable in the next.*

Banneker

What did he do except lie
under a pear tree, wrapped in
a great cloak, and meditate
on the heavenly bodies?
Venerable, the good people of Baltimore
whispered, shocked and more than
a little afraid. After all it was said
he took to strong drink.
Why else would he stay out
under the stars all night
and why hadn't he married?

But who would want him! Neither
Ethiopian nor English, neither

lucky nor crazy, a capacious bird
humming as he penned in his mind
another enflamed letter
to President Jefferson—he imagined
the reply, polite and rhetorical.
Those who had been to Philadephia
reported the statue
of Benjamin Franklin
before the library

his very size and likeness.
A wife? No, thank you.
At dawn he milked
the cows, then went inside
and put on a pot to stew
while he slept. The clock
he whittled as a boy
still ran. Neighbors
woke him up
with warm bread and quilts.
At nightfall he took out
his rifle—a white-maned
figure stalking the darkened
breast of the Union—and
shot at the stars, and by chance
one went out. Had he killed?

I assure thee, my dear Sir!
Lowering his eyes to fields
sweet with the rot of spring, he could see
a government's domed city
rising from the morass and spreading
in a spiral of lights....

Canary

for Michael S. Harper

Billie Holiday's burned voice
had as many shadows as lights,
a mournful candelabra against a sleek piano,
the gardenia her signature under that ruined face.

(Now you're cooking, drummer to bass,
magic spoon, magic needle.
Take all day if you have to
with your mirror and your bracelet of song.)

Fact is, the invention of women under siege
has been to sharpen love in the service of myth.

If you can't be free, be a mystery.

Shape the lips to an *o*, say *a*.
That's *island.*

One word of Swedish has changed the whole neighborhood.
When I look up, the yellow house on the corner
is a galleon stranded in flowers. Around it

the wind. Even the high roar of a leaf-mulcher
could be the horn-blast from a ship
as it skirts the misted shoals.

We don't need much money to keep things going.
Families complete themselves
and refuse to budge from the present,
the present extends its glass forehead to sea
(backyard breezes, scattered cardinals)

and if, one evening, the house on the corner
took off over the marshland,
neither I nor my neighbor
would be amazed. Sometimes

a word is found so right it trembles
at the slightest explanation.
You start out with one thing, end
up with another, and nothing's
like it used to be, not even the future.

Cyrus Cassells

(b. 1958)

A poet who believes in "the purgative power of a lyrical approach to the world," Cyrus Cassells writes in order to confront history and to heal the present. His first book, **The Mud Actor** *(1982), is a triptych that deals with the possibility of reincarnation. In the first sequence, the poet assumes the voice of a child; in the second, he takes on the persona of a* fin-de-siécle *Frenchman named Henri Lecroix; and, in the final sequence, he becomes a bombing victim living in the aftermath of Hiroshima. Cassells, who was born in Delaware and educated at Stanford University and the Centro Fiorenza Italian Language School, has also written a short film,* **Bayok**, *on dancer Gregory Silva. His most recent book is* **Soul Make a Path Through Shouting** *(1994), a collection of poems that has been described by Rita Dove as a "most spectacular book.... Not only are the poems enthralling—they are heartfelt, with that largeness of spirit found in great literature, possessing a vision that embraces and enriches." A former creative writing fellow at Millay Colony and Yaddo, Cassells is also the recipient of grants from the Rockefeller Foundation, the National Endowment for the Arts, the Lannan Foundation, and others. In 1992 he received the Peter I. B. Lavan Younger Poets Award from the Academy of American Poets. He currently lives in Rome.*

Tokyo Story

Here, where the sun sets
in another language,
I will ride the jammed and fabulous trains—
      every night
washed in neon, baptized
in the endless bodies. The human waves
rise and foam, and the sights
sweep by like flames. Streets
flare, handkerchiefs: the subtle women
swab their throats.
In the aisle, no breeze
but a blast of gin: volcanoes rumble
in the *salarymen.*

Whisked through a summer
of glistening rails, I'm travelling
to come clean,
new luggage, new currency, a lust

for the holy changes, the sudden faces—given
and taken away, the objects found
in a crowded car:
an old postcard
of Mount Fuji, a trampled fan, perfumed and still
beautiful, a few grains of rice
scattered from a box lunch.
Here is the late sun filling the seats
beside me, brushing the small oval
of a child's face, the bald head
of a young Buddhist priest, as slowly
they drift into sleep.
In the rhythms of my vision,
a million wires, brushstrokes flashing from the ads
in fierce designs.
Everywhere the city—its maze, its blizzards
of boldly-colored signs and steel.

Tonight paper-lamp moon's up, tent's up;
          Shinjuku's lit
like a circus midway. In a park, three boys
are slapping their thighs
                              like drums, like drums,
          like drums
to the strains of American soul. Whatever
          the language,
I know I'm snaking
through Tokyo's streets,
dives, *pachenko* parlors, hives
of lights: I'm the *gaijin*
serpent of the sushi bars and trains—where I feel
          no breeze
but a blast of gin, volcanoes
of the *salarymen*...
                              The human waves
rise and foam, and the sights
sweep by like flames.
Here, where the sun sets
in another language,
I will ride the jammed and fabulous trains.

Carl Phillips

(b. 1959)

In 1992 Carl Phillips won a Morse Poetry Prize for his first collection of poetry, **In the Blood** *(1992). After earning his bachelor's degree at Harvard University and receiving his master's from the University of Massachusetts, Phillips taught high school Latin for eight years. He has since returned to Boston to pursue his doctoral studies in classical philology. The recipient of a fellowship from the Massachusetts Artists Foundation and a George Starbuck Fellowship from Boston University, Phillips has published in such journals as* **Ploughshares**, **Paris Review**, **Callaloo**, **Kenyon Review**, *and* **Agni**.

Africa Says

Before you arrive, forget
the landscape the novels are filled with,
the dull retro-colonial glamour
of the British Sudan, Tunis's babble,
the Fat Man, Fez, the avenue that is Khartoum.
Forget the three words you know of
this continent: *baraka, baksheesh,*
assassin, words like chipped knives thrust
into an isolation of sand and night.
These will get you only so far.

In the dreams of the first night,
Africa may seem just another body to
sleep with, a place where you can lay
your own broken equipment to rest.
You have leisure to wonder at her being
a woman, at your being disappointed
with this. You come around to asking
what became of her other four fingers,
how she operates on six alone,
You wipe the sweat from
your chest with her withered hand, raised
and two-fingered, observe, as she sleeps,
how that hand casts the perfect
jackal on a wall whose color
is the same as that of the country

itself, a dark, unpalatable thing who
uses a bulbed twig to paint her lids
in three parallel zones that meet and
kiss one another. She smells of henna or
attar, or rises steeped in musk that in other
women does not stray from between the legs.
She says she has no desire to return
thin lace the air, like memory,
languidly fingers. Whose wings,
like yours where sometimes I

What Myth Is

Not only what lasts, but what
applies over time also. So
maybe, for all my believing, not

you, on either count. Any more
than this hand where it falls,
here, on your body; or than

your body itself, however good
sometimes at making—even now,
in sleep—a point carry. Not

this morning, either, that under
the heat has already begun
failing; nor, for all their pre—

Ice Age glamour—what is
mythical, at best, not myth—
these Japanese beetles that off

and on hit the window's limp
screen, fall in, even. Who
make of the trees' leaves a

thin lace the air, like memory,
languidly fingers. Whose wings,

like yours where sometimes I

see them, flash broad, green—
gold in the sun, to say bronze.
When they fold them, it's hard

to believe they fly, ever.

Harryette Mullen

(b. 1960)

Harryette Mullen is the author of three books of poetry, **Tree Tall Woman** *(1981),* **Trimmings** *(1991), and* **S*ReRM**K*T** *(1992). A contributor to such journals as* **Hambone**, **Furnitures**, *and* **big allis**, *she has also been featured in* **The Culture of Sentiment**. *By incorporating the icons and images of mass commercial culture into her verse, Mullen transcends and transforms the ordinary "thing-ness" of television commercials, supermarkets, and cars. The* **Yale Review** *has described her work as "a small extravaganza" that is "feminist, black and bluesy … sexy, alto saxophony, breezy but bruisy, quasi-flacky and mock-floozy, chic and cheeky." Mullen, who currently teaches at Cornell University, received her doctorate from the University of California, Santa Cruz, in 1990.*

Mujer De Volcanes Y Terremotos

Mujer de volcanes y terremotos,
the earth rumbles when you walk.
Man-made structures fall flat
as your footsteps announce danger.
Avenging mountain,
your anger, sudden and hot as your love,
is cleansing the earth.
Explosive woman,
when you kiss the sky with fire,
your overflow of passion
will cauterize the wounds of earth.

Restless earth,
I hear you toss and turn
on sullen nights when I am parched with heat.
Insomniac volcano,
I hear you growling in the heavy darkness.
Mountain of reckless energy,
I feel your body humming with power.
I tremble with the earth,
receiving your ceaseless vibrations.

She Landed on the Moon

She'd studied the science of motion,
applied physics to the wound
and her loneliness healed.

She landed on the moon,
alert in the snarl of machinery,
shining in complex uniform
with zippers and pockets
for emergency secrets,
a helmet to pamper her head.

Earphones played a musical wind
where not a tree was blowing.
Computers drove her there,
calculating her fall.

She landed on a soft spot on the moon,
evading the stony heart.

Emerging into braver solitude,
she walked with new gravity,
her music parting the slow silence.

Elizabeth Alexander

(b. 1962)

Elizabeth Alexander was born in New York city and raised in Washington, D.C. She earned her bachelor's degree at Yale University, her master's at Boston University, and her doctorate at the University of Pennsylvania. A regular contributor to such prestigious journals as **Southern Review**, **American Poetry Review**, **Prairie Schooner**, *and* **Callaloo**, *Alexander published her first book of poems,* **The Venus Hottentot**, *in 1990. Her poetry, which has been hailed by critics as "dazzling," "lyrical," and "intellectual," tackles both public issues and private concerns. Alexander has also contributed phototext to Houston A. Baker's* **Workings of the Spirit** *(1991). She is currently a professor at the University of Chicago.*

The Venus Hottentot

1. CUVIER
Science, science, science!
Everything is beautiful

blown up beneath my glass.
Colors dazzle insect wings.

A drop of water swirls
like marble. Ordinary

crumbs become stalactites
set in perfect angles

of geometry I'd thought
impossible. Few will

ever see what I see
through this microscope.

Cranial measurements
crowd my notebook pages,

and I am moving closer,
close to how these numbers

signify aspects of
national character

Her genitalia
will float inside a labeled

pickling jar in the Musee
de l'Homme on a shelf
above Broca's brain:
"The Venus Hottentot."

Elegant facts await me.
Small things in this world are mine.

2.
There is unexpected sun today
in London, and the clouds that
most days sift into this cage
where I am working have dispersed.
I am a black cutout against
a captive blue sky, pivoting
nude so the paying audience
can view my naked buttocks.

I am called "Venus Hottentot."
I left Capetown with a promise
of revenue: half the profits
and my passage home: A boon!
Master's brother proposed the trip;
the magistrate granted me leave.
I would return to my family
a duchess, with watered-silk

dresses and money to grow food,
rouge and powders in glass pots,
silver scissors, a lorgnette,
voile and tulle instead of flax,

cerulean blue instead
of indigo. My brother would
devour sugar-studded non-
pareils, pale taffy, damask plums.

That was years ago. London's
circuses are florid and filthy,
swarming with cabbage-smelling
citizens who stare and query,
"Is it muscle? bone? or fat?"
My neighbor to the left is
The Sapient Pig, "The Only
Scholar of His Race." He plays

at cards, tells time and fortunes
by scraping his hooves. Behind
me is Prince Kar-mi, who arches
like a rubber tree and stares back
at the crowd from under the crook
of his knee. A professional
animal trainer shouts my cues.
There are singing mice here.

"The Ball of Duchess DuBarry":
In the engraving I lurch
toward the *belles dames*, mad-eyed, and
they swoon. Men in capes and pince-nez
shield them. Tassels dance at my hips.
In this newspaper lithograph
my buttocks are shown swollen
and luminous as a planet.

Monsieur Cuvier investigates
between my legs, poking, prodding,
sure of his hypothesis.
I half expect him to pull silk
scarves from inside me, paper poppies,
then a rabbit! He complains

at my scent and does not think
I comprehend, but I speak

English. I speak Dutch. I speak
a little French as well, and
languages Monsieur Cuvier
will never know have names.
Now I am bitter and now
I am sick. I eat brown bread,
drink rancid broth. I miss good sun,
miss Mother's *sadza*. My stomach

is frequently queasy from mutton
chops, pale potatoes, blood sausage.
I was certain that this would be
better than farm life. I am
the family entrepreneur!
But there are hours in every day
to conjur my imaginary
daughters, in banana skirts

and ostrich-feather fans.
Since my own genitals are public
I have made other parts private.
In my silence I possess
mouth, larynx, brain, in a single
gesture. I rub my hair
with lanolin, and pose in profile
like a painted Nubian

archer, imagining gold leaf
woven through my hair, and diamonds.
Observe the wordless Odalisque.
I have not forgotten my Xhosa
clicks. My flexible tongue
and healthy mouth bewilder
this man with his rotting teeth.
If he were to let me rise up

from this table, I'd spirit
his knives and cut out his black heart,
seal it with science fluid inside
a bell jar, place it on a low
shelf in a white man's museum
so the whole world could see
it was shriveled and hard,
geometric, deformed, unnatural.

Boston Year

My first week in Cambridge a car full of white boys
tried to run me off the road, and spit through the window,
open to ask directions. I was always asking directions
and always driving: to an Armenian market
in Watertown to buy figs and string cheese, apricots,
dark spices and olives from barrels, tubes of paste
with unreadable Arabic labels. I ate
stuffed grape leaves and watched my lips swell in the mirror.
The floors of my apartment would never come clean.
Whenever I saw other colored people
in bookshops, or museums, or cafeterias, I'd gasp,
smile shyly, but they'd disappear before I spoke.
What would I have said to them? Come with me? Take
me home? Are you my mother? No. I sat alone
in countless Chinese restaurants eating almond
cookies, sipping tea with spoons and spoons of sugar.
Popcorn and coffee was dinner. When I fainted
from migraine in the grocery store, a Portuguese
man above me mouthed: "No breakfast." He gave me
orange juice and chocolate bars. The color red
sprang into relief singing Wagner's *Walküre*.
Entire tribes gyrated and drummed in my head.
I learned the samba from a Brazilian man
so tiny, so festooned with glitter I was certain
that he slept inside a filigreed, Fabergé egg.
No one at the door: no salesmen, Mormons, meter
readers, exterminators, no Harriet Tubman,
no one. Red notes sounding in a grey trolley town.

Kool Moe Dee

(b. 1962)

Kool Moe Dee is not only the most enduring rap star of the "old school," he is also one of the most sophisticated lyricists in contemporary music. Born Mohandas Dewese in Harlem, Kool Moe Dee began performing at house parties as an original member of the Treacherous 3. The 3's first single, "New Rap Language," also became their first hit and led to a record contract in 1982 with Sugarhill Records. After producing a compilation of the group's hit singles, Moe took time off to graduate from SUNY at Old Westbury. He then signed on with Jive/RCA in order to produce his first platinum album, **How Ya Like Me Now?** *(1987). His next album,* **Knowledge is King***, won for him an invitation to sing at the Grammy Awards, and, in 1991, Moe won one of the prestigious awards for his collaborative efforts on "Back on the Block" with Quincy Jones. His other albums include* **Old School Flava** *(1994) and the solo effort* **Interlude** *(1994). Admitting that "it's hard to rock a party when you're lyrically advanced," Moe has nonetheless remained true to his belief that rap music should express communal strength, unity, and pride—rather than be self-serving, sensationalist, and exploitative. A rising film actor and screenwriter as well, Moe plays a leading role in Mario Van Peebles's film* **Panther** *(1995); in addition, one of his seven screenplays is currently in pre-production.*

Knowledge Is King

I'm not going—I'm gone
Up up up and away and I'm on
A higher plane with a brain with a flame
Feel the fire, desire the same
Knowledge and wisdom and understandin'
Possessed by God, transferred to man in
A script or a book or a scripture that looks
Like a biblical writing
Inviting a hook
Of a song, sing along with a strong subliminal
Message divesting all men from criminal
Acts of the devil, revealed and reveled
Designed to decline the mind to a lower level
Read the holy Qu'ran or the Bible
Because it's liable to be a revival
For the weak that seek power it'll bring
Insoluble power—
Knowledge is king

Now who wants some, come git it
A battle is a test of wits and I'm wit' it
Hard beats a torch and I lit it
Set the world on fire, I did it
Now that it feels good, I'm heatin' up
I feed off knowledge, and can't eat enough
'Cause knowledge is infinite, sucker's ain't into it
Ignorance is bliss and they're kin to it
They party and dance and they don't ever glance
At a book or a look for their mind to advance
Caught in the rut, chasin' butt
Tryin' to get a dollar or a nut
Evil feeds off a source of apathy
Weak in the mind and of course you have to be
Less than a man, more like a thing
No knowledge you're nothin'
Knowledge is king

My knowledge comes from a spiritual force
Stronger than any earthly source of
Propaganda, hype, or slander
I don't believe the hype, I understand the
Media dictates the mind and rotates
The way ya think
And syncopates slow pace
Brains can't maintain
Ascertain insipid inane crass vain
Insane lame traditions
All praise fame, positions
Want be a star, drive a big car
Live bourgeois and don't know who you are
Lost in the sauce and praisin' the dollar
Whether your faith is Christ or Allah
The knowledge of God'll teach one thing
The dollar is moot
Knowledge is king

My rhymes make a weak mind anorexic
You can't hang without slang so eject it
I've selected, rhymes for records
To affect the effect of a rhyme that left it
Hangin' like a pound
That can't come down
But ya hangin' in the brain so your brain is hell-bound
Lost and found by the serpent sound
What ya don't know can't hurt—that's profound
Absurd's a better word
An ignorant fool is a real kool nerd
Your pockets are fat with an empty head
Got a little bit of fame and a name and you're brain dead
You count your dollars so ya think you're in
Ya know how to count but ya don't know when
Add history today and it'll equal the future
Repetitive mistake because the brain ain't of the future

Need knowledge to understand the concept of sacrifice
But man don't understand so we have to fight
War, killin' people we never saw before
Some don't even know what they're killin' for
Followin' rulers instead of the prophets
The wicked can rule ya but knowledge can stop it
Souls can't be controlled 'cause it's a spiritual thing
But ya got to have knowledge
Knowledge is king
Knowledge is king

Kevin Young

(b. 1970)

One of the youngest recipients ever of the prestigious writing fellowship at Stanford University, Kevin Young was born in Lincoln, Nebraska. While an undergraduate at Harvard University, he won the Academy of American Poets Prize in 1989. After graduating in 1992, Young was a Wallace Stegner Fellow from 1992 to 1994. His first book, **Most Way Home***, won the National Poetry Series Award in 1994. A member of the Boston-based Dark Room Collective writers' group, Young is also cofounder of Fisted Pick Press, a publishing venture devoted to emerging and established Black writers. His work has appeared in various periodicals and journals including* **Callaloo**, **Agni**, **Kenyon Review**, *and* **Ploughshares***.*

The Preserving

Summers meant peeling: peaches,
pears, July, all carved up. August
was a tomato dropped
in boiling water, my skin coming
right off. And peas, Lord,
after shelling all summer, if I never
saw those green fingers again
it would be too soon. We'd also
make wine, gather up those peach
scraps, put them in jars & let them
turn. Trick was enough air.

Eating something boiled each meal,
my hair in coils by June first, Mama
could barely reel me in from the red
clay long enough to wrap my hair
with string. So tight
I couldn't think. But that was far
easier to take care of, lasted all
summer like ashy knees.
One Thanksgiving, while saying grace
we heard what sounded like a gunshot
ran to the back porch to see
peach glass everywhere. Someone
didn't give the jar enough room

to breathe. Only good thing
bout them saving days was knowing
they'd be over, that by Christmas
afternoons turned to cakes: coconut
yesterday, fruitcake today, fresh
cushaw pie to start tomorrow.
On Jesus' Day we'd go house
to house tasting each family's peach

DRAMA

Bill Harris

(b. 1941)

A graduate of Wayne State University in Michigan, Bill Harris has been an associate professor in the English department there since 1993. He was previously a curator at the Museum of African American History, and he has also worked for the New Federal Theater and Jazzmobile, both in New York City. The author of numerous plays that have seen over fifty productions, Harris published his first play in book form, **Stories About the Old Days,** *in 1990. Other examples of his work can be found in* **Roots and Blossoms: African American Plays for Today** *(1991), which features the play* **Up and Gone Again,** *and in* **New Plays for the Black Theatre** *(1989), which showcases* **Every Goodbye Ain't Gone.** *Harris has also written and produced* **Trick the Devil, Slave Narrative, The Society of Men,** *and* **No Use Crying,** *among others. A poet, music critic, and essayist as well, Harris has been published in various publications including* **Callaloo, Detroit Free Press Magazine, Black Scholar, Jazz Masters Journal,** *and* **Ontario Review.** *The recipient of a Paul Robeson Cultural Arts Award and a United Black Artists Award, he has been awarded grants from the Rockefeller Foundation, the Mary Roberts Rinehart Foundation, and the Metropolitan Life Foundation.*

He Who Endures

Characters:

Shields Green (Emperor) 23
Black, unpolished.

Henry Highland Garnet 25 in first scene
42 thereafter
Black, intense. Walks with aid of cane.

Frederick Douglass 26 in first scene
42 thereafter

Voice of Conductor (scene four)

John Brown 59
White. Intense. Fiery. Carries a Bible and a pike, a lance-like weapon with a metal spear head.

Performed in one act without intermission.

Prologue and

Prologue and Scene One

SHIELDS GREEN enters pushing a flatbed handcart with two lecturns which he places DOWN LEFT and DOWN RIGHT, and a WRITING TABLE which he places UP CENTER, then wheels truck to wings, as he speaks to AUDIENCE:)

Evening. I'm Emperor. You can call me Shields Green if that makes you more comfortable.

(taking AUDIENCE into his confidence)

That ain't my real name either, but—You see, I left South Carolina in sort of a hurry—

(pause as he soberly muses for a moment, then proceeds, anxious to get back to the matter at hand)

But I don't really even get into the story till later on. What I'm suppose to be telling you about is Mr. Frederick Douglass. I'm going start back in 18 and 43. That was the year of the

(with a certain pride at the event)

National Negro Convention. In Buffalo it was. A big debate amongst us Colored people. About which way we was going to go on

(deliberate)

the Slavery Question.

(DOUGLASS and GARNET enter and take their positions at the podia)

Now, in this next part I'm going to be the Chairman—Play-acting you understand.

(with possible hidden meaning)

Have to do that play-acting sometimes—Now, remember, it's 18 and 43. The National Negro Convention it was. In Buffalo, New York. That's Mr. Frederick Douglass. And there yonder is Reverend Henry Highland Garnet.

(moving into position UP STAGE)

GARNET: *(as if continuing speech)* Rise up brothers! Rise up together. Take your liberty. Now. Let the four million that you represent rise up together and end forever the days of oppression and inhumanity. Rise up and fight. Rise up together and take your liberty now! There is no other way.

(sound of enthusiastic applause of audience of less than 100)

DOUGLASS: *(in very subdued tones in contrast to GARNET)* Reverend Garnet, may I say that just our knowledge of your being the grandson of an African chief very much impresses us with your credentials as a most militant abolitionist. But if there were even a *shred* of doubt left in any of our minds as to your militancy, your clarion-call, which I dare say, is the most militant since David Walker's famous, or infamous, *Appeal*, it has removed any doubt.

(scattered supportive applause and laughter)

GARNET: Mr. Douglass, coming from so renowned a speaker, abolitionist and man of letters as yourself, I will take your last remarks as a compliment, since, judging by the tone of your retorts during our debate over the last three days, it is as close as I am going to get to a kind word from you.

(scattered supportive applause and laughter)

Douglass: *(conciliatory)* I simply suggest, as I have, and shall continue to, that the way to end slavery is to instill, in the hearts of men, a deep and wide-spread connection of the brotherhood of the human race; that God hath indeed made of one blood all nations of men for to dwell on all the face of the earth.

(applause)

GARNET: In other words, Moral Persuasion, or "moral 'suasion," as it is more widely known. Trying to persuade a slaver to give up his slaves is like trying to persuade a rattlesnake to quit biting you.

(dropping all pretense of civility and becoming progressively indignant)

> *Mr.* Douglass, may I respectfully remind you that we are all Negroes here. Must we be continually assaulted with the pacifist views of your white friend, Mr. William Lloyd Garrison?

DOUGLASS: You say Mr. Garrison is "my friend" as if that were an accusation.

GARNET: Is it an accusation to say that a house cat gives birth to kittens, not tigers?

DOUGLASS: *(more forceful)* Gentlemen, should Reverend Garnet's message reach our enslaved brethren, and its physically forceful advice be followed, its end result would be to bring about what we were called upon to avoid: further retaliatory hardship on our unfortunate counterparts.

GARNET: *(angry, above applause)* You say, "we," Mr. Douglass, but I believe when the vote of these some seventy delegates from some ten states is taken *we* will prove your Garrisonian moral 'suasion "we" is simply an intellectual's smoke screen. This is 1843, Mr. Douglass, 1843. The position of action we are about to propose here will mark the birth of a new day. It will be a day in which *we* take *our* destiny, *and* that of our enslaved brothers, into our *own* hands! I call for the vote now!

(applause, calls for VOTE, VOTE)

DOUGLASS: *(above shouts for VOTE)* At this point in our history, voluntary conversion is the way!

CHAIRMAN/GREEN: *(gavel-rapping the audience to order, then addressing them)* Gentlemen, you, as the most powerful Negro leaders in America, are about to decide the *united* policy we will preach and follow for the coming year. The choice is very distinct and clear; whether it be moral persuasion, as Mr. Frederick Douglass has so eloquently defended, or do we heed the equally eloquent Reverend Henry Garnet's call for active resistance? An aye vote is a vote *for* Mr. Douglass' proposal. The choice is yours. I remind you that each state delegation has a single vote. The majority rules. I will now call the role.

(begins reading names of the delegates as GARNET and DOUGLASS stand together, looking out at the audience as the vote is being taken)

GARNET: There is the possibility that my speech will be published. So no matter what happens here the word will get out.

DOUGLASS: You going to publish it yourself?

GARNET: John Brown, a wool merchant from Springfield, Massachusetts.

CLERK: *(calling roll)* Frederick Douglass.

DOUGLASS: Aye!

(to GARNET)

John Brown?

GARNET: Yes. A truly different kind of white man. Very religious. He believes in and *practices* the brotherhood of all men.

CLERK: Reverend Henry Garnet?

GARNET: Nay!

DOUGLASS: *(thinking and listening to the vote)* J.W. Loguen has also mentioned this John Brown to me. Says he's not afraid to say or do anything to end slavery.

GARNET: That describes John Brown to a T.

DOUGLASS: I would like to meet him. Can you arrange it?

GARNET: *(surprised and suspicious)* I can guarantee it'll be a waste of your time to try to convert him to your Garrison way of thought.

DOUGLASS: *(with deeper meaning)* If something is needed, and it does not exist, then it must be created.

GARNET: That is the reason there are slaves.

DOUGLASS: Exactly. And if it works one way it may work the other.

GARNET: *(puzzled)* I don't see—

GREEN/CHAIRMAN: The roll is complete. The vote is 19 ayes, 18 nays.

(the sound of YEAS and BOOS)

The ayes have it. Mr. Douglass's position has carried!

GARNET: *(bitter)* And the majority rules, even if one by a single vote. So rather than demanding our freedom, like men, the one vote majority decides it's better to continue to *appeal* to their *consciences* and their *hearts.*

GREEN/CHAIRMAN: *(brings his gavel down with a bang. End of first scene)*

DOUGLASS and GARNET exit.

GREEN: *(during the following, moves WRITING DESK into place and wheels in flat bed truck with BOOKS and PAPERS for DESK; COAT RACK to represent the sitting room of a rooming house. He wheels cart off when finished)* That was 1843. We pick it up again now, 16 years later, 18 and 59. By this here time I'd escaped from bondage. I works for Frederick Douglass now. He says I works *with* him—I ain't been with him too long, but long enough to know a few things about him, not understand, mind you, but *know.* He's on this New York State speaking tour: Syracuse, Buffalo, White Plains, like that there. The thing he's speaking about is slavery, but I reckon you knows that, slavery being *the* hot question in the country still—

(pauses, then laughs ironically)

Ain't this something, me, doing, what they calls it? A recitation. In front of a audience.

(realizing it)

Kind of like Mr. Douglass does, I guess. I reckon it's funniest 'cause I didn't never get no chance to recite in school. But I reckon you knows that too from the way I talks. My ol' "massa" figured, like all them "ol' massas" does, ain't no sense in learning the mule to waltz, 'cause you ain't going invite him to the dance no how.

(with mischievous grin)

I'm dancing pretty much to my own tune now, since I left ol' massa fiddling around down in the South Carolina where he's at.

(pause as he soberly muses for a moment, then proceeds, serious again, admonishing himself)

What I ought to be telling about is what's been going on lately, like I was doing before I got all off the track. Let's see now. It's 18 and 59, August—

(losing concentration again)

—Right now, back home, they done with planting. They chopping and plowing now—

(suddenly back to the subject)

I reckon the biggest thing's happen lately, far's the Race be concerned, was the

(pronouncing distinctly)

the *Dred Scott* decision. Back in '57 it was. We still feeling the effects of that one, and *will be*. Now Mr. Douglass he could explain it better than me, with a lot fancier words and *oratory*.

(proud of his use of the word)

But see now, the Su-preme Court ruled that *no* Negro had *no* rights that *no* white man had to respect!

(pause)

No sir. No white man. Well, it didn't excite me none, 'cause that wasn't telling me nothing about the way they felt, legal or otherwise, that I hadn't knowed all along. White fellow name of Abraham Lincoln, a senator from Illinois said: "A house divided against itself cannot stand." He say, "I believe this government cannot endure permanently half slave and half free." Um hum, that's what he say. But then later on, this same white fellow turns around and says, "There is a physical difference between the ... races which I believe will forever forbid the two races living together on terms of ... equality."

(pause)

On the floor of the senate in Washington, D.C., the representative from South Carolina beat the senator from Massachusetts near about senseless after an argument over slavery. You see some white folks takes they slavery real serious. Around the same time a slave woman named Margaret Garner escaped from Kentucky with her childrens. Made it far as Ohio. But when it looked like she could see for sure they was going to be recaptured she was able to kill one of her babies sos it wouldn't have to go back to slavery.

(pause)

And after she was recaptured and was on her way back, she drowned another of her youngins,

(pause)

and herself. See, Negroes takes slavery just as serious as white folks. Right now, on the open market, I'd bring in around about $800.

(bitterly ironic)

Yeah, good buck field hand like me.

(softer and more bitter)

$800.

(pause)

Makes me about equal to a woman with a child. They cost you around the same thing, you see. Which means right now I got at least $800 worth of *goods* on a plantation in Charleston. My wife and child waiting on me to one way or another come and free them.

(looks off into the wings. Pause. Then as if acquiescing to some unspoken request)

I know you're here to be amused and not accused,

(pause)

and if I was to really go and do it up proper and give you a good picture of what's happening in the country I'd have them bring a slave out here.

(Douglass enters and stands UP CENTER. He is extremely tired)

GREEN: *(continuing, unaware of DOUGLASS)* A man whose family been sold off somewhere; or a woman whose husband run off and she don't know where or if he'll be able to get back to get her; just bring them out and let you look at them—They wouldn't have to recite or nothing—

(Douglas begins to stir. Puts his things down and look around)

GREEN: *(continuing)* But yall here more to be amused than accused, so—

DOUGLASS: *(calling, but not directly to GREEN)* Shields?

GREEN: *(pulled back from his thoughts looks around, then to audience)* Oh, there's Mr. Douglass now. I didn't even hear him come in.

(moves to join DOUGLASS)

    Evening.

DOUGLASS: Evening, Shields.

(GREEN helps him remove coat)

    Didn't I see you standing in the back of the hall during my speech?

GREEN: *(more cheerful)* Cheering and clapping right along with all the rest.

DOUGLASS: Why'd you leave? We could have come back together.

GREEN: I knowed that afterwards you was going to have to stand around and shake them white folks hands, and let them congratulate you for your fine speech. Wouldn't be nothing for me to do—

DOUGLASS: I don't find that part of it any more enjoyable than you.

GREEN: No sir. I got to congratulate you on that speech myself! You was sure giving it to them slavers.

DOUGLASS: Another speech, another convert. One by one by one. Figuring one or two a speech, and I'm talking about actual converts to the cause of abolition, not just those intelligent ones who nod in polite agreement, or the emotional ones who applaud; then leave, as indifferent to the slaves' plight as before; but, one or two *actual* converts, who will contribute substantial amounts of money and try to convert others. Figuring one or two of those per speech at say three, maybe four speeches a week, how long do yo think it will take to convert enough to actually gain a majority in order to *do* something about slavery?

GREEN: Well, ciphering ain't my strong suit, but, sometimes, just a few of the right folks in the right place, and at the right time can do a heap more than a whole bunch of the wrong ones.

DOUGLASS: The problem's not with them,

(the point and the cause of his mood)

    but with me. Here in New York white men politely call me *Mister* Douglass. But how much of what I say or they do keeps the lash off a Mississippi slave's back?

GREEN: If it's fiery white mens you be wanting at your meetings, I reckon you better hire John Brown to follow you around.

(a joke between them)

> And poor as he stay he'd probably do it for next to nothing.

DOUGLASS: *(not joining in the spirit of GREEN's comment. Searching through papers on table)* If John Brown could manage money he'd be the most valuable white abolitionist in the country.

(finding the paper he wants)

> While I was looking for some notes for that Buffalo speech I found this. On the 5th of December, in the year of our lord 1800 and 46, I delivered into the hands of Hugh Auld the sum of 711 dollars and 66 cents, and he gave me this piece of paper. This declares that he gives up the *legal right* he had to own me for life. This worn and fragile piece of paper is all that actually stands between me being a slave and a free man.

GREEN: *(after pause)* No sir, you wrong there. That piece of paper ain't got nothing to do with it.

(indicating his head)

> It's what you got up here that makes you,

(with pride)

> you and me both, freemens. 'Cause my mind was free long time before my body escaped and got itself free too. Just like you was free in your head before you ever got that piece of paper.

DOUGLASS: I've been at it for so many years. I've written and spoken and fought, and what have I really changed? There are still slaves!

GREEN: But everybody was a slave still ain't. Me for one. And you well know it. I was way down there in Charleston and I heard about

(with reverence)

> Frederick Douglass, and all you'd done. Working off your slavery and learning all you know, and raising yourself up. And just hearing about you was probably the last little something I needed to make me take off.

DOUGLASS: But what about the rest? What about your wife?

(heavy, embarrassed pause)

> Is it my destiny to just free one at a time, just as I convert one at a time?

GREEN: You just tired from all this traveling and speeching. That's all. Maybe you ought to turn in a little early. You needs your rest just like normal folks.

DOUGLASS: *(calm, but weary)* Henry Garnet was there this evening. He said he's going to stop by for a visit.

GREEN: *(chuckling)* Yall don't be visiting, yall be dueling, if you ask me.

DOUGLASS: We do have a loud friendship.

GREEN: *(to audience)* Yes sir, and he another one of them fiery ones. Him and John Brown! I'm just glad I'm on the same side they is.

(chuckling, to DOUGLASS)

> A loud friendship sure covers it. And it don't do a bit more good for yall to argue then it do to ask a blind mule to set a dinner table. 'Cause neither one of yall ain't about to change your way of thinking.

DOUGLASS: *(serious)* I have changed, Shields. Over the years. And Garnet's had a great deal to do with it. Much more then I admit to him—or to myself.

GREEN: *(coming forward to audience, leaving DOUGLASS at writing table)* I reckon we done all changed. He done changed me since I been knowing him. But he was talking about Henry Garnet prodding him along. Prodding ain't the word for it. Reverend Garnet is school educated, but still hot as fox fire. One thing Reverend Garnet did do for him though, he got him together with Captain John Brown. Back in 1847 Mr. Douglass told me. I believe Captain Brown was still in the wool business then. He been in and out of so many different businesses so many different time I reckon he don't even recollect all of them hisself.

(remembering)

> Another thing, too,

(HENRY GARNET enters behind him and moves to the "door")

John Brown wanted to publish Reverend Garnet's speech, the one he made at the National Negro Convention, you remember, back in '43.

(GARNET knocks on the "door")

GREEN: *(calling back to DOUGLASS)* I'll get it.

(to audience)

I don't think Captain Brown never did publish it though. He couldn't hardly get together enough money to feed all them 10 or 15 children of his, let alone be publishing no speeches.

(as he turns to go to door)

That were some speech though.

(he moves to door)

Reverend Garnet, I were just thinking about you.

GARNET: Emperor. How are you?

DOUGLASS: *(joins them)* Henry.

GARNET: Sorry about visiting so late. But I wanted to see you before I leave.

DOUGLASS: Leave?

GARNET: *(slightly embarrassed)* I sail for England with the morning tide.

DOUGLASS: *(surprised)* You deserting us too, Henry?

GARNET: *(angry flash)* It is not desertion.

(Pause, then calmer)

But I just couldn't pass up the chance of talking with you, for a little while anyway. Your opposition to everything I propose makes me examine what I believe. It also makes me firmer in my belief. In a roundabout way I thank you for that.

DOUGLASS: Think nothing of it.

GARNET: And I also want to compliment you.

DOUGLASS: *(mock surprise) You* compliment *me?*

GARNET: *(with a somewhat mocking tone)* You were preaching out there this evening, Frederick. That wasn't a milk and honey pacifist plea you were serving them, no sir! You sounded like me 8 or 9 years ago.

(laughing, good natured)

Another testament to the faith in the Lord and the power of prayer.

(into mock sermon delivery)

And I prayed! Yes I did. I prayed day and night for Brother Douglass to shake off the shackles of William Lloyd Garrison's non-resistance philosophy. And it took a whole lot of knee bending and hand wringing, but praise the Lord if it didn't pay off. The man orating tonight had fire in his eyes, and his heart, his words. He was calling for the slaves to *rise up*, he was calling for action! I heard about the speeches you've been making lately. I couldn't believe it! Not Frederick Douglass. Calling for *active resistance*? It's some impostor, I said, some wolf in sheep's clothing. But tonight I saw and heard for myself.

DOUGLASS: *(matter of fact)* Time comes for everything—

GARNET: *(serious)* You're devious, Fred. We all are, each in our way. We have to be, but you, Fred—You know what has always bothered me about you?

DOUGLASS: I knew the praise couldn't last too long. So, tell me, Henry. I am very interested in knowing.

GARNET: I have never been able to decide just how far you'll go.

DOUGLASS: Where? When?

GARNET: Whenever. Wherever.

DOUGLASS: Are you referring to a specific thing?

GARNET: I'm referring to every inconsistency and contradiction about you. Over the years, no matter how eloquent you were in defense of your position, or in opposition to mine, I have never been sure that what you were saying was what you were truly thinking and feeling. I have never understood or trusted you, Fred.

DOUGLASS: I apologize, Henry. I'm just a simple, uneducated man trying to do what I can to bring about the downfall of slavery.

GARNET: In the final hour, where will you be? In the vanguard where you belong, or erecting a pacifist stonewall across the path of our ultimate progress?

DOUGLASS: I will be where I am truly needed most.

GARNET: You are so good with words.

DOUGLASS: No better than you.

GARNET: I only hope that you don't forget there are weapons other than words.

DOUGLASS: My memories of slavery will not allow me to forget—

GARNET: *(defensive)* My mother was a slave ...

DOUGLASS: And your grandfather an African chief ...

GARNET: *(continuing)* ... she was killed trying to escape with me when I was a child. This lame leg of mine is a result of that effort.

DOUGLASS: And you grew up free.

GARNET: Yes!

DOUGLASS: And now you are going to further distance yourself.

(pointed)

How long did you say you were staying in England?

GARNET: *(aggressively defensive)* Here in America you have a platform. I only have a pulpit. Just as in slavery, once you've been branded a bad nigger they do whatever they can to keep you from speaking to your brothers. If I had access to the varied platforms and newspapers as you, there would be no need to go off. But, as you well know, I do not have your opportunities.

DOUGLASS: You overestimate my position.

GARNET: You have greater access and you must take greater advantage.

(a confession, like son to father)

You know how I have seen myself in relation to you?

(trying to joke, but it doesn't come off)

As a small mongrel pup nipping at your heels, hoping to keep you moving in the right direction.

DOUGLASS: More a huge pedigree loping along your own path, dragging
me along behind you.

(sincere)

We were all changed by the speech you made at the convention years
ago. Even those of us who were compelled to speak against it.
Because what you were proposing, at that time, would have
endangered the life of every Negro in America.

GARNET: *(outburst)* I always felt the majority of the free Negroes against
me were more worried about the retaliation of the white folks on
them personally than on the slaves!

*(in his passion GARNET puts too much pressure on his injured leg and almost
falls. Douglass leaps forward to help him but GARNET has caught himself and
waves DOUGLASS away)*

There's too much personal passion in my presentation. And I'm too
strange a mixture to be detached, or admired for what I am. If I
were like you; the knowledge without the education, I'd be better
off. But then you've beat me to that, too. And now that I'm leaving
for England I won't be here to nip at your heels, and that worries
me.

DOUGLASS: Of all our differences I think the major one is our beliefs as to
the role that we as "leaders" are supposed to play. I don't believe
you can expect anyone to follow you if you are so far ahead of them
they cannot see you. Neither are you likely to have much luck at
getting behind them and pushing. But if you have a way you think
they should go, go with them, beside them, amongst them,
suggesting.

(a pause as they face each other)

GARNET: *(extends his hand to DOUGLASS)* Fred.

DOUGLASS: *(shaking GARNET's hand)* Henry.

GARNET: *(turning to GREEN)* Emperor.

GREEN: *(shaking GARNET's hand)* Good luck to you over there in England.

GARNET: And you try to keep him on the right track.

GREEN: *(nods, pause, to audience)* What to do, and how to do it?

GARNET: *(to DOUGLASS)* I'd still rather be in my position than yours. At least I can say what I feel, even if not in as many places as I'd like.

(pause. He exits)

GREEN: *(to audience as DOUGLASS turns away)* Reverend Garnet went on to England,

(begins changing position of props so they represent DOUGLASS' study in his own home)

and we go on to Ithaca and Utica and Niagara Falls and Jamestown and a couple weeks later we finally get on back home to Rochester.

DOUGLASS: *(turning back, preoccupied)* Until then I had always thought it was easier for Henry, because he was always so decisive. But it's not easy for any of us, is it, Shields?

GREEN: No, it ain't.

DOUGLASS: Sometimes there are so many issues and conditions and contradictions and voices stacked up in my mind … Like bales of cotton waiting their turn on the scale. I have to sit very quietly, for a very long time, before I can hear Frederick Douglass' voice, or remember what *he* thinks or wants or feels. He has a conscience, too.

GREEN: *(sly and unsympathetic)* You could always go back to being a slave, let the white man decide everything for you.

DOUGLASS: Sometimes I wish I had the courage to take a step so bold and daring it would shock even Henry Garnet. Some action, no matter how violent, that would be the clarion call signalling to every Negro, slave and free, that the hour to strike had come.

GREEN: I reckon if something like that was possible we'd all be willing to sacrifice ourselves to it.

DOUGLASS: But I think I've become too devious for that. I suppose that's what the little bit of learning has done to me. Perhaps that is what Henry meant.

GREEN: So, till then you just got to keep on plowing along, row by row. Just like any other man.

DOUGLASS: You're just about the only somebody, outside my wife, who knows something of me other than this cursed ability to speak; or knows or cares there are certain foods which give me gas, that my back hurts if I stand too long—

GREEN: *(moving forward to audience)* Sometime after Reverend Garnet sailed for England, Oliver Brown, one of John Brown's sons, come on his father's business. The message was that Commander Brown had to see me and Mr. Douglass post haste. And if I knows of any man more full of anti-slavery passion than Reverend Garnet, it's John Brown. Slavery and Old Testament religion. If you ain't had your supper, don't get John Brown to talking on neither one of them subjects, or you'll starve to death.

(during the following, moves the writing desk UP CENTER, and arranges the two chairs side by side DOWN RIGHT as if they were a train seat)

The message was that Commander Brown is headquartered in Chambersburg, Pennsylvania, which is right up the line from Harper's Ferry, Maryland. You know, down yonder where the government got that army arsenal. Oliver tells us that the old man's getting ready to put his guerilla plan into operation from there.

(Douglas enters)

GREEN: *(continuing)* Says he got 19 men, but didn't want to do nothing till me and Douglass gets there. *(calling to Douglass as he exits)* I'll meet you after your speech. We can go to the depot from there.

DOUGLASS: *(faces audience and begins to make speech)* We must be treated as men, responsible to our enslaved brethren. The fight must be especially persistent and constant. It is obvious the slavers are running scared, the sheer desperation of their every act only serves our cause. The battle will open on fronts we never dreamed possible. No front, no method must go untried!

GREEN: *(enters with luggage. We hear train sounds)* We got to hurry we going catch that train to Chambersburg.

(they move to "train seats," sit)

GREEN: *(after riding a moment)* What you think?

DOUGLASS: *(musing)* Oliver was rather vague about specifics—but that is John Brown's nature not to reveal any more than he has to—

GREEN: How long we planning on being in Chambersburg?

DOUGLASS: Long enough to witness the launching of his plan.

GREEN: You think it's really going to happen after all this time?

DOUGLASS: *(not a direct answer)* I remember the first time I met John Brown. I thought to myself—I thought, here is this man, this John Brown, this *white man*, radical enough to say and do things with more latitude than any Negro.

(direct, as if a confession)

So I encouraged him.

(quoting himself)

If you need something, and it does not exist, you create it.

GREEN: *(probing)* Commander Brown's talked to me before—and he wants me to join his guerilla band.

DOUGLASS: *(wanting to say more)* You told me.

GREEN: *(wanting to say more)* I just wanted to make sure you knowed.

DOUGLASS: Are you going to join him?

GREEN: Depends, I reckon. On the way things go—

VOICE OF CONDUCTOR: Chambersburg! Chambersburg! Next stop Chambersburg!

(Douglass exits with suitcases)

GREEN: *(moves to audience, deep in thought)*—It depends—"No front, no method must go untried," he said one time. *(Still deep in thought, he moves to get the writing desk and chair which he places UP RIGHT. Continuing, somewhat brighter)*

Well. He we is. And I don't mind telling you that now we're here I'm getting to feel more and more uneasy about the whole thing. Gideon's Army: 19 men and boys. Don't nobody here seem to know nothing for certain sure. Some been here a couple months already. They jokes about coming ready to die for the cause, and is now bout ready to die from boredom. To keep down suspicion amongst the neighbors here abouts they ain't allowed outside lessen it's dark. Their nightly recreation is mostly the Old Man, Captain Brown, reading a chapter from the Old Testament.

(by this point the desk and chair are in place and he has moved to the audience)

(JOHN BROWN enters unnoticed by DOUGLASS. He is carrying a Bible and a pike. He sits at the desk and pantomimes writing a letter)

GREEN: *(continues above)* Only womens is the Old Man's 16-year-old daughter, and Oliver's wife. That situation don't do no whole lot for the men's morale neither—All in all, they plenty restless to kick off this little introductory raid, let the slavers know that the firm of John Brown and his Army of Liberation is open for business.

(he exits)

BROWN: *(reading over his letter)* Dear wife: We are safe and in good spirits.

The land hereabouts is truly an example of God's majesty. Often, while walking along in the fields, I am so overwhelmed by the beauty of it all, a hymn bursts from my throat, or I am compelled to bow my head and give thanks that he has chosen me to aid in the deliverance of the slaves. Since we have been here there have been at least four violent deaths involving our brothers in bondage.

This cause, and it alone, is great enough to separate us. Be strong in the faith. Pay no heed to my detractors. There are no failures or fools in the service of the Lord. And it is by the grace of God that I am here.

Tell each of the children to be good obedient children.

God be with you till we meet again—whether in Heaven, or on this earth.

(writing a line)

Your affectionate husband.

(satisfied, he stands)

Green enters, they embrace and exchange warm ad-libbed greetings)

BROWN: Praise the Lord, you're here.

GREEN: Yes sir.

BROWN: Where is Douglass?

GREEN: Over yonder cleaning up a bit from the trip. He'll be here directly.

BROWN: I praised the Lord for sending us such a man as Frederick Douglass. Over the years I watched him with a kind of reverent awe. I read his writings as faithfully as I read Judges. He not only gave me faith in the political beliefs I already had, but awakened me to innumerable others. He's a great man, Emperor.

GREEN: You is too, Captain Brown.

(to audience)

Not once or twice, but 30 times!, anti-free soldiers and the like has drawed a bead on him, some as close as me to him right now, and tried to bust a cap in him. And there ain't no scratch on him nowheres!

BROWN: Some of the boys here are beginning to have their doubts. I know the talk—It is not only my detractors that say I'm just an obsessed fanatic, and will fail at this, too.

GREEN: Maybe it's the crazy ones *ain't* obsessed with slavery's destruction.

BROWN: The instant I met him the *true* plan for the emancipation of the slaves formulated itself in my mind. He was a divine inspiration sent to me. I knew how I would use him.

GREEN: Use him?

BROWN: The final piece. The hub around which the whole wheel revolves. His presence will insure the success of this final thrust.

GREEN: You say *true* plan, and *final thrust*. I don't see—

BROWN: "Whatsoever thy hand findeth to do, do it with thy might!" What my plan involves is the wiping out of slavery. We are going to capture Harper's Ferry!

GREEN: *(shocked. Speechless for a moment he turns to audience)* The original plan Douglass knows about was guerilla style.

DOUGLASS: *(enters, as if they have been in heated conversation)* To take about 25 trained guerrillas, black and white, up in the Allegheny Mountains of Virginia and Maryland.

GREEN: Have raiding parties go down onto the various plantations thereabouts.

DOUGLASS: Encouraging slaves to escape.

GREEN: Strike and fall back into the mountains, which is like natural forts, where one man is worth a hundred trying to attack him.

DOUGLASS: The slaves can join with the guerrillas or flee to Canada.

GREEN: *(to BROWN)* Till after a while, you said, so many slaves'd run off till it'd deal slavery a serious blow, even if it didn't end it, you said.

BROWN: That was over 12 years ago.

DOUGLASS: It is suicide.

GREEN: *(to audience)* I can't believe the United States Army just going to let us walk in there and take over their little arsenal town.

DOUGLASS: Self-defense you said. In case you were attacked.

BROWN: We have no other choice. We never had any other choice.

GREEN: It don't make no more sense than a mustache on a mule—

BROWN: We must act now!

GREEN: *(to audience)* And yet, I listens to him, and he looks at me with them wild eyes of his and—

BROWN: The north is apathetic and the south set in its ways.

DOUGLASS: *(over)* You'll be walking straight into an armed fortress.

BROWN: *(continuing)* Elsewhere there is neutrality and silence.

DOUGLASS: *(continuing)* Trying to take over an Army Arsenal will be leading these simple farm boys into slaughter.

BROWN: *(continuing)*: "I have seen the affliction of my people ... and have heard their cry by reason of their taskmasters; for I know their sorrows."

DOUGLASS: *(over)* When did you conceive this plan?

BROWN: (continuing) "And I am come down to deliver them ... and to bring them up out of that land ... unto a land flowing with milk and honey ... "

DOUGLASS: Just now, or a month ago, a year, or from the beginning?

BROWN: What does that matter?

DOUGLAS: When?

BROWN: This plan was given to me.

"And I will punish the world for their evil, and the wicked for their iniquity; and I will cause the arrogance of the proud to cease, and will lay low the haughtiness of the terrible." It is the will of God. You are as responsible for it as I am.

DOUGLASS: Are you listening to yourself? You are proposing an attack, *war!*, on the government of the United States of America. It can't succeed! It will only rouse the nation *against* our cause.

BROWN: Your speeches lately have said you were ready to welcome any new method of attack on slavery. Were those your words or were you misquoted?

DOUGLASS: *(avoiding answering)* Causing such unrest and confusion so as to disrupt the economics of slavery. That was the plan.

BROWN: That was then, this is now.

DOUGLASS: It was a good plan then and now. Hurting a man's pocketbook gets his attention faster than anything else you can do.

BROWN: I know first hand what it does to a man to break him financially!

DOUGLASS: This is not about you! The slaves here about don't even know you, or your chances of succeeding.

BROWN: They know you. Your job is to tell them!, to remove those doubts. They will rise up if *you* tell them!

DOUGLASS: I can not lend my voice to an action which will lead to the certain slaughter of my people.

BROWN: Through the years you encouraged me to be bolder and bolder. This plan is the result! With you a part of it it can't fail.

DOUGLASS: Even if you capture the Ferry, the Army won't allow you to hold it long enough for word to spread.

BROWN: Hostages will be taken. I'll threaten to kill them if the Army moves in. That will give you time to get word out.

DOUGLASS: What does the government care about *hostages*? They won't allow you to hold a government facility, I don't care *who* your hostages are. It's insanity.

BROWN: What I *do* will attract them, what you *say* will control them. It is the perfect plan, my friend. I anticipated this moment from the beginning: we, shoulder to shoulder, facing the coming challenge *together*. Like brothers.

DOUGLASS: We are not brothers in life, nor could we ever be in death.

BROWN: I used you as my gauge. Now even *you* have begun to speak about revolt. All I am asking is that you say it now, but not in some safe little Northern town hall, but from here, in the eye of the storm.

DOUGLASS: I will not allow you to use me as you see fit. Go back to your original plan, John.

BROWN: The destruction of slavery is *my duty*, as it should be for *every* man capable of raising his hand or voice against it. *I* hate slavery with all my heart.

DOUGLASS: You have no corner on that market. But your hatred must be intellectual at best. You have never been a slave. I have.

BROWN: It would appear that you are the intellectual, unwilling to lift the sword against the enemies of mankind and the Lord. Instead you hang back, mincing words like the mealy-mouthed abolitionists, intellectualizing in their ivory towers. Why aren't you willing to rush forward, like the mad man they say I am?

DOUGLASS: I have one goal in life; not revenge, or financial gain, or personal glorification. It is to see each and every slave free!

BROWN: It pains me to say this, but you are an opportunist; a straw man bending which ever way the wind blows.

DOUGLASS: I suggest to you that there are two kinds of insurrection: one that results in the liberty of its participants, and another which leads to their death. I haven't suffered as I have to die a martyr swinging from a federal hangman's noose.

BROWN: *(recanting, almost a plea)* But you believe in the rightness, the righteousness of it?

DOUGLASS: What I believe is not the point. The issue here is larger than one man, or emotion, or philosophy.

BROWN: And have you appointed yourself the great overseer of the anti-slavery movement?

DOUGLASS: It appointed me.

BROWN: And is it written that an appointed leader can't fight.

DOUGLASS: *(with rising anger)* I *have* fought. Not for a cause, but for my life. I fought Edward Covey, a slave breaker in Maryland, for-my-life. A gang of ship workers in Boston who did not want me to work on their crew, I fought them for-my-life. I fought a train crew who were trying to eject me from a coach seat I had paid for. Again, I fought them for-my-life. A mob in Indiana who did not care for a speech I made, made me fight them for my life.

BROWN: Now you won't even fight with words. Is that the price a Negro pays for becoming a free man?

DOUGLASS: When I was a slave I fought the way a slave fights, out of the necessity of it. But I am no longer a slave, I am now better able to choose my battles; the prerogative of an, at least partially, free man.

BROWN: It will never be more necessary than now.

DOUGLASS: *(ironic laugh)* How paradoxical my situation is: even though I am called a free man, I am not able to do as *I* will. I envy you, John Brown, you have the luxury of singlemindedness. You can determine a self-righteous goal and march as straight to it as your abilities and convictions will take you, the consequences be damned. My position as a "leader" will not allow me to encourage my people on a course of action which may very well leave them in even worse shape than before they began it.

BROWN: You do not think I am free? Do you? That I act only for myself? That I am not a slave to a master; have not tasted His lash and scorn; pleaded to Him for mercy?

(pause, then calmer)

Frederick, we should be making final plans, not arguing.

DOUGLASS: Damn it, John, don't you see that now, here, in this place, this time, is simply not right?

BROWN: *(beginning calmly but rising in intensity throughout)* Do you understand atonement? The sins of the world can be atoned for by my *embracing* the sinner's punishment? During all of my 59 years on this, God's earth, there has not been a single year during which I or my family has not smarted mightily under the rod of our Heavenly

Father. The thing I wanted most in my early life—to study for the ministry—was denied me because of an eye infection. My *entire life* has been one of denial, and fighting the work of the devil, and of atonement. A constant struggle with sickness, poverty, lawsuits; bankruptcies, death. My mother's death; my first wife's death; 9 children in childhood. In 1837 4 died within 12 days. 3 years ago in Kansas another son, a *man* of 26, was cut down in the service of the Lord by an anti-abolitionist's bullet. I have been called a fanatic, a criminal, madman, business cheat, horse thief, an intolerant Bible-quoting bully, and a self-righteous, cold-blooded killer. And do you think I have been made to suffer all that for nothing!? There is hypocrisy in the houses of the Lord, the halls of government, and throughout the land. The times and the situation compel the implementation of my plan. The Almighty, in His infinite wisdom, has provided me with the mission and the means to bring about the emancipation of the enslaved. I am his instrument! "Vengeance is mine," saith the Lord!

DOUGLASS: *(direct)* Do you think you can win at Harper's Ferry?

BROWN: *(moving away from DOUGLASS to GREEN)* To win—Do we, as mortals, always understand what that means? Jesus sacrificed himself for the greater good, giving all it was possible to give. And you are willing to tell me He did not win?

DOUGLASS: Tell me you honestly believe you can succeed.

BROWN: With you beside me, yes! Now tell me you don't believe in the rightness of what is going to take place there in Harper's Ferry.

DOUGLASS: No.

BROWN: Because you can't allow yourself to? Or because you truly do not believe the justness of it?

(Douglas is silent)

BROWN: What if it was just you by yourself? Without the burden of your people.

(Douglas is silent)

BROWN: Otherwise you would be with me. And with God who brought me to this, my final test. And he will not allow me to fail this time.

DOUGLASS: But what about the others? Your sons? Those other young boys out there? Are you willing to sacrifice them?

BROWN: It is not a sacrifice. They believe in me. I will not fail them. And they will not forsake me—as you have—

(bitter)

You encouraged me, and then at the final hour you desert.

(sudden thought)

Is this another test, Lord?

(to DOUGLASS, suspicious)

Is this what you intended all along? Are you that calculating?

(rushing, confused)

But even if you are, and you meant for it to come to this, why won't you join now and insure its success?

(with desperation, to fight his confusion and regain his confidence)

God is my judge. God, and only God. And I have only Him to answer to. Come and pray with me.

(Douglass remains standing, as BROWN, using the pike staff to support and steady himself kneels to one knee and looks up at DOUGLASS. With a sudden strong gesture he reaches up and grasps DOUGLASS' wrist and almost pulls him to his knees. With one hand still grasping the pike and the other holding DOUGLASS' arm, BROWN lowers his head in prayer)

And the Lord looked upon Gideon, and said, 'Go in this thy might, and thou shalt save Israel from the hand of the Midianites: have not I sent thee?' And he said unto him, 'Oh my Lord, wherewith shall I save Israel? behold, my family is poor ..., and I am the least in my father's house.' And the Lord said unto him, 'Surely I will be with thee, and thou shalt smite the Midianites as one man.'

(pause. They rise and BROWN and DOUGLASS stand facing each other. BROWN offers the pike to DOUGLASS)

DOUGLASS: That is your weapon, John. I must live to aid my brothers. If you feel you must die to do it well—I can't stop you.

(turns to GREEN)

BROWN: *(forceful and bitter)* Emperor is going to join me.

DOUGLASS: *(to GREEN)* I'm going to leave for Rochester as soon as you can get our things together.

GREEN: *(moves to a position between them, favoring BROWN)* I think I'll go on with the Commander from here.

DOUGLASS: Welcome to Gideon's Army, Emperor.

(offers the pike)

(Green pauses a moment. Takes pike)

BROWN: A man who makes a decision and doesn't flip-flop like a landed fish.

GREEN: *(to DOUGLASS)* I got to go back, just like I had to leave in the first place.

DOUGLASS: *(understanding)* We must choose.

GREEN: Like they says, A man who's meant to hang won't drown.

(smiles, trying to lighten the mood)

     Maybe I'll even meet up with my old master—And get back what he's got that belong to me.

(shrugs)

     It's worth the chance.

(they shake hands warmly)

DOUGLASS: I'm going John.

(sincere)

     Your God be with you—

(he turns to exit)

BROWN: *(to DOUGLASS for benefit of GREEN)* You go!

(DOUGLASS stops at the tone and looks back at him)

BROWN: Be safe and cautious!

(sarcastic)

     Intellectual!

(DOUGLASS turns)

BROWN: Maybe someday you'll be *Ambassador* Douglass, or *Congressman* Douglass, or *Senator* Douglass.

(DOUGLASS exits)

BROWN: *(calling after DOUGLASS)* "And when Gideon perceived that he was *an angel of the Lord*,...the Lord said unto him, Peace be unto thee; fear *not*: thou *shalt not* die.

(moving toward DOUGLASS' point of exit)

I will protect you! I-will-not-let-anything happen to you! I CAN GUARANTEE THAT!! BY *GOD* I CAN!!

(BLACK.)

(we hear gun shots and screams of the wounded during short blackout)

EPILOGUE

(the tune John Brown's Body is playing softly)

DOUGLASS: *(enters carrying a telegram. He looks rumpled and worried. He takes his place at speaker's dias)* Here is the latest word from Harper's Ferry: as of yesterday morning, 17 October, 1859, John Brown and his men had seized the United States Armory and had control of all points of entry and exit to the Ferry. But by today, a company of U.S. Marines, led by

(consulting the telegram as lights reduce to a spotlight)

Colonel Robert E. Lee had arrived, overpowered the rebels, and taken control—

(bells toll throughout in contrast to the tune, which continues)

One United States Marine—killed.

Four inhabitants of Harper's Ferry—killed.

Of Commander John Brown's band, 7 escaped, and 10 killed— including 2 of Commander Brown's sons.

Commander himself was captured along with 4 of his men.

(BLACK.)

(spot immediately on DOUGLASS making a speech as music and bells continue)

John Brown, tried and found guilty of treason, was hung this morning, December 2, 1859; along with Shields Green, also known as Emperor, and others.

I personally, and the abolitionist cause generally, have lost perhaps our truest friend, and most devoted advocate. John Brown did not fail at Harper's Ferry, he took a step, a very necessary step. And by taking that step he has, almost single-handedly redramatized the plight of the slaves in the South. Through his dramatic action our consciences are once again concentrated on the misfortunes of our enslaved brethren.

Now is the time for us to *collectively* take up the torch from his fallen hand and move forward together. For it is not he who begins, but he who endures that is victorious.

(four-beat pause, then BLACK and end of play)

Alternate Table of Contents
by Theme

FAMILY AFFAIRS, COMMUNITY CONCERNS

Autobiography

Fiction

Poetry

TRICKSTERS, TROUBLE-MAKERS, TROUBLE-SHOOTERS

Autobiography

Fiction

Poetry

GROWING UP

Autobiography

IN PRAISE OF HEAVEN AND EARTH: SPIRITUALITY AND DEVOTION

SPOKEN TRADITIONS: ORAL AND AURAL

Selected Bibliography

Abrahams, Roger D. *Afro-American Folktales: Stories from Black Traditions in the New World*. Pantheon, 1985.

Adero, Malaika. *Up South: Stories, Studies and Letters of This Century's Black Migrations*. New Press: Distributed by W. W. Norton, 1993.

Adoff, Arnold. *My Black Me: A Beginning Book of Black Poetry*. Dutton Children's Books, 1994.

Allen, William G. *Wheatley, Banneker, and Horton*. Books for Libraries, 1970.

Andrews, William L. *Six Women's Slave Narratives*. Oxford University Press (The Schomburg Library of Nineteenth-Century Black Women Writers), 1988.

_____. *Classic Fiction of the Harlem Renaissance*. Oxford University Press, 1994.

_____. *African American Autobiography: A Collection of Critical Essays*. Prentice Hall, 1993.

Baker, Houston A., Jr. *Black Literature in America*. McGraw-Hill, 1971.

_____. *Long Black Song: Essays in Black American Literature and Culture*. University Press of Virginia, 1972.

_____. ed. *Twentieth-Century Interpretations of Native Son: A Collection of Critical Essays*. Prentice Hall, 1972.

_____. *Singers of Daybreak: Studies in Black American Literature*. Howard University Press, 1975, 1983.

_____. ed. *A Dark and Sudden Beauty: Two essays in Black American Poetry by George Kent and Stephen Henderson*. Afro-American Studies Program, University of Pennsylvania, 1977.

_____. ed. *Reading Black: Essays in the Criticism of African, Caribbean and Black American Literature*. Cornell University Press, 1978.

_____. *The Journey Back: Issues in Black Literature and Criticism*. University of Chicago Press, 1980.

_____. *A Many-Colored Coat of Dreams: The Poetry of Countee Cullen*. Broadside Press, 1974.

Baldwin, James. *The Devil Finds Work: An Essay*. The Dial Press, 1976.

Bambara, Toni Cade. *The Black Woman: An Anthology*. New American Library, 1970.

_____. *Tales and Stories for Black Folks*, Doubleday, 1971.

Baraka, Amiri, and Amina Baraka. *Confirmation: An Anthology of African American Women*. Quill, 1983.

Baraka, Imamu Amiri, and Charlie Reilly. *Conversations with Amiri Baraka*. University Press of Mississippi, 1994.

Barksdale, Richard, and Kenneth Kinnamon. *Black Writers of America: A Comprehensive Anthology.* Macmillan, 1972.

Barthelemy, Anthony G. *Collected Black Women's Narratives.* Oxford University Press (The Schomburg Library of Nineteenth-Century Black Women Writers), 1988.

Beam, Joseph. *In the Life: A Black Gay Anthology.* Alyson, 1986.

Bell, Bernard W. *Modern and Contemporary Afro-American Poetry.* Allyn & Bacon, 1972.

Berry, Faith. *Good Morning, Revolution: Uncollected Social Protest Writings of Langston Hughes.* Lawrence Hill, 1973.

Blackshire-Belay, Carol. *Language and Literature in the African American Imagination.* Greenwood Press, 1992.

Blassingame, John W. *Slave Testimony: Two Centuries of Letters, Speeches, Interviews and Autobiographies.* Louisiana State University Press, 1977.

Bloom, Harold. *Black American Prose Writers of the Harlem Renaissance.* Chelsea House, 1994.

_____. *Black American Prose Writers Before the Harlem Renaissance.* Chelsea House Publishers, 1994.

Brasner, William, and Dominick Consolo. *Black Drama: An Anthology.* Merrill, 1970.

Brawley, Benjamin. *Early Negro American Writers.* University of North Carolina Press, 1935.

Brooks, Gwendolyn. *Jump Bad.* A New Chicago Anthology. Broadside Press, 1971.

_____. *A Broadside Treasury, 1965–1970.* Broadside Press, 1971.

_____. *The World of Gwendolyn Brooks.* Harper & Row, 1971.

_____. *Blacks/Gwendolyn Brooks.* David, 1987.

Brown, Cecil. *Coming Up Down Home: A Memoir of a Southern Childhood.* Ecco Press, 1993.

Brown, Patricia L., Don L. Lee (a.k.a. Haki R. Madhubuti), and Francis Ward. *To Gwen, with Love: An Anthology Dedicated to Gwendolyn Brooks.* Johnson Publishing Co., 1971.

Brown, Sterling A., Arthur P. Davis, and Ulysses Lee. *The Negro Caravan: Writings by American Negroes.* Dryden, 1941; Arno, 1969.

Bruccoli, Matthew Joseph, and Judith Baughman. *Modern African American Writers.* Facts on File, 1994.

Chapman, Abraham. Black Voices: *An Anthology of Afro-American Literature.* New American Library, 1968.

_____. *Steal Away: Stories of the Runaway Slaves.* Praeger, 1971.

_____. *New Black Voices: An Anthology of Contemporary Afro-American Literature.* New American Library, 1972.

Chupa, Anna. *Anne, The White Woman in Contemporary African-American Fiction: Archetypes, Stereotypes, and Characterizations.* Greenwood Press, 1990.

Clarke, John Henrick. *Black American Short Stories: One Hundred Years of the Best.* Hill & Wang, 1993.

_____. *American Negro Short Stories.* Hill & Wang, 1966.

Cooper, Wayne F. *The Passion of Claude McKay: Selected Prose and Poetry, 1912–1948.* Schocken Books, 1973.

Courlander, Harold. *A Treasury of Afro-American Folklore: The Oral Literature, Traditions, Recollections, Legends, Tales, Songs, Religious Beliefs, Customs, Sayings and Humor of Peoples of African Descent in the Americas.* Crown Publishers, 1976.

Cullen, Countee. *Caroling Dusk: An Anthology of Verse by Black Poets of the Twenties.* Carol Publishing Group, 1993.

Dance, Daryl Cumber. *Shuckin' and Jivin': Folklore from Contemporary Black Americans.* Indiana University Press, 1978.

Dandridge, Rita B. *Black Women's Blues: A Literary Anthology, 1934–1988.* Maxwell Macmillan International, 1992.

Davis, Angela Y., and Other Political Prisoners. *If They Come in the Morning: Voices of Resistance by Angela Y. Davis and Others.* Third Press, 1971.

Davis, Arthur P., and J. Saunders Redding. *Cavalcade: Negro American Writing from 1760 to the Present.* Houghton Mifflin, 1971.

Davis, Arthur P., J. Saunders Redding, and Joyce Ann Joyce, eds. *The New Cavalcade: African American Writing from 1760 to the Present (2 vols.).* Howard University Press, 1992.

Davis, Arthur P., and Michael W. Peplow. *The New Negro Renaissance: An Anthology.* Hold, Rinehart and Winston, 1975.

Davis, Miles, with Quincy Troupe. *Miles: The Autobiography.* Simon & Schuster, 1989.

De Weever, Jacqueline. *Mythmaking and Metaphor in Black Women's Fiction.* St. Martin's Press, 1992.

Draper, James P. *Black Literature Criticism: Excerpts from Criticism of the Most Significant Works of Black Authors over the past 200 years.* Gale Research, 1992.

Dunbar, Paul Laurence. *Sport of the Gods. The African-American Novel in the Age of Reaction: Three Classics.* Mentor, 1992.

Early, Gerald Lyn. *Speech and Power: The African-American Essay and Its Cultural Content from Polemics to Pulpit.* Ecco Press, 1992–1993.

Emanuel, James A., and Theodore Gross. *Dark Symphony: Negro Literature in America.* Free Press, 1968.

Exum, Pat Crutchfield. *Keeping the Faith: Writings by Contemporary Black American Women.* Fawcett, 1974.

Fabre, Genevieve, and Robert G. O'Meally. *History and Memory in African-American Culture*. Oxford University Press, 1994.

Fabre, Michel. *The Unfinished Guest of Richard Wright*. University of Illinois Press, 1993.

Faggett, Harry Lee, and Nick Aaron Ford. *Best Short Stories by Afro-American Writers (1925–1950)*. Meador, 1950; Krause Reprint, 1977.

Ford, Nick Aaron. *Black Insights: Significant Literature by Black Americans, 1760 to the Present*. Ginn, 1971.

Foster, Frances Smith. *Witnessing Slavery: The Development of Ante-Bellum Slave Narratives*. University of Wisconsin Press, 1994.

Gates, Henry Louis, Jr., ed. *The Classic Slave Narratives (The Life of Olaudah Equiano, The History of Mary Prince, Narrative of the Life of Frederick Douglass, Incidents in the Life of a Slave Girl)*. Mentor, 1987.

Gilmore, Brian. *Elvis Presley Is Alive and Well and Living in Harlem*. Third World Press, 1992.

Giovanni, Nikki, and Virginia C. Fowler. *Conversations with Nikki Giovanni*. University Press of Mississippi, 1992.

Giovanni, Nikki. *Night Comes Softly: Anthology of Black Female Voices*. MEDIC Press, 1970.

Glaysher, Frederick. *Collected Prose/Robert Hayden*. University of Michigan Press, 1984.

_____. *Collected Poems/Robert Hayden*. Liveright, 1985.

Golden, Marita. *Wild Women Don't Wear NO Blues: Black Women Writers on Love, Men, and Sex*. Doubleday, 1993.

Gomez, Jewelle. *Forty-three Septembers: essays*. Firebrand Books, 1993.

Gounard, Jean-Francois. *The Racial Problem in the Works of Richard Wright and James Baldwin*. Greenwood Press, 1992.

Graham, Maryemma. *The complete Poems of Frances E. W. Harper*. Oxford University Press (The Schomburg Library of Nineteenth-Century Black Women writers), 1988.

Hamer, Judith A., and Martin J. Hamer. *Centers of the Self: Stories by Black American Women, from the Nineteenth Century to the Present*. Hill & Wang, 1994.

Hansberry, Lorraine. *To be Young, Gifted and Black: Lorraine Hansberry in Her Own Words*. New American Library, 1969; Samuel French, 1971.

Harley, Sharon, and Rosalyn Terborg-Penn. *Afro-American Women: Struggles and Images*. Kennikat Press, 1978.

Harper, Michael S., and Anthony Walton. *Every Shut Eye Aint Asleep: An Anthology of Poetry by African Americans Since 1945*. Little, Brown, 1994.

Harper, Michael S. *The Collected Poems of Sterling Brown*. Harper & Row, 1980.

Harper, Michael S., and Robert B. Stepto. *Chant of Saints: a Gathering of Afro-American Literature, Art, and Scholarship.* University of Illinois Press, 1979.

Harrison, Paul Carter. *Kuntu Drama: Plays of the African Continuum.* Grove Press, 1974.

Hay, Samuel A. *African American Theatre: An Historical and Critical Analysis.* Cambridge University Press, 1994.

Hayden, Robert E. *Kaleidoscope: Poems by American Negro Poets.* Harcourt, Brace & World, 1967.

_____. *Afro-American Literature: An Introduction.* Harcourt, Brace, Jovanovich, 1971.

Hill, Herbert. *Soon, One Morning: New Writings by American Negroes, 1940–1962.* Knopf, 1963.

Himes, Chester, *Black on Black: Baby Sister and Selected Writings.* Doubleday, 1973.

Houchins, Sue E. *Spiritual Narratives: Maria W. Stewart, Jarena Lee; Julia A. J. Foote, Virginia W. Broughton.* Oxford University Press (The Schomburg Library of Nineteenth-century Black Women Writers), 1988.

Hubbard, Dolan. *The Sermon and the African American Literary Imagination.* University of Missouri Press, 1994.

Hudson, Theodore R. *From LeRoi Jones to Amiri Baraka: The Literary Works.* Duke University Press, 1973.

Hudson, Wade. *Pass it On: African-American Poetry for Children.* Scholastic Inc., 1993.

Huggins, Nathan I. *Voices from the Harlem Renaissance.* Oxford University Press, 1976.

Hughes, Langston. *New Negro Poets. U.S.A.* Indiana University Press, 1964.

_____. *The Book of Negro Humor.* Dodd, Mead, 1966.

_____. *The Best Short Stories by Negro Writers: An Anthology from 1899 to the Present.* Little, Brown, 1967.

Hughes, Langston, and Arna Bontemps. *The Poetry of the Negro.* Doubleday, 1949; rev. ed., *The Poetry of the Negro, 1746–1970,* 1970.

_____. *The Book of Negro Folklore.* Dodd, Mead, 1958.

Hull, Gloria T. *The Works of Alice Dunbar-Nelson.* 3 vols. Oxford University Press (The Schomburg Library of Nineteenth-Century Black Women Writers), 1988.

Hurston, Zora Neale. *Spunk: The Selected Stories of Zora Neale Hurston.* Tuttle Island Foundation, 1985.

Jackson, Edward Mercia. *Images of Black Men in Black Women Writers, 1950–1990.* Myndham Hall Press, 1992.

Johnson, James Weldon. *The Book of American Negro Poetry.* Hourcourt, 1922; rev. and enl., 1931.

Jones, LeRoi and Larry Neal. *Black Fire: An Anthology of Afro-American Writing.* William Morrow, 1968.

Jones, Robert B., and Marjorie Toomer Latimer. *The Collected Poems of Jean Toomer.* University of North Carolina Press, 1988.

Jordan, Casper LeRoy. *A Bibliographical Guide to African-American Women Writers.* Compiled by Casper LeRoy Jordan. Greenwood Press, 1993.

Kellner, Bruce. *"Keep a-Inchin Along". Selected Writings of Carl Van Vechten About Black Art and Letters.* Greenwood Press, 1979.

Killens, John Oliver, and Jerry Washington Ward. *Black Southern Voices: An Anthology of Fiction, Poetry, Drama, Nonfiction, and Critical Essays.* Meridian, 1992.

King, Woodie, *Black Short Story Anthology.* Columbia University Press, 1972.

_____. *The Forerunners: Black Poets in America.* Howard University Press, 1976.

_____. *Voices of Color: Scenes and Monologues from the Black American Theatre.* Applause Books, 1994.

Kinnamon, Kenneth. *James Baldwin: A Collection of Critical Essays.* Prentice Hall, 1974.

Knopf, Marcy. *The Sleeper Wakes: Harlem Renaissance Stories by Women.* Rutgers University Press, 1993.

Larson, Charles R. *Invisible Darkness: Jean Toomer & Nella Larsen.* University of Iowa Press, 1993.

Last Poets (Group). *Vibes from the Scribes: Selected Poems.* Africa World Press, 1992.

Leeming, David Adams. *James Baldwin: A Biography.* Knopf, 1994.

Lewis, David L. *The Portable Harlem Renaissance Reader.* Viking, 1994.

Locke, Alain LeRoy. *The New Negro.* Maxwell Macmillan International, 1992.

Long, Richard A., and Eugenia W. Collier. *Afro-American Writing: An Anthology of Prose and Poetry.* 2 vols. New York University Press, 1972.

Mackey, Nathaniel. *Discrepant Engagement: Dissonance, Cross-Culturality, and Experimental Writing.* Cambridge University Press, 1993.

Mackey, Nathaniel, and Art Lange. *Moment's Notice: Jazz in Poetry & Prose.* Coffee House Press, 1993.

Madgett, Naomi Cornelia Long. *Adam of Ife: Black Women in Praise of Black Men.* Lotus Press, 1992.

Magill, Frank Northen, *Masterpieces of African-American Literature.* HarperCollins, 1992.

_____. *Masterplots II. African American Literature Series.* Salem Press, 1994.

Mahone, Sydne. *Moon Marked and Touched by Sun: Plays by African-American Women.* Theatre Communications Group, 1994.

Major, Clarence. *The New Black Poetry.* International Publishers, 1969.

_____. *Juba to Jive: A Dictionary of African American Slang.* Penguin Books, 1994.

Margolies, Edward. *A Native Son's Reader: Selections by Outstanding Black American Authors of the Twentieth-Century.* Lippincott, 1970.

Mberi, Antar S. K., and Cosmo Pieterse. *Speak Easy, Speak Free.* International Publishers, 1977.

McCluskey, John, Jr. *The City of Refuge; The Collected Stories of Rudolph Fisher.* University of Missouri Press, 1987.

McMillan, Terry, ed. *Breaking Ice: An Anthology of Contemporary African-American Fiction* (with a preface by John Edgar Wideman). Penguin Books, 1990.

Miller, E. Ethelbert. *In Search of Color Everywhere: A Collection of African-American Poetry.* Stewart, Tabori & Chang, 1994.

_____. *Women Surviving Massacres and Men: Nine Women Poets, An Anthology.* Anemone Press, 1977.

Mitchell, Angelyn. *Within the Circle: An Anthology of African American Literary Criticism from the Harlem Renaissance to the Present.* Duke University Press, 1994.

Moon, Bucklin. *Primer for White Folks.* Doubleday, 1945.

Mullane, Deirdre. *Crossing the Danger Water: Three Hundred Years of African-American Writing.* Anchor Books, 1993.

North, Michael. *The Dialect of Modernism: Race, Language, and Twentieth-Century Literature.* Oxford University Press, 1994.

Osolsky, Gilbert. *Puttin' on Ole Massa: The Slave Narratives of Henry Bibb, William W. Brown, and Solomon Northrop.* Harper, 1969.

Patterson, Lindsay. *A Rock Against the Wind: Black Love Poems, An Anthology.* Dodd, Mead, 1973.

Perry, Margaret. *The Short Fiction of Rudolph Fisher.* Greenwood Press, 1987.

Plato, Ann. *Essays: Including Biographies and Miscellaneous Pieces, in Prose and Poetry.* Introduction by Kenny J. Williams, Oxford University Press (the Schomburg Library of Nineteenth-Century Black Women Writers), 1988.

Plumpp, Sterling D. *Somehow We Survive: An Anthology of South African Writing.* Thunder's Mouth Press, 1982.

Powell, Kevin, and Ras Baraka. *In the Tradition: An Anthology of Young Black Writers.* Harlem River Press, 1992.

Randall, Dudley. *Black Poetry: A Supplement to Anthologies which Exclude Black Poets.* Broadside Press, 1982.

Redmond, Eugene B. *Rope of Wind and Other Stories/Henry Dumas*. Random House, 1979.

      . *Goodbye, Sweetwater: New and Selected Stories/Henry Dumas*. Thunder's Mouth Press, 1958.

Reed, Ishmael, and Cameron Northouse. *Ishmael Reed: An Interview*. Contemporary Research Press, 1993.

Reed, Ishmael, and Al Young. *Yardbird Lives*. Grove Press, 1978.

Render, Sylvia Lyons. *The Short Fiction of Charles W. Chestnutt*. Howard University, 1974.

Richardson, Willis. *Plays and Pageants from the Life of the Negro*. University Press of Mississippi, 1993.

Robinson, William H. *Early Black American Poets*. Wm. C. Brown, 1969.

Sanchez, Sonia. *We Be Word Sorcerors: 25 Stories by Black Americans*. Bantam, 1973.

Rusch, Frederik L. *A Jean Toomer Reader: Selected Unpublished Writings*. Oxford University Press, 1993.

Sherman, Charlotte Watson. *Sisterfire: Black Womanist Fiction and Poetry*. Harper-Perennial, 1994.

Sherman, Joan R. *Invisible Poets: Afro-Americans of the Nineteenth Century*. University of Illinois Press, 1974.

      . *Collected Black Women's Poetry*. 4 vols. Oxford University Press (The Schomburg Library of Nineteenth-Century Black Women Writers). 1988.

Shields, John C. *The Collected Works of Phillis Wheatley*. Oxford University Press. (The Schomburg Library of Nineteenth-Century Black Women Writers), 1988.

Smith, Barbara. *Home Girls: A Black Feminist Anthology*. Kitchen Table: Women of Color Press, 1983.

Smith, Karen Patricia. *African-American Voices in Young Adult Literature: Tradition, Transition, Transformation*. Scarecrow Press, 1994.

Stadler, Quandra P. *Out of Our Lives: A Collection of Contemporary Black Fiction*. Howard University Press, 1975.

Stuckey, Sterling. *Slave Culture: Nationalist Theory and the Foundations of Black America*. Oxford University Press, 1987.

Sundquist, Eric J. *To Wake the Nations: Race in the Making of American Literature*. Belknap Press of Harvard University Press, 1993.

Troupe, Quincy, and Rainer Schulte. *Giant Talk: An Anthology of Third World Writers*. Random House, 1975.

Turner, Darwin T. *Black American Literature: Poetry*. Chas. E. Merrill, 1969.

      . *Black Drama in America: An Anthology*. Fawcett, 1971.

      . *The Wayward and the Seeking: A Collection of Writings by Jean Toomer*. Howard University Press, 1980.

Walker, Alice. *I Love Myself When I am Laughing ... And Then Again When I Am Looking Mean and Impressive: A Zora Neale Hurston Reader.* The Feminist Press, 1979.

Washington, Mary Helen. *Black-Eyed Susans: Classic Stories By and About Black Women.* Anchor Press/Doubleday, 1975.

_____. *Midnight Birds: Stories of Contemporary Black Women Writers.* Anchor Press/Doubleday, 1975.

_____. *Invented Lives: Narratives of Black Women's Lives, 1860–1960.* Anchor Press/Doubleday, 1987.

Werner, Craig Hansen. *Playing the Changes: From Afro-Modernism to the Jazz Impulse.* University of Illinois Press, 1994.

Wideman, John Edgar. *Fatheralong: A Meditation on Fathers and Sons, Race and Society.* Pantheon Books, 1994.

Wiggins, Lida Keck. *The Life and Works of Paul Laurence Dunbar.* Winston-Derek Publishers, 1992.

Williams, John A., and Charles F. Harris. *Amistad I: Writings on Black History and Culture.* Vintage/Random House, 1970.

_____. *Amistad II: Writings on Black History and Culture.* Vintage/Random House, 1971.

Woods, Paula L., and Felix H. Liddell. *I Hear a Symphony: African Americans Celebrate Love.* Anchor Books, 1994.

Wright, Lee Alfred. *Identity, Family, and Folklore in African American Literature.* Garland Publishing, 1995.

Wright, Richard, and Keneth Kinnamon. *Conversations with Richard Wright.* University Press of Mississippi, 1993.

Yetman, Norman R. *Voices from Slavery.* Holt, Rinehart, Winston, 1970.

Young, Al. *Drowning in the Sea of Love: Musical Memoirs.* The Ecco Press, 1995.

Index of Author Names, Titles and First Lines of Poems

Acknowledgments

Elizabeth Alexander. "The Venus Hottentot" and "Boston Year" from <u>The Hottentot Venus</u> by Elizabeth Alexander. Reprinted by permission.

Maya Angelou. "Willie" from <u>And Still I Rise</u> by Maya Angelou. Reprinted by permission of Random House.

Louis Armstrong. Excerpt from <u>Satchmo: My Life in New Orleans</u> by Louis Armstrong. Copyright © 1954, 1982 by Louis Armstrong. Shown by permission of Prentice Hall/ A Division of Simon & Schuster.

James Baldwin. "Sonny's Blues" from <u>Going To Meet The Man</u> by James Baldwin. Reprinted by permission.

Toni Cade Bambara. "The Lesson" from <u>Gorilla, My Love</u> by Toni Cade Bambara. Reprinted by permission.

Amiri Baraka. "Preface to a Twenty Volume Suicide Note" from <u>Selected Poetry</u> by Imamu Amiri Baraka. Reprinted by permission.

George Barlow. "American Plethora: MacCorporate MacDream" from <u>Gumbo</u> by George Barlow. Reprinted by permission of the author.

Gwendolyn Brooks. "First Fight. Then Fiddle" and "The Birth in a Narrow Room" from <u>Selected Poems</u> by Gwendolyn Brooks. "The Birth in a Narrow Room" from <u>The Poetry of The Negro</u>, 1746–1949 by Gwendolyn Brooks. "We Real Cool" from <u>Blacks</u> by Gwendolyn Brooks. Reprinted by permission of the author.

Cecil M. Brown. Excerpts from "Stagolee's Memoirs" by Cecil Brown. Reprinted by permission of the author.

Sterling A. Brown. "After Winter," "Foreclosure" from <u>The Collected Poems of Sterling A. Brown</u>, edited by Michael S. Harper. Reprinted by permission of HarperCollins Publishers, Inc.

Cyrus Cassells. "Tokyo Story," by Cyrus Cassells, first appeared in <u>Quilt</u>, Issue 1. Reprinted by permission.

Lucille Clifton. "Good Times" from <u>Goodtimes</u> by Lucille Clifton. Reprinted by permission of Random House. "White Lady" and "Quilting" from <u>Quilting: Poems 1987–1990</u> by Lucille Clifton. Reprinted by permission of BOA Editions.

Countee Cullen. "The Wise," "Incident" by Countee Cullen. Reprinted by permission.

Robert Hayden. "Frederick Douglass," "The Whipping," and "Homage to the Empress of the Blues" from <u>Collected Poems</u> by Robert Hayden. Reprinted by permission of Liveright Publishing Corp.

David Henderson. "Third Eye World," by David Henderson, first appeared in <u>Yardbird Reader</u>, 1972. "Death of the Ice Queen" by David Henderson. Reprinted by permission of the author.

Chester Himes. "Headwaiter" from <u>The Collected Stories of Chester Himes</u> by Chester Himes. Reprinted by Thunder's Mouth Press.

Langston Hughes. "Harlem" by Langston Hughes. "The Weary Blues," "The Negro Speaks of Rivers," "I, Too, Sing America," and "Mother to Son" from <u>Selected Poems</u>. "Havana Dreams" by Langston Hughes. "Birmingham Sunday" from <u>The Panther and The Lash</u> by Langston Hughes. Reprinted by permission of Alfred A. Knopf.

Kristin Hunter. "The Jewel in the Lotus" by Kristin Hunter. Reprinted by permission of the author.

Charles Johnson. "Menagerie" from <u>Sorcerer's Apprentice</u> by Charles Johnson. Reprinted by permission of Atheneum Publishing Company, an imprint of Macmillan Publishing Company.

Bob Kaufman. "Walking Parker Home" and "Battle Report" by Bob Kaufman. Reprinted by permission.

William Melvin Kelley. "The Only Man on Liberty Street," from <u>Dancers On The Shore</u>. Reprinted by permission of Doubleday, a division of Bantam Doubleday Dell Publishing Group, Inc.

Jamaica Kincaid. "Girl" from <u>At the Bottom of the River</u> by Jamaica Kincaid. Reprinted by permission of Farrar, Straus & Giroux, Inc.

Etheridge Knight. "Hard Rock Returns to Prison from the Hospital for the Criminal Insane," "The Idea of Ancestry," and "Haiku" from The Essential Etheridge Knight by Etheridge Knight. Reprinted by permission of University of Pittsburgh Press.

Audre Lorde. "125th Street and Abomey" from <u>The Black Unicorn</u> by Audre Lorde. Reprinted by permission of W. W. Norton.

Nathaniel Mackey. "New and Old Gospel" from <u>Eroding Witness</u> by Nathaniel Mackey. Copyright © 1985 by Nathaniel Mackey. Used with the permission of the author and of the University of Illinois Press.

Ntozake Shange. "Rite-ing" by Ntozake Shange. Reprinted by permission of Russell & Volkening Agents.

Primus St. John. "Worship" from Dreamer by Primus St. John. Reprinted by permission of Carnegie Mellon University Press.

Joyce Carol Thomas. "Church Poem" from Bittersweet by Joyce Carol Thomas. Reprinted by permission of the author.

Lorenzo Thomas. "Wonders" and "Historiography" by Lorenzo Thomas, from Moment's Notice: Jazz in Poetry & Prose. Reprinted by permission of the author.

Melvin B. Tolson. "Lamda" and "African China" from Harlem Gallery by M. B. Tolson. Reprinted by permission.

Jean Toomer. "Esther" from Cane by Jean Toomer. Reprinted by permission.

Quincy Troupe. "Poem for My Father" from Weather Reports: New and Selected Poems by Quincy Troupe

Derek Walcott. "Omeros" from Omeros by Derek Walcott. "A Far Cry from Africa" from Collected Poems: 1948–1984 by Derek Walcott. Reprinted by permission of Farrar, Straus & Giroux, Inc.

Alice Walker. "Nineteen Fifty-Five" from You Can't Keep a Good Woman Down by Alice Walker. Reprinted by permission of Harcourt Brace & Company.

Margaret Walker. "Miss Molly Means" from For My People and "October Journey" from This Is My Century: New and Collected Poems by Margaret Walker. Reprinted by permission of University of Georgia Press.

John Edgar Wideman. "everybody knew bubba riff" from All Stories Are True by John Edgar Wideman. Reprinted by permission of Random House, Inc.

John A. Williams. "Son in the Afternoon" from The Angry Black. Reprinted by permission.

Jerome Wilson. "Paper Garden" by Jerome Wilson. Reprinted by permission of the author.

Richard Wright. "Almos' a Man" from Eight Men by Richard Wright. Reprinted by permission.

Kevin Young. "The Preserving" by Kevin Young. Reprinted by permission of the author.

Al Young. "Somebody Done Hoodoo'd the Hoodoo Man," by Al Young. Reprinted by the author.